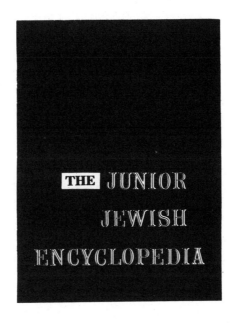

THE JUNIOR JEWISH ENCYCLOPEDIA

BUT FOR LEARNING,
HEAVEN AND EARTH WOULD NOT ENDURE

Talmud, Pesahim

"For the earth shall be full of the knowledge
of the Lord, as the waters cover the sea."

(Isaiah 11:9.)

Printer's mark used by Abraham Usque,
sixteenth century Jewish printer of Ferrara, Italy.

THE
Junior Jewish Encyclopedia

TENTH REVISED EDITION

Edited by

NAOMI BEN-ASHER   HAYIM LEAF

LOUIS L. RUFFMAN, *Educational Consultant*

JACOB SLOAN, *Editorial Consultant*

ALFRED WERNER, *Art Consultant*

SHENGOLD PUBLISHERS, INC.

New York City

ISBN 0-88400-110-5

Library of Congress Catalog Number: 84-51583
PRINTED IN THE UNITED STATES OF AMERICA

PREFACE

The history of the Jewish people has been enacted in many lands and in many ages. Its drama has been played on the stage of eternity. Its villains are enemies long forgotten except by the ageless people who suffered at their hands, and the memory of its heroes—kings and sages, men of action and men of the Word—is very ancient, and nonetheless very fresh.

The task of selecting out of the treasures of the Jewish spirit an encyclopedia of significant knowledge for Jewish youth was formidable indeed. Who ought to be included and who may be passed over? What book, what country, what battle, what act of glory or infamous massacre, what item in the long catalogue of Jewish history, culture, and civilization is not so full of meaning that some Jewish youngster might not be enriched to learn it? The task remained, however, of preparing an encyclopedia, presenting to the young mind a coherent and comprehensible picture of all of Jewish life.

The editors consulted various authorities, and tested in several schools a large sample of the material. We found that young readers are most concerned with today, with understanding the little bit of life they know. We have therefore devoted rather more attention to contemporary Jewry. This is, to be sure, a realistic perspective, for the events of the past decades—the disaster in Europe, the renaissance in Israel, the first flowering of American Jewry—have been decisive for the understanding of much of Jewish history. Our hope is that the young reader will more fully perceive the significance of the years 586 before the common era and 70 of the common era in the light of 1939-1945, the meaning of Ezra and Nehemiah in the light of Theodor Herzl, the achievement of Babylon, Spain, and Poland in the light of the unfolding promise of America.

Within the limitations of space and the vast material to be presented, the Junior Jewish Encyclopedia seeks to provide a dependable and accurate guide for the young Jew to the past and present of his people. The many photographs, drawings, and maps illustrate the individual articles, and the selective bibliographies offer the opportunity for further study of each topic. Hebrew pronunciation follows the Sephardic accent used in Israel, and the transliteration follows the form adopted by American and Israel scholars. Asterisks are used to indicate subjects which are treated separately.

The editors wish to acknowledge with thanks the generous and invaluable assistance of the following: the contributors to this volume, to whose diligent scholarship and devotion to Jewish education this encyclopedia is fitting testimony; and to Mrs. Sylvia Landress, director of the Zionist Archives, and the staff of the Archives; the librarians of the Jewish Theological Seminary of America, Yeshiva University, and the Hebrew Union College-Jewish Institute of Religion, the Jewish Division of the New York Public Library, and the staff of the Library of Jewish Information of the American Jewish Committee; and particularly, Mrs. Phillis Solomon, Miss Marion Magid, Mrs. Zeva Shapiro, and Miss Frieda Ben-Meir, who offered painstaking assistance in preparing the manuscript and reading proof. We acknowledge with gratitude the permission of the American Jewish Year Book to reprint Jewish population data and tables.

We are especially indebted to Mr. Moshe Sheinbaum, president of Shengold Publishers, for the encouragement and assistance he gave us in full measure throughout our work. To him also goes the credit of conceiving this project in Jewish education.

This is the first Junior Jewish Encyclopedia in the English language. We offer it to the reader in the hope that it will be a key to those treasures which have been the riches and the light to countless generations past.

The Editors

August, 1957
Ab, 5717

A NOTE FROM THE PUBLISHER

The reception accorded to the first nine editions of the **Junior Jewish Encyclopedia** has been extremely gratifying to editors and publishers alike. The encyclopedia has been used in homes, study groups and schools, and has been presented to students and graduates by many synagogues and religious schools of various Jewish affiliations in the United States, Canada and Great Britain. The **Junior Jewish Encyclopedia** has also received the award of the Jewish Book Council of America.

The passage of time since this book was first published, however, has necessitated considerable revision of its contents. The pace of events in Jewish history these past years has been dizzyingly rapid, and far-reaching in impact. Ever since our last edition, the Jewish world has seen the emergence of important new figures, the death of some of its beloved leaders, and a considerable shift in Jewish population, particularly in Europe, North Africa and Israel.

The tenth edition has therefore been extensively revised and updated so that it may continue to serve as a fitting contemporary vehicle of instruction and guidance for readers of all ages.

MOSHE A. SHEINBAUM

November, 1984
Heshvan, 5745

CONTRIBUTORS

IRVING A. AGUS, Ph.D.   **I.A.A.**
Professor of Jewish History, Yeshiva University, New York City.

TUVIA BANIN, Ph.D.   **S. and T.B.**
Educator, Tel Aviv, Israel.

SYLVIA SATTEN-BANIN   **S. and T.B.**
Editor, writer, Tel Aviv, Israel.

NAOMI BEN-ASHER   **N. B-A.**
Writer, educator, Newark, New Jersey.

LOUIS BERNSTEIN   **L.B.**
Rabbi, writer, New York, New York.

A. A. DAVIDSON   **A.A.D.**
Writer, New York, New York.

SHLOMO EIDELBERG, D.H.L.   **S.E.**
Assistant Professor of Jewish History, Teachers Institute, Yeshiva University, New York City.

JUDITH K. EISENSTEIN   **J.K.E.**
Musicologist, writer, Chicago, Illinois.

M. Z. FRANK   **M.Z.F.**
Journalist, Israel.

S. J. GOLDSMITH   **S.J.G.**
Editor, journalist, London.

GERTRUDE HIRSCHLER   **G.H.**
Translator, writer, editor, New York City.

SAMUEL IWRY, Ph.D.   **S.I.**
Lecturer, Oriental Seminary, Johns Hopkins University, Baltimore, Maryland.

MORDECAI KOSOVER, Ph.D.   **M.K.**
Assistant Professor of Hebrew, Brooklyn College, New York.

HAYIM LEAF, D.H.L.   **H.L.**
Professor of Hebrew Literature, Teachers Institute, Yeshiva University, New York City.

ANITA L. LEBESON   **A.A.L.**
Historian, Author, Winnetka, Illinois.

HYMAN LEWIS   **L.**
Editor, poet, London, England

EUGENE J. LIPMAN   **E.L.**
Rabbi, author, Washington, D.C.

A. R. MALACHI   **A.R.M.**
Writer, bibliographer, New York City.

CLARA MANN, M.A.   **C.M.**
Educator, New York City.

YUDEL MARK   **Y.M.**
Educator, writer, New York City.

MOSHE PRAGER   **M.P.**
Writer, Jerusalem. Israel.

HAROLD U. RIBALOW   **H.R.**
Author, Queens Village. New York.

SAMUEL ROSENBLATT, Ph.D.   **S.R.**
Associate Professor of Oriental Languages, Johns Hopkins University, Baltimore, Maryland.

LOUIS L. RUFFMAN, M.A.   **L.R.**
Educator, Orange. New Jersey.

ESTHER SALTZMAN   **E.S.**
Writer, New York City.

MORDECAI SCHREIBER   **M. Sch.**
Rabbi, writer, translator, Silver Spring, Maryland.

HILLEL SEIDMAN, Ph.D.   **H.S.**
Editor, writer, Brooklyn, New York.

MORTON SIEGEL, Ph.D.   **M.S.**
Educator, New York City.

GOLDIE WACHSMAN, M.A.   **G.W.**
Editor, translator, New York.

MEYER WAXMAN, Ph.D.   **M.W.**
Author, educator, New York City.

ALFRED WERNER, Ph.D.   **A.W.**
Editor, author, New York City.

MOSES ZALESKY, Ph.D.   **M.Z.**
Educator, writer, Cincinnati, Ohio.

ACKNOWLEDGMENTS

Our thanks are due to a great many individuals and institutions for their cooperation in the publication of this encyclopedia.

We would like to acknowledge the helpful advice of Dr. Stephen S. Kayser, former curator of the Jewish Museum, for selecting many of the reproductions and illustrations used in this volume.

We are most grateful to Mr. Isaac Yohanan and Ms. Elise Kintzer of the Consulate General of Israel for making available to us important data about recent developments in Israel and for supplying us with new illustrations from Israeli sources.

We want to express our special thanks to Mrs. Reene Kreincses for her devoted and conscientious assistance.

To Mrs. Miriam Messeloff, for her interest, criticism, and wise counsel in the preparation of this volume, go our very sincere thanks.

To the late Mr. Jack Koenigsberg, we are grateful for his constant help and encouragement. For her most gracious assistance, we thank Mrs. Emma Leaf.

Reproduced by kind permission are works by Mr. Chaim Gross, the late Mr. Ludwig Y. Wolpert, and the late Mr. Ilya Schor. Thanks go also to the Hadassah Picture Department. We are especially indebted to the American Friends of the Hebrew University, the American Technion Society, the Weizmann Institute, ORT, and YIVO, for their generous assistance.

A

AARON. Son of Amram and Yocheved of the tribe of Levi; elder brother of Miriam and Moses.* He became the spokesman of Moses in Egypt. Together the brothers appeared before Pharaoh when Aaron "cast down his staff before Pharaoh .. and it became a serpent" (Exod. 7:10). Aaron is represented as the first high priest in Israel, having officiated in the Tabernacle built in the wilderness. He became the ancestor of all the priests and high priests, thus dividing the tribe of Levi into two permanent categories: the priests, and the Levites, or servitors, in the Sanctuary. **(See also KOHEN.)**

Aaron—by Louise D. Kayser.

AARONSOHN, AARON (1876-1919). Agricultural expert and Zionist leader. When Aaron was six, his family moved to Palestine from Rumania, abandoning a prosperous business for the hardships of pioneer life. Aaronsohn showed unusual interest in nature, and was sent to study at an agricultural school in France. Upon his return, he worked as agricultural expert in various colonies. He conducted many valuable experiments to improve crops cultivated in Palestine. Aaronsohn discovered wild wheat, a special type of grain sought after by botanists the world over.

Aaronsohn went on an extensive tour throughout the United States, studying its agricultural methods. Upon his return to Palestine, he established, with the help of American friends, an experimental agricultural station in Athlit, near Haifa.* He toured the country and assembled one of the largest collections of its plant life. Aaronsohn's achievements in the cultivation and improvement of crops and trees made him the foremost agricultural expert in Palestine.

During the First World War, together with his brother Alexander and close friends, he joined the secret organization, NILI. The purpose of this organization was to aid Britain in the conquest of Palestine, in order to make possible the realization of a Jewish homeland.

At the end of the war, he set out on a political mission to England. In his way from London to Paris to the Peace Conference, his plane mysteriously disappeared. It is assumed that it fell into the English Channel on May 15, 1919.

Aaronsohn left behind him valuable botanical studies, which were published after his untimely death. A village in Israel, K'far Aaron, as well as the Agricultural Institute of the Hebrew University in Jerusalem,* are named in his honor.

H.L.

AB. Eleventh month of the Jewish civil calendar. **(See CALENDAR and FAST DAYS.)**

ABBA SIKRA (SIKARA). Leader of the extremist rebels during the Jewish uprising against Rome in 69-70 C.E. He was a nephew of Rabbi Johanan Ben Zakkai.* When the latter wanted to leave beleaguered Jerusalem* and establish a center of learning at Yavneh* in southern Palestine, Abba Sikra saw to Rabbi Johanan's safe passage through one of the city gates.

ABEL. The son of Adam* and Eve; a shepherd. When Abel's offering was accepted by God, his brother Cain grew jealous and slew him. Then the Lord asked Cain: "Where is Abel, thy brother?" Cain answered: "I know not; am I my brother's keeper?" As punishment, the Lord made Cain a "fugitive and a vagabond on the earth" (Genesis 4:1 - 4:16).

ABRAHAM (c. 1940 B.C.E.). Founder of the Jewish people, first of the patriarchs,* who discarded idol worship for the belief in one God. The Covenant* between God and Israel began with Abraham. His story is told in Genesis 11-25, from his birth in Ur of Chaldea in southern Mesopotamia, to his death and burial in the cave of Machpelah* near Hebron in the land of Ca-

"Cain and Abel." Engraving after Titian.

"And it came to pass, when they were in the field, that Cain rose up against Abel his brother, and slew him." (Genesis 4:8).

naan. Abraham was commanded by God to leave his birthplace between the Tigris and Euphrates Rivers and to settle in "the land that I will show you." He obeyed and, taking his family, set out on the long journey down to Canaan. When he came to Shehem, "the Lord appeared to Abraham and said, 'Unto your seed will I give this land!'" (Gen. 12:7.) Throughout Chapters 11:26-17:5 of Genesis, Abraham is called Av-Ram — "exalted father." Then his name is changed to **Av-Raham** —"father of multitudes"—"for the father of a multitude of nations have I made you . . . And I will establish my covenant between Me and you, and your seed after you in their generations for an everlasting covenant." As a sign of this everlasting contract, Abraham instituted circumcision of every eight-day-old man-child.

The Biblical account of Abraham brings to men a dignity new in the story of mankind. Through the covenant of Abraham, men became partners in a contract with God, obligated to serve Him in righteousness and obedience, receiving in return the Promised Land as their inheritance.

As the story of Abraham unfolds, his love of peace, sense of justice and compassion for men's suffering are shown in his acts. With great patience, he settled the disputes between the sheepherders of Lot and his own men. With great daring, he pleaded with God not to destroy the wicked people of Sodom and Gomorrah, even if there were only ten righteous men among them. In the story of the sacrifice of Isaac, Abraham's submission to the will of God was tested. As commanded, Abraham placed Isaac on the altar,

preparing to offer him up. An angel of God restrained him: "Lay not thy hand upon the lad . . . for now I know thou fearest God." Then Abraham lifted up his eyes and saw a ram "caught up in a thicket by his horns." This ram he sacrificed instead of his son. In the time of Abraham, sacrificing children to the god was a ritual common among the heathens, but the new religion of Abraham taught that God forbade child sacrifice and that human life was sacred. N.B-A.

"Sacrifice of Isaac." Ink drawing by Franz Kirzinger, 1769.

ABRAMOWITZ, SHALOM JACOB. See MENDELE MOCHER SEFARIM.

ABRAVANEL, DON ISAAC (1437-1508). Scholar, philosopher, and statesman. Don Isaac was an illustrious member of one of the most distinguished Sephardic Jewish families, tracing its origin to King David.* Born in Lisbon, Abravanel served as treasurer to King Alfonso V of Portugal.* When Alfonso died, his successor accused Don Isaac of conspiring against the king. Abravanel was forced to flee to Spain* (1483). There he served Kind Ferdinand and Queen Isabella in financial affairs of state. When the decree expelling the Jews from Spain (1492) was issued, he and other influential Jews pleaded before the court for its withdrawal, to no avail. Abravanel was offered personal exemption from the decree, but chose to flee with his people to

Naples, where he again entered royal service.

Abravanel's Jewish scholarship is shown in his excellent commentaries on the Bible.* Despite his firm faith in the divine revelation of the Bible, he saw clearly the importance of historical background in Biblical exposition. Stirred by Jewish suffering, he wrote three works to further belief in the coming of the Messiah (see MESSIANISM). As a philosopher, he upheld the principle of free will, and opposed the Greek influence of Aristotle and Plato on Jewish thought. Abravanel was survived by three distinguished sons: Joseph, a physician and scholar, Judah Leon, also a physician, and Samuel, scholar and patron of Jewish learning.   H.L.

The Death of Absalom.—From an old engraving. "And his head caught hold of a great terebinth, and he was taken up between the heaven and the earth; and the mule that was under him went on." (Second Samuel 18:9).

Tomb of Absalom.

Isaac Abravanel   Courtesy Jewish National Fund.

ABSALOM. Third son of David* by his wife Maacha, daughter of Talmai, King of Geshur. The Hebrew **Av-Shalom**—Father of Peace—is an ironic name for the son who stirred up a rebellion against his father in order to wrest the throne from him and became the lasting symbol for a rebellious child. For four years Absalom plotted secretly and then openly set up military headquarters in Hebron. David withdrew from Jerusalem.* This stratagem proved successful, for it brought Absalom out in open pursuit to "the forest of Ephraim"—a forest east of the Jordan, where David, long skilled in guerilla fighting, had no difficulty in defeating his son. As Absalom, riding a mule, fled from the field of battle, his long hair was caught in the branches of an oak tree. His mule trotted on, leaving him helplessly trapped, to be killed by David's general, Joab. At the news of this act, which he had expressly forbidden, David the King uttered a cry that has become classic as an expression of a father's grief: "O my son Absalom, my son... would I had died for thee..." (II Sam. 19:1).

ABULAFIA, ABRAHAM. See KABBALAH.

ACADEMIES, BABYLONIAN. See TALMUD.

ACCENTS. A system of signs over and under the letters of the Scriptural texts, indicating how the text is to be chanted, so as to make the meaning clear and the reading pleasant. Thus, accents serve both as musical notes and as punctuation. The signs are the same in all the books of the Bible, but they are read differently in certain passages and sections. Jews of various countries have evolved different chants for them. This system of accents is said to date back to Ezra the Scribe* (fifth century B.C.E.) and the Great Assembly.

ACOSTA, URIEL (Gabriel da Costa) (1585-1640). Uriel Acosta was born in Oporto, Portugal,* in 1585. He came of an aristocratic Marrano* family that had been forcibly converted to Christianity, received a good education, and became treasurer of a church. Yet he came to doubt the teachings of Catholicism, possibly due to the influence of a secret Jewish sect. Having no contact with Jewish life or with Talmudic scholarship, Acosta formed for himself a highly personal view of Judaism based on his reading of the Bible.* After his father's death, he persuaded his family to move to Amsterdam* and return to Judaism. There he began to express his ideas and wrote his **Proposals Against Tradition;** in 1624 he developed these ideas further in **Comparison of Pharisaic Tradition With the Scriptures.** In this book Acosta expressed his non-belief in the immortality of the soul, resurrection, reward and punishment in another world. These views aroused the active opposition of the Jewish leaders of Amsterdam and of other Jewish communities. Since Acosta's beliefs ran counter to Christianity as well as Judaism, he was brought before the Amsterdam city magistrates, who imprisoned him for a few days, fined him heavily, and condemned his book to a public burning. The Amsterdam Jewish community placed him (1618) under "the great ban" and all including his own brothers, shunned him.

In 1633, when he could not longer bear the isolation, Acosta publicly renounced his opinions only very soon to return to his own beliefs again. He visualized a religion requiring few ritual observances and was unable to remain quiet. Excommunicatd again, Acosta lived a quiet solitary life for seven years. when this existence became unbearable, he again recanted and submitted to a harrowing ceremony of repentance in the Amsterdam synagogue. Acosta could not bear to live after this public humiliation. He wrote a short autobiography defending his views and then, in 1630, this religious rebel committed suicide.

ACRE (known in Israel as Akko). On the northern hook of Haifa* Bay, the gateway to Syria.* In Canaanite times a "strong-walled" Phoenician seaport alloted to the tribe of Asher (Judges 1:31), seized alternately by Egypt* and Assyria. Since 800 B.C.E., it has served successively as a Greek and Roman port, Crusaders' fortress, Moslem battlefield, French trading center. Destroyed by the Turks, Acre was rebuilt in 1749, besieged by Napoleon, and changed hands several times until the British occupied it. In 1948 Acre fell to the State of Israel, which built a new Jewish town outside the walls. Its population of 39,000 includes Moslem, Maronite, Quaker, Druze, and Bahai minorities. With the advent of steamships, Acre has been replaced by Haifa as a major port.

ADAM. Hebrew for "man; son of the earth," male or female. In the Bible,* Adam is the first man, created "in the image of God" on the sixth day of Creation, and given by the Lord "dominion over all the earth." (For the story of Creation, see the first chapter of Genesis.)

Adam—an interpretation on a stained glass window, by A. Raymond Katz. "....Let us make man in our image, after our likeness...." (Genesis 1:26).

Section of Skylight Window at Temple Anshe Emet Synagogue in Chicago.

ADAR. Sixth month of the Jewish civil calendar. Traditionally known as a month of merriment since Purim* falls on the 14th of Adar.

ADLER, CYRUS (1863-1940). Scholar and authority on oriental civilizations and Semitic languages, and an outstanding leader of the American Jewish community. Adler was born in Van Buren, Ark., almost two years before the end of the Civil War. During the 77 years of his life, he saw the growth of the American Jewish community from thousands to five million, and played an important role in shaping its cultural life and in developing some of its great organizations. He was a founder and active member of the American Jewish Historical Society and of the Jewish Publication Society of America.* He served as president of the Jewish Theological Seminary of America* in New York and of Dropsie College (see DROPSIE UNIVERSITY) in Philadlephia. When Adler was quite young, he became instructor of Semitic languages at Johns Hopkins University in Baltimore. Between 1888 and 1909, he served as director of the Ancient East department of the Washington National Museum. At the Smithsonian Institution he served as librarian (1892-1905) and as assistant secretary (1905-08). He edited publications of Jewish learning, and one of his outstanding works is **Jews in the Diplomatic Correspondence of the United States.** He was a founder and president of the American Jewish Committee* and of the National Jewish Welfare Board. He was active in forming the Jewish Agency* for Palestine, and served as its non-Zionist co-chairman. His autobiography **I Have Considered The Days** contains an interesting profile of his time and many sketches of outstanding leaders in half a century of Jewish life.

ADLER, JULIUS OCHS (1892-1955). Newspaper executive and army officer. Born in Chattanooga, Tenn., he was educated at Princeton and joined the management of **The New York Times** after graduation in 1914. With the exception of periods of service as an officer in the armed forces during World Wars I and II, Adler was affiliated with the newspaper to the end of his life. He was elected general manager after the death of Adolph S. Ochs in 1935. The same year, he became president of the **Chattanooga Times,** another Ochs publication. Throughout his career Adler was active in the U.S. Army Reserve and in various veterans' organizations. He served as a member of the executive committee of the National Jewish Welfare Board and of numerous philanthropic, civic, and fraternal organizations.

ADON OLAM (Heb. "Lord of the World"). A hymn praising the unity, eternity, omnipotence and benevolence of God.

AFGHANISTAN. Jews have lived in Afghanistan (a Middle Eastern country lying between India,* Pakistan, and Soviet Russia*) since before the destruction of the Second Temple* in 70 A.D. There is a legend that they are descended from the Ten Lost Tribes.* Very little is known about the history of the Jewish community there. Jews have always been second-class citizens under the medieval despotism prevailing in Afghanistan. Until 1914, they were forced to live in sealed ghettos. After 1914, there was a brief period during which abuses against them were curtailed, and their lot was improved. However, in the early 1930's, largely under the influence of several hundred German technicians working in the country, discriminatory measures were renewed. Jews were required to obtain special permits for travel, forbidden to write letters abroad, excluded from the civil service and most of the professions, forbidden to engage in commerce, expelled from rural areas, and confined to the cities of Kabul, Herat, and Balkh. By the end of the Second World War, the number of Jews in Afghanistan had been reduced from about 12,000 to 5,000, largely through illegal emigration.

In 1948, with the establishment of the State of Israel, the majority of Afghanistan Jewry expressed the desire to emigrate; but the government obstructed their emigration. Between 1949 and 1970, about 4,200 Jews from Afghanistan reached Israel. By the late 1970's there were only about 200 Jews in the country.

Cyrus Adler
Courtesy The Jewish Theological Seminary of America.

To this day, there are wandering tribes on the borders between Afghanistan and Pakistan which trace their origin to the twelve tribes of Israel. They are divided into twelve large families, each named after one of Jacob's* sons. They retain some Jewish customs, such as lighting candles on Friday night and wearing Tzitzit* (fringes).

AFIKOMAN. See PASSOVER.

AGGADAH. Aggadah is that part of the Talmud* which, in complementing the legal Halakhah,* stresses its ethical and inspirational meaning. The Aggadah sparkles with picturesque similes, proverbs, and epigrams, as well as with wonderful tales. The origins of the Aggadah may be traced to Biblical times and its history was continuous to the Middle Ages. Originating in Israel, it is saturated with the atmosphere of the Holy Land. The Aggadah collections of Reb Yaakov ben Habib in the fifteenth century, entitled **Ein Yaakov,** became one of the most popular Jewish books.

AGNON, SAMUEL JOSEPH (1888-1970). Hebrew novelist. Born in Galicia, Agnon settled in Palestine in 1909, but lived in Germany from 1912 to 1923. His works are based chiefly upon traditional Jewish life in Europe. They are rich in Hasidic lore and legend, and have captured the spirit and flavor of a special way of life. Agnon's masterly prose has a charm of its own. Although abundant in realistic detail, it often has a dreamlike quality.

Among Agnon's finest novels are **Hakhnasat Kallah** ("The Bridal Canopy"), **Sippur Pashut** ("A Simple Story"), and **Oreah Natah La-lun**

("Lodging for a Night"). In **T'mol Shilshom** ("Only Yesterday") he draws upon his experiences in Palestine to create a fascinating epic. **The Bridal Canopy, In the Heart of Seas, Days of Awe** and **Two Tales: Betrothed and Edo and Enam** have been translated into English. In December 1966 he was the first Hebrew writer to receive the Nobel Prize* for Literature, an award he shared with the German-Jewish poetess Nelly Sachs.*

AGRICULTURE, JEWS IN. Now chiefly city-dwellers, the Jews spent the first two millennia of their history as a people of shepherds and farmers. Abraham* came to Canaan* in search of pasture land for his flocks. For several centuries his descendants lived a semi-nomadic life, settling down to steady farming only at the time of the conquest of Canaan in about 1200 B.C.E. Under the Judges* and during the First and Second Commonwealths, most Israelites were farmers, breeding livestock and raising wheat, barley, grapes, olives and vegetables.

The dispersion of the Jews by the Romans in the first century C.E. led to their separation from the land. In Babylonia,* most of the exiles settled in cities and earned their living in handicrafts and trade. Jews were further removed from agriculture in the Middle Ages, when most Christian princes forbade Jews to own land. Thus, by the beginning of the nineteenth century, less than .05 per cent of world Jewry were farmers.

By that time, however, a movement had arisen to bring the Jews back to the soil. Pondering the problem of anti-Semitism* and the economic distress of East European Jewry, many thinkers concluded that a return to the soil might provide a solution. In 1804, Tsar Alexander I of Russia* founded seven colonies expressly for Jewish subjects, as part of a plan for their segregation as well as rehabilitation. In the following decades several Jewish colonies were established in the Americas. Owing to lack of funds and farm experience, most of these failed. It was only in the 1880's and '90's that a number of small but successful colonies were founded in Palestine, Argentina,* and the United States.*

In 1900 the Jewish Agricultural Society was established in the United States by joint action of the Jewish Colonization Association* and the Baron de Hirsch* Fund. During the first forty years of the Society's existence, more than 13,000 Jewish farmers were assisted in the acquisition and development of land. A number of Jewish agricultural communities are located in New Jersey, Pennsylvania, and other states. The National Farm school was established in Doylestown, Pa., in

The Swedish Charge d'Affaires officially notifying and congratulating S. J. Agnon in Jerusalem on being awarded the Nobel Prize in 1966.

1896. An agricultural magazine, **The Jewish Farmer,** begun in 1908, prints agricultural information in both Yiddish and English.

During the twentieth century, the number of Jewish farmers has steadily increased, swelled by refugees from Eastern and Central Europe. In Israel, where land settlement has been the first goal of the Zionist movement, the number of Jewish farmers has risen from several hundred in 1900 to about 83,000 in 1984. (The total work force in Israel is 1,367,000.) The Jewish farm population of the United States has increased from about 300 families in 1900 to more than 10,000 in 1960. In 1979, there were about 30,000 Jewish farmers in Argentina. Colonization on a smaller scale has taken place in Brazil,* Australia,* Poland* and the Balkans.

AGRIPPA I. King of Judea (c. 10 B.C.E.-44 C.E.). Son of Aristobulus and grandson of Herod* and Mariamne, Agrippa was sent to Rome* to be educated at the age of six. He was companion to the Roman crown prince, Gaius Caligula, and shared in the gay and frivolous court life. Accused of favoring the crown prince over the reigning Emperor Tiberius, he was thrown into prison. Upon Caligula's ascent to the throne, he was released and appointed king of Galilee.

PALESTINE
OF AGRIPPA I

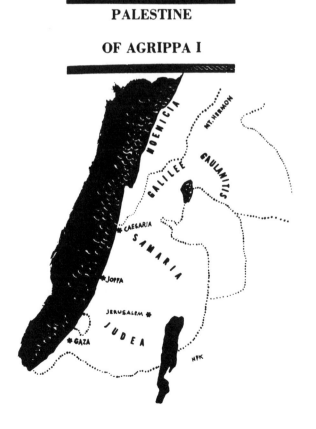

The Jews received Agrippa's appointment with great joy. Having been subjected to Roman rule for forty-five years, the appointment of Agrippa I signified to them liberation from foreign dominion and oppression. When Claudius replaced Caligula as emperor, Agrippa's rule was extended to Samaria and Judea. A brief era of peace began, which recalled the glories of the Hasmonean period. On holidays people from all corners of Palestine streamed again to the Temple.* Their beloved king participated in the festivities. (When at one time he deplored the fact that he was not of pure Jewish stock, the scholars consoled him, saying "Fear not, Agrippa, you are our brother.")

Agrippa planned to strengthen Jewish rule and eventually free Palestine from Roman yoke. The great hopes of his people for complete independence were shattered when he died suddenly in 44 C.E. while attending the Roman games in Caesarea. It is assumed that he was poisoned by enemies of the Jews.

AGRIPPA II (c. 28-93 C.E.). Son of Agrippa I, he was the last king to rule Palestine before the destruction of the Second Temple.* He was reared in the same corrupt Roman court atmosphere as his father; however, unlike his father, Agrippa II was completely alienated from his people. The Roman rulers appointed him king of the eastern provinces of Palestine and entrusted him with the care of the Temple. All of western Palestine remained under Roman rule.

When the Jewish revolt broke out against foreign dominion in 70 C.E., Agrippa urged unconditional submission to Rome. His cooperation with the hated enemy stirred the anger of the people, and together with his sister, he was forced to flee Jerusalem. He remained in the Roman camp until his death.

AGUDATH ISRAEL WORLD ORGANIZATION. Founded in 1912 at Kattowitz, Poland, for the purpose of creating a world-wide organization of Orthodox Jews. Before the Second World War, Agudath Israel was influential in many European countries, particularly in Poland, Czechoslovakia, and Germany. Its total membership was estimated at half a million.

At the first congress of the organization held in Vienna in 1923, a constitution was adopted. A world congress was to take place every five years. A rabbinical council, called Moetzet Gedolei Ha-Torah, consisting of prominent Talmudical scholars, was established to hand down decisions on Jewish law. Today, Agudah has its seat in three world capitals, London,* Jerusalem,* and New York City.*

Through a special fund, the Keren Ha-Torah, the movement has established and maintained many **yeshivot** and Talmud Torahs throughout the world. It has also promoted the Beth Jacob School system for girls in many countries, providing both religious and secular education for its students. Before the Second World war, there were 150 such Orthodox girls' schools in Poland, with more than 20,000 pupils.

Agudath Israel is active in combatting laws which interfere with traditional religious observance. It has opposed the passage of laws in Europe and the United States* prohibiting ritual slaughter. It has also compaigned against changes in the calendar which would jeopardize the observance of Jewish holy days.

From its inception, Agudath Israel has opposed political Zionism.* In the provisional and first Israel government, Rabbi Yitzhak Meyer Levin of Agudah was minsiter of Social Welfare.

Prominent leaders of Agudath Israel included the late Jacob Rosenheim (Israel), the late Rabbi Aaron Kotler (Lakewood, N.J.), and the late Rabbi Eliezer Silver (Cincinnati, Ohio).

AHAB (876-853, B.C.E.) Seventh king of Israel, contemporary and ally of Jehoshaphat, the king of Judah. Ahab married the Phoenician princess Jezebel, daughter of Ethbaal, King of Tyre. This alliance, by securing Israel's peace with a powerful neighbor, left Ahab free to resist successfully an Assyrian attack, and to win a victory over Ben Hadad II, King of Damascus.* Three years later, Ahab was slain by a chance arrow in the battle for Ramot Gilead. Elijah's* prophecy had foretold Ahab's death as punishment for tolerating the Baal* worship instituted by Jezebel, and for the lawless execution of Naboth, whose vineyard he desired.

"Ahab the Israelite" is mentioned in the "monolithic inscription" left by Shalmaneser III (858-825 B.C.E.) of Assyria. Ahab figures in the Assyrian inscription as a formidable foe commanding a force of 2,000 chariots and 10,000 soldiers.

AHAD HA-AM (Asher Ginzberg) (1856-1927). The Hebrew writer Asher Ginzberg used Ahad Ha-am, meaning "one of the people," as his pen-

name. Ahad Ha-am was one of the foremost thinkers and essayists in Hebrew literature, and the philosopher of cultural or "spiritual Zionism." Raised in a small town in the Ukraine, in a Hasidic family, he excelled in his religious studies. Later, he acquired extensive knowledge of European languages and philosophy. In 1886 he came to Odessa, which was then emerging as an important Hebrew literary and Zionist center. Ahad Ha-am took part in practical Zionist work, supporting the first colonies which had just been established in Palestine.

His first published article **Lo Zeh ha-derekh** ("This Is Not the Way") roused the Jewish public and stands as a landmark in Hebrew literature. In this article, he outlined his national philosophy, which was later further developed in the four volumes of his collected works, **Al Parashat Derakhim** ("At the Crossroads"). The fundamental thought of Ahad Ha-am's Zionist philosophy is his insistence that a spiritual and national revival must come before the return to Zion. His forceful moral personality exerted great influence on Hebrew literature and the Zionist ideal. He was the founder of the Bnai Moshe order, whose members attempted to spread Jewish national ideals in accordance with Ahad Ha-am's philosophy. In 1896 he became the editor of the leading Hebrew monthly published in Odessa, **Hashiloah,** named for a slowly flowing river as a symbol of moderation. Before the First World War, Ahad Ha-am lived in England, where he played an important role in the events leading to the Balfour Declaration. At the age of 66, he settled in Palestine, on a Tel Aviv street named in his honor.   H.L.

AHASUERUS, KING OF PERSIA. See ESTHER, BOOK OF.

AKDAMUT. See SHAVUOT.

AKEDAH (Heb. "binding"). Abraham's offering of Isaac as a sacrifice to God. (Genesis 22)

AKIBA BEN JOSEPH (c. 40-135 C.E.). Great Talmudic scholar and leader of his people. It is told that until he was forty years of age, he was an ignorant shepherd. Rachel, the beautiful daughter of a rich Jerusalemite, Kalba Sabbua, fell in love with Akiba and secretly married him. Enraged at his daughter's marrying beneath her station, her father immediately disinherited her. It was Rachel's ardent wish that Akiba study the Jewish law. They were very poor, but with Rachel's encouragement Akiba devoted many years to study in the academy. At the end of that period, he

Ahad Ha-Am

abbi Akiba   Courtesy Jewish National Fund.

returned home followed by thousands of pupils. His wife came to meet him. When his students, not knowing who she was, wanted to turn her away, Rabbi Akiba rebuked them, saying, "Let her be. Your wisdom as well as mine are due to her."

Akiba's brilliant and penetrating mind is revealed in his interpretation of the Jewish law. He assembled and edited the many teachings of previous scholars, and in arranging them by subject, laid the foundation for the editing of the Mishnah.* A great Jewish patriot, he joined Bar Kokhba* in inspiring the Jews to rebel against Roman rule, 60 years after the destruction of the Temple. Akiba saw in Bar Kokhba the Messiah (see MESSIANISM), applying to him the Biblical prediction of the coming of the Messianic redeemer of the Jews: "A star (kokhav) shall rise out of Jacob." (Numbers 24:17) The rebellion failed, however, and the Roman Emperor Hadrian prohibited, under the threat of death, the observance and study of Jewish Law. Akiba was one of the ten martyrs sentenced to be flayed to death for defying the Emperor's decree. Serene, he faced his end, accepting his fate to serve God with all his soul. While the sage recited the traditional prayer of Shema* ("Hear, O Israel, the Lord our God, the Lord is one,") he gave up his spirit. Thus he set a lasting example to the numerous Jewish martyrs in generations to come.

ALEPH. First letter of the Hebrew alphabet; numerically, one.

ALEXANDER THE GREAT (336-323 B.C.E.) King of Macedonia, conqueror of the East. Judea

was on the path of Alexander's march of conquest, but the only opposition to him there was at Gaza, which he razed to the ground. Alexander introduced Greek forms of government in his conquered provinces, encouraged the intermarriage and mixing of his own followers with the peoples he conquered, and spread the Greek language and customs wherever he went. As a result, the Greek and Oriental cultures mixed and created a new civilization — Hellenism* — which spread all over Alexander's empire. His attitude toward the Jews was friendly, and in Maccabean times, his name came to be used frequently among Jews. In Talmudic literature many legends are woven around Alexander's figure. The Hellenism he introduced into Syria* and Egypt* had a deep influence on Jewish history and on Judaism.

ALEXANDER JANNAEUS (Hebrew name Jonathan) (reigned 103-76 B.C.E.). King and high priest, son of Johanan Hyrcanos,* first of the Hasmonean dynasty to be called king, and first to issue coins stamped in both Greek and Hebrew. His wife was Queen Salome Alexandra,* sister of Simon, son of Shetah, who was president of the Sanhedrin* ("high court").

Jannaeus was a courageous warrior-king, who extended the borders of Palestine by conquering the Mediterranean coast as far as the Egyptian border; he reconquered the eastern area from Lake Huleh to the Dead Sea* and captured a number of cities beyond the eastern regions of the Jordan. He sided with the Sadducees* in their quarrel with the Pharisees.* This quarrel brought on a civil war and served to detract from the honor of king and country. During his last battle against the king of Arabia, Jannaeus suffered a severe attack of malaria from which he died. He was buried near the Damascus Gate in Jerusalem.

ALEXANDRIA. A city in northern Egypt* where a branch of the Nile enters the Mediterranean. It was founded in 331 B.C.E. by Alexander the Great,* and the city soon became a great metropolis. Alexander the Great was friendly to the Jews and Alexandria was the first Greek city to give citizenship to Jews. Under the rule of the Ptolemy kings who succeeded Alexander in Egypt, and under the rule of the Romans who defeated Cleopatra (last of the Ptolemies), the Jewish community was autonomous and prospered. Jews also held civic office and many were soldiers. The Jews of Alexandria, estimated at various times to number from half a million to a million, spoke Greek. Their Greek version of the Bible, the Septuagint,* was used in their synagogue in place of the Hebrew. The Great Synagogue of Alexandria was said to hold 100,000 worshippers. The reader had to wave a flag to indicate when the people (some of whom could not hear him) should say the responses. Such sages as Philo* lectured on Hellenistic Judaism (see HELLENISM) to multitudes of interested pagans. Nevertheless, hatred of the Jews was inflamed by such heathens as the priest Apion, against whom Josephus* defended Judaism. There were terrible riots. This hatred increased after Egypt became Christian, and Hellenistic Judaism was doomed when Christian mobs destroyed the Jewish quarter of Alexandria. Under Arab and Turkish rule, some Jews returned to Alexandria, but the center of Egyptian Jewry gradually moved to Cairo. Prior to 1956, when thousands of Jews left for Israel, Alexandria had a Jewish population of about 15,000. Today there are practically no Jews left in Alexandria. (See also EGYPT.)

ALGERIA. Jewish communities have existed in Algeria since the 1st century C.E., and have lived under Moslem rule from the 7th century onward. Refugees from the Spanish Inquisition* swelled the Jewish population in the 15th century, making Algeria an important center of Sephardic* Jewry. In 1830, Algeria became a French possession and its Jews were granted French citizenship by the Cremieux Decree of 1870. During the seven-year political struggle leading to Algeria's independence (July 1962), the Great Synagogue of Algiers was looted and many Jews were killed. Due to heavy emigration to France and some to Israel, the Jewish community shrank from 135,000 in 1958 to less than 300 today, most of whom live in Algiers (the capital).

ALIYAH. (Hebrew, meaning "going up.") In the synagogue service, an **aliyah** is the act of going up to the reading desk of the synagogue to read a portion of the Torah. In the Bible, three **aliyot** or pilgrimages to the Temple in Jerusalem were appointed for Passover,* Shavuot,* and Sukkot.* In modern times, the term **aliyah** has been used to denote immigration to the Holy Land.

ALKABETZ, SOLOMON (c. 1505-1584). Hebrew poet, Kabbalist,* and Biblical commentator. Alkabetz was born in Turkey but lived most of his life in Safed, Palestine, the sixteenth century center of mysticism.

The best known of his poems, **Lekhah Dodi** ("Come, My Beloved") is chanted in all synagogues on Friday night. In it the poet expresses the love of the Jewish people for the Sabbath Bride and their longing for Zion to be rebuilt. Legend has it that every Friday afternoon, Alkabetz and his students, dressed in the Sabbath

best, set out to welcome the Sabbath Queen. In the open field outside Safed they marched in procession in the dusk, chanting psalms and the song **Lekhah Dodi.**

ALKALAI, YEHUDA BEN SOLOMON HAI (1798-1878). Serbian rabbi who dedicated his life to the idea of establishing a Jewish state in Palestine 100 years before the modern rise of Zionism,* late in the 19th century. A forerunner of political Zionism, he proposed that the Jews obtain Palestine from the Turks through the intervention of England* and France.* He maintained that the Jews' sufferings were completely the result of their own passivity and inaction. Rabbi Alkalai also worked out a plan for redemption of land in Palestine, along the lines adopted by the present Jewish National Fund,* which came into being a century later (1901). Disappointed with the attitude of European Jewish leaders toward his ideas, he emigrated to Palestine at the age of 76, and there founded a society to resettle Jews on the land. He did not live to see his dream come true, dying in Jerusalem* at the age of 80. A few days after Rabbi Alkalai's funeral, some of his devoted followers bought the land which later became the site of Petach Tikvah, the first Jewish agricultural colony in modern Palestine.

ALLENBY, VISCOUNT EDMUND HENRY HYNMAN (1861-1936). British field marshal and veteran of many campaigns. At the outbreak of World War I in 1914, he was given command of the cavalry in France. During 1917-1918, he served as commander in chief of the Egyptian based expeditionary force of Great Britain. He invaded Palestine, captured Jerusalem,* ending Turkish resistance in his victorious battle in Samaria, Sept. 18-21, 1918. Jewish Legion troops took an active part in Allenby's Palestine campaign.

ALLIANCE ISRAÉLITE UNIVERSELLE. A French Jewish organization of international scope and influence, the first to represent world Jewry on a political basis. Founded in 1860 by a group of seventeen Parisian Jews, in protest against such anti-Semitic incidents as the Damascus affair and the Mortara case,* the alliance later expanded to world membership, becoming the central educational agency in the Mediterranean area, as well as a powerful spokesman for the interests of world Jewry. In 1862, the Alliance embarked on a program of uplifting Jews of Mediterranean Jewry by founding a network of schools in the lands of the Middle East and North Africa. It set up its first school in Tetuan, Spanish Morocco.

In 1979, the schools founded by the Alliance Israélite Universelle had an enrollment of about

Yehuda Alkalai

14,000. A very great number of Jewish children from the Middle East and North Africa have been educated in schools founded by the Alliance. In these schools, the children receive a secular as well as a Jewish education from teachers especially trained in normal schools maintained by the Alliance in Paris and Casablanca. All of the alliance schools have combatted the dread childhood scourges of trachoma, a disease of the eye, and tinea, a disease of the scalp, prevalent in the Mediterranean area; during 1950-56 some 2,000 children were cured of these diseases. The first agricultural school on Palestine soil was founded by the Alliance at Mikveh Israel* in 1869. The Alliance maintains a vocational school and a school for deaf mutes in Jerusalem.*

ALLON, YIGAL (1918-1980). Israeli army commander and Cabinet member. Born in Palestine,* he was one of the founders, and later commander in chief, of Palmach.* He subsequently played a leading role in military operations during Israel's War of Independence. A leader in the Labor Zionist and Kibbutz* organizations he was first elected to the Knesset in 1955. He was appointed Minister of Labor in 1961 and Deputy Prime Minister in 1968. He served as Israel's Foreign Minister from 1974 until 1977.

ALPHABET, HEBREW. "Alphabet"—from the Greek letters *alpha* and *beta*, themselves based on the Hebrew *aleph* and *bet*. The Hebrew alphabet has twenty-two basic letters, five of them having special final forms. Through the use of points (dots), the sounds of the following letters are changed: bet, kaf, pe, shin, tav. In Sephardic pronunciation, the tav is not changed by the dot.

According to the authorities, the Hebrew alphabet came into being around 1500 B.C.E. Before that, the Egyptians used hieroglyphs or picture writing to express ideas or objects. Then came an adaption that used some of the hieroglyphs and changed them into twenty-two sound symbols. The earliest examples of such a script come from inscriptions found in the Sinai peninsula. It is thought, however, that the first true alphabet was developed in Palestine.* All Semitic alphabets were quite similar to one another, the Phoenician being closest to the Hebrew script. The Phoenicians, a seafaring people of merchants, carried this script to many lands about the ninth century B.C.E. Various peoples took this alphabet and changed it to suit their own

language. According to their tradition, the Greeks accepted this Hebrew-Canaanite alphabet from Cadmus, the Phoenician. Cadmus is considered to be the Greek form of the Hebrew **kadmi**, or "Easterner." The oldest Greek inscriptions were written from right to left like Hebrew, and they used the twenty-two Hebrew letters in their original order and with their original names, though these had no meaning in the Greek language. All European alphabets are traced back to this common origin. North of Canaan, in the territories which formerly belonged to Assyria, the alphabetic script developed in a more cursive and square form. Following the rapid diffusion of the Aramaic language, this square script, too, came into general use. According to tradition, the Jews came in contact with this "Assyrian" or Aramaic script during the Babylonian exile in the sixth century B.C.E.; in time they adopted it, and are using it to this day. On the Maccabean coins as well as on the Bar Kokhba coins the old Hebrew script was still being copied.

THE HEBREW ALPHABET

Pronunciation	Script	Printed Letter	Pronunciation	Script	Printed Letter
m	N	מ	(Silent letter)	lc	א
m (used at the end of a word)	ρ	ם	b, v	ב,ב	ב ,ב
n	J	נ	g (as in "good")	ל	ג
n (used at the end of a word)	l	ן	d	ך	ד
s	O	ס	h	ה	ה
(Silent letter)	γ	ע	v	l	ו
p, f	ב,ב	פ ,פ	z	ל	ז
f (used at the end of a word)	ך	ף	ch (as in "Pesach")	n	ח
tz	3	צ	t	U	ט
ts (used at the end of a word)	ך	ץ	y (as in "yes")	,	י
k	P	ק	k, ch	כ,כ	כ ,כ
r	כ	ר	kh (used at the end of a word)	ך	ך
sh, s	e,e	ש,ש	l	ל	ל
t	ח	ת			

Hebrew square letters and corresponding Canaanitic

ALROY, DAVID (12th century.) Born in Chaftan, Kurdistan, Alroy declared himself Messiah to the Jews of Babylonia* and led a revolt against Persia in 1160. With his large following, he planned to capture Jerusalem* as the first step to redeeming the Jewish people. He began his campaign with an attack on the citadel of his native town, was defeated and died—possibly at the hand of his own father-in-law. For a while his memory was kept green by the **Menahemites** ("The Consolers"), a Jewish sect that revered him greatly. The folk imagination endowed his personality with great beauty and valor. In the nineteenth century, this legend-encrusted figure served Benjamin Disraeli* as the hero of his novel, **David Alroy. (See also MESSIANISM.)**

ALTERMAN, NATHAN. See HEBREW LITERATURE

AMALEKITES. A people who tried to prevent the Israelites from entering Canaan and continued to wage war against them up to the time of David. Because of their cruelty, and because Haman **(see** PURIM) was thought to be one of them, the Amalekites were branded by tradition as enemies whose "memory is to be blotted out." **(See** Ex. 17:8, Deut. 25:17, Esther 3:1.)

AMEN. "So be it," or "verily"; a Biblical word spoken to confirm the statement of another, or chanted in affirmation of a prayer. It occurs for the first time in the Book of Numbers. Amen is almost a universal word, since it is used by Jews, Christians and Moslems, alike.

AMERICA, DISCOVERY OF. Jewish participation in the discovery of America has its beginnings in the work of early Jewish astronomers, geographers, and map makers. Long before Columbus,* Jews believed that the earth was round. The Talmud* compared the world to a "ball that is thrown from hand to hand." Some centuries before Columbus, the Zohar stated that the earth revolves like a ball and "when it is day on one-half of the globe, night reigns over the other half."

Much of the background knowledge available to Columbus on the eve of discovery came from Jewish scientists. Abraham Cresques was the greatest map-maker of the fourteenth century. His **Catalan Atlas** is highly valued in the history of geography. Judah Cresques, Abraham's son, headed the academy at Sagres of which Prince Henry the Navigator, of Portugal, was patron and protector. Judah Cresques made nautical instruments and drew charts used by Henry the

Navigator. Among the Jewish scholars and scientists at the Sagres academy were two noted cartographers: Gabriel de Vallsecha of Majorca, maker of the map used by Amerigo Vespucci, and Macia de Viladestes, an expert on interior Africa and the first one to trace a road across the Sahara. Abraham Zacuto,* who improved the astrolabe used by Vasco da Gama, was a professor at the universities of Salamanca and Saragossa. He was a teacher of Columbus, and his works accompanied the great discoverer on his voyages. Columbus knew some of these Jewish scholars personally, as well as their work, and this knowledge helped pave the way for the discovery of America. Columbus is considered by some authorities to be of Jewish descent. He owed much to the Jews of Spain. Don Isaac Abravanel* befriended him; Gabriel Sanchez, treasurer of Aragon, and Luis de Santangel, chancellor of the royal household, secured financial aid for him. In the words of the historian H.B. Adams, when referring to the legend of Isabella's crown jewels: "Not jewels but Jews were the financial basis for the first expedition of Columbus." Among the crews of Columbus's three caravels were several men of Jewish ancestry. Five of these men are known by name and have been identified by scholars. One of them was Bernal, the ship's doctor who had narrowly escaped death because the Inquisition* had sentenced him for adhering to Judaism. Another, Luis de Torres, served as interpreter and made all four voyages with Columbus. De Torres was one of the two men chosen to go ashore when land was sighted.

Throughout the period of exploration in the Western Hemisphere, Jewish participants crop up. When Cabral discovered Brazil, Gaspar Judeo a Polish Jew, was a member of the expedition. One of the outstanding Brazilian pioneers was a Lisbon Marrano,* Fernando de Loronha, or Noronha, as his name was sometimes spelled. The Island of Fernando Noronha is named for him—its discoverer. Jews came to South and Central America singly and in groups. They came as Jews or secret Jews and from the first made an important contribution to the development of the new land and to commerce with European lands.

AMERICA-ISRAEL CULTURAL FOUNDATION. Agency for the promotion of cultural exchanges between the people of Israel and the United States. Originally founded in 1939 by Edward A. Norman, to unify American Jewish fund raising for educational, cultural and social service institutions, in Palestine, the organization has been known by its present name since 1957.

AMERICA-ISRAEL FRIENDSHIP LEAGUE.
Established by the Bnai Zion order, the League is dedicated to the promotion of mutual friendship and understanding between the peoples of the United States and the State of Israel through the interchange of cultural, educational, artistic and scientific knowledge between both democracies. Its program and activities are channeled through the American-Israel Friendship House in New York City. Membership is open to all, irrespective of race, creed or religion, who subscribe to its principles.

One of the ongoing projects of the America-Israel Friendship League is the High School Students Exchange Program. For a month's duration, students from Israel and America visit one another's country. They tour, study, speak about their own country, enjoy home hospitality and build lasting friendships. When they return home, they have gained new insights into themselves, their country, and the host country. The "Young Ambassadors for Peace," as they are called, come from diverse ethnic, social and religious backgrounds, but when the trip is over, they have come to appreciate the cultural similarities between the U.S. and Israel—two democratic nations built by immigrants from around the world.

AMERICAN ASSOCIATION FOR JEWISH EDUCATION. The comprehensive educational agency in American Jewish life was founded in 1938. It aims to advance instructional and professional standards, engage in research and experimentation, stimulate communal responsibility, certify teachers, provide supervisory and administrative personnel, conduct local surveys, supply educational materials, and assist other national agencies. To these ends it publishes newsletters, bulletins, curricula programs, and the widely distributed **Pedagogic Reporter** and **Jewish Audio-Visual Review**; and it sponsors the National Council on Jewish Audio-Materials. The Association organizes local and national conferences on Jewish education, and sponsors the National Curriculum Research Institute.

AMERICAN COUNCIL FOR JUDAISM. An organization which defines the Jews as members of a religious faith only, and not as a people. It was founded in 1942 by the late Rabbi Louis Wolsey of Philadelphia. From the outset, it drew its adherents chiefly from that branch of the Reform movement which was dissatisfied with the gradual acceptance of Zionism by the majority of Reform Jews. The Council waged a bitter campaign against the establishment of a Jewish State in Palestine. After the creation of the State of Israel they raised the issue of dual loyalties and dual citizenship. The Council has been charged with playing into the hands of hatemongers, as well as with encouraging assimilation. Following the Six-Day War* of 1967, the Council lost many members.

AMERICAN JEWISH COMMITTEE. Nationwide American Jewish organization, founded in 1906. At present, the membership numbers over 50,000 in eighty chapters.

The committee's objectives, as stated in its charter of incorporation are: to prevent the violation of civil and religious rights of Jews everywhere; to take action when such violations occur; to "secure for Jews equality of economic, social, and educational opportunity"; and to relieve Jews who suffer from persecution and other disasters.

In 1914 the Committee, in cooperation with other organizations, helped to organize the American Jewish Joint Distribution Committee* for Jewish overseas relief. After the First World War it assisted prominently in securing the insertion of clauses guaranteeing the rights of minorities in the treaties establishing the new states of Eastern and Central Europe.

Before and during the Hitler regime, the committee had studies made of the growth and nature or anti-Semitism, and, through its publications and representations to the United States government, alerted the public to the German outrages against the Jews. The committee continued its study of anti-Semitism in this country, and in 1949-50 published the five-volume **Studies in Prejudice,** analyzing the causes and possible remedies for prejudice.

Although the Committee initially was opposed to Jewish nationalism, a number of its leaders, particularly Louis Marshall* (president 1912-1929), were instrumental in establishing the Jewish Agency* for Palestine. In 1947 the AJC urged the United States to support the Palestine partition resolution in the United Nations.

The Committee, with the cooperation of the Jewish Publication Society of America,* has published annually (since 1909) the **American Jewish Year Book,** a handbook of information on Jews the world over. It also publishes two magazines. **Commentary,** a monthly magazine of opinion on Jewish affairs and contemporary issues and **Present Tense.**

AMERICAN JEWISH CONGRESS. The formation of an American Jewish Congress was first proposed at a New York Zionist conference held in 1914. Despite opposition, plans were completed in 1916 for the establishment of this organization "exclusively for the purpose of defining methods whereby, in cooperation with the Jews of the world, full rights may be secured for the Jews of all lands and all laws discriminating against them may be abrogated."

In 1918, the Congress resolved to send a delegation to the Versailles Peace Conference* to help secure Jewish rights all over the world.

Though the Congress adjourned "permanently" in 1920, a need was felt for it to continue, and it was revived in 1922.

During the Nazi period, 1933-45, the American Jewish Congress worked militantly against Nazism. Protest meetings, the boycott of German goods, opposition to United States participation in the 1936 Olympic Games in Berlin, refugee work of all kinds—in these and other ways, the organization labored to help European Jewry.

The American Jewish Congress worked consistently for Zionism, both before and after the establishment of the State of Israel.

In 1970, the Congress had over three hundred chapters and divisions in the United States. About half consisted of women's groups; the remainder was composed of both men and women. The total membership is approximately 50,000. Its presidents, following Nathan Straus, included Stephen S. Wise, Israel Goldstein, Joachim Prinz, Arthur J. Lelyveld, Arthur Hertzberg and Howard Squadron. The current president is Theodore R. Mann.

The program of the Congress is developed and projected by commissions in the areas of law and social action; international affairs; community relations; Jewish communal affairs; membership and organization; and finance.

Major policies are determined by its national convention of delegates. Between conventions, an executive committee administers the affairs of the organization.

The American Jewish Congress founded and still spearheads the World Jewish Congress.* It is also a member of the National Jewish Community Relations Advisory Council.

Of all its activities, the Congress has laid stress on its work in law and social legislation. It has participated in most of the famous cases before state and Federal courts involving issues of religion and the public schools, civil rights, civil liberties and related matters.　　　　　E.L.

AMERICAN JEWISH JOINT DISTRIBUTION COMMITTEE. The JDC, or "Joint" as it is universally known, was founded on November 27, 1914, to serve as the over-all distribution agency for funds collected by different American Jewish groups for overseas relief. By 1917, it was conducting its own centralized fund-raising campaign. From 1939 on, it received the bulk of its funds from the United Jewish Appeal.*

Since 1914, the JDC has spent more than 1,200,000,000 for the relief of Jews everywhere in the world. In 1979, the Committee aided more than 435,000 Jews in over 25 countries throughout the world, mainly in North Africa, the Mid-East, including Israel, and Europe. The first half century of its existence may be divided into six periods: 1. The First World War, when the Jewish refugees' status required urgent help in many parts of Europe; 2. The postwar emergency period of 1918-1920, when food and clothing had to be distributed in huge quantities; 3. The reconstruction period from 1921-1932, when JDC aided

Some of the founders and leaders of the American Jewish Joint Distribution Committee. Photograph taken on the occasion of the 40th annual JDC meeting. Seated, left to right: Adolph Held, Bernard Semel, James N. Rosenberg, Herbert Lehman, Paul Baerwald. Standing, left to right: Rabbi David de Sola Pool, Alexander Kahn, Dr. Bernard Kahn, Alex A. Landesco, Baruch Zuckerman, I. Edwin Goldwasser, and Rabbi Jonah B. Wise.

Jewish communities throughout the world to help themselves; 4. The Nazi period, 1933-1945, when Jews had to be saved from death, moved to new countries, and fed and clothed until they were self-sufficient; 5. The emergency period after World War II, when the JDC bore its greatest burdens. Tens of thousands of Jewish displaced persons (DP's) had to be helped to rebuild their lives. DP camps in Europe needed food, clothing, teachers, social workers, medical personnel—every possible kind of help. Throughout 1947, the Committee served 224,000 rations daily in the DP camps. As thousands of Jews moved to Israel, they had to be rehabilitated, taught new trades, and settled in their new land. Later, emergencies developed in Iraq,* Yemen,* North Africa, and elsewhere. In each case, JDC was needed to help Jews emigrate when possible, to supply relief on the spot when necessary. Between 1945 and 1953, the JDC aided 621,206 Jewish emigrants, of whom 504,208 settled in Israel.

In 1948, at the peak of DP period, JDC had hundreds of workers in Europe and the Middle East. It supplied relief on a previously unheard-of scale.

6. In 1960 the JDC's aid was required by some 250,000 needy men, women, and children in 25 countries of Europe, North Africa, and the Near East. In Israel, JDC-Malben provided medical, welfare, and other care for aged, ill, and handicapped newcomers. In Moslem countries, the agency gave medical, feeding, relief, cultural, and religious assistance to some 100,000 needy Jews. The emphasis in Europe was on technical and reconstruction assistance to the local population, as well as aid to migrants and refugees.   E.L.

AMERICAN MIZRACHI WOMEN. See MIZRACHI.

AMERICAN RED MAGEN DAVID FOR ISRAEL. See MAGEN DAVID ADOM.

AM HA-ARETZ. Hebrew term, literally "people of the earth," "country folk." **Am Ha-Aretz** became a derogatory phrase, meaning one ignorant and uneducated in Jewish matters. The term originated in the Biblical books of Ezra* and Nehemiah.* These two leaders urged those who returned from the Babylonian Exile with them to separate themselves from "the people of the earth," called **Ammei Ha-Aretz.** This separation was necessary to prevent the Jews from assimilating and losing their own identity. The Talmud* has many definitions of an **Am Ha-Aretz,** among them the following: "One of the multitude which knows not the (Jewish) law," and

"he who has children and does not educate them in the Law."

AMIDAH, See PRAYERS.

AMIT. See MIZRACHI WOMEN'S ORGANIZATION OF AMERICA.

AMNON OF MAYENCE. Hero of a legend that was published for the first time around 1350. This legend reflects the bloody persecutions of the Jews during the Crusades.* It tells of Amnon, a distinguished and learned man of wealth among the Jews of Mayence in Germany.* The Archbishop of Mayence continually pressed Amnon to convert to Christianity. Finally Amnon asked the archbishop for three days' time to come to a decision. At the end of this period, Amnon did not appear before the archbishop, because he regretted having giving the impression that he was considering changing his faith. As punishment, the archbishop commanded that Amnon's hands and feet be cut off. This happened just before the Jewish New Year, and Amnon, dying of his wounds, had himself carried into the synagogue on Rosh ha-Shanah* during the services. As the cantor was about to recite the **Kedusha,** or Sanctification, Amnon stopped him, saying: "Pause that I may sanctify the most holy Name." He then began the hymn starting with the words **U'netaneh Tokef** ("We will celebrate the mighty holiness of this day"); when he reached the words "and our Name hast Thou linked with Thine own," Amnon expired. The famous Rabbi Meshullam ben Kalonymus of Mayence (about 1000 C.E.) who published this poem, is considered its author. Ever since, **U'netaneh Tokef** has formed a part of Rosh ha-shanah services.

AMORA. (From the Hebrew and Aramaic, meaning "speaker or interpreter.")

The title "Amora" was given to all teachers of Jewish law in Palestine from about 200 C.E. to 500 C.E. The Amoraim continued the work of the Tannaim, the creators of the Mishnah.* After the Mishnah was edited, many new problems requiring clarification arose in Jewish law. To help solve these problems, the Amoraim explained the Mishnah, discussing its rulings and reinterpreting its decisions. Their work was eventually incorporated into what is today known as the Gemara, which, together with the Mishnah, forms the Palestinian and Babylonian Talmud.* The names of more than three thousand Amoraim are mentioned in the Talmud.

AMOS (c. 750 B.C.E.). First of the prophets known to have written down his visions, third of the Minor Prophets in the Bible.* Amos was a shepherd in the village of Tekoa nestling in the

24

hills of the kingdom of Judah. He came to nearby Bethel, the principal religious center of the northern kingdom of Israel, no doubt to sell his sheep and fruits. Amos cried out against the injustice and poverty of the masses under Jeroboam II. In pity and sorrow, he predicted the punishment of Israel and its destruction by Assyria. Turning to Samaria,* the political center of Israel, he accused the wrongdoers and warned them of the ruin they would bring on their nation. The dominant idea of Amos was justice, justice for all humanity, not only for his own nation. He was the first to see God as the universal Lord of all the nations, not only of Israel. Having been chosen God's special people, Israel must live up to a unique standard of righteousness. Amos taught also that God required of Israel not sacrifices, but justice, purity, truth. He dreamed of a future golden age of peace, when ''the exiles of my people Israel'' will return home, rebuild the wasted cities, replant the vinyards, and never be uprooted again.

Ashkenazic Synagogue in Amsterdam.

AMSTERDAM. The first Jews to settle in the Netherlands' capital were refugees from persecution in Portugal and of the Spanish expulsion of 1492. They were given religious freedom but were barred from all professions except medicine. They became active in commerce and industry, and, during the seventeenth century, they established synagogues and schools, including the great **yeshiva**, Etz Hayim.

The earliest waves of Ashkenazic* Jews came from Poland in the wake of the Chmielniki pogroms (1648). Shortly afterwards, Jews from Germany settled in Amsterdam. The entire community participated in the development of a rich cultural life. Outstanding among the many scholars of this period was Rabbi Manasseh ben Israel,* diplomat, author, and printer, who set up the first printing press in Amsterdam.

The community accorded great power to its rabbis, who opposed the study of the Kabbalah, as they did the Messianic movements. They excommunicated the religious rebel, Uriel Acosta* (1640) and the philosopher, Baruch Spinoza* (1656).

In 1796, in the wake of the French Revolution, the Jews were granted equal rights, attaining complete emancipation during the nineteenth century. They continued to play an important role in the economic life of the city, until the outbreak of the Second World War. With the Nazi rise to power in Germany in 1933, a mass migration of Jewish refugees to Holland began. When Hitler's armies entered the Netherlands, there were approximately 80,000 Jews in Amsterdam. The familiar Nazi pattern of mass deportation and atrocities against Jews was applied, destroying five-sixths of Dutch

Amos rebukes Israel's indulgence.

*"I hate, I despise your feasts
And I will take no delight in your solemn assemblies.
Yea, though ye offer me burnt-offerings and your meal-offerings,
I will not accept them;
Neither will I regard the peace-offerings of your fat beasts." (Amos 5:21-22.)*

Jewry. When the Allied armies of liberation entered Amsterdam in 1945, they found about 25,000 Jewish survivors of this once great Jewish community.

Since then, Amsterdam Jewry, with the assistance of the Netherlands government, has slowly recovered and reestablished itself. In 1977, an estimated 20,000 Jews lived in the city. Schools for children and synagogue services were functioning and serving the community. The Ashkenazi community of Amsterdam celebrated its 325th anniversary in April, 1961.

ANAN BEN DAVID. Founder of the Karaite* sect. A sharp quarrel broke out between Anan and his younger brother Hananiah (Josiah) over the office of "Prince of Exile." The Jewish leaders supported Hanaiah's appointment and it was duly confirmed by the Caliph of Baghdad. Anan protested and was arrested. While in prison he made the acquaintance of the prominent Moslem theologian Abu Hanifah, who advised him to declare himself leader of a new religious sect. Anan did so, and as a result he was freed.

Anan wrote the **Sefer ha-Mitzvot** or "Book of Commandments" (770) which became the basic text for the new sect. By recognizing Jesus and Mohammed as prophets he won the friendship of both Christians and Moslems. His sect, originally called Ananites, came to be known later as Karaites from the Hebrew "Karaim" or "[strict] readers of Scriptures." Anan died in 800, but the sect he founded exists to this day. The Karaites reject the authority of the Talmud* and base their religious beliefs on the Bible only. (**See also** KARAITES.)

ANGEL. In Hebrew **malakh,** meaning "messenger." The Bible mentions angels as spiritual beings, ministering to God and appearing to men on special missions. Angels came to Abraham* to predict the birth of a son, and to Lot to warn him of the imminent destruction of Sodom. Jacob* saw angels ascending and descending on a ladder "set up on the earth, and the top of it reached the heaven." Similarly, an angel appeared to Moses* "in a flame of fire, out of the midst of a bush." Descriptions of angels are to be found in Isaiah,* where they have six wings, and in Ezekiel. They are powerful, wise and holy, but are subject to the will of God and fulfill his commandments. While the Book of Daniel* names only the angels Michael and Gabriel, Talmudic and Midrashic literature mentions names of many angels, each one performing a specific task. In Jewish tradition a special place is occupied by the Angel of Death, the ministering angels, who give praise to the Lord, and angels appointed to guard the nations of the world.

ANGLO-JEWISH ASSOCIATION. A philanthropic organization of English Jews, with branches throughout the British empire. Founded in 1871 in conjunction with the Alliance Israélite Universelle* it shortly thereafter dissociated itself from the French organization. The Association aims to help Jews everywhere to "obtain and preserve full civic rights," "to protect those who suffer for being Jews," "to foster education of Jews particularly in the Middle East," and "to support the upbuilding of Israel." The Anglo-Jewish Association has contributed greatly to the support of Jewish schools throughout the Middle East (including Palestine) and in Shanghai. Until 1946, when it withdrew from the Board of Deputies of British Jews,* the two organizations worked together.

ANIELEWICZ, MORDECAI (1919-1943). Leader of Warsaw* ghetto uprising. In 1943, at the height of the Nazi terror, the Warsaw ghetto was populated by 40,000 Jews; 460,000 had been systematically exterminated. Unless drastic action were taken, the survivors would be led as sheep to the slaughter. The Jewish underground resolved at that moment to rise in open rebellion against their murderers.

The leader of this rebellion was Mordecai Anieliwicz. A twenty-four-year-old member of the Labor Zionist movement, Anielewicz had chosen to stay in Poland* after the Nazi conquest. Traveling from ghetto to ghetto in danger of his life, he had spent the first four years of the occupation training self-defense units among the youth.

Under Anielewicz's able and inspiring command, the ghetto factions were welded into a single fighting force. During the Passover holiday of 1943, the ghetto fighters lashed out against their oppressors. For two weeks the poorly armed and heavily outnumbered "army" battled against the air and tank divisions called in to quell the uprising. At the end of a fortnight the ghetto stood no longer. Its defenders lay in the rubble—lifeless, but to be avenged. Among them was Anielewicz; by his side, Mira, the wife who had accompanied him every step of the blood-drenched underground way.

His heroism, and that of his comrades, are commemorated in a massive monument erected at yad Mordecai, a kibbutz in Israel named after Mordecai Anielewicz.

ANTI-DEFAMATION LEAGUE OF B'NAI B'RITH. One of the nation's oldest and largest human relations organizations, ADL was founded in a corner of a Chicago law office in 1913 to combat the crude and overt anti-Semitism of the times. Its mandate was "to end the defamation of the Jewish people . . . to secure justice and fair treatment for all citizens alike."

Amos—a carving in chestnut by Don Benaron, New York.

Rooted in the spiritual heritage of Judaism and the democratic tradition of America, the agency has grown into an international organization, headquartered in New York City with 30 regional offices in this country, a European office in Paris, an Israel office in Jerusalem, affiliated offices in Latin America and Canada, and a consultant in Rome.

Both at home and abroad, the agency combats anti-Semitism and other forms of bigotry and discrimination; counteracts anti-Israel propaganda; alerts government officials and the public to threats to the democratic process; strengthens intergroup and interfaith friendship and understanding, and works generally in behalf of Jewish concerns and interests.

The security of the State of Israel is a principal concern. The League works to alert the American public to its stake in a peaceful Middle East—vital not only for Israel's security but America's strategic interests.

In this country, the agency confronts and exposes such hate and extremist groups as Liberty Lobby, the largest purveyor of anti-Semitic materials in the U.S.; the Ku Klux Klan and the Institute for Historical Review, which seeks to prove that the Nazi Holocaust was a hoax.

Two recent ADL model statutes have provided the basis of passed or pending laws in several states —one outlawing racial and religious vandalism and intimidation, another barring paramilitary operations by the Klan and other extremist groups.

In seeking "fair treatment for all citizens," the agency has fought successfully against quotas that barred Jews and other minorities from schools, jobs and housing; today, still dedicated to the merit concept, ADL opposes the reverse discrimination inherent in the use of racial quotas as the criteria for access to employment and education.

ADL enlists the support of world public opinion in speaking out against oppression of Jews in the Soviet Union, Latin America and elsewhere, and terrorist acts directed against Jewish communities in Western Europe. In this country, it prepares annual audits of incidents of anti-Semitic vandalism and violence.

Convinced that education is society's ultimate hope of eliminating prejudice, ADL has developed materials for schools to teach children to recognize and combat bigotry and help them learn about the contributions to society by Jews and other minority groups.

ADL is governed by a National Commission, representing a cross section of the Jewish community, which meets annually to chart policy and set priorities, and the Commission's National Executive Committee which meets semiannually. Regional advisory boards, comprised of local community leaders, correspond to the National Commission in their areas.

ANTI-SEMITISM. The hatred of Jews. The purpose of anti-Semitism in its active political phase is to degrade the Jews by removing their civil, political, social, economic and religious rights, and finally, by exterminating them.

The term appears to have been first used in Germany in 1879, in a pamphlet by Wilhelm Marr entitled **The Victory of Judaism Over Germanism.** That same year, Marr founded the Anti-Semitic League.

Of course, this first use of the term "anti-Semitism" was certainly not the first appearance of anti-Semitism. In the story of the Biblical Book of Esther* Haman makes use of many of the classic techniques of anti-Semitism to gain his ends: libel, false accusations, and discrimination.

After the end of the Bar Kokhba* revolt against Rome in 137 C.E., the new Christian religion rapidly developed strong anti-Semitic feelings. As Christianity came into power in the Roman Empire, the dark age of anti-Semitism began for the Jewish people. Increasingly, Jews lost their civil and other rights, and oppression became widespread.

Middle Ages.

The entire period of the Middle Ages was one of discrimination, violent persecution, and expulsions for the Jewish people, all anti-Semitic in origin. There were some relatively good periods; for example, beginning in the seventh century when Pope Gregory the Great actively opposed anti-Semitic violence. From that time until the beginning of the Crusades in 1096, the lot of the Jews in Christian Europe was tolerable. But the Crusaders, on their way to the Holy land, "revenged" themselves upon the Jews, killing thousands of men, women, and children in pogroms. Jews were blamed for having started the Black Death, an epidemic which killed off many millions of people in Europe beginning in 1348. The result was more bloody outbreaks against the Jews.

The Middle Ages did not end for the Jewish people until the end of the eighteenth century, when the spread of enlightenment, scientific knowledge, and democracy brought the breakdown of ghetto walls and the beginnings of more objective judgment and of some equality of opportunity for Jews. Nevertheless, organized and individual anti-Semitism remained everywhere— less in France, England, and the United States, more in Germany, Austria, and especially in Poland and Russia. The pogroms which erupted in Russia beginning in 1881 brought 2,100,000 Jews to the New World by 1910.

The Protocols of the Elders of Zion.

The most potent piece of anti-Semitic literature in the flood of hate-books and pamphlets which have appeared in the last century is undoubtedly the **Protocols of the Elders of Zion.** First produced by Sergius Nilus, a Russian mystic, in 1901 as an adaptation of a satire originally leveled against Napolean III by Maurice Joly of France, it was rapidly printed and distributed in various languages in Europe and later in the United States. The **Protocols** claim to be the strategic plans made by the World Zionist Congress in 1897 for the Jewish conquest of the world. Despite repeated public proof that they were forgeries, the circulation of the **Protocols** continued on a large scale until the end of Nazism in 1945.

The most fateful outbreak of anti-Semitism in history occurred in Germany* between 1933 and 1945. Adolf Hitler and his Nazi Party rose to absolute power in that unhappy country on a platform whose basis was anti-Semitism. The Jews were blamed for every German problem, and the only solution proposed to these problems was the extermination of the Jews. Hitler and his followers almost succeeded. During World War II, six million Jews were killed in crematoria and Nazi murder chambers. Poles, Hungarians, Rumanians, and others joined the Nazis in this blood bath.

Anti-Semitism in the United States.

The history of anti-Semitism in the United States may be simply charted. Before World War I, there was little organized anti-Semitism, but much quiet discrimination against Jews. A major incident occurred in 1877, when it was learned that Jews were not welcome as guests at the largest hotel in Saratoga, N.Y. This was the first open case of anti-Semitism in the United States since 1862, when General U. S. Grant had issued his notorious General Order No. 11, banning Jews from his army area. (This order had been quickly revoked by President Abraham Lincoln.)

Throughout the years, however, Jews were discriminated against in hotels, clubs, colleges, and jobs.

A Board of Delegates of American Israelites had been formed in 1859 to fight for Jewish rights. It never achieved great prominence, and merged in 1878 with the Union of American Hebrew Congregations.* The most active Jew in Washington during this period was Simon Wolf, who consulted regularly with Presidents about Jewish problems.

In 1906, the American Jewish Committee* was formed to carry on the increasing amount of activity necessary to fight anti-Semitism and to secure equal rights for Jews. Later, other organizations entered this field: the American Jewish Congress,* the Jewish Labor Committee, the Anti-Defamation League of B'nai B'rith,* local Jewish community councils, and the National Jewish Community Relations Advisory Council.

The most famous case of anti-Semitism between the two World Wars involved Henry Ford, automobile magnate, and his infamous newspaper, the **Dearborn Independent,** which reprinted the **Protocols of the Elders of Zion,** and carried on an active anti-Semitic campaign. After he had been sued for libel in 1927, Ford apologized in a public letter to Louis Marshall,* recalled all copies of the **Dearborn Independent,** and never again allowed himself to be involved in anti-Semitic activity.

During the Nazi period, the German government sponsored widespread anti-Semitic propaganda and activity in the United States. The German-American Bund achieved a fairly large membership, at least in the Yorkville section of New York, and was most vocal and vicious. It was joined by organizations and individuals like the Silver Shirts of William D. Pelley, Gerald Winrod's organization, Father Charles Coughlin of the Christian Front, Gerald L. K. Smith, and many others. They achieved a measure of success despite efforts by Jewish organizations and friendly non-Jewish groups and persons, until the outbreak of World War II, when anti-Semitism, associated with Hitler, was discredited.

Between 1945 and 1968, memories of the Holocaust kept organized anti-Semitism in the U.S. limited to a "lunatic fringe." Also, the rise and achievements of the State of Israel* helped transform the image of the Jew in non-Jewish eyes. By the 1960's American Jewry felt sufficiently secure to take a leading role in various social and civil rights causes. The "freedom marches" and similar demonstrations for Black rights enjoyed Jewish participation.

Ironically, following the assassination of Rev.

28

Martin Luther King, Jr., in 1968, part of the Black community became openly hostile to all whites, especially to Jews, who were accused of being slum landlords and who owned stores in the Black ghettoes, where poor Blacks had credit problems. Moreover, the militant segment of the Black community viewed itself as a "national liberation" movement and as such felt allied to similar movements, including the so-called "Palestine liberation" movement. Anti-Zionism became a convenient front for the new anti-Semitism. By 1979, this new anti-Semitism was becoming less vocal but Jewish leaders and institutions continued vigilant.

Theories of Origin.

There are many theories about the origin of anti-Semitism. One is religious conflict, the traditional Christian dislike for Jews because they rejected Jesus of Nazareth as the Messiah (see MESSIANISM) and, as some allege, were responsible for his crucifixion. Many persons consider this historic lie to be the chief source of anti-Semitism. Another theory maintains that the hostility is due to the fact that Jews have remained a minority refusing to lose its identity and disappear in the general population.

Neither of these theories provides a complete answer to the complicated question. We must go further, and examine some ideas which have been worked out by scientists to explain hatred and bigotry in general. The scientists have found that it is the unhappy, the emotionally sick people who tend to be intolerant. Their feelings of insecurity and inferiority breed hostility within them. They join groups through which they vent their feelings on other people, who serve them as scapegoats. Probably, anti-Semitism is due to a combination of these reasons: religious, social and psychological.   E.L.

ANTOKOLSKI, MARK (1843-1902). Russian sculptor. Born in the city of Vilna, Antokolski chose the career of sculpture against the wishes of his orthodox parents. After studying in St. Petersburg and Berlin, he moved to Paris. At the age of twenty-eight he became famous through his statue of Ivan the Terrible. He made life-size statues of such thinkers as Socrates and Spinoza, as well as fine portrait busts (among his sitters was the aged novelist, Count Leo Tolstoy). Well known is his **Christ Before Pilate:** with bowed head and bare feet, Jesus, a Jewish peasant, stands before his unseen judge. For his earliest work, **The Jewish Tailor,** made in high-relief, he received a silver medal. It shows a lean old crafts-man in cap and gabardine, sitting cross-legged in the window of his tiny shop, holding his needle against the light to thread it.

APOCALYPTIC LITERATURE. Books written during the time of the Second Temple* and shortly after its destruction (about 200 B.C.E.—100 C.E.). These books foretell future events through extraordinary and symbolic images and visions. Many parts of the Bible* such as the first chapters of Ezekiel* and Daniel,* contain apocalyptic references. Parts of the Apocrypha* belong to this group, including the Book of Enoch, Book of Jubilees, Apocalypse of Baruch, Psalms of Solomon, Book of Adam and Eve, Assumption of Moses, and others. Most of these books were created in times of danger and stress. They are full of mystic visions, prophesying Judgment Day and the coming of the Messianic Age. **(See also APOCRYPHA.)**

APOCRYPHA. From the Greek apokryphos, meaning "hidden, not recognized"; a series of books written during the last centuries B.C.E. and excluded from the Bible* when the canon* was set up, around 90 C.E. Several of the Apocrypha were written at a later date. Some of them were written in Greek, and all were generally modelled after some book in the Bible. They compromise wisdom books, such as Ben Sira,* poems, such as the Wisdom of Solomon, and prayers, such as that of Manasseh. The two historical Books of the Maccabees are a part of the Apocrypha; so also are such instructive stories as the books of Tobit, Judith, and Susanna. In the Book of Judith, the heroine rescues a whole city from a besieging Assyrian army by killing its general, Holofernes. Among the Apocrypha are also prophecies or revelations of the unknown, called Apocalyptic writings. None of these books equals the Bible in grandeur of ideas or beauty of writing. Many of them were lost altogether and forgotten by the Jews. Some survived only in Greek and were included by the early Church Fathers in the Catholic Bible.

ARAB INFLUENCE IN JEWISH HISTORY. The Arabs are a group of peoples living in Egypt, Saudi Arabia, Yemen, Syria, Iraq, Jordan, and Lebanon. They speak dialects of the Arabic tongue and are for the most part of the Islamic faith.

Jewish and Arab tradition hold that the Arabs are the descendants of Ishmael, son of Abraham.* In ancient times there were several small but highly developed kingdoms in the Arabian peninsula. Most of the Arabs, however, were camel-breeding nomads. Those mentioned in the Bible* probably wandered northward from Arabia and lived on the fringe of the Jewish settlement in Palestine.* The early Arab kingdoms fell into decay in the first centuries of the common era. It was only with the religious revolution of Mohammed in the seventh century that the Arabs emerged as a major force on the stage of history.

Scion of a wealthy merchant family, Mohammed declared himself the prophet of "the only true faith." Known as Islam,* this religion demanded faith in Allah, the "one true God," but accepted the religious writings of both Christians and Jews. Its prophets included Abraham, Moses,* the Biblical prophets, Jesus, and Mohammed. Mohammed believed it was his duty to convert all of mankind to Islam. To this end, he began a series of "Holy Wars." Leading an army of fierce desert warriors, he and his successors conquered the entire Middle East, from Egypt to Central Asia. Later, North Africa and Spain* were brought under Islamic rule. The pagan people of the conquered countries were converted to Islam, taught the Arabic language, and made subjects of a single Arab empire.

At that time the bulk of world Jewry lived within the Arab empire. When both persuasion and persecution failed to shake their faith, the Arab rulers were forced to evolve a policy of some tolerance. Jews were generally accepted as second-class citizens. But this legal definition of their status did not put an end to persecution. From time to time there were violent outbursts of hatred, often leading to massacres. Fanatic Moslem sects frequently led the onslaught. On the whole, however, Jews were much better off in the Islamic world than in Christian Europe. Though they continued to study Hebrew, Arabic became their spoken tongue. They came and went freely in the markets of the east.

By the tenth century, Jews were important in the flourishing international trade from Spain to India.* There were Jewish bankers, ministers, generals, and doctors at most Moslem courts. In addition, the Jewish community remained fairly independent, and the community head had an honored place in the government of the Caliphs.

Golden Age of Judeo-Arabic Culture.

Especially distinguished was the cultural life of the Jews during this era. Between the seventh and tenth centuries the Arabs had evolved one of the great civilizations in the history of mankind. In addition to the development and study of their own religion, Arab scholars had worked fruitfully in the fields of philosophy, poetry, language study, history, geography, medicine, astronomy, and other branches of science. Speaking Arabic and mixing freely with Arab scholars, Jews contributed to all these fields of learning. More important, they developed a culture of their own, based on their ancient traditions and on the researches of their Moslem neighbors. In Babylonia,* the heads of great Talmudic academies continued the work of their predecessors in interpreting the Jewish law. Saadiah Gaon,* head of the Jewish community in Babylonia during the tenth century, not only translated the Bible into Arabic, but also published studies in philosophy, poetry, religion, and law. In the following century, the center of Jewish life passed to Spain, and a series of brilliant figures participated in creating the "golden age" of Jewish history there. Maimonides,* a physician by profession, was one of the great masters of philosophy in his time. His great works include a codification of Jewish law and an effort to justify the Jewish religion in terms of ancient Greek philosophy. The greatest achievements of the "golden age," however, were not in philosophy, but in poetry. Living in both Christian and Moslem Spain, such poets as Judah Ha-Levi,* Solomon Ibn Gabirol,* and Moses Ibn Ezra* created some of the most beautiful poetry in the Hebrew language. Their poems treat religious and secular subjects in forms derived from classical Arabic verse. They were all learned in science and philosophy and masters of classic Arabic prose as well as of Hebrew and Jewish lore. Other poets and scholars in Babylonia, North Africa and Tunis contributed to the flowering of Jewish culture in their time.

The Golden Age of Judeo-Arabic culture came to an end with the decline of the entire Arab civilization in the thirteenth and fourteenth centuries. At that time, barbarian rulers gained domination over most of the Islamic empire. In the course of that period, the center of Jewish life passed from the shores of the Mediterranean to Europe proper. Many Jews continued to live on the shores of the Mediterranean, but they ceased to play a vital role in Jewish life. Until the rise of Jewish nationalism at the end of the nineteenth century, the Mediterranean Jews lived as a subject people among their Arab neighbors who were under the dominion of foreign powers.

The Modern Arab Revival

The nineteenth and twentieth centuries, which have witnessed the return of the Jews to Palestine and the creation of a Jewish state there, have also seen a negative change in Arab-Jewish relations. The various Arab states, which were created after the defeat of the Ottoman Turkish Empire in

World War I, have firmly opposed the return of the Jews to their homeland. This opposition flared into open warfare in 1948, when the armies of five Arab nations invaded the newly-declared State of Israel.* Despite four successive defeats on the battlefield, the Arabs did not accept the legitimacy of the Jewish state. Initial moves toward acceptance of Israel began in 1977 with President Anwar el-Sadat's visit to Jerusalem and subsequent negotiations between Israel and Egypt.*

ARABIA. The peninsula bordering on the Arabian Sea on the south, the Red Sea on the west, the Bay of Persia and Iraq* on the east. The Bible refers to the Arab crescent as the "land of the east," because it lies to the east of Palestine.* Its inhabitants are known as Arabs, and the language they speak is Arabic. The Arabic Crescent includes: Saudi Arabia, Yemen, Aden, Oman, and Kuwait. The area is estimated at about 1,160,073 square miles and the total population at about 21,000,000, composed chiefly of wandering tribes. Due to lack of rain, the land is dry and desolate.

In ancient days, before the time of Mohammed, many Jews lived in Arabia, where they enjoyed religious and economic freedom and made a significant contribution to life in that region. In the centuries preceding Mohammed the Arabian desert contained independent Jewish tribes. After Islam* conquered the lands of Arabia, attacks on Jews began. Saudi Arabia, where Islam's holy cities of Mecca and Medina are located, refuses entrance to Jews. In the other parts of the Crescent, too, religious and economic attacks were made upon Jews. Since the establishment of the Jewish state in 1948, almost all the Jews have migrated from Arabia. A small number have remained in Yemen, as well as in Aden, which was a British protectorate. The lands of Arabia opposed the establishment of the Jewish state and sent aid to Israel's enemies in their war against Israel. (**See also** ARAB INFLUENCE IN JEWISH HISTORY.)

ARAMAIC. A group of Semitic languages known as Chaldaic in their most ancient form. The earliest surviving form of Aramaic dates roughly from 900 B.C.E. The Assyro-Babylonian and Persian empires absorbed this language, and since Aramaic was closely related to Hebrew, it was picked up by the Jewish exiles in Babylonia* in the sixth century B.C.E. When they returned to Judea, the Jews brought the Aramaic tongue home with them. By 300 B.C.E. it was used in daily life, and many prayers were chanted in Aramaic. Aramaic was also the language of trade and diplomacy in the whole Middle East. Isolated

portions of the Bible (Dan. 2:46, Ezra 4:8—6:18, 7:12-26, and Jer. 10:11) are written in a West Aramaic dialect. This is also the language of the Palestinian Talmud* (except for the Mishnah,* which is in Hebrew) and of the Midrashim.* Aramaic is the language of the Babylonian Talmud and of an authorized translation of the Bible known as Targum Onkelos*—the Translation of Onkelos (second century C.E.). To this day, Aramaic is the language of parts of the Siddur* (prayer book), of the Kaddish* and of a section of the Passover Haggadah, beginning with the words "This is the bread of affliction." The **Had Gadya** ("One Little Goat"), the popular song sung toward the end of the Passover Seder, is also in Aramaic.

ARARAT. Mountain in northern Armenia, landing place of Noah's ark in the Biblical narrative (Gen. 8:4). Also a city planned on Grand Island, Niagara, N. Y., by M. M. Noah* in 1825.

ARBA KANFOT (Heb. "four corners"). A rectangular vestlet covering the chest and back, with ritual fringes (*tzitzit**) attached to its corners, in remembrance of the Biblical command that Jewish males wear a fringed garment (Num. 15:37-41). It is also called a *tallit katan* (little *tallit**).

ARCH OF TITUS. A triumphal arch overlooking the Roman Forum. It was built to celebrate the Roman victory over Judea after three years of bitter fighting, 67-70 C.E. On one of its inner panels the artist carved a scene from the triumphal procession of the victorious Roman legions. Soldiers crowned with laurel leaves are shown carrying the sacred objects they had plundered from the Temple* in Jerusalem* before destroying it. Their figures lean forward, straining against the weight of the golden table, the holy ark,* the seven-branched menorah, and the musical instruments of the Levites.* For centuries, the Jews in Rome would walk long distances to avoid passing this memorial.

Arch of Titus

ARCHAEOLOGY. Hardly any other field of knowledge has aroused greater curiosity or given more interesting returns than has archaeology (the scientific study of the material remains created by men of the past). Long before the time of the Greeks, who first coined this term, people had been digging up the past, unearthing hidden passages to burial chambers, and transmitting by word of mouth traditions regarding much earlier generations.

In the seventh century B.C.E., Assurbanipal of Assyria* was proud of his ability to decipher the writings on ancient clay tablets, and sent his scribes far and wide to collect copies of early records and documents for his wonderful library at Nineveh. Thus Nabonidus, who ruled Babylon in the sixth century B.C.E., made exploratory excavations in the age-old Ziggurat (temple tower) which loomed up at Ur (the birthplace of Abraham*). He read the foundation records of its ancient builders, and carefully carried out restorations, as told in his own inscriptions. The daughter of Nabonidus shared her father's interest, and maintained a small museum, in which objects of great importance were kept. Similarly, a royal commission was appointed by Rameses IX of Egypt to examine the physical condition of ancient tombs and pyramids. And this interest has remained unabated through the ages, down to the present day.

Modern archaeological research emerged a little more than 150 years ago, and has ingeniously called the ancient past back to life. Dead and long-forgotten tongues, buried for thousands of years in clay tablets, papyri, scrolls, and inscriptions, have now been deciphered and made to speak again. Whole cities and settlements have been found arranged one atop the other, forming artificial mounds (called **tel** in Hebrew). These mounds have been carefully excavated, sliced down like a layer-cake to reveal as many as seventeen different levels of culture. Objects of all types, secular and religious, have been found in the ruins of each layer. Even shards of pottery have been picked up and carefully restored. The different styles of shapes and decorations then provide clues for dating other objects found on the same levels. Charts of pottery vessels of almost every age and geographical area are now available and are as indispensable for the archaeologist as the stamp album for the stamp collector.

Archaeology uses both the strictest scientific methods and the latest equipment which modern science affords; electronics, aerial photography, Xrays, and radio carbon. Thus, for example, Xrays penetrate the wrappings of Egyptian mummies, locating the exact positions of jewelry and sometimes determining the cause of death. Radio-

Synagogue of Capernaum.   Courtesy Dr. Nelson Glueck.

carbon is used to determine the exact age of all organic matter.

The development of archaeology has been made possible by the teamwork of scholars and experts of many different nations and religious backgrounds. Each group, operating with its own motivation, has enabled us to see more vividly the world of the Bible* where the great prophets preached and from which sprang both Judaism and Christianity. On the other hand, the people of

A section of the mosaic floor design of the synagogue at Bet Alpha.   Courtesy Dr. Nelson Glueck.

Remains of Bet Shearim, seat of the Sanhedrin and the residence of Rabbi Judah the Prince (2nd century C.E.).

flowers, plants, and animals natural to that region.

In 1948, a young Israeli general, Yigael Yadin,* was able to surround an invading Egyptian army by following an old Roman road in the Negev known to him from his studies in Biblical archaeology. Nelson Glueck, a famous Jewish scholar, conducting a series of explorations in the Negev, has proven that hundreds of towns and settlements thrived in antiquity in an area which has for many centuries been the great wasteland of southern Palestine. He likewise unearthed King Solomon's* copper mines and refineries near Eilat,* the port at the northern tip of the Red Sea. There he found that the ancient Israelites had anticipated some of our most modern methods for refining metals.

the State of Israel* have learned that study of the Bible and of Biblical archaeology can provide them with new and important knowledge of the land which they are now reclaiming and on which they plan to build an even greater future.

Every boy and girl in modern Israel is an amateur archaeologist. Knowing the Hebrew Bible almost by heart, and equipped with maps and archaeological guide-books, children hike the length and breadth of their historic land, identifying ancient place names and ruins, and recognizing the

Marble bust found in Caesarea.

Daring military archaeologists have reopened the ancient fortress of Masada,* high in the rocks of the wilderness of Judah. This legendary stronghold—famed for the last stand of the Zealots in the desperate war against the Romans in 70 C.E. — could be seen only by aerial photography until recently. Now the labyrinth of underground passages has been laid bare, revealing implements and vessels of all types, and with interesting inscription, or **graffiti**, on the walls. Masada has become one of the great national shrines of the State of Israel.

In 1965 Yigael Yadin reported the discovery of part of the Hebrew original of the Apocryphal Book of Jubilees in Masada.

At Wadi Muraba'at near the Dead Sea,* several stratified grottoes were found to contain, amidst a mass of other relics, some coins and a number of dated personal documents (second century C.E.).

Ornament in form of man bearing candelabrum upon head at the catacombs of Bet Shearim.

Written on papyrus and crude leather, in Hebrew, Aramaic, and Greek, these documents include a letter by Bar Kokhba,* the leader of the last Jewish revolt against the Romans in 132-35 C.E. In this letter bearing the signature of Simeon ben Koseba, his authentic name, the rugged Jewish general warns his chief of staff, Joshua ben Galgola, that if the latter will not follow instructions regarding the prisoners of war and the requisitioning of private property, Bar Kokhba will fetter his legs with chains, as he has previously done to another disobedient subordinate. In 1959 an Israeli archaeological expedition assisted by army helicopters uncovered another Bar Koseba letter in a cave at Nahal Heber, in the Judean Desert.

Materially, however, Israel was always a poor nation as compared with other civilizations of the ancient world. We do not uncover here such spectacular archaeological remains as the ruins of Babylon, the Pyramids of Egypt,* or even the obelisk of Thutmose III, which can now be viewed in New York City. The ancient Israelites were a sturdy, freedom-loving people, who did not permit themselves to be forced into the slave labor which accounts for the massive structures of Babylon and Egypt. But the archaeological findings in both Palestine proper and neighboring areas throw light on perhaps the greatest and most enduring historical possession of any people, the living monument of the people in Israel, the Hebrew Bible. After the Six-Day War,* extensive excavations were begun in many parts of the country, especially in the vicinity of the Western Wall and the Old City of Jerusalem. (**See also** DEAD SEA SCROLLS.)   S.I.

ARGENTINA. Republic in southeastern South America. The first Jews arrived with early Spanish settlers in the sixteenth century. They were Marranos,* forced converts who practiced their religion in secret. By the time of Argentina's liberation from Spain in the early nineteenth century, this community had vanished. The earliest modern community was set up in 1868, but regular immigration did not begin until 1891. In that year Baron Maurice de Hirsch* founded the Jewish Colonization Association (I.C.A.)* to encourage the settlement of Jews upon the land. Swelled by wave on wave of immigrants, the community grew from 1,000 in 1890 to less than 250,000 in 1984. This represents more than half of Latin-American Jewry.

Most of Argentina's Jews live in Buenos Aires and other urban centers. About half are engaged in trade, with businesses ranging from tiny shops to huge commercial establishments. A large percentage of the remainder are workers in the leather, furniture, and garment industries. Many have entered the professions. Jews have played an especially important role in the economic life of the country. Among the ideas introduced by Jewish merchants are installment and direct sales, and the organization of cooperatives for both buying and selling. Within the Jewish community there are many cooperative banks, as well as cooperative business undertakings.

Until recently, agriculture played an important part in the life of Argentinian Jewry. The first independent Jewish farm settlement was founded in 1899 by refugees from Russia. Other settlements were established and aided by the Jewish Colonization Association (I.C.A.).* By 1940 there were 28,000 Jewish colonists on the pampas of Argentina, living in nineteen I.C.A. settlements, six non-I.C.A. settlements, and on private farms. This was one of the largest Jewish farm communities in the world. Owing to the decline of the farm economy under the dictatorship of Juan Peron, and to the tendency for children of settlers to move to the cities, the farm community has dwindled to less than 5,000.

Buenos Aires, the capital of the country, and home of most of its Jews, is one of the world's leading centers of Yiddish culture. With two Yiddish daily newspapers, three weeklies, and numerous other periodicals, it is the greatest center of Yiddish publishing today. Hundreds of Yiddish writers, artists, musicians, and scholars live in the city. To educate the young, the community maintains about seventy Jewish schools. Buenos Aires has an active Jewish theatre as well.

The capital is also distinguished by the strength of its communal organization. The Argentine-Jewish Community (**Kehilla**) of Buenos Aires is the only organization of its type in the world. With a membership of about 50,000 families, it handles all aspects of communal life for the Jews of East European origins — cultural, educational, social, and religious. It also maintains ties with the local non-Jewish communities, as well as with Jewish communities abroad. Two other organizations handle the affairs of the German and the Sephardic* Jews, who tend not to merge with the other communities. On the national level, the Delegation of Argentine-Jewish Associations (D.A.I.A.) represents all local organizations on the national and international scenes.

Zionism* is an especially powerful force in Argentina. Most of the country's Jews are either refugees or the children of refugees, and have been particularly concerned with assuring a homeland for Jews wherever they may be. Considerable sums are sent to Israel* each year, and many

"Ark of the Covenant" by Gustave Dore.

The artist depicts the return of the Ark by the Philistines who had captured it in a battle with Israel. "And they put the ark of the Lord upon the cart ... And the kine took the straight way by the way to Beth-shemesh; they went along the highway, lowing as they went, and turned not aside to the right hand or to the left; and the lords of the Philistines went after them unto the border of Beth-shemesh. And they of Beth-shemesh were reaping their wheat harvest in the valley; and they lifted up their eyes to see it. And the cart came into the field of Joshua the Beth-shemite, and stood there, where there was a great stone; and they cleaved the wood of the cart, and offered up the kine for a burnt-offering unto the Lord." (First Samuel 6:11-15.)

Argentinian youths have settled there. However, in 1979, under the military dictatorship of Rafael Videla, there was a resurgence of anti-Semitism in Argentina and thousands of Jews (los disparados) were arrested. An investigation of anti-Semitism in Argentina was conducted by various Jewish organizations. The situation of Argentine Jewry has improved since 1983.

ARK. See SYNAGOGUE.

ARK OF THE COVENANT. The Ark contained, according to tradition, the tablets on which the Ten Commandments were inscribed. In ancient times, the Ark, carried by the priests, led the people to battle. The Bible tells us that, when the Ark moved forward, Moses cried: "Rise up, O Lord, and let thine enemies be scattered." According to one tradition, the Ark was hidden under the Temple at the time of the Babylonian exile. The second Book of Maccabees relates that the prophet Jeremiah hid the Ark on Mount Nebo, where it would remain till the coming of the Messiah. The Holy Ark found in every synagogue contains the Torah scrolls used in the services. The Ark traditionally faces east, toward Jerusalem.* It is opened on special occasions when certain solemn prayers are recited. Great attention has been given to the structural beauty of the Ark, and it is usually the most decorative part of the synagogue.

ARLOSOROFF, VICTOR HAIM (1899-1933)

Zionist political and labor leader. Born in the Ukraine, Arlosoroff spent his youth and received his education in Germany.* He settled in Palestine* in 1924 and plunged immediately into the Labor Zionist movement there. He became its political expert one year later, at the age of twenty-five. A brilliant young man, he was elected in 1931 to serve on the Executive of the Jewish Agency* for Palestine where he assumed charge of the Agency's political work. When Hitler came to power in 1933, Arlosoroff was sent to Germany* to negotiate with the Nazis. Since it was the Nazi policy to expel the Jews from Germany, Arlosoroff undertook to work out an agreement permitting as many Jews as possible to leave for Palestine, where the Jewish community was eager to receive them. After preliminary negotiations with Nazi leaders, Arlosoroff returned to Palestine, where he reported to the Jewish leaders and to the British officials. But before he could resume negotiations, Arlosoroff was shot by an unknown assassin while walking with his wife on a Tel Aviv* beach. The man convicted in the act was later released by a higher court, and it was never officially determined who fired the fatal shot on that June evening in 1933.   N.B.-A.

ARMY OF ISRAEL (Tz'va Haganah L'Yisrael).

The Army of Israel (Israel Defense Forces) grew out of the Haganah,* the Jewish self-defense organization formed during the period of the British Mandate to defend Jewish life and property in Palestine against Arab marauders, and of the Jewish Brigade, which fought alongside the Allied Forces during World War II. Since its creation in 1948, Israel's army has been called upon four times to fight for the survival of the country—in 1948, 1956, 1967, and again in the Yom Kippur War* of 1973. It must be constantly on the alert to defend Israel's borders against attacks from hostile neighbors. The Army of Israel has a nucleus of career soldiers, but it is basically a citizens' army. All men from the age of 18 to 29 and women from 18 to 26 are called for regular service of up to 30 months for men and 20 months for women. Married women, mothers and mothers-to-be are exempted from the draft. Young women from strictly Orthodox homes who have religious objections to serving in the army

Israeli tankists on maneuver.

must perform national services as teachers, nurses and so on. Israeli Arabs are exempt, but Druzes are being drafted at their own request, and a number of Muslims and Christians have volunteered. Following their term of national service, men and childless women are in the Reserves until the ages of 55 and 34, respectively, and men must report each year for various periods of training. Thanks to this arrangement, able-bodied citizens can be mobilized for combat within hours if a national emergency makes that necessary.

Organization. The Israel Defense Forces include all three branches of modern armed services—army, navy and air force, and ranks are uniform throughout. They are under the orders of one General Staff, headed by a chief of staff with the rank of lieutenant-general. The General Staff consists of the chiefs of the General Staff, Manpower, Logistics and Intelligence, the Commanders of the Navy and Air Force, and the officers who command the Northern, Central and Southern regional commands into which the country is divided.

Women in the Army. The women's force, known as **Hen** (abbreviation of **Hel Nashim**-Women's Force; the word **hen** also happens to be the Hebrew for "charm"), provides non-combatant personnel such as nurses, mechanics, communication workers and many other specialists, thus freeing the men for active combat duty.

Nahal (No'ar Halutzi Lohem). This pioneer youth group combines soldiering with pioneering. After a few months of intensive military training, Nahal boys and girls are assigned to agricultural settlements for about a year to gain practical experience in farming. A Nahal group joins a frontier settlement or sets up one of its own, often in areas still too dangerous or difficult for settlement by civilians.

Israeli girl soldier in a parachutists' training course.

Gadna (G'dude HaNo'ar). The "Youth Battalions" are pre-military organizations for boys and girls between the ages of 14 and 18, supervised jointly by the Ministry of Defense and the Ministry of Education and Culture. Training is along scout lines and there are also naval and air sections. Stress is placed on pioneering and practical training in agriculture. Many developing countries, especially in Africa and South America, have formed youth movements modeled on **Nahal** and **Gadna.**

The Role of the Army in Education and Citizenship. In addition to service Israel's defense needs, the Army helps weld the many different elements of the country's population into a unified whole. Soldiers are taught the Hebrew language, Jewish history, and the geography of the country. In this manner the Army has helped new immigrants from many countries to become integrated into Israeli life. No soldier leaves the army without getting a basic education. Soldiers are also trained in trades of their choice so that they return to civilian life better prepared for the productive work that is so necessary for the continued growth and welfare of the country.

Israeli soldier in the Sinai desert during the Morning Service.

ART, JEWS IN. Jews, who regard themselves as primarily the "People of the Book," are often unaware that there were Jewish artists and architects long before the era of Emancipation. While the Second Commandment forbids the creation of such forms as can be worshipped in the pagan manner, its ban does not apply to architecture and the so-called "applied arts." There were times when the danger of a lapse into heathenism was so great that zealous men, such as the prophets, condemned all display of art rather than risk any disintegration of the faith. But there were long periods of liberal interpretation of the Biblical prohibition during which the arts could flourish.

The Book of Exodus* describes in glowing terms the beauty of the Tabernacle* fashioned by Bezalel and Oholiab, but no part of the Tabernacle has survived. Excavations in Palestine* have, however, unearthed the remains of lavishly decorated palaces and other buildings made of carefully shaped stone in the era of the Kings. Nothing remains of the magnificent temple built by King Solomon* in Jerusalem*; of the equally sumptuous temple erected by King Herod* only a

few fragments have been found. We can, however, see for ourselves the beautiful mosaic floors in ancient synagogues built after the destruction of Herod's Temple, and the superb frescoes (wall paintings) in the ruins of a small synagogue at Dura Europos, on the Euphrates river (Syria).

In antiquity, Jews were famous for goldsmithery. In the Middle Ages, however, arts and crafts flourished among Jews in those regions where for long periods there was some relief from oppression (Spain,* Italy,* Greece,* Poland,* and some Moslem countries in Asia and Africa). Jews were held in high esteem as dyers, lacemakers, bookbinders, and cartographers. They minted coins for Christian and Mohammedan rulers. Towards the end of the Middle Ages a pope forbade Jewish smiths to manufacture Christian ceremonial objects, such as goblets and crucifixes, and also barred Jews from binding any Christian religious books.

From the Middle Ages to the era of Emancipation, which begins in the eighteenth century, Jewish art was mainly ritual art for synagogues and home. The Torah Scroll was written—and sometimes illuminated (ornamented)—by special **sofrim** (scribes). Some Hebrew Bibles had beautifully ornamented pages, others were provided with initials illuminated in gold, and with full-page miniatures showing Biblical figures—Adam,* David,* and other heroes. The Passover* Haggadah* lent itself to illustration more than any other book, as it was used not in the synagogue but at home, and the religious restrictions imposed on the artist were not so severe.

The Torah mantle, generally of silk or velvet, was often skillfully embroidered by pious women. But very little religious art older than about 350 years has come down to us. Among the exceptions are some Hanukkah* lamps of brass, from North Africa and Italy.* They are probably the work of Jews. As a rule, the Christian guilds of Europe had a monopoly only over the works in the precious metals, gold and silver. The superb ritual silver objects of the seventeenth and eighteenth centuries are the works of Gentiles. While the Jewish patron gave a general description to the Christian craftsman on the construction of a particular object, he did not mind if it was executed in the style of the period, whether Renaissance, Baroque, or Rococo.

In Eastern Europe (and in the Middle East), Jews fashioned their own ceremonial objects. In seventeenth and eighteenth century Poland, Jewish carpenters and masons built synagogues; many were of wood, and, with their curved roofs, slightly resembled Chinese pagodas; others were of

The Burning Bush by Herbert Ferber—1951.

Courtesy Congregation B'nai Israel, Milburn, New Jersey.

"Balancing"—a sculpture in wood by Chaim Gross.

Dr. Chaim Gamzu, Curator of the Tel Aviv Museum, explaining a painting by Marc Chagall. Among his listeners are (left to right) Abba Eban, Zalman Shazar, Golda Meir and Mordechai Namir.

stone and some resembled fortresses. (Jews would take refuge in them in times of pogroms.) Many of these Polish synagogues were lavishly decorated on the inside with multi-colored murals in which the Jewish folk-artist gave free reign to his imagination. All these disappeared in the course of the First and Second World Wars.

Before the era of Emancipation, only a very few Jews, and those who were converted to Christianity, became painters and sculptors. This situation changed in the nineteenth century, when art schools and academies flung open their doors to anyone willing to study. The exception was Russia; hence many young Jews emigrated to enroll in the schools of Central or Western Europe, and in especially those of Paris. Some of these artists cut themselves off from their spiritual links with Judaism, making art their religion. Jews were leaders in the fight against the shopworn romantic and historical schools, guiding the rebellion in behalf of realism, open-air painting, and the understanding of the social importance of art.

These artists made portraits, painted landscapes, or created shapes in wood, metal or stone like their Gentile colleagues. Until about 1900, it was rather rare to see Jewish artists occupied with themes related to Judaism or specifically Jewish affairs. There were a few, though, who tried to translate the messages of the Jewish faith, the spirit of the holidays, the great historical traditions, into pictorial terms. After 1900, their number increased rapidly, for many of the outstanding Jewish artists of modern times have come from small Eastern European ghettoes, from Orthodox families where they received a solid grounding in the essentials of Judaism. A substantial École Juive (Jewish School) of painters and sculptors developed in Paris; New York* was another art center where gifted Jews could develop their talent freely. The tragic events of the Second World War, with the loss of six million Jewish lives, and the establishment of a Jewish state in 1948 brought many artists to the discovery, or rediscovery, of their Jewish identities.

Palestine had no art, in the modern sense of the

term, before 1906, the year when the sculptor Boris Schatz* settled in Jerusalem to establish there the Bezalel School of Arts and Crafts. In the succeeding half century Jewish Palestine, now Israel, became the center and reservoir of what can truly be called Jewish art. After 1900 Jewish artists, educators, and rabbis had cooperated to create Jewish museums all over Europe and North America; but some of the outstanding treasures were destroyed by the Nazis. Hence, it is to the relative wealth of the museums in Jerusalem, Tel Aviv,* and Haifa,* that the student of Jewish art, past and present, must turn. The Israel organization of painters and sculptors has grown to number several hundred members, including a large percentage of women. Beside painting and sculpture, Israeli artists have directed their skills towards the making of stage settings for the Hebrew theaters, the illustration of books, the designing of posters and stamps. They also fashion ritual objects in keeping with the taste of our time. The refugees from Moslem lands contribute much-needed skill in the weaving of delicate textiles and the production of fine jewelry.

Art is an international language. Unlike literature, it can be understood by everyone. Jewish art is based on the art of all other nations. But it has developed a distinctive flavor of its own, due to the artists' spiritual inheritance, and the course taken by Jewish history. It may be too early to speak of a clearly recognizable Israeli art; however, soil, climate, and living conditions will eventually influence all art created in Israel.

Among the most spectacular creations of Jewish talent are the synagogues. Until recently, architects designed synagogues in imitation of churches of different styles. There is now a new trend to develop a specific synagogue architecture, stressing both modernity and Jewish tradition, in facade as well as interior decoration. America, with the richest and largest Jewish community, has taken the lead in this trend. However, some original and admirable architectural contributions have been made in England,* Canada,* France,* and, of course, the new State of Israel.

ASARAH B'TEVET. See FAST DAYS.

ASCALON. See ASHKELON.

ASCETICISM. A regimen of self-denial to help the individual avoid temptations and distractions that hinder his spiritual development. The Nazirites* and Rechabites of the Bible, who abstained from wine, were ancient examples of asceticism. Rechabites also refrained from living in houses,

but dwelt in tents instead. In the time of the Second Temple there was an ascetic sect called the Essenes.* Fasting frequently or eating very little, wearing rough clothing, avoiding company, doing without money—these were the practices among the ascetics. The growing influence of the Zohar* and the Kabbalah* in the Middle Ages and afterwards, plus the increasingly difficult conditions of Jewish life, furthered asceticism. A practice favored by many ascetics was "putting oneself in exile." The ascetic would leave home and family for a time, in order to appreciate more fully the exile of all Jewry. Jewish authorities such as Maimonides* allowed limited asceticism for short periods, but opposed it as a way of life. A familiar ascetic figure was the **matmid,** one who devoted his days and nights to Torah study and allowed no other interests to distract him. The Mussar movement, which began in Lithuania* about 1850, had ascetic leanings. But it placed more emphasis on examination of the conscience as a means of self-improvement, than on self-inflicted suffering.

ASCH, SHOLOM (1880-1957). Outstanding Yiddish novelist and dramatist, he spent his early youth in the small town of Kutno, Poland, where he received a traditional education. At the turn of the century he dedicated himself to literary work in Yiddish and Hebrew. One of his idyllic novels of the Jewish small town, **Dos Shtetel,** attracted great attention. His later plays and novels revealed him as a keen observer and vivid portrayer of Jewish life the world over. Almost all of his important works have been translated into English and other languages: **Motke the Thief, The Three Cities, Salvation, Uncle Moses, The Song of the Valley,** and many other contemporary and historical novels and stories.

Sholom Asch

Courtesy YIVO, New York City.

Asch has treated a wide range of subjects, including the saga of Jewish struggles and achievements in Europe, America, and Palestine. He has caught the spirit of the revolutionary changes of our times; in his historical novels he has glorified Jewish martyrdom and piety. Some of his works based on New Testament figures, such as **The Nazarene**, are considered highly controversial. Two of his last novels portray the Biblical figures of Moses and Isaiah. Asch lived for many years in the United States, settled in Israel, 1956, and died while visiting London, October 1957.

ASHDOD. 4,000-year-old port on coast of Israel. Neglected over the centuries, it is now being developed into a deep sea port which, upon completion, will be the largest in Israel. The town, now numbering about 68,000, is rapidly expanding through the growth of such industries as an electric power plant, rayon factory, assembly plant for heavy vehicles, etc.

Emblem of the tribe of Asher

ASHER (Hebrew, meaning "happy or blessed"). Eighth son of Jacob.* The tribe of Asher was allotted territory from the Carmel and the lower Kishon plain as far west as the Phoenician capital of Sidon. Asher never captured Acco and Sidon from the Phoenicians, but settled largely in the Plain of Jezreel. Isaiah called their territory **Galil ha-Goyim**—"the district inhabited by many nations"; hence, this area came to be called Galilee.

ASHKELON. Ancient Mediterranean port, one of the Five Towns of the Philistines. A modern Israeli city and resort area numbering about 54,100 residents currently, it has been developed with the aid of the South African Zionist Federation.

ASHKENAZIM (Hebrew, meaning "Germans"). The name applied to the Jews of Germany* and Northern France* from the tenth century on. In the middle of the sixteenth century, the term **Ashkenazim** came to include the Jews of Eastern Europe as well. The Ashkenazim have developed a set of distinctive customs and rituals, different from those of the Sephardim,* the Jews from Spain, Portugal, the Mediterranean countries and North Africa.

ASSIMILATION. Throughout Jewish history, Jews have tended to "assimilate," or to adopt the language, manners, and customs of their neighbors, wherever they lived. At the same time, they continued to live a full Jewish life, producing great Jewish individuals and uniquely Jewish

books. Individual Jews have left the Jewish community for other groups, but the bulk of the Jewish people has remained loyal.

There were periods in Jewish history when the threat of death or exile brought the conversion of large numbers of Jews. The Marranos,* or secret Jews of Spain* and Portugal,* are examples of such forced assimilation. Under the pressure of persecution, particularly by the Inquisition,* many Jews outwardly became converts to Christianity while secretly continuing observances of their faith. This was a very dangerous practice, because the Marranos were spied upon and hunted down by the Inquisition. A few generations later, as the secret observances of Judaism dwindled or were abandoned altogether, the children of the Marranos lost all memory of their Jewish ancestry and merged with the rest of the Catholic population.

In modern times assimilation has had a more voluntary character. It first appeared on a considerable scale when the Jews of Europe began to emerge from the ghettos at the end of the eighteenth century. Drawn by the culture and science of Europe from which they had been shut off for several centuries, they were attracted by the ideals of the French revolution—liberty, equality, and the brotherhood of all mankind. The eighteenth and nineteenth centuries saw the emergence of the Jewish Enlightenment* movement, which had as its practical aim the achievement of equality or emancipation for the Jews. In its early phases, this movement found almost no price too high to pay for equality—not even the loss of Jewish identity. During the French Revolution, the relatively few Jewish leaders who spoke for French Jewry agreed on the whole with the French liberals and the ultimate aim for Jews was to disappear completely as a national group. When Napoleon convoked his Assembly of Jewish Notables or French Sanhedrin, these Jewish leaders assured the emperor that first and last they were Frenchmen first and Jews only thereafter.

In Germany,* the Enlightenment movement opened with Moses Medelssohn's* translation of the Bible* into German. This translation introduced its Jewish readers to the German language, which became a tool for acquiring modern culture. The generation that followed Moses Mendelssohn used this culture to escape from the ghetto; in their headlong rush, large numbers were lost to Judaism altogether. Having adopted the German culture and way of life, they expected to be accepted into the "brotherhood of man." Instead, they discovered that full citizenship, and social and economic advancement were possible for Jews only after baptism—the "ticket of admission to European civilization." Many took this step. Among those who explored this possibility was David Friedlaender of Berlin. He addressed an anonymous letter to Protestant clergymen, writing not only for himself but for a group of equally anonymous heads of Jewish families. These men were willing, the letter stated, to accept baptism, if it were understood that they were rationalists for whom it was a mere formality. Would the Church be willing to accept them on this condition? Naturally, the Church was not willing, and David Friedlaender's letter created an unhappy stir.

Yet Friedlaender's influence reached into Poland* and Russia.* The early Jewish Enlightenment movement in Poland and Russia had assimilationist tendencies and leaders, some of whom called themselves "Members of the Old Testament Persuasion in the Kingdom of Poland." In 1825, a rabbinical seminary that aimed at the Polonization of the Jews in Poland was actually opened in Warsaw. This seminary had the blessings of the Polish government; its purpose becomes clear when one considers that the department of Hebrew and Bible was headed by Abraham Buchner, author of a pamphlet on "The Worthlessness of the Talmud." In Russia, The Society for the Diffusion of Enlightenment was founded in 1867 in St. Petersburg. The aim of this society was most clearly expressed by its Odessa branch as "the enlightenment of the Jews through the Russian language and in the Russian spirirt."

But reaction in Germany, and persecutions and pogroms in Russia, soon disillusioned the "enlighteners." Eventually, the Jews of Western Europe were granted civic rights and swiftly transformed themselves into educated Europeans. It was no longer necessary to "assimilate" through conversion. Cultural identification with the surrounding majority was natural, particularly under American and similar forms of democracy. But the fear of being different, and the dread of anti-Semitism,* have remained as a cause of voluntary assimilation by individuals. Many Jews, ignorant of Jewish tradition and values, though remaining within the Jewish group, suffer from a lack of identification with their own people and history. The modern Jewish community has long been aware of this problem. Various ways for modern Jews to resist assimilation and identify with some element of Judaism have been advocated: religion, secular nationalism, Zionism,* and the idea of Jewish peoplehood.

ASSYRIA. The Asshur of the Bible. The North Mesopotamian empire of the city of Asshur stretched along the fertile plain on the upper Tigris River and included the towns of Kalchu and Nineveh. Assyria became a great empire after 1300 B.C.E. when it extended southward and ruled Babylon for a short period. Its drive westward continued for the next eight centuries until it controlled the whole Mediterranean coast and Egypt.* The first direct conflict between Israel and Assyria came about 854 B.C.E., when King Ahab* together with the ruler of Damascus fought King Shalmaneser III of Assyria at Karkar. Among the great rulers of this empire who figure disastrously during the next two and a half centuries in the history of Israel and Judah are Shalmaneser V, Sargon II, and Sennacherib, Esarhaddon, and Assurbanipal. King Sargon defeated Israel, destroyed its capital, Samaria, and deported the flower of Israel's population to Mesopotamia and Media. The history of Assyria as an independent empire came to an end when the Babylonians and the Medes took Asshur (616 B.C.E.) and Nineveh (612 B.C.E) and destroyed them.

ASTRONOMY. The Bible* contains a number of references to the heavenly bodies, their motions and some description of their appearance. God told Abraham* to look toward the heavens and count the stars "if thou be able to count them...So shall thy seed be." Eclipses of the sun are described in the books of Amos* and Joel.* Some of the planets and constellations are mentioned in the Bible by name.

In Talmudic times, knowledge of astronomy was important in determining the Jewish calendar.* The Jewish scholars had some knowledge of the solar system. Mention is made of the Milky Way and the comets. Rabbi Joshua was familiar with a star that appears once in seventy years—believed to be Halley's Comet. The Amora Rabbi Samuel was deeply interested in astronomy, and declared that the heavenly paths were as familiar to him as the streets of Nehardea, his home town.

In the Middle Ages the science of astronomy was one of the favorite subjects of Jewish scholars. They translated the works of Greek astronomers, especially Ptolemy's **Amalgest,** and drew up astronomical tables. The physician, Sabbatai Donnolo of the tenth century, the poet Abraham Ibn Ezra,* the great Talmudist and philosopher Maimonides,* the commentator and philosopher, Levi ben Gershom, were some of the outstanding Jewish scholars who took an interest in astronomy in the fifteenth century. The cartographer Abraham Zacuto's* astronomical charts were used by Columbus* and played their part in the discovery of America.

ATHENS. The capital of Greece had Jewish residents by the first century, C. E. Even before this time the Athenians had voted a gold crown to the high priest Hyrcanus, and later to the Herodian kings and to Princess Berenice, in gratitude for the kindly treatment of Athenians in Judea. There were many Athenian proselytes and semi-proselytes. The Talmud* has a number of stories about "the wise men of Athens." In Byzantine and Turkish times Athens decayed, and few Jews lived there. The first king of Greece after its liberation in 1830 was a German, and German Jews followed him to Athens. Sephardim* from Greece and Syria, as well as Russian Jews after World War I, increased the Jewish community. During the persecution in World War II, many Athenian Gentiles hid Jews from the Germans. After the war, survivors and remnants from other Greek Jewish communities moved to Athens. In 1984, approximately 3,000 Jews, about half of Greek Jewry, lived there.

ATONEMENT, DAY OF. See YOM KIPPUR.

AUSCHWITZ. A town in southwestern Poland, where the Germans in World War II maintained the most gruesome of all the concentration camps, in which some 4,000,000 inmates, mostly Jews, were exterminated by gas, phenol injections, shooting, hanging, hunger, and disease. **(See also** JEWRY, ANNIHILATION OF EUROPEAN.)

AUSTRALIA. Organized Jewish life in Australia began in 1828, when the Jews of Sydney formed a congregation, holding formal services in a rented building. At that time, the Jewish population of Australia was about 300. As the colonization and settlement of Australia continued, Jewish settlement proceeded apace, and soon there were organized congregations in the principal cities of Melbourne, Brisbane, Adelaide, and Perth, in western Australia. Most of the early Jewish immigrants came directly from England.* Jewish emigration to Australia was spurred by the activities of the Montefiore, Levi, and Lazarus families, influential British Jews active in the economic development of the British dominion. Later, Australia provided haven for many refugees fleeing Nazi tyranny, absorbing more Jewish immigrants in proportion to its pre-1938 Jewish population than any country except Israel. The peak of Jewish immigration was reached in 1954; it has been declining since. In 1984 there were about 75,000 Jews in Australia, most of whom lived in the six major cities, with 90 per cent concentrated in Sydney and Melbourne. The Executive Council of Australian Jewry, organized in 1944, represents the entire Jewish community of Australia, serving as its spokesman in matters of civil rights, welfare, and community status. Recent years have seen a reawakening of religious life, as well as increased interest in Jewsh education. The Zionist movement is active and well organized, with close links between the various Zionish councils and the local education boards of the Jewish schools. A number of Jews have played an active part in Australian life, including Sir Isaac Isaacs, the first Australian-born Governor General, and Sir John Monash, who commanded the Australian Expeditionary Force in World War I. Three Jewish weeklies in English and one in Yiddish are published in Australia, in addition to numerous monthlies and organizational publications.

AUSTRIA. Jews in Austria constituted one of the important communitites in Europe, with traces going back to the ninth century. Their history is one of a series of immigrations and expulsions, of a constant strugle for existence. In 1421 about 210 Jews were burned to death by the order of the Vienna Edict, while the rest were driven out. Gradually, they returned, but in 1670 there was another expulsion. At that time, a number of individual Jews were permitted to return to Austria on condition that they would not form any congregation. Among these "privileged Jews" was Samson Wertheimer, rabbi and banker to the court. In 1782 Emperor Joseph II issued his Edict of Toleration, which revoked many anti-Jewish regulations, but was opposed by Orthodox Jewry because of its interference in religious and cultural affairs, and its hidden aim of compulsory assimilation.

Following their participation in the 1848 revolutions, the Jews enjoyed a short-lived period of liberty. It was not, however, until 1867 that they attained equal political rights, which they enjoyed until the Germans occupied Austria in 1938.

Austrian Jews contributed greatly to the development of economics, science, art, literature, and the press of their country. In purely Jewish matters, they were influenced by eminent scholars whose books were accepted by Jewry throughout the world. Vienna had the largest Jewish community in Austria. Others were located in Graz, Salzburg, Innsbruck, Wiener-Neustadt and the Burgenland area.

The close of the nineteenth century witnessed the growth of the Zionist movement, due in no small measure to the fact that Theodor Herzl* made his home in Vienna and served as literary editor and correspondent for the influential newspaper **Die Neue Freie Presse.** The First World

War brought to Austria many Jews from Galicia and Hungary*; many of them remained after the war and exercised a strong influence on Jewish life in Austria. The *Anschluss* with Germany* marked the beginning of the end for Austrian Jewry in March 1938. At that time, when Austria enthusiastically welcomed the German occupation, the Jewish population there numbered 185,246. About 178,000 Jews lived in Vienna. By the end of World War II only 7,000 Jews remained: some 128,000 had fled the country, and about 50,000 were annihilated by the Austrians and Germans, many of them in the gas chambers of Auschwitz.

Currently (1984) there are about 13,000 Jews in Austria, of whom more than 9,000 live in Vienna and are registered with the Vienna Kultusgemeinde, central agency of the Austrian Jewish community. Postwar efforts of the community centered around negotiations for restitution and compensation of losses suffered under the Nazis. The Austrian Jewish community has had to contend with resurgent anti-Semitism.* Provisions for Jewish education have been lagging because of the dispersal of the children and their small numbers. Aided by the American Jewish Joint Distribution Committee,* which is extremely active in relief and welfare work in Austria, the Kultusgemeinde maintains a Hebrew school, several Talmud Torahs, and a credit cooperative.

AUTO-DA-FÉ. (Portuguese, "act of faith") (c. 1481-1810.) A tragic and justly infamous ceremony, the climax of a heresy-hunting investigation by the Inquisition in Spain and Portugal. Those condemned as heretics were led to public penance or execution, the latter usually by burning at the stake.

The auto-da-fé took the form of a procession through the main streets of the city to the public square, usually in front of a church. It was led by hooded monks who were followed by the hapless prisoners. Those condemned to death carried lit candles, wore a pointed cap on their heads and were clad in a tunic called the "san benito" upon which the "crimes" of the victims were inscribed and various diabolic symbols were painted. Priests, monks, and soldiers brought up the rear of the procession.

AVERAH. A trespass, or sinful act; the opposite of **mitzvah.*** The term does not include sin in general, but was applied to sins committed against one's fellow or against God. Judaism believes that man is not born with original sin, but rather, possesses the power of free will. "I have set before you life and death...therefore choose life..." (Deut: 30:19). Man, however, is weak, and may tend to sin; God, therefore, provides an opportunity for him to repent, and if he does so sincerely, he is forgiven. Although man may seek forgiveness at any time, it is on **Yom Kippur*** that Israel as a whole prays to God to pardon its transgressions.

AVOT. See ETHICS OF THE FATHERS.

AYIN. Sixteenth letter of the Hebrew alphabet, numerically, seventy.

AZULAI, CHAIM JOSEPH DAVID (1724-1805). Scholar and author. Azulai, known by his initials as Hida, travelled extensively all over Europe. He was sent by the Jewish community in Jerusalem* to gather funds for the poor scholars in the Holy Land. Azulai had received a thorough training in Talmud* and Kabbalah* and was endowed with a keen historical sense. He utilized his travels to visit famous libraries and to gather valuable information for his most important work, **Shem Ha-Gedolim,** in which he listed 1,500 scholars and authors and over 2,000 books written from Talmudic times to his own day.

A 15th century woodcut portraying an auto-da-fé.

BAAL. ("Ruler, possessor.") Foremost among Canaanitish gods, Baal was not the name of one particular god, but the presiding deity of a given locality. Baal, the god of rain and fertility, was killed each year by the hosts of Mot, the god of drought and death. Rain and growth ceased till the fall, when Baal came to life, bringing back the rains. In the spring, Baal married Anath, the goddess of fertility and war, returning fruitfulness to the land and its inhabitants. The Canaanites worshipped Baal with idolatry and fertility rites. The Bible records how judges and prophets fought Baal worship among the people of Israel. (See ELIJAH.)

BAAL SHEM TOV, ISRAEL BEN ELIEZER (c. 1700-1760). Founder of Hasidism.* The life of the pious "Baal Shem" (literally, "master of the name," or "miracle worker") has been the subject of so many legends and stories that it is often difficult to separate fact from fiction in it. He himself left no written works, but his sayings were collected by disciples, especially by Rabbi Baer of Mezhirich. It is known that Israel was orphaned at an early age, and raised by the community. Although deeply religious, he was not an eager student, devoting himself rather to solitary prayer and meditation. In his early life his occupations were varied; he was an assistant teacher in charge of Heder* children, a synagogue helper, a ritual slaughterer, and even a charcoal burner.

Upon his marriage to Anna Kuty, sister of the well-known scholar, Rabbi Gershon Kutower, the Baal Shem moved to an isolated town in the Carpathian mountains. There he spent long hours in communication with God and nature. Rabbi Gershon had given the couple a horse and wagon. The Baal Shem and his wife made a bare livelihood by selling one wagonload of lime to the villagers every week. It is told that on his wedding day, Israel revealed to his bride that he was a Divinely chosen Tzaddik ("righteous man") but swore her to secrecy until the time should be ripe for him to reveal himself in public. He lived in obscurity until he was thirty-six years old. Then he began to travel through towns and villages, healing the sick and performing miracles.

Israel's personality, his piety and imaginative method of expression gradually brought him fame. He became known as a man of deep religious feeling and enthusiasm, with a gift for communicating this emotion to the simplest and most ignorant person. His consideration and love for lowly people is illustrated by his comment to a disciple, "The lowliest person you can think of is dearer to me than your only son is to you." His followers' awe of him appears in a legend: Rabbi Dov Baer of Mezhirich asked Heaven to show him a man who was completely holy. He was shown a vision of the Baal Shem Tov, and it was all fire, with no shred of matter in it; it was nothing but flame.

The Baal Shem was possessed by a great longing to go to the Holy Land, but his longing was never satisfied. In 1740 he settled in Podolia, a province in the Ukraine, where many scholars, rabbis, as well as simple people, gathered around him and formed the nucleus of the Hasidic movement. Israel stressed devotion to God and dedicated prayer. He taught that joyful and enthusiastic worship, even that of an ignorant man, find more favor in the eyes of the Maker than cold scholarship and dry knowledge of the Law. These teachings had great popular appeal and the new movement of Hasidism which the Baal Shem had initiated spread like wildfire through East European Jewry.

H.L.

BABYLONIA. Ancient Asiatic land lying between the Tigris and Euphrates Rivers, now southern Iraq, the Bible* refers to this region as the land of Shinar. It is the scene of the Biblical story of the tower of Babel, built by men who aspired to reach the heavens. God's intervention caused confusion in language among the workers, who had been formerly united by one tongue. Therefore, that place was called Babel (Babylonia) from the Hebrew word **balol**, meaning "to confuse."

Babylonia was the cradle of ancient civilization and the seat of great empires. It occupies an important place in Jewish history. The capital, Ur, of the Sumerian Empire—one of the earliest in the region—was the birthplace of the patriarch Abraham.* Hammurabi, one of the most famous rulers of the region (2067-2025? B.C.E.), is known for his code of law, parts of which parallel the Biblical code. Hammurabi made Babylon the capital of his empire.

In the course of the eleventh century B.C.E. the powerful empire of Assyria* conquered all of Babylonia and destroyed the great city of Babylon. The Assyrian kings built their own capital, Nineveh. Three centuries later, the Assyrian Kings, Tiglath-Pileser IV and Sargon II, conquered the northern Kingdom of Israel, destroyed its capital, Samaria, and deported its inhabitants (the ten tribes of Israel).

A revival of Babylonian civilization was introduced by the Semitic Chaldeans (the Kasdim of the Bible). The Chaldean Empire reached its peak with King Nebuchadnezzar II, who captured Jerusalem in 597 B.C.E., destroyed it completely ten years later, and exiled all the Jews to Babylonia.

In Babylonia, the exiles of Judah probably joined the ten tribes of Israel, who had been deported by the Assyrian kings two centuries earlier. The exiles developed their own traditions and institutions. The Babylonian kings gave them wide autonomy in religious and spiritual matters, at the same time allowing them to engage freely in agriculture and trade.

After the conquest of Babylonia by Cyrus,* king of Persia (538 B.C.E.), the Jews were permitted to return to Zion. Many of them joyfully seized the opportunity to rebuild their homeland, but the majority of the exiles remained in their adopted land, Babylonia. During the succeeding centuries, under Persian rule, Babylonia became one of the greatest Jewish centers, second only to Palestine in importance and influence. Jewish communities sprang up in many parts of the land and kept close ties with the Jews in Palestine. Large numbers of Babylonian Jews made the pilgrimage to the Second Temple in Jerusalem. Many schools in Babylonia provided basic education in Jewish law. The more promising students went to Palestine to continue their studies, and later returned to spread Jewish learning throughout Babylonia.

In the year 312 B.C.E., shortly after the death of Alexander the Great,* who had conquered Babylonia, this flourishing country came under the rule of the Syrian king Seleucus Nicator. In 160 B.C.E. Babylonia was conquered by Mithridates I, king of Parthia. The Parthians, a people of Central Asia, granted the Jews equal rights and a full measure of freedom in religious matters. Babylonian Jewry was headed by an Exilarch,* a descendant of the House of David. The authority of the Exilarch was absolute and he was held in high estem by Babylonian Jewry. As the official head of his people, he made his appearance at the court of the king dressed in stately robes, riding a golden chariot, and preceded by horsemen who announced his arrival. The Exilarch had wide civil and religious powers. He collected taxes for the king's treasury from the Jewish population, and acted as the supreme judge of Babylonian Jewry. He appointed officials and judges who were responsible for maintaining law and order in the Jewish communities.

Babylonian Jewry actively supported their brothers in Palestine* in the struggle for liberation from Syrian rule during the time of the Hasmoneans. Later (69 C.E.), when th Jews in Palestine attempted to throw off the Roman yoke,

Bulls in relief on the ancient walls that surrounded the capital of Babylonia in the days of Nebuchadnezzar.

thousands of Babylonian Jews joined their ranks. They supplied the fighters with funds and amunition for their heroic resistance to the enemy. After the destruction of Jerusalem, when the centers of learning were re-established in other parts of Palestine, many Babylonian students came to the Palestinian academies to study the Law. Among the brilliant students were such great scholars as Abba Arikha, known as Rav, and Samuel Yarhinai. Upon their return to Babylonia, Rav founded the Academy of Sura and Samuel Yarhinai built up the academy of Nehardea. Other great schools of learning were established later in the Jewish centers of Pumbeditha and Mahuza. Rav and Samuel were the first Babylonian Amoraim.*

With the fall of the Parthian Empire (226 C.E.) and the rise of the new Persian rule, the Jews of Babylonia suffered great hardships. Their devotion to the study of the Law, however, did not diminish. During the period extending from the third to the sixth century, the Babylonian scholars produced the great work known as the Babylonian Talmud.*

At the beginning of the fifth century, the Byzantine empire abolished the last remnant of Jewish religious freedom in Palestine. Babylonia then became the spiritual center of all Jewry, cementing Jewish unity through intensive scholarly activity. This activity continued despite frequent persecution by the Persian rulers. At the end of the fifth century, when Persian priests were making life intolerable for Jews, a young Exilarch. Mar Zutra II, rebelled against Persian rule and established a small, independent Jewish state at Mahuza. For seven years Mar Zutra succeeded in fighting off the enemy, until he was overpowered by the superior Persian forces. Mar Zutra was captured and publicly executed.

A revival of Jewish life and learning took place

in Babylonia after the Muslim conquest of the land in the seventh century. The office of the Exilarch was restored to its full power and glory. A new period of Jewish scholarship, the period of the Geonim (see GAON), set in and lasted for four hundred years. The academies of Sura and Pumbeditha flourished again in the days of the Amoraim and their learned successors, the Saboraim. The Geonim stood at the head of the academies. Two months of the year, called the Kalla months, were devoted to popular study. Jews from all walks of life flocked to the **yeshivot** during these two months to study the Law. Thus the knowledge of the Talmud became widespread and was firmly entrenched in Jewish life.

TALMUDIC CENTERS IN BABYLONIA

Jews from all parts of the world, and especially Jews from North Africa, gave financial support to the Babylonian academies. Whenever problems of law arose, they relied upon the decisions of the Babylonian Geonim. Though Palestinian scholarship experienced a similar revival under Muslim rule, it did not enjoy the prestige conferred on the Babylonian teachers. One of the greatest Babylonian Geonim was Saadiah* Gaon, who successfully combatted the Karaite* sect, which was a threat to traditional Judaism. After Saadiah's death, the Babylonian Jewish centers began to decline. Persecution and poverty, with a general weakening of the Muslim empire, forced the closing of the renowned academy of Sura in 948; after seven

hundred years of creative activity. The office of the Exilarch was abolished. Only the academy of Pumbeditha was still in existence. In its last days it was headed by two of the foremost scholars, Sherira* Gaon and his son, Hai* Gaon. By the middle of the eleventh century, Babylonian centers had dwindled considerably. Jewish life and scholarship now moved westward to Spain,* Italy,* and Germany.*

BADHAN. (From the Aramaic,* meaning "to cheer up," "to make laugh"). A professional merrymaker, a figure dating back to the Middle Ages, whose duty it was to entertain the guests at weddings. A **badhan** was often a bit of a poet and made up and sang appropriate rhymes, on the spur of the moment, to suit the important persons he met at the weddings. One of the last **badhanim** to become well known as a popular poet was Eliakim Zunser (1836-1913). Many of Zunser's lyrics were very popular among the Jews of Eastern Europe.

BALFOUR DECLARATION. In the midst of World War I, Arthur James Balfour, British Foreign Secretary, wrote the following letter to Lord Lionel Walter Rothschild, of the Zionist Federation in England:

Foreign Office
November 2nd 1917

Dear Lord Rothschild,

I have much pleasure in conveying to you on behalf of His Majesty's Government the following declaration of sympathy with Jewish Zionist aspirations, which has been submitted to, and approved by, the Cabinet:

"His Majesty's Government view with favour the establishment in Palestine of a national home for the Jewish people, and will use their best endeavours to facilitate the achievement of this object, it being clearly understood that nothing shall be done which may prejudice the civil and religious rights of existing non-Jewish communities in Palestine or the rights and political status enjoyed by Jews in any other country."

I should be grateful if you would bring this Declaration to the knowledge of the Zionist Federation.

Yours sincerely,
(Signed) Arthur James Balfour

The three sentences of this document giving international recognition to Zionist aims were the result of three years of diplomatic negotiations reaching out from London to France,* Italy,* and the United States. The Balfour Declaration was issued with the support of the French government, and with the backing of Woodrow Wilson, President of the Untied States. Official approval came from France on February 14, 1918, from Italy on May 9, 1918, and from President Wilson in a letter to Stephen S. Wise* on August 31, 1918. The Congress of the United States voted in its favor, and President Harding approved the declaration on September 21, 1922. The Balfour declaration became the basis of the mandate for Palestine given to Britain by the League of Nations and affirmed on July 24, 1922. The news of the Balfour Declaration was received with waves of joy and spontaneous celebrations in all corners of the Jewish world, and November 2 is remembered in annual celebration as Balfour Day. (See also ZIONISM.) N.B-A.

BALTIMORE HEBREW COLLEGE AND TEACHERS TRAINING SCHOOL. Founded in 1919 in Baltimore, Maryland, the college was one of the first institutions in America to offer a full Hebrew teachers' training program. In addition to the Teachers Training School, the college conducts a four-year afternoon high-school program and adult education courses.

BAMIDBAR (Numbers). **See** BIBLE.

BAR GIORA, SIMON. One of the heroic leaders of the extremist party of Zealots who were most responsible for the Judean rebellion against Rome, 67-70 C.E. Simon Bar Giora was a man of great physical strength, boundless courage, and a thirst for power. During the siege of Jerusalem,* he fought ruthlessly not only against the Roman legions, but also against the moderate party in Jerusalem, until he was compelled by the commander of the garrison to flee the city. Bar Giora fortified himself in Masada,* mountain fortress on the western shore of the Dead Sea.* There he gathered a large army, and, with the help of the Edomites, moved into Jerusalem and massacred many of his Zealot opponents. The incessant fighting among the Zealots stopped only when Titus ringed Jerusalem in bitter siege, and Roman battering rams pounded against its walls. Then, Bar Giora fought the Romans with single-minded fury, and when the Temple was destroyed by Titus, he retreated to the Upper City. When that, too, was captured, Bar Giora hid in a cave and then tried to escape, but fell into the hands of the victorious Romans. On his return to Rome, Titus rode through its streets at the head of a triumphal procession. Behind his chariot, Bar Giora was forced to march in chains, together with the other Judean captives. Later, he was executed as one of the chiefs of the rebellion. M.Z.

Arthur James Balfour

BAR-ILAN (BERLIN), MEYER (1880-1949). World Mizrachi* leader. Born in Volozhin, Russia, Rabbi Bar-Ilan went to Berlin in 1910 where he served as general secretary of the world Mizrachi movement. In Berlin, too, he founded and edited the weekly **Ha-Ivri**. In 1913 he came to the United States, where he developed local Mizrachi branches into a national organization of which he was president from 1916 to 1926. In 1926 he settled in Palestine. Bar-Ilan was a man of tremendous energy, with an erudition and broad outlook that embraced all of Jewish life. In addition to playing a primary role in world Zionism* he edited Mizrachi's Hebrew daily **Ha-Tzofeh**, organized support for Israeli **Yeshivot** (Talmudic academies), and worked on the publication of a new edition of the Talmud.* When the First Knesset,* or parliament, convened, he was a leading representative of the religious bloc. On April 18, 1949, while pleading against the internationalization of Jerusalem, Bar-Ilan died. The World Mizrachi central building in Tel Aviv,* Bet Meir, the Berlin Forest, and the Mizrachi-sponsored Bar-Ilan University in Israel* all are named in his honor. His memoirs, written in Yiddish, **Fun Volozhin Bis Yerushalayim** ("From Volozhin to Jerusalem"), were first published in 1933.

Rabbi Meyer Bar-Ilan, left, and Israeli Chief Rabbis Herzog (center) and Uziel (right).

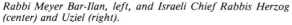

Campus of Bar-Illan University in Israel.

BAR-ILAN UNIVERSITY IN ISRAEL. Founded in 1955 as an "American University in Israel." It was chartered by the Regents of the State of New York. Bar-Ilan is the only American chartered university in Israel, with its educational and administrative operations conducted in the manner of American universities. The essence of Bar-Ilan—the quality of this university that sets it apart from all others—springs from the will of its founders to create on the holy soil of Israel a university joined to the traditional teachings of Judaism. Secular training in the arts and sciences is interwoven with religious orientation providing an environment in which the pursuit of new frontiers of knowledge is coupled with an understanding of the heritage of Judaism and a devotion to the well-being of humanity. From an initial class of 80 students, the university by 1984 and had grown to an enrollment of 12,000 men and women from Israel, the United States and about 35 other nations throughout the world. However, emphasis is on the quality of students and the University does not aspire to maximize the student body. In addition to baccalaureate programs, it now provides master's degrees in 21 disciplines and doctoral degrees in chemistry, English, general history, Hebrew literature, Hebrew and Semitic languages, Jewish history, Jewish philosophy, philosophy, physics, Talmud and world literature. Its Jacov Herzog School of Law, which was opened in 1970, is patterned after American law schools and seeks to integrate Jewish law into the analytic study of each area of the law. The university awards a number of maintenance and tuition scholarships.

BAR KOKHBA, SIMEON. Leader of the rebellion against the Romans (132-135 C.E.) His name ("son of a star") is believed to be derived from the Messianic interpretation of the prophecy, "There shall step forth a star out of Jacob." Bar Kokhba, who was also known as Simeon ben Koziba, won numerous enthusiastic followers who believed in his mission to free Palestine* from the Roman yoke. Among his supporters were famous scholars, particularly Rabbi Akiba* (who thought of him as the Messiah and changed his name from Ben Koziba to Bar Kokhba) and his host of disciples. At first Bar Kokhba and his heroic men fought guerilla-fashion against the powerful garrison in Palestine. His army grew steadily, attracting zealous fighters from all over Palestine and the Diaspora. According to legend, he tested the valor of his soldiers by requiring each to cut off one of his fingers. after the rabbis protested this needless mutilation, Bar Kokhba devised a less cruel test. Every prospective soldier was required to uproot a cedar tree while charging on horseback. Within a short time the army was strong enough to meet the Roman legions in open battle. In the two years that followed, the Jews captured ninety forts and a thousand cities and villages, including Jerusalem.

To commemorate these conquests Bar Kokhba issued coins, one side bearing his name, Simeon, and the other the legend "Liberation of Jerusalem." These successes greatly impressed the enslaved neighboring peoples. Many freedom-loving gentiles joined the Jewish army, to fight their common enemy side by side. The Roman emperor, Hadrian, fearing that the Jewish revolt would encourage a general uprising of subject countries, dispatched his best legions to quell the revolt. At the head of his legions he placed Julius Severus, the general who had distinguished himself in the campaign against Britain. Severus recaptured all the fortresses, including Jerusalem, forcing Bar Kokhba to concentrate on the mountain stronghold of Betar,* in the Judean hills.

The siege of Betar lasted a year. After a bitter struggle, the Roman legions entered the city on the ninth of AV, 135 C.E. Bar Kokhba and his men continued fighting to the end, dying with sword in hand. Legend relates that the city of Betar could have withstood a much longer siege, had it not been for hunger, thirst, and treachery from within. The number of Jewish dead reached half a million. Scores of Jews were sold as slaves. The rest hid in caves, or fled to neighboring countries. Jerusalem was renamed Aelia Capitolina, in honor of Hadrian. The subjection of Palestine was now complete, but the story of the Bar Kokhba revolt became a living symbol of Jewish desire for freedom and independence.   H.L.

BAR MITZVAH (Hebrew, meaning "son of the Commandment"). The Hebrew term refers to the boy who has reached the age of thirteen, and is expected to accept adult religious responsibilities. This "coming of age" is the occasion for a ritual in the synagogue, where on the first Sabbath of his fourteenth year, the boy is called for the first time to read from the Torah and the prophets. It is a joyous occasion, accompanied by gifts for the **bar mitzvah** boy from friends and family. Traditionally, the **bar mitzvah** boy delivers a learned speech. (Though the Bar Mitzvah is usually observed on the Sabbath, it may in fact take place any other day of the week (Monday, Thursday, the New Moon) when the Torah is read at the synagogue.)

The beginnings of this ceremony are ancient. References to the custom are found as early as the fifth and sixth centuries. **(See also CONFIRMA-TION.)**

BARSIMSON, JACOB. Pioneer American Jewish immigrant. Barsimson left Holland with a Dutch passport and arrived in Nieuw Amsterdam on August 22, 1654. He was one of the twenty-three refugees who fled the threat of the Inquisition* in Brazil* to seek asylum in the Dutch West India Company's settlement. In a lawsuit four years later he demanded and won the right to be exempt from giving testimony on the Sabbath.

BARUCH, BERNARD MANNES (1870-1965). American financier, World War I administrator of various national defense commissions, and known as "advisor to Presidents." Born in Camden, S.C., to Simon Baruch, a physician, Bernard moved with his family to N. Y. in 1881. He received his education at the College of the City of N. Y., entered a brokerage firm after graduation, and

became a very successful member of the N. Y. Stock Exchange. During World War I, President Wilson recognized Baruch's organizational abilities, and entrusted him with the task of heading various commissions to direct the war industries of the entire nation. At the end of the war, Baruch served as a member of the American Peace Commission. He served on the President's Agricultural Conference in 1922, and continued to give valued aid to American agriculture, helping to promote legislation for farm relief.

During President Franklin Delano Roosevelt's terms of office, Bernard Baruch was his confidential advisor on national problems, and is credited with planning the National Recovery Act of 1933. After America entered World War II, Baruch acted as advisor to the war mobilization director, James F. Byrnes. He also was appointed head of the fact-finding commission on synthetic rubber, and in 1944 prepared a report for President Roosevelt on war and postwar plans. In 1946 he served as U. S. representative on the United Nations Atomic Energy Commission, and presented the American proposal for the international control of atomic energy on June 14, 1946.

As a philanthropist, Baruch's interests led him to contribute large sums for the investigation of the causes of war and for possible means of preventing its outbreak. Baruch wrote articles and books on a variety of subjects. His autobiography, **My Own Story,** was published in 1957.

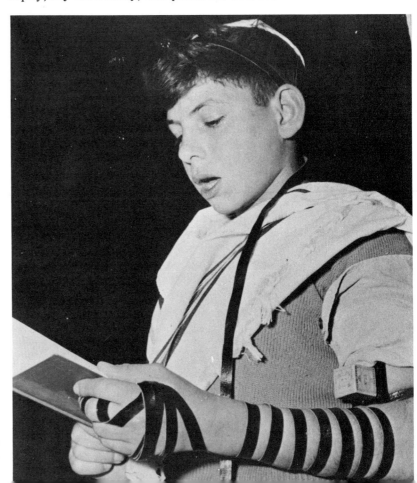

A native of Bulgaria celebrates his Bar Mitzvah in his new home in Israel.   Joint Distribution Committee.

BASLE PROGRAM. See HERZL, THEODOR.

BEERSHEBA. (From the Hebrew meaning "Well of the Oath"—Gen. 21:31-33.) Where Abraham dug a well and planted a tamarisk. The northern threshold of the Negev, on a plateau 600 feet high. In Biblical times it was a rallying place for the tribes of Israel, and until Roman and Byzantine days a prosperous caravan station on the route from Eilat to the Mediterranean. After the Arab invasion it lay in ruins for centuries. Beersheba revived briefly during the First World War when it served as the headquarters of Turkish and German armies attacking the Suez Canal. But it soon became again an apathetic Bedouin market town. Its Arab population of about 3,000 fled during the Israel War of Liberation in 1948. Since its occupation by Israel, Beersheba has developed into a bustling city with a mixed, colorful population of over 112,600 and is the administrative center of the Negev. Its new residential quarters, public buildings, schools and hospitals are set among the longest avenues and largest parks in the country. It is the site of Ben-Gurion University.

BEGIN, MENAHEM (1913-). Israeli statesman. Born in Brest-Litovsk, Russia,* he received a nationalist-religious Jewish education and studied law at the University of Warsaw.* As a teenager, he became a devoted follower of Vladimir Jabotinsky* and an active member of the Betar* (Revisionist Zionist*) youth movement. When World War II broke out in 1939 he was commander of Betar in Poland.* In 1940 he was arrested in Vilna* by the Soviet secret police because of his Zionism and sent to do forced labor in Arctic Russia. Freed by the Russians, he made his way to Palestine* in 1942. A gifted orator, writer and organizer, he became (1943) commander of the Irgun Z'vai L'umi,* and led this underground organization in the struggle against the British mandatory government. The Irgun's main aim was to sabotage British installations and make it impossible for the British to continue holding Palestine. Begin sought to attain this end without causing the death of innocent civilians, Arab, British or Jewish.

After the establishment of the State of Israel* he and the veterans of Irgun took the lead in founding the Herut party (**see also** Revisionist Zionism), a right-wing, strongly nationalist faction which he represented in the Knesset, and of which he has been the leader, without interruption, for three decades. On the eve of the Six-Day War* (1967) he joined Israel's Government of National Unity as a minister without portfolio but left the Cabinet in 1970 because of disagreement with the foreign

policy conducted by Premier Golda Meir.* In 1973 he became the leader of the Likud bloc which, led by Herut, opposed the dominant Labor alignment. In May, 1977, after almost 30 years in the opposition, Begin became Israel's first non-Socialist prime minister. He became the first Israeli prime minister to meet officially with an Arab chief of state when he met with Egypt's* President Anwar el-Sadat in Jerusalem* in November, 1977. Since that time, he has led Israel's peace negotiations with Egypt and, in 1978, following their conference at Camp David in Western Maryland, he and Sadat were jointly awarded the 1978 Nobel Peace Prize. In June 1979 Menahem Begin was reelected chairman of the Herut party. In September 1983, begin resigned as prime Minister and did not participate in the 1984 elections to the Knesset.

BEILIS, MENDEL. Central figure in the notorious ritual murder trial (1913) in Kiev, Russia. Beilis, a worker in a brick kiln, was accused of the murder of a Russian boy whose body had been found near the kiln in March 1911. Although an investigation soon established that the boy had been murdered by non-Jewish thieves, the "Beilis Affair" dragged on for over two years. The government of Czarist Russia stepped in and accused Beilis of committting this crime because the boy's blood was supposedly needed for the baking of matzos for Passover. The preposterous belief that Jews use Christian blood for such ritual purposes was held by ignorant people in Europe for many centuries. The anti-Semitic Russian government revived this belief and used the "Beilis Affair" to discredit the whole Jewish people. The atmosphere surrounding the trial was charged with hate, Russian "experts" gave false testimony, and the judges and jury were prejudiced. Yet Beilis was acquitted thanks to a brilliant team of defense lawyers and because of indignant protest of world opinion. Shortly after his acquittal, Beilis settled in Palestine,* where he lived for eight years. He came to the United States in 1924 and lived there until his death in 1934 at Saratoga Springs.

BELGIUM. Tradition has it that Jews first settled in what is now Belgium early in the 2nd century C.E. following their dispersal after the destruction of the Second Temple. But the first documented accounts place their arrival in the 4th century. Between the fourth and the seventh centuries, Jewish fortunes vacillated according to the temper of the current ruler. Under King Chilperic (561-584), they were persecuted for refusing to embrace Christianity. In the eighth and ninth centuries, they were accorded full rights and privileges, and lived amicably with their Christian neighbors. In 870 C.E., when Belgium was divided, many Jews fled after their homes had been pillaged and their property confiscated. Under Henry III and his son John I, in the thirteenth century, many returned to Belgium upon the promise that the taxes and restrictions imposed on them would be eased. Their number was swelled by an influx of French and English Jews who had been driven from their homeland. The brutal Brussels Massacre of 1370 wiped out the medieval Jewish community of Belgium. It was the climax of a series of attacks and charges against the Jews in the aftermath of the Black Death plague which decimated Europe in 1348.

Jewry did not again flourish in Belgium until the beginning of the eighteenth century, when Belgium became a part of Austria (and susequently of France and the Netherlands). In 1830 when Belgium was granted independence, a constitution was adopted granting all citizens full religious equality. For the first time, the Jews had their own communal organization, with a central council and chief rabbinate in Brussels. In 1873 Belgian Jewry was divided for administration purposes into five groups, each with its separate council of administration. All Jewish affairs were to be handled by the Consistoire Central in Brussels, which was headed by the chief rabbi, and was composed of six members from the Brussels community, as well as one delegate from each of the five councils.

When the Allied armies of liberation entered Belgium at the end of 1944, they found approximately 19,000 Jewish survivors. These were the remnant of a community which had numbered 100,000 prior to Nazi occupation in May 1940.

Like other Jewish communities throughout Europe, Belgian Jewry had been mercilessly annihilated. Altogether, about 30,000 Jews had been rescued from death, many through timely emigration, some 10,500 through the efforts of the Jewish Defense Committee of the Belgian Resistance, which provided them with hiding places or forged documents. Throughout the Nazi period, the Belgian Christian population assisted actively in the rescue of their Jewish neighbors, heedless of personal danger.

In 1977, there were about 41,000 Jews living in Belgium, of whom about 24,000 lived in Brussels and 13,000 in Antwerp, with a few small Jewish communities in Liege, Ghent, and Charleroi. Brussels Jews work in the leather, fur, glove-making, and garment industries, but the majority of Antwerp's Jews are in the diamond industry. Brussels and Antwerp, the two centers of Belgian Jewry, differ markedly. Antwerp is the center of Orthodox Jewish life, with over half of the Jewish community organizations, and 75 per cent of Jewish children attending Jewish day schools. The Brussels Jewish community is largely non-Orthodox. In March, 1959, it inaugurated a community center that planned a full program of Jewish cultural activities, intended especially to appeal to young people. The Zionist Federation of Belgium is the only organized Jewish body conducting cultural, educational, and social programs on a nation-wide basis. The federation's fortnightly **Tribune Sioniste,** is the only Jewish publication in Belgium.

BENEDICTIONS. Blessings addressed to God (Heb. *berakhot*). Tradition ascribes them to the 120 elders of the Great Synod in the time of Ezra.* A total of 100 benedictions, falling into four groups, were to be recited daily: 1) before sensory pleasures; tasting food or drink, enjoyment of a perfume, etc. 2) for the privilege of fulfilling a *mitzvah**; 3) praising Divine goodness upon hearing good or bad news, witnessing the wonders of nature, etc.; and giving thanks upon deliverance from sickness or danger (*birkat hagomel*), or upon joyous occasions and seasonal holidays (*shehecheyanu*); 4) during the daily prayers, such as the *Schmone Esre* (18 Benedictions), which include petitions for personal well-being and the welfare of the Jewish people in addition to blessings of praise and thanksgiving.

BENE ISRAEL. See INDIA.

BEN-GORION, MICAH JOSEPH. See BERDIT-CHEVSKY, MICAH JOSEPH.

52

BEN-GURION, DAVID (1886-1973). Pioneer builder of the State of Israel and its first prime minister. Born David Green in Poland,* he inherited from his father a strong love for Zion which blended with his own socialist ideals. In 1903, at the age of seventeen, he was already one of the founders of the Socialsit Zionist Party—Poale Zion—in Poland. Even as a youth, he manifested great determination to fulfill his ideals, and pursued his aims with unusual courage.

At the age of twenty (1906), Ben-Gurion went to Israel, where he worked as a common laborer, experiencing all the hardships of the young pioneer. He became active in the Galilee, which had scarcely been opened for Jewish colonization. Work was hard, and the danger of Arab attacks lurked everywhere. Ben-Gurion led in founding the Jewish self-defense movement, and took an active part in organizing the Socialist Zionist worker's movement.

When Turkey,* which then ruled over Palestine, entered the First World War, Ben-Gurion was expelled from Palestine. He came to the United States where he helped found the American Jewish Congress* and organized the Jewish Legion, which he joined as a private. In 1921, he returned to Palestine and became general secretary of the Histadrut* (General Federation of Labor), participating at the same time in other Zionist activities. In 1933, he was elected to the Executive of the World Zionist Organization, and from 1940 on he acted as its chairman.

Ben-Gurion played a decisive role in the struggle for the establishment of the State of Israel. Despite heavy pressure from the United States Department of State to postpone the proclamation of independence for Israel, he was largely instrumental in bringing it off as scheduled on May 14, 1948. As prime minister and minister of defense during the formative years of the state, he may be credited with many of its achievements. His scholarly articles and orations served the movement for years in clarifying Zionist ideals and aims. During his pioneering days, he had written: "A land is built only by pioneers who know how to give their lives to realize their ideals." He himself became the embodiment of this pioneering spirit. Ben-Gurion retired at the age of sixty-seven to the isolation of the Negev, but returned to assume leadership in 1955. He initiated the Sinai Peninsula* Campaign. He retired from the premiership in 1963 and was succeeded by Levi Eshkol.* In 1965 he broke away from Mapai and formed Rafi (Israel Labor List). He resigned from the Knesset in 1970 and retired to his kibbutz,* S'de Boker, where he engaged in study and writing until his death.

BENJAMIN (Hebrew for "son of the right hand," or, "of good fortune"). Jacob's twelfth and youngest son by Rachel, who died giving birth to him. Founder of the warlike tribe of Benjamin that settled on a stretch of land reaching up from the river Jordan* toward the hills of Jerusalem.* Saul,* the first king of Israel, was a Benjaminite.

BENJAMIN OF TUDELA (12th century). Merchant and traveler, often called the "Jewish Marco Polo." He started out from Saragossa, Spain, in 1160 and spent 13 years travelling over the greater part of the then known world before he returned home. He kept a lively diary in Hebrew, recording detailed descriptions of Jewish life in Europe, Asia and North Africa. The first English translation (1840) of his **Journeys** is esteemed highly for the historical and geographical light it sheds on the far away and little known Orient of that time. Benjamin's vivid descriptions are particularly valuable because they include information on several peoples that have since disappeared completely because they were conquered by the Tatars.

David Ben Gurion

State of Israel Bonds

BEN SIRA (c. 200 B.C.E.). Joshua ben Simeon ben Eliezer ben Sira or Sirach. Author of a book of proverbs, Ben Sira lived in Jerusalem. The Book of Ben Sira, part of the Hebrew Wisdom Literature, presents through its proverbs an interesting record of Jewish social life of that time. It includes praise of the high priest's function and of the Temple ritual. Originally written in Hebrew, the book was translated into Greek by a descendant of Ben Sira around 132 B.C.E. During the Middle Ages the Hebrew and Aramaic versions of it were lost. It was not until 1896 that most of the original Hebrew text was discovered by Solomon Schechter* among the fragments of the Cairo Geniza.*

BEN YEHUDAH, ELIEZER (1858-1922). Father of the modern Hebrew language, Ben Yehuda's life was an example of singleminded devotion to a cause—the revival of the ancient Hebrew language.*

At the age of nineteen, Ben Yehudah left Lithuania, where he had been brought up in a traditional environment, to study medicine in Paris. At first he was attracted to socialism. Later, the struggle of the Balkan countries to gain their independence made him aware of the need for a Jewish national homeland.

In 1880 Ben Yehudah decided to settle in Jerusalem* where he immediately set out to realize his cherished ideal of adapting the Hebrew language to daily use. He was subjected to ridicule by many people who considered the task impractical. It took Ben Yehudah many years of persistent work to convince the sceptics that Hebrew could be made to live again. His home was the first one in Palestine* where Hebrew was spoken to the exclusion of all other languages.

Ben Yehudah concentrated all his efforts on his monumental lifework: **The Dictionary of the Hebrew Language, Old and New,** which appeared in fifteen volumes. The final volumes, sixteen and seventeen, appeared in 1959. Numerous words for daily use were coined by Ben Yehudah and became a part of modern Hebrew. Ben Yehudah also published newspapers, composed textbooks for Hebrew schools, and was one of the founders of the Committee for the Hebrew language (now the Academy for the Hebrew Language).   H.L.

BEN-ZVI, YITZHAK (1885-1963). President of the State of Israel. He was born in Poltava, the Ukraine, where he received a thorough Jewish and secular education. In his father's house, Zvi Shimshelevitz (Shimshi), learned to feel deeply the plight of his people in Tsarist Russia.* He was influenced by Zionist and Socialist ideas in his youth, and participated actively in organizing Zionist Socialist groups (**see** LABOR ZIONISM).

Ben-Zvi was eighteen years old when he made his first trip to Palestine.* Upon his return to Russia in 1905, he joined Ber Borochov* in establishing the Socialist Zionist party, Poale Zion. This was the year of widespread pogroms in many parts of Russia. The Tsarist government, troubled by revolutions, found the Jews a convenient scapegoat and in many cases actually encouraged the attacks upon them. Ben-Zvi along with his father and brother, helped organize Jewish self-defense units. The Russian police exiled the entire Ben-Zvi family to Siberia, but Yitzhak succeeded in eluding his captors and escaped from Russia. For about two years he engaged in intensive Zionist work in Germany* and Switzerland.* In 1907 he finally reached his destination—Palestine.

On his arrival, Ben-Zvi immediately became one of the spokesmen and leaders of the Jewish workers in Palestine. He was among the founders of Hashomer,* the earliest Jewish defense force in modern Palestine. During the First World War he accompanied David Ben-Gurion* to America, where he organized first the Hehalutz* (pioneer movement) and later the Jewish Legion, which fought side by side with the British for the liberation of Palestine from Turkish rule. After the war, he returned to Palestine, where he participated in the establishment of the Histadrut,* the Palestine Workers Union, and Knesset Yisrael, the organized Jewish community of Palestine. For fourteen years, from 1931 to 1945, Ben-Zvi was head of the Vaad Leumi (National Council), the executive arm and the official representative body of Palestine Jewry.

With the establishment of the Jewish state, Ben-Zvi became a member of the Knesset,* Israel's

Emblem of the tribe of Benjamin

Yitzhak Ben-Zvi
Israel Office of Information.

54

Parliament. In the fall of 1953, he succeeded Chaim Weizmann* as the second President of the State of Israel.

In addition to his political and communal activities, Ben-Zvi has devoted a great deal of time to scholarly studies and to writing. His books on the history of the Jews in the Holy Land and on the different ethnic groups that made up Palestine Jewry are regarded as authoritative and exhaustive studies. For his **The Land of Israel Under Ottoman Rule, Four Centuries of History,** Ben-Zvi received the Bialik Prize. He died on April 23, 1963, several months after entering on a third five-year term of office. His wife, **Rahel Yanait Ben-Zvi** (1884-1979) was a well-known Labor Zionist leader, pioneer and educator in his own right.

BERDITCHEVSKY, MICAH JOSEPH (1865-1921). Hebrew novelist and essayist. Early in his youth he left his hometown in the Ukraine to study at the Yeshiva of Volozin and later at the University of Berlin. A searching student of Jewish history, he rebelled against the preoccupation with the written word and overwhelming role of study in Jewish life. He was also critical of Jewish religious tradition.

Berditchevsky's published works, under the pen name of Micah Joseph Ben-Gorion, number twenty volumes. In his novels and short stories, he deals chiefly with small-town people, describing their struggles and passions in a style that is a mixture of realism and fable. His Hasidic tales and collections of Midrashic* legends constitute a rich contribution to Hebrew letters.

BERESHIT (Genesis). See BIBLE.

BERGEN BELSEN. Nazi concentration camp near Hanover, Germany, established by the Nazis in July, 1943. Originally intended for Jews whom the German government wished to exchange for Germans in Allied territories, it became one of the infamous death camps. Anne Frank* was among the victims of Bergen Belsen. The camp was liberated by the British on April 15, 1945. **(See also** JEWRY, ANNIHILATION OF EUROPEAN; WORLD FEDERATION OF BERGEN BELSEN ASSOCIATIONS.)

BERNSTEIN, LEONARD (1918-   ). Composer, conductor and pianist. Born in Lawrence, Mass., of middle-class Jewish parents, Bernstein was educated at Harvard University and early embarked on a musical career. At 25 he was assistant conductor of the New York Philharmonic Orchestra. A year later he was named conductor of the New York City Symphony Orchestra. In 1948

he was musical director of the Israel Philharmonic Orchestra, conducting for soldiers at the front during Israel's War of Liberation.

Bernstein's numerous compositions, ranging from symphonies to scores for successful Broadway musicals, include a number of works based on traditional Jewish motifs. His first symphony, **Jeremiah,** is a moving score based on the cantillation for the Book of Lamentations*; his synagogue music has similarly rendered age-old melodic material in modern techniques.

He was professor of music at Brandeis University,* head of the conducting department at the Berkshire Music Center; and conductor of the New York Philharmonic.

BERTINORO, OBADIAH (b.1470). His name is derived from that of his birthplace, Bertinoro, in Italy. A noted Talmudic scholar, Bertinoro served as rabbi in several Italian communities. At the age of thirty-six he decided to go to Palestine.* After a long and strenuous journey, he finally reached his destination. In Jerusalem* he found about seventy Jewish families, whom he organized into a community. With the arrival of exiles from Spain,* the community grew rapidly in numbers and prestige. Bertinoro's letters describing conditions in the Palestine of that period are of great historic importance. He is, however, best known for his commentary on the Mishnah.* Its clarity of language and style, and its comprehensive presentation made it one of the most popular commentaries on that work.

BET. Second letter of the Hebrew alphabet; numerically, two

BET HAMIDRASH. Hebrew for "House of Study." Used to designate study halls for Jewish learning, the term is also used to describe one of the functions of the synagogue* in Jewish life.

Leonard Bernstein

BETAR. Strong city-fortress, where Jews made their last stand in the time of the Bar Kokhba* rebellion against the Romans (132 C.E.). Situated on a hill southwest of Jerusalem,* Betar withstood the Roman siege for over a year. The enemy finally succeeded in cutting off the food and water supplies of the besieged population. Starvation and thirst weakened the resistance of the defenders. Legend has it that the city fell through the treachery of Samaritans* (a religious sect hostile to the Jews), who disclosed its secret passages to the enemy. After a bitter and bloody battle, the Romans captured Betar, on the ninth day of Ab, in 135 C.E. Their terrible vengeance cut down the population and razed the city to its foundations. Half a million Jews perished in this last of Bar Kokhba's battles. (**See also** BAR KOKHBA: AKIBA BEN JOSEPH.)

BETAR, BRITH TRUMPELDOR ORGANIZATION. See REVISIONIST ZIONISM.

BETHLEHEM (Hebrew, meaning "House of Bread"). A town in the Judean hills south of Jerusalem, it is girdled round with olive groves, fig trees, and vineyards. Bethlehem (also called Ephrath in the Bible) was the setting of the Book of Ruth,* the home of David,* and, according to New Testament tradition the birth of Jesus of Nazareth. The architectural beauty of the Basilica, the Church of the Nativity, built in the fourth century, is still preserved. As the most important Christian shrine, Bethlehem is visited by many thousands of pilgrims, especially at Christmas time. Its population of about 10,000 consists mainly of Christian Arabs, in whose dress and features the influence of the Crusaders has been preserved.

BEZALEL SCHOOL OF ARTS AND CRAFTS. School founded in Jerusalem* in 1906 by the sculptor Boris Schatz* for the development of the arts, home industry, and crafts in Palestine.* It is named after Bezalel, the chief architect of the Tabernacle* (Exod.: 31:1-6 and 35:30). In the department of graphic arts where weaving and metal work are taught, four-year day or evening courses leading to the diploma of Master of Arts are offered. The school aims to train competent craftsmen, as well as to develop the creativity of its students and raise the cultural level of Israel. To this end, its 150 students and 20 teachers from all over the world work with vocational schools and settlements throughout Israel. The school is closely associated with the **Bezalel section of the Israel** Museum, which contains a large selection of Jewish art objects and reproductions, many of

Tomb of Rachel, on the road from Bethlehem to Jerusalem. This holy place was not accessible to Jews from 1948 until after the Six-Day War.

which are taken on tours to every corner of Israel, The Bezalel School is supported by W.I.Z.O. (the Women's International Zionist Organization) and the American Fund for Israel Institutions; it also receives a small government subsidy. In international art competitions, Bezalel students have received an average of twenty prizes a year.

Bezalel, National Museum and School of Arts and Crafts.

Chaim Nachman Bialik
Etching by Elias Grossman. Courtesy A. Kamberg Collection.

BIALIK, CHAIM NACHMAN (1873-1934). One of the greatest Hebrew poets of modern times. His father, a village innkeeper in Russia, yet a Talmudic scholar, died when the child was eight years old. The boy was placed in the care of his grandfather, a very stern old man. However, all his grandfather's restrictions and prohibitions could not stifle the energetic and spirited boy. In spite of his mischievous ways he was highly imaginative and impressionable, given to daydreaming.

Bialik was an unmistakably gifted child. At eleven, he already studied Jewish philosophic works, though most of his time was devoted to the study of the Talmud.* At sixteen, he entered the famous Yeshiva of Volozhin in Lithuania.* Later, he was to immortalize in one of his poems the yeshiva student, the **matmid,** who dedicated himself to study, excluding all worldly matters from his thoughts. During the year he spent in Volozhin, the young Bialik drew closer to Zionism* and to modern Hebrew literature.* When the Russian government closed the Volozhin Yeshiva (1891), he went to Odessa in southern Russia,* drawn by its flourishing Hebrew literary center. In an anthology called **Ha-Pardes,** Bialik published his first poem, **El Ha-tzipor** ("To the Bird"), expressing his boundless love for the old-new Zion. Other poems followed. His outstanding talent immediately impressed his readers. Here was poetry, deeply personal, yet touching the very soul of the Jewish people.

Like the ancient prophets, Bialik rebuked his people and exposed their weaknesses in fiery and sharp-edged verses. Yet the poet inspired the Jewish masses with new hope, pride and self-respect. His poem, **The City of Slaughter,** written after the Kishineff pogrom* (1903), roused the younger generation to take up arms in self-defense. Bialik linked the past with the present in his poetic works. Drawing upon the rich sources of Jewish creativity, he gave new power and meaning to age-old traditions and ideals. He imparted unusual beauty and charm to folk themes, and created wonderful poems for children. In his essays and stories, he was a master of Hebrew prose. Towering as a poet, he assumed a leading role in Jewish cultural life and became the symbol of the national revival. At his magic touch, the Hebrew language became a vital cultural force. Together with his life-long friend J.C. Rawnitzky, Bialik rearranged and paraphrased the rich treasury of Talmudic and Midrashic legend, the Aggadah.* In addition to poems, stories and the Sefer Ha-Aggadah (Talmudic legends), Bialik wrote Biblical legends. **Vayehi ha-Yom** ("It Came to Pass") recapturing their ancient charm and humor. He translated into Hebrew such world classics as Cervantes' **Don Quixote** and Schiller's **Wilhelm Tell.**

Bialik was beloved and revered while yet in Russia. After the Bolsehvik revolution, he was forced to leave the country and went to Germany.* In 1924, he settled in Palestine.* His home in Tel Aviv, a street now named after him, became a place of pilgrimage for Hebrew writers.

In 1929 Bialik visited America, and was received with acclaim. During the last years of his life, as editor, publisher, and critic, he became the guiding spirit of every Hebrew cultural and literary activity. He participated actively in the work of the Hebrew University* in Jerusalem, and the Committee for the Hebrew Language. The Oneg Shabbat gatherings in Tel Aviv, over which Bialik presided, became a celebrated institution.

The Bialik home in Tel Aviv has been preserved as a cultural center. Mossad Bialik, one of the foremost publishing houses in Israel, and Bialik prizes for the best in Hebrew literature, are symbolic monuments to his memory. The 21st day of Tammuz, the date of his death, is observed as a national memorial day in Israel.

BIBLE (HISTORY). (Taken from the Greek term **biblia,** meaning "books".) The "Torah of Moses" or the Hebrew Bible came to have many names: the Holy Scriptures, the Book of Books, the Old Testament, Divine Revelation. The Jews call it simply Torah, the Hebrew word for "Teaching" and also "Law." The Bible consists of three sections: The Five Books of Moses (Pentateuch), Prophets, and Writings.

Canon: Sometime during the first century, the final decision was made as to which sacred books

Facsimile of a poem in Bialik's handwriting

were to be considered part of the Holy Scriptures, or the Biblical canon. The word "canon" or "standard," that was applied by the scholars to the holy books, comes from the Greek **kanones,** or models of excellence.

Influence of the Bible: For the Jew, the Bible has been the source of life, growth, and survival. He read in it the record of his people's spiritual progress, from Abraham, the first to reject the belief in many gods, to the prophets and their momentous vision of God as the loving Father of all creation. When the Jews were expelled from Palestine* and became wanderers on the face of the earth, the Bible became a way of life and a Jewish "portable homeland."

The influence of the Bible was not limited to Judaism, but has extended to two daughter religions: Christianity and Islam.* Mohammed, the creator of Islam, was so deeply influenced by the Bible that at first he thought of himself as a new prophet of Judaism. His mind was so filled with Biblical stories that he traced his descent to Ishmael, son of Abraham* and Hagar. The theology of the Koran, the sacred book of Islam, shows Mohammed's debt to the Bible and to Judaism. As Mohammedanism spread, the Bible influenced many peoples in the East.

When Christianity came into being it took over the Hebrew Bible, with the addition of the New Testament. Western civilization, as it took shape, absorbed the Hebrew Old Testament ideas. Such Biblical ideas as those of the common origin of man, of the equality of men before God and the law of mercy and of the right of all men to knowledge, filtered down only gradually to the common man in the Christian world. For at first the Bible was known only to priests and to the few learned men who could read its ancient Greek and Latin translations. But the Renaissance movement, the invention of printing, and the religious reformation, spread learning and knowledge of the Bible to ever larger and larger numbers of people.

As they read the Bible, the people began to apply its ideas to their own lives.

> "When Adam delved and Eve span,
> Who was then the gentleman?"

This was the old English rhyme that John Ball used in a speech to the rebels of the Wat Tyler Insurrections in 1381. And the rough peasant and worker audience of John Ball understood very well this Bible-inspired view of the equality of all men.

Bible Translations: The first translation of the Bible was the Septuagint,* a Greek translation for the Jews of Alexandria* began in the middle of the

third century B.C.E. and continued to the end of the next century. During the second century C.E., a series of new Greek translations were made by the Christian Church Fathers. Then came the first great translation into a West European tongue, the Latin Vulgate version of 382. This became the official Bible of the Roman Catholic Church. Each age produced its own Bible translations in hundreds of languages, all over the world. The Jews themselves found the need to make translations; after the Septuagint came the Aramaic* translations by Onkelos* and by Jonathan Ben Uziel. The great scholar Saadiah Gaon* (tenth century) made one of the most successful Arabic translations. A Persian translation appeared about four hundred years later. By the middle of the fifteenth century, Europe saw the first Bible printed from wood blocks. It was an inexpensive illustrated Bible known as the Poor Man's Bible, and under its many pictures of Biblical scenes were short explanations in Latin and in the local vernacular. The Renaissance and the Reformation brought new translations to western Europe. Martin Luther's German translation of 1534 exerted great influence. In France,* Roman Catholic scholars published the important Douay Version in 1610. Perhaps the greatest and most influential translation was the English King James Version of 1611. The beauty of its language came close to the spirit of the Hebrew Bible. The King James version became an instrument that formed noble minds and inspired great works of music and literature. New translations, by Jews and non-Jews, are still being produced. To this day, scholars search the ancient Hebrew texts as they are discovered, (see DEAD SEA SCROLLS) compare the translations with the originals, and correct errors. The Bible by now has been translated into 1,108 different languages, and missionary linguists are planning additional translations into 2,000 dialects for primitive peoples in the most distant corners of New Guinea, Africa, Southeast Asia, and for the Indians of South America.

Bible in American History: The influence of the Bible in the early history of the United States* cannot be overstated. The Puritans lived by the Bible. They looked upon themselves as God's chosen people, like the ancient Israelites, and in the New England colonies they formed their "Holy Commonwealth." They actually felt their church to be a continuation of the Covenant* between God and the Jews. For the early Protestants of New England, the Old Testament was the supreme authority, and in the colleges where their sons trained for the minsitry, the Bible was studied in the original Hebrew. Records of births, deaths,

The Second Isaiah Scroll, one of the seven Dead Sea Scrolls in possession of the Hebrew University of Jerusalem, before unrolling.

and marriages were kept in the family Bible. Every day a chapter from it was read aloud to the household. American pioneers gave Biblical names to their towns and villages: e.g., Jerusalem in the State of Washington, Jonah in Texas. The New England settlers based the political laws governing their colonies on the Scriptures. Forty-six of the forty-eight laws in the Body of Liberties which they drew up in 1641 were based on the Hebrew Bible. It is no wonder that when the Liberty Bell rang out in July 1776 to announce the Declaration of Independence, a verse from the Bible was engraved on that bell. "Proclaim liberty throughout the land unto all the inhabitants thereof" (Lev. 25:10).

The influence of the Bible on Western literature and art cannot be told in few words. From earliest times, the storytellers and poets, the sculptors and the painters have drawn from the Bible the themes for their books and poems, for their statues and pictures. The libraries and museums of the Western World are filled with works of art inspired by the Bible. And in the great concert halls where men listen to musical translations of the Bible, from Handel's oratorio **Israel in Egypt** to Ernest Bloch's* **Schelomo** rhapsody. The books, the works of art, and the music are only some ways in which men recognize the Bible as a great spiritual heritage for all mankind.

N.B.-A.

BIBLE (STRUCTURE). The first section, the Pentateuch, contains five books of Moses.* Genesis,* Exodus,* Leviticus,* Numbers,* and Deuteronomy.* The second section, Prophets,* is itself divided into two parts, the Former Prophets, and the Latter Prophets. The Former Prophets, are actually historical books relating the story of the Jewish people from the death of Moses to the destruction of the kingdom of Judah. They consist of: Joshua,* Judges,* Samuel I, Samuel II, Kings I, and Kings II. The Latter Prophets are likewise subdivided into two parts: the three Major Prophets, and the twelve Minor Prophets. The Major Prophets are: Isaiah,* Jeremiah,* and Ezekiel.* The Minor Prophets are: Hosea,* Joel,* Amos,* Obadiah,* Jonah,* Micah,* Nahum,* Habakkuk,* Haggai,* Zephaniah,* Zechariah,* and Malachi.* The third section, Writings, consists of three subsections. The first is Writings proper, which contains: Psalms,* Proverbs,* and Job.* The second is Scrolls: The Song of Songs,* Ruth,* Lamentations,* Ecclesiastes,* Esther,* and Daniel* (a book of prophecy). The last subsection is the Historical Writings: Ezra,* Nehemiah,* Chronicles I,* and Chronicles II.*

BILU. First pioneers to go to Palestine after the pogroms of 1881 in Russia.* The name "Bilu" is an abbreviation of the Hebrew **Bet Yaakov Lekhu Venailkho**—"O House of Jacob, come, and let us go forth" (Isaiah 2:5). The Bilu was made up largely of university students, who were fired with the ideal of serving as the trail-blazers of Palestine settlers. Their program called for the "encouragement and strengthening of immigration and colonization in Eretz Israel through the establishment of an agricultural colony, built on cooperative-social foundations." Their final aim was the "politico-economic and national spiritual revival of the Jewish people in Palestine."

The first Bilu group which came to Palestine in 1882 consisted of twenty members. They endured many hardships in the land that had been desolate for generations. They began their work at the agricultural school of Mikveh Israel.* The director of the school tried to dissuade them from dedicating their life to a "hopeless cause." Most of the pioneers, however, preferred their spade and hoe to a professional career, and they founded one of the first colonies, Rishon Le-Zion,* and later Gederah. The Bilu endured hunger, poverty, and Arab hostility, serving as an inspiring example for the future builders of Israel.

Leah Hervet, one of the Biluim who founded Gedera, reminiscing with her granddaughter.

BIRKAT HAMAZON. See PRAYERS.

BIROBIDJAN. Far-Eastern province of the Soviet Union, north of Manchukuo, bordering the Amur River. The region was set aside by the Soviet government for Jewish colonization on March 28, 1928. On May 7, 1934, Birobidjan was officially declared an autonomous Jewish region. Yiddish was to be the official language of the area in all educational, cultural and legal institutions. Jewish Communists and Communist sympathizers the world over hailed the project as a great Soviet contribution to the solution of the Jewish problem. However, the experiment proved unsuccessful. In contrast to Israel, this desolate region held no national appeal to the masses of Jews. Information about Jewish life in Birobidjan is currently very difficult to obtain. However, it is estimated that of the 40,000 who originally settled there, only 15,000 Jews remain, a small minority of the total population. Since the end of World War II, the Soviet government has made no effort to implement its plan of establishing a Jewish autonomous region in Birobidjan. The Yiddish schools have been liquidated and but one synagogue remains, without a rabbi.

BIUR HAMETZ. See PASSOVER.

BLOCH, ERNEST (1880-1959). Composer. Son of a Geneva clockmaker, Ernest Bloch studied in his native Switzerland and in Germany. **Macbeth,** an opera performed in Paris in 1910, gained him immediate critical acclaim. In 1916 he came to the United States, where he spent the rest of his life. A great part of Bloch's work, which is distinguished by passionate intensity of feeling and free play of melody, has been devoted to compositions on Jewish themes. These included **Israel,** a symphony; the **Baal Shem Suite; Schelomo;** and **Avodat Hakodesh** ("Sacred Service"), an oratorio based on the Sabbath synagogue service. Even his works on non-Jewish themes—such as **America, Helvetia** and **Evocations**—have been said to be essentially Jewish in spirit.

BLOOD ACCUSATION. The false charge that Jews eat Gentile blood in connection with holiday rituals, particularly on Passover.* This dreadful falsehood has been hurled at Jews in various places since the twelfth century. Popes, Christian scholars, and judges have denounced the libel, yet there are about 200 cases of this accusation on record. Often, Jews were tortured to make them "confess their guilt." As late as the nineteenth century, thirty-nine such cases occurred in Europe and in the Near East. One of the most notorious cases of blood libel was the Beilis* case in 1911.

In 1928, this monstrous libel turned up even in

Ernest Bloch

G. Schirmer, music publishers

the United States, when a Christian child disappeared in Massena, N.Y., and some officials actually asked the rabbi whether ritual slaying was part of the Yom Kippur* observance. This case so shocked the nation that the organization later to be known as the National Conference of Christians and Jews issued a statement declaring, "There is no custom...among Jews anywhere ...which calls for the use of human blood." The Nazis tried to give the charge additional circulation, but in recent times it has died out. What makes the accusation especially absurd is the fact that the Bible* (Lev. 17.10, Deut. 12.16, I Sam. 14.32-34, etc.) expressly forbids the consumption of blood, and the dietary laws* are replete with rules about the scrupulous removal of blood from meat.

BLUM, LEON (1872-1950). French statesman, three times premier of France.* Socialist leader and writer. The father of Leon Blum was a wealthy Alsatian merchant whose four sons grew up with a good Jewish background. Young Leon studied law and at the age of twenty-two was already recognized as a poet and writer of distinction. The Dreyfus* case stirred Blum deeply, and he became active in the defense of the Jewish officer accused of treason by the French Army. In the course of this work (1896), he met Jean Jaures, the famous leader of the French Socialists. Under the influence of Jaures, Blum joined the Socialist movement, and by the end of World War I he had become the outstanding leader of the Socialist party. From 1919 onward, Blum served in the Chamber of Deputies almost continuously. From 1936 to June 1937 and again in 1938, he was premier of France.

Under the threat of the growing Nazi power in Germany,* the French Socialist Party joined the

Communists in a Popular Front coalition during the late 1930's. Blum successfully opposed all efforts at a merger with the Communists. During World War II, when Nazi Germany ruled France through the puppet Vichy government, Blum was imprisoned and brought to trial for treason in Riom. With remarkable courage, Leon Blum faced his accusers as "a Socialist among Facists, a Jew among anti-Semites," and turned accuser himself. He so effectively showed that the appeasers were the real traitors of France that the Vichy government stopped the trial. Blum was transferred from the French prison to a German concentration camp; at the approach of the Allied armies, he was sent to a camp in Italy.* The remarkable man, then in his 70's, managed to keep alive until the Allied victory brought his freedom in 1945. France immediately put him into public service again, and in the spring of 1946, he came to the United States on a mission for his country. In December of that year, he again became premier of France.

Leon Blum always indentified himself closely with Jewish causes, and repeatedly aided Zionism.* In 1929, he appeared in Zurich and participated in forming the enlarged Jewish Agency for Palestine.* The **halutzim*** of Palestine were grateful to Leon Blum. On November 10, 1943, while he was behind the barbed wire of a concentration camp, a kibbutz* in northern Galilee* was named after him, Kfar Blum.   N.B-A.

BLUVSTEIN, RACHEL. See RACHEL.

B'NAI B'RITH. On October 13, 1843, twelve German Jews living in New York City* met together to form what they called a **Bundes Brueder,** or "Brothers of the Covenant." Patterned after other lodges of the day, it had a ritual, regalia, and benefits in the form of insurance and mutual aid. It later became known as the Independent Order of B'nai B'rith, and finally, after 1930, as B'nai B'rith.

B'nai B'rith's membership in the United States

stands at 550,000 men, women and youths, in addition to many hundreds of members in Aleph Zadik Aleph and B'nai B'rith Girls, its junior affiliates. It is organized into somewhat autonomous local lodges, women's chapters, and district grand lodges. The supreme lodge establishes general policies for the order.

Over the years, B'nai B'rith has supported, in whole or in part, the following institutions: Bellefaire, an orphan home in Cleveland; the Jewish Children's Home of New Orleans, the Touro Infirmary of New Orleans; the Jewish Orphan Home of Atlanta (Ga.); the Home for the Aged at Yonkers, N.Y.; the National Jewish Hospital at Denver (Colo.); the Leo N. Levi Memorial Hospital at Hot Springs, Ark.; the B'nai B'rith Orphanage at Erie, Pa.; and the B'nai B'rith Home for the Aged at Memphis, Tenn.

B'nai B'rith has always been interested in advancing the rights of Jews, and working with government and other groups to combat anti-Jewish agitation at home and abroad. Today these activities, together with B'nai B'rith's concern for the democratic rights of all people, center in its Anti-Defamation League,* formed in 1913.

Cultural and educational activities are emphasized by B'nai B'rith, both in local lodges and on a national scale, through speakers, bureaus, cultural programs and publications. The **National Jewish Monthly,** published under various names since 1886, has the largest circulation of any Jewish journal in the English language. B'nai B'rith sponsors an extensive adult education program, featuring the annual Wildacres Institutes for adults, held at various camps in the United States.

There are affiliates in thirty-seven countries, including Israel.

B'nai B'rith Hillel Foundation. A network of cultural, religious and social centers for Jewish college youth. The first Hillel Foundation was set uo at the University of Illinois in 1924 to make Jewish life and culture vital and meaningful to college youth. Taken up as a national project by B'nai B'rith in 1925, the Foundation now maintains 150 foundations, 161 counselorships, 3 chairs of Judaic study in 314 colleges in the United States, Europe, Israel and Latin America. In addition, it has established four professorships of Judaic studies in American universities. Hillel campus programs include cultural, religious, fellowship, community service, personal guidance and interfaith activities. To stimulate discussion and understanding of Jewish life and thought, the foundation is engaged in publishing a series of Hillel Little Books. **What Is the Jewish Heritage,** by Ludwig Lewisohn,* was the first.

B'nai B'rith Youth Organization is the youth division of B'nai B'rith, a national Jewish fraternal organization. The first B'nai B'rith youth groups were founded in Omaha, Nebraska, in 1924. Known as Aleph Zadik Aleph, they quickly took root throughout the midwest, and by 1925 were incorporated as a national branch of the adult organization. In 1927, the B'nai B'rith Girls (ages range from fifteen to twenty-one) were formed as a sister organization to the AZA. About fifteen years later, to satisfy the needs of college students and young war veterans, the B'nai B'rith Young Adults was founded. All three groups, joined in the overall Youth Organization since 1949, conduct programs designed to familiarize young Jews with their heritage and to prepare them for active participation in Jewish and general community life. In addition to discussions and study groups dealing with specifically Jewish affairs, Youth Organization concerns itself with problems of social welfare and citizenship, and conducts a broad program of leisure-time sports and social activities. There are over 30,000 members in 1,200 units in 15 countries.

BNAI ZION. A non-political American Zionist Fraternal Organization founded in 1908 by a group of Jewish leaders headed by Dr. Judah L. Magnes, Dr. Joseph Barondess and Dr. Stephen S. Wise. Dedicated to the three principles of Americanism, Fraternalism and Zionism, it now numbers a membership of some 35,000 Jewish families organized in over 200 chapters in various parts of the United States. Through its Foundation it has established and funded close to 50 constructive and life saving projects in Israel, including Kfar Bnai Zion, considered one of the most successful agricultural settlements (Moshav) with over 500 residents, the Artists' colony at Ein Hod, a chain of medical clinics, sports centers, and diagnostic and rehabilitation institutions. The Bnai Zion Homes for retarded children in Rosh Ha'Ayin and in Kfar Hashwedi in Jerusalem, now care for some 700 children. Additional major projects assumed in recent years include the Beit Halochem Rehabilitation Center for Disabled Veterans, the Haifa Medical Center (Rothschild), the Kupath Cholim Meuchedet in Jerusalem and the Beth Hatefutsoth, the Jewish Museum of the Disapora, in which the main auditorium was named for Bnai Zion.

Its prime projects in the United States is the promotion of America-Israel Friendship. In 1973 it established the America-Israel Friendship House in New York City. It also numbers an active National Women's League and a growing young Leadership Division known as TAMID with scores of youth chapters in New York, Florida and Los Angeles. In 1981 the 120-year-old Jewish Fraternal Organization BRITH ABRAHAM, affiliated with Bnai Zion.

United States Ambassador to the United Nations Jean Kirkpatrick receiving 1984 America-Israel Friendship Award at 76th annual Bnai Zion Award Dinner in New York City. Left to right: Paul Safro, chairman of the Bnai Zion Foundation; Sidney Wiener, national Bnai Zion president; Meir Rosenne, Israel's Ambassador to Washington; and Mel Parness, national Executive vice-president and national secretary of Bnai Zion.

Its monthly publication "Bnai Zion Voice" is edited by Ernest E. Barbarash. Benefits include medical, health and life insurance. As part of its cultural program Bnai Zion grants annual scholarship and medal awards to students of universities and high schools for proficiency in Hebrew.

BOARD OF DEPUTIES OF BRITISH JEWS. Founded in 1760 when, following the accession of George III (1760), the Sephardic and Ashkenazic communities agreed upon the creation of a joint body to represent English Jewry at court.

The board is organized on a synagogal basis and functions through committees. In addition to the administrative committees, specific committees deal with Israel affairs, charities, education, **Shehitah*** (ritual slaughter), and Jewish defense against anti-Semitism.*

BOARD OF JEWISH EDUCATION OF GREATER NEW YORK. The world's largest central agency for Jewish education, BJE conducts extensive and varied services for Jewish education. BJE conducts extensive and varied services for Jewish school teachers, principals, parents and students from the early childhood level through high school. These services include a network of

Tomorrow's doctors are busily at work examining their teddy bear while attending one of the Jewish early childhood programs serviced by the Board of Jewish Education of Greater New York (BJE).

62

Jewish Teachers' Centers; guidance ot schools' production of multi-media materials; **World Over** magazine; scholarship aid to students; nutrition education; family education; and art and music programs for children.

BOHR, NIELS (1885-1962). Born in Denmark, Bohr was one of the originators of the modern atomic theory. For his research in this field, he was awarded the Nobel Prize in 1922. Bohr's investigations of the fissions of uranium paved the way for the modern atom bomb and atomic energy. From 1943 to 1945, he took an active part in the preparation of the atomic bomb in Los Alamos.

BOKHARA. A region in central Asia, now part of the Soviet republic of Uzbekistan. Bokhara is the home of an ancient and colorful Jewish community, which believes itself descended from the Ten Lost Tribes* of Israel. Its ancestors are known to have come from Samarkind and other areas in Persia, where the Jews have lived since the destruction of the First Temple.* The early records of Jewish life in this tiny country were destroyed during the invasion of the Huns in the thirteenth century. The Bokharan community is still Judeo-Persian in culture. It possesses a considerable literature in Tadjik, a Persian dialect which its members still speak. Until the conquest of Bokhara by Russia in the nineteenth century, the community was completely cut off from the rest of the Jewish world. In 1893, to escape persecution by the Tsar, a number of Bokharans

A Bokharan Jew, by E.M. Lilien.

settled in Jerusalem. This settlement has grown, but the bulk of Bokharan Jews—about 30,000—remain in the Soviet Union, where they earn their livelihood in the production and sale of textiles. More than other Jewish communities in Russia, they have been able to withstand the pressure of Soviet policy to give up their age-old traditions.

BOLIVIA. Republic in South America. Total population (1984) 5,755,000, Jewish population, 1,000. Jews were active in exploiting Bolivia's rich silver mines during the early period of Spanish colonization in the 1500's. All of them were Marranos,* Jews who had been forced to convert to Catholicism, and who practiced Judaism in secret. This community was stifled by the Inquisition,* which was established in 1570. From that time until the rise of Hitler, very few Jews lived in Bolivia. Between 1933 and 1939, however, Bolivia was the only country which did not restrict the immigration of Jews. As a result, 10,000 refugees from Germany settled there. Most of them were completely unprepared for the life of this underdeveloped country. To ease the situation, Socobox, the Bolivian Colonization Association, was established. About 200 Jews did settle in a farm colony at Villa Sacaba, and other colonies were planned. But the majority of the refugees did not take root. When an economic slump set in during the late '40's, more than half of the immigrants left for Argentina and Chile. Most of those who remain live in La Paz and Cochabamba, where there are Zionist, philanthropic, and youth organizations, as well as some Jewish schools. Education is one of the community's chief problems, since the public schools are sectarian and Catholic in spirit. As a result, there has been an increase in religious education, and a one-day-a-week school has been established in La Paz. Bolivia's Jews keep in touch with world Jewry through the World Jewish Congress,* in which they are represented by the Central Jewish Committee of Bolivia, a government-accredited agency.

BONDS FOR ISRAEL. The Israel Bonds program in the United States was inaugurated by Ben-Gurion* in 1951 to help develop Israel's economy. The more than $6,700,000,000 in bond sales since then has contributed to Israel's outstanding economic progress.

The money put into bonds is not donated, but lent to the State of Israel.* The funds are for economic development, for building factories and farms, roads and railways, harbors and homes, power stations and pipelines. These funds provide the Israeli economy with the long-term, relatively cheap capital needed for basic investment.

BOROCHOV, DOV BER (1881-1917). Labor Zionist leader, writer, and Yiddish philologist. Ber Borochov was born in a small Ukrainian town and received a good Jewish and general education. When quite young, he joined the Russian Social Democratic Party from which he was expelled for his independent views. He became active in the Zionist movement, joining the Poale Zion* in 1905. Because of his activities, Borochov was arrested by the Russian police and made his escape from the country in 1907. He came to the United States in 1914, where he continued to be active in the Labor Zionist movement. He edited **Der Yiddisher Kempfer** and other publications and wrote books on Yiddish philology. His important theories on Socialism and Zionism* were published in 1937 in **Nationalism and the Class Struggle,** a Marxist approach to the Jewish problem. Borochov returned to Russia after the Revolution in 1917, and died there shortly afterward. On April 3, 1963 his remains were reinterred in a cemetery on the shores of Lake Kinneret.* The coffin was attended by Zalman Shazar* and the eulogy was given by David Ben-Gurion.*

Ber Borochov was one of the founders of the World Confederation of Poale Zion (1907), and Labor Zionism* owes much to him. He formulated theories fusing Zionism and Socialism, and his ideas served greatly to win the sympathy of many labor and socialist circles for the Jewish upbuilding of Palestine.

BRAININ, REUBEN (1862-1939). Hebrew writer and critic. One of the first to introduce into Hebrew writing modern European literary standards and values. At the beginning of the century Brainin was one of the foremost figures on the Hebrew literary scene. After living for some years in Vienna and Berlin, he came to America in 1909. For a short time, he edited a Hebrew weekly **Ha-Dror** ("The Swallow"), and the monthly **Ha-Toren** ("The Mast"). Brainin contributed to the Yiddish press in the United States. He published biographies of Herzl,* and of the classical Hebrew writers Mapu* and Smolenskin,* and wrote extensively on European literary figures.

BRANDEIS, LOUIS DEMBITZ (1856-1941). American jurist and Zionist leader. Born in Louisville, Ky., he received his early education at a private school in Louisville and an academy in Germany. He had very little formal Jewish training in his childhood.

In 1877, Brandeis, at the age of twenty, was graduated from the Harvard Law School with the highest honors in its history. He began his private law practice in St. Louis, but soon settled in

Boston where he lived and practiced law for about forty years. In law, Brandeis distinguished himself as "the people's attorney." He defended the citizens of Boston against the monopolies and unethical practices of public utilities companies. Brandeis's defense of the common man against the encroachments of "big business" continued throughout his career. His book **Other People's Money,** influenced President Wilson deeply; in 1916 he appointed Brandeis to the Supreme Court of the United States where he served for twenty-three years. His judicial opinions exerted a profound influence on American constitutional law. Brandeis often joined Justice Oliver Wendell Holmes in minority dissenting opinions. These historic opinions changed American thought on social problems. Brandies's belief in the need for legal change to meet the new conditions of industrial society, and for public regulations to protect the public interest, foreshadowed the social legislation of the New Deal in the 1930's.

In 1910, Brandeis's interest in Jewish life was awakened by his contact with the Jewish garment workers of New York, when he served as mediator in a strike. His active participation in Zionism* dates to the period closely preceding the First World War. As chairman of the Provisional Committee for General Zionist affairs, 1914-1918, he strengthened the World Zionist movement that had been disrupted by the war. He was influencial in obtaining American approval of the Balfour

Louis Dembitz Brandeis
Courtesy
Brandeis University.

64

Declaration.* A businesslike Zionist, Brandeis stressed the practical aspects of the rebuilding of Jewish Palestine.* He helped found Palestine Economic Corporation, and played an important part in the encouragement of the investment of private capital in Palestine. As a result of a disagreement with Chaim Weizmann* on the proper methods to be employed in developing Palestine economically, he resigned from his Zionist offices in 1921. Brandeis remained, nevertheless, a devoted Zionist all his life, and was often consulted on important policy matters.

BRANDEIS UNIVERSITY. Founded in 1948 and located in Waltham, Mass., Brandeis University is the first Jewish-sponsored nonsectarian institution of higher learning in the Western Hemisphere. Named after the late Supreme Court Justice Louis Dembitz Brandeis,* it admits students without regard to race, color, or religious affiliation. Its first president was Abram Sachar, a Jewish scholar, and a former national director of the Hillel Foundation of B'nai B'rith.*

The religious requirements of Christians and Jewish students are respected in planning the school calendar and in the dining hall.

In October 1955, Brandeis University dedicated a modern group of three chapels, for students of the Catholic, Jewish, and Protestant faiths. This is a departure from the usual college practice of having a single non-denominational chapel.

BRAZIL. A federal republic; the largest country in South America. Brazil, which was discovered by Portugal* in 1500, was the home of the first organized Jewish community in the New World. Large numbers of Marranos,* forced converts who observed their Jewish faith in secret, arrived early in the sixteenth century. They prospered in commerce and industry, but at the price of denying their Judaism publicly. Only when the Dutch conquered Pernambuco in 1630 were the Marranos able to declare their faith. Their congregations were enlarged by Jews from Holland, the West Indies, and North Africa. So extensive was their trade that Pernambuco came to be known as "the port of the Jews." This happy interlude ended when the Portuguese recaptured Dutch Brazil in 1654, and expelled the Jews from the country. Most of the Brazilian Jews fled to Holland. Small groups found refuge in Surinam and Curacao in the Dutch West Indies. Twenty-three boarded a ship which bore them to New Amsterdam, where they became the nucleus of the famous Portuguese-Jewish community of New York.*

So effective was the Portuguese persecution that for the next 175 years there was no indication of

Students in Feldberg Lounge at Brandeis University.

Jewish life in Brazil. After Brazil achieved its independence from Portugal in 1824, however, a small community of Marranos revealed its Judaism in Belem, far from the capital. Later in the century, two other small communities were founded in Brazil. Yet it is only at the turn of the 20th century that the "modern" community may be said to begin. At that time, the Jewish Colonization Association* began to encourage European Jews to emigrate to Brazil and settle on farms. The farm colonies were not very successful. Most of their members settled in cities and founded communities there. These communities were enlarged by new immigrants, especially after the United States began to restrict its own immigration in 1924. Because of the opportunities it offered to newcomers, Brazil became the home of the second largest Jewish community in Latin America. Totaling (1984) 100,000, it is second only to the Argentinian settlement of 250,000. Between 1957 and 1959 Brazil received some 3,000 immigrants from Egypt and 700 from Hungary.

The Brazilian Jewish community is a prosperous one. Most of its members are merchants or manufacturers; the remainder are largely skilled craftsmen. The large majority live in Rio de Janeiro and Sao Paulo, but there are Jews in every major city in the country. Since 1951 all sectors of the Jewish community have been represented in the World Jewish Congress* by the Confederation of the Jewish Societies of Brazil.

The cultural activities within the community are varied. There are three Yiddish newspapers and many Jewish periodicals in Portuguese. The larger communities have Jewish school systems and elaborate community organizations. Zionist feeling runs high, especially since the creation of the State of Israel.* Educators from Israel play a large part in running the Jewish schools in Rio and Sao

Paulo, although non-Zionists have their own schools. In addition, teachers from most of the Jewish schools are regularly sent to Israel for training. In 1954, an Israel-Brazilian Cultural Institute was inaugurated under the chairmanship of Brazil's foreign minister. It grants scholarships to Brazil's students who wish to study in Israel, and has set itself the task of popularizing Brazilian literature in Israel and Israel literature in Brazil. Another cultural institution of note is the Jewish-Brazilian Institute of Historical Research, which studies the history of the Jewish community in Brazil.

BRENNER, JOSEPH CHAIM (1881-1921). Zionist pioneer and Hebrew novelist, first attracted attention with his stories of the grim life in poverty-stricken small towns of Russia. His larger novels, **Ba-Horef, Mi-Saviv La-Nekudah,** are stories of the futile strivings of Jewish youth to improve their lot in Czarist Russia. In his later novels, he describes life in Palestine. Brenner lived

Joseph Chaim Brenner

for several years in London and edited there a Hebrew monthly, **Ha-Meorer** ("The Awakener"). He settled in Palestine in 1909, and there, deeply influenced by A.D. Gordon,* followed Gordon's ideas in advocating a just society and a life close to nature. Brenner advocated friendly relations with the Arabs and himself lived and mingled freely with them. Ironically, he was killed in an Arab riot on May 1, 1921. One of the largest agricultural settlements, Givat Brenner, bears his name.

BRODETSKY, SELIG (1888-1954). Mathematician, Zionist leader. Brought to England from Russia at the age of five, Brodetsky was for many years a professor of mathematics at the Universities of Bristol and Leeds. In 1921 he attended his first Zionist Congress; he was elected to the World Zionist Executive in 1928. Brodetsky was president of the Board of Deputies of British Jews* and of the Zionist Federation of Great Britain from

Selig Brodetsky

1940 to 1949, and served as president of the Hebrew University in Jerusalem from 1949 until 1951.

BUBER, MARTIN (1878-1965). Jewish philosopher and scholar, who exerted great influence on Jewish and Zionist thought in Western Europe. He was born in Vienna. Most of his works are in German, some in Hebrew. From 1916 to 1924 he was editor of **Der Jude,** a leading publication of Jewish thought, philosophy, and religion, published in Berlin. Buber's religious philosophy has its roots in an ethical and social approach to man's place in the world. Together with Franz Rosenzweig, he translated the Bible into German.

Buber delved into Jewish mysticism and published collections of Hasidic tales, in which he brought to light the beauty and thought of Hasidism.

After the rise of Nazism, Buber settled in Palestine. In 1938 he became professor of social philosophy in the Hebrew University of Jerusalem. He was the recipient of many honors from postwar Germany, including the Honor Prize of the City of Munich (1960). Other honors included the Albert Schweitzer Medal (1964).

Martin Buber

BUCHENWALD. Town in Germany. In 1937, the Nazis established a concentration camp there to provide slave labor for factories in central Germany. In November, 1938, 10,000 German Jews arrived in Buchenwald and by 1944, the figure rose to nearly 100,000. Among the prominent political prisoners was the former French premier, Leon Blum, who was liberated by American troops on April 11, 1945. Many inmates died of hunger, disease and maltreatment. (See also JEWRY, ANNIHILATION OF EUROPEAN.)

BULGARIA. According to documentary evidence, Jews lived in Bulgaria during the second century C.E. In 379, while it was still a Roman province, there were anti-Jewish disturbances in Bulgaria. In the eighth and ninth centuries, the Bulgarian Jewish communities grew in numbers and in influence, and in 967, many Byzantine Jews settled there. The growth of the Jewish centers continued, and by the end of the twelfth century the Jews controlled Bulgarian trade with Venice. Their position was even more favorable under the rule of King Ivan Alexander. In 1335, this ruler married the Jewess, Sarah, who on her baptism took the name Theodora. Her son, Ivan Sisman III came to the throne in 1346, and continued his mother's friendly attitude to the Jewish population.

Bulgaria was conquered by Turkey in 1389, and soon became a haven for Jewish refugees from the Spanish Inquisition.* Since then, the majority of Bulgarian Jews have been Sephardim.* Anti-Jewish outbreaks resulted when Bulgaria became an independent state in 1878 and thousands of Jews were expelled. Sporadic outbreaks of anti-Semitism* resulted in continued emigration from the country. During the Second World War, the Nazis exterminated the majority of the Jews of Bulgaria. Of the few Jews who survived at the end of the war, the majority emigrated to Israel in the mass exodus of 1949. At the Fifth Conference of the Jewish People's Communities held in Sofia on April 20, 1952, it was reported that there were some 7,676 Jews in Bulgaria. Of these 4,259 lived in Sofia. All Jewish schools had been closed in 1948, when the Jewish Scientific Institute in Sofia and the Jewish Library and Reading Room were taken over by the municipal government. By the law of May 19, 1951, Jewish communities became lay institutions, and those with fewer than fifty Jews were ordered dissolved. In 1984 there were less than 3,400 Jews in Bulgaria.

BUND. Jewish Socialist Party, founded in Russia in 1897. Its influence was especially strong among the Jewish workers in densely Jewish population centers such as those of Warsaw, Bialystok, Minsk, and Vitebsk. A militant group, the Bund worked for the overthrow of the Russian Tsarist government, organizing demonstrations and strikes. Arrests and deportations of its leaders followed. Some Bundists escaped to the United States and became active in the Jewish socialist movement in America. During the pogroms following the unsuccessful Russian revolution in 1905, the Bund took part in organizing Jewish self-defense, and bravely repelled the attackers.

After the Russian Revolution in 1917, a part of the Bund joined the Jewish section of the Communist party. Those who did not were persecuted by the Soviets. In Poland,* the Bund showed considerable strength between the two World Wars. It established schools, conducted cultural work in the Yiddish language, organized youth groups and workers' cooperatives.

Initially, the Bund bitterly opposed Zionism and considered it a "bourgeois Utopia." It was equally antagonistic to Hebrew as the Jewish national tongue. Remnants of the Bund are still active in America, Israel,* and some European countries.

BURG, YOSEPH (1909-   ). Israel political leader. Born in Germany, he settled in Palestine in 1939. He has been a member of the Knesset* since its establishment in 1949. A leader of Mizrachi* and Ha-Poel ha-Mizrachi, he served as Minister of Health, Minister of Posts, Minister of Social Welfare and Minister of Interior. In 1979, he was nominated to head the Israel delegation that negotiated with Egypt* on the autonomy for the Arabs in the West Bank and Gaza.

In August 1984, he presided as the oldest member of the newly elected Knesset's opening session.

BURLA, YEHUDA, See HEBREW LITERATURE.

CABALAH. See KABBALAH.

CAHAN, ABRAHAM (1860-1952). Socialist leader and founder and editor of the influential Yiddish newspaper, the New York **Jewish Daily Forward.** He was educated for the rabbinate in his native Russia, but soon turned toward radical and socialist views. Upon his arrival in America in 1882, he found a fertile field for his ideas among immigrant Jewry. Cahan worked actively as labor organizer, lecturer, and editor of various Yiddish periodicals. In 1902 he became the editor of the **Forward**, a post he held till his death. A talented writer, he published successful short stories and novels in English, with **The Rise of David Levinsky** particularly notable. In this work Cahan achieved a description of the problems of his generation that has been recognized as a classic of immigrant literature in the United States.

Abraham Cahan   Courtesy Jewish Daily Forward.

CALENDAR. The Jewish calendar is based on the changes of the moon, and not on those of the sun, as is the general calendar. There is a new moon every twenty-nine or thirty days. Twelve such months make up the normal Jewish year. This method of figuring created differences between the solar, or sun year, of 365 days and the Jewish or lunar year of 354 days. To make up for this difference the Jewish leap year has an additional month after Adar,* called Adar Sheni (Second

Camp Massad, Pennsylvania.

Adar). The second Adar month comes every third, sixth, eighth, eleventh, fourteenth, seventeenth and nineteenth year.

In ancient times, before astronomical calculations were made mathematically exact, the people of Judea watched the skies for the appearance of the new moon. As soon as the new moon was spotted by witnesses, bonfires were lit on the hilltops to speed the news. Burning torches signaled from mountain to mountain, beginning with Jerusalem's Mount of Olives and on as far as the Babylonian* frontier. In the Holy Land the Sanhedrin* (highest legislative and judicial council) fixed the dates of the holidays and the festivals, and fast messengers relayed the information as far as Babylonia. By the middle of the fourth century, persecutions had made conditions in Palestine very difficult and uncertain. It was probably then that the head of the scattered Sanhedrin, Hillel II, introduced a final and fixed calendar. He published the mathematical and astronomical information for it and made it possible for all Jewish communities in the Dispersion to use this knowledge. This removed the uncertainties from the date of the Rosh Hodesh, the New Moon, and of the first of the year from which the dates of all holidays are set.

N.B-A.

CAMPS, JEWISH. American Jewish boys and girls of school age are afforded many opportunities for a summer of constructive relaxation at day camps and away-from-home camps. There are very many fine camps in all parts of the United States and Canada which provide the Jewish camper with residence accommodations, athletic facilities, kosher cuisine and variegated programs of activity. These camps are either privately owned or sponsored by communal agencies such as Y.M.H.A.'s or by **yeshivot.**

67

However, there are a number of camps which are exceptional in that they provide the normal advantages of camping life, and add a program of comprehensive Jewish instruction and Jewish religious experience in pleasant and relaxing surroundings. The young people who spend their vacations in these camps return better informed Jews as well.

The three best-known camps are Cejwin, Ramah, and Morasha. Cejwin, in Port Jervis, N.Y., was the pioneer of Jewish educational camps, and was founded in 1919.

Ramah camps are located in Wisconsin, Pennsylvania, Connecticut, California, Ontario (Canada), New York, and Israel. Ramah also conducts an annual teenage study program in Israel and a training institute for future counselors. Organized by the Jewish Theological Seminary of America* in 1947, Ramah offers a Jewish educational program conducted in Hebrew, with formal instruction in classical Hebrew texts. The religious outlook is that of Conservative Judaism. The educational program is directed by the faculty of the Seminary's Teachers Institute. Ramah camps are attended by some 3,000 youngsters in the U.S. and 500 in Israel, and have a staff of 2,000.

Very much like Ramah and Cejwin is Camp Yavneh in the Boston area. There are also a number of Yiddish-speaking camps which offer a rich program of special activities in Yiddish language and culture.

The Federation of Jewish Philanthropies runs 16 camp sites in New York, New Jersey, and Pennsylvania. Some 6,500 youngsters attend Federation camps. The best-known is Surprise Lake Camp in New York.

In recent years Orthodox groups—religious Zionist organizations, the Agudath Israel World Organization, yeshivot (Lubavitch Movement, Torah Vada'ath, Yeshiva University, etc.), and Beth Jacob Schools—have set up camps of their own, where a full program of religious training is offered alongside regular camping activities. The largest of these camps is Morasha in Pennsylvania, established in 1964.

Every year, hundreds of Israeli counselors come to the United States to work with youngsters in Jewish camps throughout the country.

CANAAN. Son of Ham and grandson of Noah*; ancestor of seven Canaanite tribes, sometimes identified with the Phoenicians. In the Biblical account, Canaan, the coastal plain west of the Jordan, is the land God promised to Abraham. "Unto thy seed will I give this land" (Genesis: 12:17).

CANADA. The British Dominion of Canada is somewhat larger in area than the United States including Alaska. Yet its population is only about one-tenth that of the United States. In 1984 the Canadian population numbered over 24,000,000. Of these, about 310,000 are Jews. About 100,000 live in Montreal and about 125,000 in Toronto.

Until 1760, Camada formed a part of a vast French colony in which very few Jews had been allowed to settle. In 1763, however, the British defeated the French and established British rule over the country. Several Jews had served as officers in the British army. One of them, Aaron Hart, settled in Trois Rivieres ("Three Rivers"), a small town in the province of Quebec. Later, his son, Ezekiel Hart, was elected to the legislature of Lower Canada. His political opponents objected to his being seated in the legislature because, being a Jew, he refused to take the prescribed oath "on my faith as a Christian." The law was on their side; but in 1829 it was amended to extend the same political rights to Jews as to Christians. In 1832 the Jews were granted full political equality —twenty-five years earlier than in England.

The growth of the Jewish community in Canada was very slow until the middle of the nineteenth century; until then it had consisted almost entirely of Sephardic Jews who arrived from England, Holland, and from various countries in the Americas. These early Sephardic settlers played a leading role in developing the new country, pioneering in such enterprises as transatlantic shipping, transatlantic cables, fishing, street-railways, and mining. By 1768 there had been enough Sephardic Jews to enable them to found a congregation. They named it Shearith Israel ("Remnant of Israel"), which was also the name of the oldest Jewish congregation in the United States.

Study encounter at B'nai Brith Hillel Foundation's Summer Institute at Camp B'nai Brith in the Poconos, Pa.
Courtesy B'nai B'rith.

Beth Tzedec Congregation—Toronto, Canada.

In the middle of the nineteenth century, a large number of German Jews came to Canada. Being Ashkenazic Jews, they did not feel at home in the Sephardic synagogue. Therefore, in 1858, when their numbers were sufficient, the German and Polish newcomers in Montreal founded the first Ashkenazic congregation in Canada.

With the great Jewish emigration from eastern Europe beginning in the 1880's in the wake of persecution and anti-Semitism,* large numbers of new arrivals reached Canada. Since pioneers were needed to develop Canada's vast unsettled areas, the government offered the newcomers such inducements as free land, equipment, and financial help. Moreover, many of the immigrants were under the influence of the "back to the soil" movement among the Jews of Europe. The arriving immigrants were therefore encouraged to choose agriculture as their new way of life in Canada. The first Canadian Jewish farm settlement was founded in 1882. Baron Maurice de Hirsch* of Paris, and the Jewish Colonization Association (ICA),* which he founded, helped to settle Jews on Canadian soil. Other immigrant Jews became artisans, instrumental in developing industry in Canada. The modern clothing industry, for instance, having been built up by Jews in the United States, was gradually introduced into neighboring Canada as well. First Montreal and later Toronto became Canada's garment centers.

The Jewish community of Montreal is the oldest and largest in Canada. While the majority of Montreal inhabitants speak French, the Jews belong to its English-speaking minority. The majority of the Jewish children attend the "Protestant," that is, English-speaking schools, and the Jewish taxpayers pay their school taxes into the "Protestant" panel. An attempt in 1923 and 1924 to create in Montreal a separate Jewish tax-supported school system failed because the higher courts found it to be unconstitutional. Education in Canada, as in the United States, is under the authority of each province and not of the Federal government. The law provides that those who do not wish either of the two prevailing types of education, the Catholic or the Protestant, may conduct schools of their own choice. Many Jewish parents in Canada prefer to send their children to private all-day schools. In Montreal, sixty per cent of all the Jewish boys and forty per cent of all the Jewish girls attended some type of Jewish school. The largest number of children, almost 50 per cent, attended Jewish all-day schools.

M.Z.F.

Mt. Sinai Hospital in Toronto.

CANON. See BIBLE.

CANTONISTS. Jewish children in Russia conscripted for military service. In 1827, Czar Nicholas I extended military service to include Jews. The Russian conscripts served in the army for twenty-five years, beginning at eighteen. Jewish children, however, were taken at the age of twelve and placed in "canton" or district, schools for six years of preliminary training. They were sent as far away from any Jewish settlement as possible, and every effort was made to convert them to Christianity. Many of the cantonists did not survive the cruel treatment in these schools; many saved themselves by conversion. For this reason, the Jews did everything in their power to keep their children from being taken into the Russian army. To meet this evasion, the government simply compelled the heads of each Jewish community to produce the community's quota of children. The rich often tried to buy substitutes for their children, while informers and professional kidnappers added to the terror and demoralization within the Jewish communities. This state of affairs lasted for 30 years until Alexander II abolished the system in 1857.

CANTOR. See HAZAN.

CANTOR, GEORGE (1845-1918). German mathematician. Born of a converted family of Jewish extraction, he was the founder of the theory of sets, which revolutionized modern mathematics.

CARDOZO, BENJAMIN NATHAN (1870-1938). United States Supreme Court justice. Born in New York City into a family of Sephardic* Jews, Cardozo was graduated with high honors from Columbia College, and in 1891 received his degree in law from the Columbia University Law School. He practiced law in New York, and was elected justice of the Supreme Court of the State of New York in 1913. President Herbert Hoover appointed Cardozo to succeed Oliver Wendell Holmes as Associate Justice of the Supreme Court of the United States in 1932.

Cardozo was a trustee of Columbia University; a member of the Board of Governors of the American Friends of the Hebrew University; and a member of the executive committees of the National Jewish Welfare Board and of the American Jewish Committee.*

Cardozo also distinguished himself in legal literature. His books include **The Nature of the Judicial Process, Paradoxes of the Legal Sciences,** and **Law and Literature.** In his writings, he always

Benjamin N. Cardozo   Courtesy Fallon Publications.

endeavored to reconcile the law with the spirit and the needs of the times.

CARIGAL, HAYM ISAAC (1733-1777). Rabbi and scholar, born in Palestine. During the course of Carigal's wide travels, he met Ezra Stiles, a Protestant clergyman and president of Yale College, in Newport, R.I. Stiles' diary contains many references to Rabbi Carigal and the Jews of Newport. Stiles studied exegesis or critical Biblical interpretation with Carigal, and the two men corresponded after Carigal left. The Hebrew correspondence is preserved in the library of Yale University.

CARTOGRAPHY. See AMERICA, DISCOVERY OF.

CENTRAL CONFERENCE OF AMERICAN RABBIS. The oldest of American rabbinic associations (about 1,100 members), founded for Reform rabbis by Isaac Mayer Wise in 1889. A leading spokesman for Liberal or Reform Judaism, the CCAR publishes the Union prayer books, the Union hymnal, a home prayer book, proceedings of its annual conventions, reports of its commissions, and other volumes. Since 1954, the conference has had a permanent office in New York City. Membership includes Reform rabbis in every part of the world.

CHAGALL, MARC (1889-   ). Painter, born in a small town near Vitebsk, White Russia. As a young man Chagall settled in France. He is the most eminent member of the École Juive ("Jewish School") of Paris which, through modern pictorial means, transferred to canvas recollections of the Jewish past. Judaism, as he experienced it in his hometown, has always been a strong source of inspiration to Chagall. Chagall draws and paints Jewish figures with a bold imagination, and with little concern for realistic detail. Some of his pictures are like strange dreams in which all objects appear topsy-turvy, without concern for logic or perspective. One of the early surrealist painters. Chagall used floating figures in his painting as his personal symbol for the liberation of the spirit through love or art. Among his best known paintings are the vibrantly colored canvasses of **I and My Village, Over Vitebsk, The Betrothed, Rabbi of Vitebsk, Rabbi with Torah,** and **The Green Violinist.**

Chagall has also painted murals, ballet and theatre settings, and costumes. He has illustrated the **Fables** of La Fontaine, the **Arabian Nights,** and Gogol's **Dead Souls.** His etchings illustrating the Bible appeared late in 1956. A group of stained-glass windows symbolizing the tribes of Israel were commissioned by Hadassah* and installed in the synagogue of the Hebrew University-Medical Center on the outskirts of Jerusalem. He executed a mosaic wall for the lobby of the new (1966) Knesset building and two murals for the new (1966) Metropolitan Opera building in New York.

CHAIN, ERNEST BORIS (1906-1979). Biochemist, discoverer of the curative properties of penicillin, and its adapter for use on the human body. Chain was born in Berlin of Russian-Jewish parents, and came to England in 1933. He worked at Cambridge and Oxford universities and was subsequently Director of the Instituto Superiore di Sanita in Rome. He returned to England to become professor of biochemistry at the Imperial College of Science and Technology, London.

CHARITY. The Hebrew word is **tsedakah,** meaning "righteousness," or "justice," since helping the needy is considered a duty. In Biblical times, when the Jews were a farming people, they gave charity by letting the poor glean, that is, gather the grain dropped in harvesting. (**See** Ruth 2: 2-16.) According to Biblical law the corners of the field were to be left unreaped for the poor, who also had the right to all sheaves found uncollected. A tithe, or tenth, of all farm produce was offered to charity; untithed food could not be eaten. Biblical law required that the tithe be distributed to the needy, particularly "to the stranger, the fatherless and the widow."

By Talmudic times each community had a **kuppah,** or charity fund. The community had absolute power to levy taxes for this purpose. From the **kuppah** the community's poor were given money for fourteen meals per week. Distinguished members of the community were collectors for the **kuppah,** and a board of three men was responsible for allocating its moneys. Some rabbis divided charity into seven categories: feeding the hungry; clothing the naked; visiting the sick; burying the dead and comforting mourners; ransoming captives; educating orphans and housing the homeless; and providing dowries for poor brides.

The lending of money without interest, helping the non-Jewish poor in the community, and giving the preference to women and students were all part of the system of Jewish charity. Maimonides* listed eight degrees of charity: the lowest was to give grudgingly; the highest to help a person to become self-supporting.

Charity was also an important act leading to the pardoning of personal trangressions or sins. The Yom Kippur* service states that "repentance and prayer and charity avert the harshness of God's decree." The Jew believes that if one asks God to have pity upon one's own misfortune, one must have pity for the misfortune of others. Charity is therefore distributed on the eve of Yom Kippur in atonement for one's sins. Because charity is considered as effective in redeeming the souls of the dead as well as of the living, alms are also generously distributed at funerals.

Gifts to the poor are not merely associated with mournful occasions and with fear of punishment. Rather, they are a basic principle of Judaism, and are offered on joyous occasions as well. Thus, the merry Purim* festivities include the custom of **mishloah manot,** the sending of gifts to the poor, and it is customary to raise **maot hittim** ("wheat money") before Passover.* This money is used to provide **matzot,** wine and the other ritual needs of the holiday for those who cannot afford them. Similarly, the Passover Seder ceremony includes an invitation to "all the poor to come and eat." In Eastern Europe it was common for the poor to be invited to all ritual celebrations.   A.A.D.

CHILE. Republic on the west coast of South America. Total population (1984), 11,500,000. Jewish population, 20,000. Like other Spanish colonies of South America, Chile had a flourishing Marrano* community in the sixteenth and seventeenth centuries. But whereas the Inquisition* succeeded in suppressing such communities elsewhere, Chile is still the home of a remnant of its colonial Jews: the Sabbatarios, descendants of Marranos who fled to the interior to escape the Inquisition, survive in the mountain province of Cautin. Nothing was known of them until 1919, when a letter requesting admission to the South American Zionist Organization revealed their presence in the country. Investigation disclosed that, despite intermarriage with Spaniards and Indians, and total lack of contact with other Jewish communities, they had preserved a number of Jewish customs and beliefs.

Aside from the Sabbatarios, however, the entire colonial community was lost. Jewish life in Chile was renewed only after 1810. when the country gained independence and offered guarantees of religious freedom. The first communities were small. At the time of World War I, there were about 3,000 Jews in Chile. Most of these were Sephardic Jews from Macedonia and the Balkans. The waves of immigration from Eastern and Central Europe in the decades that followed, increased the number of Jews to 30,000, and made Chile's Jewish community the fourth largest in Latin America. It is also the most highly organized. The Central Committee of the Jewish Community of Chile coordinates the activities of all local organizations, represents Chile's Jews in the World Jewish Congress,* and is recognized by the government as the spokesman for the community.

The Jews in Chile are mainly engaged in trade, crafts, and small industry. They are more active in national political life than are Jews in other South American republics. The degree of their cultural integration is shown by the fact that **Nosotros,** the leading Jewish periodical of the country, is published in Spanish, rather than Yiddish or Hebrew. Yet the Jews of Chile have shown great concern over Israel, and the Zionist Federation, a central organization of all Zionist parties, is active in the Central Committee of the community. C.M.

CHINA, PEOPLE'S REPUBLIC OF. Chinese Jewry consisted of two communities. The Oriental group believed that its forbears reached China after the destruction of the First Temple* (586 B.C.E.). Early Chinese documents indeed mention Jewish traders several centuries before the Common Era. Much later, in the fourteenth century, Marco Polo wrote of influential Jews at the court of Kublai Khan. After 1650 this community, which had preserved its religious traditions for over 2,000 years, declined rapidly. By the middle of the nineteenth century its last synagogue—a beautiful pagoda-like structure at Kai-fung-foo—had disappeared. Today, only a handful of "native" Jews remain. Owing to intermarriage and possibly to conversions in the past, they are indistinguishable in appearance from their Chinese neighbors. The Western community in

China was founded in the 1840's, when China was opened to western trade. Its ranks were swelled by refugees from Europe during the Nazi era. During World War II several well-known European **yeshivot** (Talmudical academies) had branches in the coastal cities of China. The greater part of the refugee community emigrated to Israel after 1948, although many reached the United States and Latin America.*

CHRONICLES. The first and second Books of Chronicles form the last book of the Bible.* Chronicles retells the history of the Jewish people from Creation to the close of the Babylonian exile. It omits the history of the northern Kingdom of Israel,* concentrates on the history of the Kingdom of Judah* and stresses the priestly duties and Temple* ritual.

CIRCUMCISION. Performed upon the Jewish male child on the eighth day of his life. In Genesis 18: 10-18, God commands Abraham* to circumcise the foreskin of all males of the house as the sign of the covenant between God and the children of Abraham. It has become a basic law among Jews. In times of persecution, Jews risked their lives to fulfill the commandment. Traditionally the ceremony is performed by a trained **mohel** ("circumciser"), the child being held by an honored guest, the **sandek** ("godfather"), who occupies a seat designated as Elijah's chair in honor of the prophet Elijah.* This custom stems from the belief that the prophet is witness to the ritual. The circumcision ceremony is an occasion for rejoicing and feasting, accompanied by special blessings and prayers.

COCHIN, JEWS OF. See INDIA.

COHEN. See KOHEN.

COHEN, HERMANN (1848-1918). German philosopher. The son of a cantor in a small Jewish community, he attended the Rabbinical Seminary at Breslau for a few years. However, he left the Seminary and instead devoted himself to the study of philosophy. In 1876, he was appointed professor of philosophy at the University of Marburg. At this time, Cohen entertained little interest in Judaism, and devoted himself entirely to the development of his philosophic system, a modification of the system of Immanuel Kant.

The anti-Semitic outburst of the historian, Treitschke, in 1880, stirred Cohen's Jewish consciousness and he made an attempt to defend his people. An essay on **Love of Fellowman in the Talmud,** written as a reply to a query of a court about the Jewish attitude towards morality, drew him still closer to Jewish matters. From that time on, Cohen wrote many essays on Jewish subjects which were later collected in three volumes. He also wrote a work on the Jewish religion called **Die Religion der Vernunft** ("The Religion of Reason"). In these works, he formulated his philosophical and ethical principles of Judaism. He dwelt especially on the high value of the Messianic idea—the hope for the triumph of good at the "end of days."

COHEN, MORRIS RAPHAEL (1880-1947). American philosopher. Born in Minsk, Russia, he was brought to America by his parents in 1892, at the age of twelve. He studied at City College, Columbia, and Harvard, from where he received his degree of Doctor of Philosophy. Cohen taught at City College for thirty-six years, at first mathematics, and from 1912 to 1936, philosophy.

Of his numerous works, the leading ones are **A Preface to Logic and Scientific Method** and **Reason and Nature.** In addition, Cohen wrote many essays on the philosophy of law and was the editor of the "Modern Legal Philosophical Series."

For a number of years he was inclined to socialism and was active in the Socialist movement. Cohen's interest in Jewish affairs came late in his life. Instrumental in founding the Conference on Jewish Relations in 1933, he served as its president for a number of years.

COLOMBIA. A republic in northwestern South America. Marranos*—converted Jews who practiced the faith of their fathers in secret—lived in Colombia during the sixteenth and seventeenth centuries. Their community was suppressed by the Inquisition* established in 1910. During the 1850's Sephardic Jews from Curacao settled in Colombia. They were joined by immigrants from Greece, Rumania, and Turkey after World War I, and by refugees from Germany and East Europe during the 1930's. Colombia, whose total population (1984) is 29,000,000, is the home of 7,000 Jews, most of whom live in the cities of Bogota, Baranquilla, Cali, Cartagena, and Medellin. Each of these has its own synagogues, religious schools, and charitable organizations.

COLUMBUS, CHRISTOPHER (1491-1506). Discoverer of America. Doubt exists as to the birth date and birthplace of Columbus. Scholars like Rabbi Meyer Kayserling (1829-1905) have uncovered a Marrano* family in Spain whose family names resemble those of the parents and other relatives of Columbus. The Spanish form of Columbus's name is Cristobal Colon, and Vicente Blasco Ibanez asserted that Columbus was a Spanish Jew whose family name was Colon. Another authority, Salvador de Madariaga, had written a biography in which he states: "It is always in this mental region that we find Colon: the border-line between the two faiths. The problem of the converted Jew, but also the problem of the Jew who remains unconverted." Columbus knew no Italian and named places in the New World after Spanish landmarks. Presumably, therefore, he was of Marrano* descent. He had Jews in his crew, and was befriended by powerful Marranos in Spain, to whom he wrote letters bewailing his treatment. Columbus claimed descent from the dynasty of King David. His son, Ferdinand, stated that his father's "progenitors were of the blood royal of Jerusalem, and it pleased him that his parents shall not be much known."

COMMUNITY. See KAHAL.

CONCENTRATION CAMPS. See JEWRY, ANNIHILATION OF EUROPEAN.

CONFIRMATION. Group synagogue ceremony in which boys and girls graduating from elementary religious school publicly mark their attachment to Judaism. Originating in Germany, confirmation was introduced in the United States in 1847 and now takes place in all Reform, most Conservative, and some Orthodox synagogues. It is celebrated on the holiday of Shavuot, to signify that the graduates confirm their loyalty to the Torah, which, according to tradition, was given on Shavuot.

CONGRESS, ZIONIST. Meetings of Zionists from all over the world. The first Zionist Congress was called by Theodor Herzl* and met in Basle, Switzerland,* in August, 1897. It was the first representative Jewish assembly since Judea was conquered by Rome and the Jews dispersed all over the world. Modern political Zionism was formulated there in the Basle Program.* Thereafter, Zionist congresses met periodically and conducted the business of the Zionist movement throughout the world. (**See also** ZIONISM.)

CONSERVATIVE JUDAISM. See JUDAISM.

COPLAND, AARON (1900-   ). Composer, pianist, conductor and author. One of America's leading musicians, Copland has distinguished himself both as creative artist and as intrepreter of modern music. His work as a composer has developed from a dry, ironic modern idiom to more simplified melodic treatment. In both phases he has made striking use of American jazz and folk motifs. His **Vitebsk, Study on a Jewish**

Melody, and **In the Beginning,** a choral setting on the theme of Creation, are works on Jewish motifs.

CORDOVERO, MOSES. See KABBALAH.

COSSACK UPRISING. See LITHUANIA; also GERMANY.

COSTA RICA. A republic in southern Central America. Costa Rica's Jewish community was founded by settlers from Curacao in the 1890's. Immigrants from Europe have since swelled its number to 2,500 in total population of 2,020,000. The Ashkenazic* (East European) majority and Sephardic* minority have separate organizations. The Central Zionist Organization is the representative Jewish body of that community.

COUNCIL OF FOUR LANDS. See KAHAL.

COVENANT. In Biblical times a contract or agreement of friendship between men or nations was completed in a ceremony in which the two parties passed between the two halves of an animal sacrifice. (Genesis 15:9-11.) In the Biblical covenants between God and Israel, a sign accompanied each renewal of the contract.

When God made a covenant with Noah* after the flood, He set the rainbow as a sign that "the waters shall no more become a flood to destroy all flesh." (Gen. 9:13-15.) In the covenant God made with Abraham,* giving to him and to his children the land of Canaan* for "an everlasting possession," circumcision* was the sign. (Gen. 17:10.) When the Lord renewed the covenant with the Children of Israel at Sinai, His sign was the Sabbath.* (Exod. 31:13.) In the Bible, the Torah* itself is called "the Book of the Covenant," the stone tablets with the Ten Commandments "the tablets of the covenant," a reminder that Israel's part of the contract was faithfulness to God and righteous behavior toward men.

CRACOW. A city in Poland which dates the origins of its Jewish community back to the 14th century, when its Old Synagogue was erected. The Jewish community of Cracow became noted for its learning and creativeness, its well-established traditions and its individual style. From 595 on, the Jewish community of Cracow enjoyed full autonomy.

Among the renowned rabbis who were the pride of the Jewish community of Cracow were: Jacob Pollack, who introduced the "pilpull"* method into the study of the Talmud;* Moses Isserles, who wrote a commentary and supplement to the Shulhan Arukh;* Joel Sirkis, the suthor of **Bayit Hadash,** a volume on Jewish law; and Yom Tov Lippman Heller,* who wrote a commentary on the Mishnah.

During the nineteenth century Cracow won the distinction of having two of its rabbis, Berush Meisels and Simon Sofer (Schreiber), elected as members of the Austrian Parliament. In the course of the twentieth century Zionism gained great influence in Cracow due in part to the leadership of its noted rabbi, Joshua Thon, a member of the Sejm or Polish Parliament.

When the Germans occupied the city, they put to death all of its Jewish inhabitants who failed to make their escape. Thus was destroyed a famed Jewish community, which had existed for over six hundred years. H.S.

CRÉMIEUX, ISAAC ADOLPHE (1796-1880). Statesman and champion of French democracy and equal rights for the Jews of France.* Crémieux devoted all his life to furthering these aims. He was instrumental in the abolition of a degrading oath which all French Jews had been forced to take when appearing at court. Admitted to the bar in 1817, he became an outstanding orator, lawyer, statesman, and defender of human rights.

Deeply aroused by the blood accusation* against his fellow Jews in the Damascus affair, Crémieux actively intervened on behalf of the unfortunate victims. This close contact with the misery of Oriental Jewry led him to form the Alliance Israélite Universelle* to promote their welfare. He became president of this important organization and retained the post for life. In the turbulent political scene of 19th-century France, he held various government posts, including that of minister of justice, and in 1873 was made senator for life.

CRESCAS, HASDAI (c. 1340-1412). Spanish rabbi, statesman, and religious philosopher. The Talmudic scholarship of Hasdai Crescas was so highly valued that in his own day he was called simply "the **Rav** (teacher of Saragossa." Crescas' statesmanship was recognized when he served the Royal Court of Aragon, yet this did not save him from tragedy. His son was killed during the black year of 1391, when Spanish mobs, stirred up by the eloquence of a monk, raged in many cities and gave the Jews a choice between death or giving up their faith. Crescas is best remembered for his philosophical work **Or Adonai,** "Light of the Lord." This book described the major beliefs of Judaism as faith in God's guidance and in Jewish destiny. Hasdai Crescas opposed the philosophy of Aristotle and stressed his belief in man's free will. He is considered the last original Jewish thinker of the medieval period, and his work influenced deeply the 17th-century philosopher Baruch (Benedict) Spinoza.*

CRIMEA. Peninsula in the Soviet Union, on the eastern shore of the Black Sea. Jews first settled there during the time of the Second Temple,* over two thousand years ago, and possibly even earlier. Their numbers grew under Roman rule. Old Jewish inscriptions discovered in Crimea indicate that a substantial and prosperous Jewish population existed there at the beginning of the common era. From the 8th to the 9th centuries, the Khazar* Kingdom flourished in the Crimea. First a pagan nation, the Khazars embraced Judaism at a very early period in their history. This period of an independent Khazar state ended in 1016, when the Russians and Byzantines united to defeat the Khazars.

Jewish communities survived the Tatar invasions in the 13th century. In later periods, prosperous Jewish tradesmen from the Crimea opened routes of commerce to Turkey, Russia, and Poland.* When Tsarist Russia annexed the region in 1784, most of the Jews were artisans and small traders. In addition to the Jewish population, Crimea had substantial Karaite* communities. This sect, founded by Anan ben David during the 8th century, rejected Talmudic tradition, adhering only to the Biblical law.

In 1924, the Soviet government set aside some of the arid land of this area for Jewish colonization. A number of Jewish families who had lost their means of livelihood because of the government ban on private enterprise emigrated to the Crimea. A special organization, Komzet (Commission for the Rural Placement of Jewish Toilers), supervised the colonization. The American Joint Distribution Committee (JDC)* extended financial and technical help to the settlers through the Agro-Joint. Before World War II, there were about 80,000 Jews in the Crimea, out of a total population of over one million. 25,000 of the Jews engaged in agriculture. During the Nazi occupation, all the Jewish colonies were destroyed, and most of the Jews perished. Only a small number returned to their homes after the war. H.L.

CRUSADES (1096-1291). The Crusades were a series of Christian wars designed to free the Holy Land from Moslem rule. They were uniformly tragic in their effects upon the Jews. Crusaders were exempted from the payment of their debts to Jews. Inflamed to hatred against the "unbelievers" by both church and state, the armies of Crusaders— often little better than armed mobs—began their "holy war" by massacring Jewish communities in France,* Germany,* and England. Some Jews were forcibly baptized, others were killed for refusing baptism, still others were slain without being offered the opportunity of choice. The Emperor Henry IV permitted the enforced converts to live as Jews again. A few bishops and archbishops tried to protect the Jews of their districts, but their efforts generally failed. In the Holy Land itself, the few surviving Jewish communities were almost entirely destroyed by the Crusaders. What the pagan Romans had left undone, the Christians completed. The afflicted European communities met the attacks in different ways. The Jews of Treves submitted to forced baptism (and later renounced it); those of Cologne tried in vain to hide; those of Worms, Speyer, Mayence and York took their own lives; those of the French city of Carentan died fighting. Rashi,* who was in Troyes (France) during the First Crusade, escaped injury. His grandson, Rabbenu Jacob Tam, was badly wounded—almost killed—in the Second Crusade. Many of the **kinnot**—poems of lamentation—composed in memory of the victims are still recited on the Fast of the Ninth of Av. As a result of the Crusades, tens of thousands of Jews were massacred, some communities were completely wiped out, and others never recovered their strength. Jewish trade with the Orient was broken, and Jews were forced more and more to earn their living by usury. Above all, the suspicion, prejudice and hatred fanned against them became deep rooted and lingered on for centuries in the popular mind. A.A.D

CUBA. Until the 1959 revolution which ended in the transformation of Cuba into a socialist state by Fidel Castro, the Jews in Cuba numbered 10,000. Less than 700 Jews remain (1984) in a population of over 10 million. Cuba won freedom from Spain in 1898 as a result of the Spanish-American War. In the sixteenth century, Marranos,* forced converts who practiced Judaism in

Jewish Community House in Havana, Cuba.

secret, came to Cuba to escape persecution in other parts of Spanish America. For a short time they prospered, playing an important part in developing Cuba's sugar industry. Finally, the Inquisition,* which sought to wipe out all non-Catholic faiths, reached the island, and the Marrano community disappeared. Although religious persecution ceased in 1783, it was not until Cuba gained her independence that Jews began to immigrate in fairly large numbers. The first to come were Jews from the United States, who formed an independent community. At about the same time, many Sephardic Jews from Turkey and Morocco arrived. The influx of East European Jews began only after 1924, when the United States shut its doors to immigrants. Strict immigration laws passed in the 1930's prevented the further growth of the community. Today about half of Cuba's Jews are descendants of the Sephardic immigrants; the rest are divided between a "North American" and an East European community.

CUP OF ELIJAH. See PASSOVER.

CUSTOMS, JEWISH. Traditionally, a custom **(minhag** in Hebrew) is a practice which, though not based on Biblical or Talmudic law, has become, through long observance, as sacred and binding as a religious law. Customs have played an important part in the development of **Halakhah,** or Jewish religious law. The rabbis, seeking to achieve unanimity of practice and usage, established many customs of different times and places as laws. Many Biblical laws, such as circumcision,* began as customs before they became law. "The custom of Israel is law," (Tosafot) is a familiar comment.

Customs may vary from place to place, and the rabbis maintain that one must follow the local custom, and that sometimes a custom may even override a law. Sephardic and Ashkenazic Jews vary in many of their customs, such as Hebrew pronunciation, the text of some prayers, and holiday observances. Reform Jews have instituted new customs, such as the confirmation* ceremony on Shavuot.* M.Sch.

CYPRUS. An island at the eastern end of the Mediterranean Sea. It comprises an area of 6,188 square miles, and has a population of close to half a million, consisting chiefly of Greeks and Turks. Cyprus is mentioned in the Bible under the name of Kittim.

During the Maccabean period there were Jews living on Cyprus. Alexander Jannaeus* fought the king of Cyprus and conquered him. In the time of Trajan, the Jews of Cyprus took an active part in the revolt against Rome.* As a consequence, the Jewish Cypriots were exterminated, and for many years Jews were forbidden to live on the island. At the advice of Don Joseph Nasi* (the "Prince"), the Turks captured the island in 1571 from the city-state of Venice. In 1878, during the time of Lord Beaconsfield (Benjamin Disraeli*), the island became a British Crown Colony in 1925. In 1960, Cyprus gained its independence.

Several attempts have been made by the Jews of Cyprus to start farm settlements, but they have failed. In the 1930's a number of families moved from Palestine* to Cyprus, and engaged there in the citrus fruit trade. After the Second World War the British established detention camps on Cyprus for Jewish refugees who tried to enter Palestine illegally. In 1977 about 30 Jews lived on Cyprus.

CYRUS. (Sixth century B.C.E.) One of the great conqueror-kings of the ancient world, and founder of the Persian Empire. When this Median prince took Babylon in 539 B.C.E. he found there the Jews who had been led into captivity by Nebuchadnezzar fifty years earlier. Cyrus permitted them to return to Palestine, and named Zerubbabel, grandson of Judea's last king, as governor of Jerusalem. He assigned a military guard to escort Zerubbabel to his capital. The returning exiles carried with them the plundered vessels of the Temple and funds for its reconstruction. Both were gifts of the emperor.

CZECHOSLOVAKIA. A republic in central Europe, bounded by Poland and Germany on the north and west, respectively, and Hungary and Austria on the east and south respectively. The state is composed of the districts of Moravia, Silesia and Slovakia (Slovakia the district of "Carpatho-Russia in Subcarpathian Ruthenia" was ceded to Russia in 1945).

The beginnings of the Jewish community in Moravia and Bohemia date back to the tenth century. The first place in which Jews settled was evidently a suburb of the capital city, Prague, and from there they spread to other cities in the land. Their numbers increased when they were joined by Jews who were fleeing from the cruel attacks of the Crusaders in the countries of western and southern Europe. Until the middle of the fourteenth century, the Jews prospered in the region, engaging in agriculture and various trades.

In the middle of the fourteenth century the Jews of what is now Czechoslovakia suffered persecution and exile. They were accused of poisoning wells and desecrating the bread of the Holy Communion. The religious war which broke out at this time between the students of Jan Hus and the Catholics brought further suffering to the Jews. In the year 1542, disaster was narrowly averted when Pope Pius IV persuaded King Ferdinand I to cancel the edict ordering the Jews of Prague out of the city. After each tragic disturbance, the Jewish community rebuilt its life, and the community became famous for its outstanding scholars. Among these were Rabbi Judah Loew* (Maharal),* scholar and saint, and Rabbi Yom Tov Lipman Heller,* author of a commentary on the Mishnah.

The country was for many years the cause of controversy between certain Slavic and German tribes. After continuous battles between the Slavic and the German rulers in the middle of the seventeenth century, it fell to the Hapsburg crown and became a part of the empire of Austro-Hungary. In 1918, Czechoslovakia again won her political independence.

The new republic, established after the First World War by Thomas Masaryk, granted its Jewish citizens equal rights in practice as well as in theory. In 1938, there were about 400,000 Jews living in Czechoslovakia, in a general population of about 15,000,000. The Jews were represented in the government, in civil service, in the armed forces, in the Parliment, in trade and commerce, and in the professions. A national-cultural Jewish life developed there, and numerous **yeshivot** and Hebrew schools flourished. Carpatho-Russia, was, between the two World Wars, an important center of Hasidism.* Many Jews there engaged in farming. Some of the most famous Czecholovak communities were: Prague, Brno, Bratislava, Moravska Ostrava and Mukacevo. In the 1930's Czechoslovakia absorbed many Jewish refugees from Germany.

The Munich Pact of 1938, under which large areas were surrendered to Nazi Germany, brought tragedy to the Jews of Czechoslovakia. In the area which was ceded to Germany, Czech Jews were persecuted, as their co-religionists throughout the German Reich. In 1939, the Germans occupied Czechoslovakia, nullified her independence, and turned her into a puppet state. Some Czechoslovak Jews managed to emigrate to other countries, including Palestine, but large numbers suffered the fate of millions of other Jews, and were exterminated in the infamous death camps.

After the Second World War, the republic of Czechoslovakia was re-established and its Jewish citizens were granted equal rights. But nearly all of the communities were without Jewish residents. In 1946 the Communist regime came into power, and most of the remaining Jews left. In 1984 the Jewish population in Czechoslovakia was estimated at about 8,500; most of the Jews live in Prague and several other large centers. There are no **yeshivot** or Hebrew schools in Czechoslovakia, no Jewish cultural or national activity; emigration is impossible.

S.E.

Silver Gilded Kiddush Cup, 1610, Czechosolvakia.

D

DALET. Fourth letter of the Hebrew alphabet. Its numerical value is four.

DAMASCUS. The Syrian city "half as old as time." When Abraham* fought King Chedorlaomer for the liberation of Lot, he pursued Chedor-laomer to Hobah which is north of Damascus (Gen. 14:15). For briefs periods on and off, beginning with David,* Jewish kings ruled this capital of Aram. Finally it fell to the Assyrian empire of Tiglat-Pileser in 732 B.C.E. (I Kings 16:9). Ruled at different times by almost every aggressive power of the Mid-East, Damascus fell to the Arabs and became their imperial city in 635 C.E. In 1516 C.E., the Ottoman Turks held Damascus as one of their important ruling centers. It continued as such until the First World War. The Jewish settlement of Damascus has been almost unbroken from the time of King Herod* (40-4 B.C.E.) to the present. After World War I, Arab nationalism made life difficult for the Jews, and they began to move away, mostly to Israel. Of the 10,000 Jews in Damascus in 1940, only about 3,000 poor, small tradesmen and artisans remained in 1979.

DAMASCUS AFFAIR. In 1840, while Syria was under Egyptian rule, the Jewish community of Damascus* was accused of killing a Franciscan friar, Father Tomaso, in order to use his blood for ritual purposes. Influenced by the French consul, Ratti Menton, an inquiry was undertaken by the local governor. Jewish leaders of the community were arrested and tortured. One died in prison, eight others were condemned to death. Isaac Adolphe Crémieux* of France and Sir Moses Montefiore* of England came to Alexandria to plead with the ruler Mehemet Ali. They succeeded in obtaining the release of the prisoners as well as an expression of Mehemet Ali's disbelief in the charge against them. Meanwhile, Turkey had recovered control of Syria, and Crémieux and Montefiore proceeded to Constantinople, obtaining from the Sultan Abd al Majid a denunciation of the blood accusation* as a base falsehood. The same document, the **Hatti Humayun,** removed some of the disabilities governing Turkish Jews.

DAN. Jacob's fifth son, founder of the tribe known for its fighting men. The tribe of Dan settled in the area around Ekron in the south of Canaan and up along the coast north of Jaffa. Dan is also the name of a settlement established later by Danites in the north near the headwaters of the Jordan. The modern Kibbutz Dan was established in 1939 near the site of its ancient namesake.

DANIEL, BOOK OF. The Book of Daniel is in the section of the Bible* known as Writings. The book tells the story of the prophet Daniel. He was taken captive to Babylon and trained for the king's service. He became a favorite of King Belshazzar and interpreted his dreams. When the mysterious writing "Mene, mene, tekel upharsin" appeared on a wall in the King's palace during a feast, Daniel explained that it foretold the downfall of the king. As a punishment, he was cast into a lion's den but was miraculously saved from death. This story, written in Aramaic,* occupies the first six chapters of the book. The last six chapters, written in Hebrew, are mystic revelations about the end of days—the day of judgment in which the wicked world powers would be destroyed and the Jewish people restored to its home.

DANIEL DERONDA. A novel by George Eliot published in 1877. It tells the story of Daniel Deronda, English-born and completely unaware of his Jewish ancestry, who finds his way back to Judaism and tries to recreate a Jewish state in Palestine. Written twenty years before Herzl's*

The feast of Belshazzar—the handwriting on the wall.

Emblem of the tribe of Dan

The Jewish State, Daniel Deronda makes a passionate plea for the "revival of the organic center" for the Jewish people.

DAVID (c.1000-c.960 B.C.E.). The second king of Israel. A shepherd lad, David, the youngest son of Jesse, was taken from grazing his father's sheep near Bethlehem* in Judah* and brought to court to soothe King Saul.* David played his harp to calm the king when he was depressed by an "evil spirit," and Saul took a liking to David. A very deep friendship also developed between David and Saul's son, Jonathan. When the Philistine* giant Goliath taunted and challenged Saul's army, David killed the giant with a stone from his slingshot. He distinguished himself in battle, and married Saul's daughter Michal. The disturbed king grew jealous of David's popularity, and repeatedly tried to kill him. David became a refugee, hiding from Saul in the mountains and later among the Philistines. Yet he managed not to fight on their side when the Philistines faced Saul in battle on Mt. Gilboa and defeated him. David mourned the death of Saul and of his beloved friend Jonathan, in a beautiful elegy (II Samuel 1:17-27).

Long before Saul's death, the prophet Samuel had anointed David secretly, and now Judah—his own tribe—chose him king. The other tribes had crowned Saul's son, Ishbaal, and a civil war resulted that lasted two years. On the death of Ishbaal, David was acclaimed king over all Israel and ruled for forty years.

Under David's reign, the tribes of Israel were really united and became a nation. He defeated the Philistines so soundly that they were not heard from again for centuries. He subdued the surrounding Canaanite peoples, including Aram and its capital Damascus* in the north. By defeating the Edomites in the south, David gave the Israelites an outlet to the Red Sea at Ezion-Geber. David's crowning achievement was the capture of Jerusalem* from the Jebusites; he made this ancient city, sitting up on the rocky heights of Zion, the capital of Israel. There he built a splendid new tabernacle to which he brought up the Ark of the Covenant.* Thus David made Zion the center of worship and the holy city of religious pilgrimage. Jerusalem came to be called the City of David, the heart of his kingdom. David extended the boundaries of Israel to an area never again attained, except for a short period under the Hasmoneans.

King David suffered much grief. In old age his greatest sorrow was the rebellion and death of his beloved son Absalom.* David died at the age of seventy-one, the beloved hero of his people leaving the throne of Israel to his son Solomon.* He is remembered as a great warrior, as a loyal friend, and as the erring king who bowed with meekness to the prophet's reprimand.

David is remembered as the "sweet singer of Israel" author of the Psalms* (Tehillim), the son of Jesse from whose stem the Messiah would spring to lead scattered Israel back to Zion.

N.B-A.

DAVID, TOMB OF. The Bible relates that David was buried in Jerusalem (I Kings 2:10). Though the site of the tomb is not certain, it is placed at the south of old Jerusalem, on what is (erroneously) called Mount Zion. Between 1948 and 1967, when the Western Wall was not accessible to Jews, pilgrimages were made to the tomb on Mount Zion.

DAYAN, MOSHE (1915-1981). Israeli soldier and statesman. Born in Kibbutz Degania "A," he received his early education at Nahalal, a settlement which his parents helped found. He joined Haganah when still a boy. After the Arab disturbances in 1936 Dayan first served as an instructor in the Supernumerary Police Force and later with General Orde Charles Wingate's* Special Night Squads. In 1939 he was arrested by the British authorities and sentenced to 5 years in prison but was released after only 2 years. He resumed his service in the Haganah, and fought in the Syrian border area. In the invasion of Syria (then held by Vichy France) by the Allied forces, Dayan was seriously wounded, losing an eye.

In the War of Independence, Dayan commanded a battalion on the Syrian front. During the siege of Jerusalem he served as military commander there. He participated in the Rhodes Armistice talks with the Kingdom of Jordan and served with the Mixed

Moshe Dayan

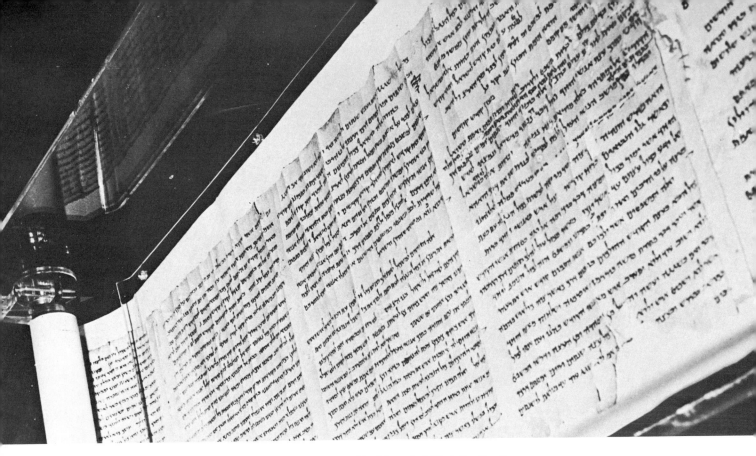

The Manual of Discipline Scroll

Armistice Commission. After attending a course of military studies in England he became (1953) Chief of Staff of the Israeli army with the rank of Major General, a position he held during the Sinai Campaign of 1956. He was released from active service in the Israeli Defense Forces in 1958. He was elected to the Knesset,* and served as minister of agriculture from 1959 to 1964. In 1967 he was appointed minister of defense. He played an important role in the planning of the stategy that brought Israel* victory in the Six-Day War.* He left his post when Golda Meir's government resigned in 1974. In 1977 he quit the Labor party to become Israel's foreign minister under Menahem Begin.* In this position he has played a key role in the negotiations between Israel and Egypt* initiated by the visit of Egypt's President Anwar el-Sadat to Jerusalem in November, 1977. He is the author (1965) of **Diary of the Sinai Campaign.**

DEAD SEA. The lowest and heaviest inland sea in the world is a long band of smoky blue water, forty-seven miles long by nine and one-half miles wide, in the deepest pit of the Jordan depression, and fed by the Jordan and Arnon rivers. Compressed between the mountains of Moab in the east and the Judean hills in the west, the Dead Sea was the stage for the tragic Biblical drama of Sodom and Gomorrah's destruction for their sins. Its historic character is reflected in its numerous names: in Hebrew the Salt Sea, in Arabic the Sea of Lot; it was the Asphalt Sea to Josephus Flavius, and the Dead Sea to the Greeks, who believed that nothing could live in it, though microscopic life has recently been discovered in its silt. Its waters are so heavy that they hold the human body buoyant. The first attempt to tap the treasures of this "fluid mine" was made before World War II, when two plants were set up at northern and southern ends. The northern plant was destroyed by the Arabs in 1948, but the second, at Sodom, has been restored by Israel for the exploitation of its millions of tons of salt, potash, bromides, and other minerals. There is a winter health and pleasure resort near this sea whose many moods have haunting beauty despite its bleak shores and grim rampart of cliffs.

DEAD SEA SCROLLS. Ancient Biblical manuscripts discovered, in the spring of 1947, by Arab Bedouins in the Qumran caves at Ain Fashka on the northwest shore of the Dead Sea.* Part of a hidden library consisting of many hundreds of fragments and scrolls, seven invaluable leather manuscripts were salvaged still wrapped in linen and enclosed in earthen jars. Briefly, they contain: 1) The Book of Isaiah, in its entirety, written in fifty-four columns. This copy differs in some details from the Masoretic text in the Hebrew Bible; 2) A second Isaiah Scroll, containing most of Chapters 38-66, is closer to the Bible text. This second copy was acquired by the Hebrew University in Jerusalem through the efforts of the eminent archaeologist, Eliezer L. Sukenik. He also published the first accounts of his findings in two volumes. After many difficulties all seven scrolls came into the possession of the State of Israel;* 3) A Midrash* on the Book of Habakkuk,* consisting of a commentary on "the end of the days" and of the imminent visitation of God pronounced by the "Teacher of Righteousness," prefaced by verses from the Biblical book of Habakkuk; 4) **The Manual of Discipline,** in two fragments, is a "constitution" of a religious sect, probably the Essenes, setting forth the righteous way of life and admonishing the members of the sect to battle for truth and virtue; 5) **The War of the Sons of Light and the Sons of Darkness,** presumably a manual on the conduct of war on the religious and the military level. The "Sons of Light" are defined as "the sons of Levi, the sons of Judah and the sons of Benjamin," while the "Sons of Darkness" include "the bands of Edomites, Moabites...Philistines,* the bands of Kittim of Ashur" and the "Kittim of Egypt." The latter, in the opinion of Professor Sukenik, refer to the Seleucids in Syria* and Ptolemies in Egypt.* These were the adversaries confronting the Jews and Judea. The armed combatants mentioned in this croll are archers, slingers, horsemen, and charioteers; 6) **Thanksgiving Psalms,** four leaves of leather, include about twenty psalms and are very similar to those of the Bible. Five of these psalms were published by Professor Sukenik. They are composed in verse of a rather loose rhythm, with inspiring contents and profound religious feeling; 7) The **Aramaic Scroll,** previously thought to be the lost Apocalypse of Lamech, now called the Genesis Apocryphon, is written in Aramaic and contains some chapters from the Book of Genesis,* plus folklore material.

The dating of the Dead Sea Scrolls has aroused a stormy debate among scholars. The scrolls are generally accepted, on the basis of archaeological evidence and the Hebrew script, as dating from the first century B.C.E. Further exploration of caves in the vicinity where the Dead Sea Scrolls were discovered has produced other fragments of Biblical scrolls. Of particular interest to archaeologists are the "copper scrolls," which are now known to contain a mysterious account of a unique inventory of buried treasures totaling tons of gold, silver, and precious vessels.   M.K.

DEBORAH. Prophetess and judge of Israel who held court "under the palm tree of Deborah, between Ramah and Bethel on the mountain of Ephraim." When Yabin, King of Chazor, oppressed the Children of Israel, Deborah summoned Barak to lead the tribes in the battle of Megiddo against the Canaanites. Deborah planned the strategy which brought Barak victory, though the Canaanite general, Sisera, had "nine hundred chariots of iron." She celebrated this victory with a stirring ode of thanksgiving (Judges 4 and 5).

DECALOGUE. See TEN COMMANDMENTS.

DENMARK. Jews have lived in Denmark since 1622, when King Christian IV invited them to migrate from Holland to his country. Enjoying civic rights and the friendship of the rulers, they concentrated chiefly in the capital city, Copenhagen. Danish Jews engaged widely in commerce, and a number of them attained wealth and influence. By the eighteenth century, leading Danish Jewish families had established close ties with the world of secular Danish culture.

The Jewish community of Denmark was the largest in the Scandinavian countries, but it was very small in proportion to the general population. Nevertheless, the Jews of Denmark have played a very significant role in that country's culture, especially in literature, art, science, music, and also in the world of finance.

Deborah

During the First World War, Copenhagen served as a haven for many refugees from Eastern Europe. But on April 9, 1940, the Germans occupied Denmark. When they attempted to persecute the Jews there, both the government and the people of Denmark raised a great cry of protest and succeeded in preventing the maltreatment of their Jewish neighbors. In 1943, when the Danish people learned of Gestapo plans for the deportation and annihilation of Danish Jewry, they organized a broad plan of rescue: all the Danish Jews were secretly gathered at the ports and smuggled in ships and boats of every description to Sweden.* Both the Swedish and Danish governments supported this humanitarian operation, which came to be known as Little Dunkirk. As a result, the Germans seized no more that 467 aged men and women who were deported to Theresienstadt. This example of brotherly love was the only organized non-Jewish rescue operation of Jews during the entire Nazi period.

After the war, virtually all Danish Jews who escaped to Sweden were repatriated. In 1977 there were 7,500 Jews living in Denmark, of whom over 90 per cent lived in Copenhagen, the seat of the country's only Jewish congregation. Danish Jews were active in the textile industry and in publishing and book selling. There was a Jewish elementary school in Copenhagen in existence since 1850, which offered a general education as well as religious instruction. The Danish Jewish community was pro-Zionist and actively interested in Israel affairs.

DEUTERONOMY. A Latinized version of the Greek word meaning "repetition of the law"; the fifth book of the Bible, called in Hebrew Devarim ("Words") after the second word of the opening verse of the book: "These are the words which Moses* spoke unto all Israel on this side of the Jordan, in the wilderness." The book is thought to be identified, in part, with the book of the Torah found in the Temple during the reign of King Josiah (638-608 B.C.E.). It retells the story of Israel from the time of the exodus from Egypt.* This Book is also termed in Jewish tradition as **Mishneh Torah,** a "repetition of the laws" given in the books of Exodus* and Leviticus. Many of the ethical ideas found in the earlier books of the Pentateuch* reach their loftiest form in Deuteronomy. The book closes in noble verse as Moses bids farewell to the people and gives his blessings to the tribes one by one.

DIASPORA. See GALUT.

DIETARY LAWS. Code of law restricting the foods Jews may eat, and controlling the preparation of permitted foods. According to the story of Creation (Gen. I: 29) all fruits and vegetables may be eaten. The Bible separates animals into clean—**tahor**—and unclean—**tameh** (Leviticus 11). Israel, as a holy people, is allowed to eat only the flesh of "clean" animals, mammals which chew the cud and have cloven hooves. The rabbis have restricted the birds considered fit for food, since it has been very difficulty to identify all those mentioned in Leviticus. All permitted animals, before they may be eaten, must be ritually slaughtered. Since the eating of blood is forbidden, the meat must be soaked and salted to withdraw as much blood as possible. It is not permissible to use the hindquarter of cattle unless certain veins are removed. If the animal is sick, or if after slaughtering the vital organs show signs of fatal disease, the animal becomes "unclean." Fish which have both scales and fins may be eaten, but shellfish, reptiles and insects, etc., are forbidden.

The products of "unclean" animals and their milk or eggs are also "unclean." In several places the Bible commands "Thou shalt not seethe a kid in the milk of its mother" (Ex. 34:26; Deut. 14:21). From this has come the command to separate meat and milk foods to the extent of using separate utensils for their preparation and serving. Explanations for the dietary laws are manifold. It is assumed that some of the laws are hygienic in origin. Historically, they were extremely important in helping the Jewish people maintain their identity; they have added a measure of sanctity to their daily lives and have prevented the Jews from intermingling too freely with gentiles.

DISRAELI, BENJAMIN, FIRST EARL OF BEACONSFIELD (1804-1881). British statesman and author. He was born in London to a Jewish family proud of a long line of ancestors who had come to England* after having been driven out of Spain* by the Inquisition.* Benjamin was twelve when his father, Isaac, a well-known writer,

Benjamin Disraeli

withdrew from his Sephardic congregation. Isaac had his son baptized because of the political and social discrimination practiced against Jews in England at that time. Yet Benjamin Disraeli never lost his pride in his Jewish ancestry. After completing his education, he spent three years traveling in southern Europe and the Near East. The impressions of his travels, particulary of the Holy Land, never left him. In Disraeli's books all the heroes go to Palestine for inspiration. One of his novels, **David Alroy,** is the romantic story of the twelfth-century Jewish revolt against Persia led by Alroy, who planned to reconquer Jerusalem* for the Jews.

Benjamin Disraeli had a trigger-quick wit, and some of his clever novels, beginning with **Vivian Grey** (1826), were amusing satires which made him the idol of London society. Disraeli's career in British politics was remarkable. His political novels, pamphlets, and speeches helped reshape the Conservative Party, and his influence continued for a long time, after his death. He served, for a time, as leader of the House of Commons, and twice as chancellor of the exchequer. In 1868, and again from 1874 to 1880 he was prime minister. During these years, his policies at home reflected Disraeli's sympathy with the working class, and resulted in a number of progressive health, housing, and factory laws. He consistently supported the struggle for obtaining the vote for Jews, despite opposition from his own party. However, it was his foreign policy that was particularly outstanding. Dusraeli obtained for Britain a controlling interest in the Suez Canal in Egypt.* He arranged to have Queen Victoria proclaimed Empress of India, and brought about the cession of Cyprus* to Great Britian. Through these and similar acts he enlarged and strengthened the power of the British Empire. His policies and courtliness brought him Queen Victoria's deep affection, while his swift repartee and his political and diplomatic victories made Benjamin Disraeli one of the most fascinating figures of the nineteenth century. For the people from whom he sprang, Disraeli had a rare tenderness and respect. Of them he wrote: "that is the aristocracy of nature, the purest race, the chosen people."

N.B-A.

DIZENGOFF, MEIR. (1861 - 1936). Zionist leader and mayor of Tel Aviv.* Joining the Zionist movement in the 1880's, Dizengoff visited Palestine several times before settling there in 1905. In 1909, he laid the cornerstone of Tel Aviv, the first all-Jewish city, and was elected its mayor in 1921. His devoted efforts were important in making Tel Aviv a flourishing city of 100,000 by the time of his death in 1936.

DOMINICAN REPUBLIC. Republic occupying the major eastern section of the Caribbean island of Hispaniola. Before 1940, few Jews settled in the Dominican Republic. Those who did assimilated rapidly. Suddenly, for a brief period, it became one of the few points of light on the darkening horizons of European Jewry. At a time when most nations were severely restricting immigration, Generalissimo Rafael Trujillo announced that the Dominican Republic would open its gates to Jewish refugees. Speaking at an inter-governmental conference on refugees at Evian, France,* in 1938, Trujillo offered full economic assistance and "equality of opportunities and of civil, legal, and economic rights" to all colonists. A farm colony was immediately established at Sosua in the Dominican Republic, and plans were made for transferring refugees from Europe. The outbreak of World War II, however, interfered with the project. Communications were difficult, and Jews could not escape from the countries under Nazi domination. Only 1,200 managed to reach the Dominican Republic. Of these, some 300 stayed on after the end of World War II. The total Jewish population (1977) was 200, living in Sosua, and Ciudad Trujillo. There is one synagogue in each of these cities. The Jewish Congregation of the Dominican Republic is the central Jewish organization recognized by the government.

DREYFUS, ALFRED (1859-1935). The only Jewish officer on the French General Staff, he became the center of what was to become one of the most famous cases in legal history, and a crucial point in the battle against anti-Semitism* in the modern world. In 1894, a French court-martial convicted Dreyfus of treason on the basis of documents alleged to have been written in his hand. Two years later, fearing that the army would be discredited, the government suppressed evidence that Dreyfus was not guilty, and that the real spy was one Major Ferdinand Esterhazy, another member of the general staff. In 1897, however, the issue was brought into the open, and the case became the center of a conflict that was to embroil French politics for a decade. Those who insisted on Dreyfus's guilt were both politically reactionary and openly anti-Semitic; winning the majority of voters to their side, they vanquished the liberal forces in the elections of 1898. The following year, however, a new prime minister permitted a second trial. Because Dreyfus's innocence was common knowledge, it was expected that he would be acquitted. Nevertheless, the court found him "guilty with extenuating circumstances," and sentenced him to ten years' imprisonment. Although he was pardoned by the President of France soon after, the battle for

84

Dreyfus's exoneration continued. Finally, in 1906, the Supreme Court of Appeals cleared the prisoner, and Dreyfus was reinstated as a major in the army. His exoneration represented not only victory over anti-Semitism in official circles, but the final defeat of monarchical and clerical elements in French politics; it led to the separation of church and state in France. The Dreyfus affair has been treated in several books; two movies have been produced on this theme, including **The Life of Emile Zola** (1936).   B.H.

DROPSIE UNIVERSITY. Founded in 1907 in Philadelphia through the will of Moses Aaron Dropsie, Dropsie University is one of the institutions of higher Jewish learning in America. It is a non-sectarian, non-theological postgraduate institution, specializing in the science of Judaism. It offers courses leading to degrees of Doctor of Philosophy, Doctor of Education, and Master of Arts. Dropsie consists of three divisions: the inter-related Hebrew and Semitic studies in the Department of Hebrew and Cognate Learning; the School of Education, with parallel courses in New York City; and the Institute for Israel and the Middle East, which trains qualified personnel for government, social, and educational agencies in the United States and Israel. Dropsie issues a number of scholarly publications, including the **Jewish Quarterly Review.**

DRUZES. Followers of a religious sect which split off from Islam* in the 11th century. Most of them live in Syria,* Iraq,* Iran* and Lebanon,* from where they came to Palestine.* The Druzes in Israel are loyal citizens of the Jewish state.

DUBNO, MAGGID OF. See MAGGID OF DUBNO.

DUBNOW, SIMON MARKOVICH (1860-1941). Russian Jewish historian. Dubnow developed his own interpretation of Jewish history, claiming that the spiritual powers of the Jewish people and their unity were preserved by the organized Jewish community during the two thousand years of the dispersion. Dubnow believed that the unity of the Jewish people did not depend upon a national territory, nor upon an independent state. This unity was kept alive by communal organizations, within whose framework Jewish culture and religion had continued their growth for two thousand years after the Dispersion. He therefore believed in cultural autonomy and self-government for the Jewish communities. Dubnow's theories of Jewish nationalism resulted in the formation of the Jewish Peoples Party in Russia* in 1906. At the

Versailles Peace Conference* after World War I, Dubnow's theory of Diaspora Nationalism motivated the demand for minority rights for the Jews of Eastern Europe. Dubnow's **History of the Jews of Russia and Poland** was translated into English, and has been of considerable influence on the writing of Jewish history.

His general **History of the Jewish People,** in ten volumes, was published in 1901.

S. Anski

DYBBUK (Hebrew root, "attachment"). Name given to the soul of one deceased, usually evil, which has entered a living person in order to find its salvation. The belief in the transmigration of the soul is ancient; mention of it is made in the Talmud. The books of the Kabbalah* gave this belief widespread circulation. Special rites (exorcism) were prescribed to drive out the evil spirit. By the use of holy names and assurances of salvation, certain "miracle workers" were believed to be capable of inducing the **dybbuk** to leave. S. Anski made use of the legend in his famous play, **The Dybbuk.**

Simon M. Dubnow (center of photo, with cane), on his usual Sabbath walk in Kovno, shortly before his capture by the Nazis.   Courtesy Anita L. Lebeson.

E

EBAN, ABBA (1915-   ). Israeli statesman. Eban was born in Capetown, South Africa, on February 2, 1915, to Solomon Myer, a businessman. When Abba was still an infant, his father died and his mother brought him to England. When he was six years old, his mother married Dr. Isaac Eban, a radiologist. Abba Eban gew up in England,* his home influences making him a Zionist in earliest childhood. He was educated at Cambridge University, where he studied Hebrew, Arabic, and Persian. Having distinguished himself in these subjects, he remained in Cambridge to teach them in Pembroke College. During the Second World War, he enlisted in the British Army, became an officer within five months, and was assigned to Cairo headquarters. A part of Eban's duties included flights to Palestine* in order to stimulate the Jewish war effort there. In Cairo, he met a young student at the American University who became his wife in 1945.

Eban settled in Jerusalem* where his special background was utilized by the Jewish "shadow government" of the country during the closing days of the British Mandate. In 1947, he was appointed liaison officer with the United Nations Special Commission on Palestine. After the proclamation of the State of Israel in 1948, Eban pleaded successfully for the admission of Israel to the United Nations. One of the most eloquent spokesmen on the international scene, he served with distinction as head of the Israeli delegation to the United Nations. In 1950 he also became Israel's ambassador to the U.S. In 1953 he was deputy chairman of the UN assembly. From 1958 until 1966 he was president of the Weizmann Institute of Science.* In 1960 he was appointed Minister of Education and Culture, in 1963, Deputy Prime Minister, and in 1966, Foreign Minister of the State of Israel, a post he held until the fall of Golda Meir's government in 1974.

ECCLESIASTES. The Greek name for **Kohelet.** The seventh book of Writings in the Bible. The suggested Hebrew meaning for the author's name —Kohelet—is "the Assembler." One of several Wisdom books, the central idea of **Kohelet** that "all is vanity" is expressed in pithy sayings. Written mostly in prose, it has passages of great poetic beauty.

ECUADOR. Republic on the northern Pacific coast of South America. There are about 1,000 Jews in a population of 8,800,000. In Spanish colonial times Ecuador was the home of Marranos,* forced converts to Catholicism who practiced their Jewish faith in secret. The Marrano settlement disappeared, and nothing is known of it. In the twentieth century, Jews from Europe founded a new community in Ecuador consisting of two distinct settlements, one in Quito and one in Guayaquil. Each is separately affiliated with the World Jewish Congress.* Each settlement has Zionist groups and a B'nai B'rith* organization, but educational facilities are poor. In recent years, there has been a tendency for Jews to emigrate to other South American countries.

EDOMITES. Small tribe in southern Palestine, conquered and forcibly converted to Judaism by Johanan Hyrcanus.*

EDUCATION IN JEWISH HISTORY. In many ways, Jewish history is the story of the education of a people. From the beginning, many of the great Jewish leaders were also great teachers who spoke to the world through the Jewish people. When the world was young and its mystery and wonder fresh in the mind of man, the patriarch Abraham* thought about its mystery and wondered about its Creator. He discarded his father's idols, and began to teach his tribe to believe in one God. Thus, the founder of the Jewish people was also the first teacher in Jewish history. Moses,* the Lawgiver who led the people to freedom, was called **rabbenu**—our teacher. He taught the children of Israel during the years of wandering in the wilderness, and he appointed times when the whole people were to come together and study. When the Children of Israel settled in the Promised Land and were ruled by judges, there were no schools, but knowledge was handed down by word of mouth from father to son, from mother to daughter. The Judges,* priests, and Levites* taught the people to reject the idols of their Canaanite neighbors and to follow the laws of Moses. Then, the greatest teachers of all time, the prophets of Israel, brought to the people a lofty vision of God, and

Abba Eban and David Ben-Gurion, Prime Minister of Israel, leaving the Secretariat Building at the United Nations; seen with them are members of the Israeli delegation to the U.N.— May, 1951.   Courtesy Unations.

taught that to serve Him, men must love peace and justice and act rightly toward one another.

A knowledge of reading and writing seems not to have been uncommon in Israel's earliest days. Gideon,* the fifth of the Judges, wanted some information during one of his military expeditions. He therefore got hold of a simple boy who knew enough to "write down for him the princes of Sukkot, and the elders thereof, seventy and seven men." Perhaps the earliest formal schools in ancient Israel were those that trained the priests and Levites in the complicated laws and rituals of bringing sacrifices and of conducting the Temple* services. By the sixth century B.C.E., after the return from the Babylonian exile, scribes or **soferim** had become the teachers of the people, who were required to come regularly to the Temple courts for instruction. Synagogues,* or houses of prayer, then sprang up all over Judea; they served as schools, also. Around 75 B.C.E., Simeon ben Shetah,* the head of the Sanhedrin* (a judicial and legislative body), established a system of high schools in all large towns for boys of sixteen and upward. Less than 100 years later, the high priest, Joshua ben Gamala, set up a system of elementary schools in every town for all boys from the age of five. The historian Josephus Flavius* boasted that in Jerusalem alone there were more than 300 schools for children.

Education came to be of utmost importance in the life of the people. After the destruction of the Second Temple by the Romans, the rabbis taught that study, like prayer, was a form of worhip and a substitute for sacrifices. During the Talmudic period in Babylonia,* the rabbis set up a complete system of education. It began at the age of five or six and was a lifelong process. Few details were overlooked, and there was even a place for athletics. In the sixth century C.E., one rabbi stressed that twenty-five pupils were the ideal number for a class. If there were 40 children, he urged that an assistant teacher be engaged, and for 50 he advised two teachers. The **Bet Ha-Sefer** or

A child of the hara (ghetto) in Tunis, learning Hebrew.

"House of the Book," was the Bible school for the youngest children. At ten they were expected to enter the **Bet Talmud** or **Bet Ha-Knesset** ("House of Assembly") for the study of the Talmud.* These schools also taught languages and mathematics; such subjects as astronomy, botany, and zoology were required for certain Talmudic studies.

The highest schools of this system were the great academies of Babylonia,* where the scholars studied and created the Talmud. One great teacher, Abba Arikha, founded an academy at Sura that lasted, with brief interruptions, for eight centuries. The academy at Sura was never idle or empty. Scholars who had to work all day studied there in the early morning and the late evening. In March and September, when there was little work in the fields, the Sura academy held **Kallot,** or seminars, for farmers and business men. There were even scholarships for worthy students who could not afford to take two months off from work and travel to attend the Kallot in Sura.

The education system begun in Palestine and developed in Babylonia moved with the people wherever they went. By the eleventh century, persecution and intolerance had driven the Jews out of Babylonia. The great centers dwindled and almost disappeared, and the Jews set up new communities in Spain* and Italy,* France* and Germany.* New subjects of study were added to the system, others were subtracted, without changing its core. In twelfth-century Arab Spain, philosophy and Arabic were added to the studies in the higher schools. In Italy the new subjects were Latin, Italian, and logic. To escape the bloody path of the Crusades,* the Jews began to migrate from Germany to Poland in the twelfth century. The **Kahal,** or community organization in Poland, was a strong one. Education was made compulsory for children from six to thirteen years

Religious education begins at the age of three for these children of very religious families in Jerusalem.

Children of Kibbutz Hulata in Galilee studying art.
Zionist Archives and Library, New York City.

of age, and the system was controlled by a board of study called the Hevra Talmud Torah. This **hevra** prescribed the studies for the **heder,*** or elementary private school, as well as for the Talmud* Torah, the community free school. The **yeshiva,** or Talmudic academy, was also supervised by the **hevra,** and the head, or Rosh Yeshiva, was selected by them. During the sixteenth, seventeenth, and eighteenth centuries, when Jewish life became constricted and was limited to the ghetto, education, too, narrowed, and languages and sciences were no longer studied. These subjects were reintroduced during the Haskalah,* or enlightenment period. Education for girls was not required at any period. Yet the woman of outstanding abilities usually managed to get an education. The ordinary woman shared deeply the general reverence for learning, and often made great sacrifices that her sons might become scholars.

During the twentieth century, Orthodoxy turned its attention to providing formal Jewish education for girls and women. One of the outstanding movements working to this end is the Beth Jacob movement, which was founded by Sara Schenirer in Cracow* in the early 1920's and has since spread all over the world.

The average Jew could always read and write, since even the poorest child could get an elementary education. For the brilliant young students who had no means of support, the community provided food and shelter, so that they might be free to devote themselves completely to study at the **yeshiva.** As a result, ignorance was rare among Jews. During the Middle Ages, when even princes and nobles were illiterate, the Jewish community had many scholars, and honored them above other men. Until recent times, Jewish education was considered a lifetime process: the young studied all day, the adults studied during their leisure hours, evenings, Sabbaths, and holidays. And when Jews dreamed of Paradise, study held a place in their vision.   N.B.-A.

Due to a shortage of books in Yemen, many children studied from one book, and learned to read upside down.

EGYPT. North African land of the pyramids and the Sphinx. Its capital is Cairo, its principal port Alexandria.* Egypt is an agricultural country, its main crops being cotton, rice, and wheat.

Egypt's recorded history goes back to about 4000 B.C.E. A close neighbor of Palestine,* Egypt has been linked with the Jews and their history from the very beginning. The patriarchs all stayed in Egypt for various periods of time. The bondage in Egypt and the Exodus* mark the beginnings of Jewish history. Historians believe that the first Hebrew migration to Egypt probably took place during the rule of the Semitic Hyksos dynasty of the eighteenth to sixteenth centuries B.C.E. The Tel El-Amarna tablets, discovered in 1887, show that the Pharaohs had set up governors in many towns of Canaan, evidence of their domination of the country. One of the Amarna tablets is a letter from the ruler of Jerusalem.* In it, he complains to Pharaoh that the Habiru, or Hebrews, are invading and conquering the land.

Relations between Egypt and the Jewish people continued throughout the period of the Jewish Monarchy. Solomon* married an Egyptian princess and made a trade treaty with Egypt. After Solomon's death, when the northern tribes broke off and established their own kingdom, the Pharaoh Shishak came to their aid by attacking Jerusalem.* Two centuries later, Josiah, King of Judah, died in battle (608 B.C.E.) at Megiddo* when he tried to block the march of Pharaoh Necho through his territory. Josiah's son, Jehoahaz, ruled Judah for only three months. The Egyptians deposed him and set his brother Jehoiakim on the throne.

After the First Temple* was destroyed in 586 B.C.E., the exiled prophet Jeremiah* found Jewish colonies in Upper and Lower Egypt. Papyri discovered in Elephantine, an island on the Nile, describe the life of a Jewish colony there and tell of its Jewish temple in the fifth century B.C.E. After Alexander the Great* conquered Egypt (333 B.C.E.), Jewish immigrants streamed into Egypt, where they prospered and established themselves under Hellenist rule. The Alexandrian Jewish community grew until in time it numbered almost one million members; in Alexandria, a great Hellenistic Jewish civilization developed. (**See** HELLENISM.) Jews spoke Greek and tried to work out a viable compromise between Jewish and Greek culture. The philosopher Philo* is the best known representative of this movement. During the Syrian oppression of Judea, the refugee High Priest Onias founded a Temple in Heliopolis, a city near the Nile. During this period (the third century B.C.E.), the Bible, translated into Greek at Alexandria (the Septuagint* version), came to exert a great influence, serving both the Jews of the Hellenistic period and the rising Christian Church.

At the same time, the security of Egyptian Jewry was threatened by a great deal of anti-Jewish feeling among the Greek population. Sometimes Greek riots and attacks on the Jewish community had to be stopped by the governing Roman authorities. Developments in Judea also influenced the security of Egyptian Jewry. Refugees from the Judean revolt against Rome stirred up a Jewish rebellion in Egypt in 72 C.E., and again in 115-117 C.E., when Alexandrian Jewry was massacred.

As the Roman Empire became Christianized, the situation of Egyptian Jewry deteriorated. In 415 C.E., Alexandrian masses, inflamed by Bishop Cyril, broke out in violent riots and forced hundreds of Jews to undergo baptism. During the following two centuries, the Alexandrian Jewish community dwindled in importance. It was not until the Arab invasion of 639 that the situation improved slightly. Under Moslem rule, the community, centered mainly in the new city of Cairo, became Arab in character and culture. Documents found in the Cairo Genizah* (storehouse of worn-out books), describe in great detail the life of the community. Though the traditional Moslem code treated the Jews as inferiors, Jewish cultural life reached a high level. Saadiah Gaon,* the greatest scholar of his day, was a native of the Fayyum in Egypt. The Jewish community came to be governed by an exilarch,* and significant academies of learning were established. Except for the period of bitter persecution under Caliph Hakim (995-1021), conditions were favorable. When Maimonides* arrived in Egypt in 1165, the great scholar found an appreciative Jewish environment. Maimonides became court physician to the Sultan Saladin, and a number of his great works were written during this period. Maimonides took a leading part in Jewish life in Egypt, and his descendants were dominant there for a long time.

After the Turkish occupation of Egypt in 1517, the Egyptian Jewish community managed to sustain itself, but did not achieve economic or cultural advancement. It was not until the opening of the Suez Canal in 1869 that economic prosperity and western influence reached the Jewish community, then numbering about 75,000. A number of Jews became wealthy business men, and even pashas and senators. The majority, however, remained poor peddlers and craftsmen, segregated in the Jewish quarters of Alexandria and Cairo. During the First World War (1914-1918), many Jews from Palestine* fled to Egypt to escape Turkish persecution. Their influence and the development of Arab nationalism stirred Egyptian Jewry from its lethargy. They began to migrate to Palestine and Europe, and the community declined. Many Egyptian Jews who had European citizenship also suffered because of the general anti-European reaction of the period, and because an anti-Zionist policy had been adopted.

After the establishment of the State of Israel* in 1948, the position of the Jews in Egypt became increasingly difficult. Jews were arrested and robbed. After the Sinai Campaign of 1956 President Gamal Abdel Nasser passed a law which in effect deprived all Zionists of Egyptian citizenship. Jews were imprisoned and expelled for security reasons. Large numbers of Jews were able to immigrate to Israel by way of Europe.

In 1967 and again in 1973 (see Six-Day War and Yom Kippur War) Egypt went to war against Israel with the avowed aim of destroying the Jewish State. In November, 1977, Anwar el-Sadat, who had succeeded Nasser as president of Egypt in 1970, took the world by surprise with the announcement that he would be willing to visit Israel and discuss the possibility of peace with the Jewish State. He arrived in Jerusalem late on November 18, 1977, and on the next day addressed the Knesset.* This marked the beginning of peace negotiations between Egypt and Israel. In September, 1978, Sadat met with Israel's prime minister Menahem Begin* under the auspices of U.S. President Jimmy Carter at Camp David, Md., to draw up a framework for a peace treaty. A formal peace treaty, the Camp David Accords, was signed in 1979 by Menahem Begin, Anwar Sadat, and Jimmy Carter. However, Sadat was assassinated in October 1981 by Arab fundamentalists who opposed his policy of Israeli-Egyptian rapprochment. Despite the treaty, relations between Israel and Egypt have remained strained under the leadership of Sadat's successor, Hosni Mubarak. No other Arab states, aside from Egypt, have entered into a formal peace treaty with Israel.

Egypt's Jewish population at the time of the establishment of the State of Israel was about 90,000. In 1984 there were about 250.

EHRLICH, PAUL (1845-1915). German scientist. His discovery of the method of staining the white blood cells, his research in the field of bacteriology, and particularly his discovery of a drug to cure syphilis, made him world famous. The originator of modern chemotherapy, in 1908 he shared the Nobel Prize in medicine and physiology with Elie Mitchnikoff.

EICHMANN, ADOLF. (See JEWRY, ANNIHILATION OF EUROPEAN.)

EILAT (Heb. "terebinth"). Seaport on the Gulf of Eilat (or Aqaba), a finger on the Red Sea, where the borders of Israel,* Egypt,* Jordan and Saudi Arabia meet. About 950 B.C.E. Solomon* built the twin cities of Eilat and Ezion Geber for his navy and copper industry. With the discovery of a sea route around Africa to India, Eilat was abandoned. Developed by Israel as a seaport-window to East African and Asian markets, Eilat now boasts a population of 19,600 and its growth continues. The nearby Timna copper mines are expanding production and the port is growing. Eilat is also a winter resort, noted for its coral reefs and exotic tropical fish.

EINSTEIN, ALBERT (1879-1955). Theoretical physicist. The most outstanding physicist of modern times, Albert Einstein was almost as revered for his honesty, humility, and humanitarianism as for his theories about the nature of the universe. Born in Ulm (Germany), he received his scientific education in Switzerland, where he was naturalized in 1901. While working at the Patent Office in Berne, he prepared four scientific papers which gained him international acclaim before he was twenty-six. In the years that followed, Einstein lectured and taught in Prague, Zurich, Leyden, and Berlin. In 1916 he published his famous general theory of relativity, which has been described as "the greatest intellectual revolution since Newton"; six years later he was awarded the Nobel Prize for his work on photo-electric effects. With the rise of Hitler to power in 1933, he left Berlin, where he had held a distinguished position since 1914, and settled in the United States. From 1933 until his death in 1955, he served as professor of theoretical physics at Princeton's Institute of Advanced Studies.

Albert Einstein   Courtesy Yeshiva University.

90

In 1939 Einstein called the attention of President Franklin Delano Roosevelt to the possibilities of atomic warfare; his own theories played a crucial part in unbinding the energies of the atom. It was, in fact, the great irony of Einstein's life that his work for the advancement of man's understanding of the world in which he lived had also, and in hitherto unimaginable degree, advanced man's capacity for deadly warfare. Having experienced anti-Semitism* early in life, and, realizing the evils of Prussian militarism, Einstein had early become a crusader for peace and harmony in human relations. He did not hesitate to speak out against injustice. After the First World War, he headed the International Committee for Intellectual Cooperation of the League of Nations, withdrawing in protest against the League's failure to take strong measures against Italian Fascism. As the clouds of Nazism gathered over Germany, Einstein spoke out against anti-Semitism and the Nazi threat to intellectual freedom. In the United States, too, Einstein was an outspoken defender of freedom of thought. To the end, he advocated international cooperation, and even world government, in the hope that men might learn to live in peace. He devoted much energy during the last decade of his life to making the world aware of the great dangers threatening it, as the result of his own work in discovering the destructive potential of atomic power.

Einstein was never a practicing Jew. From the '20's onward, however, he expressed his devotion to his people by dedicating considerable effort to Zionism,* and especially to the development of the Hebrew University* in Jerusalem. He first visited the United States in 1921 on a tour with Chaim Weizmann* on behalf of the university, and sat on its board of governors until the end of his life. After the death of Weizmann, Einstein was proposed as a candidate for the presidency of the State of Israel; Einstein refused on the ground that he was not qualified to fill the position. B.H.

ELDERS OF ZION. See ANTI-SEMITISM.

ELEAZAR BEN AZARYAH. See TANNAIM.

ELIEZER BEN HYRCANUS. See TANNAIM.

ELIJAH. The prophet Elijah the Tishbite lived at the time of Ahab (875-854 B.C.E.), the king who "did what is evil in the eyes of the Lord." Ahab married the Phoenician princess Jezebel and permitted her to build an altar and sanctuary to Baal* in Samaria.*

The Biblical story of Elijah—from his first startling appearance before the king, prophesying drought in the land, to his end, when he is whirled

to heaven in a chariot of fire—established the image of the prophet for ages to come. A gaunt figure clothed in goatskin, Elijah prophesies drought and disappears into the desert to be fed by the ravens. When the punishing drought comes, the people cry out for rain. Yet the king does not forbid the idol worship, and Elijah challenges the priests of Baal to prove that theirs is the true god. The dramatic public duel on Mt. Carmel between Elijah and the 450 priests of Baal ends in the humiliation of the latter. The Lord answers Elijah's prayers. The king and people see a fire descend from heaven to consume the offering on Elijah's altar. Then a heavy rain falls and the drought is ended. (I Kings, chapter 18)

Still the struggle goes on. Elijah must flee from the anger of Queen Jezebel who threatens his life. Ahab desires the fine vineyard of Naboth, who refuses to sell it. Jezebel has Naboth executed on false charges. When Ahab comes to take posession of the dead man's vineyard, Elijah appears before him and cries out: "Hast thou murdered and also taken possession?...In the place where the dogs licked the blood of Naboth shall the dogs lick thy blood, yes thine also." (I Kings 21:19.) Elijah predicts a grim end for Jezebel and the punishment of the Kingdom of Israel.* Hazael, the king of Aram, will make war upon Israel, and only the "seven thousand" who "did not bow down to Baal" will survive.

But in the closing verses in the Book of Malachi,* the stern figure of Elijah begins to grow milder. Here, Elijah is portrayed as the prophet who will descend from heaven before the great Day of the Lord, to bring peace to the earth. Elijah's appearance to usher in the Messianic age is spoken of in the Talmud.* When the Talmudic masters had a difference of opinion and could arrive at no decision, they tabled the discussion by deferring it "till the appearance of Elijah the prophet." Since the time of the Talmud, Jewish literature and legend have presented Elijah as comforter of the poor and the suffering. He appears miraculously when the need is greatest; he reveals himself to mystics—students of the Kabbalah*—and to Hasidic wonder rabbis to teach them to reveal the secrets of the future. To this day, at the Seder table on Passover,* a special cup is filled with wine in honor of the prophet.

N.B.-A.

ELIJAH BAHUR (1469-1549). Scholar and grammarian, born Elijah Levite in the village of Ipsheim near Nuremberg, Germany. Elijah was a linguist noted for his Bible research. He settled in Italy, where he composed the grammar entitled **Ha-Bahur,** and also **Ha-Mesorah,** a book on the symbols of chanting. In Rome he associated with humanist scholars. His friends and students included various churchmen, who studied grammar and Bible with him. Elijah transcribed a number of Hebrew manuscripts for prominent church leaders. He served also as proofreader in the Daniel Bamberg publishing house of Venice. Elijah was among the first to translate from the Hebrew into Yiddish, which was then beginning to develop as a language.

ELIJAH, GAON OF VILNA (1720 - 1797). Great Talmudist and revered spiritual leader of Lithuanian Jewry. Tradition has it that at the age of ten he was already well-versed in the Talmud,* and had outgrown the need for instructors. The title "Gaon" was given him because of his extraordinary genius. Gaon brought a new approach to Talmud study by stressing the factual and logical interpretation of the Bible text and of the entire body of Jewish law. In brief and concise marginal notes to Talmudic and Midrashic* literature he shed light on the most difficult passages. His power of concentration and perserverance was extraordinary. It is related that for fifty years he slept no more than two hours a night. Although he gave his

Elijah, Gaon of Vilna

entire life to sacred studies, he recognized the necessity for secular learning. This recognition represented a revolutionary idea for the rabbis of his time, who generally considered worldly study as damaging to the traditional Jewish way of life. Elijah himself wrote a work on mathematics and a Hebrew grammar.

Elijah's fame spread quickly, but he remained a most unassuming and modest man. Sternly pious, he led a life of self-denial, shunning all fame and offers of rabbinical posts. He lived in seclusion on a tiny allowance granted to him and his family by the town's Jewish community. The spread of Hasidism* drew him out of his retirement. He feared that this new movement would lead its followers astray, and therefore he advocated the harshest measures against them. His most favored pupil, Rabbi Hayim of Volozhin, established a rabbinical college at Volozhin where the Gaon of Vilna's methods of study were put into practice.

ELISHA. (Latter part of ninth century B.C.E.) Biblical prophet, on whose shoulders Elijah* placed his mantle as his successor (I Kings 19:19). Elisha was the son of a wealthy landowner who lived east of the Jordan. Like Elijah, he wanted to rid Israel of Baal* worship. He therefore secretly anointed Jehu, a general in the army, as king of Israel. Jehu led a revolt against Jehoram, son of Ahab,* destroying him as well as his mother Jezebel, the idolatrous queen. Then Jehu exterminated the priests of Baal.

Elisha mingled with the people, helping them and winning their love. No other prophet in Israel is reputed to have performed as many miracles as Elisha. He is said to have divided the waters of the Jordan, to have resurrected a child, and to have healed the Syrian captain, Naaman, of leprosy. The many stories of Elisha's miracle-working reflect the people's love for the prophet who healed the sick and helped the poor. (II Kings 1-9:4; 13:14-21.)

ELISHA BEN ABUYAH (c. 80-150 C.E.). Scholar and teacher of the Law. Though he was one of the most learned men of his time, Jewish tradition regards him as a traitor and apostate. Elisha was the son of a wealthy Jerusalem family, and early excelled in both secular and rabbinic learning. He lectured at the academies of Jerusalem* and was a close friend of Rabbi Akiba,* as well as teacher and friend of Rabbi Meir.* At some time in his career, he is said to have turned to Greek mysticism, and to have informed on his fellow-Jews to the Romans. Because of this represhensible act his name is scarcely ever mentioned in the Talmud,* all his sayings being attributed to **Aher** ("the other"). Modern scholars believe that he was a Sadducee* rather than a convert to a gentile religion. This, they feel, would have been sufficient ground for his excommunication by the dominant Pharisee* faction, which demanded complete conformity during a period when the Jewish people were struggling for spiritual survival.

EL SALVADOR. Only 350 Jews (of a total population of 4,120,000 live (1977) in San Salvador, the capital of the smallest of the Central American republics. There are Zionist groups and a central, legally recognized organization, the Comunidad Israelita (Jewish Community).

ELUL. Last month of the Jewish civil calendar. Preceding the High Holy Days, it is a month of spiritual preparation and penitence.

EMDEN, JACOB ISRAEL (1697-1776). Son of a famous rabbi, Z'vi Hirsh Ashkenazi, he was born in Altona, Germany. Although a brilliant Talmudic scholar, Emden left the rabbinate to set up a printing shop in his birthplace, Altona. He was involved in a long and bitter quarrel with Jonathan Eybeschuetz,* whom he accused of secretly belonging to the movement of followers of the false Messiah, Sabbatai Zevi.* He devoted much of his life to fighting the tendencies toward mysticism among German Jews. His many works include a commentary on the Mishnah (see TALMUD) and an autobiography.

EMEK JEZREEL. See ISRAEL.

EMUNAH WOMEN OF AMERICA. Emunah Women of America is part of the World Religious Zionist Women's Organization. Organized in 1948 as Hapoel Hamizrachi Women's Organization, the name of Emunah was adopted in 1978 so as to affect a oneness with its sister countries throughout the world.

It is a national movement of 25,000 religious Zionists, encompassing 80 chapters throughout the United States. Emunah Women of America supports an extensive network of 187 institutions in Israel which includes day care centers, vocational training schools, teacher schools and children's villages. Additionally, Emunah provides social welfare services through its "Self-Help" programs for indigent and inmmigrant mothers, parental guidance programs, absorption and integration services for new immigrants, psychological counseling, community centers and aid to the elderly.

ENGLAND (UNITED KINGDOM). Island Kingdom off the northwestern coast of Euorpe. It is (1984) the home of 350,000 Jews, who make up less than one percent of a total population of almost 56,000,000.

The first Jews in England of whom we have definite knowledge were financers who followed William the Conqueror from France at the time of the Norman Conquest in 1066. By the middle of the following century, their number had grown to 5,000, with thriving Jewish communitites in London, Oxford, Cambridge, Norwich, Winchester, Lincoln, and other towns. Within another century, there were seventy "Jew Streets" in England and by the time of the expulsion from England in 1290, 16,000 Jews had to seek homes elsewhere.

During this entire period, England lived under the feudal system. As in all feudal societies, the Jews had no official rights. Officially, they were the property ("chattel") of the king. Because they paid heavy taxes to his treasury, it was in his interest to protect them. But the king was not a very kindly protector. When he was in dire need of money, he had no scruples about confiscating the property of "his Jews," or taxing to the point of bankruptcy. Despite these handicaps, English Jewry prospered for about eighty years after the conquest and suffered no serious persecution. The majority, it is true, were not rich, but some of them were great bankers and merchants who founded Talmudical academies and even wielded much influence with the king. Before a hundred years had passed, however, anti-Jewish feeling began to show itself. In 1144 a charge of ritual murder—the claim that Jews had killed a Christian for use of his blood in the Passover ceremonies—at Norwich set the pattern for oppression throughout the twelfth century. An especially violent outburst during the Third Crusade (1189-1190) finally forced Richard I (Richard the Lion-Hearted) to take up arms against the rioters. Richard also declared that anyone harming the Jews was sinning against the Crown. Later, to assure a steady flow of gold into his own treasury, he set up a special office (the Exchequer of the Jews) which registered all loans and supervised the collection of debts. Under other circumstances, this might have been a blessing. England, however, was then torn by conflict between king and barons, so that the King's Jews were naturally the target of baronial hatred. As a result, the reigns of John (1199-1216) and Henry III (1216-1277) were marked by incessant persecution and exploitation.

By the time Edward I took the throne in 1277, the Jews of England were in dire straits. Italian bankers had largely replaced them as moneylenders, they had lost the right to lease land, and the church leaders were anxious to expel them altogether. By joining with the nobility and promising Edward one-tenth of all Jewish property, they succeeded in convincing the king to take this drastic step. On the Feast of All Saints (November 1) 1290, the entire community of 16,000, penniless and with little hope of welcome anywhere, were forced to take the weary path of exile, seeking homes across the sea.

For the following 350 years and more, England hand no Jewish community. The resettlement of Jews in England took place in 1656. England was then in the throes of the Puritan Revolution, and Oliver Cromwell, the Lord Protector, believed that Jewish merchants would stimulate English trade. But the merchants of London, fearing competition from Jewish merchants, refused to accept the plan. Nonetheless, an unusual circumstance led to the founding of a Jewish community. England happened to be at war with Spain, and had ordered confiscation of all Spanish property.

Among the goods seized were those of a Marrano* residing in London. In order to regain his possessions, this man declared that he was not a Spaniard but rather a Portuguese Jew. Together with seven other Marranos he petitioned Cromwell. The Lord Protector, eager to open the country to Jews, accepted their petition. Once it was known that Jews were living openly in the city, other Sephardic* merchants settled there. Although Parliament had not approved the change, the township of London immediately permitted them to build a synagogue and sold them land for a cemetery. By 1662, there were over 100 congregants in the synagogue, and two years later, the first Jewish school was founded.

The first Sephardic settlers were followed by Jews from Germany* and elsewhere in Central Europe. By 1690, there were enough Ashkenazic* Jews to found a separate synagogue, and by 1700 there were 500 Jews in the capital. In 1760, the community, which had no political rights, founded a Board of Deputies of British Jews* to handle relations with the government. By 1753, a "Jew Bill," proposing equal rights for the Jews, had been introduced in Parliment. The bill was defeated, but the struggle for political rights had begun. At the beginning of the nineteenth century, the total number of Jews had risen to 25,000, among them a number of families noted for their wealth and accomplishments. With the general liberalization of the political and social life in England, it was inevitable that the Jews should succeed in the quest for equality. The 1832 Reform Bill granted Jews and Catholics the right to vote in parliamentary elections. Four years later the Board of Deputies of British Jews was recognized by the government. By 1858, Baron Lionel de Rothschild was admitted to the House of Commons. In 1872, the last of the handicaps was removed with admission of Jews to England's great universities.

Political and social rights were gained on the eve of another revolution in the life of English Jewry. While the battle for equality was being waged in England, the Jews of Eastern Europe were experiencing political persecution and increasing economic hardship. By the early 1880's, the situation had become so unbearable that great masses of East European Jews were forced to flee to the West. A large number settled in England. Between 1881 and 1905, when the English government imposed restrictions on immigration, between 100,000 and 150,000 Polish and Russian Jews were added to a community that in 1881 had totaled only 60,000.

Most of the immigrants settled in Whitechapel, in the East End of London. Many others found

Courtesy British Information Service.

their way to Manchester, Leeds, Glasgow, Liverpool, and other cities where Jewish communities had not existed before. The immigrants earned their living as tailors, small manufacturers, and peddlers or petty traders. They were active in establishing a ready-made garment industry. Isolated in their own districts and speaking little or no English, they tended to form communities of their own, with Yiddish newspapers, theaters, clubs, and synagogues like the ones they had known "at home." They therefore had little basis for communication with the older, well-established community. The old community, for its part, though suspicious of the newcomers, did its best to help the newcomers adjust, through the Board of Deputies and the Jewish Board of Guardians.

The adjustment of the newcomers was successful. Their children attended English schools, and within a generation, had entered into the current of English life. The drawing-together of the two communities was speeded by the fact that all of England was undergoing a social revolution. The gap between rich and poor was narrowing, and class distinctions were becoming less rigid.

Zionism* also provided a common cause for the two sectors of the community. At first the old-timers were more conservative, and less willing to exert their influence with the government on their behalf. This situation came to an end only when a group of Zionists, drawn chiefly from the immigrants and led by Chaim Weizmann,* a Russian Jew who had been naturalized in 1910, succeeded in influencing the government to grant the Balfour Declaration,* issued in 1917, and promising the establishment of a Jewish National Home in Palestine. From that time on the influence of the "newcomers" was recognized, and Zionism began to play an important part in the official life of English Jewry. During the period from 1919 to 1948, when England occupied Palestine under a Mandate from the League of Nations, the Jewish community of England was active in attempting to influence the English government in favor of the Jewish cause in Palestine.

Emblem of the tribe of Ephraim

Today, about 70 per cent of English Jewry is self-employed, chiefly in the professions and small business. Except for a brief flareup of Nazi propaganda in the 1930's and a short period of resentment against Jews during the struggle between the Palestine Jewish community and the British army in the 1940's, anti-Semitism* has not troubled the community in recent decades. England was, in fact, the only major West European country which did not suffer seriously from anti-Semitism during the Nazi era.

The center of Anglo-Jewish life is London,* home of 280,000 Jews. Jewish life in the capital centers around the United Synagogue, an organization of Orthodox synagogues headed by a chief rabbi. Well over half of all English Jews throughout the country belong to synagogues, most of them Orthodox.

Sir Jacob Epstein

Courtesy British Information Service.

ENLIGHTENMENT. See HASKALAH.

EPHRAIM. Younger of the two sons of Joseph; founder of the warlike "half tribe of Ephraim" that settled almost in the middle of the Promised Land on a narrow stretch between the Jordan and the Mediterranean. Joshua, the leader who succeeded Moses, came from the tribe of Ephraim. The first king of Israel after the division of the kingdom into two rival states, Jeroboam ben Nebat, was also an Ephraimite. So important was the part played by this tribe in the affairs of Israel that Ephraim came to be another name for the northern kingdom.

EPSTEIN, SIR JACOB. (1880-1959) Sculptor. Born of immigrant parents in New York, he decided, as a young man to live in England. His very imaginative carvings in stone were at first very much resented by the public; but, persevering, Epstein gradually gained the respect and even the admiration of the art world. In 1954, he was knighted by the Queen of England. Occasionally, Epstein found themes for his monumental sculptures in the Hebrew Bible (**Adam, Jacob and the Angel, Lucifer**). He is also widely known for his portrait busts which, dispensing with superficialities and nonessentials, analyze the sitter's personality. Those who have sat for him have included George Bernard Shaw, Winston Churchill, Jawaharlal Nehru, Albert Einstein,* and Chaim Weizmann.* In November 1959, Epstein died.

ERETZ ISRAEL. See ISRAEL, STATE OF.

ESHKOL (SHKOLNIK), LEVI (1895-1969). Israeli labor leader and statesman. Born in the Ukraine, he settled in Palestine* in 1914, where he worked in various kibbutzim and became active in HaPoel HaTzair (see **Labor Zionism**). In 1949 he was elected member of the Jewish Agency* ex-

Levi Eshkol

ecutive, head of its settlement department, and, in 1950 also became treasurer of the Agency. A Mapai member of the Knesset* since 1949, he was Minister of Agriculture (1951-52) and Minister of Finance (1952-63) before becoming Prime Minister and Minister of Defense in 1963. During his term of office the Six-Day War* broke out and he turned over the Defense portfolio to Moshe Dayan.* He reamined prime minister until his death.

ESSENES. Sect of pious, ascetic Jews during the time of the Second Temple.* Evidence of the existence of the sect dates from the Hasmonean* period. The members of the group dedicated themselves to a life of simplicity and purity. They lived close to nature, and shared in common their worldly possessions. The Essenes settled in isolated areas in the Judean desert and in the vicinity of the Dead Sea.* They eked out a modest living by cultivating the land and by their craftsmanship. Trade was prohibited, for they considered it dishonest. Similarly, they refused to produce instruments of death and destruction.

The Essenes were known for their strict observance of the ritual of daily immersion in cold water. Purity of the soul was made conditional upon purity of body. This observance gave the name **Tovle Shaharit** ("Morning Bathers") to the community. The whole community ate together. Their meals, consisting of bread and vegetables, represented a solemn ritual. Keeping absolute silence throughout their meals, they resembled priests performing their rites during the sacred services in the Temple. New members who wished to join the sect had to go through rigorous tests and initiation rites in order to prove their worthiness. Patience, perseverance, modesty, righteousness, purity of character, and above all, love of truth and readiness to aid the poor and downtrodden, were the qualities required of every candidate.

The Essenes' closeness to nature led them to recognize medicinal herbs, and they acquired a name as healers and soothsayers. The Essenes refused to divulge their secrets, rules, or knowledge even under threat of death. Although opposed to war, they hated oppression and many joined the fight against the Romans. In recent years, scrolls found in caves near the Dead Sea, revealed a rich and valuable literature of sects similar to the Essenes.

ESTHER, BOOK OF. The **megillah,** or "scroll" of Esther in the Bible, tells the story of what happened according to tradition, to the Jews of Persia. The heroine of this story is the beautiful Esther, whose Hebrew name was Hadassah, or "Myrtle." She was an orphan who lived with her wise cousin Mordecai* in the capital city Shushan. When King Ahasuerus (thought to be Xerxes, 485-464 B.C.E.) deposed Queen Vashti, he chose Esther to take her place. Neither the king nor his wicked minister, Haman the Agagite, knew that Esther was Jewish. Haman plotted to destroy all the Jews of Persia. Queen Esther, after fasting and praying for guidance, pleaded with the king and saved her people from destruction. Purim is the festival celebrated to commemorate this deliverance. The Fast of Esther is observed on the thirteenth of the month of Adar in memory of the three days the Jews of Persia fasted at Esther's request. The Purim is celebrated that evening and the following day. The Scroll of Esther is read in the synagogue on the evening and the morning of Purim.

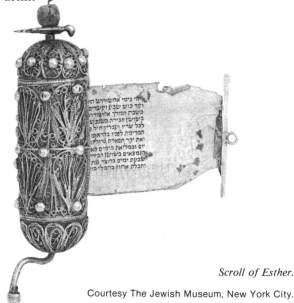

Scroll of Esther.
Courtesy The Jewish Museum, New York City.

96

ETHICS, BOOK OF. See HEBREW LITERATURE.

ETHICS (OR SAYINGS) OF THE FATHERS. A section of the Mishnah, called **Pirke Avot** in Hebrew. This book is a collection of moral and religious teachings by the rabbis who contributed to the Mishnah. One of the six chapters from the Ethics of the Fathers is read on the afternoon of every Sabbath between Passover* and Rosh Hashanah.* The original purpose for the compilation of the Ethics was to teach right conduct and to show the divine source of the traditional law. An enlarged version is the **Avot de Rabbi Natan**. The following are a few of the famous sayings:

Hillel* said: "Be of the disciples of Aaron,* love peace and pursue peace. Love mankind and draw them near to the Torah.

Shammai said: Set a fixed time for the study of Torah; say little and do much; and receive all men with a cheerful face.

Rabbi Eliezer said: Let your friend's honor be as dear to you as your own.

Ben Zoma said: Who is wise? He who learns from all men.
Who is mighty? He who controls his passions.
Who is rich? He who is content with his portion.
Who is honored? He who honors others."

ETROG. See SUKKOT.

EXILARCH. Rosh Galuta, or "Prince of the Captivity," a title held by the head of the Babylonian Jewish community until the eleventh century C.E. The Jews of Babylonia* had the right to govern themselves according to Jewish law, and the exilarch therefore had very real powers. He appointed judges and was the court of final appeal. The exilarch collected taxes, allocated them, and represented the Jewish community at the Babylonian court. Since, in addition, the exilarchs claimed direct descent from the House of David, and the office was transmitted for a thousand years from father to son, they were personages of great authority. (**See also** BABYLONIA.)

EXILE. See GALUT.

EXODUS. From the Greek, meaning "a going out." In Hebrew the second book of the Bible* is called **Shemot**—"names"—because it begins with the words, "Now these are the **names** of the sons of Israel, who came into Egypt* with Jacob."* Exodus tells the story of the Egyptian oppression of the Israelites, the appearance of Moses, the ten plagues, and the exodus from Egypt. It then describes how God revealed Himself in thunder and lightning to the Children of Israel standing at the foot of Mt. Sinai and gave them first the Ten Commandments,* the laws they were to live by, and finally the covenant or promise of the Land of Canaan. The story of the Golden Calf and the making of the Tabernacle* are in the closing chapters of the book.

EYBESCHUETZ, JONATHAN (1690-1764). Renowned rabbi and Kabbalist. Born in Cracow, Poland, he gained fame as a Talmudist early in his life. At the age of twenty-one, he became head of a **yeshiva** in Prague. His comments on the **Shulhan Arukh*** and his sermons, collected in his **Yaarot Devash** ("Forests of Honey") are classics in rabbinic literature. Because of his preoccupation with the Kabbalah* and his association with some followers of the false messiah, Sabbatai Zevi,* Rabbi Eybeschuetz was accused of sympathizing with this messianic movement. When Rabbi Eybeschuetz issued Kabbalistic amulets to ward off sickness, he was bitterly attacked by his contemporary, Rabbi Jacob Emden.* The prolonged controversy between the two famous rabbis reverberated through many Jewish communities. Rabbi Eybeschuetz was finally vindicated by his community of Altona, Germany.

Jonathan Eybeschuetz (anonymous engraving)

EZEKIEL (Hebrew, meaning "whom God makes strong"). Third of the major prophets, Ezekiel son of Buzi was a younger contemporary of Jeremiah.* He too witnessed the destruction of Jerusalem,* and Judea and went into exile to Babylonia.* Like Jeremiah, he also believed deeply in each man's individual responsibility to God. His prophecies have great poetic beauty and mystic power; the mystical concept of the Divine Chariot in the Kabbalah* drew its imagery from Ezekiel's first vision. His most famous chapter, 37, is the symbolic vision of a valley of dry bones that are resurrected and rise again as "a mighty army"—a prophecy of the rebirth of Israel.*

EZRA, BOOK OF. This Biblical book tells of Ezra* the Scribe, and how he led the Jews who had returned from the Babylonian exile to Judea, in the fifth century B.C.E.

EZRA THE SCRIBE. One of the two leaders of the return from the Babylonian captivity (5th century B.C.E.), a great teacher of the Law, and (presumably) author of the Book of Ezra* in the Bible.* About 458 B.C.E., 60 years after the Return and the rebuilding of the Temple,* the social and religious conditions in Judea had deteriorated, causing great concern among Babylonian Jewry. Ezra, a priest and learned scribe, or **sofer**, led a mission of Babylonian Jewish notables to Judea to correct this condition. He carried an authorization from King Artaxerxes to appoint officials and act as an administrator. Ezra acted vigorously; he instituted religious reforms that preserved the identity and continuity of the Jewish people. By his act, the scribes took over the responsibility of teaching the people. Ezra called an assembly of the people in the Temple courts where portions of the Torah were read out loud to them. The Levites* circulated among the people explaining the text, and the people pledged themselves to obedience. This was the first Great Assembly, an institution that continued for about two centuries. Not the least of Ezra's achievements was the custom he began of reading portions from the Torah on Sabbaths, on Mondays and Thursdays. This was a form of worship and of teaching which spread from the Temple to the synagogues all over the Land. It is no wonder that, in the Talmud, Ezra has been compared to Moses.*

F

FABLES. See HEBREW LITERATURE.

FALASHAS (meaning "exiles" in Ethiopian). A tribe of black Jews in Ethiopia. Some call themselves Beth Israel, or Israel. Most of them live in separate small villages, especially west of Lake Taana. These villages are usually located near a body of water, for the Falashas strictly observe the laws of purification, as prescribed in the Bible.

During the past hundred years Christian missionaries have succeeded in converting tens of thousands of Falashas. A minority group, dispersed throughout the land, they have not been able to withstand the overwhelming pressure of the Church. Nevertheless, many of the new "Christians" secretly observe Jewish traditions, just as did the Marranos* of medieval Spain. The Falashas today number close to 18,000. Most of them are engaged in agriculture, or in crafts such as carpentry, weaving, smithery. Few engage in commerce.

Throughout their long history (according to one tradition they came to Ethiopia after the destruction of the First Temple), the Falashas had very little contact with the main body of Jewry and were never aware of the existence of the Talmud.* They observe only the laws of the Bible. Except for a few words, they have no knowledge of the Hebrew language. Their Bible is written in Geez, one of the ancient languages of Ethiopia. Strict Sabbath* observance in accordance with the Biblical commandments is an important part of their ritual. With the exception of Hanukkah* and Purim,* they observe all the holidays, but on dates differing from those observed by Jewry at

Two Falasha boys and their teacher at Kfar Batya, a children's village near Raanana, Israel.
Courtesy Mizrachi Women's Organization of America.

98

large. At times, they perform ritual dances, and accompany their prayers with musical instruments. Until recently, they also sacrificed animals. Some of their customs were borrowed from their Christian neighbors.

The Falashas have a long history of fighting for their independence, and of defending their faith. There is no doubt that the messianic hope sustained them in their long struggle for existence. In 1862, there arose among the Falasha a messianic movement and a large group attempted to reach Israel on foot. On their way, most of them died from the plague or hunger and thirst. The rest returned to their native country.

In modern times, Jacques Faitlovich dedicated a good part of his life to extending material and spiritual aid to the Falashas, and to bringing them closer to world Jewry. He founded schools for their children in Addis Abbaba, and has also brought a number of young Falashas to Israel and other countries for education and training. Since the establishment of the Jewish state, the ties between the Falashas and the Jews of Israel have become closer.   H.L.

FARMERS, JEWISH. See AGRICULTURE, JEWS IN.

FAST DAYS. Fasting has always been a part of the profound processes of purification of the soul for the Jew. Purity of thought and action were considered the key to happiness in both this world and the next. According to Jewish belief, God keeps a strict accounting of each man's deeds, and in accordance with this record, He metes out justice. If a man wishes to ward off divine punishment, he must repent of his sins and cleanse himself of them. When he repents, he first recognizes his transgressions and confesses them to God. This may be done at all times, but is especially auspicious during the Ten Days of Awe and Repentance following the New Year. Therefore the prayers of these days include long confessions of sin and pleading for forgiveness, chanted by the congregation in unison.

In addition to confession and repentance, man must actively atone, or make up, for his misdeeds. The chief way of atoning is the fast, in which man "torments his flesh" and begs forgiveness. Yom Kippur* (the Day of Atonement) is the chief fast days, when observant Jews abstain from food and drink for twenty-four hours. Very pious Jews, however, observe additional fast days. Mondays and Thursdays are favored for this purpose, since they are the days when the Torah* is read in the synagogue. Any other day may be chosen for fasting, with the exception of Sabbath and holidays, when fasting is forbidden. When a fast

day falls on a Sabbath its observance is postponed until the next day, except in the case of Yom Kippur, which takes precedence over the Sabbath.

In addition to the fasts of purification and atonement, there are a series of fast days that are associated with mournful events in Jewish history, especially with the fall of Jerusalem and the destruction of the Temple. Since it is believed that these catastrophes were punishments for the sins of Israel, such fast days are occasions for repentance as well as mourning. They are marked by fasting and the recitation of special prayers and lamentations. Their sadness, however, is tempered by faith that the Messiah was born on the day the Temple was destroyed, and will one day come to redeem the people of Israel from the misery of the exile that began with the Destruction.

The most mournful of these fast days, and the "blackest day in the Jewish calendar," is Tisha b'Av (the Ninth of Av). Tisha b'Av is the anniversary of the destruction of both Temples—of the First by Nebuchadnezzar in 586 B.C.E., and the Second by Titus in 70 C.E. The fast lasts from

sundown of the eighth of Av to sunset of the next day. During the morning hours until noon, both work and study are forbidden. The Book of Lamentations, the Prophet Jeremiah's* outpouring of grief at the destruction of the First Temple, is chanted. Many **kinnot** ("lamentations") of later origin are also read. Some of these recall other calamities which befell the Jews on this day. Chief among these are the massacres of whole Jewish communities during the Crusades.*

An old Faith in the New World by David and Tamor de Sola Pool.   Columbia University Press.

Three other fasts are observed in commemoration of events connected with the destruction of the Temple. The Seventeenth of Tammuz marks the day on which the enemy broke through the walls of Jerusalem and entered the city. The three-week interval between the seventeenth of Tammuz and Tisha b'Av are observed as weeks of mourning. The Fast of Gedaliah, on the third day of Tishri, commemorates the assassination of Gedaliah, the governor of Judea in the days that followed the destruction of the First Temple. After Gedaliah's murder, the last vestiges of self-government were taken from the Jews. The Tenth of Tevet was the day on which Nebuchadnezzar began the siege of Jerusalem. These three fast days are observed from sunrise to sunset, rather than from sundown of the preceding day to sunset of that day itself.   B.H.

FESTIVAL PRAYERS. The services for the major festivals (Passover,* Shavuot,* Sukkot* and the High Holy Days) are contained in the Mahzor (the festival prayer book). As on the Sabbath,* the synagogue service held in the morning includes a Musaph (additional) service which describes the special sacrifices offered in the Temple in Jerusalem* on the festivals. The readings from the Torah and the Prophets are chosen to relate to the festivals. The festival service also includes special hymns (piyyutim); some of these are recited in traditional synagogues the world over, while others are chanted only in certain Jewish communities.

FINALY CASE. The case of Robert and Gerald Finaly, two Jewish orphans who had been rescued by non-Jews in France* during the Holocaust* and baptized in a Catholic children's home in Grenoble in 1948. Their parents had died in a Nazi concentration camp. A French court awarded the boys to their nearest living relative, an aunt living in Israel, but the children's home refused to give them up. In February, 1943 the children disappeared and were traced to Spain. Ten persons, including four Catholic priests, were charged with having kidnapped the children. The affair aroused much controversy in France; even some Catholics felt that the children should be turned over to their surviving Jewish relatives. As a result of the outcry from public opinion, the children were brought back to France in the summer of 1953 and delivered to their aunt who took them to Israel to raise them as Jews.

FINLAND. A European republic set between Sweden and the Soviet Union. Its population (1977) is 4,730,000 of which about 1,320 are Jews. Jews settled there under Swedish rule in the eigh-teenth century. After Finland became Russian territory in 1809, the only Jews permitted to settle were ex-servicemen and their families. There was never severe persecution as in Russia proper, but Jews suffered many restrictions. After the Finns gained independence in 1917, they granted the Jews full equality. All the Jews of Viipuri, which was annexed by Russia in the war of 1939-40, moved to Finnish territory. Finland was the only part of Europe under Nazi domination (1941-44) where Jews did not suffer from persecution during World War II. Most Finnish Jews are engaged in commerce and trades. Their small numbers and distance from other Jewish communities makes a full Jewish life difficult.

FIRSTBORN, REDEEMING OF. See PIDYON HA-BEN.

FLAG, JEWISH. The word "flag" is mentioned many times in the Bible. Each tribe had its own standard, though there is no description of the design or color. Neither is any such information available about the Jewish flags during the First or Second Commonwealth. Not until the sixteenth century does a specific Jewish flag appear. In 1524, Pope Clement VII received a mysterious visitor in Rome. He was David Reubeni,* who claimed to be a forerunner of the Messiah. He brought with him a white flag, embroidered with silver and golden letters.

In modern times, Theodor Herzl,* founder of political Zionism, suggested in **The Jewish State** in 1895 that the Zionist organization adopt a flag showing seven gold stars against a white background. The white was to signify the new and pure life, the seven stars the seven-hour workday. Instead, the Zionist movement chose a white flag with two horizontal stripes of blue and a blue Star of David* in the center—inspired by the traditional prayer shawl. By a special act of the Israeli government, on November 12, 1948, this flag became the official standard of the new state.

FOLKLORE. Traditions handed down for generations, including customs, legends, superstitions, beliefs, and folk songs current among the folk or common people.

Jewish folklore is varied and rich in content, partly because it has absorbed the folkways of many other peoples. In addition, the Jewish people's close tie to the Bible,* and the long periods of persecution and isolation, gave rise to a distinctively Jewish folklore. The Tamud* and Midrash,* as well as theological, ethical, and moral works of later centuries, contain a wealth of customs and beliefs. The legend of the Golem,* and that of the thirty-six anonymous righteous men (Lamed

Vav*), for whose sake the world survives, the tales about the Dybbuk, and the superstitions about the "Evil Eye" (Ayin-Hara), are but a few examples of Jewish folklore.

In the modern period beginning in the middle of the eighteenth century, Jewish emancipation and assimilaton* have led to the disappearance of many of these traditions. The destruction of the most vital centers of Jewish culture in Eastern Europe by the Nazis during World War II aided the process. A number of individuals and institutions have collected and published volumes on Jewish folkways. The YIVO* Institute of Jewish Research in New York and the new Yad Vashem Institute in Israel are currently making important contributions to the collection and study of Jewish folklore.   H.L.

FRANCE. The first Jews to reach France probably traveled in the wake of conquering Roman legions. Historical records show that in the seventh century, Jewish farmers, artisans and merchants had settled in most French provinces. During the reign of Charlemagne (768-814) Jews controlled the country's import-export trade. They enjoyed considerable civil and religious freedom, as well. A century later, when Charlemagne's empire began to break up, harsh restrictions were imposed. Then the Crusades,* beginning in 1096, brought persecution and often death. Entire communities were martyred for their faith. The Church brought every possible charge against them. Beginning in 1171, when all the Jews of Blois were burnt at the stake, the community was beset with blood accusations* and repeated charges that Jews desecrated Catholic forms of worship. Four years later the French king ordered twenty-four wagonloads of the Talmud burnt publicly in Paris after a "disputation" on the merits of the Jewish faith. Nonetheless, two great centers of learning flourished in medieval France: one in the northeast (mainly in Champagne) and one in the south (Provence and Languedoc). Rashi,* the "prince of Bible commentators," was perhaps the greatest French Jewish scholar.

Persecution by both church and state culminated in the decree of 1394, expelling the entire community from France. Nevertheless, scattered settlements remained, especially in the south. These grew during the following centuries, as ever greater numbers of Spanish and Portuguese refugees from the Inquisition sought haven in France. A further addition came in 1648, when Alsace, with its ancient Jewish community, was annexed by France. By the time of the Revolution of 1789, France was the home of 40,000 Jews, most of whom were forced to live in ghettos where they were deprived of all legal rights.

The revolution wrought a radical change in this respect. A decree promulgated in 1791 declared the Jews to be full citizens of France. Napoleon, however, soon curbed this freedom. Calling a "Sanhedrin"* of Jewish notables, he gained approval for a program placing the Jews directly under his control. He then proceeded to restrict the economic and political activities of the Jew. These restrictions remained in force after the emperor's downfall; it was not, in fact, until 1846 that the last of the disabilities was removed. Yet even then the battle against anti-Semitism* had not ended: as Jews began to take a prominent place in the social, cultural, and political life of France, reactionary elements in the Church and army began a campaign to undermine the Jewish position. The strength of these elements was shown in the 1890's, when the conviction on falsified charges of treason, of a Jewish army officer named Dreyfus, set off a conflict between the liberal and reactionary forces in the country. It took almost a decade, and the efforts of such men as Emile Zola,* to free Dreyfus, despite clear evidence of innocence. His exoneration, however, marked the defeat of Church and army, and the beginning of a new era in the history of France, as well as that of French Jewry.

New Jewish Geography of France

Lille 2,275 / 3,025
Amiens 140 / 340
Le Havre 265 / 765
Caen 125 / 300
Reims 350 / 450
Metz 2,800 / 3,050
Strasbourg 10,500 / 12,000
Versailles 315 615
Paris 175,000 / 250,000
Nancy 2,625 / 2,975
Rennes 0 / 150
Troyes 245 / 550
Belfort 350 / 1,600
Angers 0 / 250
Blois 0 / 175
Tours 350 / 550
Dijon 490 / 790
Besançon 420 / 695
Châteauroux 30 / 105
Poitiers 0 / 150
Mâcon 0 / 150
La Rochelle 0 / 500
Vichy 350 / 525
Lyons 6,300 / 12,300
Annecy 0 / 125
Limoges 350 / 475
Clermont-Ferrand 265 / 640
Aix-les-Bains 77 / 265
Chambery 0 / 150
Périgueux 210 / 510
Saint-Etienne 350 / 750
Grenoble 1,190 / 3,740
Valence 105 / 600
Bordeaux 3,500 / 7,250
Montauban 105 / 255
Nimes 350 / 1,100
Carpentras 55 / 155
Avignon 700 / 1,450
Nice 2,100 / 3,600
Toulouse 3,500 / 13,500
Castres 70 170
Montpellier 525 / 1,775
Aix-en-Provence 265 1,390
Cannes 455 1,055
Bayonne 420 / 570
Béziers 160 / 310
Marseilles 12,000 60,000
Toulon 525 / 1,375
Perpignan 350 / 750

The subjugation of France by Germany in 1940 brought about a revival of official anti-Semitism on a scale never before known to the country: the entire Nazi program of racism became law. Yet with the help of the French population, more Jews survived the war in France than in any other West European country. Since the war, the life of the Jewish community has returned to pre-war normalcy. Again Jews—like Pierre Mendes-France, who served as premier in 1955—have risen to eminence. There are now (1984) close to 530,000 Jews in France, many of them refugees of World War II. This figure includes those who came to France since 1961 from North Africa: 100,000 from Algeria, 30,000 from Tunisia and Morocco. Jewish life is organized in consistories, boards of one rabbi and four laymen, which concern themselves with Jewish affairs in each of the seven districts into which the community is divided. A central consistory, made up of the chief rabbi and a representative of each consistory, coordinates activities on a national level, and serves as a link between the Jewish community and the ministry of public worship. Since 1860, the Alliance Israélite Universelle* has been an important factor in the life of French Jewry, serving as a link between it and world Jewry. French Jews are active in the textile, garment, fur, leather, and jewelry industries; and have distinguished themselves in law, and medicine, journalism and banking.

FRANK, ANNE (1929-1945). Jewish Dutch girl. Hiding from the Nazis during the occupation she wrote a diary of the events and her thoughts, showing the most mature understanding. The diary was published and staged as drama in many countries.

FRANK, JACOB (1726-1791). False Messiah and leader of a sect that brought pain and strife into half a century of Jewish life. Jacob Frank spent the formative years of his life in Rumania and Turkey. Having little education, his contact, through his father, with secret followers of Sabbatai Zevi,* the seventeenth-century false Messiah, proved to be a decisive influence on his unstable personality. He assumed the role of a Messiah and went to Poland, where he proclaimed himself a reincarnation of Sabbatai Zevi. Polish Jewry was reeling from the cruel blows of Cossack pogroms and clutched at the idea of a Messiah who would save them. He began to teach the Kabbalah,* and represented himself as the reincarnation of all the prophets and messiahs that had come before him. He and his disciples of both sexes outraged the Jewish community by their immoral and unorthodox behavior; finally, the local authorities banished Frank from Poland.

Wherever Frank went, he brought trouble and calumny upon the Jewish people, including a revival of the old accusation that Jews used human blood for ritual purposes. To discipline Frank and his followers, a conference of rabbis met in 1756. They banned the Frankist sect from the Jewish community, and forbade the study of the Kabbalah by any person under thirty years of age. The Frankists appealed to the Catholic bishop Dembowsky, claiming that they were Kabbalists at war with the Talmud which was full of error and blasphemy. They hinted that their own beliefs were close to those of Christianity. The bishop summoned the rabbis to answer the charges against the Talmud in a public debate. As a result thousands of copies of the Talmud were seized and publicly burned. Eventually, Frank and a thousand of his followers were baptized. Great pomp attended these baptisms, to which Frank came dressed in magnificent Turkish robes. But the Church, which never trusted these converts, watched them closely, and later imprisoned Frank for conversion under false pretenses. The Frankist sect survived him for a time, but it no longer had any importance.   N.B.-A.

FRANKFURTER, FELIX (1882-1965). Statesman, teacher of law, United States Supreme Court Justice. He came to the United States from Vienna at the age of twelve. Educated in New York City public schools and the City College of New York, he took his law degree at Harvard University in 1906. While at Harvard he was deeply influenced by the new liberal doctrines of a group of rising lawyers that included Oliver Wendell Holmes and Louis Dembitz Brandeis.* These doctrines formed the basis of his later teachings. Upon graduation, he served as Assistant United States Attorney in New York from 1906 to 1910. As Professor of Law at Harvard (1914-1939), he exerted a profound influence on the course of American political life by training a generation of law students.

While holding the professorship at Harvard, Frankfurter served intermittently in various government departments. His brilliant plea in defense of the convicted anarchists. Sacco and Vanzetti, in 1927, earned him a national reputation and brought him to the forefront of American liberalism. During the Roosevelt administration (1933-1945), Frankfurter, and many of the young lawyers he had trained, played influential roles in drafting much of the liberal legislation of the "New Deal." Appointed to the Supreme Court in 1939, he advocated "judicial restraint" and deference to the will of the people. He resigned in 1962 because of ill health. Throughout his career he had taken an active interest in Jewish and Zionist affairs; in 1919 he was legal advisor to the Zionist delegation at the Versailles Peace Conference.*

FREIER, RECHA (1892-1984). Initiator of Youth Aliyah.* A teacher and the wife of a Berlin rabbi, she began in 1932 to help Jewish youth in Germany* perpare for agricultural life in Palestine.* After 1933 she organized similar training in other countries. She settled in Palestine in 1941.   G.H.

FREUD, SIGMUND (1856-1939). Founder of psychoanalysis. Freud was born in Austria to a scholarly, aloof father, and a vivacious mother who was usually the center of attention in the household. He graduated from the University of Vienna Medical School, and one of his earliest original research projects resulted in his discovery of the anesthetic properties of cocaine (1884). Even as a general practitioner, Freud was interested in nervous disturbances. In collaboration with Joseph Breuer, he published **Selected Papers on Hysteria** in 1895. Before these studies dealing with hypnosis as a means of studying the origins of hysteria were published, Freud had replaced the use of hypnosis with his method of "free association" which became a basic technique of psychoanalysis. In 1900, with the publication of his book, **The Interpretation of Dreams,** Freud ended his career as a general practitioner and devoted himself completely to the development and practice of psychoanalysis. His investigations into the unconscious strata of the mind helped to raise the curtain on the mysteries of the human personality, and have laid the foundations for later investigations.

Freud was the first to demonstrate the importance of earliest childhood experiences and the crucial importance of the sexual life of the individual in the development of his personality. The ideas presented in his many books were hotly rejected and disputed. Freud's work remained unrecognized in his native Austria until late in his life, the first acclaim coming to him from Germany and the English-speaking countries. After the Nazi invasion of Austria in 1938 he settled in England.

Freud was constantly aware of being a Jew, though his attitude toward Jewishness was highly complicated, both negative and positive. At a time when anti-Semitism* was widespread in Vienna, a friend asked Freud whether he ought to baptize his newborn son. Freud advised against this action. "If you do not let your son grow up as a Jew," he said, "you will deprive him of those sources of energy which cannot be replaced by anything else. He will have to struggle as a Jew, and you ought to develop in him all the energy he will need for that struggle. Do not deprive him of that advantage." Freud was a member of B'nai B'rith in Vienna.

N.B-A.

FRISCHMANN, DAVID (1864-1922). Hebrew critic, poet and novelist, born near Lodz, Poland. Frischmann achieved great fame as one of the first to introduce European ideas and values into Hebrew literature.* He revealed his keen satirical and critical sense in a pamphlet entitled **Tohu Va-Vohu,** ("Empty and Void") in which he criticized the Hebrew writers of his time for their poor taste and lack of esthetic appreciation.

Frischmann himself set an example of good taste and graceful writing in his short stories with a modern and Biblical background. Editor of some of the outstanding Hebrew magazines, he also excelled as essayist and Hebrew translator of writers such as Lord Byron, George Eliot, and Oscar Wilde.

FRUG, SIMON SAMUEL (1860-1916). Russian and Yiddish poet. Gaining recognition as a poet in the Russian language, Frug expressed in tender and moving verses the tragedy of Jewish homelessness and the age-old desire for the return to Zion. Many of his poems are based on legends of the Talmud* and on Jewish traditions. Frug also became a popular Yiddish poet, but toward the end of his life he wrote some poems in Hebrew—a language he loved and greatly admired.

Sigmund Freud

#

GABRIEL. See ANGEL.

GAD. (Hebrew, meaning "fortune.") Seventh son of Jacob,* head of the tribe of Gad, whose territory lay in the mountains of Gilead, east of the Jordan. The tribe of Gad supplied David* with some of his best warriors.

GALILEE. (From the Hebrew, meaning "district".) The northern hill country of Israel is divided into Upper and Lower Galilee; it extends lengthwise from the Emek Jezreel to the foothills of Lebanon,* and from the Mediterranean on the west to the Jordan rift on the east.

GALILEE, SEA OF. See KINNERET, LAKE.

GALUT. (Or **Golah,** from the Hebrew, meaning "exile.") The lands where Jews lived outside of the Land of Israel were called **Galut.** In early times, Galut also referred to the people-in-exile or captivity. Jewish sages called Israel's stay in Egypt* **Galut Mitzrayim** ("Egyptian captivity"). The second Galut, or captivity, that of Babylonia,* lasted seventy years, from 586 to 516 B.C.E., the year of the rebuilding of the Second Temple.* The third Exile, from the destruction of the Second Temple in 70 A.D. to the present day, is called **Galut Edom** or **Galut Ishmael.** The former refers to the Jews under Christian rule, the latter to those under Moslem dominion. A distinction is usually made between Galut, which is forced exile, and Diaspora, which is voluntary. **(See also** INGATHERING OF THE EXILES.)

GANS, DAVID BEN SOLOMON. See PRAGUE.

GAON. The title given to the heads of the Talmudic academies of Sura* and Pumbeditha* in Babylonia* between 589 and 1040. The name "Gaon" is derived from the phrase "Geon Yaakov" ("Pride of Jacob") in Psalms 47:5.

After the period of the Geonim, the title fell out of use for over 500 years; then it was used again among rabbis and scholars to describe a man of great Jewish learning.

The first Gaon was Hanan of the academy of Pumbeditha (589) and the last was Rav Hai Gaon* (1038). There were forty-eight Geonim in the academy of Pumbeditha and thirty-six in that of Sura.

The Geonim, who were known for their scholarship and wisdom, were the deciding judges in all religious matters. The Geonim also supervised the academies in their districts. Twice yearly all the academy teachers would assemble to hear the Geonim render scholarly interpretations of moot questions on the Torah* and the Talmud.* In addition, the Geonim replied to written questions sent to them from all parts of Babylonia, and from other countries as well. Responses recorded by various Geonim are still in existence. Among the most famous Geonim were: Rav Judah Gaon, Rav Saadiah Gaon,* Rav Sherira Gaon,* and his son, Rav Hai Gaon.*

GAON OF VILNA. See ELIJAH, GAON OF VILNA.

GAZA. See ISRAEL and NEGEV.

GEIGER, ABRAHAM (1810-1874). Scholar and orator. One of the founders of the Reform movement in Germany,* Geiger received a traditional Jewish education in his birthplace, Frankfurt-on-the-Main, and continued his studies in the classical and Oriental languages at Heidelberg and Bonn universities. At the age of twenty-one, he became rabbi of the Jewish community of Wiesbaden, Germany, and immediately started to introduce reforms in the synagogue services. At the same time, he embarked on a scholarly career, publishing a periodical dedicated to theological studies. In 1837, he called the first conference of liberal (Reform) rabbis in Wiesbaden; the next year, he was chosen assistant rabbi of the important community of Breslau, of which he was made rabbi a few years later. The Orthodox members separated and founded a community of their own. Geiger was also one of the founders of the famous theological seminary at Breslau, which was later taken over by the Conservative wing of German Jewry.

In his works, Geiger strove to show that Judaism has evolved throughout the generations. He considered the Jews a religious group whose mission it is to spread ethical ideas. He removed all references to Zion from the religious services and eliminated many prayers which he considered inconsistent with modern thought. Among Geiger's important works are a book on the Sadducees* and Pharisees,* and on Judaism and its history.

GEMARAH, See TALMUD.

GENERAL ZIONISM. The General Zionist programs for the development of Israel stress the encouragement of private enterprise, a unified system of Jewish education, respect for Jewish

Emblem of the tribe of Gad

tradition, and a non-dogmatic political and economic orientation. Historically, General Zionism first became differentiated as a party at the Sixth Zionist Congress* in Basle (1903). At this Congress the Socialist Zionist party, Poale Zion,* and the religious Zionist party, Mizrachi,* took up positions to the left and the right of the General Zionists.

After Theodor Herzl's* death, the leadership of the Zionist movement as a whole remained with such General Zionists as David Wolffsohn and Otto Warburg. Within General Zionism there was disagreement between the "practical" and "political" Zionists, with the former stressing settlement work over political action and the latter putting political action before settlement work. Nevertheless, financial contributions to practical Zionist work in Palestine increased, and in 1912, Hadassah,* the Women's Zionist Organization of America, was organized for the purpose of doing health work in the Holy Land. During the years 1914-1921, General Zionist leaders Chaim Weizmann,* Nahum Sokolow,* and Louis D. Brandeis* led the Zionist movement. (See also ZIONISM.)

GENESIS. (From the Greek, meaning "origin.") The first of the Five Books of Moses.* Genesis tells the story of Creation, the flood, and the patriarchs;* it closes with Jacob's* descent to Egypt* to join his son, Joseph.

GENIZAH. A literary "cemetery" for worn-out sacred books and manuscripts. A famous Genizah, which turned out to contain a treasure trove of ancient manuscripts was that of Cairo discovered by Solomon Schecter* in 1896.

GERMANY. The existence of Jewish settlements in Germany early in the fourth century has been established by historical evidence. Reference to the Jews in Cologne is found in decrees issued by Emperor Constantine. Earlier, Jewish traders had followed in the footsteps of the Roman legions who established military outposts along the northern ports of the Rhine. Very little is known about the fate of the Jews in Germany at the time of the fall of the Roman empire, and during the succeeding invasions from the East and West. During the reign of Charlemagne (771-814), the Jews engaged in commerce and trade. This wise ruler found the Jews useful to the welfare of the state and protected them against undue discrimination. His son, Louis the Pious (814-840), extended commercial privileges to the Jews. Their importance in the economic field is illustrated by the fact that on many occasions market-day was postponed from a Sabbath to a weekday in order to enable Jews to participate in it. Often, Jews were invited to settle

in particular towns in order to increase their prosperity. In the ninth and tenth centuries Jewish communities sprang up in the cities of Augsburg, Mayence, Regensburg, Speyer and Worms.

The development of Jewish economic life paralleled intensive scholarly activity. The famous family of Kalonymus, a family of scholars and poets, moved from Italy* to Germany. One of the greatest authorities on Jewish law, Rabbenu Gershom* (960-1040), called "the Light of the Exile," headed a Talmudic academy (yeshiva) in the city of Mayence, attracting students from distant countries.

In The Middle Ages.

The First Crusade* in 1096 brought about the tragic destruction of a number of important Jewish communities. A number of elegies included in the Book of Lamentations chanted on the Ninth of Av bemoan the tragedy of that period. The Second Crusade in 1146, although less severe in its effect on Jewish communities, led to a worsening of the Jewish economic position. Jews became chattels of the kings, who extended them protection against the attacks of fanatic mobs at the price of their freedom and only in exchange for a heavy tribute.

This humiliating status did not save the Jews from cruel discriminations. In the thirteenth century, the Jews were forced to wear the degrading yellow badge. They were forbidden to hold public office. Ritual murder accusations were leveled against them, even though these were denounced by Pope Innocent IV.

Persecutions of the Jews increased at the time of the plague known as the Black Death (1348-49). The Jews were accused of having caused the plague by poisoning the wells. The resulting widespread pogroms in a number of German towns caused the Jews to seek shelter in Slavic countries. In 1421, the Jews were expelled from Cologne. The Jewish population continued to be victimized during the next two centuries. Blood accusations,* confiscations of property, forced baptism, burning of Jewish books, and physical attacks were frequent occurrences. The banishment of the Jews from important centers of trade and commerce (Worms, Frankfort, Hamburg, and Vienna) continued well into the seventeenth century.

The Reformation in the sixteenth century did not radically change the position of the Jews in Germany. However, the interest of German humanists in Jewish scholarship and the emphasis of the Reformation on the Bible* resulted in some instances in better treatment of the Jewish population. The foremost defender of the Jews, Johann Reuchlin* (1455-1522), was a Hebrew scholar. He courageously fought the confiscation and the burning of Jewish books. Other humanists joined the fight against persecution. The country was divided into approximately 200 small independent states ruled by princes who had only weak ties to the Emperor. The Jewish position varied from one region to the next, depending upon the whim of the local ruler.

The Cossack uprising in the Ukraine in 1648-49, and the messianic Sabbatai Zevi* movement which followed, left their mark on the Jews of Germany. East European victims of the Cossack massacres fled to Germany, increasing the local Jewish population. The false Messiah also had followers in the Jewish communities of Germany. As late as the second half of the eighteenth century, traces of the Sabbataian movement were still evident.

The eighteenth century found the German Jews still sealed off in ghettos. They were divided into two classes, known as "protected," and "tolerated." Only a few privileged individuals fell into the "protected" category. The struggle to break out of the narrow confines of the ghetto and to become a part of German culture and society, culminated in the Haskalah* or Enlightenment movement. Under the influence of this movement, great changes took place in Jewish life. At the same time, the emancipation efforts gained support among liberal gentile scholars and authors, such as G.E. Lessing.* This movement aimed at the removal of civil and political discrimination and the granting of equal rights to the Jews as citizens of the country. The French Revolution and Napoleon's conquests brought a measure of freedom to the Jews of Germany. In the first half of the nineteenth century, the foremost champion of emancipation was Gabriel Riesser. His fight for equal rights for Jews resulted in a measure of success after the Revolution of 1848.

Emancipation and Reform.

The struggle for the achievement of equality was accompanied by great intellectual activity and far-reaching changes in the Jewish way of life. Jewish scholarship was advanced by the great historians and scholars Jost, Graetz,* Zunz,* Steinschneider, Geiger,* and many others. The quest for change in the old traditions and the adoption of new religious forms in harmony with modern thought and practices were expressed in the Reform movement. A considerable number of Jews left the Jewish fold altogether.

While the champions of religious reform were gaining ground in Germany, a new orthodoxy was strengthened by the writings and activities of Samson Raphael Hirsch and Israel Hildesheimer, head of a rabbinical seminary in Berlin. A moderating influence on Jewish life in Germany was exerted by Zacharias Frankel,* president of the Breslau

Seminary. From the middle of the nineteenth century on, the Jews of Germany made outstanding contributions to the literature, science, and economic life of the country. Jewish religion and philosophy were enriched by the works of Hermann Cohen,* Martin Buber,* and Franz Rosenzweig.

Despite their integration into the life of the country and their patriotic devotion to Germany, the Jews could not escape the plague of vicious anti-Semitism. During the First World War, 96,000 out of 550,000 Jews served in the German army, and 12,000 died on the battlefield. Yet immediately after the war, the Nazis spread the lie that the Jews had stabbed Germany in the back, causing its defeat in the war. In the 1920's there were only isolated attacks against Jews. But after the coming to power of Adolf Hitler, anti-Semitism aiming at the total destruction of the Jewish people became the avowed policy of the Nazi regime. During the first years of the Second World War, the Nazis seized the opportunity to exterminate the Jewish population of Germany and of occupied territories. Six million Jews perished in the greatest slaughter in Jewish history.

Nazi Extermination and Postwar Period.

During the early stages of Hitler's rise to power, about 60,000 German Jews managed to emigrate to Israel. Between 1933 and 1941, a total of 310,000 Jews escaped from Germany to other countries. But 130,000 were deported to the gas chambers and concentration camps of Eastern Europe. Leo Baeck, head of Germany's prewar Jewish community, survived World War II in Theresienstadt.

In 1977 there were approximately 35,000 Jews in West and East Germany. (The prewar Jewish population numbered about 600,000.) The present Jewish population of East Germany is about 700, a figure that does not include non-professing Jews. There is only one rabbi in East Germany.

On September 10, 1952, the Federal Republic of Germany agreed to pay collective reparations to Israel* and world Jewry for the crimes committed by Nazi Germany against the Jewish people.

Under the terms of the pact, reached after lengthy negotiations among the representatives of the State of Israel, the Federal Republic of Germany and the representatives of the Conference on Jewish Material Claims on Germany, Germany was to pay Israel a total of $715,000,000 in "commodities and services" over a period extending until 1962; an additional $107,000,000 was earmarked for the relief and rehabilitation of Jewish victims of Nazism outside Israel.

This agreement stirred opposition among some segments of the Jewish people, who viewed the acceptance of compensation from Germany as

morally indefensible. On the other hand, the Israeli government specifically separated this settlement from the moral issues involved in the case. It pointed out that it has assumed the heavy burden of resettling a large number of uprooted and destitute Jewish refugees from Germany and from territories formerly under German rule; Israel's claim against the Federal Republic of Germany for global recompense was intended to defray the cost of the integration of these refugees.

GERSHOM, RABBENU (Gershom ben Judah of Mayence). An outstanding scholar of the late 10th-early 11th centuries, commentator on the Talmud,* head of several academies in France* and Germany.* His learning earned him the title *"Me'or Hagolah"* ("Light of the Exile"). He was recognized as the leading Jewish religious authority in Europe and his decisions on questions of Jewish law were accepted as legally binding on all European Jews. In ca. 1000 he handed down numerous rabbinic rulings, forbidding the practice of polygamy, insisting on the consent of both parties to a divorce, prohibiting the opening of letters addressed to others, and modifying the laws relating to converts who had been forcibly baptized.

GERSHWIN, GEORGE (1898-1937). Composer and pianist. Born to immigrant Jewish parents in Brooklyn, N.Y., Gershwin had one of the meteoric careers in the history of American music. Beginning as a "Tin Pan Alley" tunester, he burst into serious music with a performance of his **Rhapsody in Blue** in 1924. After this critical success, Gershwin continued to compose for the popular stage. To the end of his life, however, he experimented with classic musical forms. His last work, **Porgy and Bess,** a "folk opera" whose score draws heavily on Negro spirituals, blues, and jazz motifs, has been acclaimed as a masterpiece throughout the world.

GET. Bill of divorcement, which by law must be drawn up at the request of the husband and presented to the wife in the presence of two witnesses. It must state that she is free to marry another. To protect the wife, the rabbis ruled that the consent of the wife is necessary for the divorce to be valid. The earliest extant form of a **get,** uncovered at the Genizah* in Cairo, dates from the year 1020.

GHETTO. The term "ghetto" has been explained variously. One explanation is that the Republic of Venice passed a law in 1516 ordering all Venetian Jews to be limited to one particular section of Venice, known as Ghetto. Another version has it that the word is derived from a Venetian workshop known as Geto, where weapons were made. Still another theory is that "ghetto" is an abbreviation of **borghetto,** meaning "suburb" in Italian. Whatever its origin, the term "ghetto" came to mean any area in any city or town inhabited only by Jews.

From the very first days of Exile, wherever in the world Jews have lived, they have kept to separate neighborhoods, by their own choice as well as by decree. In many places Jews made their living from trade, and preferred to live in the neighborhood of the marketplace or other such sources of livelihood. Their religious and social needs also caused them to settle in groups. The idea of separating the Jewish inhabitants from the rest of the population was conceived by the Catholic Church. But it was not until 1179 that the Third Lateran Council issued an edict forbidding Jews and Christians to live side by side. For a long time this decree was not carried out, but in the thirteenth century some countries began to limit the Jews to special districts. In 1239, King James I of Aragon relocated the Jews of Valencia in a specific district known as **Juderia.** In 1276 the Jews of London were assigned a special area called "Jewry." In Germany,* in the thirteenth century, Jews were limited to living in streets named **Judengasse.** In some towns in the south of France,* which were under the rule of the Pope, the Lateran decree went into effect in the fourteenth century and the ghetto in these places was called **Juiverie.** In 1555 Pope Paul restricted the Jews of Rome* to a dilapidated quarter beside the

Joint Distribution Committee.

Residents of the mellah (ghetto) evacuated to temporary shelters during the unrest in Casablanca, Morocco—1955.

Tiber river known as **Giudecca.** Later "ghettos" were instituted in other Italian towns as well, such as Toscana, Padua, and Mantua.

In the fifteenth century there were ghettos in various cities in Poland*—Posen, Cracow, Lublin, and others. Some notable ghettos were those of Amsterdam,* Frankfort-on-the-Main, and Prague.*

Generally, the ghetto was enclosed by a wall. Entrance to it was gained through an iron gate (guarded by special guards inside and out), locked at a stipulated time at night, and reopened in the morning. On Sabbaths and holidays the ghetto gates remained locked.

Because the area was so confined, the Jews living in the ghetto were crowded together. Nevertheless, their life was well organized to suit the needs of the community, and the inhabitants benefited from the freedom to conduct their own religious, civic and social life. **(See KAHAL.)**

After the French Revolution of 1789, the ghettos were dissolved one after another throughout western Europe, although the Roman ghetto continued as late as 1870.

The Nazis created a ghetto in every city they conquered where there were Jews; but they intended the ghetto to serve only as a way station in their highly organized plan of destruction of the Jews. The largest concentrations of Jews in the Nazi-created ghettos were in Warsaw,* Lublin, Lodz, Bialystok, and Vilna.

The revolt of the Warsaw Ghetto which broke out on April 19, 1943, and continued for five weeks, will remain a memorable event in Jewish history.   S.E.

GIDEON. A judge of Israel. He fought the Midianites who were oppressing the Children of Israel and defeated them decisively. In gratitude, the people offered to make Gideon king. Gideon,

however, refused immediately, saying: "I will not rule over you, neither shall my son rule over you. The Lord shall rule over you." (Judges 8:23.)

GIMEL. Third letter of the Hebrew alphabet. Numerically, three.

GINZBERG, LOUIS (1873-1953). An outstanding Talmudic scholar, Louis Ginzberg was born in Lithuania, arriving in the United States in 1899. He served as Professor of Talmud at the Jewish Theological Seminary in New York from 1902 until his death. He had received his education at the famous **yeshivot** of Slobodka and Telz and at the German universities. His important works are **Gaonica, The Legends of the Jews,** and **Students, Scholars and Saints.** Ginzberg was also one of the editors of the **Jewish Encyclopedia** published in 1901-06. His studies of the history of the Palestinian Talmud* are valuable aids in understanding the course of the development of Jewish law and life during the Second Temple.*

GLUECKEL VON HAMELN (1646-1724). Author of the **Memoirs** that have preserved in their delightful pages a portrait of Glueckel's own personality, as well as a rich description of the conditions under which Jews lived in her day. Born in seventeenth-century Hamburg, Glueckel was the wife and daughter of merchants. A capable business woman in her own right, she also managed to bring up successfully a dozen children. It was for them that she wrote her fascinating memoirs in Judeo-German. Her memoirs have been translated into German, English, and other languages.

Gideon

GOLDBERG, ARTHUR J. (1908-   ). U.S. jurist and statesman. Born in Chicago of Russian immigrant parents, he went to work at 12, but continued his studies; he earned an LL.D. and entered the practice of labor law. During World War II he served as a major in the OSS. He has been general counsel for several national unions, guided the AFL-CIO merger in 1955, and initiated labor-reform legislation and ethics codes. An expert in labor-management relations, he is respected as an outstanding arbitrator. He became Secretary of Labor in 1961 and was appointed to the Supreme Court the following year, succeeding Felix Frankfurter.* In 1965 he was appointed U.S. Ambassador to the United Nations, a position he held until 1968.

GOLDFADEN, ABRAHAM (1840-1908). One of the founders of the Yiddish theater, a playwright and artist. He organized theatrical troupes, which entertained Jewish masses in the Old and the New World for over a generation. His folk comedies and operettas are performed to this day. The songs of such plays as **Shulamit, Bar Kokhba,** and **Die Kishufmacherin** ("The Sorceress"), achieved wide popularity. At one time, there was hardly a Jewish child who was not lulled to sleep to the tune of **Rojinkes un Mandlen** ("Raisins and Almonds"). Goldfaden also published a book of Hebrew poetry. In 1887 he paid his first visit to America, where he settled in 1903. Goldfaden's plays became classics of the Yiddish stage.

GOLDMANN, NAHUM (1894-1982). World Zionist leader. Born in Poland,* he was educated in Germany* and settled in the United States in 1940. In 1923 he was a founder of the Eschkol Publishing Company in Berlin which published a German-language **Encyclopedia Judaica.** He became active in Zionism* at an early age. In 1935 he became a member of the Jewish Agency,* which he represented at the League of Nations in Geneva until 1939. He was president of the World Zionist Organization* from 1955 to 1968. In 1936 he helped found the World Zionist Congress,* of which he became acting president in 1949, serving as president from 1953 to 1977. As chairman of the Conference on Jewish Material Claims against Germany, he was largely instrumental in reaching the reparation agreement with West Germany in 1952. He was the author of two autobiographical volumes and many essays and articles in German, Yiddish, Hebrew and English.

GOLEM. A statue or image into which life is breathed by supernatural means. The word appears in the Bible (Ps. 139:16) as referring to an embryo or unformed thing. It has the same meaning in the Talmud.*

In the Middle Ages, however, Jewish superstition and mysticism gave the Golem its current meaning of a living robot.

Many famous rabbis are credited with having created golems, using various magical formulas: Rabba, Solomon ibn Gabirol,* Elijah of Chelm, and others. The most famous Golem in Jewish history, however, is the one supposedly created by Rabbi Judah Loew* of Prague (ca. 1525-1609). This Golem supposedly served the rabbi and the Jewish community as a spy and intelligence agent. He succeeded in having a group of people who were spreading false tales about the Jews arrested. It was said that Rabbi Loew used to remove the spirit of life from his Golem every Friday so that the creature would not desecrate the Sabbath.* The Golem is reputed to have crumbled to pieces; its remains, according to legend, are still in the ancient synagogue in Prague, which contains a "Golem's room."

The story of the Golem has been told many times in fiction. The most famous work in English is Pemberton's translation of Meyrink's German work. The famous Yiddish poet I. Leivick wrote a play about the Golem which has been produced frequently, and was twice made into a motion picture (1920, in Germany,* 1937, in France*).

GOMPERS, SAMUEL (1850-1924). American labor leader, founder and first president of the American Federation of Labor (1886). Samuel Gompers was born in London in 1850, came to America with his parents when he was 13 years old, and worked at his father's trade of cigar making. He pioneered in the labor movement of the United States, and reorganized the Cigar Makers International Union, which served as a model for other trade unions. Later, Gompers became one of the leading founders of the American Federation of Labor and, except for one year, he served as its president until his death. Gompers refused to participate in any socialistic and political projects, insisting that better wages, shorter hours, and other benefits were the proper aim of trade unions. He came to be recognized as a great public figure, and during World War I, served as the head of the War Committee on Labor. Gompers brought the support of the A.F. of L. to Zionism,* and was active at the Versailles Peace Conference in 1919. After his death, in 1924, Gomper's autobiography, **Seventy Years of Life and Labor,** was published.

GORDIN, JACOB (1853-1909). Yiddish playwright. Born in the Ukraine, Russia, he began in his youth a varied and adventurous career as an agricultural laborer, actor, stevedore, journalist, and founder of a "Spiritual Brotherhood." Through this organization, Gordin aimed at reforming Jewish religion and society. He came to America in 1891 with the intention of founding a collective agricultural settlement. Upon his arrival, he abandoned this plan and took to writing plays for the Yiddish stage.

For more than two decades Gordin's plays dominated the Yiddish theater. Some sixty plays issued from his prolific pen. Most of them were adaptions from classic works in world literature (Shakespeare's **King Lear,** Tolstoy's **Kreutzer Sonata,** for example). Of his original plays, **Mirele Efros** is his best known work. Melodramatic and moralizing, Gordin nevertheless exercised a valuable influence on the Yiddish theater of his day, and prepared the American Jewish immigrants for an understanding of serious drama.

GORDON, AHARON DAVID (1856-1922). Labor Zionist thinker and writer. At the age of 48, he left his native Russia and settled in Palestine,* where he eventually became a member of Degania, the first collective agricultural settlement. Gordon believed in self-fulfillment through work in the Jewish homeland. His followers and admirers were many. He was a source of inspiration and courage to his young comrades, working at their side, despite his age. His influence also extended to the next generation. Gordon expressed his ideals in many articles. He believed that close association with nature was the basis for a healthy and just society.

A Labor Zionist pioneer youth organization (Gordonia), and a cultural center in Degania have been named after him.

GORDON, JUDAH LEIB (1831-1892). Hebrew poet. No other literary personality of the nineteenth century exerted greater influence on Hebrew readers than did J.L. Gordon. Early in life, Gordon came under the influence of the two foremost poets of his day, A. D. Lebenson, and his son Michal. He began as a romantic poet, using Biblical themes. Gordon also treated tragic moments in Jewish history. Most of his historical poems are notable for their vigor and dramatic quality.

The foremost spokesman of the ideals of the Enlightenment* period in Russia, Gordon brilliantly satirized the strict rabbinical interpretations or the Law in a series of compelling narrative poems. He called upon his fellow Jews to leave their self-imposed ghetto life and avail themselves of the educational and cultural opportunities which the gentile world proffered them.

In 1875 Gordon was exiled, victim of a false accusation by the Russian government. His bitter personal experiences and the pogroms of 1881 brought about his disillusionment with the Enlightenment movement. Gordon was greatly disappointed to see Russian Jewish youth abandoning the Jewish traditions. Now he called for Jewish unity and saw great promise in a new Jewish haven in America.

Gordon ranks high in Hebrew letters as a master of style. He revealed his creative powers not only as a poet, but also as a writer of fables, novels and essays.

H.L.

GOTTHEIL, RICHARD JAMES HORATIO (1862-1936). Orientalist scholar, professor of Semitic languages at Columbia University; founder and first president of the Zionist movement in the United States. Born in Manchester, England, Gottheil came to his post at Columbia in 1886, and served as head of the Oriental department of the N.Y. Public Library from 1896 till his death.

In addition, Gottheil headed the American School of Archeology in Jerusalem (1909-1910), and served as exchange professor at the University of Strasbourg (1920-21). A pioneer in the Zionist movement of America, he was president of the organization from 1898 to 1904, serving with his skill as organizer and orator. His **History of Zionism** appeared in 1914.

GOTTLEIB, MAURICE (1856-1879). Artist. Claimed by both Poles and Jews (a small town in Galicia was his birthplace), Gottlieb was the great hope of his teachers, who acclaimed his enormous talent when he was still a boy. In his short but full life, he worked feverishly, producing masterly portraits, as wll as large historical canvasses. His most celebrated picture, **Praying Jews on the Day of Atonement,** is now in the Tel Aviv Museum. The figures are real, their expressions, their gestures convincing. In rich, yet restrained colors, Gottlieb shows the earnest, dignified men in the act of prayer, the dignified beauty of the Jewish women. The first notable canvas on a Jewish theme, **Praying Jews** paved the way for the coming generation of Eastern European artists. Gottlieb's portraits are gems of psychological penetration.

GRAETZ, HEINRICH (1817-1891). German-Jewish historian. Born in Posen, Graetz was a professor of history at the Rabbinical Seminary of Breslau for many years. Graetz lived at a time of great change in Jewish history. The ghetto walls that had sealed off the Jewish community from the rest of the world had been broken. Jews were mingling in the general life of Europe, and were working out new ways of life and thought. A movement had begun to place Jewish knowledge on a scientific and historical basis. Graetz became one of its formost leaders. He spent twenty years seeking out and studying thousands of untouched source documents, and in writing his eleven-volume **History of the Jews.** His work, completed in 1876, was a rare combination of scholarship and readability. The discovery of new documents and new archeological findings since the beginning of the century have revolutionized the study of Jewish history. The work of Graetz, however, still remains a basic source for understanding the history of the Jews.

GRATZ COLLEGE. Founded in Philadelphia, Pa., in 1897 through a grant by H. Gratz. It is the oldest existing training institution for Hebrew teachers in the United States, providing a four-year college course leading to a Bachelor of Science degree in Hebrew literature and a teacher's diploma. It also includes a preparatory and high school department, extension and in-service courses, and group leadership and summer school classes.

GRATZ, REBECCA (1781-1869). Educator noted for her beauty, charm, and good works. The memory of Rebecca Gratz has survived in several ways. Portraits of Rebecca Gratz were painted by famous artists, and her published **Letters** are rich

in descriptions of her home city (Philadelphia) and times. In 1838 she established the Hebrew Sunday School Society, the first school of its kind. It is said that she served as the inspiration for the Jewess Rebecca in Sir Walter Scott's **Ivanhoe.**

GREAT ASSEMBLY. See TALMUD.

GREAT BRITAIN. See ENGLAND.

GREECE. Jewish settlement in Greece dates back to the 2nd century B.C.E. Documents of the 12th and 13th centuries indicate the Jews were noted for their silk and dyeing industries. Greek Jewry flowered in the 14th and 15th centuries, producing many renowned rabbis and Talmudic scholars. Salonika, which became part of Greece in 1912, had been a noted center of Sephardic* Jewry. In the late 19th century 80,000 of its 120,000 inhabitants were Jewish, and Ladino* was the language of daily use. The massacres and deportations during the Nazi occupation of Greece in World War II virtually annihilated the Jewish community which has dwindled from 75,000 in 1939 to 6,000 in 1977.

GREENBERG, HAYIM (1889-1953). Labor Zionist leader, intellectual, and writer. Greenberg's career as a writer and Zionist leader began in his early youth in Odessa, Russia. In the company of the Hebrew poet Bialik* and the Zionist leader Ussishkin,* he emerged as an orator and writer on literary and philosophical themes and on Jewish ethics. After the Russian Revolution of 1917, Greenberg, then an instructor at the University of Kharkov, was arrested several times for his Zionist activities. He fled to Western Europe in 1921, and three years later came to the United States. He was the acknowledged intellectual leader of Labor Zionism* in America, serving as editor of its publications: the weekly **Der Yiddisher Kempfer,** and the English monthly the **Jewish Frontier.** During World War II, he was chairman of the Executive Council, and during the United Nations deliberations (1947) on the establishment of Israel, he helped win over many of the Latin American delegates to the Jewish cause. In 1946 he became a member of the Jewish Agency Executive and served as the head of its Department of Education and Culture in America. At his death, he was mourned as a leader of great spiritual force.

GREENBERG, URI ZVI (1895-1981). Contemporary Hebrew poet. A sensitive and imaginative poet, the rebuilding of Israel and the fate of the Jews in the Diaspora are the two major themes of Greenberg's works. Born in Galicia in a Hasidic family, Greenberg at first wrote lyric poetry. In 1924, he came to Palestine, where he identified with the pioneer builders of the land. His later poems are inspired with the vision of Jewish sovereignty over all of historical Palestine. During the Second World War, he wrote powerful and dramatic poems on the Nazi slaughter of the Jewish people. He was a member of the Herut Party. (**See** REVISIONIST ZIONISM.)

GROSS, CHAIM (1904-   ). Artist, sculptor. Born in Eastern Austria, he settled in the United States in 1921. He won a number of awards including a national sculpture prize in 1937 under the art program of the U.S. Treasury, the Silver Medal at the Paris Exposition (1937) and an award for sculpture from New York's Metropolitan Museum of Art. In 1963, he received the Medal of Merit for Sculpture (American Academy of Arts and Letters) and in 1964, he was elected a member of the National Institute of Arts and Letters.

His **Alaska Snow Shoe Mail Carrier** was chosen for the U.S. Post Office Building, Washington, D.C. (1936), and his four-foot wood sculpture **Ballerina** was exhibited at the New York World's Fair (1939-40).

His works are on exhibit in museums in Chicago, Baltimore, New York, Philadelphia, Jerusalem* and Tel Aviv.* He has published **Technique of Wood Sculpture** (1957) and **Fantasy Drawings** (1956).   G.H.

GUATEMALA. Republic in the northernmost portion of Central America. There were (1984) 900 Jews in a total population of 7,500,000. A community of Marranos,* forced converts to Catholicism who practiced their Jewish faith in secret, conducted a thriving export trade from Guatemala in the sixteenth century, when Guatemala was a Spanish colony. The Inquisition,* established in Mexico* in 1570, eventually led to the disappearance of this early Marrano community. During the 1860's a small group of German Jews from Mexico and Cuba,* as well as Sephardim* from Turkey* and France,* settled here. They have been joined by immigrants from East Europe during the past thirty years. Guatemala's forbidding climate discouraged immigration on a larger scale. Most of the country's Jews live in Guatemala City, where there is Zionist activity, a synagogue and a Jewish teacher for the youth. All organizations are represented within the Comunidad Israelita (Jewish Community).

GUENZBURG, BARON DAVID (1857-1910). Scion of a distinguished Jewish family in Russia, he was intensely interested in Jewish learning. Baron Guenzburg became a patron of Jewish scholarship, and amassed one of the largest collections of Jewish books and rare manuscripts. To serve Jewish learning, he founded an academy for Jewish studies in St. Petersburg (now Leningrad).

GUGGENHEIM FAMILY. A family of American Jewish industrialists, public servants, and philanthropists. Mayer Guggenheim (1828-1905) came to the United States from Switzerland* in 1847. By 1900 he and his seven sons controlled one of the country's great mining empires in Colorado. Simon Guggenheim (1867-1941), the sixth son, was United States Senator from Colorado from 1907 to 1913. He established the John Simon Guggenheim Foundation, with endowments of well over $10,000,000 to aid scholars and artists. Solomon Guggenheim (1861-1930), a collector of non-objective paintings, set up a fund "for the promotion of art and education in art." Daniel (1856-1930), Mayer's second son, contributed to the development of aviation. Together with his son, Harry Frank, who was United States Ambassador to Cuba* from 1929 to 1933, Daniel established a foundation for aeronautical research. Other beneficiaries of Guggenheim aid include the New York Botanical Gardens, the New York Guggenheim Concerts, the Jewish Theological Seminary of America,* and the Hebrew Union College* of Cincinnati.

HABAKKUK. The eight of the twelve minor prophets, he lived c. 630 B.C.E. In the first chapter of his book, Habakkuk foresees the Chaldean invasion of Judea. In the second, he cries out against injustice; the third and final chapter is a striking poetic prayer.

HABIMAH (Hebrew, meaning "stage"). Renowned Hebrew theater in Israel.* Founded by a group of enthusiastic young artists in Moscow in 1918. Headed by Nachum Zemach, the troupe was inspired by the idea of creating a national Jewish theater in Hebrew. In the midst of the turmoil and chaos of the Russian revolution, the Habimah prepared for its first performance. It was fortunate in securing the guidance of the great Russian directors, Constantin Stanislavski and his pupil, Eugene Vachtangov.

Habimah's first appearance in 1918 was hailed as a great artistic achievement. Theater-loving Moscow was especially impressed by the Habimah's performance of the mystic Hasidic play **Ha-Dibbuk.** Since then that play has been staged over a thousand times. Though it restricted the Hebrew language and culture, the Soviet government allowed the Habimah to perform until the troupe left the country for a tour of Europe and the United States in 1926.

In 1928, the Habimah made its permanent home in Palestine.* Its repertoire has since grown to over a hundred plays. Its artistry has been acclaimed again and again during its several tours of Europe and in its second visit to America in 1947. It is now Israel's National theater.

HADASSAH, THE WOMEN'S ZIONIST ORGANIZATION OF AMERICA. Founded in 1912 by Henrietta Szold,* Hadassah developed from a study circle of twelve women to a membership today of 370,000 organized in over 1,600 chapters and groups throughout the country, with a group in Alaska and one in Puerto Rico. The organization originally dedicated itself to the double aim of fostering Zionist and Jewish ideals in America and of doing health work in Palestine.*

In 1913, when Hadassah's two American-trained nurses arrived in Palestine, the country was suffering from a high infant mortality rate, trachoma (the dread eye disease), malaria, and other diseases that beset countries with a similar subtropical climate and primitive sewage and sanitation. The first project set up by the two nurses was a small welfare station in Jerusalem* for maternity care and the treatment of trachoma. During World War I (1916), Hadassah was chosen to provide a Medical Unit for Palestine with the financial assistance of the Zionist Organization of America* and the American Jewish Joint Distribution Committee.* In 1918, this unit established a permanent hospital in Tiberias,* took over the old Rothschild Hospital in Jerusalem and opened the first Nurses' Training School in the country. The first Infant Welfare station was opened in 1921.

From these modest beginnings, Hadassah has expanded its work step by step until its annual budget reached $39,000,000. It covered Palestine — now Israel — with a network of medical services both curative and preventive, and various forms of agricultural and vocational education.

Habimah Theatre—Tel Aviv   Israel Office of Information.

Hadassah-Hebrew University Medical Centre in Ein Karem In Jerusalem

Through the Jewish National Fund,* Hadassah has participated in the reclamation of thousands of acres of wastelands, and in afforestation. Since the initiation, in 1934, of Youth Aliyah* in Germany,* Hadassah has been its official representative in the United States. Henrietta Szold was the guiding spirit of Youth Aliyah from its inception until her death in 1945. Providing more than one-third of the world Youth Aliyah budget, Hadassah has sent to Israel over $100,000,000 for this purpose, and has helped Youth Aliyah to resettle over 250,000 young Jewish children from eighty lands.

Hadassah's Medical and Health Operations. Hadassah Medical Organization practices the principle of equality of treatment of patients regardless of race, faith, or ability to pay. Hadassah's medical and health facilities now are consolidated in a 21-building Hadassah-Hebrew University Medical Center, which was opened officially in Jerusalem in August 1961. The Medical Center includes a 500-bed teaching hospital; the Henrietta Szold Hadassah School of Nursing and Residence; the Rosensohn Outpatient Clinics, which handled more than 250,000 patient visits annually; the Adolf and Felicia Leon Mother and Child Pavilion; clinical and research laboratories; and a Synagogue, which houses the famed stained glass windows Marc Chagall* created for Hadassah. Recently completed as part of the Medical Center are the Hebrew University-Hadassah Medical School, and the Hebrew University-Hadassah School of Dentistry founded by Alpha Omega. Hadassah Medical Organization has been acclaimed for its ability to maintain the highest medical standards in Israel at times when the country was accepting immigrants from all parts of the world—people from concentration camps of Europe, from medieval Yemen* and other Middle Eastern countries, from Morocco*— who brought with them many of the diseases that have plagued their native lands for generations.

Hadassah Aid to Afro-Asian Countries. As Hadassah continues its vital pioneering and standard-setting activities to advance the health of the people of Israel, it has become an important instrument for helping the newly-developing Afro-Asian countries to meet their respective needs for medical personnel and solutions to medical and public health problems. Hadassah is helping these countries in many ways. A Hadassah team is supervising a hospital for eye diseases in Monrovia, which Hadassah was instrumental in having established by the Liberian Government.

Health Services and Preventive Medicine. The long record of Hadassah preventive medical work includes a system of visiting needy patients in their homes, mobile tuberculosis units to screen the local population and new immigrants, and projects to control malaria and typhoid. At the time the State of Israel was established, Hadassah was operating a network of 60 mother and child health stations in various parts of the country, and opened dozens more to meet the urgent needs of mass immigration. The rapid increase in population called for extension of services on a scale quite beyond the capacity of a voluntary agency. Accordingly, in 1952, the Hadassah Medical Organization transferred 102 mother and child health stations,—together with their personnel—to the Israel Government.

Vocational Education Services. The Brandeis Vocational Centers in Jerusalem include the Alice Seligsberg Vocational High School, Hadassah's Vocational Guidance Bureau, printing and fine mechanics and precision instrument workshops.

Neurim, the Rural Vocational Center at Kfar Vitkin—in the Haifa* area—is operated jointly by Hadassah and Youth Aliyah. There young people are being trained in agro-mechanics, metalwork, carpentry, vegetable growing, poultry raising, cooking and sewing. For the first time, in 1959, Arab girls living in the Triangle were permitted by their families to live and study at Neurim for six-week courses in nutrition, sewing, weaving and arts and crafts. As important as the training, is the successful establishment of friendly relations between the Arab and Jewish citizens of Israel.

Hadassah in the United States. From Hadassah's inception, its education program formed a basic part of its work. The goals of this program were to train the membership in habits of self-study. Toward this end, special techniques and materials to facilitate the study of Jewish history, the Hebrew language and literature, Zionism and Judaism, were created for Hadassah's needs within its numerous study groups. From time to time, Hadassah has also published books to fill a particular need. **Modern Palestine,** edited by the late Jesse Sampter, was issued in 1933. **The American Jew—A Composite Portrait,** edited by Oscar I. Janowsky, came out in 1942. Hadassah's latest publication (1956), **Great Ages and Ideas of the Jewish People,** edited by Leo Schwarz, was issued to provide study group leaders (and the leadership in general) with an interpretation of Jewish history and its major values. Hadassah Magazine is a monthly publication which features well-written articles on Hadassah's work and on Jewish life in Israel and the rest of the world. Through its Zionist Affairs work, Hadassah interprets Israel and its people to the American public. Through an American Affairs program, Hadassah keeps its members informed on issues at home and on democracy's role as a force for freedom and peace abroad.

Hadassah also aids Zionist youth activities in America, and sponsors an autonomous daughter organization, Junior Hadassah, the Young Women's Zionist Organization of America. N.B.-A.

HADASSAH-WIZO ORGANIZATION OF CANADA. The largest women's Zionist organization in Canada,* was formed in 1919 by women and subsequently became a Federation of World Wizo.* It now has 320 chapters in 65 centers across Canada with a membership of 17,000. In Canada it carries on fund-raising and educational activities. In Israel it supports 14 baby creches, two kindergartens, two youth clubs and the Haifa Community College, four women's clubs, and two large schools: the Children's and Youth Village at Hadassim, and the Agricultural Secondary School

and Village at Nahalal, which have graduated thousands of students to become productive citizens of Israel.

As sole agency for Youth Aliyah* in Canada, it supports and maintains the Acco Educational and Vocational Youth Village, the Magdiel Comprehensive Secondary School and Youth Village, the Nathanya Day Centre, the Child Guidance and Hadassah-WIZO Canada Research Institute in Jerusalem, and the Abe and Sophie Bronfman School in Nehalim.

Canadian Hadassah-WIZO has given the Hebrew University of Jerusalem* study centers and other facilities, and has assisted the Asaf Harofe Hospital in many phases of its development.

Hadassah-WIZO of Canada also has planted three forests in Israel through the Jewish National Fund.*

HAFTORAH (from the Hebrew, meaning "conclusion"). The section from the Prophets, recited at the conclusion of the reading from the Torah,* or Five Books of Moses, on the Sabbath,* holidays, and during afternoon services on fast days. Each portion of the Torah has a specific Haftorah of its own; there is some connection, however remote, between the Torah reading and the Haftorah. Some Sabbath days are named after the Haftorah reading, such as Shabbat Hazon ("Sabbath of Vision"), when the first chapter of Isaiah, (beginning with the words "The vision") is read.

From the Talmud* we learn that the practice of Haftorah readings on the Sabbath goes back to the first century C.E. The early Tannaim* gradually arranged for the addition of a specific Haftorah for each portion of the Torah.

HAGANAH. Defense force of the Jews in Palestine, before the establishment of the State of Israel. In 1920, in the early days of the British mandatory regime in Palestine,* the Arabs attacked the small Jewish settlement of Tel-Hai, near the Syrian border. A few defenders, headed by Joseph Trumpeldor,* held Tel-Hai but fell in its defense. The Arabs intensified their attacks. The bloody

Machinery toolshop work keeps young hands and minds busy in vocational training at the Acco Educational & Vocational Youth Village, sponsored by Hadassah-WIZO Organization of Canada.

outbreaks in Jerusalem on Passover 1920 and those in Tel Aviv in May 1921, convinced the Jews that they could not depend on the British Army for protection, but that they must organize for self-defense. Thus, despite a British ban on Jewish arms, the secret Haganah (Army of Defense) was formed during the twenties.

In 1929 an attempt was made, under the leadership of the Mufti of Jerusalem,* Haij Amin el Husseini, to undermine the Yishuv (Jewish community of Palestine). The Arabs massacred over fifty Talmudical students in the Arab town of Hebron, and killed a number of Jews in old Jerusalem and Safed, all of them unarmed and defenseless. Their attacks on the new settlements, however, were repelled by the Haganah.

The Arabs repeated their efforts to destroy the Yishuv in 1936. For thirty-two months, Arab bands harassed Jewish settlements. They caused considerable damage to property and took five hundred lives. These repeated widespread Arab attacks sped the formation of a large and powerful Jewish fighting force. First, units of Jewish special police were organized, and later Special Night Squads (SNS) were trained and led by the colorful British officer Captain Orde Wingate.* A master tactician, a Bible scholar, and a friend of the Jews, he developed commando methods to defeat the Arab bands. These SNS groups served as a training unit for the famous Palmach,* the Jewish striking force.

On the eve of the Second World War, the Haganah forces numbered close to 15,000 men. The Yishuv was ready to make its contribution to victory over the Nazis. Out of a total population of 500,000, 36,000 men and women registered for military and auxiliary services. The Palestinian Jews joined all branches of military service and gained valuable experience as sailors, pilots, gunners, draughtsmen. A Jewish Death Battalion of Commandos took part in the Abyssinian campaigns against the Italian invaders. Some units rendered outstanding service to the British Eighth Army that drove the Nazis out of North Africa.

All in all, close to 30,000 Palestinian Jews served in the Allied armed forces. On September 18, 1944, a Jewish Brigade was formed. Units of the Brigade participated in the campaigns in Italy. When the war ended, and before the Brigade was demobilized, it came to the aid of survivors from Nazi slaughter, strengthening their determination to reach the shores of the Jewish homeland.

The doors of Palestine were closed to Jewish immigrants by the British, who sought to appease the Arabs. The main task of organizing the illegal entry of Jews into Palestine fell to the Haganah. After the war, it established an "illegal" underground immigration system through which the Jews from all over Europe streamed to Palestine. A number of ships carrying Jewish immigrants to Palestine were intercepted and bitter fights ensued.

The issue of free immigration became the central point of the struggle between the British Administration and the Jews of Palestine. The British concentrated a force of 100,000 in the area to "pacify" the Jews. Searches for hidden arms were carried on day and night. Haganah leaders were arrested and sent to detention camps, but the Jewish resistance movement continued to grow.

After the partition of Palestine by the United Nations decision of November 29, 1947, the Arabs embarked on an all-out campaign to destroy the Yishuv. The armies of seven Arab states invaded Palestine. Overnight, the Haganah was transformed into the Army of Israel* and held the invading Arab armies at bay. Despite meager equipment and arms, the Israeli artillery, air force, and navy gave an excellent account of themselves, and secured the present borders of the Jewish state.

H.L.

HAGGADAH (from the Hebrew, meaning "narration"). The book containing the Passover* Seder service. Written in Hebrew with some passages in Aramaic,* the Haggadah tells the story of the exodus* from Egypt.* The original form of family observance of the Passover eve ceremony probably consisted of the eating of the Paschal lamb, followed by an informal narration of the Passover story by the head of the house. During the period of the Second Temple,* when daily and Sabbath* prayers were assuming a standard form, the need was felt for a uniform way of fulfilling the commandment of "telling" the Passover story. The first suggestions for the planning of the Seder service appear in the Talmud,* where such parts of our present-day Haggadah as the Four Cups of wine and the Four Sons are mentioned. By 200 C.E., the Haggadah had a fairly fixed form; as time went on, additional material such as psalms were added. The Passover service became so long that sometime during the Middle Ages it was divided into two parts. The first part, including the Four Questions, narration of the exodus, and explanations of symbols, was recited before the meal. The second part, consisting of the Grace after meals, psalms and songs, followed the meal. To make sure everyone understood the Haggadah, it was translated into many languages, and often illustrated with Biblical scenes and pictures of the Seder service. Many editions of the Haggadah have been written and printed in many lands. The earliest manuscript available is of the thirteenth century; the earliest extant printed Haggadah carries the date 1505.

shopping section, interspersed with parks and gardens. Mount Carmel, with its splendid forests, its terraces of Persian gardens, and its white villas, commands a matchless view of the city, the sea, and the broad sweep of the bay, with snow-capped Mount Hermon in the hazy distance.

Haifa is not mentioned in the Bible,* and is referred to only casually in the Talmud* as a fishing village. Herzl* called it the "city of the future" when it was still a small Oriental town of twisted streets. Until recent times it was cast in the shade by its rival Acre.*

Its first Jewish community consisted of Moroccan and Algerian Jews who settled there in 1833. Once, it was linked with Damascus by the Hedjaz railway, and later to Cairo. Haifa's growth has been phenomenal, spurred by the construction of the deep sea harbor by the British mandatory government. When the British departed in 1948 the Jewish population took over the city, which has become the metropolis of northern Israel.

The city of Haifa has two institutions of higher learning, the Technion* and the University of Haifa.

HAI GAON (939-1038). Head of the academy of Pumbeditha, Babylonia,* Hai Gaon was the foremost authority of Talmudic law in his time. He was the last of the Geonim in Babylonia. In addition to his vast knowledge of Jewish law, he was familiar with Greek philosophy and Arabic literature. Hai Gaon wrote poems and commentaries on the Bible.*

HAITI. The only French-speaking republic in South America, Haiti occupies the western third of a Caribbean island lying between Cuba* and Puerto Rico.* Several Spanish Jewish families settled in Haiti in the sixteenth century. They were driven out when the French, who did not favor Jewish colonists, took the island from the Spanish in 1683. Because the predominantly Negro republic of Haiti does not favor white immigration, few Jews have settled here. A number arrived during World War II. In 1984, there were 100 Jews in Haiti, out of a total population of 5,104,000. All are engaged in commerce. There is no organized Jewish community in the republic.

HALAKHAH. The term applied to Jewish law, as interpreted by the masters of the Talmud* and later authorities. The entire legal framework of Jewish tradition, especially the Mishnah and rabbinic laws, are known as Halakhah, as distinguished from the legendary and narrative portions of the Talmud, called Aggadah.*

HA-LEVI, JUDAH (1085-1142). The greatest Hebrew poet of the Middle Ages. Born in Toledo, Spain,* when it was under Christian rule, he went to study at the academy of Isaac Al-Fasi in

HAGGAI. One of the minor prophets in the Bible.* He encouraged Zerubbabel,* governor of Judea after the return of the Jews from the Babylonian exile, and urged the rebuilding of the Temple.* Haggai's prophecy that the Second Temple would be more beautiful than the first was fulfilled.

HAIFA. Israel's principal port, situated where the mountains meet the sea, has (1984) a population of 226,100. The city extends over the foot, slopes and crest of Mount Carmel. Greater Haifa also includes Haifa Bay between the Kishon and Naaman rivers, with its oil refineries and heavy industries, as well as a chain of suburbs and villages. The lower city, fringing the harbor, is the mercantile center. Hadar Hacarmel is the residential and

Haifa Harbor

Haifa after dark—seen from Mt. Carmel.

Lucena, near Cordova, in Moslem Spain. Having acquired an extensive knowledge of the Talmud,* philosophy, Arabic literature, and medicine, he returned to his native town, where he was a practicing physician.

In his youth, Judah's joy of life was expressed in the poems he composed on love and the beauty of nature. Few Hebrew poems can rival the gracefulness, style, the brilliance of expression, and also the tenderness found in the best of his poetry. His religious poems, on the other hand, are radiant with nobility of spirit and longing for the living God:

Oh Lord, where shall I find Thee?
All-hidden and exalted is Thy place;
And where shall I not find Thee?
Full of Thy glory is the infinite space.

But his deepest passion and burning love he reserved for Zion; only in the land of Israel's glorious past could the poet find peace and fulfillment:

My heart is in the East,
But I am in the uttermost West,
How then can I taste what I eat,
And how can food to me be sweet?

Judah realized his dream. He set out first by boat to Egypt,* and thence to Palestine.* This trip enriched Hebrew literature with ardent and powerful songs of the sea. Legend has it that when Judah reached the ruins of the Temple,* and he knelt at the Wailing Wall,* an Arab horseman trampled him to death under his horse's hooves.

Many of Judah's poems became part of the Jewish prayer book. He also exercised great influence on Jewish thinking by his philosophic work, **The Kuzari.** In it, he attempted to prove the Jewish religion superior to any of the philosophic systems known in his time. Unlike Jewish philosophers before him, Judah Ha-Levi does not find it necessary to reconcile the Jewish religion with philosophic thought. For him, Jewish tradition needs no confirmation by reason; ethical perfection is best attained by religious observance. **The Kuzari** was written in the form of a discussion at the court of the king of the Khazars* among representatives of the three major religions: Judaism, Christianity, and Islam. The king is finally convinced of the superiority of the Jewish religion. **The Kuzari** also stresses the intimate bond between the Jewish people and the Land of Israel, expressing the thought that "Jerusalem* will be built when the children of Israel strongly desire it."   H.L.

HALLEL (Hebrew, meaning "hymns of praise"). Consists of Psalms 113-118, which were sung by the Levites* in the Temple* in Jerusalem* on Suk-

kot,* Passover,* Shavuot,* and (later) Hanukkah.* Hallel became part of the synagogue morning service for those days and for New Moons as well. During the chanting of Hallel on Sukkot the **lulav** ("palm branch") is wavd. Some congregations recite Hallel on Passover after the evening service, and it is also part of the **Seder** (Passover service). **(See also PRAYERS.)**

HALUKKAH. (Hebrew for "distribution.") A system for the support of Jews in Palestine* with funds raised abroad. The tradition of subsidizing Palestinian Jews goes back to Talmudic times, when higher institutions of Jewish learning received such support. Systematic **halukkah** began in 1600, when fairly large numbers of Jews settled in the Holy Cities of Jerusalem,* Safed, Hebron, and Tiberias* to pray for the coming of the Messiah. Lacking means of support, they sent messengers **(meshulahim)** to raise money in the Diaspora. During the nineteenth century **halukkah** contributions came from the entire Jewish world. When the Zionist movement replaced Messianic longings with the ideal of self-help, **halukkah** fell into disrepute. It still exists, but its scope has been reduced to a minimum.

HALUTZIM (Hebrew, meaning "pioneers"). The term came into widespread use after the First World War, when Joseph Trumpeldor* helped found the Hechalutz movement in Russia.* Inspired by the ideal of rebuilding Palestine* as a Jewish homeland, the **Halutzim** came from countries ravaged by war and revolutions. To reach their goal, the Russian **Halutzim** traveled dangerous roads over the Balkan lands and Caucasian mountains. The **Halutzim** made up the bulk of the Third Aliyah or immigration, to Palestine from 1918 to 1924. They undertook the most difficult tasks, building roads, draining swamps, and establishing colonies.

The first World Conference of the Hechalutz movement took place in Carlsbad, Czechoslovakia, in 1921. The movement established **hakhsharot,** or training farms, in many countries, particularly in Poland and other East-European nations. The farms prepared the young **Halutzim** for agricultural life in Palestine. There they were taught Hebrew and given deeper knowledge of their people's history. Before the Second World War, Hechalutz members numbered in the tens of thousands. At the present time, Hechalutz organizations exist in North and Latin America, North and South Africa, and several European countries.

HAM (Hebrew, meaning "warm or hot"). Second

son of Noah, whose descendants are described in Gen. 10:6-20 as inhabiting the southernmost regions of the earth.

HAMAN. See PURIM.

HANUKKAH. The Feast of Dedication and the Feast of Lights, which falls on the twenty-fifth of Kislev* and lasts for eight days. It marks the rededication of the Temple* by Judah Maccabee in 165 B.C.E. after his victory over the Syrians who had defiled its sanctuary. Tradition relates that Judah could find only a single cruse of oil which had not been contaminated by the enemy. Although it contained only enough oil to light the menorah* for one day, a miracle took place, and it burned for eight. Therefore, candles are lit throughout the holiday—one on the eve of the first day, two on the eve of the second and so forth, until eight are kindled on the last evening.

A feast of liberation symbolizing the victory of the few over the many and of the weak over the strong, Hanukkah is one of the gayest Jewish holidays. Gifts are given to children at candle-lighting time, and it is customary to play with a small top—the dreidl—inscribed with the Hebrew letters N, G, H, and S. These stand for the words **Nes Gadol Hayah Sham,** which means "A great miracle happened there."

In the synagogue, the Torah* is read every day of Hanukkah, and Hallel* ("Hymns of Praise"), consisting of Psalms 113-118, is chanted. One of the hymns sung after the candles are lit is **Maoz Zur,** known in English as "Rock of Ages." The prayer of **Al Ha-Nissim** ("For the Miracles..."), which recounts the story of Hanukkah, is added to the Eighteen Benedictions and to the usual order of Grace after meals.

The story of Hanukkah, which tells of the evil decrees of Antiochus Epiphanes against the Jews and the triumph of the Maccabees* over their enemies is related in the Book of the Maccabees of the Apocrypha.* The second book contains the

A guard of honor of Israeli scouts carrying the Hanukkah Torch of Freedom ascends steps to Mt. Zion in Jerusalem, on the last leg of the traditional run from Modin.

120

story of Hannah and her seven children who refused to bow before an idol and suffered a martyr's death at the hands of Antiochus' henchmen.

HARBY, ISAAC (1788-1828). Critic, playwright, precursor of Reform Judaism. Born in Charleston, S.C., Harby received a thorough classical education, studied law, and became a journalist. His critical essays and dramatic plays brought him considerable reputation. In 1824 he organized the Reform Society of Israelites, which sought to make changes in the traditional synagogue service. This organization lasted less than a decade; but it pointed the way to the later Reform movement in American Judaism.

HASDAI IBN SHAPRUT. See SPAIN.

HASHOMER (Hebrew, meaning "the watchman"). From the very beginning of modern Jewish settlement in Palestine (1882), the settlers were exposed to attacks by their Arab neighbors. They resisted vigorously, and the Arabs soon realized that they faced a new type of Jew. Unlike their predecessors who had come to Palestine only to pray and die, the new settlers refused to be intimidated by physical threats. The very names of some of these early heroic defenders of the Jewish settlements became legends: Abraham Shapiro, Judah Raab, Abu Yusuf, Mendel Kopelman, Sender Hadad. They and others like them often fought the Arab marauders single-handed. At the same time they learned Arabic, studied Arab ways of thinking and living, and succeeded in establishing friendly relations with their Arab neighbors.

The first organized self-defense group was established in Palestine in 1907. The initial meeting was held in the one-room apartment of Yitzhak Ben-Zvi,* President of Israel from 1953-63. The few young men assembled decided that the protection of the settlements should be in the hands of the Jews themselves, instead of hired Arabs, who often plotted with the attackers. The valor of this group of watchmen, which called itself Hashomer, soon became famous throughout Palestine. Each member dedicated himself to the protection of life and property, as well as of the honor of the Yishuv, or Jewish settlement.

Galloping on their thoroughbred horses along the narrow paths of the Galilee mountains and valleys, the Shomrim were romantic figures. They paid a heavy price for their daring. Many of them fell fighting off armed marauders. They were also among the first to establish frontier settlements in Palestine—K'far-Giladi in the north was an outstanding example.   H.L.

HASIDISM. Religious movement which began in the 18th century. At that time, life for the masses of Jews in the Ukraine and southern Europe was bitter and difficult. Jewish communities were destroyed or annihilated by the Cossack and peasant uprisings. Stark poverty prevailed among Jews. Economically helpless, they were unable to acquire much learning. The scholarly rabbis and community leaders looked down upon the illiterate and semi-literate masses who spent their lives in poverty and ignorance.

To the common people who craved spiritual uplift, the personality and teachings of Israel Baal Shem Tov* offered new hope and dignity. The "Baal Shem," (ca. 1700-1760) founder of the Hasidic movement, placed prayer and faith on an equal level with scholarship and knowledge of the Law. Hasidism, therefore, appealed greatly to these "forgotten" Jews, for no longer did they have to feel inferior to the scholar. Even the ignorant person, the Baal Shem taught, could find grace in the eyes of God if he prayed in purity of heart, with devotion and enthusiasm. Hasidism also introduced the idea of serving God with joy and happiness. It was opposed to excessive mourning and fasting as weakening to both the body and the soul.

The Hasidic movement encouraged a close bond among its followers. Mutual trust and companionship fostered a spirit of brotherhood. In the center of the closely knit group stood the Zaddik, or righteous man, the spiritual leader of the community who had reached a close union with God. He served as an intermediary between the Heavenly Power and man. His disciples' admiration for the Zaddik and the faith in his powers were boundless. The Hasidim believed that through his prayers the Zaddik could alter the decrees of God and even perform miracles. The position and ability of the Zaddik were believed to be hereditary. This trust and loyalty in the leader was at times carried to excess, and obscured the true meaning of Hasidism.

The Hasidic movement spread rapidly through the Ukraine, Poland,* Galicia, and penetrated even the fortress of Jewish scholarship, Lithuania.* The stress on prayer by the new popular movement; its lesser emphasis on Talmudic study; the creation of separate houses of prayer, with some changes in liturgy; the extreme reliance on the Zaddik, and the inspired singing and dancing which was new to traditional services of the time—all of these deviations aroused bitter opposition from the **Mitnagdim,** as the opponents of Hasidism were called. The opposition to the movement spread to many communities. Rabbis and leaders were alarmed at the rapid growth of Hasidism. The memory of the tragic Sabbatai Zevi* affair contributed to the rabbis' fear that Hasidism might cause a rift in Judaism. The greatest rabbinical authority of the eighteenth century, the Gaon Elijah of Vilna,* shared this distrust of Hasidism. In a letter to all Jewish communities in Lithuania, he urged an all-out campaign against the Hasidic movement. This internal conflict at times took on very ugly forms; false accusations were made to the governmental authorities, opponents were excommunicated, and even physical violence was not uncommon.

Numerous disciples of Ber of Mezhirich established themselves as Zaddikim in their own right. They settled in various towns where they gained followers and influenced large numbers. Each one of them left his individual mark on Hasidism. Prominent among the famous Hasidic rabbis was Levi Yitzhak of Berditchev (1740-1809). His love for the individual was the predominant facet in his personality. In many moving prayers, he appealed to God to put an end to the suffering of the Jewish people. His devotion

The Hasidic Rabbi of Ger accompanied by his son and followers.

Member of the Habad (Lubavitch) Hasidic Movement helping visitors to Western Wall in Jerusalem put on phylacteries.

Yet, all these persecutions did not stop the advance of Hasidism. The more conservative rabbis and leaders finally realized that the new movement did not represent a real threat to Jewish unity. Hasidism, on the other hand, recognized the value of the study of the law, while yet retaining its own character and appeal to the Jewish masses. In fact, Hasidism today is associated with extreme Orthodoxy. Hasidim often wear distinct garb and many are opposed to secular studies.

After the death of the Baal Shem Tov, the movement was led by his disciple, Rabbi Dov Ber of Mezhirich (1710-1772), also known as the great Maggid* ("preacher"). His "court" at the small town of Mezhirich became the center for the movement. Thousands of Jews flocked there to benefit from his wisdom and learning. His position as a scholar, preacher, and mystic contributed greatly toward the popular spread of Hasidism: eventually, it all came to influence scholars as well.

to the simple people, and his kindness and understanding for the weaknesses of human nature became the subjects of numerous legends.

Another great disciple of Dov Ber of Mezhirich was Shneour Zalman (1748-1812), known as the Rabbi of Ladi. He introduced to Hasidism a more rational concept of Judaism, based on a profound knowledge of the Talmud* and the Kabbalah,* the teachings of Jewish mysticism. In the **Tanya** Shneour Zalman formulated the three bases of his form of Hasidism: Wisdom, Understanding, and Knowledge (**habad**). Shneour Zalman emphasized scholarship as one of the pillars of Hasidism. He was among those falsely denounced for plotting against the Russian government. He was imprisoned, and was not released until his innocence had been clearly established. The branch of Hasidism begun by Shneour Zalman eventually became known as the **Habad** or **Lubavitch** movement. **(See also SHNEERSON.)**

One of the most original and creative Hasidic teachers was Nahman of Bratzlav,* the grandson of the Baal Shem. Close to nature and poetic, he preached the doctrine of simple and direct faith. For a short time he lived in Palestine, and for the remainder of his life, cherished a burning love for Zion. Nahman was a master of parable and fairytale. In these he displayed a rich imagination and a deeply moral personality.

Hasidism branched out in different directions and assumed various forms. The movement produced great teachers who enriched Jewish values and exerted great influence on the spiritual life of the Jews for two hundred years. Pinkhas of Koretz, Elimelekh of Lizhensk, Jacob Yitzhak of Lublin ("The Seer"), Mendel of Kotzk, and many others were leaders who extended the influence and scope of Hasidism. To this day, Hasidism remains a vital force among Jews the world over. Many Hasidic rebbes who survived the Nazi Holocaust have resettled in the United States and Israel* and have established new communities there. In modern times, Hasidism has served as a source of inspiration for such non-Hasidic literary masters as J. L. Peretz,* M. Y. Berditchevsky,* Sholom Asch,* and S. J. Agnon.* Jewish culture as a whole owes a great debt to the movement. Almost every form of artistic expression—the stage, music, dance—have used Hasidic themes and motifs.   H.L.

HASKALAH (Hebrew, meaning "enlightenment"). Great social and cultural changes began to take place in Western Europe in the eighteenth century. Men like Montesquieu, Voltaire, and Locke in France and England began to question the existing authority of Church and state and the prevailing social order. They introduced new concepts of freedom, religious tolerance, equality and reliance on reason rather than on tradition. These ideas ushered in a new era of rationalism or enlightenment.

During the early Enlightenment period, Jewish life in most European countries was still enclosed in the ghetto.* As a result of generations of persecution and isolation, Jews differed from their neighbors not only in religion and education but also in language, dress and habits. The hostile attitude of the gentile world forced the Jew to seek security and peace within his own group. As the Enlightenment movement began to strike root, the educated Jews in Prussia, and those who held high economic and financial positions, clamored for equal rights. They sought to abolish the degrading and discriminating laws directed against them.

Believing that emancipation was at hand, they sought to break down the ghetto walls; many broke with Jewish religious traditions as well.

More and more Jews began to participate in the cultural and literary life of Germany.* Berlin became the center of the Jewish Enlightenment movement. The leading spirit of this group was Moses Mendelssohn,* who began as a poor rabbinical student and gained fame as a German author and philosopher. Mendelssohn sought to bring the Jews closer to European culture and the European mode of living, without giving up their own cultural and religious values. Under his guidance and inspiration there was a short-lived revival of Hebrew language and literature.

But by the beginning of the nineteenth century, a large part of German Jewry was well on the road to assimilation.* From Germany, the Enlightenment moved first to Galicia and later to Russia.* In both countries, the Jewish masses followed their traditional way of life, and outside influences had little effect. Hence, they turned inward to the development of Jewish literature, enriching it with new forms and ideas. Rabbi Nachman Krochmal* in Galicia, Yitzhak Ber Levinson, Abraham Mapu,* Judah L. Gordon and Peretz Smolenskin* in Russia, were the outstanding leaders of the Haskalah movement.

In Eastern Europe, the Haskalah movement developed a national purpose and a practical approach to the Jewish problem. It proposed that the Jews improve their economic condition by engaging in agriculture and other useful trades. It also called for the inclusion of secular subjects in Jewish schooling and the loosening of rabbinical restrictions. On the whole, the movement aimed at striking a happy medium between faith and enlightenment. The Orthodox Jews, however, were frightened by the assimilation and even conversion that had resulted from the Haskalah movement in Germany. They opposed very effort to institute innovations and bring about changes in traditional Jewish life.

With a few exceptions, the writers of the Haskalah were the forerunners of the Jewish national revival which took place after the Russian pogroms in 1881. This revival later gave rise to the Zionist movement, which finally culminated in the establishment of the State of Israel.*   H.L.

HASMONEANS. See MACCABEES.

HA-TIKVAH (Hebrew, meaning "The Hope"). The national anthem of Israel.* Written in 1878 by the poet Naphtali Herz Imber,* and set to

הַתִּקְוָה

Kol - od be - le - vav p'ni __ ma

ne-fesh ye-hu - di ho - mi - ya u-le-fa - te miz - rach

ka - di - ma a - yin le-tzi - yon tzo - fi — ya

od lo av - da tik-va - te - nu ha____ tik - va

h'not al - pa — yim li - h'yot am chof - shi

be - ar - tze-nu be e - retz tzi yon vi - ru sha la - yim

music by Samuel Cohen, it was adopted as the Zionist national anthem early in the 20th century. Since then, it has been accepted by Jews throughout the world. **Ha-Tikvah** expresses the eternal hope of Israel to live as a free nation in the land of Zion. When the State of Israel was established in 1948, **Ha-Tikvah,** with a slight change of the wording in its last two lines, became the national anthem.

HAWAII. Admitted as the fiftieth state of the United States, August 21, 1959. There are over 5,500 Jews in Hawaii, most of them in Honolulu. The majority came to the Islands during the past twenty years. Community life centers around Temple Emanu-El. The Temple conducts a religious school and adult education courses.

HAZAN. Originally,* at the time of the Talmud,* the **hazan** was a caretaker of the synagogue and a functionary at the religious ceremonials. Today the term **hazan,** or cantor, is applied to one who chants the religious services at temple and synagogue.

Modern cantorial music had its origin in the work of the Jewish Italian rabbi and composer, Salomone Rossi. Salomon Sulzer, Louis Lewandowsky, and many other hazanim in the nineteenth century helped develop the cantorial music used extensively in the synagogue to this day.

HAZAZ, CHAIM (1898-1973). Born in the Ukraine, Chaim Hazaz settled in Palestine in 1931. He won early recognition as a major novelist with his portrayal of life in the Jewish small town during the Russian revolution and civil war of 1917. One of the great masters of Hebrew prose, his range of writing embraces Jewish life in many countries and generations. One of his penetrating satirical novels on the life of Yemenite Jewry has been translated into English and published as **Mori Said.**

HE. Fifth letter of the Hebrew alphabet; numerically, five.

HEBREW ARTS SCHOOL FOR MUSIC AND DANCE. School of Hebrew music and dance in New York City. Established in 1952, it offers to students of all ages courses in the music of the Jewish people, the songs of modern Israel, instrumental music by Jewish composers, prayer modes, Biblical chants, as well as the dances of the various Jewish communities. The program of the school also includes publication of the Hebrew Arts Music series, public concerts, concerts at schools and a Music Teachers' Institute. The director, who also helped found the school, is Dr. Tzipora H. Jochsberger.

HEBREW COLLEGE, BOSTON, MASS. Founded in 1921 to expand the scope of a teachers' training school set up in Boston in 1918. Currently located in Brookline, Mass., the college, in addition to the teachers' seminary, maintains a Hebrew high school, a training program for Sunday school teachers, extension courses for adults (The Hebrew Forum), a graduate faculty, a summer camp, a library, and a publishing house. Its faculties offer programs of study leading to degrees of Bachelor, Master, and Doctor of Hebrew Literature.

HEBREW LANGUAGE. Hebrew belongs to the northern group of Semitic languages, which also includes Aramaic,* Assyrian, Arabic, and Syriac. Most of the ancient peoples in the lands adjoining Palestine—the Moabites, Amorites, and Edomites —seem to have spoken a common language.

The ancient Ugaritic tablets (14th century B.C.E.) found in the city of Ugarit, in Northern Syria, and the Moabite Stone of King Mesha (9th century B.C.E.) are both written in Hebrew or in a closely related dialect. Although Hebrew underwent many modifications in the course of generations, it has retained its ancient structure and character. It is basically the same language today as it was over 3,500 years ago, in the days of the

Patriarchs.* The rich literature of the Bible* has preserved for us some of the ancient forms of the language as well as its basic characteristics.

The Hebrew alphabet* consists of twenty-two letters, all consonants. Vowel signs were invented much later for easier reading; they are placed underneath and above the consonants. However, even in ancient times, some of the letters, such as Aleph, He, Vav and Yod, served the purpose of vowels. All the Hebrew parts of speech and word forms are based on a root, which generally consists of three letters. This root is expanded by means of prefixes and suffixes, as well as by changes in sound or vocalization. A verb may be used in several and sometimes even in all of the seven conjugations which give the language its flexibility.

Biblical Hebrew is distinguished by its simplicity and directness. It is vivid and expressive, lending itself beautifully to the poetic form. At the same time, it has few abstract forms, adjectives, and adverbs.

During the Babylonian Exile (586 B.C.E.) the development of Hebrew was marked by the ever-increasing influence of the Aramaic language on Hebrew grammar and vocabulary. During the period of the Second Temple,* Mishnaic Hebrew came into being. The language of the Mishnah* essentially follows the rules of the Biblical Hebrew, but it is enriched with new words and grammatical forms. Greek and Latin terms were assimilated and given Hebraic form. The language became more descriptive and was now better equipped to express ideas, both practical and abstract.

Although Hebrew was not used again as an everyday language until the growth of modern Zionism in the 19th century, it continued as the language of prayer and literature. The Jews at all times displayed love and affection for Hebrew as their holy tongue, in which the Bible was written and the Law proclaimed. It was a reminder of the days of their independence and glory. Throughout the ages, poets, scholars, philosophers, grammarians, and translators all contributed to the development of Hebrew. In the Middle Ages, Hebrew was influenced by Arabic. The scientific works translated into Hebrew from the Arabic enriched the Hebrew vocabulary and increased its power to express new ideas.

The revival of the Hebrew literature and language took place in the nineteenth century. This revival was marked in the beginning by a return to Biblical Hebrew. But in the course of time, it was recognized that classical Hebrew required expansion and modification, if it was to be used as a modern tongue. It became necessary to

The Holy Scriptures, including the Book of Exodus and the Book of Isaiah, published in Paris, 1544.

coin new words and expressions, and to adapt old ones for modern needs.

In the 1880's, Eliezer Ben Yehudah* pioneered in the revival of Hebrew as a spoken language. His example was taken up enthusiastically by many followers. Hebrew-speaking groups were formed throughout the world. A mass of technical and scientific terms in all fields of human endeavor were created. The ancient tongue has displayed remarkable adaptability to modern needs. Today, Hebrew keeps pace with the steady progress of science and technology. It is the living language of the State of Israel.*   H.L.

HEBREW LITERATURE Hebrew literature from the Biblical days to the present embraces a period of approximately 3,500 years. The Bible,* the cornerstone of the Jewish religion, its laws and ethics, has been the source of inspiration for Hebrew literary activity throughout Jewish history. The monumental works of the Talmud* and Midrashic* literature are interpretations of the Bible, or works stimulated by it.

The books of the Bible were not the only spiritual and literary treasures of this early period in Jewish history. The Bible itself mentions the Book of Wars of the Lord, The Book of the Righteous, and the Chronicles of the Kings of Judah and Israel, all of which have been lost in antiquity. It is likely that many more such epic works have similarly disappeared.

The period following the return of the Jews from Babylonia* and the re-establishment of the Jewish Commonwealth witnessed the revival of Hebrew literary activity. Many works followed the pattern and character of the Bible. Because they were of a later period, these works were not deemed worthy to be included among the sacred books of the Bible. Most of the Apocrypha,* as these books are called, were written in Hebrew and represent a link between the Bible and the subsequent Midrashic literature. Parts of the original Hebrew text of one of the Apocryphal Wisdom books, Ben Sira,* have recently been recovered. All the other Apocrypha have come down to us in their Greek,

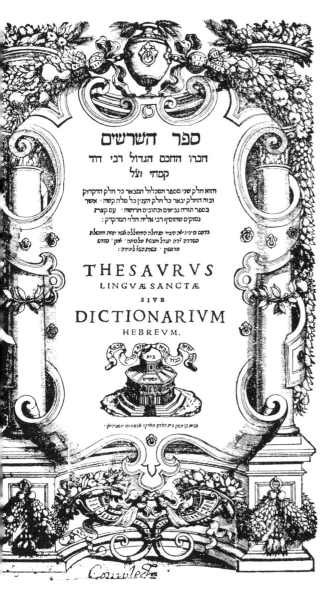

Latin and Syriac translations. Of great historical and literary value are the recently found Dead Sea Scrolls*—the oldest Hebrew manuscripts in existence.

The Talmud is mainly a compilation of Jewish law, remarkable in its encyclopedic scope and character. It reflects Jewish creativity for nearly a thousand years. The Aggadic* parts of the Talmud are rich in stories, legends, moral and ethical instruction, parables, songs, prayers, dramatic dialogues, and fanciful, symbolic visions of the world-to-come, or of the Messianic times.

Geonic Period.

After the close of the Talmud (about 500 C.E.), its laws, enactments, and discussions were further interpreted and extended during the Geonic period in Babylonia (from the seventh to the end of the eleventh century C.E.). One of the outstanding works of the period is **Halakhot Gedolot,** a compilation of laws attributed to Judah Gaon in the eighth century. Some of the Geonim produced historical accounts (such as the Letter of Sherira Gaon*) as well as works on grammar, and liturgical poetry. Hai Gaon* and Saadiah Gaon* employed the poetical form even in explaining the Law. They also composed meditations or prayers in which lofty thoughts and delicate emotions mingled with deep religious fervor. The Masorites, who arranged (the "Masoretic") the Bible text (**see** MASORAH), were active primarily during the Geonic period in Palestine. The punctuation and vocalization of the Biblical text took place around the eighth century. The chief authority in this field was Aaron Ben Asher.

Liturgical poetry flourished in Palestine from the sixth to the eighth century. However, a number of moving prayers and poetical passages have come down to us from earlier times. An example of these is the Sabbath* prayer, **El Adon** ("God the Master"). The early liturgy was still under the influence of the poetic majesty and simplicity of the Bible. Representative religious poets of that period were Jose ben Jose, Yannai, and Eliezer Kalir. The latter was particularly prolific. His style is most flowery, introducing new forms and coining new Hebrew words. The liturgical poets drew on the legends and teachings of the Talmud and Midrashim, as well as the Bible, for themes. Jose ben Jose is remembered for his imposing portrayal of the Yom Kippur* service in the Temple* before its destruction. A further development of liturgical poetry took place in Italy during the tenth and eleventh centuries. This poetry, generally striking a plaintive note, bewailed the bitter lot of the persecuted Jew and pleaded with God to save his people. A number of these poems, hymns and lamentations are recited on fast days* and days of mourning.

The Hebrew scholars in Italy also produced historical works. One of these, called **Yosippon,** was based on the historical masterpieces of Josephus Flavius.* The **Sefer Ha-Kabbalah,** by Abraham Ibn Daud (1110-1180) was another important historical source which traced the development of rabbinic tradition and scholarship. In the eleventh century Nathan ben Yehiel Ha-Romi completed a comprehensive dictionary of the Talmud and Midrashim. In the tenth century, works on medicine were contributed by Sabbatai Donnola, who drew extensively on the knowledge of the Greeks.

Golden Age in Spain.

In the beginning of the tenth century a great revival of Hebrew literature took place in Spain.* The patronage of Hasdai Ibn Shaprut, a physician and chief counsellor to the Caliph, stimulated the

"Book of Principles," by Joseph Albo, published in Rimini, Italy, in 1522.

spread of Jewish learning and creativity. This was the opening of a new era, called the "Golden Age of Spain." Stimulated by Arab scholarship, Jewish scholars contributed to all fields of Jewish literature and the sciences, including poetry, grammar, philosophy, astronomy, mysticism, medicine, and Biblical and Talmudic commentary.

The foremost grammarians — among them Menahem, Jonah Ibn Jannah, and Judah Hayyuj —formulated the rules of the Hebrew language, its structure and character. Outstanding poets, such as Samuel Ha-Nagid,* Solomon Ibn Gabirol,* Judah Ha-Levi,* and Abraham and Moses Ibn Ezra,* introduced new and secular themes to Hebrew poetry. They sang of battles, love, wine, friendship, and travels—often with satirical and humorous overtones. In the Dark Ages, when Jews were subjected to constant persecution and suffering, the Hebrew poets of Spain opened new horizons of beauty and thought. However, the greater part of their poetry was dedicated to religious themes and to the passionate plea for the restoration of the Jewish people to Zion. Judah Alharizi, thirteenth-century author of **Tahkemoni** ("Academy"), a collection of stories in rhyming prose, was one of the last representatives of the Golden Age in Spain.

While Jewish philosophic works were as a rule written in Arabic, many were translated into Hebrew by members of the Ibn Tibbon* family. The most influential of the philosophic works include **Emunot Ve-Deot** ("Beliefs and Opinions") by Saadiah Gaon; **Moreh Nebukhim** ("Guide for the Perplexed") by Maimonides;* and the **Kuzari** by Judah Ha-Levi. Each one of these books had overwhelming influence on Jewish religious thought. Other works of note in philosophy and ethics are **Mekor Hayyim** ("Fountain of Life") by Solomon Ibn Gabirol, and **Hovot Ha-Levavot** ("The Duties of the Heart") by Bahya Ibn Pakuda.* Levi ben Gerson, also known as Gersonides (1288-1344), an adherent of Aristotelian thought, defended the philosophic principles of Maimonides in his **Milhamot Adonai** ("Battles of the Lord"). **Or Adonai** ("Light of the Lord") by Hasdai Crescas* (c. 1340-1412) and Sefer **Ha-Ikkarim** ("Book of Principles") by Joseph Albo (1380-1440) explained the fundamental principles of the Jewish faith, defending it against Christian and rationalistic criticism. The latter three philosophic works were written in Hebrew.

Studies in Bible, Talmud, Mysticism and Ethics.

Throughout the ages, commentaries on the Bible and the Talmud were rich and fruitful fields of Hebrew literature. Some commentaries of the Bible stem from the days of the Tannaim.* The greatest contribution toward the understanding of the Bible

and Talmud, especially the latter, was made by Shelomo Yitzhaki (Rashi*). The literal, or factual interpretation of the Biblical text preoccupied many of the commentators. The most distinguished of these were Samuel ben Meir, Rashi's grandson, Abraham Ibn Ezra*, and David Kimhi*. Other scholars wrote ethical, philosophical and even mystic interpretations of the Scriptures—e.g., Nahmanides,* Gersonides, and Don Isaac Abravanel.*

"Great Laws," the first code to give a detailed list of the 613 precepts which are included in the Torah.

The Zohar, Mantua, Italy, 1560.

Numerous works dealing with all phases of Talmudic study have been produced since the final editing of the Talmud. These include codes of Jewish law and responsa, or rabbinical discussion of particular religious and legal problems. The Tosafists, who came after Rashi and were active in the twelfth and thirteenth centuries, continued the process of expanding and advancing the knowledge of Talmudic law. Keen reasoning power, thorough knowledge of the vast Talmudic literature, and exhaustive discussion of the principles of Jewish law, characterize the commentaries of the great Polish scholars in the sixteenth century. Outstanding were Solomon Luria (Maharshal), Rabbi Meir of Lublin (Maharam), and Samuel Edels (Maharsha). Their works together with those of their predecessors (Alfasi,* Rabbi Hananel of Kairwan, Rashi, Nissim ben Reuben of Gerona, known as Ran, and the Tosafists) are published with every edition of the Talmud.

Since the thirteenth century, study of Kabbalah,* the mystic trend in Judaism, has produced a variety of literary works. The Zohar,* the principal book of Kabbalah, stimulated the creation of a rich literature of mysticism in the sixteenth century. Even so literal an interpreter of Jewish law as the great codifier, Rabbi Joseph Karo, came under the spell of the Kabbalah; together with other mystics, he sought to hasten the coming of the Messiah.

With the expulsion of the Jews from Spain in 1492 and the formation of new centers of learning in Poland,* Jewish creativity became limited to Talmudic studies. In the **yeshivot** of Poland a system of study known as **pilpul*** evolved. A rich rabbinic literature of responsa accumulated. Ethical works, expressing the pietistic spirit of the times, became extremely popular. The new books of morality included **Menorat Ha-Maor** ("Candelabrum of Light") by Isaac Aboab, **Reshit Hokhma** ("The Beginning of Wisdom") by Elijah de Vidos, and **Shevet Musar** ("The Rod of Instruction") by Elijah Ha-Kohen.

Italy,* however, saw the development of a more secular literary tradition. Dante's **Divine Comedy** was the model for such Hebrew works as the sonnets and **Ha-Tofet Ve-Ha-Eden** ("Hell and Eden") by Immanuel of Rome, which found many imitators. Immanuel's influence extended well into the seventeenth century, when Moses Zacuto (1625-1697) composed the first Hebrew drama.

Enlightenment Period (see HASKALAH).

New "enlightened" social and political ideas emerged in the eighteenth century. Under the influence of the Enlightenment movement, Jews began to call for a reappraisal of traditional Jewish values. There was the feeling that the strictness of Jewish religious organization isolated the Jew from his environment. In Germany,* a group of **Maskilim,** or "enlightened" Jews, undertook to revive the Hebrew language and literature, under the leadership of Moses Mendelssohn.* In 1784 they began to publish a Hebrew monthly called **Ha-Meassef** ("The Gatherer"). In the course of time **Ha-Meassef** became a quarterly and then an annual journal. Finally, as the German Jews forsook Hebrew for the language and culture of their native land, it ceased publication altogether.

Earlier, the Italian Moses Hayim Luzzato* (1707-1747) had ushered in a new phase of Hebrew literature. Though he was deeply religious, his plays were worldly in their approach to man and nature. He was followed by the poets David Franco-Mendes; Naphtali Herz Wessely (or Weisl), author of **Shire Tiferet** ("Poems of Glory"); Shalom Hacohen and Shlomo Levinson (or Lewisohn), a poet and scholar of note who set forth his appreciation of beauty in a masterful poem, **Ha-Melizah Medaberet** ("Poetry Speaks"). Perhaps the most noteworthy contribution of the early **Maskilim** to Hebrew scholarship was Mendelssohn's **biur,** ("translation")—a new, more scientific and rational interpretation of the Bible.

During the second period the Enlightenment centered in Galicia, a province of Austro-

Hungary, where the Jews clung to their traditional way of life. Here the new ideas of the **maskilim** were bitterly opposed by the pious, especially the Hasidim. Outstanding among the Hebrew authors, some of whom developed the satiric novel to combat their opponents, were Joseph Perl and Yitzhak Erter.

This period was also noteworthy for its important scholarly contributions. Solomon Judah Rapoport produced some important scholarly works based on historical research. **Moreh Nebukhe Ha-Zman** ("Guide for the Perplexed of Our Time"), by Nachman Krochmal* represented an historical approach to the development of the Jewish spirit and religion that greatly influenced subsequent Jewish philosophy and scholarship. At about the same time, Samuel David Luzzato* produced scholarly essays on the Bible, the Hebrew language, and philosophy. In contrast to most of the other Enlighteners, Luzzato advocated strict adherence to Jewish traditions and considered the ethical teachings of Judaism superior to any philosophical system of thought. Jewish scholarship was greatly enhanced by the five-volume work by Isaac Hirsch Weiss on the history of Talmudic literature—the most comprehensive work of its kind, tracing the origin of Jewish law from the Bible to the end of the fifteenth century.

Russia.

By the middle of the nineteenth century, modern Hebrew literature had begun to develop in Russia.* One of the first of the modern Hebrew authors, Isaac Baer Levinsohn, advocated the introduction of secular studies and the teaching of trades in the Jewish school system. Brief texts on general and Jewish history, geography, and biography, in a modernized Biblical Hebrew, were written by Mordecai Aaron Ginzburg (1796-1846) and Kalman Shulman (1819-1899). The first significant Hebrew poet in Russia, Abraham Dov Levinsohn (Adam Ha-Kohen, 1794-1878) composed reflective poetry. The lyric genius of his son, Micah Joseph Levinsohn (1828-1852), was expressed in tender, lyrical poems bearing the tragic foreboding of his early death. His greatest contribution to Hebrew verse consists of six Biblical narrative poems expressing the conflicts of universal human emotions. His poems on Biblical themes were matched only by Abraham Mapu's* popular novels describing the glories of Israel in Biblical times.

The leading spirit of the Enlightenment in Russia was J. L. Gordon.* Toward the end of his life Gordon, who had been in the forefront of the battle against the old stultifying ghetto traditions, admitted his disappointment with the results of the Enlightenment. The greatest poet of his day, Gordon enriched all forms of Hebrew verse: historical, narrative, and satirical. During the same period, Hebrew novelists often subjected the contemporary Jewish scene to scathing criticism. The greatest of these novelists, Peretz Smolenskin* and Reuben Asher Brodes (1851-1902), ridiculed the ignorance, narrow-mindedness, and backwardness of Jewish life. The Hebrew press which emerged at the end of the 1850's joined in the struggle for the spiritual and social emancipation of the Jewish people. The Hebrew periodicals, **Ha-Melitz** ("The Advocate"), **Ha-Carmel** and **Ha-Tzefirah** ("Daybreak"), spread the ideas of the Enlightenment throughout Eastern Europe.

The pogroms of 1881 in Russia hastened the disillusionment of the "Enlighteners." M. L. Lilienblum,* formerly a leader in the fight for change in Jewish religious life, the novelist R. A. Brodes, and some of the Hebrew writers who had been attracted to Socialism now turned to Jewish nationalism.

The 1880's were a transitional period in Hebrew literature. The theme in the Hebrew poetry of the period was the yearning for Zion. N. H. Imber,* K. A. Shapiro, a true and pure lyricist, M. M. Dolitzky, and M. Z. Maneh, all sang romantically of Zion. But the period was also a turning point in the revival of the Hebrew language. Eliezer Ben Yehudah* became the advocate of spoken Hebrew. Very few believed that the language of the Bible could again come alive. Soon, however, Hebrew-speaking groups sprang up all over the Diaspora. The Hebrew press grew. The first Hebrew daily, **Ha-Yom** ("The Day"), made its appearance in 1886. Writers and literary critics of note, such as Nahum Sokolow,* David Frischmann,* and Reuben Brainin,* contributed greatly to the modernization of Hebrew literature.

Renaissance of Hebrew Literature.

Mendele Mocher Sefarim* (Shalom Jacob Abramowitz) opened new horizons for the realistic novel. Mendele, who had begun his literary career in the Enlightenment period, ushered in a new era in the Hebrew language and literature at the end of the 1880's. He realized that Biblical Hebrew was inadequate for portraying present-day life in its great variety. Mendele therefore drew upon the rich stores of the language in the Mishnah, Midrash, and the literary sources of the Middle Ages, to create a vigorous new Hebrew.

Mendele was followed by two important figures: Ahad Ha-Am,* the brilliant essayist and pleader for a spiritual center in Palestine, and Chaim Nachman Bialik, the poet who best ex-

pressed the essence of East European Judaism. Saul Tschernichowsky,* Jacob Cohen, and Zalman Shneur,* three of Bialik's contemporaries, each left an individual and distinctive mark on Hebrew poetry: Tschernichowsky through mastery of form, Cohen in lyrical verse, and Shneur in his striking nature poems.

The poetry of David Shimoni,* Jacob Fichman, Yehudah Karni (1884-1948), and Jacob Steinberg (1886-1948), was considerably influenced by Bialik. Yet each of these poets succeeded in striking an individual note and in making his own, unique contribution as a critic of great persuasion and charm. Shimoni sang of the **halutz** and portrayed the new life in pioneer Palestine in his romantic and appealing idylls, while Karni is one of the most colorful poets of Jerusalem.*

The 1890's and the beginning of the twentieth century saw the rise of the realistic modern Hebrew novel. Joseph Chaim Brenner,* S. Ben-Zion, Isaiah Bershadsky, described the bitter poverty and despair prevalent in the Jewish towns of Eastern Europe. The short novel achieved artistic perfection in the masterly works of Uri Zvi Gnessin, Gershon Schoffman, and Itzhak Dov Berkowitz. Berkowitz skillfully translated most of the works of Sholom Aleichem, * the great Yiddish humorist, into Hebrew. The Hasidic tale, as well as the life of the simple folk, were reproduced in classic style by J.L. Peretz,* Micah Joseph Berditchevsky,* and Judah Steinberg. Hasidic lore was also the subject of philosophic and historic essays and works by Hillel Zeitlin* and S.A. Horodetzky. The philosophic Hebrew essay reached its height in the writings of Jacob Klatzkin (1882-1948).

In the years immediately preceding the First World War, the Hebrew writers who emigrated to Palestine continued to write of the Old Country. These writers included Dvorah Baron, Samuel Joseph Agnon,* Asher Barash,* and Abraham Aaron Kabak. Kabak is the author of a number of historical novels, the most famous of which deal with the life of the mystic Solomon Molkho,* and with Jewish life in the nineteenth century.

Hebrew Literature in Israel.

After the Second World War, the new State of Israel* became the center of Hebrew literature. The new life in Palestine produced a number of romantic and realistic novels from the pens of Moshe Smilansky, A. Reubeni, Dov Kimhi, and Avigdor Hameiri. The latter, a poet and novelist, was born in Hungary and served as officer in the Austrian army during the First World War. His short stories and novels dealing with his war experiences are gripping accounts of human cruelty, degradation, and suffering. Later arrivals to the Holy Land were Chaim Hazaz,* a novelist of deep insight and brilliant style, Yehudi Yaari, Yitzhak Shenhar and Israel Zarhi. Yaari describes the new immigrant and his impressions of the new land. Shenhar combines sober realism with lyric undertones, and his stories have a clever satirical twist. Zarhi, who died young, reflected the life of the first settlers in his novels.

Born is Israel, Yehudah Burla describes in his novels the life of Oriental Jews, often with much warmth and local color. One of his best novels, **The Adventures of Akavyah,** is the life story of the son of a Turkish-Jewish family, who grows up in the mountains of Anatolia and meets with strange adventures before reaching Jerusalem. Fate, passion, and romance are the interesting ingredients which makes up most of Burla's fascinating stories. One of his historical novels centers around the life of Rabbi Yehuda ben Solomon Hai Alkalai.*

Hebrew poetry was enriched between the two World Wars by the works of Yitzhak Lamdan (1889-1954) and Abraham Shlonsky* (1900-1973). Lamdan is best known for his dramatic poem **Massadah.** This poem became a symbol for a generation of pioneers who sacrificed their lives for the upbuilding of the land. For the last twenty years of his life, Lamdan was also editor of the excellent monthly, **Gilyonot.** Shlonsky is a versatile modern poet and a masterful translator. Noteworthy also are Rachel Bluvstein's **(see RACHEL)** tender, lyrical songs; Sr. Shalom's mystical and nationalistic verses, the modern poetry of Nathan Alterman and Leah Goldberg, and the quaint Hasidic poems of Shimshon Meltzer. Other poets of note are Yokheved Bat-Miriam and Anda Amir-Pinkerfeld.

A number of Hebrew writers were active between the two World Wars outside Palestine. Mattathias Shoham, brilliant poet and dramatist, probed into the roots of Jewish faith and destiny. Hayim Lensky (1905-1935) struggled to break out of his isolation in Soviet Russia to sing of a new life in poetry which is a mixture of traditionalism and modernism.

New talents in the field of poetry and the novel have appeared in the last two decades. These are native Israelis who grew up during the turbulent years of building the land and developing a new culture, and who fought in the War of Independence. The varied experiences of the young generation of Israelis are reflected in the deeply lyrical novels of S. Yitzhar, in the works of Moshe Shamir, who has written a notable historical novel on King Alexander Jannaeus,* and in the writings of Igal Mossinsohn, Aaron Meged, and Natan and David Shaham.

Modern Hebrew literature in Israel numbers fine scholars, essayists, and critics. Prominent are Ezekiel Kaufman,* Eliezer Steinman, Gershon Shalom, and Joseph Klausner,* to name only a few.

In the 1960's and 1970's there emerged a new generation of poets and novelists of note. Some of them have already left their mark on Hebrew letters. Their works in translation have gained recognition for their craftsmanship and imagination in many lands.

Among these talented poets, Yehuda Amichai ranks as an innovator. His use of everyday language in his poetry, his ironic imagery, and existentialist intellectual and emotional posture have created a new trend in Hebrew poetry. Other poets, who are highly individualistic, and yet express national and social experiences are Amir Gilboa, Chaim Gury, Abba Kovner, Dan Pagis and the American-born T. Karmi.

Among the novelists Hanoch Bartov, Binyamin Tammuz, Yehudit Handel, Amelia Kahana-Carinon, Yitzhak Oren, David Shachar, M. Tabib and others are exponents of the generation that saw the establishment of the State of Israel and expressed the mood of the people ranging from tragedy to elation, from doubt to resolution.

More perplexed and complex are the characters and themes in the works of talented young writers such as Yoram Kaniuk, Yitzhak Orpaz, Amos Oz, Pinchas Sadeh, A.B. Yehoshua, and in the poetry of David Avidan, Dalia Ravikovitz, T. Ribner and N. Zach. Still active are the older experimental poets, such as Yonatan Ratosh and Avot Yeshurun.

Lyrical and introspective, Aharon Appelfeld is one of the foremost younger novelists, who is preoccupied with the Holocaust and its effect on the people who lived through it.

S. Yizhar

Modern Hebrew Literature in America.

Modern Hebrew literature assumed significance in America on the eve of World War I, with the arrival of a number of young poets. The best known of these were B.M. Silkiner, Ephraim A. Lisitzky, A.S. Schwartz; later came Hillel Barli, Israel Efros, and Simon Ginzburg. These poets were under the influence of their great contemporaries in Eastern Europe: Bialik, Tschernichowsky,

Uri Zvi Greenberg   *Nathan Alterman*

Shneur and others. This influence was especially pronounced in their earlier works, which, in theme as well as in form, were rooted in the classic Hebrew tradition.

Nevertheless, the influence of the New World was not absent from their work. B.N. Silkiner was inspired by American Indian lore, to write his poem **Mul Ohel Timura** ("Opposite the Tent of Timura"). This was a unique experiment in Hebrew poetry. Silkiner succeeded in capturing the mood and rhythm of Indian life and struggle during the period of Spanish rule. The tragic beauty of a declining people and its culture held particular appeal for the Hebrew poet, who himself derived his spiritual strength from an ancient and distant past. The lot of the Indians also found sympathetic expression in the poetic works **Medurot Doakhot** ("Dying Campfires") by E.A. Lisitsky and **Wigwamim Shotkim** ("Silent Wigwams") by Israel Efros. Lisitzky also drew from the rich primitive folklore of the Negro in America, in his **Be-ohole Kush.**

The influence of American motifs is evident in the poetry of Simon Halkin, Abraham Regelson, and Garbriel Preil. Reflecting both Hebrew and American culture, their poetry has had a refreshing and invigorating effect on Hebrew verse in America. Four other poets, the late A.Z. Freidland, Eisig Silberschlag, Moshe Feinstein, and Reuben Avinoam (Grossman, who was born in America but emigrated to Israel) wrote poems of classical structure. In these, they achieved mastery of narrative and lyrical forms.

The Warsaw poet and essayist Aaron Zeitlin (1898-1973) arrived in the United States on the eve of World War II. By that time, he had already gained fame as a Hebrew and Yiddish poet, publicist, and dramatist. Another American Hebrew poet, Barukh Katzenelson, now lives in Israel. The few poems he wrote on the American scene are in the same warm vein as is the rest of his delicate poetry. In contrast, bold and direct expression and stark realism characterize the poetry of Abraham Zvi Halevi.

The American Hebrew Novel.

The Hebrew novel did not make its appearance on American soil until the First World War. Abraham Soyer wrote novels on Jewish traditional and early immigrant life. S.L. Blank describes realistically his native Bessarabia and his adopted country, America. Harry Sackler and the prolific Johanan Twersky produced many historical novels. Much soul-searching and probing into the inner life of the younger generation of American Jews characterize the two novels by Simon Halkin: **Yehiel Hahagri** and **Ad Mashber** ("Until the Crisis"). L.A. Arieli left a series of absorbing and searching novels which were recently published. Jewish life in America has also served as the theme for Reuben Wallenrod's novels. Isaiah Rabinowitz has produced a book of subtle and interesting stories in his collection **Nerot Dolkim** ("Burning Candles").

Essays and Literary Criticism.

The literary essay has generally been a fruitful field in Hebrew literature. Menahem Ribalow* published five volumes of literary criticism. Some of the authors who made important contributions to the field of Hebrew literary criticism in America were S.B. Maximon, Dr. S. Melamed, Abraham Goldberg, and Abraham Epstein. An important place in Hebrew creativity in America was held by Nissan Touroff. He was one of the first to write on psychology in Hebrew.

A group of scholars ventured into the field of the essay, literary criticism and publicistic work. Among the best known was the late Rav Tsair (Hayim Tchernowitz), former editor of the monthly **Bitzaron.** M.R. Malachi, the writer-bibliographer, has also written informatively on a number of Hebrew authors. M. Ch. Amishai (pen name of

Hebrew Pen Club, New York, 1940. Front row, left to right: Menahem Ribalow, Moshe Feinstein, Zvi Scharfstein, Hillel Bavli, Nissan Tourov, Abraham Epstein, Isaac Rifkind, Abraham Goldberg. Center row, left to right: Yekutiel Ginsburg, A. Dominitz, A. S. Schwartz, Simon Bernstein, Shlomo Hillels, Menahem Glen, Gabriel Preil, A. R. Malachi. Third row, left to right: I. Berger, S. Z. Zetzer, Y. Ovsel, Y. Y. Wohl, A. S. Orleans, Daniel Persky, L. A. Arieli, M. Maisels.

Moshe Maisels) wrote an important philosophic work in two volumes, entitled **Mahshavah Veemet** ("Thought and Truth"). Daniel Persky was popular for his column in the **Hadoar,** Hebrew weekly published by the Histadruth Ivrith.*

H.L.

HEBREWS. From the Hebrew Eber, the descendant of Shem and the forefather of Abraham.* **Eber** also means "the region beyond" as in Joshua 24:2, **Ever ha-Nahar**—the country "on the other side" of the river (Euphrates, Abraham's birthplace). Hence, the Canaanites called the people who migrated from beyond the Euphrates— **Hebrews.** In the Bible, the people usually called themselves **Israelites.** They used the term "Hebrews" mainly when speaking to foreigners, or when opposing other nations. Early Greek and Roman writers used only the term "Hebrews"; later writers also used the expression "Jews."

HEBREW UNION COLLEGE-JEWISH INSTITUTE OF RELIGION. Reform rabbinical seminary founded in Cincinnati in 1875 by Isaac Mayer Wise. After two earlier failures, Rabbi Wise succeeded in starting the school under the auspices of the Union of American Hebrew Congregations, which he had helped establish in 1873. Meeting first in the basement of Rabbi Wise's

Isaac Mayer Wise
First President of the Hebrew Union College.

Hebrew Union College, Cincinnati, Ohio campus.

Alfred Gottschalk
President of the Hebrew Union College (1

Temple Bnei Jeshurun, the school graduated four rabbis in its first class (1883). Since its founding the school has ordained over 1879 Reform rabbis, of which 72 are women.

Merged in 1950 with the Jewish Institute of Religion in New York, the school, now known as HUC-JIR, has four campuses: (1) Cincinnati (which includes the American Jewish Archives); (2) New York (the Jewish Institute of Religion building); (3) Los Angeles and (4) Jerusalem.* The New York and Los Angeles campuses include schools for the training of cantors and religious teachers: in addition, the Los Angeles campus has a training school for those desiring to become professional workers in American Jewish community agencies. The president of HUC is (1979) Dr. Alfred Gottschalk.

HEBREW UNIVERSITY OF JERUSALEM. A teaching and research institute, its six Faculties—Humanities, Science, Social Science, Medicine, Law and Agriculture—and Schools of Education, Economics, Dentistry, Pharmacy, Social Service Work, Graduate Library School, Oriental Studies, Institute of Jewish Studies and School of Public Administration serve the practical needs of Israel and act as a cultural center for all Jewry. In time, the University will also serve the entire Middle East region.

The Hebrew University's total enrollment of graduate and undergraduate students for the current academic year is about 18,000. Its faculty of about 2,500 men and women is drawn, as is the student body, from almost every part of the world. The University's Magnes Press has issued many distinguished publications.

The idea for a Hebrew University was first proposed in 1897 by the mathematician, Professor Hermann Schapira* of Heidelberg. Thus, the University idea, born in the very infancy of Zionism, developed simultaneously with this movement. At the 1913 Zionist Congress in Vienna, it was decided to form the University of the Jewish People. Then and there, David Wolffsohn, former president of the World Zionist Organization,* contributed $25,000 toward its foundation. The first meeting of the University Committee (Professor Paul Ehrlich, Frankfurt; Otto Warburg, Berlin; Baron James de Rothschild, London; Martin Buber*; Ahad Ha-Am* and Chaim Weizmann*) was to be held in Paris and was called for August 4, 1914. This meeting never took place for on that day World War I broke out. In the midst of the war, while Palestine was still under Turkish control, a villa and a portion of the University site on Mount Scopus were purchased from its London owner, Lady Gray Hill. Four months before the end of the war, on July 24, 1918, the cornerstone of the University was laid on Mount Scopus by Chaim Weizmann in the presence of General Allenby,* commander of the British Forces in Palestine.

The Hebrew University was opened by Lord Balfour, on April 1, 1925 at a memorable ceremony in the natural amphitheatre of Mount Scopus. At this inauguration, the first Institutes of Biochemistry, Microbiology and Jewish Studies were already housed in the rebuilt Gray Hill villa. The Faculty of the Humanities followed in 1928; Biological Sciences in 1931 and Science in 1935.

The Wolffsohn Memorial of the Jewish National and University Library, and the Hadassah Hospital, erected in 1939, were among the key University buildings which crowned Mount Scopus until Israel's War of Liberation in 1948, in

A new building on the Hebrew University campus at Givat Ram.

Courtesy American Friends of the Hebrew University.

which many of its students gave their lives. Cut off from the New City of Jerusalem by the fighting, the area of Mount Scopus was demilitarized after the Armistice.

Until its reoccupation by Israeli forces in 1967, the Mount Scopus campus stood untenanted except for Israeli guards who were changed every two weeks. The road leading from Jerusalem to Mount Scopus was controlled by the Jordanians.

After a year of disruption, the University was reorganized in the New City, in Terra Sancta College, and in some 50 other scattered quarters. In 1949, the Hebrew University-Hadassah Medical School* was opened, and of necessity also scattered in several buildings. The considerable overcrowding and discomfort imposed severe hardships on instructors and students alike, and in 1954, construction was begun on a new University campus at Givat Ram, to the west of Jerusalem. The new campus was not intended to supersede, but rather to complement, that on Mount Scopus. In 1970 the University used both the campus at Givat Ram and that on Mount Scopus, which has been rebuilt and expanded. The Faculty of Agriculture is situated in Rehovot.

The first president of the Hebrew University was the late educator, Dr. Judah L. Magnes,* who headed the University for almost 25 years. A Board of Governors of distinguished scholars and laymen of Israel, the United States, and from a number of other countries in the world, give active service to the University, as do the American Friends of the Hebrew University who act as foster alumni, supporting it with funds and educational know-how.   N.B-A.

The Hebrew University, Jerusalem. Above, the Mount Scopus campus. Below, the new campus at Givat Ram.

Amphitheatre of the Hebrew University, Jerusalem—1970. Prime Minister Golda Meir (seated at dais) receiving an honorary degree. Seated at the table, left to right: Samuel Rothberg, chairman, the Board of Governors; President Zalman Shazar; Mrs. Meir; Avraham Harman, president of the University and Prof. Jacob Katz, Rector. The speaker is Prof. Arthur F. Burns, economic advisor to President Nixon, who also received an honorary degree on that occasion.

HEDER (Hebrew, meaning "room"). Since the sixteenth century, possibly even earlier, the term has been applied to one of the most important institutions in Jewish life—the traditional school.

The program of the **heder** included learning the Hebrew alphabet, reading, and the study of the Bible with Rashi's* commentary. The Talmud* was studied next. The fundamental aim of the **heder** was preparation for individual study of the Talmud and its commentaries. The **heder** was on the whole a private enterprise, usually comprising one room in the house where the rabbi lived. The school year was divided into winter and summer terms.

By the end of the nineteenth century, the **heder** had fallen into disrepute. More and more parents began to demand modern teaching methods and facilities, as well as the inclusion of secular subjects. The **heder metukan,** or modernized **heder,** which was established in Russia at the beginning of this century, aimed to correct some of these shortcomings.

HEIFETZ, JASCHA (1901-   ). Violin virtuoso. A child prodigy, Heifetz entered the Royal Society of Music in Vilna, Russia, before he was four. His first concert was held two years later; by the age of nine he was appearing with the great orchestras of Europe. Enthusiastic response to his New York debut in 1917 led him to settle in the United States. Although Heifetz's technique was perfected before he was eighteen, his career has shown continuous musical development. His own experiments in composition are believed to have contributed to this development. More than sixty years after his first public appearance, Heifetz is still considered one of the most brilliant violinists on the concert stage.

HEINE, HEINRICH (1797-1856). One of the greatest German poets. The French Revolution, which started eight years before Heine's birth, shook the ghettos* of Germany,* influenced Heine and made him a poet of liberty. Trained to be a banker, he failed dismally, preferred to write poetry. An unrequited love for a cousin affected him deeply and became a recurrent theme in his poetry. Sent to Goettingen to study law, he obtained his degree only after baptism, because the University of Goettingen did not grant degrees to Jews. Bitterness entered Heine's soul and made his pen razor sharp. He never practiced law, went off to travel, and wrote his exquisite **Harzreise** ("The Harz Journey") in 1826. Heine's brilliant political satires attacked tyranny in high places. A pamphlet against the nobility made him a fugitive from Germany. He settled in Paris where he lived

and wrote until his death. The last ten years of his life he spent on his "mattress-grave," suffering agonies from a crippling disease.

Heine's lyrical poems are beloved masterpieces of world literature. Even the Nazis, who burned his books, could not erase the love of these poems from among their people. Since the Germans persisted in singing **Die Lorelei,** it was reprinted without the author's name. Heine's baptism was never more than an expedient. He called it the "admission ticket to European civilization." His work is full of references to his Jewishness and Judaism—sometimes tender, sometimes ironic. Heine's Jewish sensitivity emerges as tense drama in the unfinished novel **Rabbi of Bacharach;** it flashes with superb irony in the play **Almansor** whose Moslem character disguises Jewish themes. Heine's **Hebrew Melodies** contain some of the best Jewish poems ever written outside the Hebrew language.   N.B-A.

HELLENISM. The Greek civilization of antiquity. It was the policy of Alexander the Great* to introduce the Hellenistic culture in the vanquished countries of the Near East. Adopting elements of the Near Eastern cultures, Hellenism lost much of the pure Greek spirit. However, it held a great attraction for the conquered peoples, who were fascinated by the Greek language, arts, and science, and the Hellenist cult of the perfection of the body. Judaism alone of the cultures of the Near East opposed Hellenism. The Greek belief in many gods, and Hellenistic sensuality, conflicted with Jewish monotheism and strict morality. The struggle between Hebraism and Hellenism came to a head in the Maccabean rebellion. Hebraism was victorious, the Judeans regained their independence, and the spread of Hellenism was checked in Judea.

Heinrich Heine

The large Jewish communities in the Hellenistic kingdoms in Asia, particularly those of Alexandria* and Antioch, were deeply influenced by Hellenism. They became largely Greek-speaking, and the Bible* was translated into Greek (the Septuagint*) for their use. A Graeco-Jewish philosophy developed, of which the interpretation of the Bible by Philo* of Alexandria is outstanding. The traces of Greek influence remain in some of the Jewish Wisdom literature (Apocrypha) of this period, and in such words as synagogue, sanhedrin, and parnas, which passed into the language spoken by Jews.   M.W.

HELLER, YOM TOV LIPMAN. See PRAGUE.

HEREM. In the Bible this term applied to that which is accursed, put under a ban, and therefore not fit for use. Later it came to have the meaning of excommunication or expulsion from the community. The person upon whom the **herem** was pronounced was cut off from all social and trade relations with his fellow Jews. In extreme cases the offender was denied such basic Jewish rights as marriage into a Jewish family, circumcision for his children, or even a Jewish burial. However, only when the religious authorities felt that the future of Judaism was at stake were they moved to resort to such extreme measures. Such was the case in the seventeenth century, for example, when the **herem** was pronounced on the followers of the false messiah—Sabattai Zevi.*

It was during and after the Middle Ages that the **herem** was used extensively by religious authorities to ensure obedience to their religious decisions. The most celebrated **herem** was that introduced by Rabbenu Gershom* which forbade Jews under pain of excommunication from taking more than one wife in marriage, or divorcing a woman against her will.

In later centuries the powerful weapon of the **herem** was sometimes needlessly resorted to by the rabbis.

HEROD THE GREAT (c. 73-4 B.C.E.). King of Judea. Son of Antipater and grandson of Antipas, rulers of Edom. Antipater was the friend and advisor of Hyrcanus II. When the Romans conquered Palestine,* Antipater was appointed to an important political post. As a result of his influence, his son Herod became governor of Galilee. Herod married Mariamne, granddaughter of Hyrcanus, in order to be related to the Hasmonean family. He was friendly with the Romans and won their favor by his devotion. In the year 40 B.C.E., the Roman Senate crowned him king of Judea.

The Jews hated Herod because he was an Edomite and a friend of their Roman enemies, and because he did not respect the Jewish religion. He waged war against Antigonus, the son of Aristobulus of the house of the Hasmonean dynasty who demanded the throne of Judea for himself. In this battle (37 B.C.E.) Herod captured Jerusalem,* put Antigonus to death, and destroyed the Hasmonean house. He showed no mercy even for his own wife and children whom he ordered killed some years later.

Herod deprived the Sanhedrin* of its executive powers, but allowed it to function in religious matters. With the Romans' permission, he extended the borders of Palestine from Damascus* to Egypt,* developed foreign trade, and built Samaria and Caesarea. An achievement that brought him fame was the rebuilding of the Temple (20-19 B.C.E.) which he decorated lavishly. He had beautiful buildings constructed in Jerusalem, too. Nevertheless, the people's hatred of the tyrant was not lessened by these acts. Legend has it that, feeling death at hand, he commanded his men to execute a number of Jewish leaders the day he died, in order to lessen the popular joy at his passing. This final act of cruelty, however, was not carried out.   S.E.

HERTZ, HEINRICH (1857-1894). German physicist, a pupil of the German scholar Helmholtz. He became world-famous through his experiments on the propagation of electrical waves. These experiments proved the electro magnetic theory of light that had been developed in 1865 by the British physicist Maxwell. Hertz's work paved the way for the era of electronics, culminating in the discovery of wireless telegraphy, radio, and television.

HERTZ, JOSEPH HERMAN (1872-1946). Chief Rabbi of the British Empire from 1913 to his death. Born in Hungary, he was twelve years old when he came to America. As the first graduate of the Jewish Tehological Seminary* in New York, Hertz served as a rabbi in several congregations of America and South Africa before he accepted the position of Chief Rabbi of the British Empire.

Hertz was one of the leaders of the Mizrachi Organization in England.* He assisted in obtaining the Balfour Declaration* in 1917, which proclaimed Palestine* as a Jewish homeland. During the Second World War, he worked untiringly to save Jews from death in Nazi-occupied lands.

Of his written works, the best known are **The Book of Jewish Thoughts,** a translation and commentary on the Five Books of Moses and a translation and commentary on the prayerbook.

HERZL, THEODOR (1860-1904). The founder of modern political Zionism* was born in Budapest to a well-to-do intellectual Jewish family. Herzl received a good education at the University of Vienna, was admitted to the bar in 1884, and shortly afterward turned to writing. He became a journalist and playwright, particularly famous for his feuilletons, a special type of literary column.

In 1891, Herzl became the Paris correspondent of the **Neue Freie Presse,** the leading liberal newspaper of that day. All his life, he had met with anti-Semitism* from fellow-students and professors, in books and in life. In Paris he thought to rid himself of this burden by writing a play on anti-Semitism—**The New Ghetto.** But at this time the Dreyfus* Case occurred; it shocked Herzl and changed the whole course of his life. As a newspaper correspondent, Herzl attended the trial and discovered that it was not Dreyfus the army captain, but Dreyfus the Jew who was being tried. Deeply shaken, Herzl, the spectator, became a man of action. He proposed a solution to the problem of anti-Semitism: the creation of a Jewish State. He started to put his ideas down on paper, and at the same time tried to put them into action. While writing his **Judenstaat** ("Jewish State"), he began to search for financial support and leadership. Herzl first approached the philanthropist Baron Maurice de Hirsch.* Hirsch dismissed the idea as

"fantastic." Then Herzl wrote to Albert Rothschild of Vienna and got no reply at all. His own paper, the **Neue Freie Presse,** refused to print a single word about a Jewish state. The first one to give him encouragement in 1895, his year of crisis, was Max Nordau,* the Paris physician who was famous as a writer and social philosopher.

In 1896, Herzl's **Judenstaat** was published. He turned to Baron Edmond de Rothschild* of Paris, who refused to accept the responsibility. Meanwhile the popular response grew and in January 1897, Herzl issued a call for a Zionist congress. The first Zionist Congress* met in Basle, Switzerland on August 27, 1897.

The congress was attended by 204 delegates from 17 countries. Herzl stood before them, a magnetic figure, and told them that "Zionism was the Jewish people on the march." He reported his efforts to get the approval and assistance of European nations for the formation of a Jewish state in Palestine* by obtaining a "charter" from Turkey.* He had seen and won over the Duke of Baden, uncle of Kaiser Wilhelm II. He had been to Constantinople, and had negotiated with important Turkish ministers, and he had been received in audience by King Ferdinand of Bulgaria. In London, he had won over the Jewish masses and had interested Israel Zangwill,* the writer. Finally, to provide a forum that should serve as the voice of Zionism, he founded with his own funds the journal **Die Welt.**

אִם תִּרְצוּ אֵין זוֹ אַגָּדָה

If you will it—it is no legend.

During three days of deliberation, the first Zionist Congress created the World Zionist Organization* and formulated the Basle Program, stating that "Zionism aims to create for the Jewish people a home in Palestine secured by public law." For this purpose the congress decided to obtain the necessary backing of various governments as a legal foundation for the Jewish homeland. Herzl was elected president of the World Zionist Organization. The next (and last) seven years of his life were years of feverish work. At the next five Zionist Congresses (1898-1903) over which he presided, the policies and institutions of the movement were hammered out, the Jewish Colonial Trust-the Zionist banking arm—and the Jewish National Fund*—its land purchasing agency—were established. Herzl conducted far-flung diplomatic negotiations, was received in audience by the German Kaiser

Theodor Herzl

Wilhelm II, by Sultan Abdul Hamid of Turkey, and by British statesmen. In the midst of it all, he wrote the novel **Altneuland,** a Utopian vision of the Zionist state. To obtain a promise of diplomatic support in Turkey, Herzl traveled to Russia, where he was received by two key members of the government, the Minister of the Interior, Vyacheslav von Plehve, and Finance Minister Sergei Witte. In his travels through Russia, Herzl saw the dreadful suffering of the Russian Jews, who were subjected to periodic pogroms. He was so deeply affected that he decided to accept the British offer of Uganda in East Africa to serve as a temporary asylum for Russian Jewry.

In August 1903, Herzl presided over a Zionist Congress for the last time. He had built well; this time 592 delegates attended, and the democratic temper was clearly demonstrated. The Uganda project was rejected after painful sessions. The delegates would have the ancient Land of Israel or nothing, and the Zionist movement seemed badly split. Herzl continued working for a "charter" for Palestine. In January 1904 he was received by the king of Italy, Victor Emmanuel III, who responded favorably. Pope Pius X, however, gave Herzl a clear "no." In April 1904 Herzl met with Zionist executives and made every effort to unify the movement. Worn out, his heart failing, he attended some of the sessions with an ice pack under his frock coat. On July 3, he died, but the work he had begun was carried forward by others. Fifty years after the first Zionist Congress, the State of Israel* was proclaimed (May 14, 1948). Over a year later, the coffin with Theodor Herzl's remains was flown from Vienna to Israel. The author of the **Jewish State** was laid to rest on Mt. Herzl in Jerusalem on August 17, 1949.   N.B-A.

HERZLIAH GYMNASIUM. Hebrew high school in Tel Aviv. When the Herzliah Gymnasium, or high school, was opened in 1906 in Jaffa, Palestine, it was considered a daring experiment. At that time it was still considered impractical to use Hebrew as a language of instruction, especially in the teaching of science. Hebrew had not been spoken for generations; most people thought it inadequate for modern usage. The Herzliah Gymnasium proved to be a great success. Its founders, who included Ben Zion Mossinsohn, Chaim Boger (Bogratchev), and J.L. Matemon-Cohen, set about preparing modern textbooks and coining new Hebrew words for all scientific terms.

The Herzliah Gymnasium became a national institution and contributed to the growth of Tel Aviv. Students from all over the world converged upon the newly built all-Jewish city of Tel Aviv, when the school moved from the ancient city of Jaffa.   H.L.

HERZOG, CHAIM (1918-   ). Israeli soldier and statesman. Born in Belfast, Ireland, the son of Rabbi Isaac Halevi Herzog,* he immigrated to Palestine in 1935 and obtained a thorough schooling in religious and secular studies. In 1939, he enlisted in the British army and participated in the liberation of the concentration camps in 1945. He returned to Palestine in 1947 and rejoined the Haganah.

Upon formation of the Israel Defense Forces in 1948, Herzog served as chief of military intelligence until 1950 and was appointed defense attaché at Israel's embassy in Washington (1950-1954). He was Israel's leading political and military commentator, in both Hebrew and English, during the 1967 Six-Day War and the 1973 Yom Kippur War.

From 1975 to 1978, Herzog was Israel's ambassador to the United Nations and publicly tore apart the U.N.'s "Zionism is racism" resolution in 1975. A noted writer on political, military, and economic affairs, he became Israel's fifth president in 1983, succeeding Yitzhak Navon.   G.W.

HERZOG, ISAAC HALEVI (1888-1959). Chief Rabbi of the State of Israel. Born in Lomza, Poland he acquired a thorough schooling in Talmud* and secular studies, specializing in law, philosophy and Oriental studies. In 1925, Herzog became Chief Rabbi of Ireland, where he gained the respect and love of all classes of Jewry. In 1936 he was elected Chief Rabbi of Palestine, and he remained Chief Rabbi until his death. A profound scholar, Rabbi Herzog took an active part in the life of his people and land. After the end of the Second World War, he devoted all his energies to saving the remnants of European Jewry. He made special efforts to save from forced conversion Jewish children who had been hidden in Christian homes and churches during the war.

Herzog published important works in Talmudic and Rabbinical studies, including five volumes on **The Main Institutions of Jewish Law.**

HESS, MOSES (1812-1875). Political leader, writer, and forerunner of modern Zionism. He was born in Bonn, Germany,* and died in Paris. Hess came of a wealthy Jewish family and his own grandfather taught him Bible* and Talmud.* As a youth he was attracted to the study of philosophy, and later participated in the Socialist movement, with Karl Marx* and Freidrich Engels. Then he turned to Ferdinand Lassalle and became active in the workers movement. After the failure of the 1848 Revolution in Germany, Hess settled in Paris, where he began to study the problem of the Jewish people and to think about its destiny. He published his thoughts in a small book, **Rome and Jerusalem** (1862). In it he wrote that Jewish national consciousness could not be erased, as the German Jewish Reform movement was trying to do. Mankind is made up of many nations, and small peoples have a right to an equal place in the family of nations. Every cultural historical group has something of its own to contribute to world civilization. The Jewish people, too, have much to contribute. The only solution to the Jewish question is the settlement of Palestine,* which should be under the protection of some European power. The ideas in **Rome and Jerusalem** came to be a basic part of Zionist thinking, and for them Moses Hess is remembered.

HET. Eighth letter of the Hebrew alphabet; numerically, eight.

HIAS. See UNITED HIAS SERVICE.

HILLEL (c. first century B.C.E.). Talmudic authority. Born in Babylonia,* he came to Palestine to study Law. His fame as a brilliant scholar grew, and he became the leader of the Pharisees* and head of the liberal school of interpretation of the Jewish law.

Moses Hess

Many legends are told about Hillel's devotion to learning, simplicity, and modesty. In his youth, he was a poor laborer, spending a large portion of his earnings on his tuition. Once, when he lacked the price of admission to the house of study, he climbed to the roof, and, through the skylight, listened to the discussions of the rabbis. He became so absorbed that he did not mind the snow which almost covered him completely. Half-frozen, he was finally noticed by the scholars inside, taken down, and revived.

In his interpretation of the law, Hillel's first consideration was the welfare of the people. He established regulations which were aimed at reconciling the ancient law with new conditions. One of these, the "prosbul," made it possible for the poor to borrow money at the approach of the seventh, or sabbatical year, when people were reluctant to lend money, since all debts were cancelled during that year.

There is a tradition that Hillel was a descendant of the House of David. His saintliness and scholarship earned him the love and respect of his countrymen. King Herod* appointed him head of the Sanhedrin.* He remained spiritual leader of the Jews for a period of forty years. His utterances reveal his nobility of character. His love of peace was great; he said: "Be of the disciples of Aaron,* loving peace and pursuing peace, loving thy fellow creatures, and drawing them close to the Torah." His tolerance is illustrated by the story of the heathen who asked Hillel to teach him all of the principles of Judaism while he stood on one foot. Hillel replied: "Do not unto your neighbor what you would not have him do unto you; this is the whole law, the rest is commentary."

As contrasted with his great opponent Shammai,* Hillel stands out as the liberal interpreter of Jewish law. H.L.

HILLEL FOUNDATION. See B'NAI B'RITH.

HIRSCH, BARON MAURICE DE (1831-1896). Financier and philanthropist. Son of a titled and wealthy family, he became one of the richest men in Europe by investing his inheritance in railroads, banking, and other industries. When his plan to improve the deplorable condition of the Russian Jews failed to receive the approval of the Tsar, he formed the Jewish Colonization Association* in order to resettle Jews in various parts of the world and to establish colonies in North and South America, particularly Argentina.* Hirsch believed that the condition of the Jews could be greatly improved if they were to become farmers and industrial workers in less densely populated areas of the world. To this end, he established agricultural and industrial schools in both Europe and the New

World. Baron de Hirsch gave billions of dollars to charitable causes, regardless of religion or creed. In 1887, his only son died. "I have lost my son but not my heir," he said. "Humanity is my heir."

HIRSCH, SAMSON RAPHAEL (1808-1888).

German rabbi, champion of neo-Orthodoxy. Born in Hamburg, Hirsch received a thorough Jewish education, as well as secular training at the University of Bonn. He held rabbinical positions in Germany and Moravia until 1851, when he became rabbi of the Israelite Religious Society of Frankfort-on-the-Main, where he spent the rest of his life. The Frankfort group had seceded from the general Jewish community to form an independent Orthodox congregation. Hirsch was violently opposed to the Reform movement, and advocated the separation of his followers from any community where Reform Judaism had gained the upper hand. Due to his initiative, the German Parliament later (1876) legalized the secession of the Orthodox Jews from the Jewish community. In 1836 Hirsch published his **Nineteen Letters,** an uncompromising defense of the institutions and laws of Judaism, and a statement of his theories on neo-Orthodoxy. In opposition to the German Reform movement, Hirsch maintained that the acceptance of Biblical and Talmudic authority was absolutely necessary to a true understanding of Judaism. He felt what was needed in Judaism was not the abolition of traditional authority, as the Reform movement advocated, but rather the reinterpretation and spiritualization of the traditional laws and practices to give them deeper meaning and significance in the modern world. Hirsch founded a day school which combined a thorough Jewish education with modern secular training. Hirsch's educational philosophy was based on Verse 2 of Chapter 2 of the Ethics of the Fathers: "It is well to continue Torah studies with a worldy occupation" **(Torah imderekh eretz)**. He established a monthly journal to publicize his ideas, and found time to defend the Jews against anti-Semitic attacks. He published **Horeb** (a book on the religious duties of the Jewish people in exile), and voluminous commentaries on the Pentateuch* and the Book of Psalms.* A commentary on the Jewish prayer book, based on his writings, was published after his death. Most of his writings have been translated into English. Hirsch believed that the Jews were a group of co-religionists whose nationhood did not depend on land, but on the Jewish tradition and who would regain their land only upon the coming of the Messiah. After his death a small group of his adherents based their opposition to political Zionism* on Hirsch's concept of Judaism.

HISTADRUT HA-OVDIM (GENERAL FEDERATION OF JEWISH LABOR IN ISRAEL).

Founded in 1920 by the representatives of 4,500 Jewish workers in Palestine,* the Histadrut has grown to be the most powerful non-governmental institution in Israel, an institution unique in the history of labor movements. David Ben-Gurion, Yitzhak Ben-Zvi,* and Joseph Sprinzak were among the early founders and leaders of the organization.

By 1979 the Histadrut membership was over 1,450,000. Each member pays dues to the federation, and receives in return full medical coverage through Kupat Holim—the Workers' Sick Fund— old age and disability benefits, the right to participate in all its cultural and social activities, and to vote in elections.

On joining Histadrut, the worker automatically becomes a member of the General Cooperative

Executive Headquarters of Histadrut, Tel Aviv.

Courtesy Histadrut.

Association of Israel, founded by the Histadrut to facilitate the growth of new industries. To it belong most of Israel's consumers' and producers' cooperatives. About 25% of Israel's GNP is attributed to Histadrut's owned and centrally-managed enterprises.

Most workers also belong to one of 35 trade and industrial unions affiliated with the Histadrut. These unions include both skilled and unskilled laborers, as well as professional, academic and clerical workers. Through coordination of bargaining policy, the Histadrut has striven to maintain uniform standards throughout Israel.

Nationally, the Histadrut has been active in preparing labor legislation for consideration by the Knesset* (Parliament). Histadrut also maintains local labor councils in towns and villages; a Working Women's Council; a Working Youth Organization; an Agricultural Workers' Center; and Shikun Ovdim, which builds low-cost homes for workers and their families. Its cultural activities include publication of two daily newspapers, **Daver,** and **Omer**, a publication for newcomers; Ohel, a full-scale repertory theatre; Hapoel, a national sports organization; a publishing house; vocational and general schools for both children and adults; libraries; and a department for the organization of lectures, concerts, discussion groups, etc. Since the establishment of the State of Israel in 1948, the Histadrut has accepted Israel's Arabs for membership in its unions; the Israel Labor League, an all-Arab union, is a Histadrut affiliate. To facilitate the integration of Arabs into the economic and cultural life of Israel, the Histadrut maintains a special Arab Department.

Na'amat. More than half the membership of Histadrut are women organized in Na'amat as well as in their own trade unions. Irgun Imahot (Association of Working Mothers) is the voluntary arm of Na'amat, with its own program of community service. A special section for Arab women's activities has been instrumental in im-

Members of a cultural delegation from Israel in 1955. Left to right: Dr. B. Ben-Yehudah, Professor Simon Halkin and Dr. Reuven Avinoam, with leaders of the Histadruth Ivrith in America, Samuel J. Borowsky (second from right) and Mrs. Zahava Sheinbaum (Shen).

proving the status of its members, both economically and socially.

Working with its sister organization, Pioneer Women,* in 12 countries throughout the world, Na'amat provides 60% of all social services for the women, youth and children of Israel. (**See also** PIONEER WOMEN.)

HISTADRUTH IVRITH OF AMERICA. National organization for Hebrew culture. It was founded in 1916 in New York, with the participation of outstanding Zionist leaders who had escaped from imprisonment in Turkish Palestine* and had come to America for the duration of the First World War. Among them were Eliezer Ben-Yehudah,* David Ben-Gurion,* Yitzhak Ben-Zvi,* Rabbi Meir Bar-Ilan,* and Shmaryahu Levin.*

To acheive its aim of spreading the knowledge of the Hebrew language among American Jews, the Histadruth Ivrith sponsors a number of cultural and educational activities. Since 1921, it has published the Hebrew weekly **Hadoar,** with two supplements: **Hadoar Lanoar** for children, and **Musaf Lakore Hatzair** for youth and adults. Both are illustrated nad vowelized.

The Histadruth Ivrith helped to introduce Hebrew as a living language in the public high schools and colleges and in special courses for adults. It has organized Hebrew-speaking clubs

Bellinson Hospital—one of the hospitals built and maintained by Kupat Holim, Histadrut health organization.

for young people, and subsidizes Massad, a Hebrew-speaking summer camp, established in 1942.

Histadruth Ivrith branches carry on intensive cultural activities throughout the United States. In addition, the organization arranges for public meeting and concerts, and supports the Hebrew Arts Foundation.

Since the establishment of the State of Israel in 1948, the Histadruth Ivrith has stressed the need to establish a cultural bridge between American and Israel Jewry. The executive secretary of the Histadruth Ivrith in the early '50's was Zahava Sheinbaum. She dedicated all her talents, and ability to this task. Mrs. Sheinbaum was among the 58 passengers killed when an El Al airliner was shot down by Bulgarian fighter planes in July, 1955.

HOFETZ HAIM (c. 1837-1933). Scholar, author, and one of the prominent leaders of Polish Orthodox Jewry. Born Israel Meir Kahan (or Kagan) in Zhitil, Poland, he derived his byname from his book **Hofetz Haim** ("He Who Desires Life"), a treatise against slander. Rabbi Kahan founded a **yeshiva** in Radin and, refusing important rabbinical positions, devoted his time to writing and teaching. When World War I erupted, he was active in raising funds for the support of Polish and Russian Jewry. Often he interceded in their behalf before the Russian governemnt. In 1930 he protested personally to the Polish government against government interference with Jewish religious and economic rights. A man of great erudition, he was the author of thirty books on Jewish ethics and law. **Mishnah Berurah,** a six-volume treatise on Joseph Karo's* **Orah Haim,** is a highly valuable manual for rabbis today.

HOLLAND. See NETHERLANDS.

HOLOCAUST. See JEWRY, ANNIHILATION OF EUROPEAN.

HONDURAS. The first Jews to reach Honduras were East Europeans who came from other Latin American countries in the 1920's. Today (1977) there are 200 Jews in Honduras, whoses total population is 2,830,000. Almost all live in Tegucigalpa, the capital, and engage in trade. **(See** LATIN AMERICA.)

HOROWITZ, VLADIMIR (1904-   ). Concert pianist. Born in Kiev, Russia, Horowitz studied music at the conservatory in his native city. He performed his first solo concert in 1921, making his United States debut seven years later. He settled in New York, and in 1933 married Wanda Toscanini, daughter of the famous conductor. A great interpreter of classical music, Horowitz has appeared with outstanding orchestras everywhere. His numerous recordings have made his name a household word.

HOSEA (c. 784-725 B.C.E.). First of the minor prophets. He lived in the turbulent idolatrous northern Kingdom of Israel* when it was at the height of its power under the rule of Jeroboam II. Hosea's prophecies thunder against moral, religious, and political evils as offenses against God. He predicted the doom of Israel as punishment for its idol worship and social injustice. Yet he loved his people and saw visions of its restoration after the punishment. Then, a reconciliation between man and God would come about, a reconciliation arising out of God's love of Israel and of all humanity. Hosea's all-consuming ideal is love; in striking phrases he compares God to a loving father and faithful husband.

And I will betroth thee unto Me forever;
Yea I will betroth thee unto Me in righteousness,
and in loving kindness, and in mercy.
And I will betroth thee unto Me in faithfulness,
an thou shalt know the Lord.

This triple betrothal (Hosea 2:21-22) is recited by the observant Jew when he puts on his tefillin* (phylacteries) each morning. As he winds the thong of the hand phylactery three time around his middle finger he pledges himself anew to the three-fold ideal first pronounced by Hosea.

Vladimir Horowitz   Courtesy RCA Victor Red Seal.

HOVEVE ZION (Hebrew for "Lovers of Zion"). An East European, 19th-century organization for the settlement of Jews in Palestine. A direct reaction to the widespread pogroms in Tsarist Russia* it grew out of the thinking and writing of a few men and from scattered colonization societies that began to spring up in the 1860's. The Hoveve Zion federation was organized formally at a conference in Kattowitz, Silesia, in November 1884. **(See also ZIONISM.)**

HUBERMAN, BRONISLAW (1882-1947). Violinist. Huberman began to study the violin in his native Warsaw at the age of six, and made his first public appearance a year later. Continuing his studies in Berlin under the great Joseph Joachim, Huberman made a number of triumphant world tours before he reached his majority. As a violinist, Huberman used his brilliant technical mastery not for showmanship, but for imaginative artistry. He pursued a successful career until Hitler's rise to power in 1933. In 1936 he visited Palestine, where he conceived the idea of founding a Palestine Symphony Orchestra. Owing to his unstinting efforts, the orchestra was founded, and Arturo Toscanini conducted its first concert in December 1936. This was the forerunner of the Israel Philharmonic Orchestra.

HUNGARY. Jews lived in Hungary as far back as Roman times, when the area was part of the Roman province of Dacia. Conquest of the land by invading Magyars (897), spelled for the Jews continuous plunder and persecution at the hands of Catholic kings. Under Turkish rule (1526-1686) the situation of the Jewish populace greatly improved. Austrian domination, however, again changed their circumstances for the worse. France Joseph II (1741-1790) emancipated the Jews, but his decree was carried out only partially. A number of Jews fought on the side of Hungary against Austria in the revolution of 1848.

At that time there was a severe struggle between the Orthodox and the Reform elements of Hungarian Jewry, which led to a split in 1871. Three congregational groupings emerged: Orthodox, Reform, and "status quo." Modern Hungarian Jewry has been characterized by sharp contrasts: on the one hand extreme piety; on the other, extreme assimilation,* even to the point of conversion to Christianity.

By the beginning of the twentieth century, Hungarian Jews were occupying important positions in the economic and cultural life of the country, in the arts, the press, and the sciences. However, the interval between the two World Wars was marked by the growth of anti-Semitism.*

Before the Second World War ended, the Germans had occupied Hungary. In the summer of 1944 they transported 400,000 local Jews to Auschwitz.*

The end of the war found some 120,000 Jewish survivors in Hungary, of whom about 80,000 lived in Budapest. The Jewish community, like the rest of the population, was in dire economic straits. In addition, anti-Semitism was no less virulent than at the height of the Nazi terror. When Hungary came under Soviet domination in 1948, Jews suffered especially from directives aimed at eliminating middle-class elements from the nation's economy. Although official Communist doctrine forbade anti-Semitism, an unusually high percentage of Jews were included in the mass deportations of "undesirables" from the larger cities begun in 1951 and continued into 1952. The Hungarian Zionist movement was outlawed. All contact with Western Jewry and Israel was severed. Emigration was barred. The American Jewish Joint Distribution Committee,* responsible until 1953 for most welfare and economic aid to the Jewish community, was forced to leave. The Hungarian uprising of October-November 1956 was accompanied by some anti-Jewish acts, and 18,000—20,000 Jews fled the country, streaming mainly into Austria. The Jewish population (1984) numbers about 60,000. There is a rabbinical seminary and Jewish schools are functioning.

HUPPAH. See MARRIAGE CUSTOMS.

HYRCANUS, JOHANAN. Of all the Hasmonean rulers who re-established and strengthened the independence of Judea, Johanan Hyrcanus was the most successful. A son of Simon the Maccabee, Hyrcanus ruled from 135 to 104 B.C.E. His defeat of the allied Samaritans and Syrians and conquest of their cities ended forever the threat of Syrian rule and extended the borders of Judea to the west and to the north. Hyrcanus turned next to the south and conquered the Edomites, forcing them to accept Judaism.

During his thirty-year rule, the Second Jewish Commonwealth attained its greatest independence and power. At the end of his rule, he came into conflict with the Pharisees,* one of the two political parties that had developed in Judea. The Pharisees wanted to deprive him of his position as high priest, but this group paid heavily for their opposition to Hyrcanus, who drew closer to their opponents, the Sadducees.*

I

IBN EZRA, ABRAHAM (1092-1167). Hebrew poet, philosopher, and Bible commentator. Born in Toledo, Spain,* he travelled widely, visiting Italy,* France,* England,* North Africa and the Middle East. Ibn Ezra contributed greatly to the spread of Arab-Jewish culture among the Jews of Western Europe. He suffered poverty and often complained bitterly about his lot, in biting satirical poems. His Bible* commentaries are distinguished by their logical and penetrating interpretation of Biblical language and content. Of considerable importance also are his books on mathematics, philosophy, astronomy and Hebrew grammar. Ibn Ezra's grammatical works were translated into Latin. In contrast to most of the Jewish scholars in Spain, he wrote his works in Hebrew, rather than Arabic.

As a poet, Abraham Ibn Ezra does not measure up to the stature of the great Hebrew masters during the "Golden Age" in Spain. Yet some of his liturgical poems possess depth of feeling. He composed remarkable hymns on creation and on the qualities of angels. His poetic darts of ridicule and wit strike at the root of human weaknesses. Ibn Ezra's contrasting qualities are revealed in his truly moving religious poetry on the one hand, and the rhymed riddles and puzzles—the product of a keen and quick-witted mind—on the other. A number of his liturgical poems are included in the traditional prayer book.

IBN EZRA, MOSES (c. 1070-1150). Hebrew poet and contemporary of Judah Ha-Levi,* Moses Ibn Ezra came of a famous Jewish family in Granada, Spain.* At first he was fascinated by the beauty of nature and the pleasures of life. After experiencing rejection and disappointment in love, he took to wandering. He wrote so many religious poems pleading for forgiveness that he became known as "Hasallach," or the penitential poet. Ibn Ezra made excellent use of the riches of the Hebrew language in his secular and religious poetry. He was a master of form and literary technique. His book **Shirat Yisrael** (The Poetry of Israel) is of great value for the study of Hebrew poetry and the Arabic influences upon it.

IBN GABIROL, SOLOMON (1021-1058) Medieval Hebrew poet and philosopher. Born in Malaga, Spain,* he was orphaned while yet a child. At sixteen, his genius had already become evident. The tragic experiences of his short life—poverty, illness, and loneliness—are reflected in his subtle and pessimistic poems. His outstanding creative intelligence is revealed in his philosophical works as well.

Many of Ibn Gabirol's poems, or **piyyutim,** became part of Jewish religious liturgy. His **Keter Malkhut,** a paean to the greatness of God, is recited on Yom Kippur* Eve.

As a penetrating philosopher, Ibn Gabirol influenced both Christian theology and Jewish mystic thought. His philosophic work **Fons Vitae** ("Source of Life") was originally written in Arabic and later translated into Latin. The work was for centuries attributed to "Avicebron"; it was not until the middle of the nineteenth century that a Jewish scholar, Solomon Munk, discovered a fragmentary Hebrew translation by means of which he was able to prove that Avicebron was actually Ibn Gabirol.

Ibn Gabirol's end is surrounded by mystery. An envious Arabic poet was said to have murdered him, and to have buried his remains under a fig tree. To the astonishment of all, the tree bore unusually beautiful fruit. The king questioned the owner about his marvelous tree until he broke down and confessed his crime.

H.L.

IBN JANNAH, JONAH (990-1050). Scholar and Hebrew grammarian. A physician by profession, he practiced medicine first in Cordova, Spain. When the Berbers destroyed Cordova he settled in Saragossa.

Ibn Jannah's primary interest, however, was the study of Hebrew grammar. He wrote two important books, one on the grammatical construction and the other on the sources of the Hebrew language, which are classics of their kind. These books were translated from the Arabic into Hebrew by Judah Ibn Tibbon.*

IBN PAKUDA, BAHYA BEN JOSEPH. (1st half of 11th cent.). Philosopher and **dayan** (rabbinical judge) of Saragossa, Spain,* Ibn Pakuda is best known for his classic book on Jewish ethics, **Hovot ha-Levavot,** or "Duties of the Heart." Little is known about his life, except that he was deeply learned and well acquainted with both Arabic and Jewish philosophical and scientific writing. In his work he urges man to love and accept God with his heart. Yet man must also exercise his reason in order to understand his obligations in this world. Ibn Pakuda believes that gratitude to God for His marvelous universe requires us to live ethically. Ibn Pakuda also wrote several beautiful hymns and poems; especially noteworthy is the "Admonition" to his soul that begins with the verse from the Psalms, "Bless the Lord, O my soul."

144

IBN TIBBON FAMILY. This famous family came from Spain* and lived mostly in Southern France* during the twelfth and thirteenth centuries. They are best known as translators of Arabic works into Hebrew. In doing this they accomplished two great tasks: 1) they enriched the Hebrew language by creating new words and expressions for philosophic and scientific terms previously unknown in Hebrew. 2) They made available the works of outstanding Jewish philosophers and scholars to a wider public which could not read Arabic.

The following are outstanding members of this family:

1) Judah Ben Saul (1120-1190) who practiced medicine at Lunel in Southern France. Among the works he translated were **Emunot Vedeot** ("Beliefs and Opinions") by Saadiah Gaon;* **Hovot ha-Levavot** ("Duties of the Heart") by Bahya ibn Pakuda,* and the **Kuzari** by Judah Ha-Levi.*

2) Judah ben Samuel (1150-1230). Most important of all translators. He rendered into Hebrew the **Moreh Nebuchim** ("Guide to the Perplexed") by Maimonides,* and other works of this great scholar and philosopher. Judah corresponded with Maimonides, discussing various problems that arose in connection with the translations.

3) Moses ben Samuel (1240-1283). Practicing physician in Provence. He also translated some of Maimonides' works: his commentary on the **Mishnah** (Peirush Hamishnayot), **Sefer Hamitzvot** and **Milot Hahigayon** ("Terms of Logic"), as well as scientific and philosophic works from the Arabic.   H.L.

IMBER, NAPHTALI HERZ (1856-1909). The author of **Ha-Tikvah,*** Imber was a poet and an incurable wanderer. He left his home in Galicia when quite young and roamed all over Europe. In 1878, he wrote **Ha-Tikvah** ("The Hope"),* a poem of nine stanzas expressing the Jewish longing to return to the Land of Israel. **Ha-Tikvah** is now the national anthem of the State of Israel.* Imber lived in Palestine from 1882 to 1887, when he went to Europe and England. Later he came to the United States and traveled all over the country, writing Hebrew poems and articles for many Jewish magazines. He died in New York.

IMMANUEL BEN SOLOMON OF ROME (1270-1330). Hebrew scholar and satirical poet. Immanuel, named Ha-Romi because he was born in Rome,* came of a rich and distinguished Jewish family. In his youth, he studied the Talmud as well as mathematics, astronomy, medicine and languages. He served as secretary to the Jewish community of Rome, and excelled as an orator. However, Immanuel's biting tongue made him many enemies and he was forced to resign his position. Shortly afterward, he lost all his possessions and took to wandering. Immanuel's best known work, **Mahberot Immanuel,** is a collection of poems written in narrative sequence. The section entitled "Tofet and Eden" is modeled after Dante's **Divine Comedy.**

Immanuel also wrote in Italian, and was one of the first to introduce the sonnet into Hebrew poetry. Some Talmudic scholars were critical of his writings, because of the frivolous and irreverent nature of some of the passages in his **Mahberot.**

INDIA. A republic in southern Asia. India's (1984) 4,300 Jews fall into three distinct groups: the Bene Israel (Sons of Israel), the Jews of Cochin, and a series of loosely organized communities from Persia and the west.

The Bene Israel, largest of the groups, speak Maharati, wear Indian dress, and are divided into caste-like groups of "black" and "white" Jews which have separate synagogues and do not intermarry. They believe they settled in the Bombay District in about 175 B.C.E., after the Maccabean uprising in Palestine. When first discovered by the West about two hundred years ago, they knew no Hebrew and owned no prayer books. **Shema Yisrael,** one of the few prayers they remembered, was recited at all their religious ceremonies. Several thousand of them have emigrated to Israel.

The second largest group of Indian Jews is of Iraqi origin, lives predominantly in Bombay and Calcutta, and is mainly engaged in commerce. They are the descendants of the Jews who followed their leader David Sassoon from Iraq to India in 1832 where he founded the house of Sassoon,* well known for its great wealth and generous contributions to Jewish charitable causes.

A third group of Indian Jewry, consisting of the Cochin Jews, live in Cochin and other cities on the Malabar Coast. They came from Persia and the Arab countries during the early Middle Ages. They spoke Malayalam, the language of the Dravidians, India's original inhabitants. Hebrew, however, was

A Rabbi and his family in Karachi, India.

Courtesy Hazel Greenwald.

Operation "Magic Carpet" in which an entire Yemenite community was transported by planes to Israel—1949-50.

known, and used in their strictly Orthodox religious ritual. The first written record of Cochin Jews is a copper inscription dated 1020 C.E., in which the maharajah of the district grants privileges of nobility to the head of the community. The "white," "black," and "brown" Jews of Cochin all believe they stem from exiles who left Palestine in 70 C.E., after the destruction of the Second Temple. It is more probable that the "black" Jews arrived in India after the Moslem conquest of Persia in the seventh century, and that the "whites" came after the expulsion from Spain in 1492.

The smallest group is of European origin, and consists of refugees who emigrated to India to escape the Hitler persecutions in Germany in 1933.

The Jews of India live in comparative freedom and security. Many of them have risen to high ranks in the armed services; others have prospered in business and the professions.

INGATHERING OF THE EXILES (in Hebrew, Kibbutz Galuyot).

The hope for the reunion of the people of Israel in the land of Israel is fundamental to the prophetic idea of redemption. "The redeemed of the Lord shall return and come with singing into Zion; and joy shall be upon their head." (Isa. 51:11)

For centuries Jewish prayers echoed the fervent desire for the ingathering of the exiles. "Sound the great trumpet for our freedom . . . and gather us from the four corners of the earth."

But it was not until the rise of the Zionist movement that the reunion of Israel became a reality. Unfortunately, only a small portion of Jewry was privileged to return to Zion before the Nazis exterminated 6,000,000 European Jews.

After the establishment of the State of Israel* on May 15, 1948, the ingathering of the exiles assumed undreamed-of proportions. The Israel government and its people flung open the gates of the new State. The inalienable right of every Jew to enter Israel and become an Israeli citizen was given legal form in "The Law of the Return." The greatest number of Jews came during the first five years of Israel's existence. From mid-May 1948 to the end of 1982, 1,722,000 Jews came to Israel from all five continents and from over eighty countries. The entire Jewish communities of Bulgaria, Iraq, and the majority of the Jews of Czechoslovakia, Libya, Poland, and Yugoslavia came to Israel. Until the middle of 1979, about 140,000 Jews came from the Soviet Union.

This ingathering created the problem of absorbing and integrating members of many different communities into one united, strong nation. By 1979, 31 years after the establishment of the State, Israel had made considerable progress in solving this problem.   H.L.

INQUISITION. The special courts set up by the Catholic Church to check the spread of heretical opinion among the faithful. The first such courts were set up in the 13th century. It was most active, however, in Spain, where it was begun in 1480. In time, the dreaded activities of this agency of the Church came to be directed mainly at ferreting out Jews who had been forcibly converted to Christianity, and were found to be secretly observing the practices of Judaism — the Marranos.*

It is estimated that in the three-and-a-half centuries during which the Inquisition was active (roughly from 1480 to 1821), about 400,000 Jews were brought before these ecclesiastical tribunals; 30,000 were put to death. Punishment was carried

Immigrant from Hadramaut, southern Arabia, learns vegetable gardening from a Rumanian fellow immigrant.

THE FLIGHT FROM THE INQUISITION

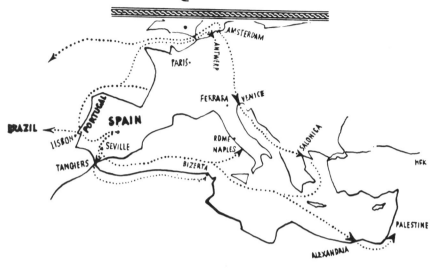

out in public squares, to serve both as a warning and a demonstration of "the glory of the Church." Hence, an inquisitorial execution was known as **suto-da-fe***—an "act of faith." Most notorious of the inquisitors was Thomas de Torquemada, who was largely responsible for the edict issued by Ferdinand and Isabella of Spain on the Ninth of Ab 1492, expelling all Jews from Spanish territory.

IRAN. Iran, the ancient Persia, included at its height of power, Asia Minor, Mesopotamia, Babylonia,* and the mountainous lands east and south. Jews first came under Persian rule in 539 B.C.E., when King Cyrus* conquered Babylonia. The Judean captives, exiled to Babylonia after the destruction of the Temple* in 586 B.C.E., welcomed the Persian rulers. Forty thousand of them returned to Judea and rebuilt their homeland. For the two centuries of Persian rule, the Jewish communities of Persian Babylonia flourished, and close links were maintained with the communities of Judea. In later centuries, when the Persian Empire fell successively under Greek, Parthian and Arab domination, Jews continued to live in its territories, notably in the Babylonian cities of Sura and Pumbeditha, where great academies flourished and where the immense work of compiling the Talmud* was completed in 500 A.D.

During the twelfth century, there were large Jewish communities in the cities of Isfahan, Shiraz, and Hamadan, which are a part of present-day Iran. Under the Safavid Dynasty (1499-1736), Jews suffered severely from discriminatory measures against them. Many converted to Islam,* living secretly as Jews. Some fled to Afghanistan* and

A Jewish child of the Teheran ghetto, holding "loaves" of Persian bread, virtually her only staple food.

Joint Distribution Committee.

Palestine,* where their descendants are still to be found. The Kadar Dynasty (1795-1925) continued the harsh anti-Jewish policy of the Safavids. They considered the Jews ritually unclean, humiliated them, and taxed them heavily. Under this treatment, the Jewish community went into decline. In the latter half of the nineteenth century, the lot of Persian Jewry improved somewhat when the Jews of Western Europe interceded on their behalf. In 1898, the first school of the Alliance Israélite Universelle* was organized at Teheran. Today, the Alliance conducts a network of twenty-one schools throughout Iran, and these have contributed greatly to raising the cultural and economic standards of Persian Jewry. Since May 15, 1948, there has been a mass emigration of about 60,000 Persian Jews to Israel. Emigration is still continuing at a slow pace. Under the Shah, Reza Pahlevi, the Jewish community was estimated at 70,000 in 1979. In 1984, there were about 30,000-35,000 Jews, the majority in Teheran. Other Jewish centers are Shiraz, Isfahan, and Hamadan. Only a handful of Iran's Jews are in comfortable circumstances. Many, particularly in the smaller towns and villages, live in conditions bordering on destitution.

Since the triumph of the Ayatollah Ruholla Khomeini's Islamic Revolution in 1979, the 2,500-year-old Jewish community of Iran has experienced a dramatic decline. Zionism, defined on the basis of

ties with Israel, is regarded as a crime punishable by death. At present, the outlook for Iranian Jewry is uncertain.

IRAQ. Jews in Iraq constitute the oldest Jewish community in the world aside from Israel. Iraq, the Babylonia* of the Bible* and the Talmud,* was the Jews' first land of exile, to which they were driven from Palestine by Nebuchadnezzar after he had destroyed the First Temple, in 597 B.C.E. The Babylonian Talmud* was composed there. The series of wars which occurred in the course of centuries had their effect on the local Jewry: due to the repeated unrest and disorder in the country, the Jews were steadily emigrating to India and to Persia, where they created their own communities. These communities, known as Baghdad Jews, still exist today.

In the seventh century, Arabs conquered the country. Under the rule of Harun-al-Rashid (786-809), the scholars and leaders of the Talmudic academies began to make contact with the various Jewish communities in Europe. Their influence extended to the Jewries of both Europe and North Africa.

In 1534 Turkey conquered that area which today comprises the land of Iraq, and continued to rule it until 1917, when Great Britain won it. In 1932 the independent kingdom of Iraq was established. Both under the British mandate and under Iraqi sovereign rule, the Jews lived in comparative freedom. A considerable number enjoyed prosperity and even wealth, especially in the capital city of Baghdad. About 50,000 Jews resided there, representing approximately 20% of the population.

Spiritually the Jewish community in Iraq had deteriorated since its original growth and development. The Alliance Israélite Universelle* played a very significant educational role in Iraq, by founding a broad network of schools early in the twentieth century.

In 1948 the outbreak of the Arab war against the newly established State of Israel was marked by "legal" plunder and persecution of Iraqi Jews. The "great exodus" of Jews followed in 1951-1952. Of the 130,000 Jewish inhabitants who were in Iraq in 1948, less than 350 have remained. The remnants of the Iraqi Jewish community are settled mainly in Baghdad. Anti-Jewish feeling has heightened with unrest in the Middle East. The Jews have lost property rights, and mass trials have been held to uncover "Zionist spy rings." Jewish cultural and religious life is at a standstill, with all Jewish periodicals banned, seventy synagogues in Baghdad's Old City closed down, and five Jewish clubs taken over by the government without compensation. The property of all Jewish emigres is ad-

ministered by a special government department.

IRELAND. The earliest evidence of Jewish settlement in Ireland is a grant made in 1232 to a certain Peter de Rivall, giving him "custody of the King's Jews in Ireland." In 1290 Irish Jews, like their English brethren, were expelled from Ireland and did not return until around 1655, during the days of Oliver Cromwell and the Commonwealth. It was then that the first Sephardic* community was founded in Dublin; Jewish settlement in Ireland has been small but continuous ever since.

Of Ireland's 2,000 Jews, most live in Dublin, the capital city of Eire, the Irish Free State. They are mostly small shopkeepers and tradesmen. The clothing and furniture industries were introduced into Ireland by Lithuanian immigrants. Dublin, with its two large and four small synagogues, its charitable organizations and Talmud Torah, is the center of religious and cultural life of Irish Jewry. More than half of Northern Ireland's Jews live in the capital city of Belfast, whose present Jewish community was founded in 1870. An earlier Jewish community was founded there a century before, but later dissolved.

IRGUN Z'VAI L'UMI. Underground military force organized by the Revisionists* in April 1937, to combat the repressions of the British administration in Palestine and the growing rule of Arab terror. The Revisionists were impatient with the policy of restraint practiced by Jewish leaders in Palestine* in the face of constant Arab attacks. The Irgun was guided by two fundamental principles: 1) A Jewish State had to be established in the immediate future; and 2) Every Jew had a natural right to come to Palestine.

The Irgun believed the time ripe for military action in order to achieve the legitimate aim of establishing a Jewish State. The Irgun's symbol— a hand gripping a rifle over a map of Palestine that included eastern Palestine—began to appear on all the organization's posters.

In 1938 a member of the Irgun, Shlomo Ben Yosef, was accused of attacking an Arab vehicle in retaliation for the numerous killings of Jews. He was sentenced to the gallows. Ben Yosef became a symbol of the determination of Irgun members to fight to the death for the cause of Jewish liberation.

When the Second World War broke out and the free world was engaged in a deadly struggle with the Nazi armies, the Irgun committed its small force to fight the common enemy on the side of the British. The first Irgun commander, David Raziel, was killed in 1941 in a commando operation in Iraq. The command of Irgun was then taken over by Yaakov Meridor, and later, in 1943, by Menahem Begin.*

In February 1944, the Irgun called for the end of the British mandate, the freeing of Palestine from "foreign domination," and the immediate establishment of a provisional government. The British began a ruthless campaign to destroy the Irgun. Several hundred of its members were arrested and exiled to Eritrea, a British colony in Northeast Africa. The arrests swelled to thousands after the Irgun blew up the King David Hotel, the administrative offices of the Palestine (British) government. Each Irgun exploit was countered by an act of British repression. In the spring of 1947, Dov Gruner and four other members of Irgun were hanged at the Acre prison.

Though the Jewish Agency and the Haganah* frequently condemned Irgun for its extremist policies, there was a short period after World War II when Haganah and Irgun cooperated in the struggle against the British. This happened when the British Labor party, on coming to power in 1945, failed to fulfill its pre-election promises to open Palestine without restrictions to survivors of the Holocaust. To allegations that Irgun was a terrorist organization, Begin replied that Irgun's aim was not to cause loss of life but to hasten the British evacuation of Palestine. After the establishment of the State of Israel in May, 1948, the Irgun, numbering several thousand men, cooperated with Haganah in fighting off Arab invaders.

Open strife briefly erupted between the Irgun and Haganah (by then the official army of the State of Israel) in June, 1948, when the Irgun brought to Israel the SS. *Altalena,* a boat carrying volunteers and munitions for use in the War of Independence. Haganah claimed that it had not authorized the landing and unloading of the boat; its leaders feared that the Irgun was about to start a revolt to topple Israel's provisional government. The Irgun insisted that they had kept the Haganah informed about the boat and that the Haganah leaders with whom they had consulted had raised no objections to the arrangement. The *Altalena* was sunk by Haganah, but contrary to the fears of some, Irgun did not put up a fight against Haganah. On September 21, 1948, the Israel government ordered the Irgun disbanded. Most of its members were incorporated into the Israel army.　　　H.L.

ISAAC (from the Hebrew **Yitzhak,** meaning "laughter"); second of the three partiarchs. In his youth, Isaac had been willing to serve as a sacrifice. He married his cousin Rebecca, who bore him twins, Esau and Jacob. He prospered and the Lord renewed His promise to give Canaan to the Hebrews by telling Isaac: "Unto thee and unto thy seed I give all these lands . . . And I will cause thy seed to multiply as the stars of heaven" (Gen. 36:2, 3, 4). Isaac was 40 years old when he married. By the time his sons were grown, he was feeble and blind. Rebecca was therefore able to trick him into giving the blessing of the firstborn to Jacob instead of the unworthy Esau.

ISAAC ELCHANAN. See SPECTOR, YITZCHAK ELCHANAN.

ISAIAH (Hebrew, meaning "Help of God"). One of the greatest of the major prophets, Isaiah the son of Amoz was a Jerusalem aristocrat. Of his personal life, we find little in the Book of Isaiah. It records only that he was married, had two sons, and that his wife also had the gift of prophecy (Isa. 3:3). He lived in the second half of the eighth century B.C.E., during the reigns of Uzziah, Jotham, Ahaz, and Hezekiah; according to tradition, he was killed during the reign of Manasseh. Three major events are reflected in Isaiah's prophecies: the invasion of the kingdom of Judah* by the armies of Israel and Damascus* for the purpose of forcing King Ahaz into an anti-Assyrian alliance (734 B.C.E.); the destruction of the Kingdom of Israel* by the Assyrians (721 B.C.E.); and Sennacherib's invasion of Judah (701 B.C.E.).

Throughout this time, the small kingdom of Judah faced a two-fold danger: the risk of being swallowed up by the giant neighboring empires, and spiritual destruction through the loss of its belief in one God. Isaiah's political wisdom impelled him to advise strict isolation for Judea, and avoidance of entangling alliances with foreign nations. In chapters forty to sixty, called by some authorities the Second Isaiah, the prophet comforts the exiled, suffering, and despairing people in the great poem beginning "Comfort ye, comfort ye, My people, saith your God" (40:1-44:23).

ISLAM. Islam, or Mohammedanism, the youngest of the three monotheistic religions of our time, was founded by Mohammed, son of Abdallah, a cameldriver of Mecca, Arabia. He was born in the year 571 of the Common Era and died in the year 632. Islam's bible, the Koran, which is in its entirety the work of the founder, is based to a large extent on the Old and New Testaments, whose contents must have been transmitted to Mohammed in oral form colored by the interpretations of the rabbinic commentators and the Church Fathers. Though it incorporates elements of both Judaism and Christianity, and accepts Moses* as well as Jesus as prophets, the faith of Mohammed is closer to Judaism than it is to Christianity. It insists that there is only one God and rejects the idea of a son of God or a Trinity. It allows no sculptured figures or painted pictures to appear in its houses of worship. It forbids its communicants the eating of pork or drinking of intoxicating beverages. It subscribes to the doctrines of life after death, of a day of judgment, of reward and punishment, and of paradise and hell. Mohammed is, according to Islam, the last and greatest of all prophets, and his Koran, which in a number of places deviates from the data of the Hebrew and the Christian Scriptures, is the correct version of the Word of God.

There are today some 200,000,000 Muslims (followers of Islam), living for the most part in a belt of countries extending in a continuous line from Morocco in the west, to Indonesia in the east. Their five fundamental duties are:

1. To declare that there is no God but Allah and that Mohammed is his prophet;
2. To recite the five daily prayers;
3. To give alms;
4. To fast during the month of Ramadan (during the periods of daylight only); and
5. To make the pilgrimage to Mecca, at least once during a lifetime.

Islam is divided into sects, the two most important being that of the Sunnites (traditionalists) and that of the Shi'ites (the more mystically inclined followers of the Caliph Ali). It is theoretically tolerant towards Jews and Christians, but in practice Moselm states treat non-Muslims as second-class citizens.

The position of Jewry under Islam has on the whole been more favorable than it has been under Christian rule. During the Middle Ages, when Muslim civilization reached its height, there was often close cultural collaboration between Jewish and Muslim scientists and thinkers. At the courts of such enlightened Muslim princes as Abdurrahman of Spain* in the tenth century, Saladin the Great of Egypt* in the twelfth century, and Suleiman and Selim of Turkey in the sixteenth century, gifted Jews rose to stations of influence and eminence. That this situation, however, was neither universal nor permanent is evidenced by the fact that Moses Maimonides* was compelled by the fanatical Almohades to leave his native city, when he refused to renounce Judaism in favor of Islam.   S.R.

ISRAEL (Hebrew, meaning "one who strives with God"). The name given to Jacob* after he wrestled with the angel (Gen. 32:29); the collective name of the twelve tribes; later, the name of the northern Kingdom of Israel* (933 B.C.E.-722 B.C.E.), formed when the ten tribes seceded after the death of King Solomon. Eventually, the name came to be applied to the Jewish people as a whole. The land of their origin was known as **Eretz Israel** ("the Land of Israel"); their modern state is named **Medinat Israel.**

ISRAEL DEFENSE FORCES. See ARMY OF ISRAEL.

ISRAEL, GOVERNMENT OF. The State of Israel is a democracy and its government represents the people and is responsible to them in periodic elections. There are a number of forms of democratic government, such as the American or presidential system, and the European, or parliamentary system. The government of Israel is of the parliamentary type.

Legislature. The Knesset,* or Parliament of Israel, is the one-house legislative branch of the government. The 120 representatives to the Knesset are elected to serve four-year terms in free, secret elections. If the government fails to hold the confidence of the Knesset (**see** Executive) an election may be held before the four-year term is over. All citizens, men and women, Christians, Muslims and Jews, 18 years of age or older, have the right to vote. Both the Cabinet and the members of the Knesset may introduce new bills. A bill becomes a law after it has passed three readings and been published in the official **Reshumot,** similar to the American **Congressional Record.**

Proportional Representation. Israel has many political parties and members of the Knesset are elected according to proportional representation. This means that each party presents to the country its own list of candidates, and the voters cast their ballots not for an individual candidate but for the whole party list of its choice. The number of members each party elects to the Knesset is proportional to the percentage of the popular vote it receives. As of 1979, no party in Israel has ever received an absolute majority. As a result, several parties combine to form a working majority in the Knesset. This coalition works out a program on which it must agree and for which it assumes collective responsibility. Severe disagreements among the members of the coalition bring about resignations and the coalition loses its legislative majority. The Knesset must then be dissolved and new elections called.

Executive. The Cabinet is the executive branch of the government, and its task is to carry out and administer the laws enacted by the Knesset. Under the Israel system, the Cabinet is directly responsible to the Knesset. It has no veto power, and can continue in office only so long as it retains the confidence of the Knesset. If defeated in a vote of confidence the Cabinet must resign, and a new one must be formed. If the Knesset can not form a new Cabinet which has its confidence, it must turn to the people and call for new elections.

Prime Minister's Office. The cabinet is headed by the prime minister, who is the chief executive and exercises a great deal of power. His office coordinates the work of all the ministries and administers the civil service. The smooth and efficient working of the whole machinery of government is

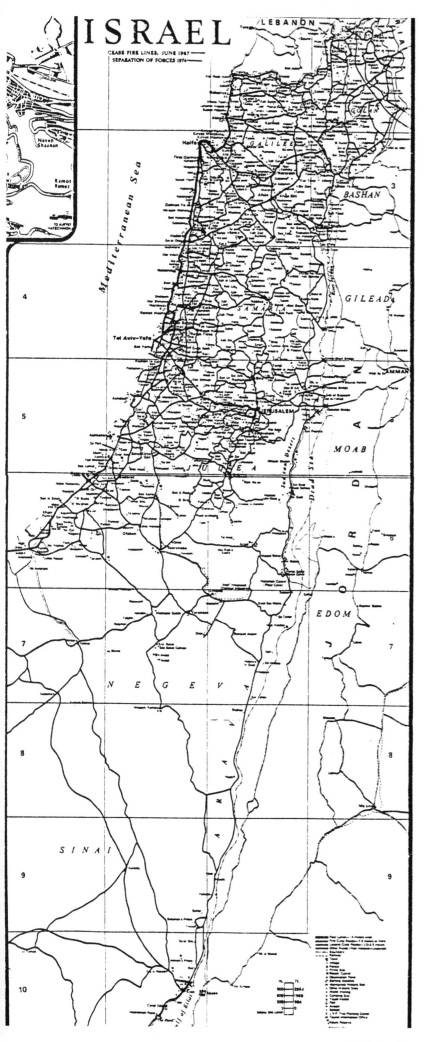

ISRAEL

CEASE FIRE LINES, JUNE 1967 ———
SEPARATION OF FORCES 1974 ———

the responsibility of the prime minister.

Presidency. The President of Israel, unlike the American President, has little actual power. Serving as a symbol of the people's unity, he is not chosen in the competitive general elections, but is elected in a secret ballot by an absolute majority of the Knesset. The president's term of office is five years, but there is no limit on the number of times he may be re-elected. The duties of the president are largely honorary. These include the task to summon a member of the Knesset (usually the leader of the majority party) to form a new government. Upon the recommendation of competent bodies, he appoints judges, diplomatic representatives, the governor of the Bank of Israel, and the comptroller. It is also in his power to grant amnesties to prisoners and to commute their sentences. Major documents, such as treaties with foreign states, are signed by the President together with the prime minister or some other competent minister.

Judiciary. Israel's judicial system is made up of two branches, civil and religious. There are Jewish, Christian, and Moslem religious courts, so that the followers of each religion come under the jurisdiction of a religious court of their own faith. Matters of marriage and divorce are under the sole jurisdiction of the religious courts.

Judicial authority is independent of the executive and legislative branches of government, as is essential in a democracy. Judges are appointed for life, and the appointments are made by the President on the recommendation of an eight-member committee. The President and two members of the Supreme Court, the minister of justice, and one other Cabinet member, two members of the Knesset selected by that entire body, and two lawyers chosen by the Bar Association, serve on that committee.

The highest court of appeal is the ten-member Supreme Court. This court sits also as a high court of justice to which a citizen may bring his complaints against the authorities, and the court acts to protect the rights of the individual citizen. The Supreme Court of Israel, unlike that of the United States, does not have the power to review laws and declare them unconstitutional, because Israel has no written constitution. Israel inherited its legal code when the state came into being in 1948. This code is a mixture of British common law, remnants of Turkish Ottoman law, decrees of the British mandatory administration, and new laws enacted by the Knesset. By a resolution passed by the Knesset on June 13, 1950, a committee on constitution and law was authorized to prepare a draft constitution. As each article of this draft constitution is completed, it must be submitted to the Knesset for approval. When all the articles are approved, they will form the state constitution.　　　　N.B-A.

Immigrants from the Soviet Union arriving in Israel during the Yom Kippur War of 1973.

ISRAEL, STATE OF. The third Jewish Commonwealth came into being on May 14, 1948, almost six months after the United Nations decision to partition Palestine into one Jewish and one Arab state. The proclamation of the State of Israel marked the climax of a half century of political Zionism* that sought to reunite the scattered Jewish people with its ancient "Promised Land."

Boundaries.

In the Bible, the boundaries of the land of Canaan, promised by God to Abraham* and his seed, extended from the Euphrates River to the Red Sea, and from the Mediterranean to the great desert in the east, a geographical and economic unit corresponding roughly to the southern horn of the Fertile Crescent. These ideal boundaries were achieved only by David;* since his time they have shifted.

Geography.

The present area of Israel is only part of the original land and is made up of three longitudinal strips: the coastal plain along the Mediterranean, the range of hills forming the backbone of the country, and the Jordan depression with its prolongation, the Plain of Araba. These strips are divided by the fertile Valley of Jezreel, which separates the mountains of Galilee in the north from the stern hills of Judea in the south, and by the Plain of Beersheba, which forms the northern boundary of the Negev. The Jordan depression follows the Jordan River from its sweet lakes in the north (Huleh and Kinneret*) to the Dead Sea* in

the south, and thence along the barren Araba to the Red Sea port of Eilat.*

Climate.

The climate of Israel varies with the altitude and with the proximity of the various regions to the Mediterranean or the desert; generally it is a Mediterranean climate, characterized by a long, hot, dry summer from April through October, and a cool rainy winter that lasts from November to April. The heaviest rainfall is in the north, the lightest precipitation at Eilat in the south. The coldest month of the year is January, and the hottest month is May or June, when the temperature is capable of rising to 98 degrees in the hill city of Jerusalem,* and as high as 120 degrees in the depth of the Jordan valley. Like the landscape of the country, the climate of Israel is extraordinarily diversified. To go from Safed to Tiberias* in the winter is to leave the shuddering cold of the hills for the sunlit warmth of spring; or, in summer, to exchange in several hours of travel the intolerable heat of Eilat for the cool afternoons of Jerusalem.

Natural Resources.

The natural resources of Israel were enriched in 1955 by the discovery of oil in the Negev.* This southern area provides the country with a large variety of minerals, ranging from copper and manganese to mica and glass-sand. The Dead Sea yields many minerals, particularly large quantities of magnesium, potash, and bromide. The variegated structure of the country affords a rich and

PALESTINE
THE TWELVE
TRIBES

TYRE

NAPHTALI

ACCHO
ASHER

ZEBULUN
MEGIDDO
ISSACHAR

MANASSEH

MANASSEH

JOPPA

DAN
EPHRAIM
BENJAMIN
GAD

ASHKELON

GAZA
JUDAH

REUBEN

KIR-HARESETH

HFK

SIMEON LEVI

diversified agriculture, with crops of grain, vegetables, and fruits. Citrus fruits provide a large part of Israel exports; there is also a wide range of products that are manufactured, processed, or finished in Israel. Not the least of the country's resources is its population, increased by constant immigration. When the State of Israel was established in May 1948, its Jewish population numbered about 650,000. In 1984 the population of Israel was approximately 4,000,000, of whom 3,400,000 were Jews. The Ingathering of the Exiles* policy has resulted in the immigration to Israel of over 1,722,000 Jews from about 80 countries.

History.

From the beginning, Israel's history was determined by its strategic situation at the crossroads of empires and of all the established routes of trade. It connected the Plain of the Nile in the south with Mesopotamia, the land of the Tigris and Euphrates rivers, in the northeast. Canaan's* harbors looked westward to Crete and Greece,* Eilat faced toward the rich lands of the south and Far East, the ancient sources of civilization. About 2300 B.C.E. Sargon I marched down from Mesopotamia and reached the Mediterranean. Later Egypt subdued Canaan, and its governors exacted tribute from the people. The earliest Hebraic association with the Promised Land occurred in the time of the patriarch Abraham, around the twentieth century B.C.E. In the Biblical story of the Covenant,* God gave the land of Canaan to Abraham and his children as an "everlasting possession." The invasion of the Israelites came in the thirteenth century B.C.E. In the Biblical story of the Exodus, Moses began the conquest of Canaan by overcoming the kings of the Amorites in East Jordan, where the tribes of Reuben,* Gad* and half of Manasseh settled. Joshua* completed the conquest, particularly of the northern hill country, dividing the land among the other tribes of Israel. But the plains and coastal regions remained settled by the Canaanites and the seafaring Philistines. These peoples were thorns in the flesh of the Israelite tribes, whom they harassed constantly so long as they remained loosely organized under the rule of Judges.*

First Commonwealth.

During the eleventh century B.C.E. the unification of the tribes into a nation began under Saul.* But it was David* who really unified the Jewish state by his decisive victories over the Philistines,* and by the conquest of the Jebusite stronghold, Jerusalem,* which he made the nation's capital. David's son, Solomon,* consolidated his father's gains; his reign marked the climax of the independent history of Israel. Solomon's empire stretched from Mount Hermon in the north to Eilat on the Red Sea, and from the plain in the east to the Mediterranean. He trained his people, hitherto only farmers and shepherds, in the arts of building, crafts, and trade. Solomon built a navy and sent his ships as far as Ophir* and Tarshish to bring back precious cargoes. But although he enriched his kingdom, the extravagance of Solomon's court and his passion for building imposed a heavy tax burden upon the people. Revolt broke out during the reign of Solomon's son, Rehoboam, and the country divided into two small kingdoms, Judah* and Israel.* The vassal states which David had subjugated now began to break free. The giant empires to the north and south awaited their opportunity to pounce. The Kingdom of Israel, though three times greater in territory and with twice the population of Judah, was the first to fall. It surrendered to the Assyrians* in 722 B.C., and most of its residents were carried off into captivity. The rest fled to Judah. As a hill country, separated from Egypt* by the desert and sheltered by Israel on the north,

Judah was easier to defend, but it fell at last in 586 B.C. to Nebuchadnezzar, king of Babylonia, who deported a great part of the population.

The conquered people of Judah did not merge with the mighty Babylonian nation, like the other peoples which had been carried off into captivity. This was because in exile they learned to value and understand the teachings of their great prophets, Isaiah,* Jeremiah,* Ezekiel,* and the others. The exiles became convinced that just as the prophecies of destruction had been fulfilled, so would the prophecy of a return to their land. And they accepted the prophetic vision of an ultimate age of peace and justice, not only for themselves but for the entire world. It was in the Babylonian exile that the people absorbed the idea of a Messiah, as described in the Book of Isaiah.

The First Return.

Thus it came about that when Cyrus* of Persia liberated the subject peoples from the Babylonian yoke in 538 B.C., a movement to return to Zion developed under Zerubbabel,* Ezra,* and Nehemiah.* In the desolated land, occupied by hostile strangers, the Judeans, as they were now called, labored with a tool in one hand and a sword in the other to rebuild the Temple in Jerusalem and a wall around the city. During the period that followed, the high priests instead of kings ruled the people, scribes took the place of the prophets as the teachers of the people, and the synagogue* developed as a permanent institution. The Persian rule ended with the conquest of the Persian empire by Alexander the Great* (356-323 B.C.E.). After Alexander's death, his empire was divided. Judea then fell first to the Ptolemies of Egypt,* then to the Seleucids of Syria.* But the Jews, too weak to resist, remained almost indifferent to the changes of overlords. Concentrating upon their inner life, they developed religious institutions and great religious books, and collected and edited the books of the Bible. It was only when Antiochus, King of Syria, tampered with their religion that the peaceable people were stirred to rebellion. Led by the Hasmoneans,* they hurled the defilers from the land in 165 B.C.E. Twenty-six years later Simon the Hasmonean declared Judea a free commonwealth.

The Second Commonwealth.

The Hasmonean dynasty not only restored the land of Israel to its ancient boundaries but also increased the population by converting the mixed population of Galileans and the Edomites* to Judaism. A powerful kingdom might have developed; but in 63 B.C.E. the Romans invaded Judea. An unequal struggle ended in the complete destruction of Jerusalem and the Second Commonwealth in 70 C.E. The fires of rebellion were rekindled from their embers by Bar Kokhba* in 132-35 C.E.

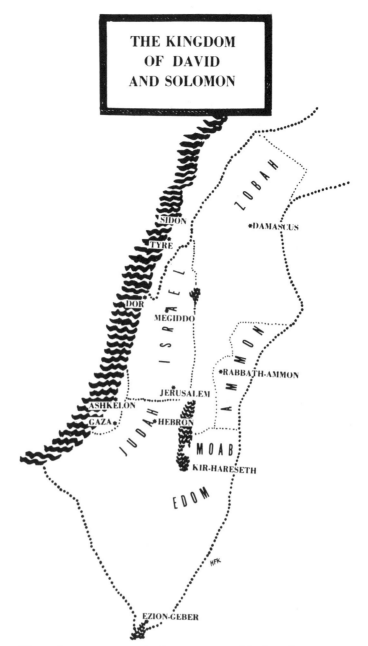

THE KINGDOM OF DAVID AND SOLOMON

Then they were quenched once more, this time for nearly 2,000 years.

The Long Night.

The land was now called Palestine* by the Romans to erase all Jewish associations, and Jerusalem was rebuilt as a soldiers' colony and renamed Aelia Capitolina. Yet the invisible chains that bound the Jews to Israel were never broken. With Jerusalem gone, a new center of Jewish study was built in Yavneh,* and a scholarly governing body, the Sanhedrin,* was created. As the Romans persecuted the tiny community, the center was moved north to Tiberias* where the Mishnah, a systematic code of law, was completed (200 C.E.). The situation worsened when Rome adopted Christianity in 320 C.E., for now the land became holy to Christians. Persecutions continued with unabated cruelty under the Byzantines of the Eastern Empire, until the Arab invasion of 636 opened the era of Islam.* The Muslims found only a few Jews in Palestine. The first centuries of

Muslim rule were marked by prosperity and a measure of tolerance. Lacking experience in civil life, the Muslims at first engaged Jews as administrators. In time, however, a decline set in as Arab power weakened. In the eleventh century the land came under the control of the Seljuk Turks, who molested the Christians and provoked the Crusades.* The hundred years of the Crusaders in Palestine, beginning in 1099, were a long nightmare to the Jewish community; nearly all the Jews of Palestine were slaughtered during the period of the Latin Kingdom of Jerusalem. This period ended when Saladin vanquished the Christians in 1187, and called on the Muslims and Jews to resettle in the land. Actually, Palestine was never completely without a Jewish population.

In 1211 the Palestine Jewish community was strengthened by the arrival of a group headed by 300 rabbis from France* and England.* Their piety was equalled only by their poverty, and their need gave rise to the system of Halukkah*—funds gathered throughout the world for the support of the Jewish community in Palestine. Still the land had no peace. In 1260 Mongol hordes poured in from the north, pillaging and murdering as they advanced, until they were halted at Gilboa. Once again the land was laid waste, and in Jerusalem there remained only two Jews. Then Rabbi Moses ben Nahman* (Nahmanides) of Gerona settled in Jerusalem. He became the father of modern Jerusalem's Jewish community; since Nahmanides' day the Holy City has never been without Jews.

In 1516, Palestine was conquered by the Ottoman Turks. About that time many of the Jews expelled from Spain in 1492 found refuge in Palestine. The Spanish Jews brought with them knowledge and skill, and one of them, Don Joseph Nasi, in 1563, attempted to create a colony of Spanish refugees in Tiberias as a starting point for the resettlement of the entire country. Some of the exiles settled in Safed, where they created a center of Kabbalah.* Until that time most of the Jewish population of Israel had been of Sephardic,* or Mediterranean origin. But with the development of the Hasidic movement in Eastern Europe, Ashkenazic* Jews began to trickle into the country. A forerunner of this movement was Rabbi Judah the Pious, from Poland, who came to Jerusalem in 1700 at the head of a group of disciples. Their synagogue was destroyed by the Arabs. Later rebuilt, it became known as the Hurva ("Ruins") Synagogue, a famous landmark until its destruction in the War of Independence (1948). As decay ate into the Ottoman Empire, the local pashas oppressed and impoverished the Jewish community of Palestine; but the community was again strengthened when a group of Hasidim from Europe settled in Safed in 1777 and later in Tiberias. These newcomers formed the nucleus of the present Ashkenazic community of Israel. They were followed at the beginning of the eighteenth century by groups of "Mitnagdim"—opponents of Hasidism*—who flocked to Jerusalem; later, more Hasidim settled in Hebron. Between 1827 and 1875, the philanthropist Sir Moses Montefiore* tried to help the Jewish community by constructive projects. The French Alliance Israélite Universelle* set up an agricultural school at Mikveh Israel* in 1870 and trade school in the cities. These efforts were the beginning of the modern resettlements of the country.

The Lovers of Zion and the First Aliyah.

The pogroms in Russia* and growing anti-Semitism* in Western Europe, in an age when liberalism was being paid lip service, finally brought Jews to the conviction that as a nation, the only road open to them was the road back to Zion. Out of this conviction developed modern Zionism.* In 1882, a year after the murderous attacks upon the Jews in Russia, the movement of **Hoveve Zion*** ("Lovers of Zion") developed. The object of this movement was the acquisition of land in Palestine and the promotion of Jewish settlement there. The newcomers founded Rishon-Le-Zion* (in 1882) and later Zikhron Yaacov. Among the first settlers of thee colonies were the Bilu,* a group of young Jewish students from Russia who founded Gedera in 1884. The settlers of the First Aliyah* endured terrible ordeals resulting from their own ignorance of agriculture, as well as from malaria, excessive poverty, and the hostility of their neighbors, until most of them were taken under the wing of Baron Edmond de Rothschild,* of Paris. This great philanthropist did more than any other individual man for the practical resettlement of Palestine.

Celebrating the 70th anniversary of the founding of Zikhron Yaacov in 1952.

Political Zionism and the Second Aliyah.

It was not until 1897 that political Zionism was formulated by Theodor Herzl,* the father of the idea of the Jewish State. He rekindled the national fervor of the Jews throughout the world, and set in motion a chain of events that culminated fifty years later in the establishment of the State of Israel. Between 1904 and 1914, the Second Aliyah, consisting mainly of young people, came streaming to Palestine from Russia* and Poland.* Though comparatively few in number, it was the settlers of the First and Second Aliyot who laid the agricultural, economic, and political foundations of modern Israel. Each new village was in fact a cell of the future state. The settlers waged a struggle against primitive conditions, hostile neighbors and Turkish obstructionism.

The Balfour Declaration* and the Rebuilding of the Land.

The First World War, in which Turkey was allied with Germany* and Austria,* seriously set back the movement of Jewish upbuilding and resettlement. Much of the Jewish population was deported, and starvation and epidemics harried the remainder. Then came the issuance of the Balfour Declaration in 1917, promising a national home for the Jews in Palestine. On a great upsurge of hope, the Third Aliyah established new agricultural cooperatives. The Fourth Aliyah was composed mainly of tradespeople, manufacturers, and business people with some capital for investments. Tel Aviv* and Haifa* grew in population and many new industries were established. School systems and hospitals were developed, and the Jewish community of Palestine organized itself for democratic self-government. The Keren Kayemet, or Jewish National Fund,* provided the land for the Halutzim,* and the Keren Hayesod, the Palestine Foundation Fund, provided the credit and other forms of assistance for the new immigrants.

A reversal in British policy, due partly to the recurrence of Arab outbreaks, was reflected in the shearing away of Transjordan from the area of the Jewish national home, in 1922. The mid-1920's saw economic and political setbacks. Arab hostility to Jewish settlement of Palestine was inflamed by Arab leaders. The British administration either did not see, or closed its eyes, to the threatening danger. In 1929, Arab riots broke out in Jerusalem, Hebron, Safed, and in other parts of the country; Jewish lives and property were destroyed. In this new political situation, the British whittled down further the original meaning of the Balfour Declaration. The major provisions of the Passfield White Paper cut down Jewish immigration drastically, and stopped altogether the purchase of agricultural land by Jews. A storm of protest and indignation from Jews and non-Jews alike broke

This Danish girl came to Israel as a volunteer farm worker and married a member of a kibbutz.

out. As a result, the worst features of the Passfield White Paper were modified.

The situation in Palestine quieted down, and there were no further serious Arab disturbances until 1936. The country escaped the world-wide economic depression, and progressed. Fleeing from the lengthening shadow of the Nazi terror in Germany, thousands of Jews came into Palestine. This was the Fifth Aliyah of 1933-1939, when 300,000 newcomers were absorbed by the Jewish community. In addition, 55,000 adolescent children of the Youth Aliyah* came into the country. These immigrants had to adjust quickly to a new climate, a new language, Hebrew, to new jobs, and to a people for whom hard menial work was part of their "Religion of Labor." In the meantime, Arab riots broke out anew. From 1936 to 1939, Arab terrorists attacked Jewish settlements, burned fields and forests, and murdered and intimidated Arabs friendly to Jews. British counteraction against the terror was neither consistent nor forceful enough. Nor would the British permit the Haganah,* the

The Knesset building in Jerusalem.

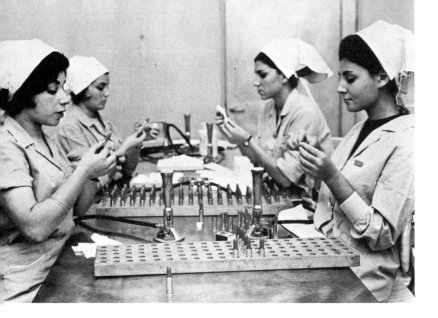

British Labor Government that 100,000 Jewish survivors of Nazi concentration camps be admitted without delay into Palestine. The British suggested, in reply, an Anglo-American Committee of Inquiry, to which President Truman agreed. This committee subscribed to the recommendation to admit 100,000 immigrants forthwith, but the British again rejected it. Matters came to a head in the United Nations, which decided in November 1947 to partition Palestine into separate Jewish and Arab states. The Arabs reacted to this announce-

The vineyards of Judea and Samaria provide the grapes for the wine industry of Israel.

Jewish militia, to protect the settlements. A period of self-defense and of "illegal" immigration followed; this activity was intesified during the Second World War, when the Jews of Palestine strove to save as many Jews as possible from the fires of Europe. At the same time, the Jewish settlement contributed actively to the Allied war effort, serving not only as a source of industrial supplies but also as a fighting force in North Africa and in the European campaigns.

By the end of the war the Jewish population of Palestine had risen to 500,000 as against 1,000,000 Palestine Arabs. The resurgence of Jewish national aspirations after the war was opposed by the British, whose vacillation further encouraged Arab opposition. Numerous commissions were sent to investigate the Palestine situation and make recommendations. President Harry S. Truman recommended in a pesonal message to the newly elected

ment by attempting to terrorize the Jewish community through attacks on settlements, ambushes on roads, and sabotage in cities. The British administration began to disintegrate, although it had undertaken to function until May 15, 1948. But, despite the prevailing chaos and terror, the Jews of Palestine did not panic. They kept the situation under control through their self-defense organization, the Haganah, forerunner of the Army of Israel.*

The Third Commonwealth.

On May 14, 1948, the State of Israel was proclaimed in Tel Aviv. Ten minutes after the proclamation, President Truman extended **de facto** recognition to the new State. The five surrounding Arab states immediately attacked Israel from the

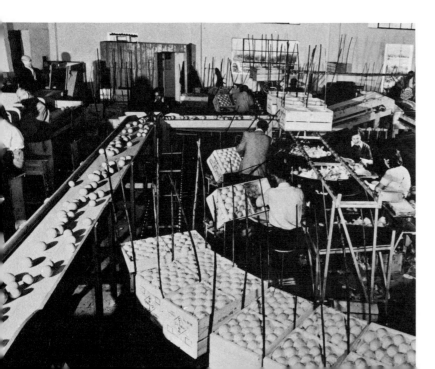

Oranges and other citrus fruits are among Israel's major export products.

land, sea, and air. Urged on by their leaders, who told them that they could all return after the Jews had been driven out, most of the Arab population fled the country. Eventually, however Israel's enemies were driven off, and an armistice was signed in 1949. After that time, an uneasy peace prevailed in the area. Notwithstanding political tensions, a fierce Arab boycott, and sporadic border "incidents," the new republic made remarkable progress. Schools and universities have helped to weld together a multilingual mass of immigrants from every continent in the world into a Hebrew-speaking community. The number of agricultural settlements has increased to over 700. New industrial crops have been introduced. Agricultural development has been paralleled by industrial expansion. New sources of water and oil have been tapped, the Huleh swamps have been drained, and water has been piped from the Yarkon River to the thirsty Negev.* Though still beset by meanacing enemies and struggling in a morass of problems and difficulties, economic, political and cultural, Israel is again a nation and a land, the Third Commonwealth of the Jewish people.

This basic unity was demonstrated effectively in a few autumn days in 1956. Israel's long borders had been subjected for years to sabotage, pillage and murdering raids, particularly by "fedayeen" (commandos) from Egyptian bases and from the Gaza strip. Harassed beyond endurance, Israel undertook a lightning four-day campaign on October 29, 1956, which resulted in the conquest of the Sinai Peninsula and of the Gaza strip. The enormous quantities of arms and material, as well as documents captured by the Israeli Army, revealed that the area was being prepared as a springboard for an Egyptian assault on Israel. Following a United Nations request, Israel withdrew its army from Sinai and Gaza.

When these attacks, or Israel's retaliations, were brought before the Security Council of the United Nations, Israel never received justice, primarily because of the constant hostility of the Soviet Union, which could use the veto right to block the passage of any decision that would displease the Arab governments.

The situation steadily deteriorated until, in June 1967, Israel struck back at the hostile Arab nations surrounding her (see SIX-DAY WAR). This war, which took less than a week, ended in a brilliant victory for Israel. However, the Arabs refused to make peace with Israel and even to recognize her existence. On Yom Kippur, 1973, Egypt and Syria launched an attack on the country (see YOM KIPPUR WAR). Following the cease-fire imposed by the United Nations, the United States made strenuous initiatives toward a permanent peace in the Middle East.

The Diamond Exchange Buildings on the Ramat-Gan Highway.

Courtesy Israel Office of Information.

On May 29, 1974, Syria, the most implacable of Israel's enemies, agreed to sign a disengagement pact with Israel under terms similar to those agreed upon by Israel and Egypt. On June 5, 1974, the agreement between Israel and Syria was signed in Geneva.

None of these agreements, however, even remotely implied a full peace and Arab recognition of Israel's existence.

In May, 1977, an important political change took place in Israel. The Labor Alignment which had led Israel's governing coalition without interruption since the establishment of the state suffered an electoral defeat and was replaced by Likud, a non-socialist parliamentary block led by Herut, successor of the right-wing Revisionist movement in Zionism. Menaham Begin,* became prime minister. In November of that year Begin became the first Israeli prime minister to meet officially with an Arab chief of state when Egypt's President Anwar el-Sadat paid a surprise visit to Jerusalem to discuss the possibility of peace with Israel. At a meeting at Camp David, Md. in September, 1978 between Begin and Sadat under the auspices of U.S. President Jimmy Carter, a framework for a peace treaty between Israel and Egypt was drawn up, and on March 26, 1979, the two countries signed a peace agreement in Washington, D.C. Under this treaty, which promised the establishment of normal relations between Israel and Egypt, Israel returned to Egypt the entire Sinai peninsula which Israel had occupied in the Six-Day War. As of mid-1979, none

Concert of the Israel Philharmonic Orchestra at Mann Auditorium, Tel Aviv.

of the other Arab countries has shown willingness to make peace with Israel or even to recognize her existence, but it was hoped that if subsequent negotiations between Israel and Egypt went well, these other countries might be persuaded to follow Egypt's example so that peace will come to Israel and the entire Middle East. (**See also** LEBANON.)

ISRAELS, JOSEPH (1824-1911). Artist. this Dutch Jew was among the first painters to free his palette from the influence of the dark studio and to execute his sketches in the open air. He was also among the first to capture the spirit of the common people, the humble fishermen in little villages, to paint them at work and at leisure, in happiness and grief. Israels painted many Jewish subjects; notable among them is **A Son of the Old People** (a sad old-clothes dealer sitting before his modest shop), and **The Old Scribe,** based on a sketch he made while traveling through Tangier, North Africa.

ISSACHAR (Hebrew, meaning "reward bringer"). Fifth son of Jacob* and Leah; ancestor of the tribe that settled on the west bank of the Jordan near the Sea of Galilee.

ISSERLES, MOSES. See SHULHAN ARUKH.

ITALY. Italy's Jewish community is the oldest with a continuous history in Europe. During the second century B.C.E. there were Jewish farmers and traders in Rome,* Naples, Venice, and other cities.

For several hundred years they shared the rights that Rome liberally granted to members of conquered nations. When Christianity became the state religion in the fourth century, these privileges were revoked. Restrictions were relaxed, however, after the fall of Rome. By the ninth century Jews were playing an important part in the commercial life of Italy. In addition to trade, they worked in all the handicrafts and professions; it was only later that Jews were forced into the field of money-lending. During the early Middle Ages, the prosperity and freedom of the Jews permitted the establishment of great academies of learning at Bari and Otranto, where Italian Jewish grammarians, Talmudists, philosophers, physicians, and poets became famous.

Although many of the decrees which plagued other medieval Jewries had their origin in Rome, Italian Jewry was long spared their enforcement. Not until the thirteenth century did Pope Innocent III succeed in implementing discriminatory measures. Yet even these measures, and the popular outbreaks that became frequent in the following centuries, did not succeed in crippling the economic and cultural life of the Jews. Italy was then organized in independent city-states; Rome did not have the power to enforce its decrees in the powerful commercial centers where Jewish merchants contributed to the wealth of the community. In addition, the Renaissance spirit of tolerance had already been born. Papal Rome herself found room for a thriving center of Jewish culture. Immanuel ben Solomon of Rome* (ca. 1270-1330) dedicated Hebrew verses to his friend Dante; scholars like Pico della Mirandola, studied Hebrew with Jewish colleagues in the faculties of medicine, law, and philosophy at the great Italian universities. Between 1230 and 1550, poets, scholars and philosophers writing in Hebrew, Latin, and Italian created a "golden age" of Jewish learning paralleled only in Muslim Spain.*

By the middle of the sixteenth century, the flowers of this renaissance began to fade. Italy was torn by civil strife, and fell prey to French and Spanish invaders. The Spanish Jews who had swelled the Italian community after their exile from Spain in 1492 were overtaken by the Inquisition,* which accompanied the Spanish invaders to Italy. Rome herself, threatened by the Reformation in the north, adopted the fanatical tactics of the Spanish Inquisition to stamp out heresy at home. The expulsion of the Jewish community from Genoa was the first sign of the change. Soon after, Pope Julius III (1550-1555) ordered the Talmud* burned in the streets of Rome, and nearly succeeded in expelling the Jews from the Eternal City. His successor confined the Jews of the Papal States to ghettos. As part of a campaign to convert the Jews to Catholicism, the entire community was forced to attend special church sermons.

Many Jews fled from Rome; those who remained suffered from discrimination. The leadership of Italian Jewry then fell to the communities of Venice, Ferrara, and Mantua. A printing press was founded at Mantua, where a new edition of the Talmud appeared in 1590. Also published were popular and scholarly works by men like Azariah dei Rossi of Ferrara. (See ROSSI, AZARIAH BEN MOSES DEI.) Within several decades, however, Spanish and Austrian invaders decimated the communities of Ferrara and Mantua as well, leaving the Jews of Venice to bear the burden of Jewish culture. For a century and a half Venetian Jewry produced a line of distinguished scholars and poets. The last and greatest of these was Moses Haim Luzzato,* Kabbalist, linguist, scholar and poet. Leghorn (Livorno), where the Jews had some autonomy until the nineteenth century, remained a center of Kabbalistic learning throughout.

Napoleon's conquest of Italy in 1797 was the first step in the emancipation of Italian Jewry. As in France,* he convened a "Sanhedrin" to organize the affairs of the Jewish community, and proceeded to grant full civil rights to the Jews. Napoleon's defeat, and the strong reaction that followed, lead to a revival of the Inquisition. The nationalist movement, which sought the liberation of Italy from foreign rule and the unification of its many states, soon provided a rallying point for Jewish hopes. Espousing the cause of civil rights for all, it drew many young Jews to its ranks. With the final unification of all Italy under King Victor Emmanuel II in 1870, Jews were again granted full citizenship.

The Jews of Italy were grateful for their freedom. Having fought valiantly for her independence, they remained ardent patriots, and threw themselves vigorously into public life. Within a short time they were finding important positions in government, politics, and society. The urge to take full advantage of their newly acquired rights was so strong that large sections of Italian Jewry began to lose touch with the Jewish community. Intermarriage became common, especially among the upper classes, and the number of conversions was great. Though closely organized communities remained, and scholars maintained the "enlightened" tradition of Jewish scholarship established by Samuel David Luzzato* earlier in the century, the threat of assimilation was serious.

But the period of unrestricted freedom was short-lived. The Italian Fascist movement was founded in 1919; in 1923, Benito Mussolini came to power. At first Mussolini fought the anti-Semitic elements in his party, which was supported by many influential Jews. In the hope that the ties of Italian Jews with other Mediterranean and Balkan Jewish communities would be of use in his plan for imperialist expansion, he encouraged Zionism,* and helped German-Jewish refugees settle in Italy. When Hitler came to power in 1933 Mussolini took a stand against Nazi anti-Semitism. By 1936, however, Mussolini found himself in need of German aid for his Abyssinian war, and began to adopt the Nazi racist doctrines. By the outbreak of the Second World War, Jews had been banned from the army, government service, professions, and many branches of trade. Jewish schools, which Mussolini had encouraged and subsidized, were closed; all large-scale Jewish businesses were confiscated, and Jews were forbidden to hold land of any value. Toward the end of the war, when the Italian defense system had broken down and German troops moved into the country, Hitler proposed the deportation and destruction of Italy's Jewry. Official anti-Semitism* had never struck deep roots among the people, however, and the Italian Jews found protection among their neighbors. Then the Allied forces invaded, and the war was over before Hitler's plan could be executed.

With the overthrow of Mussolini, Jewish rights were restored. After the war, Italy was the temporary home of over 35,000 refugees, all but 1,500 of whom have left for Israel and other countries. Because of its location, Italy was for a while the chief sailing point for "illegal" immigrants on their way to Israel.

Today there are approximately 39,000 Jews permanently settled in Italy — a little below the prewar total. They are organized under the law of 1930 which requires that all Jews affiliate with the official Jewish community, to which they pay taxes. Rome has the largest concentration, with 10,000; Milan follows with 9,000. The rest of the Jewish population is scattered in twenty-one other cities, only six of which have communities of more than 1,000. This dispersion again raises the problem of assimilation*—a problem which community leaders hope to solve by means of an intensive educational program. The educational system now includes Jewish day schools in eight cities, a rabbinical seminary in Rome, and special courses for Hebrew teachers. In Rome, a vocational training school is maintained by ORT.* A monthly magazine is published by the community. There is an active Zionist organization, and close ties are maintained with Israel.*

In recent years, Italy has been almost completely free of anti-Semitic activities, and Jews have again achieved prominence in national life. Writers like Alberto Moravia, Paolo Milano and Carlo Levi are leading literary figures. Jews are prominent in the professions and several branches of the economy. As the result of conditions during and after the war, there is a preponderance of peddlers and petty tradesmen.   B.H.

IYAR. Eighth month of the Jewish civil calendar. This month falls during the Omer.* Israel's Independence Day is celebrated on the fifth of Iyar.

J

JABOTINSKY, VLADIMIR (ZEEV) (1880-1940). Writer, founder of Revisionist* Zionism.* Vladimir Jabotinsky came of an assimilated Jewish family in Odessa, Russia. He studied law and was steeped in Russian literature. In his student days he won recognition as a Russian writer and orator. Yet at the age of 25, he was already a leading figure among Russian Zionists. During the early part of World War I, he served as war correspondent in France for an important Moscow newspaper. When Turkey* entered the war in 1915 and drove many Palestinian Jews into exile, Jabotinsky conceived the idea of a Jewish Legion* which would fight on the side of the Allies and help capture Palestine* from the Turks. In his efforts to establish such a legion he approached the British, Italian, and French authorities. Success came finally in June 1917, when the British officially announced the formation of Jewish battalions to serve with the British Royal Fusiliers in the Palestine campaign. Jabotinsky, who enlisted as a private, was the only foreigner to be made an honorary lieutenant by the British during World War I.

Vladimir Jabotinsky
by Elias Grossman. Courtesy Zionist Revisionists, New York.

After the end of the war, Jabotinsky remained in Palestine, and in 1919, when the country was threatened with Arab riots, he joined Pinhas

Jacob's Dream, from an old engraving. "And he dreamed, and he beheld a ladder set up on the earth and the top of it reached to heaven; and behold the angels of God ascending and descending on it." (Genesis 28:12).

Russian and from English, French, and Italian into Hebrew. Jabotinsky was a master of prose in English, French and Yiddish. As an orator he was dramatic and incisive, with a magnetic personality.

N.B-A.

JACOB (from the Hebrew, meaning, "One who supplants another"). The younger of the twin sons of Isaac* and Rebecca; third of the Biblical patriarchs.* Jacob bought the family birthright from his elder brother, Esau, "for a mess of pottage," and with his mother's help received the blessing of the firstborn from his father, whose eyes were dimmed by age. Jacob then fled from Esau's anger to his mother's father, Bethuel, in Padan Aram. On his way he slept in a field with a stone for his pillow, and dreamed a strange dream: he saw a ladder reaching up to heaven, and angels ascending and descending it. God promised Jacob that he would inherit the land upon which he had slept. When Jacob arose in the morning, he called the place Bethel, meaning "House of God."

In Haran, Jacob served his uncle Laban for 20 years, marrying Laban's two daughters Leah and

Rutenberg in organizing a Jewish self-defense corps. On April 4, 1920, Arab rioters attacked the Jewish quarter in old Jerusalem,* and the self-defense corps tried to defend the area. The British arrested them and later tried them before a military court. Jabotinsky and twenty comrades were sentenced to twenty years' imprisonment. There was great public protest, and after three and a half months in the Acre prison, Jabotinsky was freed. He returned to England* and joined the Executive of the World Zionist Organization.* On this body he differed sharply with its leader, Chaim Weizmann,* whom he considered too conciliatory toward Britain, and resigned in 1921. In 1925 he organized the Revisionist Zionist party. His program pressed for the speedy creation of a Jewish state on both sides of the Jordan. The last years of Jabotinsky's life were shadowed by the rise of Hitler to power in Germany* and by the beginning of World War II. He who had fought the British for so long because they obstructed the realization of the Jewish homeland in Palestine now pleaded for a Jewish army to fight by the side of England against Hitler. He died in 1940, before the formation of the Jewish Brigade.

Jabotinsky was a brilliant, versatile writer in six languages. He wrote a novel, **Samson the Nazirite,** and translated voluminously from Hebrew into

Jacob in the house of Laban.

Rachel; then he started back to the land of his fathers. He took with hm his wives and children, his flocks and rich possessions. On the banks of the river Jabbok he wrestled all night with an angel and received the name of Israel.* His brother Esau came to meet him, and Jacob made peace with Esau. Later, on the way to Bethel, God appeared to Jacob and confirmed his promise to give him the Land of Canaan as an inheritance. There, too, his beloved wife, Rachel, died giving birth to his twelfth and youngest son, Benjamin.* Jacob lived in Canaan with his twelve sons and prospered, till grief came to him in his old age: his favorite son, Joseph,* disappeared, having been sold by his envious brothers as a slave to Ishmaelite traders, who took him to Egypt.* Eventually Jacob and his sons settled in Egypt, where Joseph had become Pharaoh's second-in-command. Jacob died in Egypt in his one hundred and forty-seventh year. His body was borne to Canaan, where he was buried in the patriachial burial place, the cave of Machpelah.*

JACOBI, KARL GUSTAV JACOB (1804-1851). German mathematician, born of Jewish parents. Along with the Norwegian, Abel, Jacobi established the theory of elliptic functions. Jacobi was one of the greatest mathematicians of all time.

JAFFA. Biblical Joppa. Situated on a steep rocky promontory 116 feet above the sea, it was Israel's* oldest seaport and the natural outlet for Jerusalem,* with whose fate it was linked. King Hiram of Tyre floated the cedars of Lebanon* down to Jaffa for the building of Solomon's Temple.* From Jaffa the prophet Jonah* set out for Tarshish. Although allotted to Dan* during the conquest of Canaan, Jaffa did not become a Jewish city until after the Maccabean* victory. Ships from Jaffa played a part in the Bar Kokhba* insurrection against Rome. Jaffa figures in the history of the Crusades* and in Napoleon's invasion. Its modern

Jewish community dates to the early nineteenth century. Jaffa remained, however, an Arab town with a Jewish minority until captured by Israel in 1948 and incorporated into Tel Aviv.* Most of the Arabs fled, leaving only 4,000 behind. The city has become a center for the new Jewish immigrants. The "Jaffa orange" developed in the costal area of Israel is internationally famous.

JAPAN. A constitutional monarchy consisting of four main islands, and many smaller ones, lying off the northeast coast of Asia. By the ninth century C.E., Jewish merchants from the West were trading in Japan, but no permanent colony had been established. Legends that some Japanese clans are of Jewish origin may refer to the descendants of these early visitors. After Japan was opened to the West by Commodore Perry in 1854, Jews came there from Europe, Turkey,* Iraq, and India.* The first synagogue was built in Nagasaki in the 1890's. It belonged to Russian Jews. A Sephardic* colony was soon settled in Kobe, and is still there. Yokohama was settled next, then Tokyo. Jewish refugees from Germany arrived during the 1930's. At first there was no anti-Semitism,* but Japan's signing of the Axis Pact with the Nazis brought familiar trouble. Many Polish and Lithuanian Jews, including the entire Mir yeshiva, en route to the Americas were caught in Japan by World War II. They were sent to the Hongkow ghetto in Shanghai. Although some Jews left Japan at the end of the war, others entered when the Communist conquest of China* imperiled Jewish life there. The arrival of American Jewish chaplains to serve the occupation forces stimulated Japanese interest in Judaism. Several Japan-Israel Friendship Societies were formed. In 1984 there were 800 Jews in Japan.

JAVITS, JACOB K. (1904-   ). United States Senator, attorney. Javits grew up on New York's Lower East Side, of immigrant parents. After receiving a law degree from New York University in 1926, he was admitted to the New York State Bar in 1927, and practiced law in New York until his appointment as special assistant to the chief of the Chemical Warfare Service. He began his political

Senator Jacob K. Javits with Rabbi C.H. Lipschitz, U.S. Ambassador to Israel Kenneth B. Keating, and the late President Lyndon B. Johnson.

Jeremiah Proclaims the Law—sixteenth-century French engraving by C. P. Marillier. "Then the Lord said unto me, Proclaim all these words in the cities of Judah, and in the streets of Jerusalem, saying, Hear ye the words of this covenant and do them." (Jeremiah 11:6).

career in 1946, when he was elected to the United States House of Representatives from New York City's 21st Congressional District. In 1954, Javits was elected New York State Attorney General, and in 1956, United States Senator from New York. Throughout his career, Javits has favored increased foreign aid, national housing, and rent control legislation. He has drafted a Selective Immigration Act establishing an immigration quota based on skills of prospective immigrants rather than their national origins. Javits has taken a consistently pro-Israel stand. He is a member of the Board of Overseers of the Jewish Theological Seminary of America.*

JEREMIAH (c. 626-585 B.C.E.). The second of the major prophets, his book is a masterpiece of Biblical literature. Jeremiah, son of Hilkiah, a priest of Anathoth, witnessed the tragic events in the history of Judea* that ended in the destruction of Jerusalem* and in the exile to Babylonia.* His prophecies foretell the doom of his people as punishment for their sins. Jeremiah envisions a universal God governing all mankind, forgiving even those sins that had been "written with a pen of iron and a point of diamond." The people will survive only if they uphold justice, and each person is responsible for his own acts. At the end of days the Lord will bring the people of Israel back from their captivity, and a righteous Israel will dwell in safety in its own land (Jer. 33:14-16).

JERICHO (Hebrew, meaning "the Moon City" or "Fragrance"). Also called the City of Palms in the Bible. Situated five miles north of the Dead Sea,* Jericho is a rich tropical oasis in the salt encrusted plain, nourished by the springs of Elisha and other rivulets. It is 820 feet below sea level. The key to Jerusalem and all Canaan* from the east, it was stormed by Joshua* and all the succeeding conquerors attacking the land from that direction. Destroyed and rebuilt many times, modern Jericho stands on the foundation of the Crusaders' city. It is now a small town where a thousand farmers live in mud huts. Orange groves and banana trees replace the balsams, sycamores, and palms of antiquity.

JERUSALEM. The capital of Israel, ever since David* established his throne there about 1000 B.C.E., and the Holy City of Judaism, from the time David had the Ark of the Covenant* borne in triumph into Jerusalem and Solomon* built the Temple* to house it on Mount Moriah. Jerusalem has also been called Zion, the citadel of justice and faith, since the days of the prophets Isaiah* and Jeremiah.*

Fall of the Walls of Jericho. (18th century engraving).

Modern Jerusalem State of Israel Bonds.

The city is situated in the heart of the hills of Judea, more than 2,000 feet high. It sits at the crossroads where the highway running from north to south intersects the road leading from the sea to the Jordan. A triad of hills—Zion, Moriah, and Mount of Olives—separated from the other hills by the deep ravines of Hinnom and Kidron, make Jerusalem a natural stronghold.

View of the Old City of Jerusalem.

Jerusalem's origins are lost in the mists of antiquity. It was already a center of Canaanite civilization in Abraham's* time (about 1900 B.C.E.). It was twice laid waste, once by Nebuchadnezzar of Babylonia* in 586 B.C.E., and again by Titus of Rome in 70 C.E. It was restored by the Jews 70 years after the first destruction. The Hasmoneans made it their capital and rebuilt the Temple, and Herod the Great adorned and fortified it. After the second destruction Jerusalem remained in ruins for over a century, until the Emperor Hadrian in 134 C.E. turned it into a colony for Roman veterans and renamed it Aelia Capitolina. Jews were prohibited from entering the city on pain of death. When the Romans adopted Christianity, however, they not only restored Jerusalem's ancient Hebrew name but made it the highest altar in the Empire. The city became the mystical center of Christendom, particularly after the Church of the Holy Sepulcher was erected by the Emperor Constantine in the fourth century.

In 637 C.E. came the invasion of Islam, and the third monotheistic religion now added its mosques to the skyline of the city. Jerusalem became the second holiest Muslim city after Mecca, and the seat of the famous Dome of the Rock on Mount Moriah, over the site of Israel's Temple. More tolerant than their predecessors, the Arabs allowed Jews to settle in the city. In the tenth century, the Jewish community of Jerusalem centered around the **Avele Zion** (Mourners of Zion), ascetics who bewailed the loss of Zion's ancient glories and prayed for its early restoration.

Jerusalem again fell to the Christians when the Crusaders captured the city in 1099, massacring much of the Jewish and Moslem population. During most of the twelfth century it was the capital of the Latin Kingdom of Jerusalem, but in 1187 Jerusalem was retaken by the Muslims. Thereafter, despite the heavy burden of taxation, the Jewish community found existence tolerable, except during the cruel and destructive Mongol invasions. In

1517 Jerusalem was taken by the Turks; the present walled city, with its twenty-four towers and eight gates, dates from the period of Suleiman the Magnificent, Sultan of the Turkish Empire. Until the sixteenth century, the Jewish community of Jerusalem consisted mainly of pious pilgrims who had come to die on its holy soil. After the expulsion from Spain (1492), numbers of refugees settled there under the fairly tolerant rule of the first two Turkish sultans. In the eighteenth century, 1,000 Polish Hasidim led by Judah the Pious, settled in Jerusalem.

Under the urging of Sir Moses Montefiore,* around the year 1860 the Jews of Jerusalem first ventured to step outside the protecting walls of the Old City. They built the Yemin Moshe quarter and a windmill for the grinding of grain. The colorful Mea Shearim quarter was established in 1875. The early "Lovers of Zion"* of the 1870's and 1880's settled in Jerusalem, as well as in agricultural colonies. The building of the new city with its modern residential quarters, parks and imposing public buildings began at that time. But along the dark lanes of the old city, the aged and the pious continued to live on the **Halukkah,*** funds gathered for their sustenance all over the world.

The Balfour Declaration* during the First World War, and the assumption by the British of the mandate for Palestine, occasioned changes in Jerusalem. The ancient city became the seat of the British administration governing the country, of the Jewish settlers' shadow government, and of the Palestine section of the World Zionist Organization. The Hebrew University was built on Mount Scopus; structures housing the Jewish Agency* and other Zionist institutions were erected in the New City. Arab riots shook the old city in 1929, a foretaste of the 1936-39 disturbances and of those that followed World War II.

The sponsors of the plan that partitioned Palestine into one Jewish and one Arab State originally envisioned Jerusalem as an international city, with access to the Holy Places of the various religions open to all. However, during the War of Independence of 1948, the Old City was seized by Jordanian forces and annexed by the Kingdom of Jordan. Jews were not permitted access to the Western Wall or any part of the Old City; synagogues were destroyed and Jewish graves desecrated by the Arabs. The Hebrew University campus and the Hadassah* Hospital on Mount Scopus were isolated. The Jews were confined to the New City, which, in 1949, became the seat of Israel's parliament and government. At the beginning of the Six-Day War* in 1967, Israel informed King Hussein that she would not attack Jordan if the Jordanians did not enter the war on the Arab side.

When Jordanian forces began to shell the New City of Jerusalem, the Israeli army struck back and within two days had liberated the Old City. On June 29, 1967 the two sectors of Jerusalem—the Old City and the New—were officially reunified. Since the reunification of Jerusalem, the city has grown rapidly; the ruins of the Old City are being rebuilt and many Jews have already moved into that section.

Archaeologists have been making extensive excavations in the area, particularly around the Western Wall. Currently the population of Jerusalem is about 424,400.

JEW. Derived from the Hebrew **Yehudah,** or **Judah,*** meaning "Praise to the Lord." Judah was one of the twelve tribes of Israel, descended from the fourth son of Jacob.* After the exile to Babylonia,* the term Jew came to be used synonymously with Hebrew and Israelite.

JEWISH AGENCY. Originally, the World Zionist Organization* was designated as the Jewish Agency in the mandate for Palestine given by the League of Nations to Britain and ratified in 1922. According to Article IV of the mandate, the World Zionist Organization* was the appropriate Jewish agency "for the purpose of advising and cooperating with the Administration of Palestine" in matters concerning the establishing of the Jewish national home. In order to speed the work of building, a movement began among Zionists in 1923 to obtain the support of all Jews, including non-Zionists, for the national home in Palestine. To achieve this aim, it was suggested that an extended Jewish Agency be created with a 50 per cent non-Zionist representation. This idea, actively supported by Chaim Weizmann,* had many opponents who feared that Zionism would be weakened by the non-Zionists. The discussions lasted until 1929 when at the sixteenth Congress in Zurich, the enlarged Jewish Agency was launched, and its constituent assembly met immediately. Among those who took part in it as non-Zionists were Louis Marshall* from the United States, Sir (later Viscount) Herbert Samuel* and Lord Melchett* from England, Albert Einstein* and Oscar Wasserman from Germany,* and Leon Blum* from France.* After the death of the two outstanding non-Zionists, Louis Marshall and Lord Melchett, many of the non-Zionists drifted away and the Jewish Agency Executive became almost identical with the World Zionist Executive. **(See ZIONISM.)** N.B-A.

JEWISH CHRONICLE. Anglo-Jewish weekly, founded in London in 1841 and owned by a privately incorporated company. Over the years the journal has acquired an unchallenged position as the central press organ of Anglo-Jewry.

JEWISH COLONIZATION ASSOCIATION. Founded in 1891 by Baron Maurice de Hirsch, wealthy French philanthropist, who felt that anti-Semitism* could be lessened if Jews were dispersed geographically and occupationally, especially to farm areas. This organization, best known by its initials ICA, aided immigration and agricultural projects for Jews in many places, including southern Russia, Argentina,* Brazil,* Bolivia,* Poland,* and the United States. Since 1932, ICA funds (originally more than $10,000,000) have also been used to aid refugees and to supplement the work of the Hebrew Immigrant Aid Society, the American Jewish Joint Distribution Committee,* and other groups that help immigrants.

JEWISH DEFENSE LEAGUE. Militant Jewish group in the United States. Founded in Brooklyn, N.Y., in 1968, the JDL, which consists mostly of young Orthodox Jews, was originally organized to protect Jews in poor neighborhoods from physical attacks by the Blacks and Puerto Ricans in those areas. Later, under the leadership of Meir Kahane and using the slogan "Never Again" (with reference to the Holocaust), the JDL engaged in violent demonstrations and employed physical force to draw public attention to the plight of Jews in Soviet Russia and in Arab lands, and to the precarious situation of the State of Israel.* The JDL has obtained much publicity and has frequently clashed with the representative organizations of the American community.

JEWISH EDUCATION IN THE UNITED STATES. When the school year began in September 1984, about 370,000 boys and girls took their seats in the classrooms of more than 2,500 Jewish school units throughout the United States. The pupils ranged from three-year-olds in Jewish nursery schools to teenagers in Jewish high schools.

The Jews in America are in this respect following a long-standing tradition. For Jewish communities at all times and wherever they existed have made sure to give their children an adequate Jewish education. **(See EDUCATION IN JEWISH HISTORY.)**

The vast majority of Jewish children in America receive their Jewish education after public school hours. Some attend the Jewish school for only one or two years; others, for much longer periods. But the important fact is that it is possible for **every** Jewish child to receive at least a minimal Jewish education today. It is estimated that about 80 per cent of them do receive some kind of Jewish education during their school years. This is quite remarkable, because Jewish education is entirely voluntary in the United States. Nobody can force parents to send their children to a Jewish school. But since the vast majority of American Jews do so, it is because they believe, as Jews have always believed, that a Jewish education is essential if their children are to grow up to understand what it means to be a Jew and to respect themselves.

While almost all American Jews agree on the need for Jewish education, they differ among themselves as to the kind of Jewish education that is best for their children. That is why there are different types of Jewish schools functioning on the American scene. A brief description of these schools follows:

1. Congregational Schools. About 80 per cent of American Jewish children attend synagogue schools conducted by the different Orthodox, Conservative, and Reform congregations. The synagogues conduct two types of schools.

a. Week-Day Afternoon Schools, where children attend from three to five days a week after public school hours and receive from three to eight hours of instruction weekly. These are conducted largely by the Orthodox and Conservative synagogues. The Hebrew language, prayers, Jewish customs and ceremonies, Jewish history, and Bible, are the major subjects studied. These schools conduct their own children's services on the Sabbath* and holidays, and many of them also conduct a variety of club activities. The course of study covers four to six years.

b. The One-Day-A-Week School. (Sunday School) where children attend either Saturday or Sunday mornings and receive from one to three hours of instruction. These are conducted chiefly by the Reform synagogues, and more than 35 per cent of the total number of children attending Jewish schools are enrolled in this type. Jewish history, Bible,* and Jewish customs and ceremonies are the major subjects studied. More and more of these synagogues, however, are adding one or two sessions a week for Hebrew studies. Most of the Orthodox and Conservative synagogues also have one-day-a-week departments which are attended mostly by girls or by young children before they enter the weekday Hebrew school. In the Reform religious schools, the course of study usually leads up to confirmation at ages thirteen to fifteen.

2. The Yeshivot Ketanot, or All-Day Schools, where children attend for a full day, combining both Jewish studies and all the subjects covered in the general public school. This type of school offers the most thorough kind of Jewish education. Pupils receive about fifteen hours a week of instruction in Jewish studies (in the Hebrew language or Yiddish, in some instances), prayers,* the Bible in its original Hebrew, the Mishnah, Talmud, Jewish history, and Jewish laws and customs. This has been the fastest growing type of school in recent years. In 1935, there were 17 such schools in 3 communities in the whole of the United States. In 1959 there were over 230 such schools in more than 50 communities of the United States. Today there are over 500 such schools in the United States. Most of these day schools are Orthodox institutions but in recent years the Conservative movement has set up day schools also.

3. The Communal Talmud Torah is a non-synagogue weekday Hebrew school where children attend five days a week after public school hours and receive from six to ten hours of instruction weekly. The subjects covered are similar to those in the congregational weekday afternoon school. The communal Talmud Torah, which was the most flourishing type of school a generation ago, has declined rapidly in recent years and has been replaced largely by the congregational school and the all-day school. It is still found in the larger Jewish communities.

4. Yiddish Schools are sponsored by the Workmen's Circle and the Sholom Aleichem Folk Institute, national organizations which originated among Jewish socialists. In these schools, Yiddish is the language of instruction. Children attend from three to five afternoons a week, and study Yiddish language and literature, Jewish history, Jewish holidays, and the Bible in Yiddish. In some of these schools, Hebrew is taught in the upper grades. The Jewish National Workers Alliance (Labor Zionists) conducts similar schools, except that in these schools the Hebrew language as well as Yiddish is taught from the onset. These are generally small schools and only a small percentage of the total number of Jewish children attend them.

5. Yeshivot. During the 20th century, and especially with the destruction of European Jewry, yeshivot (Talmudical academies or rabbinical colleges) have assumed a place of increasing importance in American Jewish religious life. Some of these institutions were transferred to the U.S. from Europe. Among the most prominent American Yeshivot are the Yeshiva of Mir, the United Lubavitcher Yeshivot, Yeshiva and Mesivtah Chaim Berlin, Yeshiva and Mesivtah Tifereth Jerusalem and Yeshiva and Mesivtah Torah Vodaath (all in the New York area), the Yeshiva of Lakewood, N.J., the Yeshiva of Spring Valley, N.Y., the Ner Israel Rabbinical College in Baltimore, Md., and the Yeshiva of Telz in Cleveland.

History.

The various systems of Jewish education which now exist in the United States did not come into being all at once. They developed gradually with the growth of the American Jewish community. Jews came to this country from different lands, each group bringing its own traditions and ways. The schools they set up at the beginning followed the patterns they were accustomed to in their homelands, but very soon these schools were modified and changed to conform more closely with the type of schools that were growing up on the American scene.

The first Jewish school in America, the Yeshivah Minchat Areb, was founded in 1731, and was associated with the first synagogue established in New York City. It was conducted as an all-day school. At first, only the Hebrew subjects were taught, but later the general subjects (reading, writing, arithmetic, Spanish) were added. In those days, the Jewish community was responsible for the total education of its children just as every other religious group provided total education for its children. As time went on, these schools became private schools where the greatest attention was given to the general subjects and very little to the Hebrew subjects. In the early 1800's, the existing synagogue began to provide some instruction in Hebrew subjects after school hours. For a brief period (1845-1855), a number of all-day schools similar to our present-day **yeshivot** were established and flourished, but they went out of existence soon after that. After 1850, the free public school became the generally accepted type of school which attracted the greater proportion of American children, regardless of religious or racial origin. Almost all of the Jewish children attended public schools for their general education, and the Jewish school became largely a supplementary religious school.

In 1838, the first Sunday school was established in Philadelphia, and this type of school became the most widely accepted by the Jews during the last half of the 19th century. The majority of American Jews who came to America during this period were of German origin. They brought with them Reform Judaism, which began in Germany.* They minimized the importance of Hebrew, and considered that one day a week of instruction was sufficient. They patterned their Jewish religious schools after the Protestant Sunday Schools which had grown up in America.

After 1880, when Jewish immigration from Eastern Europe swelled into the millions, the **heder** entered the American scene. This was a private one-teacher school, conducted, unfortunately, by poorly trained teachers. Gradually the **heder** gave way to the Talmud Torah, also an East European type of school, but on a much higher plane. The Talmud Torah was well-organized, and provided a very rich program of instruction. Its teachers were well-trained, its textbooks on a high level, substantial school buildings were built, and Hebrew was taught as a living language. The Zionist goal of establishing Palestine as a Jewish homeland was an important part of its program. No wonder the Talmud Torah became the heart of intensive Jewish education in America, and held that position until very recently. Only since shortly before World War II have the congregational and all-day schools supplanted the Talmud Torah to a large extent. It was during the period after 1880 that the Yiddish schools also were organized.

As schools grew and became better organized, American-trained teachers were needed more and more. In 1867, the first teacher training school, Maimonides College, was established in Philadelphia. Thirty years later, Gratz College was established in Philadelphia for the same purpose. There are now fourteen recognized teacher-training schools throughout the country. However, a survey of teacher-training schools made in 1950 showed that they supply only about 25 per cent of the number of new teachers that are needed every year. This represents a serious problem for the future of Jewish education in America.

In 1910, the Bureau of Jewish Education in New York City was established by the Jewish community of that city. This was the first of the more than forty community bureaus of Jewish education which now exist in the United States. These central bureaus were established in order to meet problems which the individual schools could not handle themselves. In many instances, these bureaus of Jewish education give subsidies to schools to enable them to provide more free scholarships. They assist schools to get qualified teachers; they prepare better textbooks and other teaching materials to improve instruction; they offer expert guidance to help teachers improve their methods; and they provide many other services through which the community helps its Jewish schools to improve.

In the Jewish school of today, teachers use well prepared and colorful textbooks, workbooks, filmstrips, records, movies, and other modern teaching aids. In the Jewish classroom of today children learn not only from the book, but also through play, art, dance, and other activities.

Jewish education has spread to the summer camps.* In various parts of the country there are camps where Hebrew is spoken as a matter of course, and children actually attend classes for part of the morning. Other camps provide a rich program of Jewish educational activities, such as Sabbath services, Jewish music, dance, arts, and dramatics. Thousands of Jewish children today take their Jewish education vacationing with them and make their camp life a richer and more meaningful experience. L.L.R.

JEWISH EDUCATION SERVICE OF NORTH AMERICA. See AMERICAN ASSOCIATION OF JEWISH EDUCATION.

JEWISH MUSEUM. Located in the former family mansion of Felix M. Warburg,* presented to the Jewish Theological Seminary of America* by his widow, in memory of her husband, her father, Jacob H. Schiff,* and her brother, Mortimer L. Schiff. The present building, on New York's Fifth Avenue, was first opened to the public in May, 1947. The collections of the museum, which started in 1904, now comprise over 9,000 objects. The Jewish Museum is dedicated to the exhibition of Jewish ceremonial art and to the promotion of the visual values in Judaism. The first floor is reserved for temporary exhibits of artistic and historical merit, which change from time to time. The second and third floors are devoted to the display of part of the museum's collections of Jewish ceremonial art; while the fourth contains a display of coins, plaques and medals, as well as a Junior Gallery, of interest to young visitors. In 1963 a modern wing, donated by Mr. and Mrs. Albert A. List, was completed on an adjacent Fifth Avenue plot. It provides more room for the museum collections and serves as a showcase for young modern artists.

JEWISH NATIONAL FUND (Keren Kayemeth LeIsrael). The Jewish National Fund is the land reclamation agency for the State of Israel and the sole body responsible for the care and development of the land. Established by the World Zionist Organization* at its 5th Zionist Congress in 1901. The creation of an agency for the purpose of purchasing land in Palestine financed by small donations from the Jewish people originated with Hermann Schapira, a rabbi mathematician, who first proposed it to a meeting of the "Lovers of Zion" in 1884. He presented it again at the First Zionist Congress of 1897, and it was brought up again and adopted in 1901. Its principles were greatly influenced by the agricultural laws of the Bible. They provide that land purchased by the Jewish National Fund must remain forever the inalienable possession of the Jewish people. It cannot be sold or mortgaged but only leased to individual pioneers or groups of settlers at a nominal rental for a period of 49 years, renewable only by the original contractor.

In the early days the Jewish National Fund was the sole financial support of the WZO and in 1903 made its first purchases of land in the area of the

State Senator Hubert H. (Skip) Humphrey III (Minn.) with JNF Executive Vice President Dr. Samuel I. Cohen at the dedication ceremony of the Hubert H. Humphrey Parkway in the American Bicentennial Park outside Jerusalem, January, 1979. The Parkway is one of the many JNF special projects in Israel.

Lower Galilee. The purchasing of land soon broadened the scope of its activities to include colonization and land reclamation. Many of the first Jewish settlements in Palestine were founded with the aid of the Jewish National Fund which provided, in addition to the land, farm equipment, livestock and expert advice. It was on the basis of land holdings acquired through subsequent decades by the Jewish National Fund that the United Nations Partition Plan in 1947 was promulgated. The outlines of the State of Israel were drawn geographically in accordance with the locations of the plots of land purchased by the Fund. By 1978 the JNF land holdings covered 2,700,000 dunams on which 1,160,000 people lived, including 849 rural settlements. With the support and contributions of Jewish people the world over and they have planted 160,000 trees, reclaimed 640,000 dunams of land, built 3,800 kilometers of roads (some vital border roads greatly contributed to Israel's success in the wars of 1967 and 1973). JNF forests cover over 1,000,000 dunams of land. The JNF has also installed water supply systems to remote towns and villages, and carried out vast drainage projects, and supplied the land for many public buildings such as schools, hospitals and synagogues. The achievements of the JNF in transforming the barren soil into fertile and productive land have served as a pilot program for many other countries in Asia, Africa and Latin and South America. JNF technicians have been sent on missions to other areas in the world to instruct governments in matters of land reclamation and afforestation. The JNF is governed by a Board of Directors, elected by its General Council, and since 1922 had had its head office in Jerusalem from which it directs the activities of its network of JNF offices in countries throughout the world. The Jewish National Fund of America has its head office in New York City, and among its varied activities it maintains a Youth and Education Department which works with more than 2,500 schools across the country helping to build a sense of identification with Jewish history and tradition in the American/Jewish school children and to inspire them with a love and loyalty for their people and the state of Israel through the materials and projects it distributes and supplies.

JEWISH PUBLICATION SOCIETY OF AMERICA. The first Jewish Publication Society (JPS) was founded in Philadelphia in 1845 to counteract the influence of Christian missionaries. It failed in 1851. A second JPS closed its doors in 1873 after only two years of activity. Finally, in 1888, the present JPS was formed. Its purpose was the "publication and dissemination of literature,

scientific and religious works, and also the giving of instruction in the practices of the Jewish religion, history and literature." Its first publication was an **Outline of Jewish History,** in 1890, its first popular success: Israel Zangwill's **Children of the Ghetto,** appeared in 1892. In the latter year a new translation of the Bible began to be planned—a task that was not completed until 1917. Beginning with the 1960's, the JPS has been issuing new translations of the books of the Bible. Beginning in 1899, the JPS published the **American Jewish Yearbook,** now prepared by the American Jewish Committee,* with the JPS collaborating in its distribution. Several important series have been published by the JPS. These include the Schiff Memorial Library of Jewish Classics; a Historical Jewish Communities series; a series of commentaries on the Bible; and a series of children's books. The editors of the JPS have been Henrietta Szold,* Solomon Grayzel, Chaim Potok, and Maier Deshell.

JEWISH THEOLOGICAL SEMINARY OF AMERICA. A seminary of Conservative Judaism, for the training of rabbis, teachers and cantors. Founded in 1887 with a class of seven students, its program now includes projects for the advancement of Jewish scholarship and research. Rabbi Sabato Morais, first Seminary president and H. Pereira Mendes, its co-founder, were also its first instructors. In 1902, Solomon Schechter* was brought from Cambridge University in England* to become the second president of the Seminary. The establishment of the Seminary Library by Judge Mayer Sulzberger* came under Schechter's auspices, and he transformed the Rabbinical School into a graduate institution. Upon Schechter's death in 1915, Cyrus Adler* succeeded to the presidency. The Seminary moved into its

The Jewish Theological Seminary of America, New York City.

new buildings on Morningside Heights in New York City, which it occupies at the present. Since 1940, Louis Finkelstein became president of the Seminary in 1945, after becoming chancellor. The

Sabato Morais
First President of the Jewish
Theological Seminary.

Gerson D. Cohen
Chancellor of the Jewish
Theological Seminary (1977).

Seminary chancellor in 1979 was Gerson D. Cohen. Among the activities launched by Finkelstein was the Institute for Religious and Social Studies, which aims "to develop a keener awareness of the unique contributions which the various religious traditions have made to the advancement of civilization."

Besides the Rabbinical School, the Seminary includes a Teachers Institute, Cantors Institute, Seminary College of Jewish Studies, Seminary College of Jewish Music, and the Seminary School fo Jewish Studies. The University of Judaism in Los Angeles is the West Coast branch of the Seminary. In 1952, the Seminary Israel Institute was established as a joint project of the Seminary and the Jewish Agency,* The "Eternal Light" program on radio, "Frontiers of Faith" on television, and exhibits at the Jewish Museum* are special projects launched by the Seminary. In over nine decades of its existence, it has graduated more than 1,000 rabbis and about the same number of teachers, who serve synagogues and schools throughout the United States and Canada.*

The Rabbinical Assembly of America is the organization for rabbinical graduates of the Seminary and other Conservative rabbis.

Members of the Jewish War Veterans picket the Egyptian Consulate in New York—1957.

JEWISH WAR VETERANS OF THE UNITED STATES.

An organization composed of Jewish men and women who have served in the armed forces of the United States. The JWV is an outgrowth of the Hebrew Union Veterans Organization, which was founded in 1896 by seventy-eight Jewish veterans of the Civil War. Since membership was limited to veterans of the Civil War, over the years its membership became depleted, and the remnants were ultimately absorbed into the Hebrew Veterans of the War with Spain, organized as an independent veterans' group after the Spanish-American War. After the First World War this organization changed its name to Hebrew Veterans of the Wars of the Republic, in order to include all veterans of all wars. The organization adopted its present name in 1929.

The Jewish War Veterans has its headquarters in Washington, D.C. and a post in every major city and in many of the suburbs throughout the United States. It is the official representative of Jewish soldiers and sailors confined to the various hospitals for veterans under the care of the United States Veterans' Administration. It aids the families of deceased Jewish veterans to obtain benefits to which they are entitled. It officially represents American Jewry at patriotic functions. In its program to promote Americanism, the JWV is on the alert against ideologies which pose a threat to American freedom. Each year it presents an award for Americanism.

JEWRY, ANNIHILATION OF EUROPEAN (THE HOLOCAUST).

In the Jewish people's long history of martyrdom, the catastrophe that eventuated from the six years of Nazi conquest in Europe between 1939 and 1945 was unprecedented in suffering and death. The Jewish people lost 6,000,000 victims, or two-thirds of its European community.

On February 24, 1920, an ex-corporal in the German army named Adolf Hitler and a group of professional anti-Semitic agitators, including Julius Streicher, Alfred Rosenberg, and Gottfried Feder, met in a Munich beer hall and founded the National Socialist Party. (Streicher and Rosenberg were later sentenced to death by hanging by the International War Crimes Tribunal at Nuremberg in October 1946. Hitler escaped the world's verdict by committing suicide in his private bunker in beleaguered Berlin at the end of April 1945.)

Nazi Program. The core of the National Socialist Party (Nazi) program was the racist doctrine that "only he in whose veins German blood flows" might be considered a citizen of Germany, and therefore "no Jew can belong to the German nation." The Nazis shouted that "anti-Semitism* is the emotional foundation of our movement; every member of the Nazi party is an anti-Semite."

Hitler, the Fuehrer, or dictatorial leader, of the

climax of Nazi barbarism directed against Jewish culture occurred with the notorious burning of the books, when hundreds of works by Jewish and anti-Nazi authors were put to the torch in a gigantic bonfire in the square before the famed Berlin Opera House on May 10, 1933.

In its second phase (1938-1944), Nazism burst the bounds of Germany and embarked on a war of conquest against all of Europe. During these years, as country after country fell before the Nazis, the character of the war against Judaism changed from one of hate propaganda to one of organized mass murder. Men and women, the children and the aged, were hurled into the gas chambers and crematoria of the death camps.

The diabolical Nazi blueprint for the annihilation of European Jewry from 1939 on was systematically conceived and carried out in two stages. First came the physical isolation of the Jews in ghettos, concentration camps, and special forced-labor camps, all hermetically sealed off from the outside world. This stage began in 1939 with the Nazi occupation of Poland and lasted until June 1941, when Germany attacked Soviet Russia. Second was the systematic mass murder of the entire Jewish population of all Nazi-occupied areas by means of mass executions before open graves, convoys of hermetically-sealed boxcars, and specially constructed death-factories like Auschwitz, Treblinka and Maidanek, in which millions were methodically gassed and then cremated. This stage lasted from the summer of 1941 until the Nazi collapse in the spring of 1945.

Typical of what was happening in Germany during the pre-war stage of the anti-Semitic program (1933-1939) was the Nazi crusade against German-Jewish scientists and intellectuals. Despite their brilliant record of achievement and high international standing (within the ranks of German Nobel Prize winners, Jews numbered 25 per cent, although only one per cent of the German population was Jewish) Jewish professors were hounded from the universities, Jewish doctors from the hospitals, and Jewish scientists from the laboratories. The internationally known refugees who sought haven at this time in America and other free nations were received with open arms and urged to carry on their interrupted work. Later, many of these scientists were to lend vital assistance to the free world in the decisive battle for strategic and military superiority over Nazi Germany.

Although the war against Jewry continued constant and unrelenting, the Nazis attempted at all times to mask their real intentions. In Nuremberg in 1935, for example, when the first of a series of anti-Semitic laws was passed depriving Jews of equal citizenship rights, and forbidding intermar-

Nazi Party, announced his anti-Semitism as well as his inhumanity, proudly: "Yes, we are barbarians! We want to be barbarians! It is an honorable title. We shall rejuvenate the world! This world is near its end...We are now at the end of the Age of Reason...The Ten Commandments have lost their validity. Conscience is a Jewish invention. It is a blemish, like circumcision...There is no such thing as truth, either in the moral or in the scientific sense...We must distrust the intelligence and the conscience, and must place our trust in our instincts...And was not the whole doctrine of Christianity, with its faith in redemption, its moral code, its conscience, its conception of original sin, the outcome of Judaism? The struggle for world domination will be fought entirely between us, between Germans and Jews."

This, then, was the double aim of the Nazi revolution—to destroy both the Jew and the spirit of Judaism—and, simultaneously, of Christianity. The Nazi regime came into power in Germany* in 1933. It trained its weapons, during the first, pre-war phase (1933-1939), on the Jewish spirit. Christianity, as a "product of Judaism," suffered persecution and harassment at the same time. The

ROMANIA
50.0%

POLAND
85.0%

LATVIA
89.5%

CZECHOSLOVAKIA
82.5%

GERMANY
81.0%

BULGARIA
14.0%

FRANCE
30.0%

BELGIUM
44.4%

ITALY
26.3%

LITHUANIA
90.0%

GREECE
80.0%.

YUGOSLAVIA
73.3%

AUSTRIA
66.6%

HOLLAND
60.0%

HUNGARY
49.5%

SOVIET UNION *(Occupied Zone)*
71.4%

riage between Jews and non-Jews, Nazi leaders declared that they asked of the Jews nothing more than peaceful withdrawal "to their own areas" and cessation of intermingling "with alien peoples." These same pious protestations later accompanied the creation of the ghettos.

The Ghettos. After the Nazis occupied Poland, their first move was the isolation of the Jews from the rest of the Polish population. In February 1940, the Ghetto* of Lodz (renamed Litzmanstadt by the Nazis) was set up, to be followed in October by the Warsaw* Ghetto. Determined to preserve to the very end the pretext of "legality," the Germans set up "Jewish Councils" or governing bodies, and a system of Jewish police within the ghetto walls. All these devices were intended to prove that the ghettos enjoyed a measure of "Jewish autonomy," to cloak their real function as death traps for Polish Jewry, for which they had been designed from the beginning. To allay suspicion, Nazi leaders pointed out to the world that in fact they were doing nothing worse than reviving an old medieval institution—providing separate living areas for the Jewish population. But the electrified barbed wire surrounding the ghetto walls told a different story, as did the heavily armed Nazi patrols on constant watch at the ghetto gates. And whereas the Jew of the Middle Ages had unrestricted freedom of movement

Maps and figures on the Nazi extermination of Jews during World War II, courtesy American Jewish Congress.

QUITTUNG ÜBER FÜNFZIG KRONEN

50

WER DIESE QUITTUNG VERFÄLSCHT ODER NACHMACHT
ODER GEFÄLSCHTE QUITTUNGEN IN VERKEHR BRINGT,
WIRD STRENGSTENS BESTRAFT.

50

outside of the ghetto walls by day, the penalty for leaving a Polish ghetto without official permission at any time was instant death.

Within the ghetto walls, hunger and privation held sway. Because of unspeakably cramped living conditions, epidemics were rampant. And the ghetto population was constant prey to attacks of indescribable cruelty at the whim of its Nazi overseers. Yet despite these hardships, the ghettos displayed a remarkable vitality and almost unbelievable capacity for survival. Cultural and religious activities of all kinds animated the underground life of the ghetto. Moving dramas of devoted selflessness were played out within its walls. And, in perhaps the most sublime triumph of the human spirit to be written in the annals of any people, the Jews of the Polish ghetto, tortured, doomed, and alone, summoned up the magnificent courage to rise in revolt against their Nazi jailers.

Camouflage and deception were also characteristic of the mass murder of European Jewry, which the Nazis disguised as "the final

Money especially printed by the Nazis for the Theresienstadt Ghetto in Bohemia, where they tried to preserve the illusion of an autonomous Jewish community.

solution to the Jewish question." The infamous Nazi death camp at Auschwitz was disguised as a labor camp with numerous factories and workshops. Over the entrance-gate was emblazoned in huge letters the slogan: FREEDOM THROUGH WORK. The transports which daily drove into the center of the camps, bearing victims from all corners of Nazi-occupied Europe, were falsely identified as part of the "Resettlement Project for Colonization in the East." And the gas chambers with crematoria-ovens were disguised as public baths for the purposes of disinfection.

The Balance Sheet of Annihilation. Statistics on the Jewish catastrophe are indicated in the accompanying table and diagram, published by the World Jewish Congress.* It should be noted that the only unclear part of the record refers to the fate of the Jews of the Soviet Union. No official estimate of Jewish losses suffered there has yet been made.

The diagram representing the percentage of

Founding of Kibbutz Lochamei Hagetaot (Ghetto Fighters) near Naharia on Monday, April 18, 1949—the sixth anniversary of the Warsaw Ghetto Uprising. Itzhak Zuckerman, one of the ghetto leaders, addresses the gathering.

Zionist Archives and Library, New York City.

The late Zivia Lubatkin, one of the surviving leaders of the Warsaw Ghetto uprising, who settled in Israel.

Jewish losses in individual countries warrants closer scrutiny. Significant differences are apparent—as for example the disparity between the 14 per cent loss suffered in Bulgaria* and the 90 per cent toll in Latvia and Lithuania.* The Polish figures particularly demanded clarification. Deducting from the total number of Polish survivors the more than 200,000 who were temporarily evacuated by the Russians to a point deep within the heart of Soviet territory out of reach of the Nazis, the proportion of the victims who remained in Poland becomes more than 90 per cent —the highest toll of all European Jewry. Individual political, social and technical factors also affected the fate of Jews in different countries. In Hungary,* for example, the Nazis were thwarted in their attempt at the total annihilation of the Jews by the heavy losses they suffered at the war front. In other countries, such as Italy,* France,* and Belgium,* the non-Jewish population helped rescue its Jewish neighbors. These acts of generosity were most frequent in the cases of rescue of children. Unusual instances of individual heroism occurred in nearly all the occupied coun-

"A brand plucked out of the fire" (Zechariah 3:2). A child rescued from the Nazi Holocaust.

Jewish orphans found among the survivors of the notorious Buchenwald murder camp and brought to Israel.

tries. Unfortunately, only Denmark* organized mass resistance to the annihilation of its Jewish citizens.

At the end of 1942, when the Nazi conquerors invaded Denmark, and proceeded to set in motion their war of Jewish extermination, King Christian X registered instant protest. He threatened to abdicate; when the Nazis made it known that henceforth every Jew was to be identified by a yellow arm band bearing a Star of David, King Christian announced that he would be the first to don the badge of Judaism. Finally, just as the Gestapo—the dread German secret police—had completed their plans for dealing with the Jews without Danish assistance, there occurred perhaps

Kibbutz Lochamei Hagetaot (Ghetto Fighters).

A display at the museum of Kibbutz Lochamei Hagetaot. Musical instruments made by Nazis out of captured Torah scrolls, and the yellow stars worm by the Jews in Europe during the Nazi occupation.

the noblest example of human solidarity to be recorded in the annals of the period. Of the 6,500 Danish Jews officially marked for death by the Nazis, approximately 6,200 or 95 per cent, were secretly smuggled out of Denmark into Sweden with the help of a special rescue fleet of small Danish fishing ships. Between September 26 and October 12, 1942, the Danes rescued all but a few hundred Danish Jews from the gas chambers.

M.P.

Survivors. Each of the Jewish survivors of the catastrophe owed his life either to a freak accident, or a chain of fortunate coincidences. The Nazi murder-decree against the Jews lasted, in effect, until the final moment of the war. Soviet troops entering Poland* in 1944 seized the death camp Maidanek, near Lublin, while it was still operating its ultra-modern machinery for murder intact for the world to see. In April 1945, when the victorious Allied armies under General Eisenhower marched into Germany, they succeeded in taking the still-functioning camps at Dachau, Buchenwald, and Bergen Belsen* by surprise, and in freeing the not-yet-cremated remnant.

The full extent of the Jewish tragedy came to light only with the final collapse of Nazism and the Allied liberation of Europe. Gradually the survivors began to emerge from their hiding places to make their stories known. There were Jews who had been living in concealed underground bunkers, women who had lived as "Aryans" on forged documents, children, mainly orphans, who had been sheltered in monasteries or among kind-hearted Christian neighbors, and brave men and women who fought the Nazis as partisans in the forests of Poland.

In May 1960, Adolf Eichmann, one of the cruelest masters of the Nazi extermination system, was captured in Argentina* by Jews and brought to Israel* for trial. After lengthy hearings in 1961, he was convicted and executed in May, 1962.

JEWS' COLLEGE. A rabbinical seminary in London, England, it is the main agency for training Orthodox rabbis, cantors, and teachers in Great Britain. The college, founded in 1855 by Chief Rabbi Nathan Marcus Adler, has been incorporated into the University of London. According to the constitution of the college, the chief rabbi of Great Britain is always its president. The college library, particularly rich in items on Anglo-Jewish history, is larger than that of any other European theological seminary.

JOB. Third book in the Biblical section, Writings. The theme of Job is divine justice, and the problem discussed is "Why do the righteous suffer?" Job of Uz, a good man, suddenly has a series of terrible misfortunes: he loses his wealth, his children die, and he becomes ill with a loathsome disease. Three of his friends, Eliphaz, Bildad, and Zophar come to console him. They assume that his troubles have come to him as punishment for his sins, and urge Job to confess his guilt and accept his suffering as God's righteous judgment. Job insists that he is innocent, and, in the discussion with his friends, he pours out the bitterness of his soul. Finally a fourth friend, Elihu, son of Barachel, scolds Job for lack-

"Job," by Ben Zion.

ing trust in God. The book has a happy ending. Job learns that men cannot really understand the mystery of the Lord's ways, when God speaks to him "out of a whirlwind" and then restores his health and happiness. Job has sons and daughters and lives to be 140. The magnificent poetic description of Job's trials and his patient faith, together with the majestic descriptions of Divine power, make the Book of Job the greatest of the Wisdom books in the Bible.*

JOEL. Second of the minor prophets in the Bible.* The Book of Joel calls the people of Judea to repent because the Judgment Day is at hand. It ends with the promise that the enemies of Israel will be overturned, Jerusalem* and Judah will be restored, and God will dwell in the midst of His people once again.

JOHANAN BEN ZAKKAI (first century C.E.). Religious leader. A student of Hillel* and a member of the Sanhedrin,* Ben Zakkai advocated a policy of peace with the Romans.

The Talmud* relates that during the siege of Jerusalem* no one was allowed to leave the city except to bury the dead. Ben Zakkai instructed his disciples to carry him in a coffin across the city walls. There he met the Roman commander, Vespasian, who granted him permission to open a Talmudical academy at Yavneh.*

At Yavneh, Ben Zakkai continued the work of the Sanhedrin, instituting laws and regulations which exerted a lasting influence on the development of Jewish spiritual values.

JOHANAN OF GUSH HALAV (John of Gischala, first century C.E.). One of the leaders of the Judean rebellion against Rome, 66-70 C.E., Johanan was a man of frail body and peaceful habits. An attack on his town forced him to take up arms, and transformed him into one of the fiercest opponents of Roman tyranny. After Gush Halav fell to the Roman legions, Johanan fled to Jerusalem* with several thousand followers. There he joined in the ruthless struggle between the peace party and the Zealots, who favored war. Only after Titus had already laid siege to Jerusalem did Johanan join forces with Bar Giora,* another Zealot leader, for defense of the capital. After five months of heroic fighting, Jerusalem was taken by sheer force of numbers. Johanan was among the last to be captured. He was forced to march in Titus's triumphal entry into Rome, and was later sentenced to life imprisonment as a rebel.

JOINT DISTRIBUTION COMMITTEE. See AMERICAN JEWISH JOINT DISTRIBUTION COMMITTEE.

JONAH (Hebrew, meaning "dove"). Fifth and perhaps most familiar of the minor prophets in the Bible. The first two chapters of the book of Jonah tell how, unwillingly, the prophet set out on his mission to save the people of Nineveh, how he was swallowed by a great fish, prayed for salvation, and was spewed out safely on the shore. The third chapter tells how Jonah obeys the word of the Lord and prophesies the destruction of Nineveh because of its wickedness, and how the people repented. The final chapter describes Jonah's displeasure because God forgave the people of Nineveh and his prophecy of destruction did not come true. It also tells how the Lord taught Jonah the meaning of mercy and forgiveness.

JORDAN (Hebrew, Yarden). Israel's largest river, flowing into the Red Sea. It was the original natural border between Palestine* and Transjordan.

JORDAN, HASHEMITE KINGDOM OF. Modern name for kingdom of Transjordan,* which was formed in 1922. In 1948 Jordan annexed the territory on the West Bank* originally assigned in 1947 for a new Arab state under the United Nations partition resolution, and also occupied the Old City of Jerusalem.* In 1967 Israeli forces occupied Jerusalem and the West Bank territory.

JOSEPH (Hebrew, meaning He [i.e. GOD] will add). Son of Jacob* and Rachel. The favorite, he was given "a coat of many colors" to wear. Both a dreamer and an interpreter of dreams, Joseph aroused the jealousy of his brothers and was sold as a slave to an Egypt-bound caravan. In Egypt he gained a position of authority on the estate of his master, Potiphar, but was imprisoned because of a false accusation by Potiphar's wife. His old skill at interpreting dreams brought his release from prison and his rise to the office of Pharaoh's viceroy and governor of Egypt. The dramatic re-

Joseph and His brothers; an eighteenth century engraving. "And Joseph said unto his brethren: I am Joseph; doth my father yet live? And his brethren could not answer him" (Genesis 45:3).

union with his family, who came down to Egypt during the years of famine in Canaan, the comfort he brought to his father who had thought Joseph dead—these form the final chapter in his story. Joseph was not forgotten by his people. Years later, when they fled Egypt to return to their Promised Land, they took Joseph's embalmed body along on their forty-year journey to Canaan and gave him final burial near Shechem. Rabbinic tales and Jewish folklore have spangled the Joseph story with numerous legends. Folk plays on the theme of his life came into being as traditional entertainment for Purim,* to be performed by strolling players or the townspeople themselves. The imagination of mankind has been gripped by the story, and countless dramas and tales have been written about Joseph, culminating in Thomas Mann's great trilogy, **Joseph and His Brothers.**

JOSEPHUS FLAVIUS (c. 37-c. 105). Soldier and historian. Born in Jerusalem,* Joseph ben Mattathias came of a priestly family and was educated in the schools of the Pharisees.* At the age of twenty-six he was sent on a mission to Rome, where he remained for two years at the court of Nero. Returning home in 65 C.E., Josephus found the country in open rebellion against Roman rule. Entrusted with the command of Galilee,* he fortified its cities against Vespasian and his invading Roman legions. From the beginning, Joseph's loyalty was suspected by Johanan of Gush Halav,* the leader of the extremist Zeolot party, and the feud between them was bitter. Vespasian invaded Galilee in 67, and conquered the fortresses one by one. In Jotapata, Josephus held out for three months. When the garrison was captured, Josephus saved his life by surrendering. He won his way into Vespasian's good graces by predicting that he would become emperor of Rome. The prediction came true, Vespasian returned to Rome to mount the imperial throne, and Titus took over command of the war in Judea. During the siege of Jerusalem, Titus used Josephus to urge the Jews to surrender. After the fall of Jerusalem, Joseph accompanied Titus to Rome, and was rewarded by the favor of the Flavian emperors, Vespasian and Titus. In gratitude, he took their name and called himself Josephus Flavius. Josephus appears to have been torn between his inescapable Jewishness and his need to please the Romans. He turned to writing and wrote first **The Judaean Wars** (against Rome). Then he wrote the **Antiquities of the Jews,** a history glorifying the Jewish people. In **Against Apion,** a reply to the Alexandrian schoolmaster and anti-Semite Josephus passionately defended

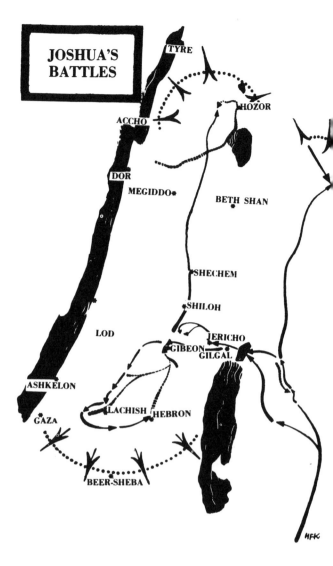

JOSHUA'S BATTLES

the Jews against slander. **Vita** is the autobiography that Josephus wrote to answer the charges made against him by another Jewish historian, Justus of Galilee. The writings of Justus on the Jewish revolt have been lost. The books of Josephus have survived, and serve as the only source of knowledge for a good part of the Jewish history of that period.   N.B-A.

JOSHUA (Hebrew, meaning "the Lord will help"). According to the Bible,* Joshua, the son of Nun, was chosen by Moses* to be his successor. Joshua led Israel* across the Jordan in about 1400 B.C.E., conquered the Jericho* fortress and defeated the six hostile Canaanite tribes. After six years of battle, he began the division of the conquered territory among the tribes. The Book of Joshua is the sixth in the Bible, following immediately after Deuteronomy;* it tells the story of the conquest and division of Canaan,* and ends with Joshua's farewell address and death.

JOSHUA BEN HANANYAH. See TANNAIM.

JUDAH (Hebrew, meaning "Praise to the Lord"). Fourth son of Jacob,* born of Leah; founder of the tribe of Judah, whose emblem was the lion. Just as Judah came to be the leader of all the sons of Jacob, so the tribe of Judah took the leading role in the life of the people. Much of Chapter 15 in Joshua is devoted to a description of Judah's territory, which extended from the end of the Salt Sea in the south to the Great Sea in the west and was crowned with Jerusalem* on its heights. Judah was also the name of the southern kingdom, which included the tribes of Judah, Simeon,* and part of Benjamin.* This kingdom came into being after the northern tribes had seceded at the death of Solomon,* forming their own northern kingdom of Israel.*

JUDAH HA-LEVI. See HA-LEVI, JUDAH.

JUDAH, KINGDOM OF. The name of the southern kingdom which included the territory belonging to the tribes of Judah,* Simeon,* and part of Benjamin.* The kingdom of Judah came into being after the northern tribes had seceded from the House of David* at the death of Solomon,* forming their own northern kingdom of Israel.

JUDAH MACCABEE. See MACCABEES.

JUDAH THE PRINCE. (Yehudah Hanasi. About (135-222 C.E.) Also called "Rabbi" and "Rabenu ha-Kadosh" (our Holy Rabbi). His life work consisted of editing, compiling and classifying the Mishnah,* or the entire body of Jewish oral law which had been accumulated during the the preceding four centuries. He arranged the Mishnah in six sections, each one dealing with a particular set of laws, and this work exerted a crucial influence on the development of the religious, cultural and social life of the Jewish people.

Judah the Prince was born on the day when Rabbi Akiba* died, an occurrence symbolic of the continuity of Jewish scholarship. A descendant of Hillel,* who established a famous school of interpreters of the Law, he succeeded his father as "Nasi" or head of the Sanhedrin,* the highest legislative and judicial council of the time.

His preoccupation with Jewish law did not prevent the great Rabbi and scholar from acquiring a thorough knowledge of the Greek language and culture. But it was his vast knowledge of Jewish law which earned him the recognition of all the scholars of his time. His learning as well as his wealth added dignity and splendor to his leadership of the Jewish people as head of the Sanhedrin. Even the Roman authorities respected his station. His house resembled a royal court. Yet Rabbi Judah himself was a modest and self-denying person, highly responsive to the needs of his fellowmen. In time of famine, he distributed his wealth freely to the poor. His main interests lay in learning and in his students whom he loved deeply. "I learned much from my teachers," he once said, "much more from my comrades, and most of all from my students."

Judah the Prince lived first in Bet Shearim and then in Zippori, Galilee. He was the last of the Tannaim,* closing a great period of Jewish scholarship.

H.L.

JUDAISM. Judaism is based on the Bible,* each age reinterpreting and redefining the Biblical laws. The Talmud is the result of such a process of interpretation. Changing conditions and circumstances resulted in further interpretations by the rabbinic authorities of every generation. Hence, Judaism never froze into a fixed and rigid philosophy. It was always more concerned with the practice of the commandments regulating man's relations with man and with God.

Orthodox Judaism.

The way of life that adheres to the traditional aspects of Judaism came to be called "Orthodox" in the early nineteenth century, when Reform and Conservative Judaisms, which differ somewhat from the original tradition of Judaism, developed. Orthodox Jews continued to follow the laws, customs, and ceremonies prescribed in the Shulhan Arukh.* This code of Jewish law, however, deals only with obligatory practices. In addition, there are many customs which have grown up over the ages. These customs have been so hallowed by time and tradition that they now have almost the binding force of law for the communities in which they are practiced. Numerous collections of such customs have been made, and many of them have become an organic part of Jewish life.

At the very center of the Orthodox way of life lies the idea that God chose His people Israel from among the nations, and bestowed His law upon them as a symbol of this love. In receiving the Torah,* the Jews took upon themselves the task of becoming "a nation of priests and a sacred folk" by dedicating themselves to fulfilling the ideals of justice and holiness embodied in the Law. For the Orthodox Jew, the Law embodies all the rules for the good life. When he acts according to the letter and spirit of the Law, the Jew realizes the will of God, and reflects upon the goodness of God and the love lavished by Him upon Israel and all

Emblem of the tribe of Judah

180

mankind. In fact, a large number of customs and ceremonies observed by the Orthodox Jew serve directly to remind him of this love.

Conservative Judaism.

The history of Conservative Judaism began with the Historical School of Jewish Learning founded by Zechariah Frankel in Germany* in 1850. Frankel held that Judaism was a living spirit which had undergone many changes in the course of its long history, as it adjusted itself to the changes in its surroundings. The Historical School he initiated aimed to use modern scientific methods for the study of the Jewish past. So long as every effort was made to preserve and understand the Jewish tradition, Zechariah Frankel believed that in the future as in the past, changes in customs or ceremonies would come of themselves and be in the spirit of Judaism, as well as in that of the environment.

A leader of this school of thought was Sabato Morais, a founder of the Jewish Theological Seminary of America.* When Solomon Schechter* assumed the leadership of the Seminary, Conservative Judaism in America was greatly strengthened. Schechter felt that "Universal Israel" had always permitted differences of opinion because of the all-embracing unity of Judaism, past, present, and future. This unity, together with tradition and scholarship constituted, he believed, a fertile soil for the growth of a program for Conservative Judaism. The religious movement known as Reconstructionism* was first formulated by a member of the Jewish Theological Seminary's faculty Dr. Mordecai M. Kaplan.

Reform Judaism.

Early Reform Judaism was rooted in the period of political emancipation and cultural adaption of European Jewry, extending from the middle of the eighteenth through the nineteenth century. Israel Jacobson, in the German province of Westphalia, was perhaps the first leader to express the current desire for modifications in Judaism. He introduced a number of changes into his synagogue: a mixed choir, a few prayers recited in German, and a sermon in German.

When he moved to Berlin in 1815, Israel Jacobson instituted these innovations in a new synagogue founded by him and the banker Jacob Beer. It was, however, the scholar Abraham Geiger* who laid the ideological foundation for Reform Judaism. Geiger saw Judaism as an historical, developing faith, and rejected basic beliefs and practices which he believed were contradictory to modern scientific thought.

The first to found Reform institutions in America was Isaac Mayer Wise. The principles he advocated formed the basis for the Pittsburgh Platform adopted by a conference of rabbis in 1885. These principles emphasized the prophetic ideas of the Bible, and declared some of the Biblical and Talmudic regulations no longer applicable. The Platform separated the Jewish religion from Jewish nationalism, and rejected a return to Palestine and the belief in a personal Messiah. For the Messianic era of peace and perfection it substituted the hope for a perfect world achieved by cultural and scientific progress. Reform Judaism conceived of the Jews as a group with a mission to spread godliness in the world. A revision of these principles took place in 1937 at the meeting of the Central Conference of American Rabbis in Columbus, Ohio. The conference defined Judaism as the "historical religious experience of the Jewish people," thereby including not only the Jewish belief and ethic, but also its traditional culture and peoplehood.

JUDGES. (12th and 11th centuries B.C.E.) The Book of Judges spans the period from the death of Joshua* to the time when Saul* was anointed king. The conquest of Canaan* under Joshua had been incomplete. The tribes of Israel had not reached the coast which remained occupied by the Phoenicians* and the Philistines.* In the Great Plain the unconquered fortresses of Taanach, Megiddo, and Beth-Shean were ranged as a formidable barrier separating the tribes of Dan* Asher,* Zebulun,* Naphtali, and Issachar* in the north, from Manasseh, Ephraim* Benjamin,* and Judah* in the south. Aloof across the Jordan, Reuben* tended its sheep, and Gad dallied in Gilead. The physical separation, as well as the nature of tribal society, prevented the Judges from effecting the unification of the people, even though they were popular heroes. During their era, Mesopotamian enemies from the north, the Moabites from across the Jordan in the south, and the nomad Midianites from Sinai, subjugated the Israelites for varying periods of time. In such times of crisis, the Judges were called to leadership by the people and their battles eventually extended Israelite mastery of the Land. There were sixteen Judges; two of them, Deborah* and Samuel,* were also prophets, and one, Eli, was a priest, while Samson* was a folk-hero rather than a military or religious leader. Another kind of battle characterized the period of the Judges—the battle of Israel's religion of one God against the fertility and nature gods of Canaan. In both these struggles, the Judges were the leaders of the people.

N.B-A.

OTHNIEL, son of Kenaz, the first to judge Israel after Joshua's death ruled . . . . 40 years

EHUD, son of Gera, who fought the Moabites and ruled Israel for . . . . 40 years

SHAMGAR, son of Anath; he led the Children of Israel against the Philistines . . . . 40 years

DEBORAH, the prophetess who guided Barak to victory over the Canaanites . . . . 40 years

GIDEON, son of Yoash who defeated a host of Midianites with 300 men . . . . 40 years

ABIMELECH, son of Gideon, the only judge to gain leadership by treachery . . . . 3 years

TOLA, son of Puah, who judged Israel for . . . . 23 years

YAIR, the Gileadite; he judged the people for . . . . 22 years

JEPTHAH, son of Gilead, who defeated the Ammonites and ruled for . . . . 6 years

IBZAN of Bethlehem judged the people for . . . . 7 years

ABDON, the son of Hillel, ruled for . . . . 8 years

SAMSON, son of Monoah, who fought the Philistines singlehanded and
ruled for . . . . 20 years

ELI, the priest, ruled the people from the sanctuary at Shiloh for . . . . 40 years

SAMUEL, the prophet, the last to judge Israel before it became a kingdom under
Saul . . . . 41 years

K

KABAK, A.A. See HEBREW LITERATURE.

KABBALAH (Hebrew, meaning "tradition"). Jewish mysticism. Kabbalah was an attempt to fathom the mysteries of God and Creation; the Kabbalists developed a complete philosophic system during the Middle Ages. The Talmud* contains mystical interpretations of the Biblical story of Creation. With the appearance of the Zohar* in the thirteenth century, the study of the Kabbalah gained great popularity. Among the earliest mystic works are the **Alphabet of Rabbi Akiba** and **Sefer Yetzirah** ("The Book of Creation") attributed to Abraham.* The **Sefer Yetzirah** attaches great mystic power to numbers, and enumerates the ten **sefirot,** or diven emenations, which later assumed great importance in the Kabbalistic system. God, the "En Sof" (Infinite One), makes His divine existence known by means of these ten emenations. The first sefirah is called **Keter** ("Crown"). The others follow in this order: **Hokhmah** ("Wisdom"); **Binah** ("Intelligence"); **Hesed** ("Mercy"); **Din** ("Judgment") or **Gevurah** ("Strength"); **Tiferet** ("Beauty"); **Netzah** ("Victory"); **Hod** ("Glory"); **Yesod** ("Foundation"); and **Malkhut** ("Kingdom").

Jewish mysticism attracted to itself remarkable personalities, some of whom considered themselves to be Messiahs. Abraham Abulafia (1240-1291), who regarded himself as a forerunner of the Messiah, even attempted to convert the Pope to Judaism.

Kabbalistic teachings gained in intensity and scope in sixteenth-century Safed. This town, in upper Galilee* in Palestine,* became a center of Jewish mysticism; its foremost teachers of Kabbalah included Isaac Luria (1534-1572). A practical, or miracle-working mystic, Luria claimed that the secrets of Creation had been revealed to

him by the prophet Elijah.* Luria believed that human beings could attain identification with the Divine Spirit through intense concentration, or **kavvanah.** This theory was described by Luria's disciple, Hayim Vital in his book **Etz Hayim** ("The Tree of Life"). Another famous Kabbalist, Moses Cordovero, formulated Kabbalistic teachings in a philosophic system. His contemporary, Isaiah Horowitz (1555-1625) interpreted the teachings of Judaism in the light of Kabbalah. He sought, with the other inspired mystics of his generation, to hasten the coming of the Messiah.

The teachings of the Kabbalah contributed to the rise of Messianic hopes and, in time, influenced Hasidism* profoundly. Jewish folklore thrived on the Kabbalah's poetic and magical elements.

H.L.

KADDISH (Hebrew meaning "santification"). One of the most ancient prayers in the Jewish prayer book, generally recited in the synagogue* during religious services. It became popular as the mourner's prayer. Kaddish is traditionally recited in the presence of a **minyan,** or quorum of ten adult male Jews. The essential part of the prayer is the verse from Psalm 113 in its Aramaic version: "Let His great name be blessed forever and to all eternity." The Mourner's Kaddish is recited for eleven months and on every anniversary of the relative's death.

The so-called Rabbinical Kaddish is recited at the close of a lesson, or the completion of the study of any portion of the Talmudic law.

The Kaddish glorifies the name of the Lord, reaffirms faith in the establishment of the Kingdom of God, and calls for peace in the house of Israel. Beautiful and stirring melodies accompany the reciting of the Kaddish on the High Holy Days of Rosh ha-Shanah* and Yom Kippur.*

KAF. Eleventh letter of the Hebrew alphabet; numerically, twenty.

KAFKA, FRANZ (1882-1924). Writer, born and died in Prague. Franz Kafka was a strange genius whose short life was very unhappy. From his youth onward he lived only for his writing. Kafka's family life was very difficult; he never succeeded in gaining his father's approval, nor did he agree with his father's views. Kafka never married. His first engagement was broken after several years, when he became ill with tuberculosis. The second time he fell in love, the girl was forbidden to marry him. This personal unhappiness, and Kafka's Jewishness, are thought to be reflected in his novels, stories, and aphorisms (or sayings). Outstanding among his writings are

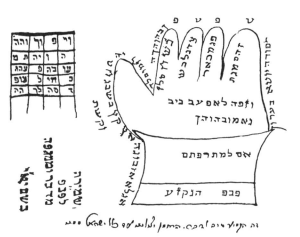

Symbolic representation of the Kabbalistic doctrines.

America, The Trial, and **The Castle.** These novels, as well as his other works, have a strange poetic beauty, an eerie, dream-like quality. Yet they continually startle the reader into recognizing reality, and disturb him with the hero's hopeless, tragic fate. Literary critics have written a great deal about the philosophy, the symbols, and the meaning of Kafka's work. They, however, agree mainly in rating him a great literary artist.

KAHAL. (Also **kehilla,** Hebrew meaning "community.") During the Middle Ages, Jewish localities were organized into communities with considerable power to govern themselves. The pattern for the Jewish community had developed over the ages in Palestine* and in Bablyonia,* and was continued with some changes in the West. The community derived its power to manage all the Jewish affairs and institutions of the Jewish community from several sources. First was the inner obligation and need of the Jew to live according to Talmudic religious and civil law. Therefore every Jew was a member of his community with definite rights and duties that could not be taken away from him. Secondly, the Jewish community was granted power by the non-Jewish world to conduct its own affairs and enforce its rules. The feudal barons, kings, and princes of the Church who "owned" the Jews living in their various domains, held the **kahal** responsible for a tax placed on the Jewish community as a whole. The Christian governments throughout the Middle Ages followed the same practice. The community officials, consequently, had the authority to decide how much individuals were to be taxed.

The term "kahal" came to be applied to the local governments of the Jewish communities in Lithuania,* Poland,* and Russia* during the sixteenth century. The head of the **kahal** was called the **rosh ha-kahal,** or the **parnas,** and had considerable authority and prestige. He was assisted by **gabbaim,** or overseers—usually seven. The **kahal** had its own courts of law to which Jews turned in all disputes. The community had the right to enforce its decision by means of imprisonment, by flogging (no more than thirty-nine lashes), and by temporary or permanent excommunication (**herem***). **Herem** was the most dreaded punishment, because it meant being barred completely from contact with any other Jew, including members of one's immediate family.

Life within the **kahal** proceeded according to age-old tradition. Public life revolved around the synagogue, since not only religious worship, but meetings and weddings also took place there. The community school, or Talmud Torah, open to the poorest, was housed in some part of the synagogue. Often, the hostel, or **hekdesh,** provided by the community for strangers, was located in a synagogue annex, as was the public bathhouse or **mikveh.** Public charities in the community were well organized, and no Jew was ever left without help. Learning was highly valued, and illiteracy was rare. Most of the officials served without salary, and were usually chosen for their learning. For a time, the rabbi also served without salary, and was the religious authority, the teacher, and the guide of the community. Between 1580 and 1764, the **kahal** reached a high form of development in the Council of the Four Lands. Delegates of the communities from Great Poland, Little Poland, Podolia and Galicia met, at first once and later twice a year, to regulate the affairs of the people. N.B-A.

KALISHER, Z'VI HIRSCH (1795-1874). Rabbi, scholar, and early proponent of Zionism.* Born in Poland, Kalisher was the first outstanding Orthodox rabbi to preach that Judaism permitted Jews to work actively for the Zionist cause: that Jews were not restricted only to waiting and praying for the coming Messiah. In his Hebrew pamphlet, **The Quest for Zion** (1862), he outlined methods for the settlement of Palestine. His pioneering effort actually resulted in the organization of the first Palestine colonization society. His pamphlet influenced a French organization, the Alliance Israélite Universelle,* to establish the Mikveh Israel* Agricultural School in Palestine.* He influenced eighty Jews, in 1866, to buy land there for an agricultural settlement in Palestine.

KARAITES. This Jewish sect was founded late in the eighth century by Anan ben David.* Karaism rejected the rabbinic tradition of Talmudic law, and based its religious life on the literal interpretation of the Bible.*

Anan ben David was a nephew of the deceased Exilarch* of the Bustanai dynasty, and aspired to this high position. The Geonim, highest religious authorities in Babylonia,* doubted Anan's devotion to Talmudic law and appointed instead his younger brother, Hananiah. Angered by the rejection from the Geonim, Anan proclaimed openly his opposition to the Talmud.* His followers rebelled against the Talmudic tradition. They were influenced by the great controversy raging in Islam* at that time, between traditionalists and their opponents. When Anan's supporters increased in numbers, he became head of the new religious sect which later came to be known as Karaism, from the Hebrew "Karaim" or (strict) readers of the Scripture.

Anan recognized the authority of the Bible only. He urged his pupils to search in the Scriptures for the true or literal interpretation of the law. By their strict adherence to the Biblical text the Karaites defeated their own purpose. As time went on, the Karaite teachers engaged in hair-splitting interpretations of the Bible no less than the rabbinical authorities whom they criticized. Much confusion resulted from the varied and often conflicting interpretation of Karaite scholars. In many instances the Karaite restrictions were more severe than those of the Talmud. They prohibited the use of light on the Sabbath day altogether, and were even more rigorous in observance of the laws of ritual cleanliness and fasting.

The debates between the Talmudists and Karaites stimulated Jewish scholarship. The defense of traditional Judaism required a thorough knowlege of the Bible and the Hebrew language. Jewish philosophic thought was also mobilized in defense of tradition.

Between the ninth and twelfth centuries Karaite communities were established in Babylonia, Persia, Egypt,* and Palestine.* In the thirteenth century great numbers of Karaites settled in the Crimea in Russia,* and from there they spread to Lithuania* and Galicia. During the last few centuries the Karaites have turned away more and more from the rest of the Jewish community. In order to avoid the restrictive measures of the Tsarist regime in Russia, directed against the Jews, Karaites tried to prove that they were not Jews.

Before the Second World War, there were about 12,000 Karaites, most of them in the Crimea. The Karaites have at all times professed a love for Zion.* Since the establishment of Israel,* many Karaites from Egypt have settled in the Holy Land. They have founded several settlements, and have tended markedly to draw nearer to other Jews.   H.L.

KARO, JOSEPH BEN EPHRAIM (1488-1575). Famous Talmudic scholar, author of the **Shulhan Arukh,*** core of Jewish law. Orthodox Jewish life for the last four hundren years has been regulated by the **Shulhan Arukh.** Born in Toledo, Spain, Karo was forced to go into exile with his parents when only four years old. After much wandering, the family finally settled in Turkey,* where he received his education. Karo acquired his greatest fame in Safed, Palestine,* which at that time became a center for the study of the Talmud* and of Jewish mysticism (Kabbalah*). In this city, high on the mountains of upper Galilee, Karo founded a **yeshivah** and wrote most of his books. Before compiling the **Shulhan Arukh,** he spent many years in the writing of **Bet Joseph,** a commentary on the **Arbaah Turim,** an earlier code of Jewish law composed by Jacob Ben Asher. Other works by Joseph Karo are **Kesef Mishneh,** a commentary on the famed Maimonides* Code. Joseph Karo, himself steeped in the Kabbalah, greatly influenced his students, many of whom were famous Kabbalists.

KASHRUT. See DIETARY LAWS.

Ephraim Katzir

KATZIR, EPHRAIM (1916-). Professor, biochemist and biophysicist, fourth president of Israel. Born in Kiev, Russia, he was brought to Palestine* by his parents at the age of nine years. A graduate of the Hebrew University,* in 1949 he was appointed Acting Head of Department of Biophysics in the Weizmann Institute of Science* at Rehovot, and in due course its substantive director. From 1966-1968, he was Chief Scientist to the Ministry of Defense. He has written extensively on proteins and such natural products as nucleic acids and is a member of a number of national and international societies. In 1966, he was the first Israeli to be elected to the United States National Academy of Sciences. He was president of the State of Israel from 1973 to 1978.

KATZNELSON, BERL (1887-1944). Writer, editor, Israel labor leader. Honored for many years as the "conscience" of Israel labor, Katznelson came to Palestine from Russia in 1909. In 1920, after working for many years as an agricultural laborer and serving in the Jewish Legion* during the First World War, he was instrumental in founding the Histadrut,* the Israel Federation of Labor. Five years later he established **Davar,** the Histadrut daily, which he edited to the end of his life. A founding member of

Mapai, the Israel labor party, he was active in public life as a member of the executive committees of the Histadrut, the Jewish Agency,* and the World Zionist Organization.* During the late 1930's Katznelson was a strong partisan of "illegal" immigration. Recognizing the imminent danger to European and world Jewry, he was an active supporter of the underground, which smuggled Jews out of Europe and into Palestine.

KATZNELSON, YITZHAK. See HEBREW LITERATURE.

KAUFMAN, YEHEZKEL (1889-1963). Hebrew philosopher and scholar. He was born in the Ukraine, Russia, and educated in Talmudical academies and European universities. In his comprehensive sociological study called **Golah Ve-Nekhar** ("Exile and Alienhood"), Kaufman points out that the problem of Jewish nationalism is unique in character and historical development and therefore requires a solution of its own. His eight-volume history of the Jewish religion, **Toldot Ha-Emunah Ha-Yisraelit,** is an exhaustive and analytical work on the development of Jewish religious thought and practices. Kaufman was professor of Biblical research at the Hebrew University* in Jerusalem.*

KEREN HAYESOD. See ISRAEL, STATE OF and ZIONISM

KEREN KAYEMET. See JEWISH NATIONAL FUND.

KETUBAH. Jewish marriage contract listing the details of the marriage agreement, with particular emphasis on the promise of the husband to provide for his wife, both during the marriage and in case of divorce. The oldest **ketubah** preserved dates from the fifth century, though the Aramaic form used today probably dates only to the twelfth century. The margins of many **ketubot** were artistically ornamented with designs and Biblical verses.

KHAZARS. A people of Turkish origin who lived in southern Russia* and adopted the Jewish religion in the eighth century. Originally the Khazars were only a very small nomadic tribe, but by allying themselves with stronger tribes of Arabs, Russians, and Byzantines, and by constant warfare, they succeeded in establishing an empire that stretched from the steppes of Eastern Europe and from the Volga Basin to the Chinese frontier. In 960, Hasdai Ibn Shaprut, Jewish scholar and physician to the Caliph of Cordova, received a letter from King Joseph of the Khazars. It told a

THE KHAZAR KINGDOM

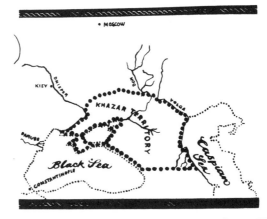

remarkable story. Some centuries before, King Bulan of the Khazars had asked the religious leaders of the Jews, Christians, and Mohammedans to explain their religion to him. Most impressed by the description of the Jewish faith, Bulan adopted it for his entire kingdom, and invited Jewish scholars to establish schools for the instruction of his people in the Bible,* Talmud,* and Jewish ritual. Bulan's successors took Jewish names and encouraged the practice of the Jewish religion within the country. Fascinated by the story, and grasping at the possibility of obtaining a land of refuge for persecuted Jews, Hasdai entered into correspondence with King Joseph, and learned about the country of the Khazars. At

Illuminated Ketubah, by Sol Nadel. Commissioned for the marriage of Mr. and Mrs. Maximilian Solomon, Toronto, Canada.

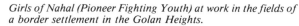

Girls of Nahal (Pioneer Fighting Youth) at work in the fields of a border settlement in the Golan Heights.

the conversion of the Khazars to Judaism has been interpreted variously. Some scholars call it a fable; others claim that only the ruling class adopted Judaism. Fascinated by the story, the medieval poet, Judah Ha-Levi,* described the philosophic discussion between King Bulan and the three religious leaders in his book **Ha-Kuzari.**

KIBBUTZ, KVUTZAH (Hebrew for "group," "collective"). Forms of communal settlement in Israel. The early **halutzim,*** or pionerrs, established the **kibbutz** on the principle of complete

Member of a kibbutz looking after chickens. The chicken in the picture is wearing glasses to prevent its pecking other chickens.

a time when much of Europe was fanatically bigoted, the Khazars had established a rule of tolerance. The King's palace was located on the Volga River near the site of modern Astrakhan. The Khazar capital conducted a flourishing trade in grains, hides, and fruit. Unfortunately, early in the eleventh century, Russian attacks destroyed the Khazar kingdom completely. The people were scattered throughout Crimea, Hungary* and even Spain;* most of them adopted Christianity, and they disappeared as a separate group. The story of

equality. The members of each settlement own its property in common. Every member has one vote in the assembly which manages the settlement. All members must work, and hired labor is employed only in times of crisis. Women share fully in the life and work of the community. Children are cared for by trained people, in separate houses. Their parents come for them immediately after work, and spend their free time, evenings, and Sabbaths with them.

The **kibbutz** and the **kvutzah** differ in several ways. The **kvutzah** has fewer members, and

Farming in a border village under the protection of guards.

originally was more often devoted solely to agriculture. Both types trace their origin to Degania, "mother of **kvutzot**," which was founded in 1909. The large **kibbutz** appeared many years later, when the number of immigrants flowing into the country rose. It was felt by some that larger units would better serve the need of the country. Industrial enterprises were introduced to increase employment opportunities, lessen the dependence of the settlements on the cities, and raise the standard of living. At present, virtually all **kibbutzim** and **kvutzot** belong to one of three national federations. These federations coordinate the activities of their members in such matters as marketing, education, culture, credit, and relations with the government and other outside groups.

KIBBUTZ GALUYOT. See INGATHERING OF THE EXILES.

KIDDUSH (Hebrew, meaning "sanctification"). The prayer of sanctification, that ushers in the Sabbath* and major holidays; it is primarily a home ceremony. The Biblical commandment, "Remember the Sabbath day to keep it holy," is observed in a number of ways. The Kiddush ceremony acknowledges the holiness of the day. The table is set with two covered loaves of **hallah**—twisted Sabbath loaves—in memory of the double portion of manna given the children of Israel for the Sabbath during the wanderings in the desert. The head of the house lifts the wine cup, and, reciting the Kiddush in the presence of the family, welcomes the Sabbath "Blessed art thou, O Lord Our God, King of the universe, who...in love and favor has given us Thy holy Sabbath..." Kiddush may be recited over hallah alone, although it is customary to use wine to "gladden the heart" so that the Sabbath or holiday is greeted with joy. For the benefit of wayfarers who were lodged in the synagogue, Kiddush was recited also there, after the evening service, a custom which has survived to this day. Special Kiddush goblets fashioned of fine gold and silver, and patterned in skillful design, were frequently used for this ceremony.

KIDDUSH HA-SHEM (Hebrew, meaning "sanctification of God's Name"). This term was applied to the act of martyrdom in Jewish history, especially during the Middle Ages, at the time of the Inquisition,* and during the Cossack massacres led by Bogdan Khmelnitzky in the Ukraine in 1648. **Kiddush Ha-Shem** also defines an act that brings honor to the Jewish people. The opposite of **Kiddush Ha-Shem** is **Hillul Ha-Shem,** desecration of God's Name.

KIMHI, DAVID (1160-1235). Hebrew grammarian and Biblical commentator. Kimhi provided Biblical students with logical, grammatical explanations of difficult words and passages. His grammatical works, encyclopedia, and **Book of Roots** were translated into Latin and used extensively by Christian scholars. Kimhi ably defended his faith in debates with various Christian scholars.

KINGS, BOOK OF. In the Bible,* the First and Second Books of Kings cover the history of the kingdoms of Israel* and Judah,* from Solomon,* 970 B.C.E., to the destruction of Judah by Babylonia in 586 B.C.E. Beginning with the last days of King David,* one dramatic story follows another. After Solomon's brilliant reign and the building of the Temple* in Jerusalem,* war split the country into two separate kingdoms, that of Israel in the north and Judah in the south. The story of the Kingdom of Israel spanning the years between 993-721 B.C.E. follows. Throughout his life the prophet Elijah* battled against Israel's idol worship; he was followed by the prophet Elisha who continued this struggle. In its close to three centuries of existence, the northern kingdom never managed to rid itself of idol worship. After describing the fall of the northern kingdom, the Book of Kings continues with the southern Kingdom of Judah whose capital was Jerusalem and whose center of worship was the Temple. Great prophets came to Judah, taught its people, and prepared and strengthened them for the time of their defeat and exile in 586 B.C.E.

KINNERET (Sea of Galilee). A harp-shaped sweet-water lake in Israel. 13 miles long and 7½ miles wide at its broadest point. Surrounded by the hills of Galilee and Golan, and dominated by the white-capped Hermon, Kinneret has the beauty of an Alpine lake. With its low altitude (640 feet below sea level), it has an almost tropical climate; its fertile shores, according to the sages, are the "doors to paradise." A rich fishing ground, Kinneret is encircled by towns and villages, including Tiberias,* Kfar Nahum (Capernaum), Migdal, Ginossar, and Ein Gev.

KISLEV. Third month of the Jewish civil calendar. Hanukkah* falls on the 25th of this month.

KISSINGER, HENRY ALFRED (1923-   ). U.S. political scientist and statesman. Born in Fuerth, Germany,* the son of Orthodox Jewish parents, he came to the U.S. as a refugee in 1938. After serving in the U.S. Army during World War II, he completed his studies at Harvard University, where he subsequently served as faculty member,

working primarily in the fields of government and international affairs. He was consultant to the U.S. Arms Control and Disarmament Agency from 1961 to 1967 and to the U.S. Department of State from 1965 to 1969. From 1961 to 1962 he was an advisor on national security affairs to President John F. Kennedy. In 1969 he became National Security Advisor to President Richard M. Nixon, and from 1973 to 1977 served as Secretary of State, the first foreign-born person and the first Jew in U.S. history to hold that office. In 1973 he received the Nobel Peace Prize (together with Le Duc Tho of North Vietnam) for his efforts to bring about peace in Vietnam. Following the Yom Kippur War* of 1973 he initiated a cease-fire between Israel and her Arab neighbors, and shuttled back and forth between Israel, Egypt,* Syria* and Jordan to effectuate troop disengagements on Israel's fronteirs with Egypt and Syria.   G.H.

KLAUSNER, JOSEPH (1874-1958). Hebrew scholar, writer and historian. As a youth of fifteen in Odessa, Russia, Klausner dedicated himself to the task of modernizing Hebrew.

He has published books in Hebrew on a variety of subjects: literature, philosophy, philology, history, and Oriental studies. He was editor of one of the finest Hebrew publications, **Ha-Shiloah,** for over twenty years, and has served as professor of modern Hebrew literature at the Hebrew University* in Jerusalem* since its establishment in 1925. Klausner was chief editor of a Hebrew encyclopedia, of which 31 volumes have already been printed. his two studies on the rise of Christianity, **Jesus of Nazareth** and **From Jesus to Paul,** are available in English translation.

KNESSET. Parliament of Israel. **(See** ISRAEL, GOVERNMENT OF.)

KNESSET ISRAEL (from the Hebrew, meaning "assembly of Israel"). In Jewish literature the term stands for the Jewish people. Knesset Israel was the official organization of the Jewish population in Palestine* under the British mandate. It was represented by the Asefat Ha-Nivharim, or parliament, which elected a national council (Vaad Leumi). Knesset Israel in Palestine achieved a measure of self-government in social, educational, cultural and, through the Rabbinical Council, in religious affairs as well.

KOF. Nineteenth letter of the Hebrew alphabet; numerically, one hundred.

KOHELET. See ECCLESIASTES.

KOHEN (Hebrew, meaning "priest"). Aaron,* the elder brother of Moses,* was the first high priest and the ancestor of all the priests and high priests who performed the sacrificial rites and conducted services in the Sanctuary. According to the Bible, the tent of meeting, or Tabernacle,* was built by the Israelites in the wilderness after their exodus from Egypt.* It was the first sanctuary in which a **kohen,** or priest, served the Lord (Exod. 25:8). There Aaron brought the offerings of the people in the desert. When he performed the services in the Tabernacle, Aaron wore priestly robes called the **hoshen** and **ephod.** On the shoulder-pieces of the **ephod** were two stones on which the names of the twelve tribes of Israel were engraved. On his chest, Aaron wore a breastplate made of gold, blue, purple, and scarlet yarn set with precious stones (Exod. 28).

When the Children of Israel settled in the Land of Canaan,* the priests, like the rest of the tribe of Levi,* received no portion of land, because they were completely dedicated to the service of the Lord. Instead, Biblical laws assigned to them a part of levitical taxes paid by the people, and some of the voluntary offerings from the crops and produce. Certain portions from the sacrifices and first fruit offerings were also set aside for the priests.

The Tabernacle rested in Shiloh (almost in the center of the land). Eli, the priest, officiated there for forty years and served as Judge of Israel. In the time or King David,* the role of the priest assumed new importance in the life of the people. Religious worship became centralized in Jerusalem,* the new capital of the nation. When King Solomon* built the Temple,* gleaming with gold and bronze, high on Mt. Moriah, Zadok served there as high priest, and his son Azariah after him. For a thousand years, this position passed from father to son in the family of Zadok. As the centuries passed, triumph and disaster followed in turn, changing the life of the nation. The First Temple was destroyed, then rebuilt by the people come home from exile. The priests were the teachers and the leaders of the people at that time, and their power was very great. As foreign empires came and went, they interfered with the life of the people, with worship in the Temple. Corrupt Greek and Roman governors ignored the required religious qualifications for priests, and set up puppet high priests, who bought their high place with gold. Then the Second Temple also was destroyed, and the people were scattered in the lands of the dispersion, where prayer took the place of sacrifices. The **kohanim** went into exile with their people, and many retained their identity by the surname **Kohen**. The spelling of the name has varied at different times and in different countries. Cohen, Coen, Cahn, Cahen, Cohan, Cahan, Kagan, Kahn; or Cowen, Kohn, Kann, and Katz (from the initials of **kohen tzedek**—priest of justice)—all these identify members of a family whose ancestors acted as priests in the Sanctuary. Descendants of the original **kohanim** still rise up in Orthodox synagogues during the holiday services, cover their faces with prayer shawls, and bless the people with the triple benediction of the ancient priests of Israel.   N.B-A.

KOHLER, KAUFMAN (1843-1926). Rabbi, educator and leader of Reform Judaism. This descendant of a family of rabbis was born in Fuerth, Bavaria, in 1843. He studied in Frankfurt-am-Main under the Orthodox philosopher, Samson Raphael Hirsch.* Later, he came under the influence of the famous Reform leader, Abraham Geiger,* who urged him to go to America. He arrived in the United States in 1869 and held Reform pulpits in Detroit, Chicago, and New York. Kohler convened the conference of 1885, which drew up the "Pittsburgh Platform"—a statement of Reform views which retained its influence until the late 1930's. He introduced Sunday services into his temples. Kohler was President of Hebrew Union College* and of the Central Conference of American Rabbis.* He also served as editor of the Jewish Publication Society's* 1917 Bible translation.

KOHUT, ALEXANDER (1842-1894). Rabbi and scholar. Ordained in Hungary, Kohut arrived in New York in 1885, and became one of the founding fathers of Conservative Judaism in America. He is best know for his exhaustive Talmudic dictionary, and work in behalf of the Jewish Theological Seminary of America* with Sabbato Morais. The Alexander Kohut Memorial Foundation, established in his memory, has contributed 8.000 books to Yale University to set up an Alexander Kohut Memorial Library of Hebrew and Rabbinic books. In addition, the foundation has created an Alexander Kohut Publication Fund for the printing of Semitic texts, and an Alexander Kohut Research Fellowship in Semitics at Yale.

KOHUT, REBECCA BETTELHEIM (1864-1951). Educator and communal worker. Brought to America from Hungary* as a child, Rebecca Bettelheim studied literature and history before her marriage to Alexander Kohut in 1887. After his death in 1894, she embarked on a long career as lecturer, author, educator, and communal worker. She founded the Kohut School for Girls,

and served as president of the first World Congress of Jewish Women and of the National Council of Jewish Women. Her writings include **My Portion,** an autobiography.

KOL NIDRE. See YOM KIPPUR.

Rabbi Abraham Isaac Kook

Courtesy Musaf Lakore Hatzair (Hadoar Weekly).

KOOK, ABRAHAM ISAAC HACOHEN (1865-1935). Great religious thinker and famous Chief Rabbi of Palestine. Born in a small town in Latvia, he studied at famous **yeshivot** (Talmudic academies), and became known as a brilliant Talmudic scholar when very young. He served as rabbi in several important Jewish communities. He also gained renown for his knowledge of Jewish mysticism (Kabbalah*), Hasidism,* and

Rebecca Kohut

Drawing by Isaac Friedlander.

religious philosophy. He was among the few religious leaders of his time who saw in the return to Zion the fulfillment of a basic doctrine of Judaism.

In 1904, he became Rabbi of Jaffa,* thus realizing his wish to settle in the Holy Land. After the First World War, in 1922, he was chosen Chief Rabbi of the Ashkenazic Jews in Palestine. In Jerusalem,* he founded his Yeshivah Merkaz-Harav. He wrote and published distinguished Talmudic works and philosophic-poetical essays. He identified himself with the pioneers and exerted a great influence on the young generation. His devotion and tolerance endeared him to all the builders of Palestine, the freethinking as well as the Orthodox. Every pioneer was close to his heart. When criticized for his tolerance of the irreligious Halutzim,* he gave this characteristic reply: "When the Holy Temple* existed, it was forbidden for a stranger or even an ordinary priest to enter in the Holy of Holies. Only the High Pirest was permitted to enter it, and that but once a year during the Day of Atonement...However, when the Temple was being built, any worker engaged in the enterprise would go into its innermost chambers in his ordinary work-clothes."

KOSHER. See DIETARY LAWS.

KOVNO. See LITHUANIA.

KREBS, SIR HANS ADOLF (1900-1981). Whitley Professor of Biochemistry at Oxford University since 1954. He was born in Hildesheim, Germany, and was educated in that country. Appointed lecturer in medicine at the University of Freiburg, Bavaria in 1932, he had to give up his post and emigrate to England* with the advent of the Nazis. There he was first demonstrator in biochemistry at Cambridge University and afterwards professor and head of the biochemistry department at the University of Sheffield. He shared the 1953 Nobel Prize in Medicine for his discovery of the citric acid cycle, which describes the chemical stages of oxidation of foodstuffs in living organisms. He is one of the 600 Fellows of the Royal Society, the highest distinction for any scientist in the world. His knighthood followed the Nobel Award.

KROCHMAL. NACHMAN (1785-1840). Hebrew philosopher and scholar. Born in Galicia, Krochmal shared his profound wisdom with students attracted by his philosophy of Jewish history. After his death his teachings were published in his **Guide for the Perplexed of the Age.**

Like Maimonides,* Krochmal sought to reconcile Jewish religious thought with modern ideas. He believed that the Jewish people had survived because it was endowed with an "absolute Spirit" —one which was universal and immortal. Krochmal stimulated the Jewish people to think of themselves, once again, as a nation.

KURDISTAN. "The Land of the Kurds" is not a separate country, but is divided among Turkey,* Iraq* and Iran.* Kurdistan stretches along the south shore of the Caspian Sea. The land is mountainous, with few roads. The Kurds are Moslems, ruled by semi-independent tribal chiefs. Many Christian Armenians and Assyrians lived there at one time, but their numbers were greatly reduced by massacres committed by the Kurds. Kurdish Jews according to an old legend came to Kurdistan from Palestine* in the time of Ezra,* several centuries before the common era. They still speak Aramaic* a dialect closely related to the language of the Gemara (**See** TALMUD). Once they were nomads like the local Moslems, but later they settled down like the Kurdish Christians. Kurdistan has always remained uninfluenced by Western civilization. The Jewish occupations included farming and fruit growing, shop-keeping, peddling, and handicrafts. Thousands of Kurdish Jews have gone to Israel, where their tall, stalwart figures, their beards and turbans, have become a familiar sight.

KVUTZAH. See KIBBUTZ.

L

LABOR ZIONISM. Socialist Zionism originated at the close of the nineteenth century and had to struggle for followers among Jewish socialists who objected to Zionism as a "reactionary movement." The Jewish socialists saw the solution of the Jewish problem in a Utopian world that socialism aimed to create for all people. The first Jewish leader to differ with the Marxist idea was Moses Hess,* who held that the Jewish people had the right to a place in mankind's family of nations. As the Socialist Zionist movement grew, it had to make its way against socialist ridicule and opposition. Two men, Nachman Syrkin* and Ber Borochov,* were the leaders in this struggle. Syrkin saw in Socialist Zionism a modern expression of the Hebrew prophets' teachings of justice for all men. He founded the first Poale Zion ("Workers of Zion") group in London (1903). Borochov felt that the special problem of the Jewish masses could be solved only in a Jewish Socialist commonwealth in Palestine.* At a conference in 1906, the various Russian Poale Zion groups adjusted their differences, and formed the Jewish Social Democratic Party, Poale Zion of Russia.* This body united with the Poale Zion groups of Austria* and America in 1907 to form the Poale Zion Party as an autonomous body within the World Zionist Organization.*

The Labor Zionists came to Palestine as the famous pioneering Second Aliyah (1904-1914), which established agricultural cooperatives, and organized the self-defense that guarded Jewish colonies from Arab attack. Before World War I, the Labor Zionists were divided into two parties: Poale Zion and the Hapoel Hatzair ("The Young Worker"). The personality and "religion of labor" gospel of Aaron David Gordon* exerted the greatest influence on both groups. The Poale Zion leaders in Palestine included David Ben-Gurion,* Yitzhak Ben-Zvi,* and Berl Katznelson.* In 1929, Poale Zion and Hapoel Hatzair merged to form Mifleget Poale Eretz Israel ("The Party of the Workers of Israel"). For decades Mapai, the initials by which this party is known, was the largest political party in Israel.

Another socialist Zionist party, the Hashomer Hatzair ("The Young Guard"), originated in Vienna during World War I. Later it spread to Eastern Europe; many of its members emigrated to Palestine, where they dedicated themselves to pioneering on the land. Hashomer Hatzair established a network of **kibbutzim*** (agricultural cooperatives), some in the most dangerous outposts in Palestine. During World War II (1942),

they formulated a program calling for the establishment of an independent bi-national state in Palestine with parity for Arabs and Jews. In 1948, the Hashomer Hatzair merged with two other groups: Ahdut Avodah which had broken off from Mapai, and Left Poale Zion. These three groups joined to form the Mifleget Ha-Poalim Ha-Meuhedet ("The United Workers' Party") best known by its initials, as Mapam.

N.B-A.

LABOR ZIONIST ALLIANCE. This organization is a result of a unification that took place in October 1972 of three elements of the Labor Zionist Movement in the United States: The Labor Zionist Organization of America (Poale Zion); the Farband-Labor Zionist Order; and the American Habonim Associations, an adult group of former members of Habonim the Labor Zionist youth organization.

The Poale Zion was the first organization of Socialist Zionists in the United States. Begun in 1903 in New York City, the Poale Zion platform called both socialism and Zionism reactions to "the intolerable conditions in Jewish life." Its program included trade union and mutual aid activities, participation in Zionist fund raising, and affiliation with the World Zionist Organization. A school system, later to be known as the Jewish Folk Schools, was organized, and a fraternal order for mutual aid—the Farband-Jewish National Workers Alliance—was established. In 1912, the Palestine Workers Fund was created, and became one of the major Poale Zion activities.

Outstanding among the Poale Zion intellectual leaders and theoreticians of this period were Nachman Syrkin,* who settled in the United States in 1908, Ber Borochov,* who came on repeated visits before his death in 1917, and Hayim Greenberg,* who came to America in 1924.

The Gewerkshaften (Trade Union) Campaign of the National Committee for Labor Israel was launched by Poale Zion in 1923, to enlist the sympathy and active interest of American trade unions in aiding the workers of Palestine. One consequence of the campaign was the Haifa* trade school, Amal, set up through the generosity of the International Ladies Garment Workers Union in 1946.

In 1925, the Women's Organization for the Pioneer Women in Palestine was founded as an outgrowth of fund-raising work for a girls' training farm in Palestine. Since then, the Pioneer Women have been an integral part of the Labor Zionist movement in America. In 1931, the Poale

Zion were united with the Zeire Zion, a younger element in American Labor Zionism.

The League for Labor Palestine was organized in 1932, to appeal largely to the business and professional elements within American Jewry that were in sympathy with the work of the Histadrut* in Palestine. Among the important educational activities of the league was the founding in 1934 of the periodical **Jewish Frontier**. In 1946, the continuous process of fusion and the melting down of ideological differences typical of American Jewish life resulted again in another merger of two Labor Zionist Organizations: the Poale Zion and the League for Labor Palestine. The Labor Zionist youth movement has followed a similar pattern. The Young Poale Zion Alliance was organized in 1920. Its youth branch, Habonim, became a separate organization in 1935. In 1940 the two groups joined Gordonia, a pioneer youth group, to form a new organization, Habonim—Labor Zionist Youth.   N.B-A.

LACHISH. A Canaanite city kingdom conquered by Joshua* in 1230 B.C.E. and alloted to Judah. A rice, corn, vine, and olive-growing area lying astride the main trade routes to Egypt* and Mesopotamia, Lachish was coveted and fought for by Israel's neighbors. Later it was the scene of Samson's* triumphs and David's* victory over Goliath. Lachish was a link in the chain of fortresses which King Rehoboam built to guard the southern approaches to Jerusalem. It was attacked by Sennacherib and then by Nebuchadnezzar, as corroborated in the Lachish Letters discovered in 1935. After fourteen centuries of neglect, the 125,000 acres of the Lachish area on Israel's southern border are now being rehabilitated through agricultural settlement. Three training camps have been set up to prepare future settlers, and eight villages have already been established.

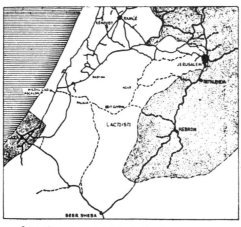

Location plan of Lachish development area.

LADINO (Judeo-Spanish). When the Jews left Spain* in 1492, the Spanish language was on the verge of change. The old form of the language is preserved today only in the Jewish dialect called Ladino. It is also called Spaniolish or Castiliano. It is spoken by Sephardic* Jews in Turkey,* the Balkans, part of North Africa, in Israel,* and the Americas. Over 20,000 persons in New York City speak Ladino. From the beginning, Ladino included Hebrew words. Later, it picked up Arabic, Turkish, Greek, French, and Italian words. It is usually printed in Rashi* script; but in Turkey and Israel a few newspapers print Ladino in Latin letters. Spanish scholars often visit the Sephardim* to collect old Spanish songs and sayings. Though many books and newspapers have been printed in Ladino, it has not been so creative a language as Yiddish.*

LAG B'OMER. See OMER.

LAMDAN, YITZHAK. See HEBREW LITERATURE.

LAMED. Twelfth letter of the Hebrew alphabet; numerically, thirty.

LAMED VAV TZADDIKIM (Hebrew, meaning "thirty-six righteous men"). The secret saints for whose sake the world survives. These "secret saints" are the center of many stories and mystic legends, all of them based on the saying in the Talmud* by Abbaye that there are at least thirty-six righteous men in every generation. The outstanding qualities of the "secret saint" are piety and modesty so great that he hides his learning and earns his bread by physical labor. According to this legend, before one of the Lamed Vav dies, another is born, and so the sinful world is saved from destruction.

LAMENTATIONS. The third of the five scrolls in the Writings section of the Bible.* Its author, according to tradition, is the prophet Jeremiah.* Lamentations consists of five beautiful elegies or poems of mourning lamenting the fall of Jerusalem* and the destruction of the first Temple.* The first four elegies are written in alphabetic acrostics, that is, each verse opens with a letter of the alphabet, in consecutive order. Lamentations is chanted in the synagogue on the ninth day of the month of Ab—the day of the destruction of the Temple, in 586 B.C.E.

LANDAU, SAMUEL HAYIM (1892-1928). Religious Zionist leader and philosopher. Born in a Hasidic family in Poland,* he rose at an early age to a high position of leadership in religious

Zionism.* He worked untiringly for Hapoel Hamizrachi, as well as for Hehalutz and Zionist fund-raising, at first in Poland and later (1925) in Palestine. Landau was the founder of the movement within religious Zionism that stressed Torah Ve-Avodah (traditional Judaism and Labor).

LATIN AMERICA. All of the Western Hemisphere south of the United States-Mexican border and north of Antarctica, including South America, Central America, Mexico and the islands of the Caribbean. This large and variegated portion of the globe is known as "Latin" America because of the mark left upon it by its Spanish and Portuguese colonizers, who spoke "Romance" languages, or tongues derived from Latin. Spanish or Portuguese is still spoken in most Latin American countries.

Columbus, it will be recalled, had ventured to cross the Atlantic in search of the "Indies." He believed that by sailing westward he would discover a sea route to India, home of silk, spices, elephants, gold and all the "riches of the Orient." Instead, he stumbled on the Americas, which he believed to be the "West Indies." It was soon realized however, first that this was neither India nor the Indies, but a "New World" no less rich and exotic than the fabled Orient. Within thirty years this "New World" was overrun with Spanish and Portuguese adventurers intent on exploiting the wealth of their newly discovered empire, which they came to call "New Spain."

As colonists settled in the Americas, a thriving traffic sprang up between "New Spain" and the mother countries. Ships bore rich ores to Europe and returned with manufactured goods for the colonies. Soon it was discovered that the riches of the New World lay not in metals alone. Sugar, tobacco, coffee, and other items that could be grown in the fertile valleys and tropical islands of the Americas commanded high prices on the markets of the old world. Trade boomed.

Among the masters of this trade were Marranos,* Spanish Jews who had become converts to Catholicism rather than go into exile or be burned at the stake. For 1492, the year Columbus* discovered America, was in other respects a great year in the annals of Spain—and a dread one in those of the Jews. In that year, King Ferdinand and Queen Isabella, Columbus's patrons, had finally expelled the last Moorish invaders from their land. Declaring Spain a "Christian kingdom," they had banished all Jews from their dominions. Only those Jews who accepted Catholicism could remain. Most chose exile. A good number, however, were baptized, but continued to practice the faith of their fathers in secret. Such Jews were known as Marranos, or "new-Christians," and were the special object of persecution by a branch of the Church known as the Inquisition.* Seeking to escape the watchful eye of the Inquisition, many such Jews had emigrated to the colonies. Experienced in trade and management, they prospered almost beyond belief. Within a few decades, Marrano communities flourished in Argentina,* Peru,* Bolivia,* Mexico,* Brazil*—in fact, wherever Spanish or Portuguese colonists had settled. In Brazil, they were pioneers in the sugar-growing and refining industry; in Bolivia, they monopolized local shipbuilding; elsewhere, they engaged in international commerce.

But their prosperity was not long-lived, for the long arm of the Inquisition soon reached out to the New World. Established in Peru in 1569 and Mexico in 1570, it succeeded in time in destroying virtually all Marrano settlements within its reach. In Mexico, even Don Luiz de Carvajal, governor of a province, was burned at the stake. Peru alone had thirty-four **autos-da-fe*** (acts of faith) between the establishment of the Inquisition there and its abolition in 1806. Today, the only known survivors of the Old Marrano Communities are the **Sabbatarios,** descendants of Chilean Marranos who escaped to the interior and intermarried with Indians and Spaniards, and a community of 3,000 in Mexico who claim similar descent.

Not all the Marranos of New Spain and New Portugal were lost, however. By the time the Inquisition was in full swing, there were some places of refuge for Jews in the New World. England and Holland,* the two great mercantile powers of the seventeenth century, were not long in demanding a share of trade in the Western Hemisphere. By force and by treaty they gained a number of colonies in Latin as well as in North America. It was to such colonies that persecuted Marranos could flee. Thus, when Portugal* in 1654 expelled the Brazilian Jews who had confessed their true faith during a brief period of Dutch rule, the exiles made their was to other Dutch colonies in the Americas. Twenty-six of them reached what was then the Dutch colony of New Amsterdam, forming the nucleus of the first Jewish congregation in New York.* Others found their way to Surinam (Dutch Guiana), Curacao, Jamaica and other colonies held by either the British or the Dutch. There they founded communities which survive to the present day—the oldest with continuous history in the Western hemisphere.

These settlements, looking back three hundred years and more make up a historically important but numerically insignificant part of Latin American Jewry today. For the bulk of the approximately 400,000 Jews who now live in Latin America are either immigrants themselves, or the

194

children of immigrants who arrived less than 100 years ago.

The modern immigration began in the nineteenth century, after most Latin American countries had gained their independence. The first to come were traders and merchants, chiefly from the Sephardic* communities of the Balkans and the Middle East. After 1890 the pace of immigration quickened. Encouraged by the Jewish Colonization Society (I.C.A.),* an organization which believed that the sufferings of the Jewish people might be eased by a return to the soil, several thousand newcomers settled on farm colonies in Argentina and Brazil. The greatest influx, however, came between the First and Second World Wars. After the United States curtailed immigration in 1924, the stream of newcomers from Eastern Europe was directed to Latin America. During the 1930's thousands of German Jews, fleeing Nazi persecution, settled there. Partly because of the pressure of this immigration, and partly because of Nazi propaganda, most Latin American countries closed their gates to refugees in the mid 1930's. Only after World War II did they again open their doors to limited numbers of refugees and displaced persons.

Bringing new skills and great initiative, these Jews played an important role in the development of Latin American commerce and industry. Most of the immigrants settled in cities, where they pursued their old occupations: trade, manufacturing—especially of textiles, furs, furniture—and crafts. New business techniques included installment and direct sales—techniques which extended consumer markets to include even the poorest. To the field of banking they introduced "peoples' banks"—cooperative institutions which lend small sums at low rates of interest.

The various Latin American communities vary widely in size, organization and problems. Argentina, the largest settlement, has 233,000 Jews in a highly organized community. All the organized settlements participate in the World Jewish Congress.* Although most communities are clearly subdivided into Sephardic, Ashkenazic (East European) and German Jewish sectors, these subsectors generally unite to participate in national Jewish organizations.

One problem shared by most of the settlements is anti-Semitism,* which appears from time to time. During the 1930's and 1940's Nazi agents actively fomented hatred against the Jewish population, but their efforts were only partly effective. Since the end of World War II, the problem has become less acute. One sign of the change is the favorable attitude of most Latin American governments toward Israel.* This is reflected in their voting record in the United Nations. Such countries as Argentina have favored Israel in matters of trade.

Having suffered persecution in their lands of origin, and sometimes in their new homes as well, Latin American Jews are for the most part ardent Zionists. Almost all communities have Zionist organizations, through which they have made considerable contributions to the development of Israel. There are **halutz (see** HALUTZIM) ("pioneer") movements in the larger communities, and there has been some immigration to Israel. In some countries, the Jewish schools are under Zionist control.

Education is one of the chief concerns of Latin American Jewry. Except in Mexico City, the teacher shortage is acute. However, Latin American Jewry has experienced a flowering of Jewish—especially Yiddish—culture. Hope for its continuance depends on the education of the younger generation. Only time will tell.

Emma Lazarus

LAZARUS, EMMA (1849-1887). American poet. Born in New York, member of a highly placed Sephardic* family, this gifted poetess eventually brought her considerable talent to Hebraic themes. News stories of bloody persecutions of the Jews in Russia,* followed by contact with refugees in New York, inspired her prose and animated her poetry. "The New Colossus," which she wrote on a single sheet of paper, is now inscribed on a plaque imbedded in the Statue of Liberty. The last lines of the poem constitute an invocation of welcome to the immigrants.

Give me your tired, your poor,
Your huddled masses yearning to breathe free.
The wretched refuse of your teeming shore,
Send these, the homeless, tempest-tost to me,
I lift my lamp beside the golden door!

LEBANON (Hebrew, meaning "white," after its snow-capped peaks). An independent republic since 1944, Lebanon occupies a mountain range that runs almost parallel with the Mediterranean, north of Israel, for about 100 miles, rising at its highest point to 10,000 feet. The country is divided by the Coelesyria (or El Baka) Valley into Lebanon on the west and Anti-Lebanon on the east. Lebanon was famous in antiquity for its cedar forests (long since destroyed by reckless cutting), which provided timber for the First and Second Temples in Jerusalem. Its present (1984) population of about 2,650,000 includes a Christian (Maronite) majority, Moslems, Druzes, and a small number of Jews.

The Jewish community is approximately 400, most of whom live in Beirut, the capital. It has a large degree of autonomy in internal affairs under a statute passed in 1952. Although Lebanon participated in the Arab invasion of Israel in 1948, Lebanese Jewry has enjoyed better treatment than any other Jewish community in the Arab World. There is nonetheless a complete ban on travel and emigration, and Jews are excluded from army and government positions.

During the Six-Day War,* Lebanon did not participate in the fighting. However, two and a half years later, Palestinian Arab guerillas began to infiltrate into Lebanon and to use the southern part of the country as a base for raids into Israeli territory. When it became obvious that the Lebanon government was unable to put an end to these attacks, Israel retaliated in the areas from which the guerillas operated.

In 1982, Israel launched Operation Peace for Galilee, designed to secure its southern border from terrorist infiltration from Lebanon, where the PLO became, in effect, a state within a state. As a result of the war, the PLO was ousted from Beirut and their military base in Lebanon was destroyed, creating hopes for a unified Lebanon and the possibility of an Israeli-Lebanese peace treaty in 1983. This treaty was abrogated by Lebanon in 1984, owing to internal Moslem and Druze pressure and Syrian opposition. In mid-1984, both Israeli and Syrian troops were still stationed in Lebanon.

LEESER, ISAAC (1806-1868). American religious leader. A rabbi and founder of Maimonides College in Philadelphia, Isaac Leeser came to the United States while still in his teens. He continued his studies, and became a journalist and editor. In 1829 he became rabbi of Congregation Mikveh Israel in Philadelphia, where he introduced the English sermon into synagogue services. He was opposed to Reform, and carried on a strenuous campaign for the preservation of traditional Judaism. His work and thought were reflected in the pages of **The Occident,** a magazine he edited for twenty-six years. His Bible translation of 1853 served American Jewry as the accepted English version for more than fifty years.

LEGION, JEWISH. During the First World War the Turkish government persecuted the Jewish community in Palestine,* many of whom had migrated from Russia* and were hence considered "enemy aliens." During 1914 alone, 12,000 Jews fled Palestine to find refuge in Egypt.* These refugees felt that the time had come for the Jews to take an active part in liberating their homeland. Under the leadership of Joseph Trumpeldor,* a Jewish unit, the Zion Mule Corps, was founded in March 1915 and served with the British in the Gallipoli Expeditionary Force. This corps' record for bravery helped break down British resistance to the establishing of a Jewish Legion. Such a legion, the Royal Fusiliers, was organized in 1917, in London, after much effort by Vladimir Jabotinsky.* On June 5, in 1918, the mobilization of a Jewish Legion began in America. David Ben-Gurion,* later Prime Minister of Israel, Yitzhak Ben-Zvi* and Pinhas Rutenberg were the chief architects of the Legion movement in America. The Jewish Legion numbered 5,000, and was a part of the British Army that wrested Samaria, Galilee, and Trans-Jordania from the Turks. Another 5,000 men were due to join them, but the Armistice was proclaimed before their arrival.

LEHMAN, HERBET HENRY (1878-1963). United States legislator, statesman. His early career was in the banking business. During the First World War he became special advisor to the Secretary of War and, later, aid to Franklin D. Roosevelt, then Secretary of the Navy. In 1928 he was elected Lieutenant Governor of New York State, and succeeded Roosevelt as Governor in 1932, an office he held for ten years. During the depression years that began in 1929, Lehman's liberal legislation in such fields as welfare and labor brought economic stability to the state. In 1949 he was elected to the United States Senate, where his liberalism was expressed in his opposition to the McCarran-Walter immigration bill, his

Herbert H. Lehman
Photo by Pach Bros.

196

support of sending arms to Israel* and the settlement of Jewish claims in Austria.* He served actively in the Senate until his retirement in 1956. For more than half a century, Lehman's numerous philanthropic activities included interest in child welfare institutions, hospitals, and vocational schools. He was a trustee of the Jewish Theological Seminary,* a director of the National Conference of Christians and Jews, and affiliated with the American Jewish Committee.* In addition to honorary degrees from numerous educational institutions, Lehman received awards from the Sidney Hillman Foundation and the Four Freedoms Foundation, in recognition of his service to the cause of civil liberties.

LEIVICK, HALPERN (1888-1963). Yiddish poet and playwright. Born Levi Halpern, he spent his youth in White Russia,* where he participated in the revolutionary movement. For this act, young Halpern was sentenced to four years of hard labor and life-long Siberian exile by the Tsarist government. He succeeded in escaping to America in 1913.

In his Russian prison, Leivick wrote his first poems. His tendency toward symbolism and visionary writing became evident in his later poems and plays. Deeply lyrical, Leivick's poetry is dedicated to the idea of social redemption for his own people and of all mankind. In his plays **Der Goilem** ("The Golem*"), **Kaiten** ("Chains"), **Shmates** ("Rags"), and others, he cries out against social injustice and human suffering. His plays have been presented on the Yiddish stage, and in Hebrew translation by the Ohel and Habimah* theatres in Israel.

LESSING, GOTTHOLD EPHRAIM (1729-1781). German (non-Jewish) dramatist, peot, and critic, and one of the most influential writers of his time. His plays were widely performed and of lasting influence. They usually had underlying ideas that Lessing wanted to impress on his generation. At that time, the Jews of Germany* were deprived of civil rights and were considered inferior and incapable of being noble or generous. Lessing wrote a play, **Die Juden,** about a Jew who saves the life of a baron and refuses to accept any reward. This play aroused a controversy as to whether such a Jew could possibly exist. It also brought the author a letter from Moses Mendelssohn,* then an unknown student in a Berlin garret. A few years later, Lessing met the young philosopher and a life-long friendship developed between them. Lessing's battle against religious bigotry was suppressed by the authorities, and some of his writings were confiscated. He then decided to see if "they would

Halpern Leivick
Courtesy YIVO, New York City.

let me preach undisturbed from my old pulpit—the stage." He therefore wrote **Nathan der Weise,** ("Nathan the Wise") (1779), a plea for religious tolerance and a protrait of his friend Moses Mendelssohn, the Jewish philosopher. This drama helped considerably in the eighteenth-century movement to break down prejudice against Jews.

LEVI. Third son of Jacob* and Leah. The tribe of Levi received no allotment of land in Canaan,* because it was set apart to conduct the worship of God. Instead, the Levites received for their maintenance a portion of the tithes brought by the worshippers to the Tabernacle of Sanctuary. **(See also KOHEN.)**

LEVIATHAN. Legendary sea creature, described in several places in the Bible, and particularly in Job 40:25. The Talmud* and Midrash describe the leviathan as a huge fish coiled around the entire globe, and reserved for the feast of the righteous in the world-to-come.

LEVI ISAAC OF BERDICTCHEV. See HASIDISM.

LEVIN, SHMARYAHU (1867-1935). Writer, orator and Zionist leader. Born in Russia,* Levin from his earliest youth, was active in the Hoveve Zion* ("Love of Zion") movement. He dreamed of being an engineer, then of becoming a pioneer on the soil of Palestine,* and set out to make his way there. At the last moment, his father persuad-

Shmaryahu Levin

ed him to return and enter the family business. Drawn back gradually to his studies, Levin went to Germany* and obtained his doctoral degree from the University of Koenigsberg. With the coming of Theodor Herzl,* the founder of political Zionism, Levin's Zionist work increased in scope. His position as government-appointed rabbi in important Russian cities, and later as director of a school in Vilna, enlarged his opportunities for such service. He also participated in the movement to obtain equal rights for the Jews in Russia; in the short-lived first Russian Duma, or parliament, Levin was outstanding among the twelve elected Jewish delegates. When the Duma passed a resolution denouncing the government's policy of oppression and secret sponsoring of pogroms, the Tsar dissolved it. Levin was no longer safe in Russia, and left on a Zionist mission to the Unites States. In America, his oratory electrified Zionist audiences, and the razor edge of his wit persuaded many who were previously opposed or apathetic to Zionism* to aid in the upbuilding of Palestine. World War I found Levin in the United States, where, as a member of the World Zionist Executive, he was active in Zionist leadership. After the war, he settled in Palestine, living in Haifa* till his death in 1935. Levin's four-volume memoirs are a facinating record of his life and time. N.B-A.

LEVINSOHN, ADAM HACOHEN. See HEBREW LITERATURE.

LEVINSOHN, ISAAC BAER. See HEBREW LITERATURE.

LEVINSOHN, MICAH JOSEPH. See HEBREW LITERATURE.

LEVITES. Descendants of Levi,* third son of Jacob. From the age of twenty years to fifty, the Levite was consecrated to render service at the Sanctuary where the Israelites worshipped God by bringing sacrifices to the altar. They were gatekeepers and caretakers of the sanctuary and its furnishings; they were judges, teachers of the Law and scribes, temple musicians, and assistants to the priests. Since the tribe of Levi had received no land in Canaan, the Levites were assigned the revenues from forty cities as well as certain tithes from all crops and produce. They assisted the prophet Samuel* at Shiloh in the Tabernacle* services and in teaching the people. In the First Temple,* built by Solomon* in Jerusalem,* they were the musicians and the singers, and performed all the menial tasks as well. When the Temple was rebuilt after the Babylonian exile, the Levites led the joyous procession at the dedication festival. When Ezra* and Nehemiah* instituted the Great Assemblies and read the Law to the people, the Levites circulated among them explaining and teaching its meaning. To this day, when all traces of the various tribes of Israel have long been erased by the centuries, the tradition of descent from the Levites is still handed down from father to son. At synagogue services, a Levite is called up to the reading of the Torah second, after a **kohen*** (priest).

LEVITICUS. (From the Greek, meaning "relating to the Levites.") The third of the Five books of Moses. It contains a manual for Levites, the priestly ritual of sacrifices, the Code of Holiness, rules regarding charity, marriage and laws governing many other phases of life.

LEVY, ASSER (d. 1681). His full name was Asser Levy van Swellem. He was one of the original band of twenty-three pilgrims who came to New York in 1654. From a penniless immigrant he rose to be a substantial citizen, a man of property and importance in the community. He initiated several lawsuits which resulted in the clarification of Jewish rights in New Amsterdam. Notable among these was the right to stand guard along with fellow-burghers, rather than pay a tax to be exempt from military duty. A novel by Louis Zara, **Blessed Is the Land,** commemorates Levy's life and accomplishments.

LEVY, URIAH PHILLIPS (1792-1862). United States naval officer. He led the crusade to abolish flogging as a form of discipline in the United States Navy. Levy's opposition to this and other accepted practices, as well as his Jewishness, made him a target of petty persecution, abuse, imprison-

Uriah P. Levy, from the collection of Capt. N. Taylor Philips.

ment, and six courts-martial. Finally vindicated by an official court of inquiry, he rose in rank from cabin boy to commodore and flag officer of the United States Navy, in the Mediterranean, under President Abraham Lincoln. In March 1943 the Navy honored the memory of Uriah Phillips Levy by naming a destroyer after him.

LEWISOHN, LUDWIG (1883-1955). American novelish, critic, and outstanding writer on modern Jewish problems. Born in Germany, he was brought to the United States as a child. Of his upbringing he wrote: "Like all Jewish youngsters educated wholly in the traditions of the West, I had heard and knew little of that heritage of mine—mine apparently whether I wanted it or not—except in terms of contempt and contumely." Under the influence of his early environment, his first love was German culture; his first jobs were teaching German at the universities of Wisconsin and Ohio. During this period (1904-1919) he wrote stories, novels, and criticism of German literature and drama.

Between 1920-24, Lewisohn served on the editorial staff of the magazine, **The Nation.** During that perioed, a great inner change transformed Lewisohn from an assimilated Jew to one deeply absorbed in his Jewishness. He began to lecture and write on Jewish subjects, visited Palestine,* and became an active Zionist. His first autobiographical volume, **Upstream** (1922) documented the author's spiritual and intellectual development from childhod to manhood. The next three books published between 1924 and 1932, **The Creative Life, Citites and men,** and **Expression in America,** developed Lewisohn's belief that literature may not be seperated from life. These volumes were highly esteemed in the literary

world. Beginning with **The Island Within** (1928), Ludwig Lewisohn emerged as primarily a Jewish writer. In **The Island Within,** as in another autobiographical volume, **Midchannel,** he analyzed the problems of the assimilated Jew, the difficulties of intermarriage, and the spiritual enrichment that flowed from a rediscovery of Judaism. The last years of Lewisohn's life were spent at Brandeis University, where, as Professor of Comparative Literature, as a Jew, a Zionist, and a literary stylist, he influenced young minds.

N.B-A.

LIEBERMANN, MAX (1847-1935). Artist. A native of Berlin, he followed in the footsteps of Joseph Israels* and painted Dutch themes. In Amsterdam he was attracted by the same colorful ghetto scenes that had fascinated Rembrandt.* Since he chose to paint such "ignoble" subjects as peasants working in a potato field, and women plucking geese, he met with much opposition in the Germany of Emperor William II. In his old age, however, Liebermann became very famous, and was called to paint the portraits of outstanding statesmen, educators, and civic leaders. These portraits are notable for their realistic vigor. He served as president of the Prussian Academy of Arts from 1919 until the Nazis ousted him in 1933.

LILIEN, EPHRAIM MOSES (1874-1925). Artist. Born in Galicia. Lilien became the leader of the new Jewish art movement in Berlin in 1902. He came to Paelstine* in 1907, and while there taught at the Bezalel School of Arts and Crafts* in Jerusalem.* A master of black and white drawings, he has left numerous sketches of Jewish life throughout the world. Lilien was an ardent Zionist, and emphasized the cultural motif in Zionism.

Ludwig Lewisohn

"The Miracle" by Jacques Lipchitz.

LILIENBLUM, MOSHE LEIB (1843-1910). Writer, leader in the Enlightenment movement and early Zionist. Born in a small town in Lithuania,* he was steeped in the Jewish tradition. While still very young, he headed a Talmudical academy in his hometown. Yet he joined the ranks of those "enlightened" Jews who tried to introduce reforms into Jewish life. Lilienblum's criticism of some traditional beliefs and practices aroused the anger of the Orthodox. Shielded for a time from the persecution of his townspeople by his friends, he eventually left his hometown.

Lilienblum's desire for secular education brought him to Odessa. There, disillusioned by the lack of spiritual values, he wrote a revealing account of his life called **Hatot Neurim** ("Sins of Youth"), in which he struck at the evils of ghetto life. After the pogrom of 1881 in Russia,* Lilienblum favored Jewish settlement in Palestine.

LIPCHITZ, JACQUES (1891-1973). Sculptor. Born in a small Lithuanian town, he migrated to France,* whence he fled during the Second World War to the United States, where he lived. He has drawn much inspiration from the Bible,* and from his own experiences as a Jew. When he made the bronze, **Jacob Wrestling with the Angel,** he associated Jacob's name with his own first name. He explained: "Man is wrestling with the angel; it is a tremendous struggle, but he wins, and is blessed." Other pieces of Jewish interest include **The Prayer** (an old man performing the **kapparot** ceremony) and **The Miracle,** a tribute to the new state of Israel (a figure, arms raised, facing the Tables of the Law, out of which grows the seven-branched candelabrum). Toward the end of this life he became interested in the Lubavitch Hasidic movement. **(See** HASIDIM; SHNEERSON.)

LIPSKY, LOUIS (1876-1963). Zionist leader and writer. He was born in Rochester, N.Y., in 1876, and educated at the Rochester Free Academy and Columbia University. From 1930, Lipsky was president of the Eastern Life Insurance Co. of New York. His work as a gifted journalist introduced him into Jewish public life. Lipsky served as editor and columnist for various publications, including the **New York Morning Telegraph, Reader Magazine,** and **Associated Magazine.** In 1899 he founded the **Maccabaean,** editing this monthly official Zionist publication until 1918, when it was transformed into the weekly **New Palestine.** Lipsky's two-volume collection of **Stories from Jewish Life** was published in 1927. In these, as in his other writing, Lipsky's clear and pungent style compels the interest of the reader.

Lipsky was active in the American Jewish Con-gress from its inception in 1918, and he was largely responsible for founding the World Jewish Congress.* He served as a member of the Jewish delegation to the Versailles Peace Conference* in 1919, and as writer, orator, and parliamentarian, participated in every phase of American Zionist life from the beginning of the twentieth century. Lipsky achieved recognition as one of the foremost thinkers in American Zionism and served as President of the Zionist Organization of America* from 1921 to 1931. Lipsky supported the policies of Chaim Weizmann,* was co-founder (1929) and member of the enlarged Jewish Agency for Palestine* and was elected a life-member of the World Zionist Executive. During the period between 1949 and 1954, he served as chairman of the Zionist Emergency Council, and was the honorary chairman of the American Zionist Council until his death. Lipsky's last book, **A Gallery of Zionist Profiles,** was published in 1956.

Louis Lipsky

200

LITHUANIA. Soviet Republic on the Baltic Sea. Bounded by Latvia, Poland,* and Prussia. In the 13th century, Lithuania gained its independence from Russia. It became a grand duchy, including all of White Russia and parts of the Ukraine. Jews settled there in the 14th century. They came from Germany* and Poland, and were treated well by the local pagan rulers. Most of these Jews were farmers, artisans, and managers of estates. During this period, intermarriage between the ruling families of Lithuania and Poland drew the two countries closer, bringing Lithuania under the influence of Catholicism, and reversing the favorable treatment of the Jews.

In 1495, the Grand Duke Alexander expelled the Jews from the country. The expulsion edict remained in force for eight years. After returning in 1503, the Jews resumed their respected place in the economic life of the country. By the middle of the sixteenth century, the influence of the Chruch and the enmity of the lower nobility again made themselves felt, and laws restricting Jewish dress and occupations were passed. The political union of Lithuania and Poland in 1569 brought no marked change in the Jewish position. On the whole, the rulers of the country protected the Jews from excessive restrictions. The Jewish population enjoyed a measure of self-rule within their own communities.

From 1623 to 1764, Jewish religious, economic, and social life was regulated by the Council of Three Lands, within which the important Jewish communities of Lithuania were represented. During the years of the Cossack uprisings which began in 1648 and were led by Chmielnicki, thousands of Jews were slaughtered and many of the Jewish communities in Lithuania destroyed. A partial healing of the wounds inflicted by the Cossacks came in the following century. The Jewish community of Lithuania became a center of Jewish learning. Great influence on the spiritual life of the Jews was exerted by Rabbi Elijah, Gaon* of Vilna. His pupils, especially Hayim of Volozhin, were the founders of famous Talmudical academies, or **yeshivot,** in the land. Lithuanian Jewry played an important role in the dispute between the Hasidism and their opponents, the Mitnagdim. **(See** HASIDISM.) The bulk of Lithuanian Jewry remained aloof from the Hasidic movement, and was primarily devoted to the study of the Talmud.*

During the second half of the nineteenth century, Lithuania became fertile ground for the growth of the Haskalah* or Enlightenment movement. Here, modern Hebrew literature flourished and produced some of the greatest Hebrew writers, among whom were Micah Joseph Levin-sohn, Abraham Mapu,* and J. L. Gordon.* Later in the nineteenth century, the Zionist movement, as well as the Socialist Bund* found numerous followers among Lithuanian Jewry. During the same period, due to economic hardships and Tsarist persecutions, a large number of Lithuanian Jews emigrated to America, South Africa,* and other countries, where they established flourishing Jewish communities.

After World War I, Lithuania became an independent republic. In 1919, the Lithuanian government appointed a Ministry of Jewish Affairs and granted the Jews full cultural autonomy. The Jews enjoyed these rights for five years, then they were curtailed and economic restrictions instituted. However, the Jews retained some of their cultural autonomy and developed a government-supported school system, using Hebrew and Yiddish as the languages of instruction. Lithuania also remained a center of Talmudic study. **Yeshivot** continued to exist in Slobodka, Telz, Panevezsh, and in a number of other cities.

At the outbreak of the Second World War, close to 170,000 Jews (about 7% of the general population), lived in Lithuania, 40,000 of them in Kovno, the capital of the country. In 1940, Lithuania was annexed by Soviet Russia, only to fall into the hands of Nazi Germany in the following year. In 1942, mass murders of the Jews were carried out with the help of the local populace, until almost all Lithuanian Jews were wiped out, save only those few who had managed to flee to other countries.

After the Second World War, Lithuania was incorporated into the Soviet Union. Precise statistics as to the number of Jews at present are not available. A 1956 report by a Lithuanian emigrant placed the number of Jews in Vilna and Kovno at 40,000. Information of Jewish cultural, religious, and educational institutions in Soviet Lithuania is virtually non-existent, although it is known that a few synagogues still function in the cities of Vilna and Kovno. H.L.

LITERATURE, HEBREW. See HEBREW LITERATURE.

LITERATURE, YIDDISH. See YIDDISH LITERATURE.

LOD. See LYDDA.

LOEW, JUDAH BEN BEZALEL (c. 1525-1609). Talmudic scholar and astronomer in Prague. He was greatly interested in science, an uncommon pursuit for a rabbi of his time. Rabbi Judah's advanced views were evident in his many books, where he criticized the state of Jewish education, and expressed ideas which centuries later came to be known as Zionism.* Known in Jewish scholarship as the Maharal, he published about twenty books of which the most famous is a commentary on Rashi.* He was considered an extraordinary person, and many legends are woven around his personality. The most famous of these tells about the creation of the Golem,* an automaton made of clay and brought to life by the Maharal's use of the secret name of God. According to this legend, the Maharal used the Golem during times of stress to save the Jewish community from persecution and evil decrees. As soon as the Golem had fulfilled his mission, the Maharal would return him to his lifeless state. The legend of the Golem has been the theme of many poems, novels, and plays. In Hebrew, it has been ably used by David Frischmann,* and in Yiddish the play **Der Golem,** by H. Leivick,* has been a favorite on the stage. A film has also been made on the subject.

Jewish folkore is rich with anecdotes about the wisdom of the Maharal, and the miracles that he performed. His interest in alchemy was probably at the root of his fame as a miracle-maker. Rudolph II of Austria,* who himself took an interest in astronomy, hoped to become wealthy by the use of alchemy. He summoned the Maharal, and they met on February 16, 1592, and spent a number of hours in conversation. A statue of the Maharal was erected in front of the city hall of Prague.   A.R.M.

LONDON. Jews resided in England's capital as early as the Norman Conquest in 1066—if not earlier. For religious and security reasons they lived as a compact community in one special part of the city, whose site is still remembered by the name of one of the City of London's oldest streets—Old Jewry.

There was little peace for Jews in those early times. As money-lenders they were hardly likely to endear themselves to the barons who were in their debt or to peasants, who, urged on by fanatical priests, blamed the Jews for their woes. However, as the property of the king—the "king's chattels"—the Jews were under royal protection. But this was withdrawn when, after a series of extortions, the Jews were expelled by Edward I in 1290.

A new and happier chapter began with the readmission of Jews in 1656 under Oliver Cromwell. The handful of Sephardim,* originally from Mediterranean lands, who lived in London at that time, at fist met for worship in their small synagogue in Creechurch Lane. However, with the arrival of more Sephardim from Holland, a larger synagogue was erected in 1701 at Bevis Marks. It still stands today, and is cherished as the mother synagogue of the Jews in England.

In the wake of the Sephardim came the Ashkenazim from Central Europe, and they too set up their special house of worship at Duke's Place, where they met for prayer as early as 1690.

London has always been the home of England's Jewish communal institutions; the Board of Deputies of British Jews,* the elected representative body of British Jewry, founded in 1760; the Jewish Board of Guardians, (1859); the United Synagogue (1870); Jews' College (1855); the Anglo-Jewish Association (1871), and a whole network of educational, social, and philanthropic institutions. London is also the seat of the Chief Rabbinate of the British Commonwealth, the Jewish Colonization Association* (ICA), the Maccabi World Union, and the Sephardi World Federation. London's first Jewish Lord Mayor was Sir David Salomons, elected in 1855. The Lord Mayor elected in September 1960 was a Jew, Sir Bernard Waley-Cohen. London's famous school was the Jews' Free School, demolished by enemy action in the Second World War, as was the old and beloved Ashkenazic Great Synagogue at Duke's Place.

Today (1984) the Jewish population is given roughly as 300,000, out of a total population in the whole of London of about 7,000,000. The mass of immigrants came from Russia and Poland from 1882 onwards, fleeing Tsarist pogroms. They settled largely in the East End of the metropolis. These immigrants were largely repsonsible for developing the tailoring, cabinet making, fur trade, and kindred industries. In recent years, the Jews have moved into the outer suburbs of London. (**See also** ENGLAND.)

LOPEZ, AARON (c. 1731-1782). Born in Portugal, Lopez came to America with his wife and child and settled in Newport, R. I. He became a successful merchant esteemed by the entire community. Denied naturalization by Rhode Island, he was the first Jew to be naturalized in Massachusetts. Lopez owned many ships which, together with his personal fortune, he placed at the disposal of the American Revolution.

LOST TRIBES. The ten tribes that composed the Kingdom of Israel.* When Sargon, King of the Assyrian Empire, completed the conquest of the Kingdom of Israel in 722 B.C.E., he led most of the population into exile. Ever since then, the ultimate fate of these exiles has been the subject of innumerable theories and legends. The Talmud* presents contradictory opinions. One maintains that the ten tribes were assimilated and merged with the peoples among whom they lived. Another opinion holds that they survived and joined the exiles from Judea (sixth century B.C.E.) who returned to their homeland in the time of Exra* and Nehemiah.*

Medieval Jewish writing is full of references to one or another of the Lost Tribes. Some of the travelers of the Middle Ages, notably Eldad the Danite, claimed to have visited among them. Eldad claimed to have found these tribes in North Africa. Some of them, he said, were called the "sons of Moses" and lived guarded by the Sambatyon,* a river made impassable six days in the week by its stone-throwing, turbulent waters. To this day, Yemenite Jews and the Bene Israel of Afghanistan* claim to be descended from the ancient Israelites. Various theories have identified the Tatars, the holy Shindai class of Japan,* and the American Indians, in turn, as the Lost Tribes. The most popular of these theories, claiming more than a million followers in England* and the United States, identifies the people of the British Isles as the Lost Tribes.   N.B-A.

LUBAVITCH HASIDIM. See SHNEERSON.

LUDWIG, EMIL (1881-1948). Biographer, novelist and playwright. Born Emil Ludwig Cohen, in Germany, he began his career as a lawyer. At the age of twenty-five he turned to literature, achieving fame with a series of biographies which include lives of **Jesus, Bismarck, and Lincoln.** In 1932, on the eve of the Nazis' seizure of the German government, Ludwig became a citizen of Switzerland. Several years later, the Nazis burned all his books. During World War II Ludwig lived in the United States.

The critical biography, which stresses character (psychology) rather than history, is considered Ludwig's outstanding creative achievement.

LULAV. See SUKKOT.

LURIA, ISAAC. See KABBALAH.

LUZZATO, MOSES HAIM (1707-1746). Scholar, mystic, poet, and dramatist. Born in Padua, Italy,* Luzzato acquired great knowledge of the Talmud,* as well as of classical and modern languages and literature. As a young man, he immersed himself in the study of Jewish mysticism, or Kabbalah.* This preoccupation led him to believe that the secrets of the Torah* had been revealed to him by an angel. The rabbis in Italy saw in his fantastic visions the dangerous possibili-

ty of a new Messianic movement. Still upset by the Sabbatai Zevi* tragedy, they prohibited Luzzato, under threat of excommunication, to study Kabbalah. Consequently, Luzzato moved to Amsterdam,* where he worked as a diamond polisher. In his spare hours, he wrote poetry, as well as works of scholarship, mystic philosophy, and ethics.

An innovator in Hebrew literature, Luzzato was particularly effective in his allegorical dramas. His classic style, use of symbolism, and ethical thinking, exerted considerable influence.

In 1743, Luzzato settled in Safed, Palestine, the city of the mystics. A few years later he fell victim to a plague in Acre.

LUZZATO, SAMUEL DAVID (1800-1865). Hebrew scholar, thinker, and poet. He was born in Trieste to a poor but learned carpenter. Luzzato devoted his entire life to the study of philology, literature, philosophy and history. Great Jewish scholars, among them Zunz,* Geiger,* and Graetz,* drew on his vast knowledge.

Luzzato was also a religious thinker and a poet of note. Living at a time when assimilation threatened Jewish traditional life, Luzzato stressed the superiority of Judaism. In a number of articles and poems he expressed his hope for the restoration of Zion and his great love for the Hebrew language.

His life was spent in poverty, and his wife and gifted son died at an early age. Nevertheless, Luzzato's misfortunes did not deter him from his studies. As a teacher of Bible,* history, and religious philosophy at the Rabbinical College at Padua, Italy, he carried on a vuluminous correspondence with Jewish scholars the world over. Published after his death, his letters filled nine volumes and served as a great reservoir of knowledge in all fields of Jewish literature, from Biblical to modern times.

LYDDA (Lod). Ancient town situated southeast of Tel Aviv,* on the road to the Judean hills, Lydda had a considerable population after the Jewish return from Babylonian captivity (537 B.C.E.). It served as an important commercial center between Damascus* and Egypt.* The Romans called it Diospolis, "the City of God," and burned it down during the Bar Kokhba* revolt. In the second and third centuries, Lod was known for its Talmudical academy. It was conquered by the Israel Army during the War of Independence in 1948. Israel's largest ariport is now located near the town.

M

MAABARAH. Transition camp or temporary village for new immigrants in Israel.* This type of village was evolved in 1950 as a means of dealing with the vast numbers of immigrants who streamed into the country after the establishment of the state. In 1948 and 1949 they were received in huge reception camps maintained by the Jewish Agency,* which supplied them with their basic

Social worker at a maabara.

Immigrant from Bucharest at Holon Maabara.

Israel Office of Information.

necessities. It was soon found that the complete dependence and enforced idleness of many thousands of people, often extending over a period of months or years, not only constituted an

intolerabe economic burden but also had a demoralizing influence on the immigrants themselves. **Maabarot** were therefore set up in large towns or in development areas where employment was available. Each family was provided with a hut or tent, and some essential equipment, and offered an opportunity to work for a living. By the end of 1952 there were 111 **maabarot,** with a population of 230,000, extending from Galilee* to the Negev.* But as many of these villages were a blemish on the landscape and a reproach to the national conscience, efforts were made to convert them into more attractive permanent settlements or to resettle the **maabarot** dwellers in new modern housing areas. By the late 1950's nearly all the **maabarot** had either been liquated or turned into permanent settlements.

Transition from temporary to permanent housing.

Israel Office of Information

MAARIV. See PRAYERS.

MACCABEE, JUDAH. See MACCABEES.

MACCABEES. The name of the priestly family of the Hasmoneans from the town of Modin in Palestine.* The Maccabees led the struggle (167-160 B.C.E.) against Antiochus Epiphanes, the Seleucid King of Syria,* and succeeded in freeing Judea from Syrian oppression. The family consisted of the father Mattathias, and his five sons: Johanan, Simon, Judah, Eliezer, and Jonathan. Judah was nicknamed Maccabee or "The Hammer", i.e., the hammer that pounded the Syrian forces. Later, the whole family came to be known as the Maccabees.

The Seleucid rulers of Syria engaged in a campaign to establish their empire over the lands that had originally been conquered by Alexander the Great.* They wrested control of Judea from Egyptian rule, and then tried to force the Greek culture and religion on the Jews. In the year 167 B.C.E., when Antiochus prohibited the practice of Judaism and the Temple was desecrated, the peaceful farmers of Judea were transformed into warriors. Led by Mattathias and his sons, they rebelled against the Syrians. Few in number, untrained and poorly armed, they fought for a year as guerillas in the hills and mountain passes of Judea. When Mattathias died in 166 B.C.E., Judah took over leadership. The little army of farmers repeatedly defeated the trained legions sent against them, captured arms and supplies, and grew in numbers. In several successful battles, the Maccabeeans achieved great victory against

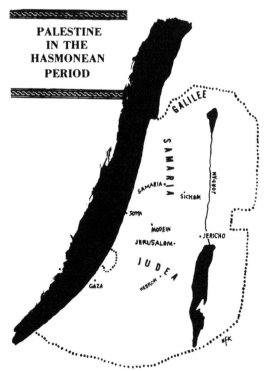

**PALESTINE
IN THE
HASMONEAN
PERIOD**

overwhelming odds. In the year 165 B.C.E., they entered Jerusalem. Then the Temple was cleared and worship restored. This is the origin of the festival of Hanukkah.*

To secure their victory, the Maccabeeans undertook expeditions against hostile neighbors who aided the Syrians in the past and might be expected to do so again when the Syrians returned to the attack. In one of the ensuing battles, Eliezer was killed, crushed by a war elephant he had stabbed. Another brother, Johanan, fell in a battle with an Arabian tribe. In 160 B.C.E., when the Syrians returned in a new attempt to conquer Judea, Judah Maccabee, with 800 men, faced a huge Syrian force and died in battle. Johnathan succeeded Judah, carried on the struggle with the Syrians, and succeeded in strengthening Judea and in widening its boundaries. In 143 B.C.E., he was treacherously killed by a Syrian general who had posed as his friend. Simon, the last of the five Maccabee brothers, was elected by the people ruler and high priest. Beloved by the people, Simon governed them and served as their high priest, leaving the military activities to his sons when he became old.

M.W.

MACHPELAH. Cave near Hebron. When Sarah died, Abraham* purchased it from Ephron the Hittite (Genesis 23). It became the burial crypt of the patriachs* and matriarchs* and a place of pilgrimage. Long held as a Moslem shrine, admission was denied to non-Moslems until after the Six-Day War.*

MAGEN DAVID (Hebrew, meaning "shield of David"). The six-cornered star made by combining two triangles is a very ancient and widespread symbol. Many ancient architectural ruins carry the engraving of this Hebrew seal. The third- or fourth-century synagogue dug up in Capernaum, Israel, has not only the six-pointed Magen David upon it, but also the rarer five-pointed Seal of Solomon.* In 1345, the Emperor Charles IV permitted the Jews of Prague* to use a flag bearing "the Shield of David and the Seal of Solomon" upon a red field. In modern times, the Shield of David with the word Zion in the center became the symbol of Zionism* and the State of Israel.*

MAGEN DAVID ADOM (MDA) (Hebrew meaning, "Red Shield of David"). Israel's emergency medical, health and disaster service was authorized by the Knesset on July 12, 1950 and entrusted to carry out the functions assigned by the Geneva Convention as the National Society equivalent to other Red Cross Societies. MDA cooperates with the International Red Cross in disaster areas throughout the world.

American Red Magen David For Israel (ARMD) is the sole support arm in the United States of MDA. A member organization with chapters throughout the country, it educates and involves its members in activities of MDA, raises funds for MDA's emergency medical services, including collection and distribution of blood and blood products for Israel's military and civilian population: supplies ambulances, bloodmobiles, mobile cardiac rescue units serving all the hospitals and communities throughout Israel; supports MDA's 73 emergency medical stations and helps provide training equipment for voluntary paramedical corps.

MAGGID (from the Hebrew, meaning "to tell"). Intinerant preacher. The **Maggid** was a folk-preacher who used Biblical and Midrashic* quotations, parables, and stories, to preach morality and repentance. Traveling from town to town, the **Maggid** attracted great masses with his chanting oratory. Although he was often not too scholarly, his influence was more widespread than that of scholars and rabbis.

Outstanding among **maggidim** were Jacob Kranz (the Maggid of Dubno*) in the eighteenth century; and Moses Isaac ben Noah Darshan (the Kelmer Maggid), and Rabbi Jacob Joseph of New York, originally the Maggid of Vilna, in the nineteenth century.

MAGGID OF DUBNO (JACOB KRANZ) (1740-1804). Popular preacher, one of the best loved personalities in East European Jewish life. The fables of the Maggid of Dubno always had a moral or ethical message, and were enjoyed by young and old, scholar and layman alike. Elijah, the Gaon* of Vilna, was very fond of his sermons.

MAGNES, JUDAH LEON (1877-1948). Rabbi, community leader, and educator. Magnes played an important role in the organization of Jewish community life in the United States during the early years of this century. He was secretary of the Federation of American Zionists between 1905 and 1908, and was director of the New York **Kehilla,** or community, from 1909 to 1922. After World War I he was called to organize the Hebrew University* in Jerusalem.* Settling in Jerusalem, Magnes served as president of the University from 1925 to his death in 1948. In Palestine,* he was one of the leaders of the movement, which called for a bi-national (Arab-Jewish) state in Palestine.

MAHARAL. See LOEW, JUDAH BEN BEZALEL.

Israeli soldiers giving blood in the Golan Heights.
Courtesy American Red Magen David for Israel.

MAHLER, GUSTAV (1860-1911). Conductor and composer. He was born in Bohemia and baptized as a child. Mahler served as conductor at the opera in Prague,* Hamburg, and at the Imperial Opera in Vienna. For a number of years, he conducted German opera at the New York Metropolitan Opera House, and from 1909 to 1911 he was the conductor of the New York Philharmonic. When he died in Vienna, the Czechs, the Austrians, and the Jews alike laid claim to him as a great son.

Gustav Mahler wrote many songs and nine symphonies. The greatly enlarged orchestra needed to play Mahler's works was the cause of much controversy. His second, third and fourth symphonies have choral sections as last movements, and the eighth—the "Symphony of the Thousands"—is a choral work almost throughout. Mahler was one of the greatest composers of modern times.

MAHZOR (from the Hebrew, meaning "cycle"). A book of prayers, hymns, and liturgic poetry; more generally, the prayer book for the High Holy Days and Passover,* Shavuot* and Sukkot.* There were several versions of the Mahzor, each following the customs and traditions of a different locality: the Roman Mahzor, based on the sixteenth-century Mahzor Romaniya, which originated in the Byzantine Empire; the Ashkenazic Nusah of German Jews; and the Mahzor Sephardi, compiled during the early part of the Middle Ages by Spanish Jewry. Today, the two accepted tests are the Ashkenazic and Sephardic versions.

MAIMON, (FISHMAN) JUDAH LEIB (1876-1962). Scholar and leader of religious Zionism.* Born in Bessarabia, he was inspired at an early age by the ideal of the return to Zion. In

206

Rabbi Judah Leib Maimon
Courtesy Musaf Lakore Hatzair
(Hadoar Weekly).

1913, Rabbi Maimon and his family settled in Palestine,* and he began to take an active part in the rebuilding of the land. He was appointed Minister of Religions in the first Cabinet of the State of Isarael.* Rabbi Maimon was head of the Rabbi Kook publishing house, and editor of the scholarly monthly, **Sinai.** He published many important volumes dealing with the Jewish holidays, Zionism, law, and monographs on famous personalities. He possessed one of the largest private collections of books of Jewish interest.

MAIMONIDES (1135-1204). Jewish philosopher, religious thinker, and physician. Few have attained the heights of thought and scholarship scaled by Maimonides (Moses ben Maimon, or Rambam). His genius revealed itself in many fields of spiritual and scientific activity: in law, philosophy, medicine, astronomy, and logic. He wrote many extraordinary scholarly works, and was the acknowledged head of the Jewish community in Egypt* and the revered leader of all Jewry. His authority extended as far as the distant land of Yemen; to this day, Yemenite Jews pay homage to his memory in their prayers.

Maimonides was born in Cordova, Spain,* where his father, Rabbi Maimon, was the religious head, or **dayan,** of the community. He was only thirteen years old when Cordova was conquered by the Almohades, a fanatic Muslim sect. His family was forced to flee; after much wandering, they reached Fez, Morocco.* All through this troubled period, Maimonides continued his studies. In Fez, he published a letter addressed to Jews who were forced to accept the Islamic faith, urging them to observe secretly the Jewish commandments. When Yemenite Jews were bitterly persecuted, Maimonides wrote to them the famous **Iggeret Teman** in which he advised his distant brethren not to despair, for all persecutions are a challenge to prove the truth and purity of the Jewish faith.

Maimonides' outspoken and courageous leadership endangered his position in Morocco, and he and his family were forced to flee again. he remained briefly in Palestine. In 1165 he left for Egypt, where he settled in Fostat near Cairo. He carried heavy obligations as head of the Jewish community, and court physician to the Vizier Al-Kadi al Fadil and later to the Caliph Al Fadal. Yet Maimonides still devoted much time to study.

Even during his lifetime Maimonides was held in the highest regard. His commentary on the Mishnah and his great code **Mishneh Torah,** are truly the work of a genius. The code is divided into fourteen books and embraces the entire field of Jewish law. The **Mishneh Torah** is written in clear, rich and precise Hebrew. In the first of these volumes Maimonides explained the foundations of the Jewish religion and its principles in the light of reason and logic. To explain further the philosophic principles of Judaism, he wrote, in Arabic, a **Guide for the Perplexed.**

Maimonides (Rabbi Moses ben Maimon)

Maimonides influenced the spiritual development of his people throughout the generations. His **Guide for the Perplexed,** and attempt to bring philosophy into harmony with religion, has been translated into many languages. It has exerted great influence not only on Jewish thinkers, but also on Christian theologians and philosophers. Maimonides was enshrined in folk legend and the people of Tiberias erected a tomb in his memory. The inscription upon it reads: "Here lies our master Moses be Maimon, Mankind's Chosen One." H.L.

Sign at the entrance of an exhibit of Maimonides work.
Mosad Ha-Rav Kook.

רבינו משה בן מימון (רמב״ם)

נולד בקורדובה אשד בספרד
ערב פסח ד תתניה

נפטר בפוסטאט אשד במצרים
כי מסבת ד תתקסה ה

הובא לקבורה בטבריה

MALACHI. The last of the Biblical prophets; he is considered by some traditional authorities to be an anonymous prophet, because "Malachi" means "my messenger." Malachi lived in Jerusalem* toward the middle of the fifth century, B.C.E., perhaps fifty years after the rebuilding of the Temple by the returned exiles from Babylonia. Malachi stresses obedience to ritual and Law; his prophecies teach the universality of God and the natural worth of all human beings.

MANGER, ITZIK. See YIDDISH LITERATURE.

MAOT CHITTIM ("Wheat money"). The collection of money before Passover* to provide poor Jewish families with **matzot,** wine, and other holiday needs. This was considered a very important religious obligation. Societies were often set up for this purpose.

MAOZ ZUR. See HANUKKAH.

MAPU, ABRAHAM (1808-1867). Hebrew novelist. The first original Hebrew novel, in the Enlightenment period, entitled **Ahavat Zion** ("Love of Zion"), appeared over a hundred years ago in 1853. Abraham Mapu, the author of this novel, opened a new era in the history of Hebrew letters.

Born in Slobodka, Lithuania, he grew up poor in material things, but rich in Jewish knowledge. In accordance with the custom of that time, he received a religious education only and soon acquired a reputation as a prodigy in the study of Talmud.* In later years he studied Latin and modern languages as well. At the age of twenty-two, he began to work on his historical novel, **Ahavat Zion,** completing it 23 years later. The charm and beauty of the Biblical style, the idyllic scenes of life in ancient Judea, the refreshing naivete—all these qualities appealed to Jewish youth oppressed by ghetto life in Tsarist Russia.

MARRANOS. The term for Spanish and Portuguese Jews and their descendants who were forced to accept Christianity, but continued to practice Judaism in secret and, in a number of cases, passed on their secret beliefs from generation to generation. The Inquisition,* in its relentless investigations to root out those not true to the Church, tortured many Marranos till they admitted their heresy and were then burned at the stake. Those New Christians, as they were called, who were not exposed as secret Jews were nevertheless despised, and remained continually under suspicion. When the Jews were expelled from Spain in 1492, many

escaped to Portugal* and Spanish South America; but there too, large numbers of Marranos met martyrdom at the hand of the Inquisition. Other Marranos found refuge in Holland, France,* Italy,* and North Africa. There they immediately reverted to Judaism openly, or remained secret Jews, sometimes for several hundred years, until they felt it was no longer dangerous to declare themselves openly. In the course of centuries, Portuguese descendants of the early Marranos lost or forgot their connections with Judaism, yet still retained a number of Jewish customs. These they practiced in secret, often believing the secrecy itself to be part of the custom. During the nineteenth century, considerable numbers of such secret Jews were found in northern Portugal and the Balearic Isles. Although they were assimilated into the Christian communities, they observed various Jewish customs and holidays. The Marranos of Belmonte, for example, lighted Sabbath candles, fasted on Yom Kippur,* and refrained from eating swine (on the Sabbath and holidays only!). An international committee for Portuguese Marranos, formed during the 1920's, aided some Marranos to return to Judaism openly.

MARRIAGE CUSTOMS. Marriage is one of the most sacred and joyous of Jewish ceremonies. Traditionally, the marriage rites begin with the drawing up of a contract between the bride and groom and their families. This serves as an engagement. On the Sabbath before the wedding itself, the bridegroom is called up to the reading of the Torah,* as is the father of the bride. Traditionally, bride and groom fast on the wedding day.

The wedding cermony takes place under a **huppah,** or canopy, which represents the home. It is traditionally held in the open air. Preceded by the reading of the marriage contract (**ketubah**), the

"Jewish Wedding," by Joseph Israels.

Ceremonial wedding ring,
sixteenth century.
Courtesy Sidney L. Quitman.

ceremony consists of a series of benedictions thanking God for establishing the family, for creating man in His image, and for the joy of the wedding festivities. After the first benediction, the bridegroom places a ring on the finger of the hand of the bride and says, "Thou art sanctified unto me with this ring in accordance with the Law of Moses and Israel." After the benedictions, which end with a prayer for the happiness of the bride and groom and for the rebuilding of Jerusalem,* the bridegroom breaks a glass. This is done to bring to mind the destruction of the Temple* and of Jerusalem, which must not be forgotten even on the most joyous occasions.

Among certain Orthodox Jews, the festivities last for a whole week. Special benedictions for the happiness of bride and groom are said each evening, concluding with a feast on the seventh day.

B.H.

MARSHALL, LOUIS (1856-1929). World Jewish leader. A brilliant constitutional lawyer, Louis Marshall made his mark in civic and national affairs as a member of a slum investigation committee in New York and as chairman of the Commission of Immigration of the State of New York. A tireless worker for the underprivileged, he took a forthright stand on Negro rights. He championed conservation and preservation of wild life. A founder and president of the American Jewish Committee,* chairman of the executive board of the Jewish Theological Seminary of America,* Marshall also spearheaded the work of the American Jewish Joint Distribution Committee.

In 1919 he was a member of the United States Jewish delegation to the Versailles Peace Conference* after World War I, and it was he who drew up the resolution for Jewish minority rights in Eastern Europe. These rights were extended to other minorities and incorporated by the Peace Conference into the treaties with a number of European countries. When the enlarged Jewish Agency* for Palestine was organized in 1929, Louis Marshall was one of the leading non-Zionists to become a member of its executive body.

Louis Marshall   Courtesy Mr. James Marshall.

MARTINIQUE. One of the Windward Islands in the West Indies. It has been ruled by France* since 1635. Three hundred Brazilian exiles who settled there in 1654 formed the largest Jewish community Martinique has ever known. They were expelled in 1683. During World War II refugees from Europe arrived but were not allowed to establish themselves.

MARTYRS, TEN. After the unsuccessful revolt of Bar Kokhba* (132-5) against Roman rule, a new and bloody chapter in Jewish history began. Hadrian, the Roman emperor, attempted the spiritual destruction of the Jewish people. On the penalty of death, he forbade the study of the Torah.* Jews were not permitted to practice the most fundamental laws of their religion. Sabbath* observance, celebration of holidays, and circumcision* were forbidden.

Jewish scholars were the major target of this persecution. However, they braved death rather than submit to Roman oppression. The story of their courageous stand and martyrdom became embodied in legend. The foremost scholars and leaders of their people, they defied the Roman decree and continued to teach the Torah to their students. Among these martyrs were Rabbi Akiba ben Joseph,* Juda ben Bava, and Hananiah ben Teradion. While enduring a slow agonizing death, the martyrs proclaimed their faith in God. It is related that the executioner of Hananiah ben Teradion was so moved by the spirit of the sage that he did everything possible to spare him suffering. Moved to remorse by his victim's saintly bearing, the executioner himself leaped into the flames, atoning for the cruel task he had been forced to perform.

Thereafter, the heroic death of the ten scholars served as a symbol of martyrdom. Their faith and fortitude gave countless Jews the strength to sacrifice their lives "for the sanctification of the name of God."　　　　　　　　　　　　　H.L.

MARX, KARL (1818-1883). Economist, thinker, and founder of scientific socialism. Born to a German-Jewish family, Marx was destined to become one of the leading revolutionary thinkers of modern times. Exiled from Germany for political activity in 1845, he went to Paris, where he joined revolutionary Socialist circles. There, in collaboration with Friedrich Engels, he wrote **The Communist Manifesto** (1848) calling upon the workers to rise in violent revolution against their capitalist oppressors. Exiled from France and then again from Germany, Marx settled in London, where he devoted his lfe to the development and exposition of his theories of history and society, and to the organization of an international workers' movement.

Marx believed that labor was the source of all economic value, and that the profits of an employer (a "capitalist") therefore constituted "theft." In Marx's theory, capitalism not only led to the mulcting of the worker and his impoverishment, it also led to the perversion of human nature, which Marx believed to be essentially good. Because Marx held that all history and culture were determined by economic conditions, he favored a world revolution, which would give labor its due and permit the "rehumanization" of man. **Das Kapital** ("Capital"), setting forth his economic theory, was his most important work, and later became the handbook of both the Socialist and Communist movements. Its assumptions, were the basis for early economic policy in the Soviet Union.

Marx was baptized at the age of six, a practice common among German Jews who were ambitious for their children, and in his future years he avoided involvement in Jewish life. Only one article, **Zur Judenfrage** ("On the Jewish Question"), dealt directly with Jewish affairs.

MASADA. Ancient fortress in the Judean wilderness, famed for the last stand of the Zealots in the war against the Romans (70 C.E.). In recent years it has been the site of much archaeological activity. In 1965 Prof. Yigael Yadin* of the Hebrew University reported that an expedition led by him had discovered a large piece of scroll belonging to the long-lost Hebrew original of the Book of Jubilees, one of the most important of Apocryphal* writings. (**See also** ARCHAEOLOGY).　　　　　　　　　　　　　　G.H.

MASORAH (from the Hebrew, meaning "tradition"). The literary activity centering around the text of the Bible.* This activity took place in Tiberias* in Palestine* during the eighth century. The result of this labor was a standard text of the Bible.

The Massoretes, or scholars who devoted themselves to establishing the Masoretic text, introduced the division of the Biblical books into chapters and verses—lacking in the original text—and set down the correct pronunciation of Biblical words—often unclear because vowel and accent marks were unknown in early times. They compiled spelling lists and introduced a system of vowel and accent marks which enabled every Jew to read and study the Bible. The Masoretic activity was brought to a close at the beginning of the tenth century by the last of the Masorites, Aaron ben Asher.

MATRIARCHS. The collective name for the wives of the three patriarchs,* Abraham,* Isaac,* and Jacob.* Sarah, Rebecca, Leah, and Rachel were the matriarchs, or mothers of the people of Israel. On Sabbath* and holiday eves, it was customary for fathers to bless their daughters: "May the Lord make you like unto Sarah, Rebecca, Rachel, and Leah."

MATTATHIAS. See MACCABEES.

MATZAH. Unleavened bread. (**See** PASSOVER.)

MEGGIDO. An ancient Palestinian city in Emek Jezreel, at the foot of the Samarian hills. Strategically located on the ancient highway linking Egypt* in the south of Israel to Syria and Assyria in the north, Meggido was the scene of many battles until the fourth century B.C.E, when the city was abandoned. Joshua* subjugated the Canaanite king of Meggido (Joshua 12:21); later Solomon* fortified the town, and established a garrison of horsemen there. During the period of the Kings, ending with Josiah (II Kings 23:29), numerous battles were fought in and around the city. Meggido has become a Christian symbol of war, and it was believed that at the "end of days"

210

the final war between Good and Evil would be carried on there (Battle of Armaggedon). During the World War I campaign for the Holy Land, General Edmund Allenby* and his British forces defeated the Turks near this spot. The **tel,** or mound, which is all that remains of Meggido, has been the subject of archaeological diggings since 1903, the most significant excavation being that of the Rockefeller expedition of 1926-39. The excavations have exposed seven layers of ancient cities, built one over the other, the earliest probably dating back to 3500 B.C.E. Early Canaanite altars and Solomon's stables, in a remarkable state of preservation, may be seen among the ruins of Meggido.

MEGILLAH (Scroll). A book written on a single roll of parchment, as distinguished from **sefer,** a larger book mounted on double rollers. Each of the following five books of the Bible is called a **megillah:** Song of Songs,* Ruth,* Lamentations,* Ecclesiastes,* and Esther;* collectively they are known as the **megillot.** The proper noun, megillah, refers primarily to the Scroll of Esther. Written by hand in illuminated script, and often decorated with colorful border designs, **megillot** were kept in cases of carved wood and figured on filigreed silver. Examples of **megillot** dating back to the thirteenth century may be found in many museums.

MEIR BAAL HA-NES (Meir the Miracle Worker). Charity boxes in Jewish homes for the poor in the Holy Land bear his name, because of his repute as a performer of miracles.

MEIR, GOLDA (1898-1979). Labor Zionist leader and Prime Minister of Israel (1969-74). She was born Gold Mabowitz to a carpenter in Kiev Russia. The Mabowitz family came to the United States in 1906 and settled in Milwaukee, where Golda grew up and taught school. A Zionist since her early youth, she married Morris Myerson on the condition that they go to Palestine* to settle as pioneers. Arriving in Palestine in 1921, they joined the kibbutz* Merhavia, where Golda was trained to become its specialist in poultry raising.

Golda Myerson's public career began with her work as secretary of the Women's Labor Council. This work involved her in shuttling between Palestine and the United States, and developed her remarkable skill as administrator, organizer, propagandist, and fund raiser. These abilities were recognized by the Histadrut,* the General Federation of Labor in Palestine, and Golda Myerson was appointed to its executive committee. She served the Histadrut ably in a variety of executive posts, heading the Workers' Sick Fund, and

Golda Meir   Israel Office of Information.

organizing the unemployment insurance system by persuading the workers to tax themselves for this purpose. Golda's versatility enabled her to raise, single-handed, the capital to finance Nachshon, the Histadrut harbor installations in Tel Aviv.* In retaliation for resistance to its immigration policy, the British arrested the top leaders of the Jewish community in Palestine (June 29, 1946). The imprisoned Moshe Sharett* was then replaced by Golda Myerson as head of the Jewish Agency* Political Department.

She was one of two women who signed Israel's Declaration of Independence in May, 1948, and became Israel's first ambassador to Russia.* She was enthusiastically welcomed by the Jews of Russia. Because of her experience in labor relations and in social insurance, she was recalled to Israel in 1949 to become minister of labor in Prime Minister Ben-Gurion's* first cabinet. In this capacity, she served until June, 1956, when, upon the resignation of Moshe Sharett, Golda Myerson assumed the office of Minister for Foreign Affairs. In keeping with the established practice that foreign service officials Hebraize their names, she changed her last name to Meir. Mrs. Meir was succeeded as Minister of Foreign affairs by Abba Eban (1965).

When the Mapai, Ahdut HaAvodah and Rafi parties officially merged early in 1968, Mrs. Meir was elected secretary general of the new party. She held this office until 1969 when she succeeded the late Levi Eshkol* as Prime Minister of Israel. As

Prime Minister she paid several official visits to the United States as the guest of President Richard M. Nixon. In 1974, following the Yom Kippur War,* she resigned from the government and was succeeded as Prime Minister by Yitzhak Rabin.*

MEIR OF ROTHENBURG (1215-1293). Scholar and poet. Renowned rabbi in Western Germany. At the age of sixty-six he fled with his family from the persecutions of the German rulers, with the intention of going to the Holy Land, but was arrested on the way and returned as a prisoner to Germany. Emperor Rudolph of Hapsburg demanded from the Jews a large sum for the liberation of their beloved leader. Although the Jews were ready to pay the money, Rabbi Meir refused to be ransomed, in order not to establish the precedent of redeeming imprisoned Jewish leaders. Rabbi Meir died in prison, and again the Emperor demanded a heavy ransom before yielding the rabbi's body for Jewish burial. Fourteen years later, a wealthy Jew ransomed the body on condition that he himself be buried beside the remains of the venerable rabbi. To this day, one can see in the Jewish cemetery of Worms the double grave with a single tombstone marking the resting place of the rabbi and his loyal follower.

MEIR, RABBI (second century, C.E.). Greatest of Rabbi Akiba's* disciples, this second-century Tanna figures prominently in the Mishnah. All laws in the Mishnah, whose authorship is not specified, are ascribed to Rabbi Meir. Although second only to the head of the Sanhedrin* in scholarship and rank, Rabbi Meir earned a modest living by copying holy scrolls. He had a keen legal mind, and the imaginative side of his nature was expressed in legends, fables, and parables. It is said that he composed three hundred fox fables. All except three of these have been lost.

Rabbi Meir was a pupil of Elisha Ben Abuyah,* who later strayed from Judaism. Unlike other sages who forsook this once revered teacher, Rabbi Meir continued to benefit from his learning, and tried to bring Elisha Ben Abuyah back to Judaism. Rabbi Meir had an abiding, deep love for the land of Israel and for the Hebrew language. He said: "One who lives in the land of Israel and speaks the holy tongue is assured of his share in the world to come." H.L.

MEISELS, DOV BERISH (1798-1870). Chief Rabbi of Warsaw,* Polish patriot. He took part in the Polish rebellion of 1863. A street in Warsaw was named after him.

MELCHETT, LORD (SIR ALFRED MOND) (1868-1930). English industrialist, chemist, and

Lord Melchett   Courtesy British Information Service.

Zionist leader. He was the head of the Imperial Chemical Industries of London,* one of the largest of its kind in the world. In his youth, Lord Melchett studied law and participated actively in the economic and political life of Britian. For seventeen years he was a member of Parliment; during the First World War he served as Minister of Health and Labor. In 1917, Lord Melchett was attracted to Zionism* and worked closely with Louis D. Brandeis* for the economic development of Palestine. He was at one time president of the English Zionist Federation and Joint Chairman of the Jewish Agency. A colony in Palestine, Tel-Mond, is named after him. His son, Lord Henry Melchett (1898-1949) was president of the Maccabi World Union, and wrote several books, one of which, **Your Neighbor,** expounds the ideals of Judaism and Zionism.

MEM. Thirteenth letter of the Hebrew alphabet; numerically, forty.

MENASSEH. Older son of Joseph.

MENASSEH BEN ISRAEL (1604-1657). Rabbi and author. In 1655, when England was a Republic under the rule of Cromwell, the Lord Protector, a strange figure with a strange case to plead appeared in London.* He was Menasseh ben Israel, a Lisbon-born rabbi who had settled in Amsterdam* and become famous throughout Europe for books on religious and other subjects. In 1650 he had written **Esperanza de Israel** ("Hope of Israel"), a treatise arguing that the Messiah would not come until Jews had been scattered to the four corners of the earth. Oliver Cromwell, convinced by the argument, had invited Menasseh to discuss the return of Jews to England,* whence they had been banished in 1290. Menasseh pleaded eloquently, but a Whitehall convention rejected his plan. A Jewish community was nonetheless founded in 1656. Menasseh died a year later in Middelburg, Holland. His face is known to us from a portrait by his friend, Rembrandt, the greatest Dutch artist of his day.

MENDELE MOCHER SEFARIM (ABRAMOWITZ, SHALOM JACOB) (1836-1917). Pioneer Hebrew and Yiddish writer, best known by his pen-name, Mendele Mocher Sefarim (Mendele, the Bookseller). Born in a small town in White Russia, he received a traditional Jewish education, studying for a time at a Talmudical academy. At seventeen he was persuaded to join an adventurous traveling beggar, who promised the youth an eventful life in faraway places. His travels through the populous Jewish towns in southern Russia furnished the material for Mendele's realistic novels, **Fishke der Krumer,** and others. Abramowitz began his literary career in the Haskalah* (Enlightenment) period and he successfully adapted from the German into Hebrew a work on natural history. In 1857 he published articles urging the improvement of Jewish education. His Hebrew novel, **Fathers and Sons,** deals with the clash between the old and new generations, and completes the first cycle of his literary career. In his second period, Mendele chose to write in the vernacular, or spoken language of the people, Yiddish. In his novels, **The Little Man, Meat Tax,** and **The Mare** he introduced the social reform motive, criticizing the

Mendele Mocher Sefarim (Shalom Jacob Abramowitz).

community for exploiting the poor. In **The Travels of Benjamin the Third** and his other works, he revealed himself as a sharp satirist, ridiculing the pettiness, narrow-mindedness, and ignorance of the small town inhabitant. In masterly fashion he described the stark poverty of the Jewish masses, mixing, as Dickens did, humor with compassion. Mendele created a new Hebrew and Yiddish literary style, making full use of the rich, hidden treasures of the language and contibuting to its revival. His works present a vivid picture of Jewish life in the first half of the nineteenth century. Odessa, where Mendele had lived since 1881, became an important Hebrew literary center. Mendele's influence was far-reaching. Chaim N. Bialik,* one of the foremost Hebrew poets, prided himself on being among Mendele's disciples. H.L.

MENDELSSOHN, MOSES (1729-1786). Philosopher, and founder of the German Jewish Enlightenment movement. Born in Dessau, the son of Mendel, a Torah scribe, young Mendelssohn received a traditional Jewish education in Bible** and Talmd.* One of his early teachers introduced Moses to the study of Maimonides.* This study influenced him deeply, and formed his taste for philosophy. Coming to Berlin at the age of fourteen, he studied mathematics, Latin, Greek, and philosophy and became a master of German prose. At a time when German Jews were still locked in their ghettos and required special permits to live in Berlin, Moses Mendelssohn became widely known as a German writer on philosophical subjects and on the theory of art. His home became the meeting place for many of the cultural leaders of his day, both Jewish and non-Jewish.

Moses Mendelssohn tried to break down the walls of the ghetto from both the inside and the outside. He wanted Jews to learn the German language as a gateway to the knowledge of the outside world. And he wanted Jewish children to learn manual trades. With the help of wealthy friends, he opened a free school in Berlin where Jewish boys were trained in manual occupations, and were taught some German, in addition to Bible and Talmud. Mendelssohn set himself the task of translating the Pentatuech* and the Psalms* into German. Eventually he published this German translation in Hebrew letters by the side of the original Hebrew text. The influence of this Bible translation was enormous. From it many Talmud students learned the German language and went on to the study of general European culture. The Haskalah or Enlightenment movement in Germany and Eastern Europe is usually dated back to this translation.

MOSES MENDELSSOHN.

To breach the walls of the ghetto from the outside, Mendelssohn wrote his **Jerusalem.** At publication, some parts of this book were attacked by Christians and Jews alike. In **Jerusalem,** he outlined his ideals of religious and political toleration, separation of church and state, and the equality of all citizens. At the same time he pleaded with the Jews to hold on to their "particularism," and to the absolute authority of Jewish laws. Mendelssohn used his literary friendships to prevent the placing of new restrictions upon the Swiss Jews, and he tried to save the Jews of Dresden from expulsion. He induced Christian Wilhelm Dohm, a Prussian aristocrat, to write an essay urging that Jews be granted civil rights. Mendelssohn's devoted friendship with the famous author Gotthold Ephraim Lessing. also contributed to the eventual emancipation of the Jews in Germany.* Lessing wrote a highly successful play **Nathan Der Weise** ("Nathan the Wise") which was a portrait of his friend Moses Mendelssohn, and a powerful plea for religious tolerance. N.B-A.

MENDELSSOHN-BARTHOLDY, FELIX
(1809-1847). Composer, pianist, and conductor. His grandfather was Moses Mendelssohn,* the Jewish philosopher whose work opened the period of emancipation in Jewish history. Abraham, the father of the composer, was a banker who wanted to spare his children from social and other forms of anti-Jewish discrimination. He therefore had them baptized as Lutherans. "That is the form of

religion of most cultured men," said Abraham Mendelssohn. To further cover up his son's Jewish origin, he took the additional surname of Bartholdy. Yet Felix often dropped the "Bartholdy" from his signature, and in the world of music his work is known simply as "Mendelssohn's." He retained a sincere and positive regard for Judaism, and there are many references in his correspondence to his Jewish identification.

A child prodigy, Mendelssohn began composing at the age of eleven, and wrote some of his greatest work at the age of seventeen. Some of his works **(The Midsummer Night's Dream,** the **Scotch** and **Italian** symphonies, and the **Hebrides** and **Meeresstille** overtures) rank among the great musical masterpieces of the world. Mendelssohn's music is characterized by a fusion of the classic and romantic styles. The religious element of his nature appears in his psalms, motets and oratorios. His oratorio, **Moses,** was only discovered in recent years. Mendelssohn's inspired oratorio **Elijah** is as dramatic as an opera. N.B-A.

MENDES, DONNA GRACIA (1510-1569).
Financier, philanthropist, and patron of Jewish learning. She was born to a family of Marrano* or secret Jews in Portugal,* and named Beatrice de Luna. Beatrice married the banker Francisco Mendes of Lisbon. She was only twenty-five when her husband died, and she became the head of the Mendes banking house with far-flung business interests, including an important branch in Antwerp. Life for Marranos in Portugal was becoming very dangerous because of the Inquisition.* She gathered up her family, including her daughter and her nephew Joao Miguez, and left for Antwerp, sailing in her own sloop.

In Antwerp she joined her brother-in-law Diego Mendes in managing their business. The family had a very high social position. Donna Gracia's responsibilities were great, and after the death of Diego in 1545, they became even greater. Her beautiful daughter Reyna was sought in marriage by many young nobles, and the firm refusals aroused the justified suspicion that the Mendes family were secret Judaizers who would not intermarry with Christians. Before the authorities could act, Donna Gracia fled with her family to Venice, a way station to Turkey* where they would be free to practice Judaism openly. In Venice she was denounced to the authorities, who imprisoned her and confiscated her fortune. The king of France,* in debt to the Mendes Bank, used his piety as a pretext for not paying his debt.

Her nephew, Joao Miguez, managed to obtain the help of the Turkish sultan, Suleiman the

Magnificent, and Donna Gracia was released. She was permitted to settle in Ferrara, a haven of refuge for Jews under the rule of the Dukes d'Este. Here Donna Gracia threw off the disguise of Christianity, and became Hannah Nasi, a devoted Jewess. In Ferrara she brought together a conference of Marrano notables to organize their flight to freedom, and used her great wealth to help finance this movement. She was interested in Jewish learning, and became a patroness of Jewish scholars. When Abraham Usque of Ferrara published the first translation of the Bible* into Spanish, a special edition was dedicated to Gracia. This edition became the Bible from which generations of Marranos relearned their Judaism. Finally, in 1552, the Nasi family was permitted to leave for Turkey. They settled in Constantinople where Gracia built her home—the Belvedere. She also built a synagogue, and set up a Hebrew printing press in her own home. The Belvedere became a haven for Jewish scholars, a practice continued by her daughter Reyna after Gracia's death.

Shortly after the family settled in Constantinople, Reyna married her cousin Joao Miguez who had taken the name Joseph Nasi when the family returned to Judaism. After he husband's death Reyna continued to house the printing press which issued many important Hebrew books.

N.B-A.

MENORAH. Candelabrum. There were seven branches in the original oil **menorah** used in the Tabernacle* (Ex. 25:31) and later in Solomon's* Temple.* It is this **menorah** that Titus is said to have carried away after the destruction of the Temple and that is pictured in bas-relief on the Arch of Titus in Rome. On Hanukkah,* an eight-branched **menorah** (plus a **shammash,** or servant-candle) is lighted to commmemorate the Maccabean victories. This **menorah** is frequently silver, bronze, or brass, and decorated with elaborate representations of animals and flowers.

MERON. A village in upper Galilee,* mentioned in the Bible as the site of Joshua's* victory over the Canaanite* kings. Rabbi Simeon ben Yohai took refuge in a cave at Meron to escape a death sentence imposed by the Romans during Bar Kokhba's* uprising in the second century C.E. After Bar Kokhba's victory Rabbi Simeon founded an academy and synagogue there. When the Kabbalists* began settling in nearby Safed during the sixteenth century, they instituted the custom of visiting his tomb on Lag b'Omer (**see** OMER). This custom has been revived in modern times. Today thousands of pilgrims from all parts of Israel* stream to Meron to celebrate the holiday

with song and dance, as well as prayer and meditation. Bearded **Hasidim*** in dark gabardines, Oriental Jews in native costume, and tow-haired young Israelis join arms to dance around great bonfires in this most colorful of folk festivals.

MESSIANISM. The belief that the Jewish people and all humanity would be led to a golden age of perfect justice and universal peace by a Messiah, an ideal king and a perfect man. The Hebrew **mashiah** means "one anointed with oil," the ancient way of dedicating a man to a special service or office. "Mashiah Adonai"—the Anointed of God—was a title of honor given in the Bible* to the kings of Israel.* The prophet Samuel* anointed both Saul* and David* as kings. The high priest Zadok and the prophet Nathan anointed Solomon king of Israel at David's request. The prophets described the Messiah as a divinely appointed man, an ideal ruler who would lead the world in righteousness and in peace.

When the Persians would not permit a descendant of David to rule Judea, the people began to dream of a time when an anointed king from the House of David would again sit on the throne of Israel. The more Judea was oppressed, particularly by the Roman empire, the stronger grew the belief in the coming of the Messiah who would bring salvation and freedom to the Jewish people while the Roman empire would be replaced by the Kingdom of God on earth.

When Judea fell in 70 C.E. and the Temple* was destroyed, the longing for the Messiah among the Jewish people was intense. In their last revolt (132-35 C.E.) against Rome, they were led by Simeon the son of Koziba. The aged Rabbi Akiba* called Simeon "God's Anointed" or Messiah, and changed his name from Bar Koziba to Bar Kokhba,* "the son of a star." Defeated again, the people yearned for the Messiah more than ever and his figure began to be surrounded with mystery. Instead of a human Messiah he became a divine deliverer and a being with supernatural powers. His coming would be announced by the prophet Elijah.* A forerunner would appear first—the Messiah son of Joseph. The first Messiah would defeat Israel's enemies, Gog and Magog, and prepare the way for the Messiah, son of David. Then the dead would rise again, the Day of Judgment would begin, and the righteous would be rewarded.

During the long centuries of exile, the Jewish people continued to dream of the Messiah and of the return to Israel. Many false Messiahs arose, mystics who really believed in themselves, and impostors who took advantage of the people's despair. Each false Messiah brought suffering and

Main entrance of the Jewish Sport Center, Mexico City.
Photo Guillermo Zamora.

disillusion in his wake, yet each new "Messiah" found many followers anxious to believe that the Return was at hand. (For false Messiahs, **see** ALROY, DAVID: MOLKHO, SOLOMON; REUBENI, DAVID; SABBATAI, ZEVI.)

N.B-A.

MEXICO. A federated republic in North America. Early in the sixteenth century, Mexico was a center of activity for Spanish conquistadores, intent on exploiting the wealth of Montezuma's empire. With them had come a group of Marranos,* or secret Jews. The Marranos quickly prospered in commerce and thus aroused the hositility of their neighbors. As early as 1528, a Marrano shipbuilder was burned at the stake. But systematic persecution began only in 1570, with the establishment of an Office of the Inquisition.* By 1820, when the Inquisition was abolished, the Marrano community had disappeared. Its only remaining trace are several thousand Indians who live in Mexico City and claim Marrano descent.

The modern community, composed chiefly of East European Jews, was founded in the nineteenth century. In 1984 there were about 38,000 Jews in Mexico, an increase of 18,000 since 1940. Immigration has been limited since 1950. The vast majority of the Jewish population lives in Mexico City, but there are active communities in Guadalajara, Monterrey, and elsewhere. Mexican Jews, living in freedom and equality with their neighbors, have become shopkeepers, manufacturers, and artisans. A small number have entered the professions. They have formed many synagogues, Zionist organizations, local charity activities, B'nai B'rith* lodges, and youth groups.

Mexico City is especially noted for its Jewish schools, in which about 85 per cent of the capital's Jewish children are enrolled. There are a number of all-day schools, combining the Jewish and general studies. The pride of the system is the Colegia Israelita de Mexico, where Spanish, Yiddish, and Hebrew are taught from the elementary school through the college levels. Its Faculty of Philosophy and Letters, founded in 1952, is affiliated with the National University of Mexico. The Albert Einstein school is a non-sectarian institution built by the Jewish community and presented to the government to aid its school construction program.

The Mexico Jewish press is also worthy of note. There are three publications of Jewish interest; one in Yiddish, one in Spanish and Hebrew, and one in Spanish. The Encyclopedia Judaica Castellana, a Jewish encyclopedia in Spanish, with special emphasis on Latin American Jewry, was published in 1952. (**See also** LATIN AMERICA.)

216

*Silver mezuzah
by Jehudah Wolpert.*

MEZUZAH (Hebrew, meaning "doorpost"). Case containing a rolled parchment inscribed with several passages from Deuteronomy (6:4-9 and 11:13-21), affirming the unity of God and teaching the love of God. This case is attached to the right doorposts of the entrance and each room in Jewish homes in accordance with the Biblical commandment, "And thou shalt write them on the doorposts of thy home" (Deut. 6:9). The parchments are kept in decorative cases which are slightly open to reveal the word **Shaddai** (Almighty) written on the back of the parchment.

MICAH (c. 730-705 B.C.E.). Sixth of the minor prophets. A peasant from tiny Moreshet in Judah,* Micah cried out against the social corruption of the cities, the injustice of the rulers, and the wrongs done to the poor. He predicted the destruction of the Temple* and of the beloved city, Jerusalem.* Reminding the people of God's love for Israel, he pleaded with them to live with justice and kindness, and prophesied that in the "end of days" universal justice would emanate from Zion and fill the world.

MIDRASH (from the Hebrew, meaning "to search"). A particular manner of interpreting the verses of the Bible,* developed mainly in Judea during the period of the Second Temple.* The Jewish sages were convinced that the words of the Bible lent themselves to many interpretations, each interpretation intended for men of a particular level of understanding and culture, as well as for a particular age and circumstance. The sages contemplated and discussed some of the greatest and most profound ideas of mankind. They were anxious, moreover, to teach these exalted ideas to the average and ordinary men and women of the towns and villages of Judea. On Sabbaths* and holidays they would preach in the synagogues, using the verses of the Bible as their text, and revealing many profound interpretations of these verses. So that their ideas might be understood by the people, they used illustrative parables, imaginative stories, and poetic interpretations of the verses. In their sermons, the sages also discussed those problems that deeply troubled the people. After the burning of the Temple and the destruction of the Jewish state, the sages strove to heal the wounds of the people, raise their spirit, and restore their courage. They extolled the greatness and power of God, His abiding love for His people, His sympathy for their suffering, and His promise of a glorious future.

The sages preached on the verses of the weekly portions, to which pertinent verses from other parts of the Bible were added. Most of their sermons were lost, but the finest of them were often repeated and zealously guarded in the memories of many devoted students. Eventually (beginning with the fourth century) many of the sermons were collected and written down, as books of **midrashim**. Today we possess over one hundred, the most important of which are:

1. **Midrash Rabbah** (The Great Midrash), which consists of collections of **midrashim** on the Five Books of Moses and the Five Scrolls (Song of Songs,* Ruth,* Lamentations,* Ecclesiastes,* and Esther*). Each collection was edited by a different man and at a different time, from the sixth to the twelfth century C.E.; they were the most popular collections of **midrashim**, and have been widely read by Jews the world over.

2. **Midrash Tanhuma,** a more homogeneous collection of **midrashim** on the Five Books of Moses, in which the preachings of Rabbi Tanhuma (a sage of the fourth century) predominate.

3. **Pesikhtot,** two collections of lengthy sermons delivered on special Sabbaths (the ones before Passover,* and before the High Holy Days).

4. **Yalkut Shimoni,** a collection of **midrashim** on all the books of the Bible. This collection was edited in the thirteenth century, and consists of material taken from many early collections of **midrashim** now lost to us.

5. A number of briefer **midrashim**, such as: Pirke D'Rabbi Eliezer on the first nine chapters of Genesis;* Midrash Shohar Tov on Psalms; Midrash Mishle, on Proverbs; Midrash Shemuel, on the books of Samuel;* and Midrash Lekah Tov on the third, fourth, and fifth Books of Moses, and on the Book of Ruth.   I.A.A.

MIKVEH ISRAEL (Hebrew, meaning "Gathering of Israel"). Agricultural school southeast of Tel Aviv.* It is approached by an avenue of stately palms, and surrounded by orange orchards, vineyards, vegetable gardens, and cornfields. It was the first and for many years the only agricultural school in Israel, originally for boys only, and was established in 1870 by the Alliance Israélite Universelle,* in response to an appeal to help Jews in the Holy Land learn a productive occupation. The eucalyptus tree, which the Arabs called "the Jewish tree," was first introduced at this school. The Bilu* settlers came to Mikveh Israel to learn how to handle the plough and the **turia** ("mattock").

MINHAG (Hebrew, meaning "custom"). Although a **minhag** is not specified in either Bible* or Talmud,* Jewish law, Jewish tradition considers it no less binding than a law. The Talmud

Students at the Bnei Akiva Yeshiva.

Religious Zionists of America—Mizrachi-Hapoel Hamizrachi.

states that one should not depart from the accepted **minhag.** A number of laws based on **minhag** are included in the Shulhan Arukh,* the code of Jewish laws and observances.

MINYAN. The term describing the quorum of ten adult Jewish males traditionally required for congregational services.

MISHNAH. See TALMUD.

MITZVAH (Hebrew, meaning "commandment"). An obligation or duty taught by the Torah and by rabbinic law; a good deed. Traditionally, there are 613 commandments contained in the Torah, 248 affirmative ("thou shalt") and 365 negative ("thou shalt not"). The Jews regarded these as representing a desirable way of life and an opportunity for fulfilling one's duty to God and his fellowman. By performing a meritorious act, such as giving charity, a person is said to have "earned a mitzvah."

MIZRACH (Hebrew, meaning "the place where the sun rises," "the east"). Traditionally Jews have always faced east, toward Jerusalem,* when praying. Therefore it was the custom to hang a picture or ornament to mark the eastern wall in their homes or synagogue. These illustrations, of plants and animals mentioned in the Bible,* were often handsome examples of folk art.

MIZRACHI. Religious Zionist movement. Mizrachi's slogan is "The land of Israel for the people of Israel according to the Torah of Israel." Although religious leaders who believed that they could find common ground with secularists had been part of the Zionist movement since its inception in Basle in 1898, religious Zionism as a political party first made its initial appearance on the Zionist scene on March 4, 1902 when Rabbi Isaac Jacob Reines* convened the Mizrachi conference in Vilna. The Fifth Zionist Congress, in 1901, had urged that the Zionist organization conduct a kind of secularist educational program to which religious Jews took sharp exception. The Mizrachi rallied many religious Jews to its banner and fought secularism within the Zionist movement.

The Mizrachi soon had active branches wherever Zionism* took root. It became particularly active in education; Mizrachi's network of religious schools eventually became part of the Israel government's religious school system. The Mizrachi Organization of America built and sponsored Bar Ilan University,* the first religious institution of higher academic learning in Israel.

When the State of Israel was proclaimed,

Mizrachi was represented in its provisional and first governments by Rabbi Judah Leib Maimon (Fishman).* Four members of the first Knesset represented Mizrachi.

Mizrachi was formally organized in the United States after 1913, although groups existed even earlier. The first national convention was held in Cincinnati in 1914 following an intensive tour of the country by Rabbi Meyer Bar Ilan,* who eventually became the president and leader of the world Mizrachi movement. Affiliated with the Mizrachi Organization of America are the Mizrachi Women, who have concentrated on

Laying pipelines in a kibbutz.

Religious Zionists of America—Mizrachi-Hapoel Hamizrachi.

Beth Zeiroth Mizrachi—a vocational high school in Tel Aviv.
Mizrachi Women's Organization of America.

218

education and child care, and B'nai Akiva, the Mizrachi Youth Organization.

Hapoel Hamizrachi (the Mizrachi Worker) came into being in 1922, when religious young people began to arrive in Palestine in increasing numbers. Highly idealistic, they formulated under the guidance of Rabbi Samuel Hayim Landau, a program based on the slogan of **Torah Ve-Avodah** (Torah and Labor). Despite the hardships and discrimination it suffered because of its religious principles, the movement grew rapidly both in Israel and abroad. It worked with the Mizrachi in the world Mizrachi movement. In 1955, it merged with Mizrachi to form one united religious party within Zionism.

In its labor activities, Hapoel Hamizrachi cooperates with other labor parties, has a contracting office, a construction company, a large banking institution, a sports organization, and one of the finest youth organizations in Israel.

Hapoel Hamizrachi is particularly proud of its collective settlements. Its first Moshav, Sde Yaakov, was founded more than fifty years ago in the Emek Jezreel. Kibbutz Hadati, Hapoel Hamizrachi's organization of religious collective settlements played an important role in Israel's defense and growth. The valiant stand of Kfar Etzion and the other settlements in the vicinity of the Hebron hills saved Jerusalem from the Arab armies during a difficult period in 1948. Hapoel Hamizrachi has been a member of the Israel government ever since the State was established in 1948.

The unification of Mizrachi and Hapoel Hamizrachi was decided on at a convention of the World Mizrachi Organization held in Jerusalem in August, 1955. The formal merger of the two movements in the United States took place in January 1957, but in the United States Mizrachi and Hapoel Hamizrachi still maintain separate women's organizations; the Hapoel Hamizrachi women's organization is known as Emunah.* The merged party, Mizrachi-Hapoel Hamizrachi, Religious Zionists of America, favors legislation to preserve traditional Jewish law in Israel. It endeavors to safeguard Jewish laws relating to marriage and divorce, and the limitation of pig breeding and selling in Israel. It seeks to protect the rights of religious newcomers to Israel.

MIZRACHI WOMEN'S ORGANIZATION OF AMERICA.
Orthodox Zionist women's organization in the United States whose primary goal is to help Israel* and its people build, develop, and generally improve the living and working conditions in the country in the spirit and framework of traditional Judaism. The Mizrachi Women's Organization supports a network of children's villages, vocational high schools, settlement houses, after-school club centers, and nurseries. Here the children, newcomers, and citizens of Israel can live, study, play and learn trades in an atmosphere that emphasizes an Orthodox way of life. The organization established the first settlement house in Jerusalem, the first vocational high school for girls in Israel, then Palestine, the first religious community center in Haifa,* and has been a leader in setting new standards for preschool to Golden Age groups. Founded in 1925, American Mizrachi Women are organized into more than 425 chapters in 35 states and the District of Columbia.

MOHILEVER, SAMUEL (1824-1898). Outstanding Russian rabbi, a founder and leader of the Zionist movement. Mohilever founded the first Hoveve Zion* society in Warsaw in 1882, at a time when Orthodox opinion frowned on any active attempt to bring about the return to Zion. In 1891, Rabbi Mohilever visited Baron Maurice de Hirsch* and successfully pleaded with him to found Jewish agricultural settlements in Palestine* instead of Argentina.* When Theodor Herzl* began to work for political Zionism,* Mohilever delivered a stirring message to the first Zionist Congress,* in 1897, supporting Herzl.

Rabbi Samuel Mohilever

MOLKHO, SOLOMON (c. 1500-1532). False Messiah, born in Portugal,* died in Mantua, Italy. Molkho was born a Christian, Diego Pires, to parents who were Marranos*—secret Jews. When David Reubeni,* who was considered a forerunner of the Messiah, came to Portugal, Diego fell under his spell completely. He gave up a government post, and openly returned to Judaism. He had himself circumcised and renamed Solomon Molkho; then he left Portugal secretly and went to Salonika, Turkey.* He studied the Kabbalah* and was drawn to Safed, a Kabbalist center in the Holy Land. Influenced greatly by Joseph Karo* and the Safed Kabbalists, Molkho predicted that the Messiah would come in 1540.

Molkho was deeply mystical and came to believe in his mission as a Messiah, winning many followers. Italy, seat of the Pope, seemed to him the very place to begin his mission. He came to Ancona in 1529, where despite opposition from some Jewish leaders, he preached to admiring congregations. Disguised as a beggar, he went to Rome, managed to see Pope Clement VII, and prophesied that the Tiber would flood its banks and that an earthquake would shake Portugal while comets showered from the sky. On October 8, 1530, the Tiber actually overflowed and on January 26, 1531, Portugal was indeed shaken by an earthquake and a comet appeared in the sky. The Pope was impressed by this visionary, and protected Molkho even when some of his writing was found offensive to Christianity. He was condemned to death by the Inquisition,* but the Pope helped him escape. Molkho joined Reubeni in Venice and went with him to Ratisbon in 1532. Carrying a banner inscribed with initials of the Hebrew words, "Who is like unto Thee, O Lord, among the mighty," they appeared before Charles V, Emperor of the Holy Roman Empire, to persuade him to call the Jews to arms against the Turks. The Emperor put them both in chains and had them sent to Italy. There Molkho was immediately condemned by the Inquisition* as a renegade from Catholicism and sentenced to burn at the stake. Molkho refused to return to the Church and died in the flames of an **auto-da-fe**.* Charles V had Reubeni sent to Spain, where he was turned over to the Inquisition. (**See also** MESSIANISM.)

N.B-A.

MONASH, SIR JOHN (1865-1931). General and engineer. Born in Melbourne, Australia,* to Jewish emigrants from Austria, Monash took degrees in arts, law and engineering at the University of Melbourne. After a brilliant career in engineering, he enlisted in the Victoria militia, where he advanced rapidly. During World War I he was named commander of the Australian forces on the Western Front, with the rank of lieutenant general. Thus, he became the first Jewish general in the English army. After the war, Monash was active in Australian Jewish life, and in 1928 was elected President of the Anzac Zionist Federation. His many foreign military honors include the United States Distinguished Service Medal.

MOND, SIR ALFRED. See MELCHETT, LORD.

MONOTHEISM. Belief in one God. According to the Bible, Abraham* was the first to teach the unity of God. The early history of the Jewish people is the story of their struggle to break away from the worship of the local Canaanite gods, and to become whole-hearted monotheists. Moses* proclaimed the unity of God in the **Shema,*** and "Hear, O Israel, the Lord our God, the Lord is One" became the cornerstone of Jewish doctrine. All the prophets pleaded with the people not to relapse into idolatry. Strangely enough it was during their exile in Babylonia,* the home of idol worship, that the Jewish people wholeheartedly accepted monotheism. In Maimonides'* 13 articles of faith, God is defined as being without "any form whatsoever." The unity of God is proclaimed in daily prayer; it is the climax of the Day of Atonement service, and it is the last confession made by the Jew on his deathbed. Monotheism also became the central doctrine of Christianity and Islam.

MONTEFIORE, SIR MOSES (1784-1885). English Jewish philanthropist and community worker.

Sir Moses Montefiore

Courtesy Library of the Jewish Theological Seminary.

220

By the age of thirty-seven, he had amassed a fortune as a stockbroker and was able to retire. Henceforth, he devoted himself completely to Jewish affairs. The Jewish community in Palestine* was foremost among his interests. Montefiore bought land for agricultural enterprises, and encouraged Jewish settlement. He endowed hospitals, established the first girls' school in Jerusalem,* helped to provide almshouses, and built synagogues. Montefiore visited Russia twice (1846, 1872), intervening on behalf of oppressed Russian Jewry with the Tsar. He traveled to Egypt* and Constantinople to intercede in the Damascus affair,* and also undertook missions to Rome, Morocco,* and Rumania.* He was the most beloved Jewish leader of his day, and his picture hung in Jewish homes the world over. Queen Victoria knighted him (1837), and the same year he was elected Sheriff of London. Montefiore remained devoutly Orthodox in belief and practice throughout his life. Many places and institutions bear his name: Zikhron Moshe near Jerusalem, Shkhunat Montefiore near Tel Aviv,* and Montefiore Hospital in New York, to name just a few.   H.L.

MONTREAL. See CANADA.

MORDECAI (5th Century B.C.E.). Mentioned in the Book of Esther,* Mordecai was a cousin and guardian of a young woman named Esther whom King Ahasuerus chose to be his queen. After the king's chief minister, Haman, received the king's permission to destroy the Jews, Mordecai enlisted Esther's help and succeeded in thwarting the plan and having Haman executed.

MORGENTHAU, HENRY SR. (1856-1946). Diplomat and financier. Brought to the United States from Germany in 1865, Morgenthau studied law but made his fortune in real estate. A supporter of Woodrow Wilson, he was named Ambassador to Turkey* in 1913. After the First World War, he headed two United States commissions on refugee problems. His last years were devoted to writing. Morgenthau's works include **All in a Lifetime,** an autobiography.

MORGENTHAU, HENRY JR. (1891-1967). American statesman and agricultural expert. The son of Henry Morgenthau, Sr.,* he was called to Washington by President Franklin Delano Roosevelt to head the Farm Credit Board. He was soon named Undersecretary of the Treasury, and then promoted to the Secretaryship. He played a key role in the recovery of the United States from the economic depression of the 1930's, and in its

mobilization for the Second World War. After his retirement from public office he became active in Zionist fund raising. In 1947 he was named General Chairman of the United Jewish Appeal,* and in 1951 became Chairman of the Board of Governors of the Bonds for Israel* drive. Kibbutz **Tal Shahar** ("Morning Dew"), in Israel, is named for Morgenthau.

MOROCCO. The Jewish community of Morocco dates back to the period before the destruction of the Second Temple* (70 C. E.). Under Roman rule, the Jews suffered continual harassment. This ended temporarily with the fall of the Roman Empire, when the Vandal King Generich permitted Moroccan Jews equal citizenship. They engaged in navigation, maritime commerce, vinegrowing, and agriculture, and flourished for a time. But the era of prosperity soon ended. Under Arab rule during the tenth century, there was an upsurge of Jewish cultural and religious life. Such famous Talmudic scholars as Isaac Alfasi and Moses Maimonides* lived in Morocco. The notorious **mellahs** (ghettos) whose cramped and twisted streets came to symbolize Moroccan Jewish degradation to second-class citizenship, were originally instituted in the thirteenth century to protect the Jews from attack by Muslim mobs. These ghettos have continued into the twentieth century.

The expulsion from Spain* in 1492 brought a great influx of Jews to Morocco, where they introduced European traditions of art, culture, and commerce. The Jewish community witnessed another cultural resurgence in the sixteenth century, when Morocco became the home of many noted Jewish scholars. But the Jews remained second-class citizens, always subject to Moslem violence. War with France* and Spain (1884-1859) further inflamed Moslem fanaticism, and the mellahs became the scene of brutal, unprovoked attacks. With French and Spanish occupation of

Henry Morgenthau, Jr.
Courtesy United Jewish Appeal.

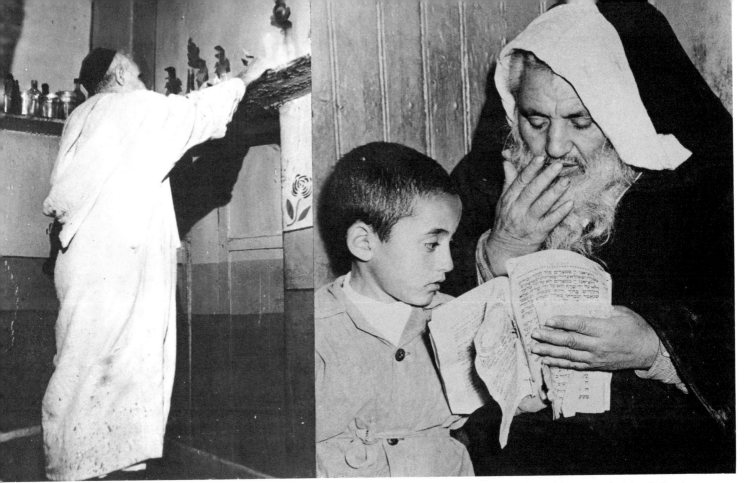

rabbi lights the Sabbath eve candles in primitive synagogue
f the Casablanca mellah (ghetto).

Teaching the Passover Haggadah at a primitive heder in
Casablanca, Morocco.

Joint Distribution Committee.

Morocco in 1912, conditions took a turn for the better. The worst abuses were ended, corporal punishment was abolished, the observance of the Sabbath* was recognized, and compulsory military service was ended.

General Arab antagonism to the State of Israel* created a rising feeling of insecurity among Moroccan Jews, which was reflected in a surge of emigration to Israel. There also was a large-scale shift of the Jewish population from villages and small towns in the hinterland to the larger cities, which offered greater protection.

In 1956, France and Spain relinquished their protectorate, and Morocco achieved its independence. In 1977 there were 18,000 Jews living in the country. Casablanca has the largest Jewish community in any Moslem country. Other important centers were Tangier, Meknes, Fez and Tetuan. A number of welfare, religious and educational institutions operate in Morocco and are aided by the American Jewish Joint Distribution Committee.*

MORTARA CASE. In 1858, church authorities kidnapped a six-year-old Jewish boy, Edgar Mortara, from his parents in Bologna, Italy.* This became an international incident, and the emperors Francis Joseph of Austria and Napolean III of France sent personal messages to Pope Pius IX pleading that the child be returned to his parents. Their requests and all other protests were rejected, and Edgar Mortara was brought up as a Catholic. The reason given by the Church was that Edgar's Catholic nurse had had him secretly baptized when he was two years old, and baptism was irrevocable. The child was never given back to his parents, and when he grew up he entered the Church as a priest.

MOSES. The "Lawgiver" who led Israel to freedom. The thirteenth century B.C.E. is considered to be the period when Moses led the Children of Israel in the exodus from Egypt.* "There hath never yet arisen in Israel a prophet like Moses, one who hath beheld His (i.e. God's) likeness." These words from the prayer book single out Moses as "a man of God," and as the greatest of all the leaders of Israel. It was he who welded the Children of Israel into a nation and gave them a divinely inspired law—the Torah*—to set the Jewish nation apart as a "kingdom of priests."

The details of Moses' career are vividly record-

The Burning Bush—old engraving. "...And the angel of the Lord appeared unto him in a flame of fire out of the midst of a bush..." (Exodus 3:2).

dian where he joins the household of Jethro, the priest, whose daughter Zipporah he takes for a wife. She bears him two sons, Gershom and Eliezer.

It was while tending the flocks of his father-in-law that Moses received his first call from God; it comes from a burning bush. He is assigned the task of liberating the people, and accepts it, though with some reluctance.

With his brother Aaron, who acts, as his spokesman (for Moses is a stammerer) he appears before Pharaoh, whom he orders to free the Children of Israel from bondage. Pharaoh's consent comes only after the infliction of ten plagues. The hurried exodus of the Children of Israel from Egypt is followed by the miraculous crossing of the Red Sea. Free at last, the people of Israel now journey into the desert to receive the Ten Commandments at the foot of Mt. Sinai, and to enter into an eternal covenant with God.

But the habits of a long-enslaved people are not easily broken. In the absence of Moses during his forty days' encounter with God in the craggy solitudes of Mt. Sinai, the old superstitions and beliefs assert themselves with the making of a golden calf. Besides, the trials of desert life demoralize the people. They lose faith in themselves and in their leader Moses, and their constant murmurings soon turn into open rebellion. This seals their fate. They are condemned to wander in the desert for forty years, by the end of which time a new generation will have grown up to undertake the conquest of the land of Canaan. Even Moses has to share this fate, dying at the desert's edge in sight of the promised land. On the seventh of Adar he ascends Mt. Nebo for a last look at the land, then, Jewish tradition has it, Moses dies by "the kiss of God."

Thus ends the life of the greatest of all prophets, called "the lawgiver," "the servant of God," and (most popularly) **Moshe Rabbenu**—"our teacher

ed in the pages of the Bible.* Of the five books that bear his name (the Pentateuch), four recount the story of his leadership. The third child of Amram and Yocheved of the tribe of Levi,* his birth in Egypt is surrounded by secrecy as is his death in the wilderness near Mt. Nebo—"no man knowing his burying place."

To escape Pharaoh's cruel decree ordering every Hebrew male child to be cast into the Nile, Moses was hidden by his mother for three months after his birth, then he was placed onto an ark of bulrushes by the river's edge, with his sister Miriam keeping watch at a distance. There he was discovered by the daughter of Pharaoh, who took pity on the child and, through the clever prompting of Moses' sister Miriam, engaged the child's mother to act as nurse. Brought up as an Egyptian prince in the palace of Pharaoh, Moses never forgot his Hebrew origin, for his mother reared him in the faith and traditions of his people.

Moses' zeal for justice finds dramatic expression when he kills an Egyptian taskmaster for assaulting a Jew. When the news of this act reaches Pharaoh, Moses flees for his life to Mi-

The Prayer of Moses Against Amalek—eighteenth-century engraving. "But Moses' hands were heavy...and Aaron and Hur stayed up his hands" (Exodus 17:12).

Moses." He dies, at the age of 120, in the prime of his powers—"his eye was not dim, nor his natural force abated."

The tremendous personality of Moses impressed itself upon Israel in its formative years and shaped its maturity. The people learned to live by his laws and wrote great books about them. They revered the qualities of Moses' character, his loving kindness, strength and humility, his wisdom and modesty. And they wove innumerable legends about his life. The peoples of the world shared with Israel the reverence for Moses, and the "Five Books of Moses" gave direction to the civilization of the West.   L.

MOSES BEN NAHMAN (1195-1270). Also known as Nahmanides, or Ramban. Born in Gerona, Spain, he was one of the outstanding Talmudic scholars and Bible* commentators of the Middle Ages. Nahmanides' fame rose when he brilliantly defended the Jewish faith in one of the forced religious disputes between Christians and Jews. The dispute took place at Barcelona, Spain,* in 1263. Nahmanides was compelled to participate in it under order of King James I of Aragon. "Has the Messiah already arrived, or is he yet to appear and redeem the world from its state of misery and suffering?" was one of the central themes of the debate. The King conceded the success of the great Jewish scholar, who presented winning arguments in support of the Jewish religion. This enraged his adversaries, the Dominican priests, who accused him of insulting the Christian faith. Forced to leave Spain, Nahmanides came to Palestine* in 1267, settling first in Jerusalem* and later in Acre, where he founded a Talmudical academy. Finding very few Jews in Palestine, Nahmanides issued a call to his brethren in other countries and urged them to come and settle in the Holy Land.

Nahmanides was recognized as the foremost authority on Jewish law. His commentary on the Bible continues to be highly regarded for its profound interpretations, based on reason and deep legal knowledge. A physician by profession, and versed in philosophy and science, Nahmanides also engaged in the study of mysticism or Kabbalah.*

MOSHAV. Form of cooperative agricultural settlement in Israel. As distinct from the kibbutz,* each member of the moshav has his own home and a plot of land worked by himself and his family. However, all marketing of produce and purchase of supplies is done cooperatively, and some of the farm machinery is owned by the village as a whole. The **Moshav Shitufi** is run along lines midway between a kibbutz and a moshav.

MUSIC, JEWISH. The Jews began to compose music when the Israelites were still wandering tribes in the desert. Our earliest ancestors sang with joy when they discovered water and good grazing for their flocks. They beat rhythms on simple drums and tambourines. They blew their crude rams' horns when they were attacked by marauders, or when they wanted to summon an assembly of the tribe. Settling in the land of Canaan,* they sang songs of triumph, of mourning, their vineyard songs, their love songs. What is more, they had among them professional musicians and singers who knew how to play the more sophisticated instruments of the Middle East— strings, wind, and percussion—and who were trained to perform the elaborate music of the Temple service.

All of this ancient music has been lost. It was created long before people had discovered a way of writing music. We can only guess at what it may have been like: first, by studying wall paintings and friezes which have remained from ancient times in Egypt, Babylon, and Rome; second, by studying the names of instruments mentioned in the Bible* and their derivations. The Bible, particularly Psalms* and the Song of Songs,* is also a good source for the words of many ancient songs.

After the destruction of the Second Temple,* "professional," or "art" music dwindled in

224

Jewish life. Synagogue songs may have contained some fragments of the Temple chants. Carried by word of mouth, from generation to generation, into many far-flung lands, the chant changed further. Still, the fact is that we can find similarities in the chants of Jews as far apart geographically and culturally as Germany,* North Africa and Yemen. Probably the oldest music still in use in synagogues is the Biblical chant, the melody in which the readings from the Torah,* the Prophets, and the special scrolls are chanted on Sabbaths* and Festivals in the synagogue.

At some point in the very early Middle Ages, these chants were written down for the Bible text, in a very primitive sort of musical sign language. The symbols are vague, so that people in different parts of the world sound them differently. Besides, the same set of signs are sung differently in connection with the various sections of the Bible. In other words, even in the tradition of the East European Jews, for example, the melody of the Torah or Pentateuch chant sounds quite different from that of the prophetic chant; the Book of Esther* and the Song of Songs* are chanted still differently.

Another heritage from the distant past is the prayer chant, which is the basis of our cantors' improvisations. **Nusah** is the Hebrew name for these chants. A particular **Nusah** consists of a series of short melodic phrases within a particular scale. We must remember that, beside the major and minor scales of our comparatively modern European music, there are a number of other scales which one can find by playing on only white notes on the piano, beginning at any note. There are special **Nusahot** (plural of **Nusah**) for special occasions, or for special ideas found in the prayers. The cantor (**see also** HAZAN) uses the musical phrases, but is free to elaborate on them, to weave his own individual decorations of sound around the bare outlines. Some of these chants may indeed be descendants of Temple song. Others are believed to have been composed by unknown composers in the Middle Ages, in the days of the troubadours and minnesingers of Europe.

In Germany and East Europe, the Biblical and prayer chants became part of the folk song of the people. Conversely, wherever Jews lived, their folk song took on the color of the country. Folk songs were usually sung in a vernacular, that is, in a language of everyday life. There are a number of such languages—usually a combination of Hebrew with the language of the country: Yiddish,* Ladino,* Judaeo-Arabic, etc. Also, even when Jews lived in ghettos, they could not help hearing tunes, the drinking songs, the soldier songs, the balalaikas or the fiddles of their Gentile

"Hasidim." Water color by Saul Raskin.

neighbors. Sometimes they consciously took over those tunes and put their own words to them. Sometimes the Jews unconsciously imitated them. Always stamped something of their own character on the tune they adopted. Wherever Jews lived, it has been religious folk songs that have lasted longest: Sabbath table songs (**Zemirot**), wedding songs, and the songs of the Passover* Haggadah.*

One particular sect of Jews that arose in the eighteenth century created a very unique type of religious folk song. The **Hasidim** believed that one did not need learning to get a feeling of direct contact with God. They believed that one of the best ways to get that feeling was through music—particularly, through songs without words. Words, they thought, chained one to Heaven. Their songs, usually accompanied by dance movement, were sometimes meditative, sometimes gay. Frequently they would gradually progress from quiet concentration to the wildest ecstasy. Their songs were often a medley of original prayer chants and Slavic peasant tunes; however, they took on a religious quality.

Generally, it was not until the beginning of the nineteenth century, when Jews began to participate in the cultures of the countries of their residence, that we first encounter professionally composed music. Solomon Sulzer and Louis Lewandowski were pioneers in writing music for the synagogue, for cantors and choirs, in four-part harmonies.

They and their immediate followers were so eager to make their music sound Western that they lost almost all the flavor of the traditional **Nusah.** Later in the nineteenth century, however, with the development of Yiddish and the revival of Hebrew, interest was renewed in the traditional synagogue music. The folk song and the music of Jews in other parts of the world were studied intensively. As the twentieth century dawned, a movement of young Jews in Russia* attempted to create a "national" Jewish music. At the same time, a new folk music was growing up in the first settlements of Jews in Palestine.* This folk music was at first very much like that of Russia and Poland.* At the same time a beginning was made in the composition of new synagogue music in the United States. Some of the composers of this music have come here from Europe, others are native born and trained. Much of the music, though written in the style of our own day, has its roots in the ancient chants.

Folk song continues to be created in Israel,* where melodies of Eastern and Oriental Jews have added their exotic flavor to the earlier Slavic tunes of the Land. To a great extent, however, the songs of Israel are now composed in folk style by somewhat more professional composers. Also, a completely new "art" music is growing up; symphonic, chamber, choral and song music, is written by practicing composers. Some of these composers have received all of their training and much of their experience in Europe. A new generation of composers, however, has received it basic training in the music conservatories of Israel, or under Israeli teachers. Both the folk and the professional composers have been greatly influenced by the music of the Oriental Jews, who have been pouring into the country in recent years. Using the instruments of the symphony orchestra, and the technique of harmony and counterpoint developed in the Western world, they are writing music in which we can hear the oudh, the shepherd flute, the different kinds of drums and tambours, the strange nasal singing, and the odd offbeat rhythms of the Orient. Only a small portion of this music has been published and can be found in the United States. Still less has been recorded. If we take the pains to accustom our ears to the folk song which has been published and recorded, and to become familiar with the music of the modern composers of America and Europe, we shall enjoy the new professional music of Israel immensely.

J.K.E.

MYSTICISM. See KABBALAH.

NAHMAN OF BRATZLAV (1770-1811). Hasidic leader. Among the remarkable personalities produced by Hasidism,* Nahman of the town of Bratzlav, in the Ukraine, is outstanding. A grandson of the founder of the movement, Israel Baal Shem Tov,* his unique gifts became evident in childhood. He was still very young when followers began to flock to him to listen eagerly to his interpretation of Hasidic philosophy. He taught them to pray joyfully, and yet to devote time to contemplation. Aside from his Hasidic works, he created imaginative and original fairy tales.

Unlike other Hasidic rabbis, Rabbi Nahman did not establish a dynasty. Followers of his teachings are to be found all over the world, especially in Israel. They revere his memory, and mark the anniversaries of his death with a special observance.

NAHMANIDES. See MOSES BEN NAHMAN.

NAHUM. Seventh of the minor prophets. The Book of Nahum, in the Bible,* describes in beautiful poetic language the downfall of Nineveh and the Assyrian empire. Excavations of Nineveh make it evident that the prophet knew well the city whose destruction he painted in colors so vivid.

NAHUM OF GIMZO. See TANNAIM.

NAMES, JEWISH. Proper Names. In Biblical times, a name expressed some thought or emotion. In the story of Creation, Adam named his wife Eve (Havah) meaning "Life" in Hebrew, because she was the "mother of all living." When Rachel bore her first son, she named him Joseph—Hebrew for "he will add"—saying: "The Lord will add to me another son." Sometimes the name was a compound of two related words. The Hebrew **Ab** ("Father") was combined with a variety of words: Abishai—"Father-of-a-gift"; Abner— "Father-of-light"; Abraham—"Father-of-multitudes"; and Absalom—"Father-of-peace." The Hebrew **Ah** or brother, was variously fused to make: Ahijah—"Brother-of-God"; Ahinadab— "Brother-of-nobility"; Ahitub—"Brother-of-goodness." **Ben,** the Hebrew for "son," is part of Benjamin—"Son-of-the-right-hand" or of "good fortune," and Reuben—"Behold-a-son;" while **Bat,** "daughter," is in Bathsheba—"Daughter-of-the-oath." Often the divine names **El, IAH, Jeho,** and **Shaddai** were contained in proper names. **El** was combined to make: Eldad—"Beloved-of-God"; Elkanah—"God-created"; Bezalel—"In-the-shadow-of-God"; and Israel—"Warrior-of-

God.'' Most familiar is the use of **Iah,** as in Isaiah—"Help-of-God," and Jeremiah—"Whom-God-raised-up." **Jeho** is found in the names: Jehoiadah—"Whom-God-favors"; Joab—"God-desired"; and Jonathan— "God-given." Finally, **Shaddai** was used to make Ammishaddai—"Kindred-of-God," and Zurishaddai—"God-protected."

People were also named after animals and plants: e.g., Arieh—"Lion," Deborah—"Bee," Jonah—"Dove," Rachel—"Ewe," Tamar—"Palm Tree." The custom of naming children after deceased relatives, especially grandparents, was adopted after the Babylonian exile; later, among the Hasidim* it was customary to name the boy after a deceased **tsadik,** a Hasidic rabbi. Sephardic Jews name their children after living grandparents; among Reform Jews, the son often bears the father's name with the addition of Junior, as among the Christians.

The use of foreign names, first found in the later Biblical period (e.g., Esther* derived from Ishtar, and Mordecai* from Marduk), became more prevalent in Talmudic and medieval times. Some of the names in Jewish history that bear witness to contact with Greek and Roman civilizations are Antigonus, Symachus, Tarphon, Marcus, Justus, and Titus. The Greek name Alexander was shortened in time to Sander and Sender, while Phoebus became Feivel or Feivish—names that persist in Yiddish to this day. Beginning with the Greek-Hellenistic period, when the records show us Judah-Aristobulus, Salome-Alexandra, Simon-Peter, and Saul-Paul—dual names, one Jewish and the other non-Jewish, became popular under the influence of foreign cultures.

This is still the custom today: Jewish children as a rule receive one name typical of the country in which they live, and one "Jewish" (i.e. Yiddish or Hebrew) name.

In our own days, the tendency is to retain a likeness in sound to the Jewish name: Arthur-Aaron, Hyman-Hayim, Bella-Beile, Rose-Reizel. The Hebrew name for a boy is usually bestowed at the circumcision ceremony, while a girl is named soon after birth; among the German Jews, the giving of the civic name was marked by the so-called **Hollekreisch** ceremony on the fourth Sabbath after birth. The first child is named after someone in the father's family; the second child, after someone in the mother's. Sometimes a child is given two Hebrew (or "Jewish") names to satisfy the wishes of both parents.

The influence of the Kabbalah* is felt also in the naming of children. People who have been dangerously ill are given additional names such as Hayim (for men) and Hayah (for women). Hope for good health is expressed by the name Raphael

("God heals"), Azriel ("God is my help") invokes divine aid, and Alter or Alte ("Old One") expresses the wish for a long life. Yiddish contains the largest variety of names, both male and female, adopted from the Hebrew and European languages. Thus the Hebrew Brakhah become Brokhe in Yiddish, Israel becomes Isser, Jacob Koppel, Mordecai Motel, Rebbeca Rive, and Zipporah Feiga (one is the Hebrew, the other Yiddish, for "bird"). French and Spanish names also became Yiddishized: Belle becomes Beile, and Esperanza Sprinze. The Italian name Angelo turns up as Anshel, and Benedetto as Bendet. A few of the German transformations are Braun to Bryna, Enoch to Henach, Hirsch to Hertz, Freude to Frade, Fradl, or Freidl. From Czech we have Bohdanka becoming Badane and Benes Beinish. The Russian Dobra becomes Dobre in Yiddish, Khvala Khvoles, and Zlata Zlate; the Polish Czarna becomes Charne.

Among Yemenite and other Arabic-speaking Jews, the influence of Arab names is apparent; e.g., names like Aminah, Asisah, Barhun, Dunash, Faradi, Gamilah, Hassan, Masudah, Nogema, Yahiah, Yaish. Under the influence of Zionism,* the use of Biblical names has increased, and new Hebrew names have developed, particularly in the State of Israel:* e.g., Amikam—"My-people-has-risen"; Arnon—"Torrent"; Eran—"Awakened"; Raanan—"Verdant"; Shaanan—"Peaceable"; Uzzi—"My-strength"; and Yigal—"God-will-redeem" for boys. The new names for girls include Adinah—"Delicate" or "Noble"; Aviva—"Spring"; Geulah—"Redemption"; Nitza—"Blossom"; Nurit—"Light"; Tikvah—"Hope"; Zahavah—"Goldie"; Zionah and Galilah are adaptations of Israel place names.

Laws prohibiting Jews to use non-Jewish names were in force in Prussia, Bohemia, and Tsarist Russia in the nineteenth century. A decree in Nazi Germany,* published in August 1938, suggested the use of 276 typical Jewish names (185 for males and 91 for females) for Jewish children born after that date. Among these were such humiliating male names as Ahab and Ahasuerus—wicked Biblical kings, Assur—the nation that defeated Israel; Chamor, Esau, Korah, Laban and Lot—ignoble Biblical personalities; Moab, another enemy of Israel; and Orev, a crow. Two wicked queens, Athalaiah and Jezebel, and the ludicrous Chinke and Driesel were Nazi-prescribed names for the females. Under this decree, Jewish males were ordered to add the name of Israel and females were to take the additional name of Sarah in case their names did not proclaim their Jewish lineage.

Under the influence of the Bible, many Hebrew names came to be used by Christians, either in their pure Biblical form (Aaron, Abner, Abigail, Adah, Beulah) or in a derivative form (Ann, Anna from Hannah, John from Yohanan, Elizabeth from Elisheba, Mary and Maria from Miriam).

Surnames. Jewish family names are of recent origin, and until 1800, a person's second name would often be taken as his family name; e.g. Aaron Samuel—Aaron **ben** (Hebrew for the son of) Samuel. In the early Middle Ages, **Cohen** and **Levi** or their Hebrew abbreviations, Katz (from the initials of Kohen Zedek"—"Priest of Justice"),—and **Segal** (from "S'gan Levi"—"Levitical Head"), are mentioned. Names such as Aaronson, Abramson, Hirschenson, Jacobson (with their Slavic forms Aronovsky, Abramsky, Hirshovsky, Yakubovsky, or Aronovitsh, Abramovitsh, Hirshovitsh, Yakubovitsh) originated from the use of the father's name. The elimination of "son" restored such names to their anglicized forms, Aaron, Abrahams, Hirsh, Jacobs, while the addition of "mann" to the Hebrew or Yiddish proper names created surnames like Abermann (from Abraham), Heymann (Hayim), Koppelmann (Jacob), Mosesmann, Nachmann, Saulmann, and Urimann.

The majority of Jewish family names in Europe (60 to 65 per cent) are of geographic derivation, the oldest among them being Spiro, Mintz, Horowitz, Liebshitz, and names ending in "burg" (Friedburg, Maidenburg, Ruttenburg, Warburg). A small percentage denotes occupations, such as: Buchbinder, Drucker, Goldschmidt, Hutmacher, Kirzhner, Lederer, Milner, Schneider, Tischler; or Jewish communal functions, like: Chazan ("Cantor"), Lehrer ("Teacher"), Magid ("Preacher"), Parnes ("President"), and the obvious Singer. Abbreviations are also common: Asch from Eisenstadt, Bach from Bayit Chadash ("Newhouse"), Bahrav from Ben Ha-rav ("Rabbi's Son"), Back from Ben Kedoshim ("Son-of-Saints"), Barash from Ben Rabbi Shimon ("Son-of-Rabbi-Simon"), Shatz from Sheliah Tzibur ("Public Pleader"), Zakheim from Zera Kodesh Haim ("Seed-of-Holiness").

Among the Jews in the United States there is a tendency to anglicize their family name, and a name such as Katzenelenbogen, one of the oldest among European Jews, may be changed to Katenel, Katzen, Katz or Kat—ultimately to become Kay. In the State of Israel, the translation of a name into a Hebraized form is very popular. Thus, Gutstein becomes Eventov, Lichtstein become Maor or Even-Ur, Goldberg becomes Har Zahav, Friedberg becomes Har Shalom, Friedman becomes Ish Shalom, Derbarimdiker becomes Rahman or Rahamim, Florentin becomes Perahiah, Diamant becomes Yahalom, Rosen becomes Shoshan, Stock becomes Sedan or Zmorah, Shertok becomes Sharett, Treger becomes Amos.
M.K.

NAPHTALI (Hebrew, meaning "my struggle"). Tenth son of Jacob. The tribe of Naphtali was war-like in its early days; it was allotted territory north and west of the Sea of Galilee.

NASI, JOSEPH (c. 1510-1579). Jewish statesman, banker, and merchant. Born in Portugal,* Joseph Nasi came from a historic family of Spanish aristocrats, the distinguished Nasi-Mendes family. Some of them were among the refugees from Spain* (in 1492) who settled in Portugal. Forced to adopt Christianity in 1497, they became Marranos,* or secret Jews, and Joseph's Marrano name was Joao Miguez. When he was about fifteen years old, Jospeh was taken by his widowed aunt, Gracia de Mendesia, to Antwerp, where there was less religious prejudice. In Antwerp, also, they came to be suspected of observing Judaism secretly, and fled to Venice. When Venice expelled all Marranos from the city and arrested Donna Gracia, the influence of the powerful Nasi-Mendes banking and financial house extended to Turkey. Joseph was therefore able to get the help of Sultan Suleiman the Magnificent in obtaining freedom for his aunt. When she was released, Donna Gracia, her daughter Reyna, and Joseph settled in Constantinople, and threw off the disguise of Catholicism. Joseph married his beautiful cousin Reyna, and after Suleiman's death he entered the service of Sultan Selim. He was a favorite at court, and his influence was greater than that of the Grand Vizier. In gratitude for the success of his policies, Selim made Joseph Nasi Duke of Naxos and Prince of the Cyclades. He also gave him a grant of the city of Tiberias in Palestine. Joseph Nasi gathered up 200 Jewish refugees from the Inquisition* in Italy and brought them to Tiberias* in his own ships. Into this colony he introduced mulberry trees for silk cultivation. The results of this sixteenth-century experiment in agricultural settlement of the Holy Land are not recorded. One of Joseph Nasi's spectacular policies was dictated by the desire for revenge. He pressed the Sultan into declaring war on Venice; the result was the capture of Cyprus by the Turks.
N.B-A.

NATIONAL CONFERENCE ON SOVIET JEWRY. See RUSSIA.

NATIONAL COUNCIL OF JEWISH WOMEN. As the oldest major Jewish Women's organization in the United States, The National council of Jewish Women has a history of pioneering advocacy and community service projects in the United States and Israel for more than 91 years. Over 100,000 mem-

Emblem of the tribe of Naphtali

Both mother and children learn from NCJW Research Institute's HIPPY (Home Instruction Program for Preschool Youngsters) program. Serving 1,400 families in Israel, the home-based program trains mothers from educationally disadvantaged backgrounds to teach their children (ages 4-6) skills essential to success in school.

bers in 200 Sections nationwide, implement the mission of the organization, which in the spirit of Judaism, is dedicated to furthering human welfare in the Jewish and general communities, locally, nationally and internationally.

Currently, NCJW maintains five Priorities: children and youth; women's issues; Israel; the aging; and Jewish life. The organization offers a myriad of programs and projects in each Priority. For example, NCJW's Court Appointed Special Advocate (CASA) project, implemented by its Sections, provides volunteers as advocates for children in the foster care system.

NCJW's commitment to Israel dates from 1947 when it helped establish the School of Education at the Hebrew University of Jerusalem. In 1968, it established the NCJW Research Institute for Innovation in Education at the Hebrew University which currently promotes education and social welfare for the educationally disadvantaged through research and service projects. NCJW's Ship-A-Box project provides packages of educational material for disadvantaged children.

NATIONAL FEDERATION OF TEMPLE SISTERHOODS. The women's division of the Union of American Hebrew Congregations,* the central organization of Reform Judaism in America. Organized in 1913, the organization has a membership of about 120,000 women in 640 sisterhoods. Functioning groups are also found in Canada, the United Kingdom, Cuba, Panama, Australia, and Union of South Africa. Through program material, study courses and projects, the Federation assists its members to serve the synagogue, to gain Jewish knowledge, and to translate religious ideals into practical expressions of concern for humanity. The Federation provides scholarships and aid to students at the Hebrew Union College—Jewish Institute of Religion,*

helps to promote and support the youth activities program of the Union of American Hebrew Congregations, and subsidizes institutes for religious school teachers and laymen. It grants rabbinic fellowships to students from overseas, to enable them to serve congregations belonging to the World Union of Progressive Judaism after ordination and graduation. To further interfaith awareness and understanding, the sisterhoods conduct institutes on Judaism for church women to acquaint them with the traditions, ritual and philosophy of Judaism.

NATIONAL FEDERATION OF TEMPLE YOUTH. The National Federation of Temple Youth—called NIFTY—represents teenagers affiliated with Reform synagogues in the United States. Approximately 20,000 adolescents belong to NIFTY in twenty-one regions. Members in the various regions are encouraged to attend conclaves, to participate in leadership institutes, and to help in NIFTY projects. The national organization seeks to exert a direct influence on the individual members through its Mitzvah Program. A Mitzvah Kit details the projects of the individual groups, and forms the basis for the major part of teenage activity. The program includes various activities of NIFTY in Israel.

NATIONAL JEWISH WELFARE BOARD (JWB). The central agency of the Jewish Community Center movement, the JWB has 470 Jewish community centers with field service, program aids, advice and guidance on personnel selection and training, and problems relating to administration. These centers serve many thousands of persons, in addition to their more than 900,000 members, through cultural, recrea-

The Jewish Book Fair at the Jewish Community Center of Detroit. These book fairs are conducted locally by the Jewish Community Centers under the auspices of the National Jewish Welfare Board.

tional, camping, youth and athletic programs.

In 1917 the JWB was authorized to care for the welfare of Jewish servicemen. During and after the Second World War, the JWB was a constituent member of the United Service Organizations (USO). It assumed the responsibility for providing chaplains, prayer books, educational services and materials, and kosher food for Jewish soldiers in the armed forces, as well as for arranging for Sabbath and other religious observances.

NATIONAL WOMEN'S LEAGUE OF THE UNITED SYNAGOGUE OF AMERICA. Now known as the **Women's League for Conservative Judaism.** An organization of women belonging to sisterhoods of the Conservative synagogues throughout the United States and Canada. Founded in 1917 by Mrs. Solomon Schechter,* the organization totals over 800 sisterhoods, with a membership of more than 200,000 women affiliated with the Jewish Theological Seminary of America.*

The goal of Women's League is to bring the ideas of Conservative Judaism to the attention of the American Jewish woman. For this purpose, the organization fosters study cources, Judaism-in-the-home Institutes, and synagogue libraries. It publishes books for children, education and program kits, a magazine called the **Outlook,** and a bulletin called **Leaguenotes.** The organization sponsors a comprehensive Leadership Training Program to prepare leaders for local sisterhoods. Its Social Actions Committee seeks to give the American Jewish woman a better understanding of her civic responsibilities. The League helps to support the Jewish Theological Seminary of America* through the Torah Fund. It is one of the sponsors of the United Synagogue Youth, and cooperates with other organizations in civic welfare and Israel projects.

NAVON, YITZHAK (1921-   ). Israel educator, public servant and fifth president of the State of Israel.* Born in Jerusalem* of an old Sephardic* family, he studied at the Hebrew University,* then taught at elementary and secondary schools. He also served as director of the Arabic department of Haganah.* In 1949 he joined Israel's foreign service. Later, he was political secretary first to Moshe Sharett* and subsequently (1952-63) to Prime Minister David Ben-Gurion.* In 1965, after serving two years with the Ministry of Education, he was elected to the Knesset.* In 1978 he was elected president of the State of Israel, the first Sephardic Jew and native-born Israeli to hold that office. He has written books and stories on the folklore of Sephardic communities, one of which, **The Sephardic Orchard,** has become a popular musical in Israel.

NAZARETH. An Israeli town of about 69,000 inhabitants. It is the principal Arab city in Israel; most of its inhabitants are Christian with a Moslem minority. Nazareth nestles in a secluded glen in the hills of lower Galilee, in the shadow of Mount Tabor, and overlooking the great Plain of Jezreel. The home of Jesus as a child and young man, Nazareth has many beautiful churches, monasteries, and sacred sites, including the Fountain of the Virgin.

NAZIRITE. One who, in Biblical times, vowed to abstain from various pleasures for a limited period of time and dedicated himself to God. The Nazirite was not allowed to drink wine, go near a dead body, or cut his hair (Numbers 6). Samson* was a Nazirite, and caused his own downfall by allowing Delilah to shave his head (Judges 11:17). The Nazirite assumed vows for a period of not less than thirty days, at the end of which he brought a sacrifice at the Temple. Although a section of the Talmud* is devoted to the laws of the Nazirite, Jewish tradition discouraged man from placing personal restrictions on himself and placing himself apart from society.

NAZISM. See JEWRY, ANNIHILATION OF EUROPEAN.

NEGEV. The southern and still largely empty part of Israel,* over 4,000 square miles in area. It has a desert climate, hot and dry by day, cold and humid by night. The Negev is the largest compact territorial block in Israel. It is made up of parched uplands and plateaus, with elevations of up to

Yitzhak Navon

Bird's eye view of the Negev.

Forbidding rocks guard the winding road through the southern Negev to the Red Sea.

3,000 feet, scarred by rugged canyons and wide dry river beds.

A peculiar feature of the landscape are the strikingly colored cirques, great mortars, some a thousand feet in depth, surrounded by high ridges, usually cracked by a single trench. The coastal margin of the Negev is carpeted with fertile loess soil, interspersed with glittering sand dunes. For many centuries the Negev was a forsaken wasteland. Yet its surface is strewn with the ruins of cities and villages, such as Eilat* and Haluza, Avdat and Shivta, with relics of terraces, dams, and pools dating back to Nabatean, Roman, and Byzantine times. These were stations of the ancient trade routes and the mining cities of Solomon.* Today the dry lands of the Negev are slowly coming to life and taking on color. New settlements are springing up, to which many immigrants are now being directed; sheep ranches are being established and crops are being cultivated with the aid of water piped from the Yarkon River. Underground water sources are being tapped, and copper mining resumed at the ancient sites. Such minerals as phosphates and kaolin are being successfully exploited.

T. and S.B.

NEHARDEIA. See BABYLONIA.

NEHEMIAH, BOOK OF. Eleventh book in the **Ketuvim** or Writings section of the Bible.* It relates the history of Nehemiah, son of Hacaliah, who was the cup-bearer of Artaxerxes II, King of Persia (c. 446 B.C.E.). When news of the bad condition of the returned exiles in Jerusalem* reached Nehemiah in Susa, he obtained a commission from the King to return to Judea as its governor. One of Nehemiah's first tasks was to lead the people in rebuilding the walls of Jerusalem, while defending themselves from attacks by the Samaritans.*

Nehemiah inspired the builders to defend themselves as they worked: "one of his hands wrought in the work and in the other he held his weapon." Together with Ezra the Scribe,* Nehemiah reinsituted the festivals and observances that preserved the identity and continuity of the Jewish people.

NEILAH (Hebrew, meaning "closing"). Final service of Yom Kippur.* Traditionally, the recital of this prayer indicated that the gates of heaven were about to close and judgement would be passed on the fate of man for the coming year. The Neilah service dates back to the third century, and is one of the most solemn portions of Jewish liturgy.

NETHERLANDS. Jews began to settle in Holland in 1322, but in the latter part of the fourteenth century they were driven out. However, in the fifteenth century, Jews and Marranos* began to arrive from Spain in 1492 and many of the Marranos returned openly to the Jewish faith. Many of the Jewish refugees had capital and initiative and their widespread contacts among relatives and friends in many countries enabled them to set up business establishments. In time they attained positions of economic importance. Later, in the seventeenth century, their ranks were swelled by the arrival of Ashkenazic* Jews from Germany* and Poland.* During the seventeenth and eighteenth centuries Jewish life in Holland flourished. The Dutch communities were strictly Orthodox, and did not tolerate any act of reform or heresy. For this reason Uriel Acosta* was excommunicated (1618), as was Baruch Spinoza* (1655). Dutch Jewry enjoyed, almost without interruption, more political rights than did their fellow Jews in other European lands. Dutch Jews had independent community organizations, both Sephardic and Ash-

The Portuguese Synagogue in Amsterdam (engraving by Romain de Hooghe, 1675).

kenazic. Until the occupation of Holland by the Germans in 1940, local Jewry played a significant part in the economy, culture, and press of the Netherlands.

In 1942 the Germans herded all the Dutch Jews into ghettos and concentration camps. The largest of the latter was Westerbork, from which 117,000 Jewish men, women and children were transferred to Auschwitz* and Sobibor in Poland, where they were exterminated in gas chambers. Their possessions, factories, and businesses were plundered by the Germans. About 25,000 Jews, some of them of mixed ancestry, and others concealed in special hiding places, survived.

In 1977, the Jewish community of the Netherlands numbered some 30,000 of whom about two-thirds lived in Amsterdam. The years following the end of the war, in 1945, were taken up with recuperation—efforts to recover property and assets, to restore a semblance of order to religious and social institutions, to bring back Jewish children harbored by Christians and often brought up in the Christian faith. By the end of 1949, the remnants of Dutch Jewry had begun to take on the characteristics of a stable community. Economically, they were better off than the rest of Europe's Jewry, and self-supporting. Synagogues and schools were reopened, the work of restitution proceeded at a steady, if slow pace. The central Jewish welfare agency reported at the end of 1955, that it had some twenty-eight religious and thirty-seven private organizations affiliated with it. H.S.

NETHERLANDS ANTILLES (DUTCH WEST INDIES). Made up of Curacao and Aruba, two Caribbean islands off the coast of Venezuela. They have a combined population of 175,000.

Curacao is the home of one of the oldest permanent Jewish settlements in the New World. Jews from Holland and Brazil settled here during the 1650's and prospered in farming and trade. Their synagogue, built in 1732, is the oldest in the Western Hemisphere. The community flourished in the eighteenth century, some of its members rising to important positions in the administration of the island. Commercial decline in the nineteenth century led to a sharp drop in the Jewish population. The present community (1977), numbering 700, is composed chiefly of Sephardic* Jews, with a small East European minority. It maintains a Jewish Relief Committee and a Hebrew School.

Aruba, an island seventy-five miles west of Curacao, is the home of about 100 Jews who arrived from Europe in the late 1930's and early 1940's. An old Jewish cemetery on the island indicates that a lost Jewish community lived on it in earlier times. The members of the present community are engaged in trade or employed by the Standard Oil Company.

NETTER, KARL (1826-1882). A successful business man in London and Paris, one of the founders of the Alliance Israelite Universelle* in France, to help the persecuted Jews in Eastern Europe; he traveled widely on missions of rescue.

Netter's outstanding achievement was the founding of the agricultural school at Mikveh Israel* in Palestine,* where he died in 1882.

NETURE KARTA (Hebrew, meaning "Guardians of the City"). A group of Orthodox extremists who oppose the State of Israel* because they believe that Israel can be redeemed only through the direct intervention of God and the advent of the Messiah. In 1935 a few hundred members of Agudath Israel,* under the leadership of Amram Blau, objected strenuously to the cooperation of their organization with other Zionist groups. They broke away and formed the Neture Karta, and have not hesitated to resort to violence in support of their beliefs. The organization is very small but has supporters outside of Israel, particularly in the United States.

NEUMANN, EMANUEL (1893-1980). American Zionist leader. Brought to the U.S. from Lithuania as an infant, he was a founder of Young Judaea* and served as president of the Zionist Organization of America* from 1947-49 and from 1956-58. For more than half a century, he played an important role in the American Zionist movement as a speaker, author and organizer and was a member of the Jewish Agency* Executive from 1951.

NEW MOON (In Hebrew, "Rosh Hodesh"). A minor holiday since Biblical times. The New Moon, like the Sabbath,* is a regularly recurring celebration. Observed on the first of each month, it is marked by the reading of a special portion of the Bible* and of the Hallel.* There are also prayers asking for peace and prosperity during the coming month. In Biblical times, it was customary to celebrate the New Moon with a feast. Later, certain kinds of work were forbidden on that day.

The Jewish calendar is based on the revolution of the moon around the earth. In olden times, before the existence of a scientifically fixed calendar, the proclamation of the New Moon was a ceremony of great significance. In the days of the Temple* this proclamation, which is now recited in synagogues on the Sabbath preceding the New Moon, would be made in Jerusalem* on evidence submitted by watchmen, and would be relayed by messengers and bonfire signals to remote parts of the country.

NEW YEAR. See ROSH HA-SHANAH.

NEW YORK CITY. There was a furor in the port of Nieuw Amsterdam. The good ship **St. Charles** was furling sail for Holland, with twenty-three extra passengers. They were Dutch Jews, expelled from Brazil by the Portuguese Inquisition, who had spent their last **guilder** to cover the first lap of their voyage back to Amsterdam.* They had arranged for the rest of the ship's fare to be sent on to them in Nieuw Amsterdam. But the money had not arrived, and the ship's master was eager to sail. He could sell their personal possessions and leave them behind in town. That would just about cover expenses. The Jews thought that they might be able to leave the boat and settle in Nieuw Amsterdam, but Jews were not permitted to live in this fledgling Dutch settlement. Finally, a court decision ruled in favor of the captain: the property was to be sold at the block, and the Jews, though hardly welcome, would remain behind in Nieuw Amsterdam. Thus, in September 1654, began the history of a Jewish community that was to become the largest in the world.

The Jewish community of Nieuw Amsterdam grew slowly. Peter Stuyvesant, the peg-legged Dutch governor, was not hospitable. Led by Jacob Barsimson* and Asser Levy,* the determined settlers had to fight for every privilege. But by the time the English took the town in 1664 and renamed it New York, the Jews were citizens and engaged in trade. Though the English were more tolerant than the Dutch, it was not till 1728 that the Jewish community was permitted to build a synagogue. (It had been meeting in private homes.) Two years later, Congregation Shearith

"New Moon"—a water color by Chaim Gross.

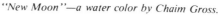

Dedication ceremony for the new building of Congregation Shearith Israel in New York City—September 1860.

Israel* was dedicated. In 1731 New York's first Jewish school was founded. In 1740, when the English Parliament made Jews eligible for citizenship in the American colonies, most of the congregants took advantage of the privilege.

During the Revolutionary War, the community, which had grown to 300, was split between Loyalists and Rebels. Establishment of the American Union wrought no great change in the life of New York Jewry. At the time of the War of 1812, it is estimated that there were 400 Jews in the city. In the decades that followed, however, the community grew by leaps and bounds, its ranks swelled by immigrants from Germany* and Central Europe. By 1840, the settlement numbered 13,000; forty years later, 60,000. Founding synagogues, periodicals, schools, and charitable organizations, the Jews of New York formed a community which, by the 1870's, could begin to claim leadership in American Jewry. After 1881, New York became the thriving center of Jewish life that it is today.

Fleeing persecution in Eastern Europe, over two million Jews came to America between 1881 and 1914; three-fourths of them lived at least for a time in New York's Lower East Side. Here they created a Yiddish-speaking world of their own, with hundreds of synagogues, schools and **heders*** (one-room schools), newspapers, theatres, clubs, political groups of every type, fraternal orders, mutual-aid societies, and the like. By 1900 there were six Yiddish dailies, and numerous weekly and monthy periodicals. As most readers knew only Yiddish, these newspapers were more than merely newspapers: they served as schools and libraries and personal guidance bureaus for hundreds of thousands of immigrants eager to find their place in a strange new world. The Yiddish theatre flourished as it never had flourished in the "old country."

However, the golden days of the East Side were numbered. America was the "land of opportunity," and the East Side soon became a squalid slum. As soon as the immigrant could afford to move to a better neighborhood, he did so. At first the majority of immigrants became peddlers or entered "sweatshops"—usually clothing factories where workers were "sweated" long hours for starvation wages. In time, many peddlers, scrimping and saving, opened small shops or factories; workers began to organize in unions to demand better conditions and a living wage. The first generation could not escape the ghetto; the second generally did. Parents struggled to educate their children, first in the high schools, then at college. The movement away from the East Side was a movement upward on the social ladder.

By the end of the 1920's, the picture of New York Jewry had changed radically. After 1924, immigration laws stopped the flow of newcomers, and the center of population passed from lower Manhattan to Brooklyn and the Bronx. By that time, too, a second generation had grown up whose mother tongue was English, not Yiddish, and who mixed more freely with the older Jewish and non-Jewish communities. A relatively large proportion of the younger generation entered the professions. Those who remained in their parents' occupations did so under new and improved conditions. Immigrants had revolutionized the garment industry, introducing new mass-production techniques. Within the industries, the great "Jewish" union organizations, such as the International Ladies Garment Workers founded in 1900 and the Amalgamated Clothing Workers established in 1913, bolstered by national and state labor laws, assured their members a decent return for their labor.

With gradual "Americanization" of immigrants, and their integration into American life, a new phase began in the history of American Jewry. The early immigrants had kept together, founding institutions to satisfy their immediate needs. But now it was necessary to educate a new generation, and to organize a community which could sustain the traditions of Jewish life. Effort to organize the sprawling mass of New York Jewry into a single comprehensive community organization **(kehilla*)** were made early in the century: between 1909 and 1922 such a **kehilla** did function under the chairmanship of Judah Magnes.* Although the kehilla plan collasped, areas of cooperation were found. A Bureau of

PURIM

A Purim Ball in New York City—1879.

Jewish Education, later absorbed by the Jewish Education Committee, continued to function after the kehilla's failure; so did the Federation of Jewish Philanthropies formed in Brooklyn in 1906, and a similar federation founded in Manhattan in 1917. In 1937, the two federations merged to form a single Greater New York Federation. Similarly, Zionist activities and the need to unite in defense against Nazi-fomented anti-Semitic groups in the 1930's required the participation of the entire community.

The Jewish community, as it emerged in the 1940's, tended to be organized around independent synagogues, community centers, **landsmanschaften** (organizations of people from the same town in Europe), and some independent Zionist organizations. In the 1950's ever-greater numbers of Jews moved to the surburban areas of New York. The synagogue became the basic unit of affiliation, with community and nationwide organizations working through synagogue groups. But individual Jews also continued to belong to other communal organizations: labor groups, fraternal orders, and the like.

At present (1984) the home of about 1,750,000 Jews in a total city population of almost 8,000,000, New York is undoubtedly the center of Jewish life in America. All national Jewish religious, national and cultural organizations maintain offices in the city. There are many Jewish day schools at the elementary level, and a large number of full-time high schools. A number of Hebrew high schools offer courses in Hebrew in the afternoons and Sundays, and many public high schools also teach Hebrew as a foreign language. A number of colleges in New York have departments of Jewish studies. Yiddish groups support a network of afternoon schools at the elementary and high school levels. The majority of children, however, receive their Jewish education in synagogue-affiliated afternoon and Sunday schools. New York's Jewish publications include two Yiddish dailies, a Hebrew weekly, and dozens of English language weeklies and monthlies put out by various organizations and denominations. (See also UNITED STATES, HISTORY OF JEWS IN.)

NEW ZEALAND. A British dominion comprising two large and many small islands in the Pacific Ocean, southeast of Australia.* New Zealand has about 4,000 Jews in a total population of 3,125,000.

A few adventurous Jews settled in New Zealand a few years before British rule was established in 1840. The first group arrived with the first transports of immigrants from England.* In 1843 they founded the dominion's first Jewish community at Wellington. A second community was established at Auckland in 1859, and a third at Dunedin, in 1862.

The New Zealand Jewish community remained one of the smallest in the world until the discovery of gold in the Otago district (1861) swelled the settlement more than ten-fold: while there were 65 Jews in the country in 1851, 1,247 arrived in 1867 alone. The later growth of the community was restricted by the dominion's severe immigration policies.

The early settlers braved the backland wilds to trade with the aborigines. Others went into dairy and sheep farming, or sought to exploit the gold fields. At present, however, over 90 per cent earn their living in commerce, 23 per cent in industry, 9 per cent in the professions, and 2 per cent in agriculture.

Auckland and Wellington have the largest communities, with Jewish populations of about 1,500 each. All four have synagogues, Zionist organizations, and literary and social clubs. Zionist interest is strong. The community is properous, and has made considerable contributions to Israel.

From the beginning Jews have played an important role in New Zealand's political and cultural life. Sir Julius Vogel served as prime minister from 1873 to 1876, and then as New Zealand's general agent in London. Sir Michael Myers served as Chief Justice of New Zealand. Jews have filled a number of cabinet and administrative posts in government, and have served in the Legislative Council.   B.H.

NILI. See AARONSOHN, AARON.

NINTH OF AB. See FAST DAYS.

NISAN. Seventh month of the Jewish civil calendar. Also considered as the first month of the religious year. (See PASSOVER.)

NOAH (Hebrew, meaning "rest"). According to the Biblical account (Gen. 6:9-9), Noah's generation, the tenth since Adam,* had become so corrupt that God decreed its destruction by a deluge. Because of his righteousness, Noah and his family, alone of all mankind, were preserved from the deluge. At God's command, Noah erected an ark aboard which he placed pairs of every living thing on earth. The flood poured down for forty days; after another one hundred and fifty days, every living creature had perished from the earth. Finally, the ark rested on Mount Ararat, and Noah came out, built an alter and offered thanksgiving sacrifices to God.

Mordecai Manuel Noah

NOAH, MORDECAI MANUEL (1785-1851). Born in Philadelphia, the son of a Revolutionary War patriot and soldier, Noah was widely read; before entering politics, he was a journalist, playwright, and visionary. He held numerous posts, including that of surveyor of the Port of New York, sheriff, and judge; he was United States Consul in Tunisia* when piracy and extortion were governmental policies in the Mediterranean world. In Tunisia, Noah studied the history and customs of the Tunisian Jewish community.

In 1820, Noah petitioned the legislature of the State of New York for a grant of land to establish a Jewish colony in the United States. Five years later, Grand Island on the Niagara River was surveyed and subdivided into farm lots. There Noah planned to establish Ararat as a city of refuge for homeless and persecuted Jews. When this project failed, Noah began to advocate the resettlement of Palestine by Jews. Despite the fanfare and theatrics associated with Noah's Ararat venture, he may be viewed as a forerunner of Zionism.*

NOBEL PRIZE WINNERS, JEWISH. The Nobel Prize has five categories, awarded annually since 1901 on an international basis from a fund established under the will of Alfred Bernhard Nobel, Swedish chemist and inventor (1833-96) "to those who, during the preceding year, shall have conferred the greatest benefit on mankind" in the fields of physics, chemistry, physiology and medicine, and literature and in the promotion of international peace. The following is a list of winners who were Jews or of Jewish descent, together with the residence or country of origin at the time they received the award.

Physics
Albert Abraham Michelson (1852-1931); American; 1907
Gabriel Lippmann (1845-1921); French; 1908
Niels Bohr (1885-1962); Danish; 1925
Gustav Hertz (1887-1950); German; 1925
James Franck (1882-1964); German; 1925
Enrico Fermi (1901-54); Italian; 1938
Otto Stern (1888-1969); American; 1944
Isidor Isaac Rabi (1898-   ); American; 1944
Felix Bloch (1905-   ); American; 1952
Max Born (1882-1970); German; 1954
Emilio Segre (1905-   ); American; 1959
Robert Hofstadter (1915-   ); American; 1961
Lev D. Landau (1908-1968); Russian; 1962
Eugene Paul Wigner (1905-   ) American; 1963
Richard Phillips Feynman (1918-   ); American; 1965
Julian Schwinger (1918-   ); American; 1965
Hans Albrecht Bethe (1906-   ); American; 1967
Murray Gell-Mann (-   ); American; 1969
Denis Gabor (1900-   ); English; 1971
Brian David Josephson (1940-   ); English; 1973
Ben R. Mottelson; Danish; 1975
Aron Penzias; American; 1978
Piotr Kapitza; Russian; 1978
Sheldon Lee Glashow (1932-   ); American; 1979
Steven Weinberg (1933-   ); American; 1979

Medicine and Physiology
Elie Metchnikoff (1845-1916); Russian; 1908
Paul Ehrlich (1854-1915); German; 1908
Robert B. Bárány (1876-1936); Austrian; 1914
Otto Meyerhof (1884-1951); German; 1922
Karl Landsteiner (1868-1943); American; 1930 ·
Otto Heinrich Warburg (1883-1938); German; 1931
Otto Loewi (1873-1961); Austrian; 1936

Joseph Erlanger; American; 1944
Ernst Boris Chain (1906-1979); English; 1945
Herman Joseph Muller; American; 1946
Tadeusz Reichstein; Swiss; 1950
Selman Abraham Waksman (1888-1973); American; 1952
Fritz Albert Lipmann; American; 1953
Sir Hans Adolf Krebs (1900-1981); English; 1953
Joshua Lederberg (1925-   ); American; 1958
Arthur Kornberg (1918); American; 1959
Max F. Perutz (1914-   ); English; 1962
Konrad Bloch (1912-   ); English; 1962
Francois Jacob (1920-   ); French; 1965
Andre Lwoff (1902-   ); French; 1965
George Wald (1906-   ); American; 1967
Marshall W. Nirenberg (1927-   ); American; 1968
Salvatore E. Luria (1912-   ); American; 1969
Julius Axelrod (1912-   ); American; 1970
Sir Bernhard Katz (1911-   ); English; 1970
Gerald Maurice Edelman (1929-   ); American; 1972
David Baltimore; American; 1975
Hard Martin Temin; American; 1975
Baruch Blumberg; American; 1976
Rosalyn Yalow; American; 1977
Daniel Nathans; American; 1978
Baruj Benacerraf (1920-   ); American; 1980

Chemistry

Adolf J.F.W. von Baeyer (1835-1917); German; 1905
Otto Wallach (1847-1931); German; 1910
Richard Willstaetter (1872-1942); German; 1915
Fritz Haber (1868-1934); German; 1918
George von Hevesy (1885-1966); Hungarian; 1943
Melvin Calvin (1911-   ); American; 1961
William Stein (1911-   ); American; 1972
Paul Berg (1926-   ); American; 1980
Walter Gilbert (1932-   ); American; 1980
Roald Hoffmann (1937-   ); American; 1981
Aaron Klug; English; 1982

Literature

Paul J.L. von Heyse (1830-1914); German; 1910
Henri Louis Bergson (1859-1941); French; 1927

Boris Pasternak (1890-1960); Russian; 1958
Samuel Joseph Agnon (1888-1970); Israeli; 1966
Nelly Sachs (1891-1970); Swedish; 1966
Saul Bellow; American; 1976
Isaac Bashevis Singer; American; 1978
Elias Canetti; English; 1981

Peace

Tobias Michael Carel Asser (1838-1913); Dutch; 1911
Alfred Hermann Fried (1864-1921); Austrian; 1911
Rene Cassin; French; 1968
Henry Alfred Kissinger (1923-   ); American; 1973
Menahem Begin; Israeli; 1978

Economics

Paul Samuelson (1915-   ); American; 1970
Simon Kuznets (1901-   ); American; 1971
Kenneth Arrow (1921-   ); American; 1972
Leonid Kantorovich; Russia; 1975
Milton Friedman; American; 1976
Herbert A. Simon; American; 1978
Lawrence Robert Klein (1920-   ); American; 1980

NORDAU, MAX (Simchah Meir Suedfeld) (1849-1923). Writer, physician, Zionist leader, and social philosopher. Born in Budapest, Hungary,* the son of a rabbi, Nordau received a sound Jewish education in his youth. He studied medicine, traveled, then came to Paris and set up practice as a neurologist in 1880. At the same time, he wrote a whole series of books of social criticism. Of these, his **Conventional Lies of our Civilization** and **Paradoxes** were the most famous and controversial.

When Theodor Herzl* came to him with the manuscript of **Judenstaat (The Jewish State),** Nordau accepted the idea immediately and became Herzl's first and most loyal colleague and closest advisor. His brilliant oratory and sharp pen were of enormous help to the young Zionist movement. Yet he steadily refused to hold any Zionist office, including that of president, offered him after Herzl's death. The last years of his life were saddened by differences of opinion with the Zionist leadership. At the Zionist Conference in London (1920), he pleaded for immediate mass immigration of half a million Jews to Palestine. He died in Paris in January, 1923. Five years later, his body was brought to Palestine and buried in Tel Aviv.

NORWAY. The earliest Jews in Norway were Sephardim. When the country came under Swedish rule in 1814, the Jews were expelled, but were permitted to return in 1851. Full emancipation was granted in 1891.

At the time of the Nazi invasion, there were some 3,500 Jews in Norway. Today (1984) there are about 950. Communal organization exists in Oslo and Trondheim, the latter being the northernmost Jewish community in the world.

NUMBERS. The fourth book of the Pentateuch in the Bible.* Its Hebrew name is **Bamidbar**—"In the Wilderness." The term Numbers, or Numeri, was chosen because of the two censuses of the Israelites reported in the book. The first numbering, or census, was taken at Sinai in the second year of the Exodus,* the second was taken on the banks of the Jordan in the fortieth year of the Exodus. The Book of Numbers contains laws given to Israel, and tells the story of the thirty-eight years the children of Israel spent wandering from Sinai to the Jordan near Jericho.*

NUMERUS CLAUSUS. ("Jewish Quota") A restriction on the number of Jews to be admitted to schools, universities, the professions, etc. Two forms of **numerus clausus** are known. The first type is based on special legislation, and thus is openly admitted. The second, or secret, type uses various devious ways to achieve the same practical results. The representative country for open discrimination was Tsarist Russia,* where, after 1887, Jews could make up from only 3 to 6 per cent of the students at higher institutions of learning. After the 1905 Revolution, the quota was abandoned in Russia, but was restored in 1908. A **numerus clausus** based on special legislation existed in Hungary after 1920.

The secret type of **numerus clausus** was used in Germany* prior to the revolution of 1918, to limit the number of Jewish university teachers; **numerus nullus** (the total exclusion of Jews) was practised in the officer corps. Poland* and Rumania* followed a practice very similar to that of the Germans. The **numerus clausus** practice of the Polish and Rumanian authorities was largely due to the anti-Semitic attitude of the non-Jewish students.   M.M.F.

NUN. Fourteenth letter of the Hebrew alphabet; numerically, fifty.

NUREMBERG LAWS. Decreed in Nuremberg on September 15, 1935, at a rally of the Nationalist Socialist (Nazi) Party. These laws were the culmination of the anti-Jewish decrees enacted since the establishment of the Nazi government in Germany. By virtue of these highly discriminatory laws, Jews became second-class citizens as compared with "Aryans," and were denied the rights of citizenship. Under these laws, persons who had Jewish grandparents, as well as persons who were married to Jews could not be classed as "Aryans." Jews were forbidden to marry Germans or persons of "Aryan" blood. Marriages of this kind were treated as null and void, and persons entering such marriages were severely punished. The Nuremberg laws practically created a Jewish ghetto* in Germany. They were abolished by the Allies after the defeat of Germany in 1945.

OBADIAH. Fourth of the minor prophets in the Bible. The Book of Obadiah, the shortest in the Bible, predicts the destruction of Edom and describes the reunion of the children of Jacob* with their historic homeland.

ODESSA. Port in Southern Russia* on the Black Sea, formerly a great Jewish center in the Ukraine.

Jews came to Odessa at the end of the eighteenth century from Poland* and Lithuania.* They participated in the rapid development of the city, and engaged in commerce and various trades as well as in the professions.

The Enlightenment movement of the nineteenth century played an important role in the Odessa Jewish community. The first Russian-Jewish weekly was published here. The weekly Hebrew newspaper **Ha-Melitz,** and a Yiddish weekly **Folksblat,** made their appearance in Odessa. By the end of the nineteenth century, the town became a center of Zionism* and of Hebrew as well as Yiddish literature.* Some of the foremost Hebrew writers, among them Mendele Mocher Sefarim,* Ahad Ha-Am,* Chaim Nachman Bialik,* and Joseph Klausner* lived and wrote in Odessa. Here also was the seat of the central committee of Hoveve Zion,* whose leaders were Leon Pinsker* and, later, Menahem Ussishkin.*

In the beginning of the twentieth century a modern **yeshiva** was founded in Odessa. Professor Chaim Tchernowitz was its head, and it produced a number of scholars and Hebrew writers.

During times of stress, waves of anti-Semitic attacks swept over the city. In the 1905 pogrom, 30 Jews were killed and many more injured. Odessa's Jewish youth joined in the self-defense movement, then an innovation in Jewish life. Odessa Jewry also suffered greatly during the civil war in 1918-1919. On the eve of the Second World War, Odessa's Jewish population was close to 160,000. Most of these were killed by the Nazis and their collaborators during 1941-1943. The number of Jews now in Odessa is not known.   H.L.

OLD TESTAMENT. The Hebrew Bible* came to be called the Old Testament to distinguish it from the New Testament of Christianity. (For the books that make up the Old Testament **see** BIBLE.)

OMER (Hebrew for "a measure," as well as a sheaf of grain). The Bible* commanded that an offering from the new barley crop be brought to the Temple.* "Ye shall bring the sheaf of the first fruits of your harvest unto the priest. And he shall wave the sheaf before the Lord, to be accepted for you; on the morrow after the Sabbath, the priest

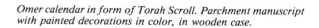
Omer calendar in form of Torah Scroll. Parchment manuscript with painted decorations in color, in wooden case.

shall wave it.'' The Rabbis interpreted ''the morrow after the Sabbath'' to mean the sixteenth day of Nisan, the second day of Passover.* New crops could not be used before an Omer had been offered from them.

Counting of the Omer (Sefirat ha-omer). In Temple times, great festivity surrounded the offering of the Omer by the farmers of Israel. Although the offering of the Omer was discontinued after the destruction of the Temple, the custom of **sefirah,** the ''counting'' of forty-nine days between the second day of Passover and Shavuot* (Festival of Weeks) has been preserved. Because of misfortunes which have overtaken the Jewish people during this time of year, it has come to be regarded as a period of mourning. For this reason, weddings and other festivities are not celebrated then. Especially associated with the **sefirah** is a plague which broke out among the disciples of Rabbi Akiba* during Bar Kokhba's uprising which took place in the month of Nisan, 135 C.E. Jewish legend tells that the plague let up on Lag b'Omer (''the thirty-third day of Omer.'') Therefore marriages may be solemnized on that day, which is celebrated outdoors and, in Israel, with pilgramages to Meron, a town in Galilee.* **(See also** MERON.)

In recent years, two special dates have been set aside during the counting of the Omer. The twenty-seventh of Nisan has been declared a memorial day for the victims of the Nazis during the Second World War. Marking the heroic ghetto uprisings which took place in 1943, the twenty-seventh of Nisan is observed with special memorial services in the synagogues. In Israel, it is the occasion for pilgramages to the memorial monuments for European Jewry. The fifth of Iyar, marking the declaration of the State of Israel* in 1948, is another special occasion. In order to permit the festivities with which Israel's Independence Day is celebrated, the chief rabbinate of Israel has exempted this day from the **sefirah** restrictions. B.H.

ONKELOS (Aquila). Author of the Aramaic* translation of the Bible.* Targum Onkelos, or the Onkelos translation, occupies a prominent place in Jewish tradition. It is printed alongside the Hebrew text of the Bible, and is consulted by Jewish commentators in explaining obscure passages.

OPATOSHU, JOSEPH (1886-1954). Yiddish novelist. Born in Poland, he was instructed by his father in ancient and modern Hebrew literature. He received his secular education at a business school in Warsaw.*

Opatoshu came to America in 1907. His first novel, which he published in 1910, aroused great interest. Some of his best-known novels are **In Polish Forests** (translated into English), **Rabbi Akiba,** and **Bar Kokhba. Rabbi Akiba** was published in an English edition, in 1954, as **The Last Revolt.**

OPHIR. Land of Solomon's* gold, located somewhere between India* and northcentral Africa. The Biblical account tells of King Solomon's ships leaving for Ophir from Ezion Geber on the Red Sea every three years, together with the ships of Phoenician King Hiram. The ships came home laden with gold and silver, peacocks, ivory, and apes. (I Kings: 9:28; 10:11; and 11:22)

OPPENHEIM, DAVID. See PRAGUE.

OPPENHEIM, MORITZ DANIEL (1800-1882). The first Jew to achieve more than a fleeting success in modern art, he became known in his native Germany* through a series of oils, ''Pictures of Oldtime Jewish Family Life.'' These paintings record with great skill and in excellent taste the activities of a typical middle-class Jewish family in the early part of the nineteenth century, with emphasis on the celebration of the holidays, bar mitzvahs, and weddings. To make photographic reproduction easy, the artist duplicated these paintings in tones of grey. As an album, this series went through many editions, some of which were also issued in the United States. Oppenheim was also noted as a portraitist. His subjects included members of the Rothschild* family, and the writers Heinrich Heine* and Ludwig Boerne.

OPPENHEIMER, J. ROBERT (1904-67). One of America's leading nuclear physicists, Oppenheimer played a major role in the development of the atomic bomb. Head of the Los Alamos Scientific Laboratory from 1943 to 1945, he was Chairman of the General Advisory Committee of Atomic Scientists from 1946 to 1952, and was a Professor of Physics at Princeton University's Institute of Advanced Studies.

ORAL LAW. See TALMUD.

ORDINATION. Ceremonial transfer of authority. In Hebrew, **semikah** or the "laying on" of hands. The Bible tells how Moses* ordained Joshua* by laying hands upon him, and thus transferring the leadership to him. (Num. 27:22-23) In the time of the Second Temple,* the members of the Sanhedrin* (the judicial and legislative body) were also ordained. The Talmud* requires two rabbis to be present when the master lays his hands upon the head of his pupil as a sign that he is now qualified to teach. **Semikhah*** traditionally refers to rabbinic ordination.

ORT. The Organization for Rehabilitation through Training is the vocational training organization of the Jewish people. It is a worldwide network whose central purpose is to help Jewish people and strengthen Jewish communities by giving them vocational and technical education. It was founded in Russia* in 1880 and has since become a global movement in Jewish life. It now operates in over 20 countries, with a student body of nearly 100,000 attending classes and workshops in over 800 training units. Its institutions include vocational high schools, advanced technical courses and schools on the junior college level, apprenticeships and pre-apprenticeship courses, factory schools and pre-vocational programs for adults. The ORT schools teach over 90 trades, covering the gamut of skills needed in modern industry: among them are agromechanics, automation, beauty culture, computer programming, dressmaking, electronics, industrial drawing, mechanics, printing, and secretarial work. The great majority of the ORT students are teenagers, both boys and girls, and ORT provides them with a complete academic secondary education as well as vocational training. ORT schools also offer courses in Jewish history; full provision for celebration of Jewish holidays; cultural and sport activities; health services; lunches and snacks; and, in many instances, dormitories and summer vacations.

A very large number of the ORT students are poor and many are immigrants and refugees; the total ORT environment—the Jewish atmosphere of the schools, the concerned teachers, and the extracurricular aids, as well as the actual schooling—give these youngsters and adults the emotional, intellectual and physical strength they need to begin building a new life. ORT's largest program is in Israel; ORT-Israel now has 78,000 students and plays an important part in building Israel's economic strength and social well-being. Other large ORT programs are in France,* where the Jewish population has grown enormously in recent decades because of immigration from North Africa; in South America, where ORT-trained technical skills offer great security in an often insecure atmosphere; and in India,* North Africa, and Iran,* where poverty often reaches abysmal depths. At ORT's center is the World ORT Union, which was founded in 1921.

ORT is represented in the United States by the American ORT Federation, (AOF) which was founded in 1922. Of the many affiliates of the AOF, the largest is **Women's American ORT,** which has 145,000 members and is the largest ORT organization in the world. Women's American ORT's major aim and purpose is to help maintain and expand the world ORT vocational education network through its membership dues and activities, but it also conducts many activities on the American scene. It performs many social services for poor and elderly American Jews. It is highly interested in promoting and improving American vocational education, and toward this end it conducts public forums and other educational events designed to acquaint the American community with the importance of good vocational schools; it also provides volunteer womanpower to work in local vocational schools as teachers' aids, office workers, etc. Women's American ORT also sponsors youth groups (ORT Youth Fellowship) for high school-age boys and girls. One of Women's American ORT's major goals is to strengthen Jewish identity among all American Jews; it works toward this goal through its sponsorship of the youth groups, through study groups conducted among its members, and through the films and literature it makes available to the American Jewish community.

Women's American ORT members speak out at a national convention.

PALE OF SETTLEMENT. Certain districts of Tsarist Russia* in which Jews were given the right to live. They were not permitted to live elsewhere because the Russian government claimed it wanted to "protect" the Russian people from Jewish influence. The definite restrictions confining Jews to the Pale of Settlement in White Russia were made in 1791. Thereafter, the Polish and Lithuanian provinces that Russia acquired in the three partitions of Poland (1772-1795) were also included in the Pale Settlement. Until 1910, this policy of restricting Jewish rights of residence continued; sometimes the Pale was enlarged, at other times a given city or village was withdraen from the Pale. Restrictions, changing from time to time, were placed on Jews living inside the Pale as well. They were forbidden to lease lands or keep taverns in villages; double taxes were levied upon them, and they were barred from higher education. It was only after the overthrow of the Tsarist goverment by the 1917 revolution that the Pale of Settlement was finally abolished.

PALESTINE. The area of which part is now occupied by the State of Israel was called Palestina by the Greeks and Romans after the Philistines* who lived in the southern coastal region. During the period of Turkish rule, the area was known by the Arabic form Falastin or Filestin. The League of Nations mandate used the term Palestine to refer to an area to the west and to the east of the Jordan River which was bounded by Lebanon* in the north, Egypt* on the southwest and by Syria,* Iraq* and Saudi Arabia on the east. Subsequently the term was applied only to the part of Palestine that lay west of the Jordan. With the establishment of the State of Israel* in 1948 Palestine ceased to exist as a geographic unit.

PALLIÈRE, AIMÉ (1875-1949). French pro-Zionist. Born in Lyon as a Catholic and intended for the priesthood, he was drawn to Judaism at the age of 20. He had been influenced by his studies with Rabbi Elijah Benamozegh of Livorno. Because he believed that there was no basic contradiction between the tenets of Judaism and Catholicism, he lived the life of a practicing Jew without ever renouncing Christ or formally converting to Judaism. In his work as a writer and lecturer, he sought to bring the two faiths together. He became an ardent Zionist and was active on behalf of the Jewish National Fund in France.* Pallière's best-known work is an autobiography, **The Unknown Sanctuary.**

PALMACH. (Abbreviation of Hebrew **Plugot Mahatz,** meaning "shock troops.") In the underground defense force of the **Haganah,*** before the establishment of the State of Israel,* the Palmarch was the strongest group. Its members, recruited mainly from the agricultural settlements, high schools and the Hebrew University,* were thoroughly trained for commando warfare. Organized in 1939, they carried out missions of incredible daring. They rescued thousands of Jews from Nazi Europe, running the British blockades of Palestine* in the "death ships" of the "illegal immigration" period. During the chaotic period when the British were prepared to abandon Palestine, the Palmach guarded the settlements and highways; in the War of Independence its members bore the brunt of the Arab attack. A large proportion of them lost their lives in action; in 1949 Palmach was absorbed by the Army of Israel.*

PANAMA. A republic occupying the Isthmus of Panama, a narrow neck of land which connects Central and South America. Panama was a province of Colombia until it declared its independence in 1903. The Panama Canal Zone, which stretches for five miles on either side of the Canal, is under the jurisdiction of the United States. The first Jews to reach Panama were merchants. Because of the unhealthy climate and living conditions most of them fled the Isthmus. The small permanent community which remained was enlarged only when the United States began building the Panama Canal in 1904. Today (1984) there are about 2,500 Jews in the country, out of a total population of 1,940,000. They are engaged in the dry goods and entertainment industries, as well as in petty trade. The majority lives in Panama City, but there is a small community in Colon, the Pacific terminus of the Canal. Both communities maintain synagogues and are affiliated with the World Jewish Congress.* The National Jewish Welfare Board* maintains a center for Jewish personnel in the Canal Zone, where only military units and Canal employees may live.

PARAGUAY. Republic in South America. Immigrants from Turkey,* Russia,* Germany,* and France established a small Jewish community in Paraguay at the turn of the century. Refugees from Nazi Europe swelled its ranks to 2,200 by 1940. Lack of economic opportunities led most of the refugees to emigrate after World War II. The Jewish community of Paraguaynow (1984) numbers about 700 out of a total population of 3,268,000. It maintains three synagogues, none of which has a rabbi, as well as Zionist and youth groups.

PARIS. Capital and largest city of France.* Jews have lived in Paris since at least the sixth century. In the twelfth and thirteenth centuries, the city was a center of Jewish learning, and the home of a famous Talmudic academy. By the fourteenth century repeated persecutions had weakened the community; it was finally banished with the rest of French Jewry in 1394. Jews continued to live in Paris illegally, however. In 1791, they finally gained civil and residence rights. By 1800, there were 3,000 Jews in the Paris community, many of them active in the professional and commercial life of the capital. When Napoleon organized the Jews of France in centralized "consistories," Paris became the hub of French Jewry. As the community grew, synagogues, schools, and charitable organizations were established. At mid-century, the extensive banking and commercial activities of financiers like the Rothschilds* and the Pereiras, as well as the political eminence of men like Adolphe Crémieux* had brought the community to the forefront of Parisian life. Establishment of the Alliance Israélite Universelle* in 1860, strengthened the cultural life of the settlement. The Alliance also served as an instrument for cooperation with foreign Jewries, and for rendering assistance to distressed brethren abroad.

Immigrants from Eastern Europe began to settle in Paris in fairly large numbers during the 1880's; from that time, and especially after 1910, Paris became a haven for refugees from all parts of the world. In 1860 there were 30,000 Jews in the city; in 1940, 110,000. Most of the refugees spoke Yiddish. Mixing but little with the older community, which was very "French" in culture, they created a "little world" of their own—the colorful Jewish Quarter. They founded folk universities, libraries, schools, theatres and an active Yiddish press, which in 1939 published fourteen periodicals, including two daily newspapers. Active in these undertakings were distinguished writers, scholars, and artists who continued the work they had begun in Eastern Europe. Paris was the artistic center of the world, and many of the immigrants rose to world fame in the arts. Young artists from Eastern Europe, the Balkans, Italy,* and Central Europe arrived after 1900 to study at the various academies. For years, they suffered privations, but some of them rose to world fame. French critics often referred to them as the **École Juive** ("Jewish School") of art. Outstanding among them are Marc Chagall,* Chaim Soutine, Moise Kisling, Amedeo Modigliani, Mané-Katz, and Jules Pascin.

When the Germans occupied Paris in 1940, many Jews fled to the south of France; the majority of others were deported to Poland.* Many who fled became active in the French underground.

After the war, many survivors returned. Their numbers were augmented by streams of Jews fleeing from all parts of the continent. In the past few years, a large influx of refugees from North Africa has brought the Jewish population of Paris (1977) up to 300,000. Only half this number are native French born Jews. For several years after the Second World War, international relief organizations concerned with helping Europe's ravaged and displaced Jews had their central headquarters in Paris.

Since the war, communal leaders, with the aid of foreign organizations, have striven to reorganize community life, but progress has been slow and difficult. The older community returned to its prewar patterns, but the life of newcomers, especially, has been disrupted. Many of their cultural leaders have emigrated, especially to South America, and the immigrants themselves have been involved in the problems of earning a livelihood. Most of them are engaged in trade, handicrafts and small-scale manufacturing. Many of the older community have returned to the professions and public service. The most recent development has been the migration to Paris of large numbers of North African Jews. Their adaption to French and Western Jewish life presents a challenge for the future because their integration into Western culture must not be at the expense of the traditional Jewish values they have brought with them.

PARNAS (from the Greek). The president and lay leader of a congregation. In Talmudic times a man of merit and scholarship was appointed parnas to administer congregational affairs. In later times, the office was given to men of wealth and influence. Beginning in the Middle Ages, some communities elected the parnas annually, or even monthly.

PASSOVER. The Passover (Pesach) holiday is the anniversary of Israel's liberation from Egyptian bondage. The holiday begins on the fourteenth day of Nisan and lasts for eight days. It reminds each Jew that if God had not freed his forefathers, then "he and his sons and the sons of his sons would still be slaves to Pharaoh in Egypt." Passover is also Hag Ha-Aviv, the Festival of Spring, the first of the three holidays when the agricultural population of Israel went up in pilgrimage to the Temple* in Jerusalem.* They brought an offering of barley in thanksgiving for the spring harvest. **(See OMER.)**

The **matzot** (unleavened bread) which give Passover the name **Hag Hamatzot** ("the Feast of Unleavened Bread") are eaten in memory of the unleavened bread prepared by the Israelites during

The First Plague; Dutch 17th century engraving. "...and all the waters that were in the river were turned to blood." (Exodus 7:20).

their hasty flight from Egypt, when they had no time to wait for their dough to rise. Since no leavened bread or food containing leaven may be eaten during Passover, special dishes and household utensils are used during the eight-day observance. Laws are prescribed for the cleaning or scalding in boiling water of utensils which are used throughout the year and must also be used on the holiday.

On the eve of the fourteenth day of Nisan, the ceremony of **B'dikat Hametz**—the search for leaven and its removal from the house—is performed. Inspection for **hametz** is done by candlelight, wherever food is usually kept or eaten. On the morning of the fourteenth day of Nisan, the **hametz** is burned, with the recitations of a special benediction. This observance is called **Bi'ur Hametz**—the removal or burning of **hametz**. The day preceding Passover, the fast of the first-born takes place to commemorate the "passing over" of the Israelite homes by the Angel of Death on his way to slay the firstborn of the Egyptians. In ancient times, the paschal lamb was slaughtered to recall the fact that God spared the Israelites.

While the holiday is celebrated for eight days in the Diaspora,* in Israel it is observed for seven days. The first two and last two days of the holiday are more festive than the four intermediate days called **Hol Ha-Moed** ("half-holidays"). On the first two nights of Passover, the Seder (literally, "order") is celebrated, serving as the central event of the holiday. On this occasion, the Haggadah* ("narration") is chanted, wherein are related the events of the Exodus* from Egypt and Israel's gratitude to God for its redemption is expressed.

The Seder service is one of the most colorful and joyous occasions in Jewish life. It is adorned with ancient ceremonies and symbols which recall the days when the Children of Israel were liberated from Egypt. It also evokes hopes that despite present trials and tribulations, a brighter future is in store for the Jewish people. The entire family gathers around the Seder table, on which are placed the traditional ceremonial objects. The Seder service begins with the Kiddush.* The youngest son of the household asks the "Four Questions" and all participants read the Haggadah in reply. During the Seder, traditional melodies are chanted and age-old ceremonies are

Ma Nishtana *(The Four Questions). A page from the Rose family Haggadah. Illuminated by Sol Nodel, as commissioned for Mr. and Mrs. Daniel Rose, New York.*

performed. The Seder plate, or **kaarah,** bears symbolic foods. Each one commemorates events which are connected with Passover. The roast egg stands for the festival offering at the time of the Temple; the roast shoulder bone, **z'roa,** for the paschal lamb; bitter herbs **(maror)** for the bitter lot of the Jews under Egyptian bondage; **haroset** (a mixture of ground nuts, apples, cinnamon, and red wine) represents the clay with which Jews worked to make bricks; the parsley, or **karpas** dipped in salt water, adds to the festivity for it was considered a delicacy in ancient times.

The three **matzot** which are placed on the table represent the three classes of Jews: Kohen (priest), Levi,* and Israelite. The middle **matzah** is broken in two. One half, called the **afikoman** (from the Greek, meaning "dessert"), is hidden until after the meal. It is customary for the children to "steal" the **afikoman** and ask a prize for its return. The "stealing" is an act of entertainment provided to enliven the Seder service. After the eating of the afikoman, no more food is eaten. During the seder each person drinks four cups of wine, representing the four expressions of redemption used in the Bible. A fifth cup of wine, representing **Vehayveiti**—"and I will bring you into the land..."—is the cup of Elijah,* reserved for the prophet. According to tradition, Elijah visits every Jewish house on the Seder night to herald the coming of the Messiah. The chanting of **Shir Hashirim** (Song of Songs*) adds a spring-like atmosphere at the end of the Seder service. Symbolically interpreted, it is a song of love between God and the people of Israel.   H.L.

PATRIA. The **Patria** was a French vessel that was taken over by the British Mandatory administration of Palestine* in 1940 and converted into a prison ship for the deportation (presumably to Mauritius) of 1,800 refugees. The refugees had miraculously escaped from Nazi Europe in two "death ships" which had finally stranded on the beach off Tel Aviv. Their desparate passengers were forcibly transferred to the **Patria;** but the ship mysteriously exploded in Haifa harbor, and over 250 men, women, and children were drowned. In the face of this tragedy, the remainder of the refugees were permitted to remain in Palestine.

PATRIARCHS. The Bible ancestors of the people of Israel, Abraham,* Isaac,* and Jacob,* are known as the Patriachs.

PE. Seventeenth letter of the Hebrew alphabet; numerically, eighty. With a dot it is sounded as **p;** without, it corresponds to **f.**

PEKIIN. A vil age occupied by Druzes* and Jews, situated northwest of Safed, in Israel, in a secluded, well-watered plain near the hills of Upper Galilee.* Unnoticed in their valley, Jewish farmers remained in Pekiin for centuries, successfully resisting the successive armies of invaders—Romans, Crusaders, and Bedouins. Rabbi Simeon ben Yohai* and his son Eliezer are said to have taken refuge from the Romans in a cave in Pekiin. Recently, the Jewish community has developed into a well-equipped **moshav ovdim** ("smallholders' settlement").

PENTATEUCH (Greek, meaning "five-fold"). The Five Books of Moses. **(See also** BIBLE.)

PERES, SHIMON (1923-   ). Israel political leader and cabinet Member. Brought to Palestine from his native Poland* in 1934, he was a founder of Kibbutz Alumot and from 1941 to 1945 was general secretary of the Labor Zionist Youth organization. During the War of Independence, he headed Israel's fledgling navy. In 1950 he joined the staff of the Ministry of Defense and in 1956 helped plan the Sinai Campaign. Eventually he rose to the rank of Deputy Minister of Defense, a post he held from 1959 to 1965. During those years the Defense Ministry took over Israel's armaments industry, expanded the aircraft industry, and made headway in nuclear development and research. From 1974 to 1977 he was Minister of Defense and briefly served as acting Prime Minister between the resignation of Premier Yitz-

Isaac Leib Peretz by I. Friedlander.
Courtesy YIVO, New York City.

hak Rabin* and the election which brought Menahem Begin* to the premiership. In 1979 and 1984 Peres was elected as head of the Labor Alignment in the Knesset.*

PERETZ, ISAAC LEIB (1852-1915). Yiddish and Hebrew writer. Peretz is considered one of the founding fathers of both modern Hebrew and Yiddish literature.* He was also one of the first major Jewish writers to find beauty, moral strength, and a new, as well as a happier approach to life in Hasidism.*

Born and raised in a traditional home in a small Polish town, Peretz came early in his life under the influence of the Haskalah,* or Enlightenment movement and turned to secular studies. For some time he practiced law. In his sympathy with the plight of the poor suffering masses, he was attracted to socialist ideals. His sensitivity to injustice and the social evils of the world eventually found expression in his creative writing.

His short stories brought Peretz lasting fame. They came to be considered among the classics of Yiddish literature. His tales of Hasidism and of the common people are gems of poetry and humor. In them, he glorified the heroism of humble folk, the unbounded faith of rich and poor, exalting the life of the righteous. Among the first to point a finger at social injustice. Peretz wrote in **Bontche the Silent** a folk tale of great delicacy and compassion.

For sheer beauty, delicate humor, and forcefulness, the stories of Peretz, such as **The Wondermaker,** the **Zaddik of Nemirov, The Treasure,** and **The Three Gifts** have few equals. Many of his stories have been translated into English. Maurice Samuel's **Prince of the Ghetto** is a fascinating study of Peretz and his work.

PERU. Republic on the Pacific coast of South America. Four hundred years ago, Lima, the capital of Peru, was the seat of government for most of the Spanish colonial empire in South America. It was also the home of a wealthy and flourishing Marrano* community. These Jews, who had converted to Catholicism to escape expulsion from Spain* in 1492, had fled to the New World in the hope of finding greater freedom in the practice of their original faith. Their great wealth, amassed in international trade, soon aroused the envy of the Spanish rulers. In 1569 an Inquisitorial Office was founded to detect the heretics and make it possible to confiscate their property. In the course of two centuries, by dint of thirty-four public burnings of "heretics," the Inquisition* succeeded in eradicating the entire Marrano community. In the nineteenth century (1870) Alsatian Jews settled in Lima, but they quickly assimilated. Not until the 1920's did immigrants from Argentina,* Brazil,* Turkey* and Europe succeed in establishing a permanent Jewish community. They achieved considerable success in the manufacture and sale of furniture, furs, and knitted goods, as well as in installment selling. During the 1930's, anti-Semitic propaganda spread by the German Embassy led the government to impose severe restrictions on immigration—restrictions that are still in effect. Today (1984) there are some 5,000 Jews in Peru out of a total population of 18,300,000. Over 90 percent live in Lima, the rest in small cities where there have been many mixed marriages and much assimilation.*

PESACH. See PASSOVER.

PETACH TIKVAH (Hebrew, meaning "Threshold of Hope"). Known as the "Mother of the Colonies," it was the first Jewish colony, established in Palestine in 1878 by a handful of Orthodox Jews who left their shops in the Old City of Jerusalem* to become tillers of the soil, as a first step towards the Redemption. Lacking experience, they bought 900 acres of swampland near the Yarkon River. Malaria took a heavy toll, and drove them back to Jerusalem. But reinforced by new immigrants, they returned to Petach Tikvah, built their houses at some distance from the river, planted eucalyptus trees to drain the swamps, and beat back the attacks of Arabs. Baron Edmond de Rothschild* and the Hoveve Zion* movement gave them a helping hand. The success of Petach Tikvah encouraged other settlements and attracted many workers and settlers. Petach Tikva was the first colony to introduce citriculture, or orange growing, which became the economic mainstay of Israel. It became a municipality in 1937. Today (1984) it has a population of approximately 124,000, an industrial zone with numerous factories, and a large farming community.

PHARISEES (Hebrew, meaning "separation"). One of the three parties in Palestine* during the second and first centuries B.C.E. Most of Rabbinic law, as it exists today, originates with the Pharisees, who prized the study of Jewish law as it had developed through the generations. In this they were opposed by the Sadducees,* who were literalists in that they allowed no interpretation of the law beyond the letter of the Biblical text.

It is believed that the majority of the Jewish people supported the Pharisees. It was they who instituted centers of learning and synagogues for worship. The Pharisees emphasized the importance of prayer independent of the Temple services. By teachings that strengthened the religion and morality of the individual Jew, the Pharisees prepared the Jews to withstand the trials following the destruction of the Temple and the subsequent dispersion.

The Pharisees came into conflict with two of the rulers of the Hasmonean dynasty: Johanan Hyrcanus* and Alexander Jannaeus.* They were dissatisfied with Hyrcanus's preoccupation with wars of conquest, and with the religious practices of Alexander Jannaeus. Their opposition led these kings, especially Jannaeus, to persecute the Pharisees, many of whom fled the country to escape his heavy hand.

In the New Testament the Pharisees are mentioned unfavorably. There are also some disparaging remarks about them in the Talmud.* Apparently, a few Pharisees pursued their own selfish ends under the guise of piety. There is no doubt, however, that the majority of them were true to the high ideals of their great spiritual leaders. H.L.

PHILISTINES. A seafaring people from one of the islands on the shores of the northern Mediterranean. They emigrated to the coast of Canaan* in the twelfth century B.C.E. The Philistines dominated the fertile southern coastal plain, which included five cities—Gat and Ekron in the interior, and the three ports of Ashod, Ashkelon,* and Gaza. They were the implacable enemies of Israel and continued to harass their neighbors until David* reduced them to a minor, mainly commercial role.

PHILO (30 B.C.E.-40 C.E.). Hellenistic philosopher and Biblical interpreter. Philo was a descendant of a distinguished Jewish family in Alexandria,* Egypt,* where he lived. His brother was head of the Jewish community in Egypt. Philo dedicated his life to scholarship, and acquired an extensive knowledge of literature, philosophy, and the sciences of his day. He made a pilgrimage to Jerusalem,* where he offered prayers and sacrifices in the Temple.* Philo also led a delegation of Jews to the Roman emperor Caius Caligula, to appeal against the anti-Jewish decrees of the Roman high commissioner, Flaccus of Egypt.

Philo's works include allegorical—or symbolic—commentaries on the Bible,* and **The Lives of Moses* and the Patriarchs.*** The latter work presents an interpretation of Jewish teachings in philosophical terms in an attempt to reconcile the basic ideas of the Bible with Greek thought. Philo had a great influence on Hellenized Jews who were steeped in Greek philosopy and knew very little about Judaism. His idea of the **Logos,** or the **Word,** through which God influences the world, greatly influenced the Fathers of the Christian Church, and, indirectly, Jewish mystical thought.

PHOENICIANS. The Sidonians of the Bible.* They occupied the coast of Canaan* from southern Syria through northern Palestine* up to the hills of the region that separated them from Acco (Acre*). They were organized in city-states, two of which, Sidon and Tyre, are familiar to Bible readers. Seafarers, navigators, and traders, the Phoenicians were also skilled artisans and builders. By the time of kings David* and Solomon,* their power had waned, and they had become friendly allies of Israel.* They supplied engineers and craftsmen, and floated down "the cedars of Lebanon"* in rafts for David's palace and for Solomon's Temple.* The ancient empires contending for mastery of that part of the world eventually swallowed up the Phoenician cities. The Phoenicians made valuable contributions to ancient civilization. Tyre taught the world how to make the famous purple dye, and Sidon, the beautiful blown glass. From the Phoenician tongue, a sister language of Hebrew,* the Greeks borrowed their alphabet,* which became the basis of the European alphabets.

PIDYON HA-BEN (Hebrew, meaning "Redemption of the Firstborn"). When they are thirty days old, firstborn sons pass through a festive ceremony known as **pidyon ha-ben** ("the redemption of the firstborn son"). This is based on the Biblical command that the firstborn male offspring of both man and beast be dedicated to the service of God. All children but those of priests (Kohanim) must be "redeemed," or released from this dedication. In ancient times this was done by offering a special sacrifice. Since the destruction of the Temple* it has become customary to give money for charity instead.

PILPUL. From the Hebrew **palpel,** meaning to search, or judge, or possibly from **pilpel** (literally, "pepper"), indicating the sharpness of discussion. Pilpul is an analytic method used in Talmudic

Pioneer Women/Na'amat leaders meet with President Chaim Herzog at Beit Hanassi, the official home of the President of Israel. Left to right: Gloria Elbling, national vice president; President Herzog; Phyllis Sutker, national president; M.D. Nava Arad, former secretary general of Na'amat.

study, which explores all possible sides of an argument. It was first used in **yeshivot** in Germany,* and was introduced to Poland* in the sixteenth century by the famous Talmudic scholar, Rabbi Jacob Pollack, The term pilpul is often associated with hair-splitting and unproductive argumentation.

Leon Pinsker.

PINSKER, LEO (1821-1891). Russian physician, writer, Zionist leader. The son of a Hebrew scholar, Pinsker studied medicine and settled in Odessa. In 1861 he began to publish articles favoring assimilation* and internationalism as the only solution to the Jewish problem. The Odessa* pogroms of 1871 shook his faith in assimilation,* though it was not until the great pogroms of 1881 that he completely abandoned his earlier convictions. The following year (1882) he published **Auto-Emancipation,** an extraordinary pamphlet in which he diagnosed anti-Semitism* as an incurable "disease" caused by fear of the alien, landless Jew. He prescribed "the creation of a Jewish nationality ... living on its own soil" as the only cure. At first Pinsker believed that a Jewish homeland might be established anywhere. After contact with the men and women of the **Hoveve Zion,** or "Love of Zion" movement, however, he came to think of Palestine* as the Zionist goal. Pinsker was chosen president of the Lovers of Zion societies at their conference in 1884, and served the Zionist movement until his death in 1891.

PIONEER WOMEN. The Women's Labor Zionist Organization is a world movement with sister organizations in 13 countries: Argentina,* Australia,* Belgium,* Brazil,* Canada,* Chile,* England,* France,* Israel,* Mexico,* Peru* and Uruguay,* as well as in the United States.

Pioneer Women, of the United States, was founded in 1925. Golda Meir* served as General Secretary from 1933-1934. With its sister organization Na'amat (Working Women and Volunteers)—the largest women's organization in Israel—Pioneer Women provides 60% of all social services extended to Israeli women, youth and children through its more than 1,500 installations.

Child and Youth Services. 500 day care centers and three day-night homes provide personalized care for more than 20,000 youngsters.

Vocational Education. Pioneer Women sponsors agricultural, agro-mechanical and vocational high schools, as well as vocational training courses in dental and optical technology and electronics, aeronautics, beauty culture, dressmaking, home economics, hotel services, crafts, draftsmanship and jewelry making.

Professional Programs. In addition to the Sophie Udin Graduate Library School at Hebrew University* in Jerusalem,* Pioneer Women/ Na'amat supports an annual scholarship program for women enrolled in institutions of higher learning.

Community Centers. Forty-one modern, fully-equipped centers provide vocational training courses as well as day nurseries and kindergartens for the children of working mothers.

Women's Centers. Pioneer Women operate almost 200 women's centers throughout Israel which provide opportunities for learning, counseling and relaxation. In addition, women's centers in 35 villages provide Arab, Druze and Bedouin women and girls with unprecedented opportunities for education and personal advancement.

Additional Programs. Legal aid and family counseling for war widows. Vocational training for NAHAL (**see** ARMY OF ISRAEL) girls in new border settlements.

Test kitchen for consumer protection and education in Tel Aviv.*

On the American Scene. Pioneer Women support Habonim and Dror Youth Organizations as well as Jewish cultural and educational institutions. (**See also** HISTADRUT HA-OVDIM.)

PISSARRO, CAMILLE (1830-1903). Painter of Sephardic origin, he was born on a small island in the West Indies, and as a young man emigrated to France.* There he lived for many years in great poverty, until, toward the end of his life, he became recognized as one of the outstanding landscape painters of his time. Having experienced misery himself, he often painted with warmth and sympathy peasants pushing wheelbarrows, digging potatoes, tending geese, or farm workers in coarse garments with backs bowed by labor and limbs gnarled by rheumatism. Pissarro had no spiritual links with Judaism. Toward the end of his life he was troubled by the rise of French anti-Semitism,* and the unjust condemnation of Captain Dreyfus.*

PIYUT. Liturgical poetry. **(See HEBREW LITERATURE.)**

POALE AGUDATH ISRAEL. Orthodox labor organization affiliated with Agudath Israel.* Its aim is to help rebuild Israel in the spirit of traditional Judaism. The organization encourages the preparation and education of pioneers for Israel, and solicits funds for its institutions in Israel.

Poale Agudath Israel has been instrumental in the establishment of kibbutzim and villages in various parts of Israel. There it maintains ten children's homes and two children's villages, housing over a thousand Israeli youngsters. Poale Agudath Israel takes an active part in the political life of the country and has sent three representatives to the Knesset.* It maintains educational institutions ranging from kindergartens to teachers' seminaries.

Ezra, its youth movement, is dedicated to Orthodox education and training pioneers to live on collectives in Israel. Outside of Israel, the organization is active in the United States, Canada,* England,* and other countries.

POALE ZION. See LABOR ZIONISM.

POGROM (Russian, meaning "riot"). In Russian Jewish history, particularly after 1881, the pogrom was a recurring phenomenon. All violent attacks against Jews have since come to be known as "pogroms." The Russian pogroms were a major factor in starting a wave of mass migrations of Russian Jews to the United States and to other countries.

POLAND. For several centuries of Jewish history, Poland was one of the most important countries of the world. The great-grandparents of the majority of the Jews of today were born in territories which once formed part of Poland. The traditions of modern Jews, therefore, are deeply grounded in the history, culture, and customs of the Jews of Poland. The important cultural, social, and national movements of our time— Hasidism,* Haskalah,* and Zionism*—came into their full fruition and development among the Jews of Poland.

Jews first came to Poland from Asia Minor and settled on the shores of the Black Sea at the very beginning of the Common Era. From there they spread northward. In the eighth century they succeeded in converting the ruling classes of the Khazars,* who dominated a large territory between the Volga and the Dnieper rivers, north of the Black Sea. When the Mongolians invaded Eastern Europe in 1240, many of these Jews (including many Khazars) fled to Poland and eventually settled there. Most of the Polish Jews, however came at a later date, from Germany.* They brought with them the German dialect mixed with Hebrew words which they had used in Germany for hundreds of years. This dialect developed into Yiddish,* which became the universal language of Polish Jewry.

Thus, a permanent settlement of substantial numbers of Jews began in Poland at the end of the twelfth century. Some of them became the mint-masters of the Polish kings. Since, apparently, at that time Jews were the only merchants in Poland, these mint-masters stamped their coins with Hebrew inscriptions. The Jews were very useful in the Polish economy; therefore, the kings of Poland

"The Village" by S. Yudovin

248

made a strong effort to attract large numbers of them to settle in Poland. In 1246, Boleslav the Pious issued a very favorable charter offering privileges to the Jews, based on the Charter of Privileges issued in 1244 by Duke Frederick of Austria.* This charter, which became the cornerstone of Polish Jewish legislation, allowed the Jews to organize themselves into autonomous communities, and regulated the business relationships of Jews and gentiles in a manner very favorable to the former. The charter protected the Jews against the hostile Christian clergy, guaranteed the inviolability of their life and property, and assured them protection while transporting their merchandise and while carrying on their business.

Toward the end of the thirteenth century, life became difficult for the Jews of Germany, and many migrated to Poland. In 1344, Casimir the Great reaffirmed the charter of Boleslav, and extended further privileges to the Jews of his kingdom. In the years that followed, during the Black Plague, Poland became a refuge for the Jews of Germany who were either massacred or else driven out of the towns where they resided. They began to stream into Poland in large numbers (about 50,000 German Jews migrated to Poland within a short time). Germany was practically emptied of its Jewish population, and Poland became the great center of Yiddish-speaking Jews.

Types of Polish Jews —sixteenth century.

Toward the end of the fourteenth century, Jagello, Duke of Lithuania, married the heiress to the Polish throne, and Lithuania became part of Poland. The Jews had settled in Lithuania about the same time as they had settled in Poland. The two Jewries were now united under one ruler. With but few exceptions, the kings of Poland treated the Jews well and protected them against the hostile clergy, the German merchants, and the artisans who had settled in the larger towns. Poland was an agricultural country, its land divided into large estates worked by serfs for the benefit of the nobility. the Jews served the nobility as managers of their estates, buyers and distributors of their excess farm produce, financial agents, tax farmers, and suppliers of luxury articles. Although few of the Jews became rich, they lived comfortably, married young, reared large families, and devoted a great deal of their time and energy to the study of Torah* and Talmud.*

The Jews were organized into autonomous communities, each community having full jurisdiction over its members. The Polish government levied a single tax on all the Jews of Poland. It was up to the Jews to apportion this sum among the various communities. Thus it became necessary to establish a council made up of outstanding rabbis and heads of important communities in order to repre-

sent them before the government. This council was charged with the task of negotiating the amount of the tax due to the government, collecting the tax from the various communities, and protecting the rights and interests of Polish Jewry. In the sixteenth century this representative body was known as the Council of the Three Lands, since it represented the Jews of Poland, Lithuania, and Polish Russia. In the seventeenth century a Council of the Four Lands, representing the Jews of Great Poland, Little Poland, Podolia (including Galicia), and Volhynia, was established. The members of the council met twice yearly (at the great fairs of Lublin and Jaroslav). In addition to managing communal affairs, the Council acted as the supreme court of the Jewish communities, settling all disputes and enacting all necessary ordinaces. they also supervised all elementary education and the **yeshivot** (Talmudic academies).

Jewish learning flourished in Poland. There was hardly a home where the Talmud was not studied. **Yeshivot** were established in many important cities, and the world-famous Talmudic scholars who taught there attracted hundreds of students from far and wide. among these scholars were Shalom Shakhna (1500-1558), who established the famous **yeshiva** of Lublin; Moses Isserles (1530-1572), whose notes on the **Shulhan Arukh*** made it the accepted code of Jewish law for Polish Jewry; Solomon Luria (1510-1573), author of a very important commentary on parts of the Talmud; Mordecai Jaffe (d. 1612), author of a great code of law; Joshua Falk (d. 1614), great commentator on the codes of Jacob b. Asher and Joseph Karo;* Meir of Lublin (d. 1616); Samuel Edels (d. 1631); Joel Sirkes (d. 1640); and a host of others.

Modern Period.

In the second half of the seventeenth century, the Cossack uprisings led by Chmelnicki, and subsequent wars with Sweden and Russia had catastrophic effects on the Jews in Poland. Numerous Jewish communities were completely destroyed. Tens of thousands of Jews perished; many fled to neighboring countries. When order was restored, the remaining Jews, joined by returning refugees, re-established their communal life. Through favorable legislation, King Jan Casimir helped to improve the economic status of the Jewish population in the devastated regions.

However, the recovery of Polish Jewry was not complete. They were constantly exposed to the accusations of the Church and the anger of the mob. The general anarchy which engulfed Poland in the eighteenth century further aggravated the Jewish position. Efforts of the Council of the Four Lands to reopen the once famous **yeshivot** were only partially successful. The suffering masses sought con-

Types of Polish Jews —nineteenth century.

Wooden synagogue of the nineteenth-century Polish countryside.

solation in mysticism and in illusions of redemption. The Messianic movement led by Sabbatai Zevi* stirred the imagination of considerable numbers of Polish Jews, who believed that the day of deliverance was near. Even after they were disillusioned in the false Messiah, many Polish Jews remained in the grip of mysticism. Some followed the adventurer Jacob Frank,* who proclaimed himself a successor to Sabbatai Zevi. In the middle of the eighteenth century the quest of Polish Jewry for spiritual fortitude and a glowing faith was realized in Hasidism.* The movement attracted many adherents. It preached contentment and cheerfulness and imparted a sense of importance to the simple people who were scorned or ignored by the scholars.

Throughout the eighteenth century, the Jews of Poland, which included the Ukraine and White Russia, were almost constantly terrorized by their Christian neighbors. Subjected to the hostility of the church and to the whims of local rulers and landowners, the life of the Jew was at times intolerable. The frequent blood accusations* and riots lasted until the final partition of Poland by Russia, Prussia, and Austria* in 1795. In the rebellion against foreign rule led by Kosciusko, Berek Joselovic, heading a Jewish legion in 1794, fought on the side of the Poles. In 1807, Napoleon formed part of the country into the Duchy of Warsaw, which lasted for eight years. The Jewish situation was only slightly changed during this period of time. The majority of the Jews in the partitioned provinces of Poland became part of Austria and Russia, sharing the general lot of their brethren in these two countries. The Jews of Galicia had become, in 1782, subject to the Edict of Tolerance issued by the Austrian Emperor Joseph II. This edict endeavored to foster assimilationist tendencies among Jews. Although the Revolution of 1848 secured equal rights for the Jewish population, economic discrimination lasted until the outbreak of the First World War.

A number of Jews living under Russian rule

identified closely with the Polish cause. They participated in the revolt of 1830-31, forming a regiment of their own which defended the city of Warsaw* against Russian attacks. In 1863, led by Rabbi Dov Berish Meisels, head of the Jewish community in Warsaw, they took active part in an unsuccessful attempt to overthrow Russian rule.

Due to their devotion to the cause of Polish national liberation, the Jews of Russian Poland fared poorly during the nineteenth century. They suffered at the hands of Russian oppressors and Polish oppressed alike. However, the difficult economic and political plight of Polish Jewry did not hamper its spiritual and cultural growth and advancement. In addition to being a stronghold of Talmudic scholarship and Hasidism, it became, in the second half of the nineteenth century, fertile ground for the Haskalah* or Enlightenment movement. Some of the best known Hebrew writers and scholars were active in the Jewish centers of Poland, especially in Warsaw. These included Hayim Selig Slonimski, a scientist and inventor who edited **Ha-Tzefirah,** and Nahum Sokolow.* Other scholars and writers were J. L. Peretz;* David Frischmann;* Sholom Asch;* Simon Berenfeld; Samuel Abraham Poznanski, Moses Schorr; Meyer Balban; Ignaz Schipper.

Attacks and persecution of the Jews followed the establishment of Poland as an independent state after the First World War. Minority rights for Polish Jews were secured in the peace treaty of Versailles.* With the inclusion in the new Poland of parts of White Russia and Galicia, the Jewish community became one of the largest in the world, numbering over three million. The struggle for national, economic and political rights of the Jewish

Dov Berish Meisels, Chief Rabbi of Warsaw, participated in the Polish uprising (1863) against the Tsarist occupation.

population was rigorously pursued by Jewish representatives in the Polish Sejm, or Parliament. Despite vicious anti-Semitic propaganda, economic restrictions, and the often hostile government policy, Jewish national and cultural life in Poland flourished. All parties—the Zionists, the Jewish Socialist Bund,* Agudath Israel,* and Mizrachi*—had a large following among Polish Jewry. Polish Jewry served as a main source for Palestinian pioneers. Jewish schools in which the language of instruction was either Hebrew, Yiddish, or Polish, were opened in every Jewish community by the various political and religious factions. The Yiddish press exerted great influence on the Jewish masses. There were Yiddish dailies, outstanding among them being **Hajnt** and **Moment**. There were close to two hundred periodicals in Yiddish, Hebrew and Polish, all of them devoted to Jewish affairs.

The most prominent Jewish political leaders were Isaac Gruenbaum, Joshua Thon, Leon Reich, Emil Sommerstein, and Ignaz Schwarzbart, the only Jewish representative in the Polish Government in Exile during the Second World War in London.

Just before the Second World War, the anti-Semitic movement in the country assumed a more threatening character. A new Polish party called O.N.R. openly advocated Nazi-style extermination of the Jews. Attacks on Jews became a frequent occurrence. The government concurred with the economic boycott instituted against them. Nevertheless, Polish Jewry heroically defended its rights. Even during the first few years of the Nazi occupation of Poland, when Polish Jewry was reduced to complete enslavement, it gave evidence of vitality and spiritual fortitude. The extermination of over three million Polish Jews in the years 1942 through 1945 was one of the greatest tragedies in Jewish history. Only a few hundred thousand survived the Nazi slaughter. The story of the revolt of the Warsaw* Ghetto* and the resistance of Jewish partisans and ghetto fighters in other parts of the country constitute heroic chapters in the annals of Jewish martyrdom and courage.

After the war, only about 60,000 Jews remained in Poland, thousands who survived Soviet exile and Nazi camps having fled to Israel.* Spurred by a renascence of anti-Semitism* in the new Communist Poland, another exodus began late in 1956, and over 35,000 Jews left, almost all of them for Israel. At the same time, about 19,000 Jews of Polish origin were repatriated from the Soviet Union. About two-thirds of them re-emigrated to Israel.

In 1982, there was a resurgence of anti-Semitism in Poland after the introduction of martial law. Jews were accused of being key leaders in Poland's anti-Soviet Solidarity movement. In 1984 there were fewer than 5,000 Jews in all of Poland, although some sources claim that there are tens of thousands of Jews in Poland, born after World War II, who have yet to come to terms with their Jewish identity.

POPULATION, WORLD JEWISH. Information and tables on the Jewish population, by continents and countries, are presented below. A variety of difficulties in obtaining accurate figures in some countries, as well as the extent of Jewish migrations in the last decade make some of the data only the best approximations that could be reached under the circumstances.

COUNTRIES WITH LARGEST JEWISH POPULATION
(100,000 JEWS AND ABOVE)

Rank	Country	Jewish Population	% of Total Jewish Population In the Diaspora
1	United States	5,705,000	59.3
2	Israel	3,374,300	—
3	Soviet Union	1,630,000	17.0
4	France	530,000	5.5
5	Great Britain	350,000	3.6
6	Canada	308,000	3.2
7	Argentina	233,000	2.4
8	South Africa	119,000	1.2
9	Brazil	100,000	1.1

ESTIMATED JEWISH POPULATION DISTRIBUTION
IN EUROPE

Country	Total Population	Jewish Population
Austria	7,510,000	7,500
Belgium	9,861,000	32,500
Bulgaria	8,890,000	3,400
Czechoslovakia	15,314,000	8,700
Denmark	5,122,000	6,900
Finland	4,801,000	1,000
France	53,963,000	530,000
Germany, East	16,736,000	900
Germany, West	61,666,000	33,500
Gibraltar	30,000	600
Great Britain	55,833,000	350,000
Greece	9,707,000	5,000
Hungary	10,711,000	63,000
Ireland	3,440,000	2,000
Italy	57,197,000	32,000
Luxemburg	364,000	700
Netherlands	14,246,000	26,500
Norway	4,100,000	950
Poland	35,902,000	4,800
Portugal	9,931,000	600
Rumania	22,457,000	30,000
Spain	37,654,000	12,000
Sweden	8,324,000	15,000
Switzerland	6,473,000	19,000
Turkey	45,366,000	21,000
USSR	267,697,000	1,630,000
Yugoslavia	22,516,000	5,000
Other		150
Total		2,842,700

Note: *the following tables, listing Jewish population figures in 1982, are reproduced here by special permission of the American Jewish Year Book, published by the American Jewish Committee and the Jewish Publication Society of America. These figures may differ from the figures given in some entries on individual countries, which are of more current origin and reflect the most recent Jewish migration patterns.*

ESTIMATED JEWISH POPULATION DISTRIBUTION
IN THE AMERICAS

Country	Total Population	Jewish Population
Canada	24,231,000	308,000
U.S.A.	229,807,000	5,705,000
Total Northern America		6,013,000
Bahamas	248,000	500
Costa Rica	2,271,000	2,200
Cuba	9,717,000	700
Dominican Republic	5,581,000	100
Guatemala	7,481,000	900
Haiti	5,104,000	100
Jamaica	2,220,000	300
Mexico	71,193,000	35,000
Netherlands Antilles	261,000	700
Panama	1,940,000	3,500
Puerto Rico	3,242,000	2,500
Other		300
Total Central America		46,800
Argentina	28,085,000	233,000
Bolivia	5,755,000	1,000
Brazil	121,547,000	100,000
Chile	11,294,000	20,000
Colombia	28,776,000	7,000
Ecuador	8,644,000	1,000
Paraguay	3,268,000	700
Peru	18,279,000	5,000
Surinam	397,000	200
Uruguay	2,927,000	30,000
Venezuela	14,313,000	20,000
Total Southern America		417,900
Total		6,477,700

ESTIMATED JEWISH POPULATION DISTRIBUTION
IN ASIA

Country	Total Population	Jewish Population
Hong Kong	5,154,000	1,000
India	676,218,000	4,300
Iran	39,320,000	30,000
Iraq	13,527,000	200
Israel	4,063,700	3,374,300
Japan	117,645,000	800
Lebanon	2,685,000	250
Philippines	49,530,000	150
Singapore	2,443,000	400
Syria	9,314,000	4,000
Thailand	47,488,000	300
Yemen	5,940,000	1,200
Other		300
Total		3,417,200

ESTIMATED JEWISH POPULATION DISTRIBUTION
IN AFRICA

Country	Total Population	Jewish Population
Algeria	19,590,000	300
Egypt	43,465,000	250
Ethiopia	32,158,000	27,000
Morocco	20,646,000	17,000
South Africa	30,131,000	119,000
Tunisia	6,513,000	3,700
Zaire	26,377,000	200
Zambia	5,961,000	300
Zimbabwe	7,600,000	1,250
Other		3,000
Total		172,000

ESTIMATED JEWISH POPULATION DISTRIBUTION
IN OCEANIA

Country	Total Population	Jewish Population
Australia	14,927,000	75,000
New Zealand	3,125,000	4,000
Total		79,000

JEWISH POPULATION IN THE UNITED STATES

State	Estimated Jewish Population	Total Population
Alabama	9,160	3,943,000
Alaska	960	438,000
Arizona	49,285	2,860,000
Arkansas	2,885	2,291,000
California	789,260	24,724,000
Colorado	41,765	3,045,000
Connecticut	108,575	3,153,000
Delaware	9,500	602,000
District of Columbia	30,000	631,000
Florida	479,180	10,416,000
Georgia	40,855	5,639,000
Hawaii	5,775	994,000
Idaho	505	965,000
Illinois	261,985	11,448,000
Indiana	21,360	5,471,000
Iowa	7,395	2,905,000
Kansas	11,960	2,408,000
Kentucky	12,685	3,667,000
Louisiana	17,925	4,362,000
Maine	8,185	1,133,000
Maryland	199,915	4,265,000
Massachusetts	249,045	5,781,000
Michigan	86,635	9,109,000
Minnesota	32,040	4,133,000
Mississippi	3,080	2,551,000
Missouri	85,235	4,951,000
Montana	640	801,000
Nebraska	7,850	1,586,000
Nevada	18,200	881,000
New Hampshire	5,880	951,000
New Jersey	425,180	7,438,000
New Mexico	5,305	1,359,000
New York	1,869,190	17,659,000
North Carolina	15,145	6,019,000
North Dakota	1,085	670,000
Ohio	137,785	10,791,000
Oklahoma	7,160	3,177,000
Oregon	11,940	2,649,000
Pennsylvania	408,475	11,865,000
Rhode Island	22,000	958,000
South Carolina	9,060	3,203,000
South Dakota	605	691,000
Tennessee	18,100	4,651,000
Texas	77,110	15,280,000
Utah	2,600	1,554,000
Vermont	2,465	516,000
Virginia	59,265	5,491,000
Washington	21,985	4,245,000
West Virginia	4,295	1,948,000
Wisconsin	31,295	4,765,000
Wyoming	310	502,000
U.S. TOTAL	5,728,075	231,534,000

See note on preceding page.

PORTUGAL. The history of the Jewish community in Portugal, which was founded in the twelfth century, follows the same tragic pattern as that in Spain. It begins with the Jews enjoying many privileges and holding high office in the state, and ends in enforced baptism and expulsion in 1496.

The Jews had complete charge of their own internal affairs. They were governed by the chief rabbis, to whom the state delegated much authority. For this privilege they had to pay various taxes, including a degrading poll-tax. Among the notable Jews who served the king were the astronomer Abraham Zacuto* whose astrolabe, the forerunner of the modern sextant, was used by the explorer Vasco da Gama, and Don Isaac Abravanel.*

With the expulsion of Jews from Spain in 1492 many Jews found refuge in Portugal. But here, too, tragedy was soon to overtake them. King Manoel, though friendly to the Jews at first, agreed to their expulsion as part of a marriage bargain he entered into with Ferdinand and Isabella of Spain. The Spanish rulers insisted that Manoel's marriage to their daughter be conditional on the expulsion of the Jews from Portugal. The expulsion order, promulgated in 1496, permitted the Jews to take all their property, but ordered all the young people to the be forcibly baptized. However, even the adults, on being brought to Lisbon, were not allowed to leave for other lands. They were offered the choice of being sold as slaves or baptized. Many of those who were baptized still clung to their faith secretly as Marranos.*

Today (1984) the Jewish community of Portugal consists of no more than some 600 souls. They are concentrated in Lisbon and Oporto, and are engaged mainly in the textile trade.

POTOCKI, COUNT VALENTINE (d. 1749). Polish nobleman and convert to Judaism. In the early eighteenth century, European Jewry suffered degradation and oppression. Nevertheless, Potocki was so deeply impressed by the Jewish faith that he embraced Judaism. The story is that Potocki had gone to Paris* to complete his education; there, the sight of an aged Jewish scholar studying the Bible* aroused his interest in Judaism. he persuaded the old man to teach him Bible and Hebrew. Potocki became a convert to the Jewish faith in Amsterdam*—the only country in Europe where this was permitted. Later, he returned to his native Poland* and lived with the Jews in the ghetto* of Vilna. When his identity was discovered, the Poles arrested him. Despite entreaties by his mother and his friends, he refused to return to his former faith. Instead, Potocki chose to accept a martyr's death, and was burned at the stake in 1749. The memory of this **ger zedek** ("righteous convert") was long revered by the Jews in Eastern Europe.

PRAGUE. Capital of Czechoslovakia,* home of one of the oldest and most important Jewish communities in Europe. Jews settled in Prague at the beginning of the tenth century. In 1096, at the time of the first Crusade, the Jews suffered grievously. Kings Sobeslav II and Ottokar, in the following centuries, issued laws which regulated relations between Christians and Jews. Early in the thirteenth century, the Jews settled in the Altstadt (Old City), where they built the famous **Altneuschul** synagogue, one of Prague's ancient and most celebrated landmarks. According to an old legend, this synagogue was built with some stones from the destroyed Temple* in Jerusalem.*

Despite the fact that Prague's Jewry was under the protection of the Bohemian king, they were constantly persecuted. The worst attack on the ghetto took place in 1389, when three thousand Jews were killed. The ghetto was again plundered in 1421, when the Jews sided with the Hussites who rebelled against the Catholic Church. The fortunes of the Prague Jews improved slightly in the fifteenth century. In 1527, they were permitted to display the "Jew's flag" in processions. At the same time, however, restrictions and expulsions of Jews from the city continued. But these did not deter Jewish economic and intellectual advancement. The community of Prague produced some outstanding rabbis and scholars. Among the most prominent of Prague's rabbis were Judah Loew,* known as the Maharal, and Yom Tov Lipman Heller (1579-1654), author of a commentary on the Mishnah, astronomer, and liturgical poet. David ben Solomon Gans (1541-1613) was a famous historian and astronomer who was a friend of the great astronomers Johannes Kepler and Tycho Brahe. David Oppenheim (1664-1736) was a famous collector of Hebrew books and manuscripts which are now a part of the Bodleian Library of Oxford, England.

At the end of the seventeenth century, two misfortunes befell the Jewish community—an epidemic, and a raging fire which destroyed eleven synagogues and much property. As late as 1744, Empress Maria Theresa ordered the expulsion of the Jews from Prague. Ten thousand persons were involved. They were allowed to return a few years later only after paying a heavy tax. The Haskalah,* or Enlightenment movement at the end of the eighteenth century, made a deep impression on Prague's Jewry. Many Jews began to play an important role in the intellectual life of the city and the country. The Orthodox element was

centered around Rabbi Ezekiel ben Judah Landau (1713-1783).

In 1848-1849, Prague's Jews were granted equality, and in the next century the community grew rapidly. Conditions improved further after the establishment of the Czechoslovak Republic in 1919. A number of Jewish writers in Prague achieved fame in German literature, among them Max Brod, Franz Werfel, and Franz Kafka.*

The Nazi occupation of Prague in 1939 spelled the doom of the thriving Jewish community of 35,000 souls. In 1948, the Communist government of Czechoslovakia came to the support of the newly established state of Israel,* when it was attacked by its Arab neighbors. But this did not last long, and was replaced by a violent anti-Semitic and anit-Zionist campaign, culminating in the infamous Slansky trial in Prague in 1953. The estimated Jewish population (1984) was about 2,000.

PRAYERS. The spiritual communion with God through prayer, as an important form of worship, has been part of Jewish religious experience from earliest times. In the Jewish religion, prayers may be individual or congregational, since organized religious services consisted in the offering of sacrifices. Some eloquent examples of individual prayers in the Bible* are the prayers of praise and thanksgiving offered by Moses* after the

An Israeli soldier at prayer at the Western Wall, Jerusalem.

Synagogue ornament above the cantorial lectern, by Judah Wolpert. Sheviti—"I have set the Lord always before me." (Psalms 16:8).

Israelites' deliverance from Egypt,* and the crossing of the Red Sea (Exod. 15:1-18); by Deborah* after her victory over Sisera and his Canaanite hordes (Judges 5:2-31); by Hannah after the birth of her son Samuel* (I Samuel 2:1-10); and by King Solomon* after the construction of the Holy Temple* (I Kings 8:23-53). Most psalms were also individual prayers.

The beginning of congregational services date back to the period of the Babylonian exile (586-536 B.C.E.). When the Jews returned to Judea, rebuilt the Temple, and organized community life under Ezra,* Nehemiah,* and the Men of the Great Assembly, an early form of congregational service developed. These services took place alongside sacrifices at the Temple, as well as in numerous synagogues throughout Palestine and Babylonia.* However, with the destruction of the Second Temple (70 C.E.), the dispersion of the Jewish people, and the complete elimination of sacrifices, congregational services in synagogues became the exclusive form of worhsip. Prayers were standardized by religious authorities and assembled into prayer books. In the course of centuries, new prayers were composed and incorporated into the prayer book.

The traditional Jewish prayer book is known as the **siddur,*** and the special holiday and festival prayer book as the **mahzor.*** The present prayer book consists of portions of the Bible, including

Two elders of the Casablanca Jewish community in solemn prayer at the tombs of two members of their community.

Masthead of the Hebrew daily Davar, with the headline announcing the establishment of the State of Israel.

approximately half of the psalms,* selections from the Talmud;* religious poems by medieval poets; Maimonides'* Thirteen Principles of Faith, and other prayers of benediction, petition, adoration, confession, and thanksgiving, originating in various ages.

Congregational prayers are grouped into the following services: **shaharit** (morning service), **minhah** (late afternoon service) and **maariv** (evening service). On Sabbaths* and festivals, the **musaf** (additional service) follows the reading from the Torah* after **shaharit,** and on Yom Kippur,* the **neilah** (closing service) is added at the end of the **minhah.** The **Kiddush*** (Sabbath and festival consecration service), the **Havdalah** (separating the holy day from the weekdays) and the **Birkat Ha-mazon** (grace after meals) are outstanding examples of prayers in the home.

The most important daily synagogue prayers are the **Shema*** (Deut. 6:4), which proclaims the unity and sovereignty of God; the **Shmone Esre** (or **Amidah**), consisting of eighteen basic benedictions which comprise the main portion of every service; the **Ashre** (Psalm 145), and the **Alenu,** both prayers of adoration repeated three times a day.

The great majority of prayers in the traditional prayer book are in Hebrew,* the holy tongue of the Jew. A few are in Aramaic,* a Semitic language akin to Hebrew, which the Jews spoke for many generations. (**See also** SYNAGOGUE.)

PRESS, JEWISH. Over one thousand Jewish newspapers and periodicals in about twenty-five languages appear in all parts of the world today. Of these, about 40% are published in Israel. The United States ranks second in the number of Jewish newspapers published: about 25% of the total number.

Amsterdam,* Holland, was the birthplace of the first Jewish periodical in 1678. Named **Gazeta de Amsterdam,** it was printed in Ladino,* a Spanish-Jewish dialect. Sporadic attempts were made to publish magazines for over a century thereafter, but all were short-lived. In 1841, the first issue of a weekly, **The Jewish Chronicle,** made its appearance in London. It is, today, one of the oldest and most important Jewish periodicals. In the United States, the earliest surviving weekly, **The American Israelite,** was founded in 1854 by Isaac Mayer Wise. The first Yiddish daily in the world, **Yiddishes Tageblatt,** began publication in 1885 in New York. It merged with the **Jewish Morning Journal** in 1928. The first Hebrew magazine, **Ha-Tzofeh Be-Eretz Ha-Hadasha** ("The Observer in the New Land"), edited by Zvi Hirsch Bernstein, was published in 1871.

Masthead of the first Hebrew journal in Palestine, Halbanon, which began publication in 1863.

In the second half of the nineteenth century, the Hebrew press in Russia* made great strides. In 1856, the appearance of the first regular Hebrew weekly, **Ha-Maggid,** coincided with the growth of the Enlightenment movement. Thirty years later, the first Hebrew daily, **Ha-Yom** ("The Day"), began publication in St. Petersburg, Russia's capital at that time. The two other Hebrew weeklies, **Ha-Melitz** ("The Advocate"), and **Ha-Tzefirah** ("Daybreak"), turned into dailies. With the advancement of the Zionist and socialist movements, and the development of Jewish public opinion in Eastern Europe and in particular in Russia and Poland, the Yiddish press reached widespread circulation and wielded great influence. Before the Second World War, there were Yiddish dailies in several large Jewish centers in Poland* and Lithuania,* and three dailies in the Soviet Union. With the destruction of East European Jewry, only a few Yiddish periodicals continued publication in Poland, while in Russia none exist, except for one published in Birobidjan.

In the last two decades, the number of Jewish dailies has declined, but the number of weeklies, monthlies, and other periodicals is on the increase. In Israel, in addition to the Hebrew daily press, there are daily publications in Arabic, English, Russian, French, Hungarian, Yiddish, and German. This diversity of the Jewish press in Israel reflects the great variety of linguistic and cultural background of the country's population. Israel is the only country in the world where a vibrant and diverse daily Jewish press exists. Israel's oldest existing Hebrew daily, **Ha-Aretz,** founded in 1919, is a respected liberal newspaper. It advocates a policy of moderation in political and social affairs. **Davar** is the organ of the Histadrut.* **Al Hamishmar** is the

party organ of Mapam; **Hatzofe** and **Hamodi'ah** express the views of religious parties. The afternoon newspapers **Maariv** and **Yedioth Ahronoth** reflect all shades of opinion and are the most widely read in Israel. Israel's only English daily, **The Jerusalem Post**, is a prestigious paper widely read among Jews the world over. Almost all daily newspapers in Israel publish literary supplements and popular magazines on weekends.

Only a limited number of Yiddish dailies is published outside of Israel. The United States has two Hebrew weeklies, **Yisrael Shelanu** and **Hadoar**, published in New York. The best-known Yiddish weeklies in the United States are the **Algemeiner Journal** and the **Forward**. There are two Hebrew illustrated monthlies for young people, **Olam Chadash** and **Lamishpachah**. Other monthly magazines are **Bitzaron** (Hebrew) and **Zukunft** (Yiddish).

Of the Anglo-Jewish press in America, among the most widely circulated are: (weeklies) **The Jewish Week** in New York, **The Jewish Press** in New York, **The Jewish Exponent** in Philadelphia, **The Jewish News** in Michigan, **The Jewish Advocate** in Boston, **B'nai B'rith Messenger** and **Sentinel** in Chicago; (monthlies) **Commentary, Hadassah* Magazine, B'nai Brith* National Jewish Monthly** and **Midstream**; (quarterlies) **Judaism, Tradition** and **Jewish Spectator**. The children's magazine, **Olomeinu**, published by Torah Umesorah,* is deservedly popular.

PROPHETS. See BIBLE and under names of various Biblical prophets.

PROTOCOLS OF THE ELDERS OF ZION. See ANTI-SEMITISM.

PROVERBS, BOOK OF. Written, according to tradition, by King Solomon,* Proverbs, together with Job* and Ecclesiastes,* is part of the Wisdom Literature in the Bible. It is composed of a great variety of sayings, teaching wise and moral conduct for everyday life. Some of the famous proverbs are:

"Fear of the Lord is the beginning of knowledge;
Fools alone despise wisdom and instruction.

Wisdom crieth loudly without;
In the public places she uttereth her voice,
At the corner of noisy streets she calleth,
At the entrance of the gates
In the city she sayeth her speeches;

How long, ye simple ones, will ye love simplicity?

And the scorners take their delight in scorning,
And fools hate knowledge.

The merciful man doeth good to his own soul,
But he that is cruel troubles his own flesh.

The lip of truth will stand firm forever,
But only for a moment with tongue of falsehood.

At the fall of thine enemy do not rejoice;
And at his stumbling let not thy heart be glad.
The wicked flee when no man pursueth;
But the righteous are bold as a lion.

If thy enemy be hungry, give him bread to eat;
And if he be thirsty, give him water to drink.''

PSALMS (from the Hebrew **Tehilim**, meaning "praise" or "chants of praise"). The first book in Ketuvim ("Writings"), the third division of the Bible.* The Book of Psalms is itself divided into five books, like the Pentateuch. It numbers 150 hymns, most of them ascribed to David,* some to Asaph the Musician, others to the Sons of Korah, etc. Some of the psalms are odes praising God (Hallelujahs); others are poems of thanksgiving, pilgrim songs, and mournful elegies. They vary in length, structure, and subject matter; all are beautiful and some of unsurpassed greatness. The confidence and joy of the twenty-third Psalm (beginning "The Lord is my shepard") have given gentle comfort to men ever since its creation. Psalm 104 is a nature poem that kindles the imagination with the majesty of all creation. Psalm 24, a stirring ode of praise, has been incorporated, like many other psalms, into the synagogue services. During all morning services, except those that fall on the Sabbath,* this psalm is chanted as the Torah scroll is returned to the Ark.

The psalms were knitted closely into the daily life of the Jewish people. In the synagogue, morning services end each day with a different psalm. In each community, simple men of great piety who had been unable to acquire learning joined within a **Hevra Magide Tehilim**, a "band of psalm chanters." They met daily at the synagogue and sought inspiration in reciting the **Mizmor Shel Yom**—the day's reading from the Book of Psalms—until they had completed it on the Sabbath. In folk lore there were stories about the "Psalm-Chanter," a folk hero who was the secret student of mystic lore, a modest saint who concealed his knowledge and joined the psalm-chanters daily in the house of prayer. He also joined those gathered at the bedside of the dangerously ill, and those at houses of mourning, in their recital of the psalms—a distillation of piety and a plea of mercy to Heaven. The Book of Psalms has also been read by Christians since the time of the Apostles. It has given comfort and inspiration to men during religious services and in their private devotions.

N.B-A.

PUERTO RICO. Commonwealth in the United States, occupying the easternmost island of the Greater Antilles. Puerto Rico was ruled by Spain* until ceded to the United States in 1898. Jewish businessmen and government officials arrived in the island after its occupation by the United States. Most of them came in connection with American industrial plants set up in recent years. Until 1955, when an Orthodox congregation was founded under the leadership of a rabbi from the United States, there was nor organized Jewish community life on the island.

PUMBEDITHA. See BABYLONIA.

PURIM. (The Feast of Lots) This holiday falls on the fourteenth of Adar,* commemorating a day on which the Jews were saved from their oppressors. Read on the evening and morning of the holiday, the Book of Esther* relates how Haman drew lots to determine when to put the Jews of Persia to the sword. Fortunately, Haman's scheme was foiled by the faithful Mordecai* and by Queen Esther.

Purim is celebrated with great merriment, after the fashion of the Persian Jews, who made their victory over Haman an occasion "for feasting and gladness." During the reading of the Book of

"Then the king said to Haman: Make haste, and make the apparel, and the horse, as thou hast said, and do so even to Mordecai, the Jew, that sitteth in the gate . . ." (Book of Esther.) Woodcut by Ilya Schor.

Esther, children twirl noisemakers in derision at every mention of Haman's name. Some Oriental Jewish communities even hang Haman in effigy. **Hamentaschen** ("ears of Haman") are eaten, and it is considered a "good deed" to drink wine. Comic plays, called **Purimspile,** are presented at the **seudah,** or feast, with which the holiday closes.

Purim Ball in Amsterdam—1780; an engraving by C. Philips Jacobz, from a painting by P. Wagenaar, Jr.

Among the finest of Purim customs is **mishloah manot,** the practice of sending gifts of food to friends and gifts of food and money to the poor.

The day after Purim is called Shushan Purim. This is so named because the Jews of Shushan, the capital of Persia, fought their enemies for an additional day. Many other local Purims, established for later acts of deliverance, are observed, such as those celebrated in Tiberias* (Israel), in Egypt,* Frankfurt (Germany),* Saragossa (Spain), and numerous other places. **(See also ESTHER, SCROLL OF.)**

PURITY LAWS. In addition to the dietary laws, which are partly hygienic in nature, are the ceremonies which have to do with ritual purity. The Jewish religion very literally believed that "cleanliness is next to godliness." The Bible carefully defines types of personal and ritual uncleanliness, and provides for exacting rituals of purification. These include the quarantining of persons with such diseases as leprosy, and of those considered impure because of some contamination. Persons in a state of impurity had to leave the "camp" or community, and all objects with which they came into contact required cleansing or burning. After their recovery, "unclean" individuals had to bathe in clean, "living" (running) water. Further, the Talmud* lists the **mikvah** ("ritual bath") as one of ten institutions which must be provided for wherever Jews live. Before private baths became common, regular visits to such public baths were the only assurance of personal cleanliness. Besides the visits to the **mikvah,** the washing of the hands before meals and of the feet before retiring was prescribed by Talmudic sages.

Judaism directly associates purity of body with purity of soul. The prophet Isaiah* predicts that the sins of Israel, which have been red as crimson, shall be "washed" white as snow. Similarly, the granting of the Torah* at Mount Sinai was preceded by three days of "purification." The white gowns, or kittels, worn in synagogue on the New Year and the Day of Atonement are associated with this idea. Also associated with it are the white tablecloths and clothing with which the Sabbath is received, and the white shrouds in which the dead are buried.

RABBI (Hebrew, meaning "my teacher"). The title conferred upon a religious leader and teacher. According to the famed historian Heinrich Graetz,* the title was first used during the time of the destruction of the Second Temple (70 A.D.). The term was probably introduced by the disciples of Johnanan Ben Zakkai.*

At present, a rabbi is ordained by the head or faculty of the rabbinical seminary from which he is graduated. The present functions of a rabbi consist of the religious leardership of his congregation; making decisions with regard to practical questions of Jewish law; conducting services and preaching on Sabbaths, holy days and festivals; teaching Judaism, particularly to adult groups; and officiating at important events in the life of his constituents (such as circumcision,* marriage,* and burial). In some cases, the rabbi is also the educational administrator of his congregational school. Many rabbis have excelled as scholars and authors of important works on religion. A number have also distinguished themselves as gifted orators and leaders of the community or of Jewish national and world movements, such as Zionism and Hebrew culture.

RABBINICAL ASSEMBLY OF AMERICA. See JEWIH THEOLOGICAL SEMINARY OF AMERICA.

RABBINICAL COUNCIL OF AMERICA. See YESHIVA UNIVERSITY.

RABIN, YITZHAK (1922-   ). Israeli soldier and public servant. Born in Jerusalem,* he was a member of the Palmach* and took part in the Allied invasion of Syria,* which was then under the control of Vichy France.* During the War of Independence he was in command of the Israeli

Yitzhak Rabin

forces defending the outskirts of Jerusalem. In 1949 he took part in the Rhodes armistice negotiations. He became deputy chief of staff of the Israeli Army in 1960 and chief of staff in 1964. He was responsible for the strategy employed by the Israeli army during the Six-Day War* of 1967. In 1968 he was appointed Israeli ambassador to the United States. In 1974 he joined the Israeli cabinet as Minister of Labor and succeeded Golda Meir* as Prime Minister, serving until 1977.

RABINOWITZ, SHALOM. See SHOLOM ALEICHEM.

RACHEL (1890-1931). Hebrew poetess. Few modern Hebrew poems have captured the hearts of the listeners as have those of Rachel (Bluvstein). Simplicity and sincerity shine through her poetry. It is deeply personal, yet its emotions are universal.

When Rachel came to Israel* from Russia,* at the age of nineteen, she worked as a farmhand, first in Rehovot and later in Kinneret on the shores of the beautiful lake after which that kibbutz was named. When she arrived, she did not know a word of Hebrew* or Yiddish.* Yet she mastered the Hebrew language thoroughly. In 1913, Rachel went to France* to study agriculture and was caught there when the First World War broke out a year later. Unable to return to Palestine, she decided to go to Russia, where she taught refugee children. In Russia, she contracted tuberculosis. She returned to Palestine after the war, but illness forced her to live an invalid's life for the rest of her years. No longer able to till the land, her longing and loneliness poured out in such poems as the well loved **Ve-ulai** ("Perhaps").

RAMBAM. See MAIMONIDES.

RASHI (Rabbi Solomon Yitzhaki) (1040-1105). Biblical and Talmudic commentator. In any study of the Bible and Talmud,* Rashi's commentaries are considered practically indispensable. He became a beloved figure in Jewish history. Many legends about life, piety, and saintliness are current. It is told that Rashi's father found an unusually beautiful jewel. When word of this find spread, a church dignitary became interested in buying the stone. It was to be used to decorate a holy statue. Despite the generous price offered, Rashi's father refused to sell the stone for such an idolatrous purpose, and threw the jewel into the sea. As soon as he had done so, a voice from heaven foretold that he would be rewarded with a son who would be a jewel in all Israel.

Born in Troyes, France,* Rashi spent a brief period of study in Worms, Germany,* and on his return founded a Talmudical academy in his native land. The fame of this school grew rapidly, attracting students from far and wide. In teaching Talmud, Rashi felt the lack of good commentaries to facilitate its study and undertook the exacting task of providing one.

Synagogue in Worms (Germany)

Rashi's commentary became a standard guide for every student of the Talmud. Its explanations are clear and explicit, written in a lucid Hebrew style. His commmentary on the Pentateuch* and on most of the other Biblical books are invaluable for an understanding of the Bible along traditional lines. These commentaries, in which Rashi makes full use of Midrashic* sources, have been widely used by Jewish and gentile scholars alike. They have been translated into Latin and other languages.

Rashi's three daughters all married great scholars, and it may be said that his house fathered numerous sages. Rabbi Samuel ben Meir (Kashbam) and Rabbenu Tam* were two of his famous grandsons.

H.L.

RATHENAU, WALTER (1867-1922). German industrialist and statesman and son of the engineer and industrialist Emil Rathenau. During the First World War, he organized the supply of raw materials which was of great importance to the German war effort. In 1922, he became the German Foreign Secretary, and concluded the famous agreement with Soviet Russia* at Rapallo. He was assassinated by German ultra-nationalists.

RAV (ABBA ARIKHA). See BABYLONIA.

READING, RUFUS DANIEL ISAACS, FIRST MARQUESS OF (1860-1935). Broker, jurist, and public servant. Born in London,* the son of a poor Jewish storekeeper, Rufus Isaacs spent an adventurous boyhood at sea. At the age of seventeen, he returned to England* to prepare for a career in law. At twenty-one, he became a stockbroker, and by the time he was thirty, he was one of London's most promising young lawyers. In 1913, after a dazzling career at the bar and several terms in Parliment, he was named chief justice of England—the first Jew to attain that distinction. The following year he was ennobled and, as the First Marquess of Reading, took a seat in the House of Lords. From 1921 to 1926 he served as viceroy of India*—again the first Jew to hold the post.

Rachel

Long interested in Zionist affairs, Lord Reading joined Justice Louis D. Brandeis of the United States Supreme Court in drafting an economic plan for Palestine.* This plan was presented to the

Zionist Conference in London in 1920. Elected president of the Palestine Electric Corporation in 1926, he visited Palestine and joined in the protests to the British cabinet after the 1929 riots in Palestine.

Reading, Eva Violet, Marchioness (1895-   ). Daughter-in-law of the first Marquess of Reading, and daughter of Lord Melchett.* Chairman of the National Council of Women in Britain, and President of the British ·Section of the World Jewish Congress.*

READING OF THE LAW (in Hebrew **K'riat Ha-Torah**). The reading of the Law is a distinct part of the prayer service, observed during the morning and afternoon assemblages on Sabbaths* and holidays, and each Monday and Thursday. One portion of the Five Books of Moses* is read each week, with the portions so divided that the entire Five Books are read each year. Simhat Torah ("The Rejoicing of the Law"), is the day on which the last portion of one year's cycle is read and the first portion of the following year is begun.

During the reading of the Law, the Torah* scrolls, which are written on parchment by special scribes, are removed from the Ark of the Law. Originally, the portion was read by various members of the congregation, who were "called up to the Law." Later it became customary for a special reader to chant the entire portion to a melody handed down from ancient times. The older practice, however, is preserved in the custom of "calling up" seven men, each of whom chants a blessing before the reading of each section of the weekly portion. An eighth man is "called up" for the reading of the **Haftorah,*** the short passage from the Prophets which follows the weekly portion of the Law.

Sabbaths and holidays are also the occasion for the reading of other portions of the Bible and other holy books. **Pirke Avot**, "The Ethics of the Fathers," is read every Saturday afternoon during the summer, while one of the five **megillot** (scrolls) is read on each of five holidays—The Song of Songs on Passover,* Ruth* on Shavuot,* Ecclesiastes* on Sukkot, Esther* on Purim,* and Lamentations* on the Ninth of Ab.

In the synagogue, the reading of the regular portion of Law is often followed by a **derashah** ("sermon") delivered by the rabbi or some member of the congragation. More often than not, based on the portion of the week, it generally deals with some religious or ethical subject.

B.H.

RECONSTRUCTIONISM. A religious movement which attempts to reinterpret Judaism in the light of modern life and thought without abandoning its cultural values and usages. Reconstructionism began to emerge as a movement in 1934 under the leadership of Rabbi Mordecai M. Kaplan (1881-1983). Kaplan believed that Judaism is a "religious civilization" emerging from the language, history, customs, laws, religion, art and folkways of the Jewish people. These, and the basic values they embody, can be perpetuated only through social institutions in which these entities continue to have meaning for the individuals who

An aged Yemenite Jew has become accustomed to reading the Torah Scroll upside down.

participate in them. Reconstructionism has therefore striven for the organization of closely integrated Jewish communities in America. Because it also believes that Jewish nationhood is a part of Judaism, it stresses the ties between the State of Israel* and Jewish communities in the Diaspora. In religion, it is close to Reform Judaism in its call for reexamination of religious beliefs, and to Conservative Judaism in its desire to perserve as many forms of religious practice as possible. Its work has been conducted through the Reconstructionist Foundation, formed in 1940. Its periodical, **The Reconstructionist,** has served the movement as a forum since 1935.

REFORM JUDAISM. See JUDAISM.

Isaac Jacob Reines

REINES, ISAAC JACOB (1839-1915). Scholar, teacher, founder of Mizrachi,* the religious Zionist movement. Reines was born in a small town near Pinsk, Russia. He spent his youth studying the Talmud* and was counted as one of the most brilliant students of the famous Yeshiva (Talmudical Academy) of Volozhin. When only nineteen years old, he was ordained a rabbi. Reines introduced a new method for the study of the Talmud, one in which reason and logic replaced hair-splitting. To modernize traditional Jewish education, he founded the Yeshiva of Lida. He worked actively for the Zionist cause, and in 1884, participated in the Hoveve Zion* conference at Kattowitz, where means of settling Jews in Palestine were considered. When Theodor Herzl* issued a call for the establishment of a Jewish

state, Reines became his ardent supporter. he was a fiery partisan of the rebuilding of the Jewish homeland and fought bitterly against the anti-Zionism of his contemporaries. In 1902 he founded the Mizrachi movement.

REINHARDT, MAX (1873-1943). Theatrical producer and director. Born in Baden, near Vienna, Reinhardt began his brilliant career in the theatre as a player of bit parts in Berlin. By the mid-1920's, his Grosses Schauspielhaus ("Great Theatre") had become the theatrical center of Germany.* Under his direction, it excelled in spectacular productions, and in the effective use of setting, design and color. Reinhardt's films were as famous as his stage productions. Forced to flee Germany when the Nazis came to power, Reinhardt settled in America and was active in theatrical life here. His notable production of **A Midsummer Night's Dream** was made into a film in Hollywood under his direction. Reinhardt is generally regarded as one of the leading influences on the development of both the European and American theatres.

REISEN, ABRAHAM (1876-1953). Yiddish poet and novelist. Reisen's writings have achieved world popularity. His poems and short stories abound with great love and sympathy for the life, suffering, and struggles of the simple Jewish folk in Russia and Poland. He was the literary spokesman of the Jewish Socialist Bund,* the popular Jewish radical movement at the turn of the century. Many of his poems became folk songs; in them Reisen expressed the desire of the oppressed for freedom from political tyranny, poverty, and ignorance.

Born in a small town in White Russia, in his youth Reisen wandered over all the great centers of Jewish life: Warsaw,* Berlin, Cracow, Paris, and others. Everywere he went, he engaged in literary activity, editing and publishing newspapers, journals, and anthologies. In Warsaw, he collaborated with the great Hebrew and Yiddish writer, J. L. Peretz.* From 1914 until his death, Reisen lived in New York.* He published upward of twenty volumes of verse and prose.

REMBRANDT HARMENSZOON VAN RIJN (1606-1669). This Dutch painter was the first master to show Jews not as caricatures, but as individuals endowed with human dignity. He was on friendly terms with the intellectual leaders of the Jewish quarter of Amsterdam* (where he lived for many years), and his sitters included the famous physician Dr. Ephraim Bonus, and Rabbi Saul Levi Morteira (who was Spinoza's* first teacher). In addition to the wealthy and educated Sephardic

immigrants from Portugal,* from whom he received commissions, he painted the poor refugees from Poland.* Reared in the Portestant faith, this great Dutchman was thoroughly familiar with Jewish life and lore, as indicated by his beautiful and accurate renderings of Old Testament episodes.

RESH. Twentieth letter of the Hebrew alphabet; numerically, two hundred.

RESH GALUTA. See EXILARCH: **also** BABYLONIA.

Emblem of the tribe of Reuben

REUBEN (Hebrew, meaning "Behold, a son"). Firstborn of Jacob* and Leah. In his blessing, Jacob characterized Reuben as "unstable as water" (Gen. 49:4). The tribe of Reuben were cattle-and sheep-raisers, permitted to settle on the east side of the Jordan on the condition that they continue to help in the conquest of Canaan.*

REUBENI, DAVID (c. 1491-c. 1535). False Messiah, born in Khaibar, Central Arabia, died in Spain.* Half-mystic, half-adventurer, David

Reubeni created a great stir in his time, and despite the warnings of level-headed leaders, many Jews saw in him a forerunner of the Messiah who would bring freedom to them and to the Holy Land. Reubeni arrived in Rome in 1524, and managed to get an audience with Pope Clement VII. He declared himself ambassador from his brother, King Joseph Reubeni, ruler over the descendants of the tribe of Reuben*—one of the Ten Lost Ribes*—dwelling somewhere in Tatary. He promised the Pope to raise an army among the Jews of the East and to lead it against the Turks in the Holy Land. Such were Reubeni's bearing and personality that the Pope believed him and gave him credentials to the kings of Portugal* and Abyssinia. To secure the aid of these monarchs in freeing Palestine,* wealthy members of the Roman Jewish community supplied Reubeni with money to travel in state. He came to Portugal in 1525, where King John III received him with high honors. The Marranos,* secret Jews, thought Reubeni was the Messiah and flocked around him. One of them, Diego Pires, openly returned to Judaism, took the name of Solomon Molkho* and joined Reubeni's followers. The Portuguese authorities became suspicious, and Reubeni found it necessary to leave Portugal. Continuing his fantastic career, he went to Venice where he offered the Senate an alliance with his king. The Venetian authorities had him investigated and the result was that he left empty-handed. In 1532, bearing a banner inscribed with initials of the Hebrew words "Who is like unto Thee, O Lord among the mighty?", Reubeni together with Molkho appeared in Ratisbon before Charles V, Emperor of the Holy Roman Empire. Reubeni tried to persuade the Emperor to call the Jews to arms against the Turks. Charles V put both Reubeni and Molkho in chains; eventually Reubeni was sent to Spain where he was placed in the hands of the Inquisition.* The circumstances of his death are uncertain. Reubeni's diary is now in the Bodleian Library at Oxford University. **(See also MESSIANISM.)**

REUCHLIN, JOHANN (1455-1522). Non-Jewish defender of Jews and Hebrew literature against many malicious attacks. He was an authority on Hebrew grammar and was fascinated by the mystical teachings of the Kabbalah.* Perhaps the expulsion of the Jews from Spain* in 1492 stirred Reuchlin to uphold their cause in his native Germany.* He frustrated the attempt by the Jewish convert to Christiantiy, Johann Pfefferkorn, to burn all the Hebrew books in Cologne and Frankfurt. Because of Reuchlin's influence with the Emperor Maxmilian, which he exerted in favor of the Jews, he was the butt of the attack by the

Catholic Church, and especially the Dominican orders. Reuchlin was the first non-Jew to make Hebrew an official study at a university (Tubingen).

REVEL, BERNARD (1885-1940). First president of Yeshiva College (now Yeshiva University*). Born in Kovno, Lithuania, he studied at the yeshiva of Telz, where he was ordained a rabbi. Revel came to America in 1906. Here he studied at the University of Pennsylvania, New York University, and Dropsie College,* where he obtained the degree of Doctor of Philosophy in 1911.

In 1915 Revel became president of the Rabbi Isaac Elhanan Theological Seminary. He founded the Talmudical Academy, and, in 1928, a Yeshiva College of Liberal Arts was established through his untiring efforts. He contributed articles in the fields of Semitics and rabbinic literature. A department of the Graduate School in Yeshiva University is named in his memory.

REVISIONIST ZIONISM. A Zionist party organized in 1925 by Vladimir Jabotinsky.* It called itself "Revisionist" because it felt the need for revision of the official Zionist policy toward Great Britain as the mandatory government of Palestine. The program of Revisionism included the creation of a Jewish majority on both sides of the Jordan; unrestricted mass immigration of Jews into Palestine; encouragement of middle-class immigration and of private enterprise to increase the absorptive capacity of the country; the outlawing of strikes and the substitution of compulsory arbitration during the period of national upbuilding; and the restoration of the Jewish Legion as a distinct part of the British garrison in Palestine. Brith Trumpeldor (Betar),* Revisionist Youth Organization, was part of the Revisionist World Union. The Revisionist party was a part of the World Zionist Organization* until the nineteenth World Zionist Congress* held in 1935. At that time, the Revisionist party differed so sharply with the prevailing Zionist policies that it seceded and formed the New Zionist Organization. A small group of Revisionists broke off from the parent body, and, calling themselves the Jewish State Party, remained as a part of the World Zionist Organization. In 1946, the New Zionist Organization merged with the State Party to form the United Zionist Revisionists and again became a constituent part of the World Zionist Organization. In Palestine a resistance group (against British restrictive policies and against Arab terror) grew out of Revisionism. This underground body, the Irgun Z'vai L'umi ("National Military Organization"), functioned until after the creation of the State of Israel,* when it merged with the Army of Israel.* Many of its veterans joined the Herut party, which is the Israeli counterpart of the Revisionist party.   N.B.A.

RIBALOW, MENACHEM (1896-1953). Literary critic and editor, Born in the Ukraine, he spent some years in Moscow, where he was recognized as a promising young writer. Ribalow came to America in 1921, and immediately took an active part in Hebrew life there. For thirty-two years he was editor of the Hebrew weekly, **Hadoar.** He also edited a literary annual and a quarterly journal, and published four books of criticism. For a quarter of a century, Menachem Ribalow was a leader of the Hebrew literary movement in America.

Abraham Ribicoff

RIBICOFF, ABRAHAM A. (1910-   ). Political leader, attorney. Born in a tenement in New Britain Conn., Ribicoff comes of Polish Jewish stock. His father was a factory worker in New Britain, who encouraged the boy from earliest youth to put aside money, earned at peddling papers and working in stores, toward his future education. After being graduated **cum laude** from the University of Chicago Law School, Ribicoff returned to Connecticut, was admitted to the state bar, and worked in the office of a Hartford lawyer. In November, 1938, he was elected on the Democratic ticket to the first of two terms of service in the lower house of the Connecticut General Assembly. From 1941 to 1942 he served as chairman of the Connecticut Assembly of Municipal Court Judges. Elected congressional representative from Connecticut in 1948 and 1950, Ribicoff served on the Foreign Affairs Committee. In 1954 he was elected Governor of Connecticut. He was Secretary of Health, Education and Welfare from 1961 to 1962. In that year he was elected Senator from Connecticut on the Democratic ticket.

264

RICARDO, DAVID (1772-1823). Political economist. Born in London to a family of wealthy Sephardic Jews, his marriage to a Quaker led to a breach with his family. Before he was twenty-five, Ricardo had made a fortune in the stock market. **Principles of Political Economy and Taxation,** published in 1817, won him immediate fame. The following year (1818), Ricardo turned to politics and was elected to Parliament. There, despite his early breach with Jewish life, he spoke in favor of political emancipation for Jews, shortly before his death, in 1823.

RIESSER, GABRIEL, See GERMANY.

RISHON-LE-ZION (Hebrew, meaning "First of Zion"). Founded, in 1882, by members of the Hoveve Zion* movement from Russia,* on desolate sand dunes in the plain south of Jaffa. After enduring early hardships, the village was taken over by Baron Edmond de Rothschild,* with whose aid it became a grape-growing center. In 1887 the Baron built the Rishon wine cellars, among the largest in the Mediterranean area. Later, many of the vineyards were converted into orange groves. Rishon-Le-Zion has developed rapidly, and at present is a pleasant, tree-shaded town with about 100,500 inhabitants, who are engaged mainly in the wine industry, citriculture, and various industrial enterprises.

RITUAL MURDER. See BLOOD ACCUSATION.

ROME. The Jewish community of Rome claims two distinctions: it is the oldest in Europe, dating to at least 180 B.C.E., and is also perhaps the one in which Jews have lived most continuously (with but minor interruptions) to this day. Their numbers were fairly large, even in Maccabean times. They were increased in 70 C.E., when Titus with his Roman Legions defeated Judea and burned the Second Temple.* He brought many Jewish captives to Rome, and in his train were King Agrippa II, Princess Berenice, and the historian Josephus.* After the defeat of the Bar Kokhba* rebellion in 135 C.E., captives and refugees again increased the Jewish population of Rome.

Judea may have been defeated, but Judaism was not. Conversions of Romans to Judaism must have been fairly widespread, because in 204, such conversions were prohibited by law. On the whole, Jews were persecuted less in Rome than elsewhere. About 212 to 217 C.E., Judaism was recognized as a "religio licita," a legal religion. In 590, the Pope confirmed the Jewish rights. In 855, all Jews were ordered to leave Italy,* but evidently this order was not strictly enforced, because three years

later, special clothing was introduced to identify Jews. The ebb and flow of alternate persecution and protection of Jews continued through the centuries. In 1021, Jews were persecuted; but between 1058 and 1061, the Pope opposed the compulsory baptism of Jews. In 1215, Jews had to wear a special badge; eighteen years later, a Papal bull gave Jews protection. In this same thirteenth century, the power of the Inqusition* was extended, but within a few years, another Papal bull denounced blood accusations* as false. During the first half of the sixteenth century, popes and cardinals befriended the Jews, yet in 1555, they were forced to live in a ghetto and obliged to wear the "Jewish badge" to distinguish them from non-Jews. Jews were also barred from many trades.

Through it all, Jewish life went on, and Roman Jewry produced its share of great scholars. In the eleventh century, Nathan Ben Yechiel compiled the **Arukh,** an encyclopedic work on the Talmud* vocabulary. Immanuel of Rome (ca. 1270-1330), writing under the influence of Dante, left a colorful picture of Jewish life in fourteenth-century Italy. A Jewish printing press was established in 1545 and it flourished. In 1581, the Inquisition was still active, and in 1784, a compulsory baptism ordinance was enforced.

In the nineteenth century, the Jews no longer submitted passively to persecution. When their rights as citizens, proclaimed in 1809, were later denied them again, they revolted and tore down the ghetto walls in 1829. Finally, in 1849, the Assembly granted them full civic rights. From them on, anit-Jewish manifestations diminished and the year 1907 found the Jew, Ernesto Nathan mayor of the city.

After World War I, when Mussolini's Fascist regime came to power, the Jews remained undisturbed. However, under Nazi pressure, racist doctrines were adopted. When German troops occupied the country toward the end of the Second World War, the Jewish community of Rome suffered, although they found some protection among their neighbors. At present (1984) there are about 10,000 Jews in Rome. A newly built community center and a new school building are evidence of renewed civic and educational effort, and an active Zionist organization is in close contact with the Jews of Israel.*

ROSENFELD, MORRIS (1862-1923). Yiddish poet. One of the earliest and best known Jewish poets in America, he came to the United States from Poland in 1886. His first poems, published in 1886, told of a life of toil and ill-paid labor in the "sweatshops" of those days. Rosenfeld knew the bitter lot of the working man from first-hand experience. Drawn to the revolutionary movement, Rosenfeld later wrote of Jewish national problems, bewailing Jewish homelessness, and singing songs of Zion.

A poet of vigorous expression and elemental force, Rosenfeld's poems were popular among the common people and some of them, set to music, are sung to this day. His works were translated into many European languages; a book of his poetry, **Songs from the Ghetto,** was published in English.

ROSENHEIM, JACOB. See AGUDATH ISRAEL.

ROSENWALD. An American Jewish family of wide philanthropic interests. Born of immigrant parents in Springfield, Illinois, Julius Rosenwald (1862-1932) entered business as a clothing merchant, and came to head Sears, Roebuck, the world's largest mail-order firm. At the time of his death it was estimated that he had distributed over $70,000,000 for philanthropic purposes. Negro education and housing headed a list of causes to which he contributed. Other interests of Julius Rosenwald included a program of Jewish colonization in Russia,* to which he contributed $6,000,000, an agricultural research station in Palestine* and Jewish institutions in the United States. His elder son, Lessing Julius, succeeded Julius as head of Sears, Roebuck. He is best known as the founder and first president of the anti-Zionist American Council for Judaism. William, Julius's second son, has been active in business and in pro-Israel and communal fundraising affairs. He has served as chairman of the United Jewish Appeal* for the New York district.

ROSENZWEIG, FRANZ. See GERMANY.

Julius Rosenwald

Courtesy The Rosenwald Family.

Rosh Ha-Shanah Plate—Holland, circa 1700; used on the eve of the New Year for serving apple dipped in honey.

Courtesy The Jewish Museum, New York City.

ROSH HA-SHANAH (the New Year). The cycle of special holidays begins with Rosh ha-Shanah, the New Year. Falling on the first and second days of the month of Tishri,* it introduces the Ten Days of Penitence, when Jews examine their souls and take stock of their actions. The season, beginning with the New Year on the first day of Tishri and ending with Yom Kippur,* the Day of Atonement, on the tenth, is known as "Days of Awe." The tradition is that on Rosh ha-Shanah God sits in judgment on humanity. Then the fate of every living creature is inscribed in the Book of Life or Death. These decisions may be revoked by prayer and repentance before the sealing of the books on Yom Kippur.

Also known variously as Yom Teruah (the Day of the Sounding of the Shofar), Yom ha-Din (the Day of Judgment) and Yom ha-Zikkaron (the Day of Remembrance), the holiday is highlighted by the blowing of the ram's horn **(see** SHOFAR). Sounded in the Temple* on solemn occasions, on this day the shofar reminds the congregation of the gravity of the day, and calls them to repent. It also brings to mind the sacrifice of Isaac,* the story of whose rescue from death is an example of God's mercy.

On the eve of the holiday, Jews greet each other with the words **L'shanah tovah tikatevu—**"May you be inscribed for a good year." Bread or apples are dipped in honey on the eve of the holiday to express hope for sweetness in the year ahead. To symbolize purity of heart, some men wear white robes in synagogue; these are the shrouds in which observant Jews are buried. On the afternoon of the first day, Jews go to a river or other body of running water for the **Tashlikh** ("Casting Off") ceremony, in which each man symbolically casts his sins into the water.

266

ROSSI, AZARIAH BEN MOSES DEI (1513-1578). Physician, linguist, scholar. Born in Mantua to an ancient Italian-Jewish family, at the height of the Renaissance, Rossi was one of the first to apply scientific methods to the study of Jewish history. This he did in **Me'or Enayim** ("Light of the eyes"), a scholarly work telling the history of the Jewish people from the destruction of the Temple onward. Jews and non-Jews thought it very important, and parts of it were translated into Latin.

ROTHSCHILD, HOUSE OF. Bankers and philanthropists. Meyer Amschel Rothschild (1743-1812) was the son of a German Jewish merchant. Meyer entered banking when he agreed to invest the fortune of an Austrian nobleman. He was so successful that he soon found himself in charge of the finances of several royal families. At his death, he bequeathed to his five sons a banking establishment with enormous assets and branches in several financial centers. The eldest son, Anselm Mayer (1773-1855), became the head of the Frankfort bank; Solomon Mayer (1774-1855) headed the Vienna establishment, Nathan Mayer (1777-1836) the London bank, Carl Mayer (1788-1855), the Naples Bank, while Jacob (James) Mayer (1792-1868) founded and headed the Paris bank. Because of the extent of the Rothschild family enterprises, they came to be known as the financial kings of Europe. The influence they wielded was enormous. By refusing loans to warlike governments they could help to prevent the outbreak of war; by extending credit, they helped launch educational systems in France* and Germany,* and accelerated the industrial development of many European countries.

Baron Edmond de Rothschild

Later generations of the Rothschild family gained prominence as patrons of the arts and philanthropists. Outstanding among them was Baron Edmond de Rothschild (1845-1934), who became one of the chief builders of modern Palestine.* Anonymously at first, he poured millions into the support of the early agricultural settlements in Palestine. In fact, for about fifteen years—from the early 1890's until 1905—most Jewish settlers were directly dependent on "the Baron"—or "the well-known benefactor," as he was known.

Artur Rubinstein Hurok Attractions.

RUBINSTEIN, ARTUR (1899-1982). This distinguished pianist was born in Lodz, the seventh child of a textile manufacturer. He began to play the piano at the age of three, and made his debut in a Mozart concert at the age of seven. The promising child prodigy developed into a brilliant interpreter of classical and modern music. Artur Rubinstein achieved great success on the European concert stage, coming to America for the first time in 1906. The recognition accorded him all over the world included many awards. He was elected to the French Legion of Honor and to the Brazil* Academy of Music. His love of music and his prodigious energy have often led him to give more than one hundred concerts a year.

RUMANIA. Jewish history in Rumania goes back to the fourth century. It is believed that Jews settled there in earliest times, even before the Roman conquest of Dacia (today Transylvania). In 397 C.E., the Roman emperor issued a decree granting protection to the Jewish settlers and their synagogues in Dacia.Thereafter, the fate of the Jews in the region is unknown until the early Middle Ages, when, in the eighth and ninth centuries the Khazars* conquered the region. Some three hundred years later, the famous traveler, Benjamin of Tudela,* told of a Jewish colony in Wallachia. During the Middle Ages, the country was divided into small principalities. In most of them, the Jews suffered bitter persecution. Yet they were pioneers in commerce and industry and were among the first to settle in the city of Bucharest. Some of the local rulers recognized the great contribution of the Jews to the welfare of the country, and occasionally even encouraged them to settle in their territories. Usually, however, the treatment of the Jews was inuman in its cruelty. The Cossack uprising in 1648 spread from the Ukraine to Moldavia, causing great harm to the Jewish settlers there. Nevertheless, the following century saw a rise in the Jewish population in both Rumanian provinces of Wallachia and Moldavia.

After the tumultuous Turkish rule, the two provinces were united to form an independent state, in 1859. This independence was recognized by the Congress of Berlin in 1878. According to the treaty signed at the Congress, Rumania was obligated to grant full civil and political rights to all nationalties, including the Jews. The government, however, failed to live up to the treaty. Economic as well as educational restrictions and attacks against the Jews were frequent. At the end of the nineteenth century, constant persecution forced many to emigrate to America. Some also settled in Palestine* where they founded the colonies of Rosh Pinah and Zikhron Yaakov.

Following the First World War, discrimination and anti-Semitic riots continued and spread to large Jewish communities in Bessarabia and Bukovina, which had been annexed by Rumania. A strong anti-Semitic campaign was carried on by the Iron Guard party. During the Second World War, the anti-Jewish groups cooperated with the Nazis in the extermination of Jews. Only about one-half of Rumanian Jewry survived the slaughter; some succeeded in fleeing the country and settled in Palestine. Over 200,000 Jews remained. In 1984, the Jewish population was estimated at almost 30,000.

The community has produced outstanding men, such as the scholars Moses Gaster and Solomon Schechter,* and the contemporary Yiddish poet, Itzik Manager.

Jews were permitted to emigrate to Israel* in 1958-9, but Arab political pressure has slowed down the process.   H.L.

RUSSIA. The earliest Jewish settlers in Russia were probably merchants from Byzantium, who arrived eometime during the sixth century, C.E. In the course of the eighth century Jews arrived from the land of the Khazars,* south of Russia, where Judaism had become the national religion. Jewish fugitives from the Crusades* sought haven in Russia during the twelfth century. Most of these immigrants hoped to reach Kiev, a large trading center, which linked the Black Sea zone and Asia with western Europe. In the thirteenth century the Tatars conquered Russia, checking somewhat the growth of its Jewish communities.

Since Christianity took hold of the Russian people quite late in the history of Europe (about the tenth century), the clergy and the ruling classes remained highly suspicious of the Jews, who were classed with unbelievers and considered a threat to the young Church. At the end of the fifteenth century, a strong movement of conversion to Judaism arose in Novgorod, whence it spread to some of the nobility in Moscow. This movement was ruthlessly suppressed in 1504. Thereafter, the Jews became an even greater object of suspicion among the common people of Russia, who saw them as enemies of Christianity.

From the time of Ivan the Terrible (1553-1584) the Tsars were generally fanatically anti-Semitic, and limited or prohibited the Jews' right to live in Russia (**see PALE OF SETTLEMENT**). Towards the end of the seventeenth century, there were many Jews in Muscovy who practiced their religion in secret.

With the first partition of Poland,* during the reign of Catherine II (r. 1762-1796), 100,000 Jews from Poland and what is now White Russia came under Russian rule. Their numbers and importance in commerce necessitated a revision of the official policy. When Alexander I (r. 1801-1825) came to the throne, the Jewish community (Kahal*) had received official recognition. However, Jews were still subject to much discrimination, including excessive taxation, and restricted areas of residence. During the Napoleonic wars, the Jews gained in prestige by their opposition to Napoleon, whom they regarded as an enemy of religion.

With the accession to the throne of Nicholas I (r. 1825-1855), a reaction set in. It was he who was responsible for the cruel ordinance under which Jewish children were recruited for the army, sent to the most distant regions of Russia, and forcibly converted to Christianity in the course of their military training. (**See CANTONISTS.**) This form of persecution ended with the rule of the new Tsar, the liberal Alexander II (r. 1855-1881), when the condition of the Jews generally improved. Together with the rest of the Russian population, they prospered culturally and economically, were granted new privileges and witnessed the abolition of many abuses such as serfdom.

However, a new wave of anti-Jewish antagonism and suspicion developed during the end of the nineteenth century. One of the numerous ritual murder trials on record in Russian-Jewish history occurred in 1878. (See BLOOD ACCUSATION.) In 1881, Alexander II was assassinated, and the highly anti-Semitic Alexander III came to the throne. He encouraged the popular notion that the Jews had been responsible for his predecessor's death. A long series of pogroms* began, fostered by court circles to divert the people from the developing revolutionary movement. In the winter of 1891, all Jews were expelled from Moscow. Numerous new discriminatory regulations were passed.

In 1906, as a result of a revolution in 1905, the Tsar convened the first Duma (representative assembly) in Russian history. Jewish delegates were present, and Jewish problems discussed. But on the whole, the Duma was dominated by reactionary, anti-Semitic groups. The Russian government continued to follow a policy of social and economic restrictions against the Jews. Continued persecution caused an increase in Jewish emigration. Close to one million Jews left Russia during the decade preceding the First World War, most of them heading for the United States.*

Despite its hardships, the Russian Jewish community before the First World War was the most active and numerous in the world. In the eighteenth and nineteenth centuries, such highly important movements in Jewish history as Hasidism,* Haskalah,* and Zionism,* and Jewish socialist bodies took root and flourished in Russia. World-renowned yeshivot existed in many towns. Russia was the center of Hebrew and Yiddish literary activity. Mendele Mocher Sefarim,* Sholom Aleichem,* Peretz,* Ahad Ha-am,* Bialik,* and Tschernichowsky* are a few of the great writers of the pre-Revolutionary period.

The Bolshevik Revolution of 1917 was followed by the most terrible pogroms since the Cossack uprising of 1648. The various opponents of the Bolsheviks, the counter-revolutionary leaders Denikin, Petliura, Kolchak, and others, accused the Jews of sympathizing with the Communists. Their bands of soldiers and peasants attacked Jewish communities, murdering and pillaging the defenseless population. It is estimated that between the years 1917 and 1921, one hundred thousand Jews lost their lives, most of them in the Ukraine. Over 900 communities suffered the ravages of pogroms and famine. Hundreds of thousands of children were orphaned and remained destitute.

The Soviet government secured complete political and economic emancipation for the Jews. However, the economic condition of the Jews steadily deteriorated. The curtailing of private enterprise and trade severely crippled the economic position of the Jewish population. An exodus, especially of Jewish youth, began from the small towns to larger industrial centers. To alleviate the lot of the unemployed Jews, the government encouraged their settlement in agricultural colonies. Aided by Jewish organizations from abroad, especially by the American Joint Distribution Committee,* tens of thousands of Russian Jews were settled in the Crimea and in agricultural areas in the Ukraine and White Russia.

The Soviet government outlawed anti-Semitism, yet discrimination and anti-Jewish feeling prevailed. Recognized as a national group, the Jews were allowed to form their own village and town soviets (councils) wherever they constituted a majority of the population, for example in parts of the Crimea and in Birobidjan.* In 1934, Birobidjan became a Jewish autonomous district, and was represented in the central government. Yiddish* was the primary language of instruction in a number of educational institutions, and it was the language of cultural expression in certain segments of the Jewish population. However, the Birobidjan experiment failed. Jewish religious life, like all religious life in Russia, was greatly restricted and officially ridiculed and proscribed. The government banned Zionism* and the Hebrew language* entirely. Many of the three million Jews living in Russia before 1941 assimilated rapidly into the general population.

With the outbreak of World War II, hundreds of thousands of Jews in Russian territory perished under the Nazi invasion. Facing a common enemy, world Jewry hoped the Russian Jews would be able to draw close to the Jewish communities abroad. These hopes, encouraged by a more lenient policy in the Soviet government, were destined to be shattered when the victory in the Second World War made the need for a favorable world public opinion and a "united front" less crucial for Russia. Under a new policy toward Jewish culture, the Yiddish press, theater, and literature were all but wiped out. Many outstanding writers, artists and poets were killed or banished. Autonomous Jewish life in Russia ceased to exist. The spontaneous demonstration of Jewish national feeling after the establishment of the State of Israel* was quickly suppressed by the Soviet authorities. In 1956, Jewish activity in Russia appeared to be limited to a small number of synagogues.

A small rabbinical school was permitted in recent years, and a Hebrew prayerbook appeared.

In 1984, Russia's 2.6 million Jews are served by a handful of rabbis and synagogues. Jewish ritual objects cannot be produced and are confiscated if discovered.

Between 1968 and 1983, 260,000 Jews were permitted to leave the USSR, about 170,000 to Israel; the rest went to the United States, Canada, and elsewhere. However, between 1979 and 1983, the yearly emigration for Soviet Jews was cut by ninety-five percent. In 1983, more than 382,000 Jews in the USSR wishing to emigrate did not receive exit permits. Those who wish to make *aliyah* are treated as outcasts and are often dismissed from their jobs and schools, and forced to remain unemployed. "Refuseniks" are also subject to other forms of harassment. Today (1984) eleven "Prisoners of Zion" are serving terms of imprisonment on alleged charges of treason.

National Conference on Soviet Jewry. Created in June, 1971, in the United States by 37 national Jewish organizations and hundreds of Jewish community councils and federations as a unified effort to attain freedom and equality for Russian Jews. In 1970, following a massive crackdown against some of the more activist Soviet Jews which led to a series of trials in which death sentences were issued against Jews who allegedly attempted an escape from Russia, American Jewish organizations realized that the critical nature of this problem required a coordinated effort on the part of American Jewry, and the NCSJ was formed. The Conference, enjoying a broad-base support of American Jewry and particularly American Jewish youth, highly sensitive to the plight of Soviet Jewry, has organized mass rallies and protest meetings, and exerted influence on the American government which has greatly contributed to the release of thousands of Jews from the Soviet Union.

RUTH, BOOK OF. Second of the five scrolls in the Bible, it is read in the synagogue on Shavuot,* the Feast of Weeks. It tells of Elimelech and Naomi, of Bethlehem in Judah,* who, in a time of famine, take their two sons, Mahlon and Kilyon, and migrate to Moab. There Mahlon marries Ruth, and Kilyon marries Orpah. Elimelech dies, as do Mahlon and Kilyon, ten years later. The grieving Naomi prepares to return home to Bethlehem and tells her daughters-in-law to go back to their own parents. Orpah obeys sadly, but Ruth refuses. ("Whither thou goest, will I go; where thou lodgest, will I lodge; thy people shall be my people and thy God my God.") Ruth clings to Naomi, and follows her loyally to Judah. Eventually she marries Boaz, a rich farmer of Bethlehem, and they become the ancestors of King David.* This charming idyll has been loved by countless generations.

SAADIAH GAON (892-942). Scholar, and first of the Jewish medieval philosophers. His fight against the Karaite* sect, which broke away from traditional Judaism, was decisive in preserving the unity of historical Jewry.

He was born at Fayyum, Egypt. His genius became apparent early in his life. When only twenty, he compiled a Hebrew dictionary. He also translated the Bible* into Arabic, and wrote a commentary on most of its books. At about the same time, he combatted the Karaite attack on the Talmud,* refuting all the arguments of their leader, Anan Ben David.* Saadiah's brilliant defense of the Talmud spread his fame throughout the Jewish world. Saadiah left Egypt and spent some years in Palestine.* At that time, Babylonia* was still a great center of Jewish learning. The head of the Academy of Palestine, Ben Meir, disputed the right of the Babylonian scholars to compute the calendar. Saadiah sided with the Babylonian academies, and strengthened their authority.

When he arrived in Babylonia, he was invited to become head of the ancient Academy of Sura. Saadiah accepted the post, revitalized the Academy, and re-established its fame. Unfortunately, a dispute arose between Saadiah and the exilarch,* David ben Zakkai. The exilarch succeeded in bribing the Caliph to side with him, and the Gaon was forced to hide in Baghdad for seven years. During his forced exile, he produced his most important work, written in Arabic and called **Beliefs and Opinions.** His aim was to prove that the Jewish religion is based on reason and does not contradict philosophic thought. The book exerted great influence on Jewish thought, and is one of the standard works of Jewish religious philosophy. Five years before his death, Saadiah was reinstated as head of the Academy of Sura.

H.L.

SABBATAI ZEVI (1626-1676). False Messiah, a native of Smyrna, Turkey.* When Sabbatai Zevi was still a young and impressionable Talmud student, he became so deeply attracted by the Kabbalah* that he devoted himself completely to its study. In Kabbalist circles, he learned that the year 1648 would bring the "end of days," when the Messiah, the Anointed King, would come to bring Israel back to the Holy Land. Exactly when he came to look upon himself as the Messiah is difficult to tell. It is known, however, that at the age of twenty he lived the life of a mystic, praying, fasting, and bathing in the sea even in the winter. He saw mystic visions and began to interpret the messianic passages in the Kabbalah. Handsome and magnetic, Sabbatai was swiftly surrounded by

Sabbatai Zvi (18th century engraving).

a circle of followers, to whom he revealed openly for the first time his belief in himself as the Messiah. This happened in 1648 when he was 22 years old. The Jewish community of Smyrna expelled Sabbatai and he began the wanderings that served to spread his fame far and wide. The time was ripe for him. Everywhere, the Jewish people suffered from poverty, degradation, and persecution. They longed with all their might for the coming of the Messiah who would save them, and almost everywhere there were people who believed Sabbatai was the Messiah. When Sabbatai Zevi came to Constantinople, Abraham Jachine, a self-proclaimed prophet, produced an "ancient document" prophesying Sabbatai's Messiahship. Banished from Salonika, he went to Cairo. There, Rabbi Joseph Chelebi, treasurer at the governor's court, honored him with his open support. In Jerusalem,* he was warmly received by the local Kabbalists. Sabbatai sincerely believed that he was the Messiah. He fasted and prayed, wept, and chanted psalms through wakeful nights. Sent on a mission to Cairo, he heard of Sarah, a beautiful Jewish maiden from Poland* who believed that she was the predestined bride of the Messiah. His disciples sent for Sarah, and Sabbatai married her amid great rejoicing. "Prophets" continued to spring up and to proclaim Sabbatai as Messiah, and his fame grew so great that he dared to return to his native Smyrna in 1655. There he came to the synagogue,* and amid the blowing of trumpets and the shouting of "Long Live Our King, Our Anointed One!" Sabbatai proclaimed himself as the Messiah.

His following grew everywhere, among Marranos* in Amsterdam,* among the communities of Hamburg and Venice, among the Jews of Poland, stricken by the Cossack uprisings, and in far-off Morocco* as well. In Smyrna, all business stopped, and people prepared to follow the Messiah to the Holy Land. In 1666, Sabbatai Zevi set sail for Constantinople, in full expectation that Sultan Mohammed IV would give him a royal reception as the supreme king on earth. On landing, he was arrested and taken in chains to prison. Meantime, a rival "Messiah" from Poland, Nehemiah Cohen, became a Muslim, and told the authorities that Sabbatai was plotting to overthrow Ottoman rule. Sabbatai was brought before the Sultan and given the choice of becoming a Muslim or dying. Sabbatai chose to live, took off his Jewish head-covering and put on the white turban of the Turkish Muslim. The Jewish Messiah was no more; he had assumed the name Mehemet Effendi. Sabbatai was banished to Dulcigno, a small Albanian town, where he lived until his death on the Day of Atonement in 1676. Neither his conversion nor even his death put an end to the Sabbataian movement. His imprisonment and conversion were accepted as preliminary mystic suffering before the final glory. After his death, one false messiah after another followed Sabbatai's ways. Mystic dreamers as well as imposters continued to draw followers because of the people's hunger to return to the Holy Land and because of their great longing for redemption. **(See also MESSIANISM.)** N.B-A.

SABBATH. The Jewish week is climaxed by the Sabbath, the seventh day of the week. The holiness of the Sabbath is stressed in the fourth commandment (Ex. 20:8-11), "Remember the Sabbath Day to keep it holy. Six days shalt thou labor and do all thy work, but the seventh day is a Sabbath Day unto the Lord thy God." This commandment has been given deep symbolic meaning

and great social significance. It is an everlasting sign between God and Israel: "For in six days the Lord made heaven and earth and on the seventh he ceased from work and rested." (Ex. 31:17) The Sabbath day also is a reminder of the liberation from Egyptian bondage. It has servd as a lesson to all mankind, proclaiming the need of human beings for a day of freedom from labor and for devotion to spiritual matters.

The Jewish Sabbath, likened in song and story to a queen or a bride, has given a touch of royalty to the humblest home. Its joyful family observance is traditionally marked by special prayers, three festive meals, Sabbath songs, and study of the holy writings. Mourning ceases on the Sabbath, and except for Yom Kippur,* no fast day disturbs this holy day. The house is cleaned and scoured beforehand and the family dresses in its Sabbath best. Even the poorest householder tries to provide some delicacy for the day. Fish, wine and the twisted white loaves of bread (hallah) are part of the Sabbath meals.

On Friday evening, the table is set with a white cloth. The two loaves of hallah are placed at one end and covered. Ornamental candlesticks grace the table. All preparations are completed before sundown, when the day is ushered into the home by the mistress of the house as she lights the candles and pronounces the proper blessing. In the synagogue,* the forty-fifth psalm, beginning "Come let us sing before the Lord," opens the services. **Lekhah Dodi,** song of welcome to the Sabbath Queen, composed about 1540 by Solomon Alkabetz* follows. On his return to the home, the master of the house greets the two legendary Sabbath angels (who are said to accompany every worshipper from the synagogue) with the chant **Shalom Aleikhem,** "Peace be unto you, ye ministering angels."

From the moment the candles are lit until the Sabbath is ushered out the next evening with the strains of **Havdalah** all work is prohibited; cooking, cleaning, business transactions, carrying, ex-

cessive walking, traveling, writing, kindling fires, etc. An entire volume of the Talmud* has been devoted to defining and explaining limitations set up in order to safeguard the sacredness of the day and the comfort and well-being of the individual. Despite stringent regulations, the Sabbath never was a burden to the Orthodox Jew. It has served as an endless reservoir of spiritual strength to Jewry of all the ages.

Each Sabbath has its special section of the Torah,* to be read during the morning service together with the appropriate Haftorah.* **Shabbat Bereshit,** immediately after Sukkot, begins the annual cycle of Reading the Law. A number of other Sabbaths are given special designations for one reason or another. On Shabbat Shira, in the winter months, the portion **Beshalah** (Exodus 13-17 thru 17-16), containing the famous Song of Moses* and the Children of Israel, thanking God for their deliverance from the Egyptians at the Red Sea, is read. Shabbat Hagodol is the Sabbath immediately preceeding Passover.* Shabbat Hazon (Sabbath of the Vision) before the 9th of Ab and Shabbat Nachamu (Sabbath of Consolation), directly after the 9th of Ab, take their names from the Haftorah read on these Sabbaths. Shab-

Sabbath Symbols, by Raymond A. Katz.

bat Shuvah (Sabbath of Repentance), appropriately occurs between the New Year and Yom Kippur.

On Sabbath afternoon, during the summer months, chapters from the **Ethics of the Fathers*** (Pirke Avot) are studied and discussed. Similarly, a special group of psalms, beginning with **Borki Nafshi,** are recited in the winter time.   H.L.

SABORAIM (literally, "clarifiers"). Teachers and scholars who were active about the 6th century C.E. and succeeded the Amoriam **(see AMORA*)** in clarifying the laws of the Babylonian Talmud.

Spice container. Frankfort-on-the-Main, 1550.

SACHS, NELLY (1891-1970). German-Jewish poetess. Born in Berlin, she went to Sweden with her mother in 1940 as a refugee from Nazism. Her first published work, a volume of stories and legends, appeared in 1921. From 1929-33 her verses were published in various German and German-Jewish newspapers. In Sweden she first earned her living by translating Swedish poetry into German. In her writings (all in German), she portrays in a mystical, descriptive style the sorrows of the Jewish people, its mission and its survival. In 1966 she shared the Nobel Prize for Literature with S.J. Agnon.* In the award citation, her works were described as "a testimony to Jewish destiny in times that were inhuman...Her lyrics and plays are...works of forgiveness, deliverance and peace."   G.H.

SACRIFICES. Offerings to a deity. All ancient people offered sacrifices to their gods. Some sacrifices were tendered in thanksgiving for a rich harvest, for a victory in battle, or other happy events. Some were offered in times of trouble, to appease the deity when he was thought to be angry. Others symbolized the bond between a people, a tribe, or a clan and its god. The Israelites, in Biblical times, offered up cattle, sheep, goats, doves, and farm products chiefly as a symbol of

their loyalty to God. At first such offerings could be made anywhere. Later, they were permitted only at the Holy Temple* in Jerusalem,* where priests ceremoniously slaughtered the sacrificial animals on behalf of the entire people.. The ritual was prescribed in great detail. There were "regular" sacrifices offered each morning and evening, with "additional" offerings on Sabbaths* and holidays. From these and the services accompanying them there evolved the daily morning, afternoon, evening, and holiday services that have been recited at synagogues since the destruction of the Temple. In addition, there were personal sacrifices, offered after a sin had been committed and expiated, as well as thanksgiving offerings after a vow had been fulfilled. Prophets like Amos* and Jeremiah* spoke out against the sacrificial cult. They were not opposed to the idea of sacrifices so much as to the fact that men thought they could fulfill their obligations to God by material offerings rather than by purity of heart and action. Although Jews have not offered sacrifices since the destruction of the Second Temple, Orthodox Jews have always prayed that the order of sacrifices will be restored with the coming of the Messiah and the rebuilding of the Temple in Zion.   B.H.

SADDUCEES. The second largest religious and political party in Palestine during the second and first centuries, B.C.E. Its members are believed to have been the followers of the high priests, descendants of the hous of Zadok, the high priest under King Solomon.* The Sadducees recognized the Bible* as the only source of Jewish law and rejected most of the traditions and interpretations which had developed since Ezra* the Scribe. They drew their followers from the rich and aristocratic, as well as military circles. Often, the Sadducees came into conflict with the Pharisees* in religious and political matters. In opposition to the Pharisees, they supported the wars for expansion led by Johanan Hyrcanus* and Alexander Jannaeus,* as well as the policy of forcing conquered peoples to convert to Judaism. The Sadducees, as opposed to the Pharisees, did not believe in reward and punishment after death.

The numerous differences between the two parties often led to bloody clashes. Whenever the Sadducees were in power, they suppressed and persecuted the Pharisees. After the final war with the Romans, the Sadducees disappeared. The Jewish people henceforth followed the tradition of the Pharisees.

SAFED. Capital of Upper Galilee. Many Kabbalists led by R. Isaac Luria and R. Joseph Karo settled there in the 15th century. Since then there has been a settled Jewish community in Safed. A substantial part of the city was destroyed by earthquakes and ensuing epidemics in mid-19th century. In the 1948 War of Independence, after heavy fighting, the Arabs fled. Due to its beautiful mountain location Safed is today a center of art and a popular resort city. Its population in 1984 was about 17,000.

SALANTER, RABBI ISRAEL (1810-1883). Founder of an ethical movement (Musar) which spread through many of the **yeshivot** of Eastern Europe. His modesty, kindness, and generosity became legendary. He gave away most of his meager earnings to the poor. Born in a small town in Lithuania, Israel Lipkin spent his youth studying the Talmud.* He was given to reflection and was deeply concerned with self-improvement. In his later years, he was recognized as a great Talmudic authority. His modesty was proverbial and so was his generosity. His ethical philosophy was in close agreement with that of Maimonides.* Advocating participation in worldly matters, rather than isolation from them, he sought to win back to Judaism those **yeshiva** and university students who had been influenced by the Enlightenment movement. He hoped to have them return to the study of the Torah,* and observance of its laws. It is an interesting fact that Rabbi Salanter included the Hebrew translation of Benjamin Franklin's **Poor Richard's Almanac** among the list of ethical books recommended to his students.

SALK, JONAS EDWARD (1914-   ). Medical researcher, educator. The son of a garment center worker, Salk was born in New York. Studious and an avid reader from earliest childhood, he took his B.S. degree at the College of the City of New York, and went on to study medicine at the New York University College of Medicine, assisted by fellowships in chemistry and experimental surgery. In June 1939, Salk received his M.D. degree, and interned for two years at Mount Sinai Hospital. From 1942 to 1947 he experimented with influenza vaccines at the University of Michigan as a National Research Council Fellow in epidemiology, and later as Assistant Professor in the University's School of Public Health. In 1947 he joined the staff of the University of Pittsburgh as director of the Virus Research Laboratory of the School of Medicine. While continuing his work on influenza, he became interested in finding a way to prevent poliomyelitis. He developed the Salk vaccine, made by cultivating three strains of the "polio" virus separately in monkey tissue. Thanks in large measure to the Salk vaccine the dreaded "infantile paralysis" has largely become a thing of the past.

Jonas E. Salk   Courtesy University of Pittsburgh.

SALOME ALEXANDRA. Queen of Judea, who ruled from 76 to 67 B.C.E. On his death bed, Salome's husband, the Hasmonean King Alexander Jannaeus,* appointed her to succeed him on the throne. Salome Alexandra brought peace to Judea by reversing her husband's policy and favoring the Pharisees,* who were the majority party in the country. Her brother, the learned Pharisee, Simeon ben Shetah,* served as president of the Sanhedrin,* the legislative-judicial body of the people.

SALOMON, HAYM (c. 1740-1785). American Revolutionary banker. Salomon, a native of Poland,* described himself as "Broker to the Office of Finance"; he purchased and sold on commission bank stock and bills of exchange of European governments. During the American Revolution, he provisioned the troops of General Washington, often at personal cost. Salomon lent money to many impoverished members of the Continental Congress, including James Madison. He played an important role in the crucial years of the Revolutionary War, negotiating war subsidies from France and Holland. Salomon was captured as a spy and imprisoned by the British in New York, but managed to escape to Philadelphia, where his wife and child joined him.

SAMARIA. The capital, and another name for, the northern Kingdom of Israel. (**See also** ISRAEL.)

SAMARITANS. The smallest religious sect in the world. There are about 400 Samaritans, most of whom live in Nablus (Shechem), an Arab town in the West Bank;* others are settled in the vicinity of Tel Aviv-Jaffa.

The Samaritans are historically related to the Jewish people. When the Israelite kingdom of Samaria fell in 722 B.C.E., the Assyrian conquerors exiled most of the Israelites to Babylonia.* Samaria was then resettled by members of varied Semitic groups. The few re-

Amram ben-Yitzhak HaCohen, High Priest of the Samaritans in Israel.

Failing in their plans to join or harm the Jews, the Samaritans chose Mount Gerizim, near Nablus, as their holy place, and later established a shrine there. Gerizim became the religious center of the sect. To the Ten Commandments* the Samaritans added another, proclaiming the sanctity of Mount Gerizim.

During the reign of the Maccabees,* the feud between the Jews and Samaritans became intense. At the end of the second century B.C.E., the Hasmonean king Johanan Hyrcanus, captured Samaria and destroyed its temple on Mount Gerizim. It was rebuilt in 56 B.C.E. by Gabinus, goveror of Syria.

The Samaritans shared the bitter lot of the Jews under the rule of the Roman emperors Vespasian (r. 79-81 C.E.) and Hadrian (r. 117-138 C.E.). When Palestine came under the rule of the Byzantine kings, the persecutions continued. The Samaritan temple on Mount Gerizim was again destroyed. Twenty thousand Samaritans perished in a revolt against the Byzantine ruler, Justinian I, in 572. His successor deprived them of all rights and forced many of them to embrace the Christian faith. The Arab conquest of Palestine in the seventh century and the short reign of the Crusaders* in the eleventh and twelfth centuries saw the further dwindling of their numbers. After four hundred years of Turkish rule (1516-1917), the sect had disappeared almost completely. By the end of World War I, only 200 Samaritans remained.

To this day, the Samaritans adhere strictly to the ancient traditions of their religion. Their yearly Passover* ceremonial of the sacrifice of the Paschal lamb on Mount Gerizim is a colorful event reminiscent of an old Jewish custom practiced in Jerusalem. The Samaritan Bible is written in the old Hebrew script and differs slightly from the traditional Jewish version. Like the Jews, the Samaritans recognize the 613 laws of the Five Books of Moses. They also accept the Book of Joshua,* but they reject the writings of the prophets and the oral law (Talmud*). The sanctity of Mount Gerizim is another point of departure from Jewish tradition. The Samaritans believe that the patriarchs* are buried in this mountain and that the sacrifice of Isaac* took place upon it. They also believe in the coming of the Messiah, who will rebuild the Temple on Mount Gerizim and proclaim the glory of the **Shomrim,** or "the observant," as the Samaritans call themselves.

The Samaritans possess a modest literature that includes a few works of Biblical commentary, law, theology, and history. Some of their writings date back to the fourth century. At the head of the Samaritan community stands the High Priest, whom they believe to be a descendant of Aaron,* brother of Moses.* Yitzhak Ben-Zvi,* Israel's

maining Israelites intermarried with the heathen settlers. Out of this union grew the new Samaritan sect. The Samaritans were anxious to join the Jewish group. However, conflict developed. The Jews who returned to Palestine from Babylonian captivity (537 B.C.E.) refused to accept the offer of the Samaritans to help rebuild the Temple in Jerusalem because of the differences in religious practice and belief between the two groups (the Samaritans strictly obeyed the laws of the Five Books of Moses,* but rejected the Prophets and sacred traditions of the Babylonian exiles).

Smarting at this refusal of cooperation, the Samaritans informed the Persian King Artaxerxes I that the Jews were plotting a rebellion against him. In the days of Nehemiah,* the Samaritans joined the "Arabians, Ammonites, and Ashdodites" in molesting the exiles as they built a wall around Jerusalem.

Sacrificial lamb carried by a Samaritan.

second president, wrote extensively on the Samaritans. His studies are collected in **The Book of the Samaritans.** H.L.

SAMBATYON. Legendary river whose turbulent waters did not flow on the Sabbath.* Jewish and non-Jewish writers have described similar rivers, which they have located variously, in Ethiopia, India,* and near the Caspian Sea. The Sambatyon, an actual river located in Syria,* has been pointed to as possibly connected with the fabled stream. The most famous of the tales about the Sambatyon is that of the ninth-century traveler, Eldad Hadani. He tells of visiting the Ten Lost Tribes* of Israel who dwelled on the banks of the river.

SAMSON. Son of Manoah of the tribe of Dan,* and one of the Judges* of Israel. Samson was marvelously strong, and three chapters of the Biblical Book of Judges,* are full of his great deeds, his downfall, and heroic death. According to the Bible,* Samson was a Nazirite*—a consecrated man whose supernatural strength lay in his unshorn hair. Single-handed, he fought the Philistines,* until he was trapped by Delilah, a Philistine woman. Shorn of his hair and blinded, he was imprisoned in Gaza. During one of the festivals in honor of their fish-god Dagon, the Philistines had Samson brought into their temple to "make sport before them" (Judges 16:25). By that time his hair had grown back and, with it, his strength had returned. Standing between two pillars that supported the roof of the temple, the blinded giant prayed; then, crying, "Let my soul perish with the Philistines!," he grasped the two pillars, bent them, and brought the roof crashing down upon himself and his tormentors.

SAMUEL (ca. 1100-1020 B.C.E.). Prophet and priest. He succeeded the Judges* as a leader of the people. In his old age the people asked him to select a king to rule over them and to lead them in battle. Samuel warned them against a monarchy, which would limit their freedom. When the people insisted, he chose Saul* and anointed him king. The two Books of Samuel in the Bible describe the founding of the Kingdom of Israel* and the reigns of Saul and David.*

SAMUEL HA-NAGID (993-1055). Statesman, poet, Talmudic scholar and grammarian. Born in Cordova, Spain,* he was forced by anti-Jewish persecution to flee to Malaga, where he studied both Jewish and secular subjects.

Samuel's learning and wisdom attracted the attention of the vizier, Abu-al-Kasim, who appointed Samuel his confidential secretary. On the vizier's death, Samuel became counselor and prime minister to the king of Granada. For thirty years, he had charge of the political, financial, and military affairs of the kingdom. The kingdom of Granada prospered, due largely to Samuel's discretion and sagacity.

While holding high political office, Samuel was also the spiritual leader, or **Nagid,** of the Jewish community. He supported men of letters and institutions of learning, not only in Spain, but also in Egypt,* Babylonia* and other Jewish settlements. He found the time to teach the Talmud,* as well as to write works of grammar. Samuel Ha-Nagid opened the golden era of Hebrew poetry in Spain. He was the first to write secular poetry—his unique war poems describe military campaigns vividly.

SAMUEL, MAURICE (1895-1972). Author, translator and lecturer. Born in Rumania, Samuel was educated in England and came to the United States in 1914. After serving in the American Army during the First World War, he embarked on a distinguished literary career. An ardent advocate of Zionism,* he wrote books on Israel including **What Happened in Palestine** and **Harvest in the Desert.** During the 1920's, **You Gentiles** examined the problems of the Jew in the modern world, while several studies in the 1930's examined the burning question of anti-Semitism* and its sources. In **The Great Hatred** (1940) the writer reached the conclusion that Jews are hated because they taught the world a system of morality which men have accepted as just, but have been unable to live up to. Instead of hating themselves for this failure, the anti-Semites have transferred their hatred to the people who created the moral system so difficult to obey.

In addition to a number of novels, Samuel produced many excellent translations from Yiddish, Hebrew, and German. These include most of the poetry of Chaim Nahman Bialik* and several novels by Sholem Asch.* His most popular and delightful books are probably **The World of Sholom Aleichem** and **Prince of the Ghetto.** These works combine history and biography with interpretive selections from the works of Sholom Aleichem* and Peretz.* In this way, Samuel recreated the atmosphere of these two Yiddish writers, and helped the American reader to understand the humor and pathos of works whose qualities are almost impossible to convey in simple translation. In **The Gentleman and the Jew** (1950), Maurice Samuel contrasted the pagan and Jewish ideals embodied in Western civilization. His **Certain People of the Book** (1955), retold the tales of a number of Biblical characters with a fresh enlightening approach. **The Professor and the Fossil** (1956) is an analysis and refutation of Arnold Toynbee's views of Judaism and Jewish history. **Little Did I Know** (1963) is an autobiographical work. In 1966 he published **Blood Accusation.** In these books, as in all volumes from his pen, Maurice Samuel delighted the reader with wit and humor, revealing analysis and brilliance of style.

B.H.

Viscount Herbert Samuel

SAMUEL, VISCOUNT HERBERT LOUIS

(1870-1963). British statesman. Born in Liverpool and educated at Oxford, Herbert Samuel turned to politics as a profession. He was elected to Parliament in 1902, became a member of the British Cabinet in 1909, Secretary of State for Home Affairs in 1916. From 1931 to 1935, he served as leader of the Liberal Party in the House of Commons. He was knighted and in 1937, he was made a viscount as a reward for his public services.

Herbert Samuel's connection with Zionism* began in the early stages of the First World War. He aided in the preliminary negotiations between the Zionist leaders and the British government which resulted in the Balfour Declaration.* In 1920 he was appointed first High Commissioner of Palestine* under the British Mandate. During Samuel's five years in this office, his efforts to serve as an impartial British administrator failed to please either the Arabs or the Jews. While appointing administrative officials in sympathy with the Balfour Declaration, he left others in office who were anti-Zionist, anti-Jewish, and whose very presence served to encourage Arab disorder and intransigence. Herbert Samuel's proclamation of an amnesty set free a number of prisoners arrested during Arab attacks on Jews, thus giving freedom to attackers and defenders alike. Hajj Amin El-Husseini, one of the Arab notables who led in stirring up these attacks, was later appointed by Samuel to the office of Mufti, the highest religious office of the Muslim community in Palestine. Thereafter, Husseini used all his powers to instigate anti-Jewish and anti-British strife and violence in the country.

Nevertheless, Herbert Samuel's Zionist sympathies were evident in his speech delivered when he participated in the opening of the Hebrew University* on Mount Scopus in 1925. These sympathies led him to become a member of the enlarged Jewish Agency for Palestine* when it was formed in 1929. An observant Jew, a liberal in politics, and a philosopher, Samuel was a member of the British Institute of Philosophy, and the author of such books as **Philosophy and the Ordinary Man,** and **Liberalism; Its Principles and Proposals.**

SANHEDRIN.

The name, originally Greek, applied to the higher courts of law which in the latter period of the Second Temple administered justice in Palestine according to the Mosaic law. It dealt with serious cases, both criminal and capital. Sanhedrin is also the name of a tractate of the Talmud* which deals fully with the composition, powers, and functions of the court.

Two types of Sanhedrin existed side by side: the Great Sanhedrin with seventy-one members, and several lesser ones with twenty-three. According to tradition, both were instituted by Moses, but the first reference to a functioning Sanhedrin is from 57 B.C.E. Some scholars maintain there was also a Sanhedrin with more political powers. The president was called the **nasi,** and his deputy, the **ab bet din,** and the expert or specialist on any given case, the **mufla.** The Great Sanhedrin met in the Chamber of Hewn Stone in the Temple of Jerusalem. To be valid, decisions required a majority of the votes. The Sanhedrin organized in Yavneh* after the destruction of the Second Temple was purely religious in character.

SANHEDRIN NAPOLEONIC. See FRANCE.

SAN NICANDRO. An obscure village in southern

Italy,* where Donato Manduzio, one of the few villagers who could read, happened across an Italian version of the Jewish Bible.* Manduzio became convinced that Judaism was the only true faith, and he converted most of the villagers. When the Allies entered Italy during the Second World War, some of the Jews from Palestine* serving in the British Army passed through San Nicandro. From them the villagers learned that the Jewish people still exist, and that many Jews have returned to their ancestral home. The people of San Nicandro decided to follow; after the war they migrated to Palestine, although Donato himself died on the eve of their departure.

SAPIR, JACOB HA-LEVI (1822-1885). Famous traveler and explorer. Sapir was the first Jew in modern times to rediscover the Yemenite* Jewish communities. He came to Jerusalem* from Lithuania* at the age of ten. Sapir studied at **yeshivot** in Jerusalem, and was sent to the Oriental countries to obtain support for the rabbinical institutions of Palestine. In the course of his journeys, Sapir visited Egypt,* Yemen,* India,* China* and Australia.* His two-volume Hebrew work, **Even Sapir,** contains valuable information about the conditions, history and customs of the Jews in Yemen and other distant Jewish settlements. One of his grandsons, Joseph Sapir, became Minister of the Interior in the State of Israel.*

SAPIR, PINHAS (1909-1975). Israeli Cabinet Member and public official. Born in Poland, he came to Palestine* in 1929 and early became active in the labor movement there. In February, 1948 he was put in charge of the quartermaster general's branch of Haganah.* Between 1948 and 1968, he served variously as Director General of the Ministry of Defense, Director General of the Ministry of Finance, Minister of Commerce and Industry and Minister of Finance. In 1968 he became secretary general of the Mapai party while serving in the Cabinet as Minister without Portfolio. In 1974 he became chairman of the Executive of the Jewish Agency.

SARAH. Wife of the Patriarch Abraham,* mother of the Patriarch Isaac.*

SASSOON. A family of merchants, industrialists, and public servants. David Sassoon (1793-1864), founder of the "Sassoon dynasty," was descended from an old Baghdad Jewish family. Forced to flee his birthplace in 1829, David settled in Bombay, India, where he founded a textile firm which came to dominate the Indian cotton industry. With his eight sons he extended his trading empire to China,* Japan,* and Central Asia. David was a pillar of the Bombay Jewish community and fabled for both his charity and his piety. At David's death, Abdullah (later Albert) Sassoon (1817-1897), his eldest son, assumed control of the family business. After founding Bombay's first great textile mills, Albert moved the headquarters of the firm to London.* There, together with his brothers, Reuben (1835-1905) and Arthur (1840-1912), Albert figured prominently in London society, becoming an intimate of the Prince of Wales (later Edward VII). In 1890, Albert was made first Baronet of Kensington-Gore.

Later generations of the Sassoons tended to loosen their ties with Judaism (except for one branch, which has remained strictly Orthodox), as well as to lose interest in the family business. The Sassoons achieved eminence in politics, the army, and the arts. A number married into English nobility. Among the best known of the later Sassoons were: Siegfried Sassoon (1886-   ), who gained a reputation as a poet before World War I; Rachel Sassoon Beer (1858-1927), who owned and edited two rival London newspapers at once; and Philip Sassoon (1888-1939), who rose to a high place in government.

SAUL (11th century B.C.E.). First king of Israel.* Youngest son of Kish the Benjaminite, Saul was a modest shepherd lad when the prophet Samuel annointed him as king. He defeated the Ammonites and fought successfully against the Philistines,* Moabites, Arameans, and Amalekites.* Saul's dispute with the prophet Samuel followed his defeat of the Amalekites. The prophet's public rebuke depressed the king and tragic melancholia—the Biblical "evil spirit"—clouded his mind. David,* the lad brought to soothe Saul with his music, aroused the king's suspicion, and had to flee for his life. Saul's last battle was with the Philistines in the Plain of Jezreel. Badly defeated,

Samuel anointing Saul king of Israel. "Then Samuel took the vial of oil and poured it upon his head..." (First Samuel, 10:1)

his sons slain by the enemy, he fell upon his sword and killed himself (I Samuel 8-31). **(See also DAVID.)**

SCHAPIRA, HERMANN (Zevi Hirsch) (1840-1898). Mathematician and Zionist. A frail man with a remarkable mind, Hermann Schapira, born in Russia, had turned away from a career in business to become a professor of mathematics at the University of Heidelberg. He was an accomplished Hebrew scholar and a writer for Hebrew journals. One of the early pioneers in the Zionist movement, he founded, in Heidelberg, the first Zionist society in Germany.* Schapira is best remembered as the originator of the Jewish National Fund* (Keren Kayemet le-Israel). He proposed its creation for the first time at the Hoveve Zion* Conference in Kattowitz (1884). He had worked out the basis of this plan for the purchase of land in Palestine* for the Jews through small donations from the Jewish masses. He presented this proposal again at the first Zionist Congress* in 1897, but it was not adopted till the fifth congress, in 1901—three years after Schapira's death. Another of his proposals made at the first congress was adopted at the eleventh (1913), the last congress before World War I began: it was then decided to proceed immediately with the creation of a Hebrew University* in Jerusalem.* The poet Bialik* reminded the delegates that this vision of a new house of learning in Zion came from the mind of the mathematician Hermann Schapira.

SCHATZ, BORIS (1866-1932). Painter and sculptor born in Lithuania. Schatz's works are found in many European and American museums. His statue of Matthew, the Hasmonean, is his best known work in Israel. In Paris, he assisted the great Russian sculptor, Mark Antokolsky,* and in Sofia he helped found the Academy of Fine Arts. Schatz's crowning achievement was founding, in 1906, of the Bezalel Museum* and School of Art,* in Jerusalem.*

SCHECHTER, SOLOMON (1847-1915). Scholar, founder of American Conservative Judaism. Schecter's childhood was spent in a small town in the Carpathian mountains. At the age of ten, fearing his parents would not let him leave home to study, he ran away to the **yeshiva*** of a neighboring town. Later he studied in Vienna and Berlin, and eventually came to England.* There, the wealth of Hebrew manuscripts at the British Museum in London and at the Bodleian Library of Oxford absorbed him for years. For twelve years, he taught at Cambridge University, where he was elected Reader in Rabbinics. He became Professor of Hebrew at the University

College of London in 1899. In 1896 Schechter came upon a large part of the original Hebrew of the Book of Ben Sira;* this discovery led him to visit the Cairo Genizah, a literary "cemetery" for worn-out sacred books and manuscripts. He investigated the many thousands of fragments in the Genizah, brought them back to Cambridge, and spent years sorting and studying this great scholarly treasure. The writings he published as a result of these studies brought him worldwide fame among scholars. In 1902, Schechter came to the United States to serve as president of the Jewish Theological Seminary of America.* During the fifteen years of his presidency he reorganized the Seminary and enlarged its scope. His polished English essays, particularly the three-volume **Studies in Judaism,** were widely read. Scholarly writing, brilliant lecturing, clever conversation, and a gift for coining witty phrases, won him many friends and a wide, appreciative public. N.B-A.

"Solomon Schecter," painting by C. Mielziner.

SCHIFF, JACOB HENRY (1847-1920). Financier and philanthropist. Schiff came to the United States in 1865, after receiving his general and Jewish education at the school of Samson Raphael Hirsch,* in Frankfurt, Germany, where his family had lived since the fourteenth century. He received his early business training in his father's Frankfurt brokerage house. In 1885 he became head of Kuhn, Loeb, and Co., which had a significant share in financing the expansion of railroads in the United States. Deeply hostile to Tsarist Russia* for mistreating its Jews, he consistently refused to help it obtain loans, foregoing opportunities for great profit. He was one of the founders of the American Jewish Committee* (1906) and a leader in its successful effort, in 1911, to have the United States-Russia commercial treaty abrogated because Russia discriminated against holders of United States passports. The range of his philanthropies, Jewish and nonsectarian, was immense. A Reform Jew, he nevertheless retained much of the traditional piety he had learned in his childhood, and generously supported the religious, educational, and scholarly work of all branches of Judaism. He was opposed to Zionism* insofar as it was nationalist and secularist, but he felt that Palestine* was needed as a refuge and as a spiritual and cultural center. Schiff supported educational institutions in Palestine, donating $100,000 toward the founding of the Technion* (the Haifa* Institute of Technology).

SCHÖNBERG, ARNOLD (1874-1951). Composer. One of the masters of modern music, Schönberg gained international acclaim early in Austria* and Germany* with his **Verklärte Nacht,** for strings, and the **Gurrelieder.** In the years preceding the First World War he evolved his controversial "twelve-tone principle," a theory of composition which abandoned the harmonic tonality of traditional western music. His compositions on Jewish themes include **Kol Nidre,** in the twelve-tone system; **A Survivor of the Warsaw Ghetto,** a cantata for solo, chorus and orchestra; **Moses and Aaron,** an opera; and **Die Jakobsleiter,** an unfinished oratorio. Schönberg was a teacher of genius as well as a composer and conductor. Fleeing Nazi persecution in 1934, he settled in the United States, where he was teaching at the University of California at the time of his death.

SCRIPTURE OR SCRIPTURES. (From the Latin, meaning "writing.") The Bible* came to be called the Sacred Scriptures. (**See** BIBLE.)

SEDER. See PASSOVER.

SEFIRAH. See OMER.

SEFIROT. See KABBALAH.

SELIHOT (Hebrew, meaning "forgiveness"). Prayers requesting God to pardon our sins and end our sufferings. The thousands of **selihot** were written mainly between the seventh and seventeenth centuries. Well-known writers such as Judah Ha-Levi,* Solomon ibn-Gabirol,* and Rashi,* as well as numerous anonymous poets, produced their fervent **selihot**, many bearing acrostics with the author's name. Many of the **selihot** have been incorporated into the synagogue services, particularly those of the High Holy Days.

SEMIKHAH (from the Hebrew, meaning, "laying on of hands"). The act of ordination* of a religious leader, originally performed by the ordainer's placing his hands upon the person to be ordained, probably in emulation of the manner in which Moses* ordained Joshua* (Num. 27: 22-23).

Gradually, the ceremony of the laying on of hands was abolished, and by the second century B.C.E., religious leaders were ordained simply by being awarded the titile "rabbi."

Any ordained rabbi is empowered to confer the rabbinate upon a worthy disciple by ordination. This practice has persisted in Orthodox Jewry to our day, although it has largely been replaced by institutional ordination, namely through the award of an ordination certificate by a recognized rabbinical school. In the United States today, one may be ordained as a rabbi in Orthodox Judaism by one of the numerous **yeshivot** (theological colleges) or by Yeshiva University;* in Conservative Judaism, by the Jewish Theological Seminary of America,* and in Reform Judaism, by the Hebrew Union College-Jewish Institute of Religion.*

A traditional Semikhah vests the ordained rabbi with the authority of rendering decisions in ritual matters, and in monetary disputes.

Hannah Senesch

SENESCH (SZENES) HANNAH (1921-1944). Born in Budapest, she was a high-spirited girl and a gifted poetess. At eighteen she came to Palestine, studied at the Nahalal Agricultural School, then joined the Sdoth Yam kibbutz, near Caesarea. In 1943, Hannah Senesch joined the gallant band of parachutists from Palestine* who jumped into Nazi occupied Europe on rescue missions. She was the first to cross into Hungary* from Yugoslavia,* where she landed and fought with the partisans. She was captured, tortured, and executed, at the age of twenty-three. Her poem, **"Blessed Is The Match,"** which she wrote in Yugoslavia, has been set to music.

SEPHARDIM (Hebrew, meaning "Spaniards"). Jews of Spanish and Portuguese origin. The customs, rituals, synagogue services, and Hebrew pronunciation of the Sephardim differ from those of the Ashkenazim*—the Jews of Germany and Eastern Europe. Expelled from Spain* by the Inquisition* of 1492, the Sephardim were scattered throughout the Medi erranean world, along the north coast of Africa, the Turkish Empire, and the Balkans. Wherever they went, they established the Sephardic ways and rituals. The Marranos,* or secret Jews, transported their customs to the New World. When Zionists began to migrate to Palestine at the close of the nineteenth century, they adopted the Sephardic pronunciation of Hebrew for their daily use.

SEPTUAGINT (Latin, meaning "seventy"). Greek translation of the Bible* made between 250 and 100 B.C.E. According to tradition, the translation was made in Alexandria* at the request of the ruler, Ptolemy Philadelphus, by seventy-two scholars. Working individually, they are said to have produced identical translations in seventy-two days. The Septuagint was the first translation of the Bible, and it made the Scriptures accessible to large numbers of Jews and Gentiles alike.

Because the Septuagint was translated from Hebrew texts now lost, Biblical scholars have found it invaluable in comparing translations, as an aid in the recovery of a better Hebrew text, and in interpreting difficult Hebrew passages.

SERENI, ENZO (1905-1944). Scholar, author, pioneer. Born in Rome,* son of the physician to King Victor Emmanuel III, Sereni abandoned a brilliant intellectual career to settle in Palestine* in 1926. He was the founder and moving spirit of the settlement of Givat Brenner. During World War II, Sereni organized a group of Jewish parachutists to jump into enemy territories on Jewish rescue missions. Although nearly forty, he joined the group, was caught, and was executed in Dachau in 1944.

SHAATNEZ. A fabric mixture of wool and linen. The Bible (Lev. 19:19) forbids the wearing of garments made of such compositions although the material may be used for other purposes. This prohibition follows the general laws forbidding two other kinds of mixtures: the cross-breeding of different species of animals, and the planting together of different varieties of seeds.

SHABAZI, SHALOM. (Seventeenth Century) Yemenite poet and. Kabbalist. He wrote close to 5,000 poems and songs in Hebrew and Arabic. Shabazi became almost a legendary figure, and is one of the most beloved poets of the Yemenite Jews. His poems are included in the festival and holiday liturgy of the Yemenites. A street in Tel Aviv* is named in his honor.

SHADKHAN. (From the Hebrew, meaning "mediator," or "go-between.") The **shadkhan** was a matchmaker employed by parents to arrange their children's marriages. The **shadkhan's** profession attained importance in Jewish life in the early Middle Ages. His legal position was regulated by the rabbis, and he is already mentioned in the Talmud.* Piety, modesty, and the early age of marriage among Jews tended to preserve the **shadkhan** as a go-between until recent times. In modern Yiddish and Hebrew literature,* as well as in folk stories, he is usually pictured as a ne'er-do-well, sometimes funny, sometimes downright ridiculous.

SHALOSH SEUDOT. See SABBATH.

SHAMIR, YITZHAK (1915-   ). Israel's seventh prime minister, minister of foreign affairs, Speaker of the Knesset. Born in Ruzinoy, Poland, Shamir immigrated to Palestine in 1935 and studied at the Hebrew University. He served in the Irgun Z'vai L'umi* and the Stern Group,* was arrested twice by the British, but escaped. From 1955 to 1965, he served in the Mossad, Israel's intelligence service, and was active on behalf of Soviet Jewry. In 1970, Shamir joined the Herut movement and chaired its Executive Committee in 1975 and 1977. He has served on the committees for defense, foreign affairs, and state control. In 1980 and 1981, he was minister of foreign affairs and became prime minister on October 10, 1983, following Menahem Begin's resignation.   G.W.

SHAMMAI. Talmudic scholar of the first century, B.C.E. He was the contemporary and rival of Hillel* and founder of a school named after him. Hillel was president of the Sanhedrin;* Shammai, the vice-president. The Talmud* records a number of differences of opinion between Hillel and Shammai. In most instances, Shammai and his followers were more strict in their interpretation of the law. The opinions of the School of Hillel were accepted by the sages. The stories about Shammai reveal an inflexible personality. But Shammai also preached friendliness; one of his favorite sayings was: "Welcome every man with a friendly face." Shammai and Hillel were the last of the "pairs" **(zugot)** of scholars whose teachings formed the basis of the Talmud.*

SHAPIRA, MOSHE (1902-1970). Leader of the Hapoel Hamizrachi party in Israel, member of the cabinet, was born in Grodno, Lithuania, educated at the **yeshiva** there and at the Hildesheimer Seminar of Berlin. He came to Palestine in 1925. He was a delegate to the Zionist congresses and director of the Aliyah* in the fateful years 1935-1948. From 1948 to 1953 and again in 1958 he was Minister of Internal Affairs and of Health in Israel; in 1950-1952 he was minister of Internal Affairs and of Religion. From 1953 to 1958 he served as Minister of Religious Affairs and Social Welfare. In 1967 he was Minister of Interior. He was a member of Knesset from 1949 and the leader of the Hapoel Hamizrachi faction.

SHARETT, MOSHE (1894-1965). Zionist and Israeli leader. Moshe Shertok was brought by his family to Palestine* in 1906. They settled in a village near the town of Ramle. Young Shertok (who later changed his name to Sharett) was given the opportunity to study the language, customs, and way of life of the Arabs in this village. After graduating from Herzliah* High School in 1913, he went to Istanbul, Turkey,* to study law. Sharett mastered a number of languages, which later served him in good stead in his political work. Besides Hebrew, his mother tongue, he spoke and wrote fluently in Arabic, Turkish, German, French, and English.

During the First World War, Sharett served as an officer in the Turkish army. Between the two World Wars, he took part in Zionist political work. For five years he lived in England,* where he continued with his studies and helped Chaim Weizmann* as an expert in Arab affairs. He also represented the Histadrut,* the Palestine Jewish Workers' Union at the annual British Labor conferences, winning their support of the Zionist cause.

Sharett returned to Palestine in 1924, and became a member of the staff of the daily newspaper **Davar,** organ of the Histadrut. During World War II he shared in the political work that led to the establishment of the Jewish Brigade,* which fought the Nazis and played an important part in saving and bringing the remnants of the Nazi victims to Palestine. From 1946 until the establishment of Israel in 1948, Sharett did intensive work in the United States. In the first Israel cabinet, Sharett became Minister of Foreign Affairs, and from 1954 to 1955, he served also as Prime Minister. In the middle of 1956, Sharett resigned from his post as Foreign Minister, but remained a member of the Knesset. In 1962 he was named chairman of the executive of the World Zionist General Council.

SHAS. Abbreviation of **shishah sedarim**—six "orders," or divisions, of the Mishnah. Term applied to the Talmud.*

SHAVUOT. Also known as the Feast of Weeks, it falls on the sixth day of Sivan,* just seven weeks after Passover.* The three days before Shavuot are called the "Three Days of Limitation" or "Preparation," for the people of Israel had to purify themselves for a period of three days in order to be ready to receive the Law from Mount Sinai. One of the pilgrimage festivals, Shavuot is both **Hag ha-Bikkurim** ("Holiday of the First Fruits") and **Zeman Matan Toratenu** ("The Time of the Giving of Our Torah.") In Biblical times,

Prime Minister Moshe Sharett and Moshe Dayan, Commander-in-Chief of the Army, accompany Mr. U Nu, Prime Minister of Burma, as they inspect a guard of honor in Israel—1955.

numbers of chapters in the Book of Psalms attributed to David. The custom is to prepare and eat dairy dishes on Shavuot. In recent times, Reform synagogues, as well as some Conservative and Orthodox congregations, have designated the day for the ceremony of confirmation* for children of Bar Mitzvah* age. The Shavuot service also includes the singing of a poem called **Akdamut.** This poem written in Aramaic,* deals with the grandeur of God, the greatness of His deeds, and the rewards that await the righteous in the world to come. Written in the eleventh century, **Akdamut** has a mystical theme, for which an inspiring melody has been composed.

SHAZAR, ZALMAN (1889-1974). Scholar, author, third President of Israel.* Born in Mir, Russia, and raised in a Hasidic environment, he attended the Academy of Jewish Sciences at Leningrad as well as the Universities of Freiburg, Strasbourg and Berlin. Shazar settled in Palestine* in 1924. He served as editor of the daily "Davar" until 1948, and was a leading organizer of Israel's labor movement.

Zalman Shazar was the first Minister of Education in Israel and introduced general compulsory education to the country. He has also held educational posts in the Jewish Agency* and World Zionist Organization.* Shazar was a man of wide-

offerings of the first fruits of tree and field were brought to the Temple.* Today, this aspect of the holiday is observed by decorating the synagogue* with green boughs. In Israel, Shavuot is marked by the ceremonial offering of the first fruits to the Jewish National Fund,* which holds the land in trust for the Jewish people. Because the Rabbis calculated that the Jews had received the Torah at Sinai on Shavuot, it was considered appropriate for children to begin their Hebrew studies on this day. **Tikkun Shavuot,** a collection of passages from the Bible* and other sacred books, is read on Shavuot night, while the Biblical Book of Ruth* is read after the morning service.

Tradition has it that David* was born and died on Shavuot. It is therefore customary to read Psalms* on the second evening of Shavuot. In Jerusalem,* many Jews make a pilgrimage to Mount Zion, on which, according to tradition, King David was buried. In some communities, the Jews light 150 candles in the synagogue, the

Zalman Shazar

ly varied interests and impressive scholarship. He was a gifted and persuasive speaker, and authored a number of scholarly works on Biblical archaelogy and messianic figures, which have been accorded wide acclaim. His portraits of men of letters and personalities in Jewish and general life and Zionism, are distinguished by a literary style, at once felicitous and richly poetic.

In May 1963, upon the death of Yitzchak Ben Zvi,* Zalman Shazar was elected third President of Israel and re-elected in March 1968.

In 1973 he was succeeded as president of Israel by Ephraim Katzir.*

SHEARITH ISRAEL CONGREGATION OF NEW YORK (Hebrew, meaning "remnant of Israel"). Organized in 1654 by the first Jewish pilgrims to come to Nieuw Amsterdam. Its founders had escaped from the Inquisition* in South America. The first Jewish congregation in what is now the United States, it has had continuous history of more than three centuries as a Sephardic* synagogue.

SHEHITAH. The slaughter of ritually pure animals according to Jewish law. The laws which govern slaughtering grew out of a verse in the Bible (Deut. 12:21), and are contained in the tractate Hullin of the Talmud.* The **shohet** ("slaughterer") is required to follow a special course of study dealing with these laws, and is permitted to practice his profession only upon receiving a certificate known as a **kabbalah.** The shohet employs a special knife called **hallaf,** which must be applied to a specific spot on the animal's neck. Before slaughtering, the shohet must examine his blade for flaws. To avoid causing the animal unnecessary pain, the shohet must follow strictly the rules for slaughtering; if he fails, the animal is ruled a **nevelah** ("carcass"), forbidden as food. After the slaughter, the shohet must subject the animal's inner organs, particularly the lungs, to a minute examination. The discovery of the slightest sign of disease is sufficient cause to forbid the consumption of the animal. The shehitah laws were intended to safeguard the health of the individual, and to avoid pain to the animal as much as possible.

SHEKEL (Hebrew meaning "weight"). The measure against which pieces of silver and gold were weighed for use as money. When Sarah died, Abraham* bought from Ephron the Hittite the Cave of Machpelah* as a family burial ground. In payment, he "weighed out...four hundred shekels of silver current with the merchant." (Gen. 33:12-16.) When Moses* took a census of the Children of Israel, God instructed that everyone was to give a tax of half a shekel as a "tribute unto the Lord" to use "for the service of the Tabernacle"* (Ex. 30:13). It is thought that as a unit of weight the shekel came to equal a little over sixteen grams. In Maccabean times, the shekel was a silver coin bearing inscriptions of the current ruler. In modern times, the first Zionist Congress* in 1897 established the payment of nominal dues called a "shekel." This payment, together with the acceptance of the Basle Program made any Jew or Jewess over eighteen years of age a member of the World Zionist Organization.* By means of the shekel, (then about 25 cents) the Congress aimed to create a world-wide democratic Zionist association. Thereafter, only those who paid the shekel were entitled to vote for delegates to world Zionist congresses.

SHEKHINAH (Hebrew, meaning "divine presence"). A term used to express the sense of God's omnipresence.

Though the **Shekhinah** is everwhere, it is the prophet and the righteous individual, the judge who pronounces true judgment, the charitable person, and the one who lives as well as believes his Judaism, are said to particularly attract the Divine Presence to themselves.

SHEMA. The declaration of faith in the unity of God, traditionally recited mornings and evenings: "Hear, O Israel, the Lord our God, the Lord is One." (Deut. 6:4-9.) **(See also** PRAYERS.)

SHEMINI ATZERET. See SUKKOT.

SHERIRA GAON (c. 900-100 C.E.). Babylonian sage who claimed descent from King David.* Sherira Gaon's scholarship commanded the respect of all Jewish communities. He headed the academy at Pumbeditha from 969 until his death. His letter to the Jewish scholars of Kairwan, North Africa, relates the origin of the Mishnah and enumerates in chronological order the scholars and leaders from the time of the Mishnah to his day. The work is of utmost importance, because it is a major source of information on eight hundred years of Jewish history.

SHIMONI, DAVID (1$886-1956). Hebrew poet. Born Shimonowitz in Bobrouisk, Russia,* he received both Talmudic and university training. When about twenty, he migrated to Palestine* and worked as a pioneer in the vineyards and orange groves of the Jewish settlements. Later he became a teacher.

Shimoni's reputation is based on his idylls of the new pioneering life in Palestine. Some of his topical and satirical poems became highly popular and were set to music.

SHIN. Twenty-first letter of the Hebrew alphabet; numerically, three hundred.

SHLONSKY, ABRAHAM (1900-1973). Hebrew poet. Born in the Ukraine, educated at the Tel Aviv Herzliah Gymnasium* and at the Sorbonne University in Paris.* Shlonsky's experiences as a pioneer in Palestine* are reflected in his poetry. He is a first-rate craftsman, whose poetry excels in

rich imagery and mastery of language and style. He has translated into Hebrew a number of works from world literature and is also the author of a humorous book of poems for children—**Alilot Miki Mahu** ("The Adventures of Miki Mahu").

SHMONEH ESREH. Eighteen Benedictions. **(See** PRAYERS.)

SHNEERSON. A family of Hasidic rabbis. Shneour Zalman (1748-1812), founder of the dynasty, was born in Liozno, White Russia, where he recieved a traditional Talmudic education. Won over to Hasidism,* he founded a movement known as Habad, which stressed Talmudic learning and the forms of Orthodox Judaism rather than the ecstatic mysticism of other types of Hasidism. Known as the Rabbi of Ladi, he drew many followers from among the conservative Jewish communities of Lithuania* and White Russia. During his lifetime, Habad had more than 100,000 adherents. Leadership of the movement, which has survived into the present, has remained with the Shneerson family. It passed from Shneour to his son, Baer (1774-1812), and then to his grandson, Menachem Mendel (1786-1866), whose direct descendants have remained the spiritual guides of Habad. Menachem Mendel's son, Samuel (1834-1883), settled in the town of Lubavitch; followers of Habad consequently call themselves Lubavitch Hasidim. The leadership passed to Samuel's son, Sholom Baer (1861-1920), whose son, Joseph Isaac (1890-1950), founded the World Habad movement in 1934. In the tradition of his ancestors, who had fought assimilation in

Shema, illuminated by Sol Nodel, from the collection of Mr. and Mrs. Bernard Goldberg, New York.

The oldest Hebrew Biblical manuscript in the Jewish National and University Library, Jerusalem. The text shows the third paragraph of the Shema (Numbers 15:37-41). Commentaries are given above and below the verses.

*The Lubavitcher Rebbe
Rabbi Menachem M. Shneerson.*

Tsarist Russia, Joseph Isaac refused to acquiesce to a Soviet order closing Jewish schools. For this refusal he was exiled from Greater Russia. In 1940, he settled in New York City;* here he conducted Habad activities and supervised the establishment of Lubavitch academies throughout North and South America.

The Lubavitcher movement, under the direction of the present Lubavitcher Rebbe, Rabbi Menachem M. Shneerson, is involved in all spheres of Jewish concern in communities throughout the world. It maintains regional offices and institutions around the globe with the primary purpose of promoting Jewish education in the spirit of Torah-true Judaism among all Jews regardless of background, to establish contact with, and to retrieve, alienated Jewish youth, and to promulgate the observance of the Torah* as a daily experience among all Jews.

SHNEUR, ZALMAN (1887-1959). Hebrew and Yiddish poet and novelist. Born in Russia,* Shneur began to write when he was barely fourteen years old. His creative talents were quick to develop, and as a youth of twenty he was already recognized as one of the most original and powerful poets in modern Jewish literature. His poetry appealed to the younger generation in its rebellion against convention. His novels, describing Jewish life in Eastern Europe, rank with the classic works of Mendele Mocher Sefarim* and Sholom Aleichem* in artistic achievement. His verse in English translation may be found in H. H. Fein's **Harvest of Jewish Verse** and in Edmond Fleg's **Jewish Anthology.** His novel, **Noah Pandre** appeared in an English translation in 1936.

Facsimile of one of Shneur's poems in his own handwriting.

SHOFAR (Hebrew for "horn" or "trumpet"). Traditionally the curved horn of a ram, the animal that Abraham* sacrificed instead of his son, Isaac.* In the Bible,* the shofar is blown to an-

nounce all important occasions. The blast of the ram's horn proclaimed the Jubilee* year, the beginning of the Sabbath,* the festivals and the New Moon.* The shofar is blown during the month of Elul* preceeding the High Holy Days as a call to repentance. It is an essential part of the Rosh ha-Shanah* services, and the Yom Kippur* day of fasting and prayer ends with the sound of the shofar.

Zalman Shneur

SHOLOM ALEICHEM (1859-1916). Pen name of the Yiddish writer and humorist Sholom Rabinowitz. Born in a small town in Ukraine, he displayed in his early childhood a remarkable talent for mimicry and caricature. Young Sholom was also endowed with keen sensitivity and an imaginative mind. While he liked best to play pranks on his elders, he nevertheless excelled in his studies. He was especially attracted to the Bible,* most of which he learned by heart. Later, he attended a government high school, and at seventeen he accepted a job as a private tutor. For some time he even served as a rabbinical functionary, and also engaged in business—until he lost all his money.

He then dedicated himself entirely to writing, to the great enrichment of Yiddish literature. In his hundreds of stories, novels, and plays, Sholom Aleichem mirrored Jewish life of the small towns in Eastern Europe. He reflected in his tales the wisdom and wit of his people and became their favorite writer. Universally admired, he was given rousing receptions on his visits to the Jewish centers in Russia.* He came to America twice, the last time shortly before the First World War broke out. It is said that a half million people came to his funeral when he died in New York* in 1916.

Sholom Aleichem

Sholom Aleichem created unforgettable types: Tevyeh, the milkman, Menachem Mendel, the luckless broker, and Motel, the cantor's son, whose escapades are especially endearing to young readers.

Sholom Aleichem has often been compared to Charles Dickens and Mark Twain. Much of his work has been translated into English; Maurice Samuel's **World of Sholom Aleichem** has distilled the flavor of the great humorist into one volume.

SHTADLAN (from the Hebrew "to attempt" or "endeavor"). A representative chosen by the Jewish community, or self-appointed, to plead the Jewish cause before governments or rulers. He was usually appointed because of his wealth, eloquence, or good relations with important personalities. In 1315, five such **shtadlanim** were chosen to negotiate with Philip the Fair of France* for the return of the Jews who had been expelled from the country. During the sixteenth century, another **shtadlan,** Josel of Rosheim, pleaded successfully with the nobility of Brandenburg, and the Jews were not expelled from that German state. The **shtadlan,** as an unofficial diplomat or lobbyist, continued to serve the Jewish people until he was replaced by modern professional organizations and democratically chosen communal leaders.

SHULHAN ARUKH. Authoritative code, prepared by Joseph Karo,* containing all the traditional rules of Jewish conduct, based on Talmudic sources and later opinions or decisions of the great rabbis.

Shulhan Arukh—title page of Amsterdam edition published in 1698.

Originally, the Shulhan Arukh was intended for young students who were not yet prepared to weigh the complex decisions of the authorities. However, the work suited so well the need for a methodical and easily accessible arrangement of the various laws that it became the most popular handbook for both scholars and laymen.

The Shulhan Arukh is divided, like its predecessor, the Arbaah Turim, into four parts: One summarizing the laws pertaining to prayers,* Sabbath,* and holidays; a second, the dietary laws,* laws of mourning and other ritual matters; a third, civil laws; and a fourth, the laws relating to marriage,* divorce, and similar matters.

The Code of Joseph Karo was accepted immediately by Sephardic* Jewry. Ashkenazic* scholars, chief among them Moses Isserles, amended, revised, and added many customs and practices current among the Ashkenazic Jewry. With the additions of Isserless and other commentaries, the Shulhan Arukh has been the most vital and influential book in Jewish religious life.

SHVADRON, SHOLOM MORDECAI BEN MOSES ("Maharsham"). (1835-1911) Rabbi in Galicia. He served as rabbi first in the town of Potok and then in Brezen. He is best known for his responsa, four volumes of which were published during his lifetime and three after his death. His rulings on Jewish law were widely accepted as authoritative and essential in coping with the practical problems of the time in which he was active. A modest and kindly man, he adhered stringently to the requirements of Jewish law but endeavored to reach as lenient decisions as possible in religious questions addressed to him.

SIDDUR (Hebrew for "order" or "arrangement"). The daily prayer book. Since prayer* in a synagogue* came to take the place of sacrifices in the Temple, after its destruction, the prayers in the Siddur were arranged to follow

Abba Hillel Silver visiting a maabara in Israel.

closely the order of sacrifices in the Temple. The three daily services are included in all daily prayer books, though some editions contain numerous additions, such as the Psalms* and the Song of Songs.* Many editions of the daily prayer books include the Sabbath* and Festival prayers, as well as the Haggadah* and **Pirke Avot** ("The Ethics of the Fathers"). The oldest of the prayers is **Shema** ("Hear, O Israel").* The **Shemoneh Esreh**—the Eighteen Benedictions—recited standing up and therefore called the **Amidah,** was drawn up by the men of the Great Assembly some time between the fifth and third centuries B.C.E. The **Amidah** is the most solemn of the daily prayers. Various confessions said by those who brought sacrifices to the Temple, and the Psalms chanted by the Levites,* also went into the making of the Siddur. The prayer book as we know it today is based on the one compiled c. 860 C.E. by Amram ben Sheshna, the Gaon of the Academy in Sura, Babylonia.* There is a slight difference in arrangement and in types of prayers between the Sephardic* version **(nusah)** and the Ashkenazic.* **(See also PRAYERS and MAHZOR.)**

SILVER, ABBA HILLEL (1893-1963). Rabbi, author, and Zionist leader. Brought to the United States from Lithuania as a child, Abba Hillel Silver rose to a position of leadership in American Zionism in the years of struggle that preceded the creation of a Jewish state. He prepared for the rabbinate at Hebrew Union College in Cincinnati.

In 1917 he took the pulpit of The Temple in Cleveland, Ohio, a post he held for the rest of his life. During the 1940's when Zionists were undecided whether to cooperate with England* or to oppose it on the question of Jewish statehood in Palestine,* Silver came to head the "activist" opposition faction. As chairman of the American Zionist Emergency Council from 1945 to 1948, and of the American Section of the Jewish Agency for Palestine,* he led the campaign that gained United States support for a Jewish State. From 1946 to 1948, Silver was also president of the Zionist Organization of America.* In 1956, he became chairman of the Bonds for Israel.* Silver's extensive writings include **Messianic Speculation in Ancient Israel** (1927), **Religion in a Changing World** (1930), and **Vision and Victory** (1949), his report on the Zionist struggle.

SIMEON. Second son of Jacob* and Leah. The tribe of Simeon settled in Canaan* in the territory south of Judah.* Eventually, the Simeonites merged with the dominant tribe of Judah.

SIMEON BEN SHETAH. President of the Sanhedrin* during the first century B.C.E. For nine prosperous years, during the reign of his sister, Queen Salome Alexandra,* Simeon was the leader of the Pharisees,* the majority party of Judea. The Pharisees interpreted the Law according to traditions handed down over the generations. They were opposed by the aristocratic Sadducees,* who insisted on a literal interpretation of the Biblical law. As president of the Sanhedrin, Simeon rid this legislative and judicial council of its Sadducee members. The reforms he introduced gained him the title of "restorer of the Law." Simeon was also known for his personal integrity. One story that has come down relates that Simeon once received a donkey as a gift from his students. As he mounted the donkey, he found a valuable jewel hung around his neck. His students were exultant: Now their master would be able to retire from active life and devote himself to his studies. Simeon, however, ordered them to return the treasure to the Arab from whom they had bought the animal. The Arab, he said, had sold them a donkey, and not a jewel. The students protested, but Simeon insisted, and the jewel was returned.

SIMEON BE YOHAI. See TANNAIM.

SIMHAT TORAH. See SUKKOT.

SINAI CAMPAIGN. See ISRAEL, STATE of, and SINAI PENINSULA.

SINAI PENINSULA. Situated between the two

Emblem of the Tribe of Simeon

continents of Asia and Africa, and between two seas—the Mediterranean and the Red Sea. Triangular in shape, the Peninsula is 11,200 square miles. The coastal route which runs through the Sinai, by way of el-Arish to Gaza, is one of the oldest in history. The Egyptians and Assyrians used it in ancient times, the former establishing military outposts along it. Alexander the Great* traveled it, and, in modern times, Napoleon used it on his march to Acre.* During World War I, the British Army, under the command of General Allenby,* reached Gaza through this road.

The Sinai Peninsula is mainly desert, sparsely settled by wandering Bedouins. Few permanent settlements exist because of the lack of rain and the shifting sand dunes. The largest town, el-Arish, has a population of 20,000, most of which engages in trade and agriculture. The Peninsula is rich in natural resources, which were already exploited by the ancient Pharaohs. Their limited exploitation today is due to poor means of communication and lack of water.

The Peninsula is famous because the Children of Israel traveled through it when they came out of Egypt* and made their way to the Holy Land. "In the third month after the Children of Israel were gone forth out of the land of Egypt, the same day came they into the wilderness of Sinai. And when they were departed from Rephidim, and were come to the wilderness of Sinai, they encamped in the wilderness, and there Israel encamped before the mount." (Exodus 19:1-2.)

The location of Mount Sinai, also known as Horeb, is uncertain. According to Christian tradition, it lies close to the southern tip of the Peninsula, and its peak is known as Jebel Musa ("Mountain of Moses"). It is an awe-inspiring mountain, deserving the name of "Mountain of God." Nearby is a place called Ein Musa, where, tradition has it, Moses* watered Jethro's flocks. However, the Biblical account of the routes taken by the Children of Israel through the desert does not support the claim that Jebel Musa is Mount Sinai. According to it, it is reasonable to identify Mount Sinai with Jebel Hilal, in the vicinity of Kadesh Barnea, in the northern part of the Peninsula. Jebel Hilal is only 890 feet tall, but it dominates the whole area. This region was the scene of the battle between the Israelites and Amalek in ancient times, Here, also, in the vicinity of Abu Agila, a pitched battle took place between the Israeli and Egyptian forces in the course of the four-day 1956 Sinai campaign. This battle ended with the occupation of the whole Peninsula by the Army of Israel.* However, Israel was forced to return the Peninsula to Egypt. In 1967, Egypt used the Peninsula as a staging area for a planned full-

Sinai Peninsula.

scale invasion of Israel, and in the Six-Day War* Israeli forces once again recaptured it. Following the Yom Kippur War,* part of the Peninsula was returned to Egypt and the rest of the Peninsula was returned to Egypt under the peace agreement signed between Israel and Egypt on March 26, 1979.

SINGER, ISAAC BASHEVIS (1904-   ). Yiddish novelist, and journalist. The younger brother of Israel Joshua Singer (the brothers are sons and grandsons of Hasidic rabbis), he was born in Poland and in 1935 he settled in New York, where he joined the staff of the **Jewish Daily Forward.** Beginning in the 1950's, eight novels, six collections of short stories, three volumes of memoirs and eight children's books written by Singer in Yiddish have appeared in English translations. His stories deal mostly with mysticism, love, and the conflict between piety and enlightenment; their settings are in Eastern Europe and the United States. His novels include **The Family Moskat, In My Father's Court, The Manor,** and **The Estate.** His short-story anthologies include **The Spinoza of Market Street, Short Friday,** and **A Crown of Feathers.** Among his children's books is **Zlateh the Goat.** His play, **Yentl,** was produced on Broadway in 1975. He was awarded the 1978 Nobel Prize* for Literature.   G.H.

SIX-DAY WAR. Contrary to Israel's hopes and the assumptions of her friends, Israel's withdrawal from the Sinai Peninsula and the Gaza

Strip after the Sinai Campaign of 1956 was not followed by the true peace. Emboldened by diplomatic and military support from the Soviet Union, Gamal Abdel Nasser, the president of Egypt, and his associates continued to declare their aim to destroy Israel. These threats were accompanied by increasingly serious Arab incursions into Israel from Syria,* Lebanon* and Jordan,* and Israeli border villages were constantly shelled by Arab artillery. In the middle of May 1967 Nasser began to move Egyptian troops and Russian-supplied armor into the Sinai Peninsula for an all-out invasion of Israel and summarily evicted the United Nations Emergency Force which had been stationed in Sinai and in the Gaza Strip. Next, Egypt closed the Straits of Tiran to all Israeli shipping and cargoes. On May 30, Nasser signed an anti-Israel pact with the Kingdom of Jordan and on June 4 with Iraq.* Surrounded by enemies and unable to obtain support from the United Nations and the friendly powers who had promised to guarantee her security, Israel had no other choice but to strike back at her enemies. On June 5, 1967, Israel destroyed most of Egypt's air force on the ground. With Egypt's air power neutralized, Israel's forces moved forward and by June 8 had reached the Suez Canal. In the meantime, Israeli troops had repulsed a Jordanian attack, and by June 7 had taken the sector of Jerusalem* that had been occupied by Jordan in 1948. For the first time since 1948, Jews were able to worship at the Western Wall. Next, Israeli forces stormed and occupied the Syrain fortifications in the Golan Heights which had posed a constant threat to Israeli border settlements. By June 11, Egypt, Jordan and Syria had agreed to a cease-fire.

SIYYUM. The formal conclusion of the writing of a Torah Scroll* or the completion of the study of a section of the Bible* or Talmud;* usually marked by a celebration. The custom is to hold a **siyyum** on the morning preceding the first day of Passover:* the purpose is to release the firstborn male from the pre-Passover fast.

SMOLENSKIN, PERETZ (1842-1885). Hebrew novelist and pioneer of Jewish national revival. He came from a poor Jewish family in White Russia. His restless spirit led him in his early youth to wander through the Jewish towns of Eastern Europe. He studied at intervals in **yeshivot,** and served as teacher, cantor and preacher. He later described his experiences in the foremost Hebrew novel of the period, **The Wanderer on the Paths of Life** which criticized the existing Jewish educational and communal system. It inspired young Jewish people to strive for radical changes in Jewish society.

A man of daring, courage and militant spirit, Smolenskin on the one hand fought for progress, advocating changes in Jewish life in conformity with modern ideals. On the other hand, he combated the assimilationist tendencies of the Haskalah,* or Enlightenment movement. In 1865, Smolenskin settled in Vienna, where he founded the Hebrew monthly **Ha-Shahar** ("The Dawn"), which he edited until his death. It was the best magazine of the period, and in it Smolenskin published most of his novels and articles.

SOKOLOW, NAHUM (1859-1936). Zionist leader, Hebrew writer and editor. Nahum Sokolow was an infant prodigy in Jewish scholarship and in the mastery of the Hebrew language. He became an authority on Jewish history and literature; at twenty-six he was editor of **Ha-Tzefirah**—the leading Hebrew journal of that time. Through his work on **Ha-Tzefirah** and through his numerous other writings, he became an outstanding leader of the Hebrew cultural revival. Yet only with the coming of Herzl* was he won over to Zionism.* He came to serve in the administration of world Zionist affairs, and there his knowledge of many languages was a great asset. When Sokolow became a member of the Zionist Executive, he came to London in* 1915 to participate in the diplomatic negotiations that resulted in the issuing of the Balfour Declaration* which stated that "His Majesty's Government view with favour the establishment in Palestine of a national home for the Jewish people." Throughout World War I, Sokolow traveled from London to Italy* and the Vatican, and then to France,* till he secured the approval of the British, Italian, and French powers for the declaration before its publication. In 1919 he led in the presentation of Zionist claims before the Peace Conference at Versailles.* When the Jewish Agency* for Palestine was created in 1929, Sokolow was elected its president. From 1931 to 1935 he was president of the World Zionist Organization.*

Throughout this active period Sokolow's literary output was enormous, in Hebrew, Yiddish, Polish, German, and English. The subject matter of his books and essays ranged from the scholarly to the journalistic, from a treatise on the philosopher Spinoza* to a history of anti-Semitism.* One of the many books he wrote was an English history of Zionism in two volumes. Sokolow, the linguist and the man of encyclopedic knowledge, was also a born diplomat, an even-tempered, dignified mediator. Because of these qualities, he served the Zionist movement as a traveling ambassador, from his first visit to America in 1912 to his tours of South Africa and the United States when he was past seventy. Perhaps the peak of his service came on February 23, 1919, when he stood before the Council of Ten at the Peace Conference. Five speakers were allotted for the Zionist claims presentation, and Sokolow was the first one. Chaim Weizmann* was the second speaker, and this is how he described Sokolow's effect on the Council of Ten: "From where I stood I could see Sokolow's face, and, without being sentimenttal, it was as if two thousand years of Jewish suffering rested on his shoulders. His quiet, dignified utterance made a very deep impression on the assembly."

N.B-A.

SOLOMON. Third king of Israel, son of David* and Bathsheba,* builder of the Temple,* poet and man of wisdom. His reign, like his name, was one of peace, and lasted about forty years (976-936 B.C.E.). Solomon secured peace on his southern borders by marrying Pharaoh's daughter, and kept the road to Ezion Gever with its copper mines safe and free. He used his alliance with King Hiram of Tyre, on his northwest border, to develop the arts of commerce and seafaring. Solomon wa a great administrator and builder. He erected the Temple in Jerusalem* and instituted its impressive services which were accompanied by singing and instrumental music. He built palaces, roads, aqueducts, and his wisdom became a by-word in history and in countless legends. However, his marriages to the daughters of neighboring kings introduced into the splendor of his rule the seeds of disruption. The price of Solomon's luxury was high taxation. His peace was earned at the cost of unrest, political conflict and the idol worship by his foreign wives. Yet Solomon's glory and his wisdom echo through the ages in the Song of Songs,* in Proverbs* and in Ecclesiastes,* the Scriptural works traditionally ascribed to him.

SOLOVEICHIK FAMILY. Talmudic scholars. Joseph Baer Soloveichik (1820-1892) and his son, Hayim (1853-1919), were considered the greatest rabbinical authorities in Russia.* The latter served for several years as head of the famous **yeshiva,** or Talmudical Academy, of Volozhin. Both held the position of rabbi in the city of Brest-Litovak (Brisk), Russia. Moses Soloveichik, son of Hayim, was dean of Talmudic studies, first at the **Tahkemoni** school in Warsaw,* Poland, and later at Yeshiva University in New York. Joseph Baer Soloveichik (1903-   ), who arrived in the United States in 1932, at present occupies the Chair previously filled by his father at Yeshiva University, and is one of the leading spirits in the religious Zionist movement in the United States.

Combining Talmudic scholarship with extensive secular knowledge (he received his doctorate in philosophy at the University of Berlin), he is considered one of the most brilliant and stimulating Orthodox teachers and lecturers. Rabbi Soloveichik is head of two congregations, one in Boston and one in New York.* He served as chairman of the Law Commission of the Rabbinical Council, and contributes to scholarly and rabbinical journals.

SONCINO. Small Italian town in which Israel Nathan Soncino, a learned physician, set up his noted printing press in 1483. His descendants carried on his work. The name was adopted by the Soncino Gesellschaft in Berlin, 1925, and by the Soncino Press of London,* publishers of the English Talmud and many more books of Jewish scholarly interest.

SONG OF SONGS. The first of the five scrolls in the Bible,* it is read in the synagogue service on Passover.* According to tradition, King Solomon* is the author of this series of beautiful love poems traditionally interpreted as describing symbolically God's love of Israel.

SOUTH AFRICA, REBUBIC OF. A federated republic. Its 118,000 Jews make up (1977) less than 3 per cent of a total "European" population of 4,000,000. South Africa is inhabited by another 22,500,000 Africans and Asians who play little or no part in the government of the country.

South Africa was discovered and claimed for Portugal,* in 1497, by Vasco da Gama during his voyage around the Cape of Good Hope. Holland gained control of the area in 1625. Only when England* took possession, at the beginning of the nineteenth century, were Jews able to live in South Africa.

The first Jews arrived in 1806 from St. Helena. In 1820, they were joined by a handful of co-religionists who came with 4,000 colonists sent by the English. South Africa then consisted only of the sparsely populated province of Capetown, and a vast, unexplored wilderness stretching into the heart of the Dark Continent. Inhabited by savage Zulu tribes and containing great untapped natural resources, it offered a promise of wealth and adventure to those who could face its dangers and survive. For a century, hardy pioneers hacked at its frontiers, carving for themselves private empires in mountain and veldt. Among them were enterprising Jews such as Aaron de Pass and his son Daniel, who prospered in the country's infant shipping, fishing and whaling industries, opened copper mines, founded sugar plantations, and established one of Natal's first industries. Nathaniel Isaacs and Benjamin Norden were active in the "Zulu trade"; the former was the partner and right-hand man of "empire-builder" Cecil Rhodes.

The turning point in South African history came with discovery, in the 1870's, of the world's richest gold and diamond mines, in Kimberly and the Transvaal. Bringing unprecedented wealth to the area, it drew immigrants from all over the world. These included East European Jews who migrated via England, Holland and other West European countries. The newcomers swelled the ranks of the community, going chiefly into small trade and establishing some of the country's earliest manufacturing plants. But it was the oldtimers who exploited the mineral finds: Solomon Barnato Joel came to control huge copper fields in North Rhodesia; Barney I. Barnato, who started out as a busboy in London's East End, became Kimberley's "diamond king."

With the outbreak of the Boer War in 1899, the growing Jewish community found itself fighting with distinction in two armies. The war was fought between the English, who wished to unite the country under their flag, and Dutch farmers (known as Boers) who had trekked northward at mid-century to preserve their independence. The Boers had founded the Orange Free State and the Transvaal, where Jewish farmers and traders had settled early. As in English Capetown and Natal, Jews played an important role in the commercial and political life of the provinces.

The war ended in 1902 with an English victory. Eight years later, Capetown, Natal, the Orange Free State and the Transvaal were joined in the Union of South Africa; two years after that (1912), the Jewish communitites, scattered throughout the country, joined together to form a united Board of Deputies to represent them before the central authorities. In the national life of South Africa the Jews continued to play an important role in politics, law, medicine, and the arts, as well as in the economic life. South Africa's most popular writer of English in recent times was Sarah Millin, a Jewess, whose husband, Judge Philip Millin, was one of the country's leading jurists. Jews have sat in Parliment from the outset; they have also held government positions. Jewish patrons have founded the country's leading art museums, and such artists as Irma Stern are in the first rank of South African painters and sculptors.

The wealth and earlier security of South Africa's Jews did not shield them from the serious threat of anti-Semitism* during the 1930's and 1940's. Under the influence of Nazi propaganda, the powerful Nationalist Party threatened to deprive Jews of economic and political rights. With the collapse of Nazism, this program was discarded, and the community has since been assured that discrimination will not be practiced.

South Africa's Jewry maintains strong ties with Israel.* There has been a Zionist movement in the country since the 1890's, and today the Zionist Federation is the most active organization in the community. The government of the Union of South Africa has pursued a policy friendly to Zionism* and Israel.

Jewish communal life is intensive. The first synagogue was founded in 1841, and during the nineteenth century both synagogues and Jewish schools were set up in all communities. Since 1928, a Board of Jewish Education has coordinated educational activities. Jewish education, however, is a problem with which the community is seriously concerned, as there is a shortage of both funds and adequately trained teachers. The small but flourishing Jewish press includes a number of weeklies, published mainly in Capetown and Johannesburg, the two largest communitites, with a Jewish population of 25,650 and 57,500 respectively. The Hebrew Order of David, similar to B'nai B'rith* in the United States, is active in all Jewish communities.

The entire community is represented in governmental matters by the Jewish Board of Deputies. The Board is the community's World Jewish Congress affiliate,* and is also linked with the Board of Deputies of English Jewry, and the United States B'nai B'rith, in the Coordinating Board of Jewish Organizations in the United Nations Economic and Social Council.   B.H.

SOUTH AMERICA. See LATIN AMERICA.

SPAIN. The first Jewish settlement in Spain is veiled by the mists of time. Did they come with the Phoenicians* who had established trading stations in Andalusia? This might account for an ancient Jewish tradition that Jews settled in Spain in the time of King Solomon.* However, it is evident that by the first century C.E., there were Jews in Spain, for the Christian apostle, Paul, spoke of visiting them there. During the unsettled times of the declining Roman empire, in which commerce and travel were very difficult, many Spanish Jews became farmers. They were held in respect by their neighbors, and Christian farmers sometimes called a Jew to bless their crops, as was the custom of the time. This condition could not be pleasing to the Christian clergy, and beginning with their Council at Elvira, in 303, councils passed various resolutions designed to break such peaceful relationships with Jews.

Beginning with the fifth century, during the early Visigoth rule of Spain, there was mutual trust between the rulers and the Jews, who were merchants in the large cities and owners of large agricultural estates, as well as artisans and workmen of all kinds. In 589, when the Visigoth King Recared became a Roman Catholic, the bishops obtained power to prohibit Judaism. Jews were given the choice of becoming Catholics or of leaving the country. This edict was not strictly enforced until the ruthless reign of King Sisebut (612-621). For a century and a half, the Jewish struggle for survival continued. Some Jews escaped from the country; some were forcibly converted and practiced Judaism secretly until the welcome Muslim invasion in 711.

In the five centuries that followed, under the rule of the various Muslim dynasties, and even under some of the newly formed Christian kingdoms, Jews had a large measure of religious freedom. Many who had fled the country returned in numbers. They also grew in power and entered every major avenue of life. Discrimination and persecution were sporadic and not too severely applied. Accompanying the increasing economic opportunities and growth, was a Jewish cultural development so rich that the period became known as the Golden Age of Spain. The Moorish scholars of Spain became the leaders in the science, poetry and philosophy of the Mediterranean lands. Under their influence, Jewish scholars, physicians, and grammarians, philosophers, poets, and commentators entered a period of brilliant creativity. The storied cities of Cordova, Toledo, Granada, and others were the homes of these men and great centers of Jewish learning. Among the first of these writers was Hasdai Ibn Shaprut, Jewish scholar and a patron of Jewish scholarship. Court physician to Caliph Abd-al-Rahaman in tenth-century Cordova, Hasdai was also a linguist, and served the ruler as interpreter and unofficial advisor in the conduct of affairs with foreign diplomats at the court. There were the great grammarians, from Menahem ben Saruk to Jonah Ibn Jannah, who charted the course of the Hebrew language and ordered its ways. Greatest in a galaxy of poets, Solomon Ibn Gabirol,* Judah Ha-Levi,* and Moses Ibn Ezra* distilled new beauties from the anicent Hebrew tongue. The roster of famous names that illuminates this period includes Samuel Ibn Naghdella, the grocer who became a diplomat, and Moses Maimonides,* the philosopher and commentator who went into exile because persecutions had begun to tarnish the Golden Age.

After the Christians completed their reconquest of Spain, the power of the Church in general and of some religious orders in particular grew very great. Gradually, the Inquisition closed in upon the Jews, and under its pressures, the Jewish communities suffered. Their diminished creativity resulted in the thirteenth-century Silver Age of Nahmanides,* the scholar who inclined to mysticism, Rabbi Solomon Ibn Adret, the religious teacher of Barcelona, and the codifier Rabbi Jacob ben Asher, who died in 1340. In 1480 the Inquisition* was set up as a permanent religious court in charge of discovering, judging and handing over for punishment all religious offenders. The final triumph of the Inquisition was achieved by the monk Thomas de Torquemada. Under his influence, Queen Isabella and King Ferdinand expelled the Jews from Spain in 1492.

Thereafter, the history of the Jews in Spain is the history of the Marranos,* those who had publicly accepted Christianity and secretly practiced Judaism. For centuries, the Marranos were the legitimate prey of the Inquisition, until, for all intents and purposes, it was dissolved at the close of the eighteenth century. In 1858, the Spanish edict of expulsion was dissolved, but few Jews returned to settle there. By 1904, there were enough of them in Madrid to form a congregation. Yet even then, Jews were not permitted to use a public building as a synagogue. As of 1984 the Jewish population in Spain was estimated at 12,000, concentrated mainly in Madrid, Barcelona and Seville.

SPECTOR, YITZCHAK ELCHANAN (1817-1896). Rabbinical authority and community leader. When still very young, Spector became known as a brilliant Talmudic scholar in Russia. Because of his modesty, kindness, and his deep interest in the welfare of the poor and destitute, he won the confidence and love of the Jewish masses. A lover of Zion, he lent his prestige to the initial work of redeeming the land of Israel. His support was especially valuable, because of the stubborn opposition to the Zionist ideal general at the time among religious leaders.

Rabbi Yitzchak Elchanan exchanged letters concerning Talmudic law with many rabbis in Russia and abroad. His collected letters, or responsa, were published in book form and are highly regarded by students of Jewish law. The rabbinical school of Yeshiva University,* in New York,* is named in his honor.

SPERTUS COLLEGE OF JEWISH STUDIES, CHICAGO. An institution of higher Jewish learning, founded in 1924 by the Chicago Board of Jewish Education. Reorganized in 1929 to suit the needs of a growing community it includes departments for advanced Hebrew studies, Hebrew teachers' training, general Jewish studies, Sunday School teachers' and cantors' training, and a

Women's Institute of Jewish Study. Some courses are offered in cooperation with the University of Chicago. Graduate studies lead to degrees of Master of Hebrew Literature and Doctor of Hebrew Literature. Affiliated with the College are a Summer Camp Institute, founded in 1946, and the Leaf Library and Museum.

SPINOZA, BARUCH (Benedict) (1632-1677). Philosopher. He was born in Amsterdam* to a family of Marrano refugees from the Portuguese Inquisition.* Spinoza received a thorough education in Bible* and Talmud,* and wrote a grammar of the Hebrew language. After studying the philosophy of Descartes and Giordano Bruno, he developed views for which he was excommunicated (1655) from the Jewish community. He left Amsterdam, settled in The Hague, and became an optician, grinding lenses for a living. It was dangerous for him to publish his books, since his philosophy was unacceptable to Christian dogma. To keep his freedom of thought, he lived a lonely life, refusing a professorship at the University of Heidelberg, as well as a pension from Louis XIV of France.

In his first work, **A Theological Political Treatise,** Spinoza held that ''in a free commonwealth it shall be lawful for every man to think and to speak what he thinks.'' He completed his masterpiece, **The Ethics,** in 1675, but it was not published until after his death. His philosophy, very important in Western thought, is based on the pantheistic idea: the idea that God is the universe, and everything in it is a manifestation of Him.

SPORTS. Jewish athletes have contributed their share to the history of sports all over the world, and have added to the legends of boxing, baseball, track and field, football and scores of other major and minor sports.

In the United States* in particular, where the sports world is always active and exciting, Jews have done remarkably well. In boxing, for example, there have been more than twenty Jewish boxing champions, thus carrying on an ancient tradition, for in the late 1700's, Daniel Mendoza of England* was one of the greatest and earliest Jewish boxing kings. In America, there have been equally outstanding Jewish prize fighters. Benny Leonard, who began to fight in 1912, was for nearly a decade the lightweight champion of the world, and ranks as perhaps the finest titleholder in the 135-pound class. There have been other notable Jewish lightweights, including Al Singer, Lew Tendler and Jackie ''Kid'' Berg of England, who did much of his boxing on American shores. Barney Ross, who held both the lightweight and welterweight championships, also gained acclaim

Baruch Spinoza

as one of boxing's immortals. As the social status of the Jew in America has improved, fewer boys have gone in for boxing. Yet the records show that in one of the roughest sports in the world, Jews have done as well as the best.

Fewer Jews have achieved excellence in baseball. Baseball, being a game played mainly in small towns, has not produced many Jewish stars. But those Jews who have excelled at baseball are among the top names in the game. Johnny Kling, who caught at the turn of the century and was the best receiver the Chicago Cubs ever had, has been considered one of the three or four best catchers in baseball history. And, of course, Hank Greenberg, who played first base and the outfield for the Detroit Tigers in the 1930's and 1940's, is a member of baseball's Hall of Fame and was one of the most potent home-run hitters in the annals of the sport. He hit fifty-eight homers in one year, a mark bettered by Babe Ruth and equalled only by one other man in the game. More recently, Al Rosen, who started at third base for the Cleveland Indians, became a baseball notable when he was voted the Most Valuable Player Award for 1953 in the American League by a unanimous vote, the first time any player had won such an accolade. One of the greatest Jewish baseball stars of contemporary times has been Sandy Koufax, a left-handed pitcher for the Los Angeles Dodgers. Koufax pitched four no-hit, no-run games in his brilliant carrer, which was cut short at the age of 29 by a chronic arthritic elbow. But his diamond feats won him a place in baseball's Hall of Fame, even though he had a comparatively brief career. His four no-hitters, in consecutive seasons, was a record in itself. In 11 years on the mound, he won acclaim for his remarkable fast ball and his ''unhittability.'' He won the Cy Young Award as the best pitcher of the year three times and the Most Valuable National League Player Award (rarely given to a pitcher) in 1963. He

Courtesy Bloch Publishing Company. From Harold Ribalow's
The Jew in American Sports.

also won the National League Player of the Year Award of the Sporting News in 1963-64-65. He established many strikeout records and shutout marks. He was the first pitcher to fan more than 300 batters in two consecutive years. Before that he was the first to strike out 200 men in two years in succession. Koufax also was extraordinarily effective in the World Series. He gained the record of most strikeouts in a four-game Series (23) and the most in a single game (15) against the New York Yankees in 1963. That same year he won 25 games and 26 in 1965.

Other Jewish baseball players have included: Andy Cohen, a N.Y. Giant second baseman, who succeeded the famous Rogers Hornsby; Buddy Myer, who won the American League batting title once; Harry Danning and Sid Gordon of the N.Y. Giants; Ken Holtzmann, a fine left-handed pitcher who twirled a no-hitter himself; Mike Epstein, a pretty good home-run batter; and Ron Blomberg, who showed promise of stardom with the Yankees.

Football, both amateur and professional, also has produced prominent Jewish gridiron stars. The best of them were quarterbacks, the men who called the plays and pitched the passes. Thus, Benny Friedman, great quarterback of the 1920's and later professional football player and coach at Brandeis University,* Harry Newman of Michigan, and Sid Luckman of the Columbia Lions and the Chicago Bears, are among the football greats. Many other Jews have made All-American football teams, and are remembered by fans.

Basketball once was called "the Jewish game" because of the predominance of Jewish hoop stars. But today the players are extremely tall and no longer come exclusively from metropolitan areas. Th game has been opened to black players and almost every professional team has as many blacks as whites. Still, the accomplishments of Jewish basketaball players, in college and professional ranks, is impressive. Nat Holman, once known as "Mr. Basketball," star of the Celtics, a famous professional team of the past, later was the coach of CCNY and led his clubs to many victories. The Long Island University teams, loaded with Jewish players, also won national fame. New

Hank Greenberg

York University and St. John's had Jewish stars and led their teams to prominence. Harry Boykoff was notable at St. John's and Adolph Schayes at NYU. Schayes went on to a highly successful pro career. Others who won recognition include Art Heyman, Sid Tanenbaum, Max Zaslofsky and, in more recent years, Neal Walk, the professional star and Bob Kaufmann, who has made the National Basketball League All-Star team. More notably, Red Holtzman has been a brilliant coach with the New York Knicks, and Red Auerbach was coach and general manager of the Boston Celtics.

Tennis, once a "social" sport with few Jewish players of the top rank, has undergone major changes. The professional game is now a great deal more important than the amateur sport. Nonetheless, there are not many outstanding Jews in tennis. Once Dick Savitt won the Wimbledon championship. Herb Flam was a member of the U.S. Davis Cup team. Tom Okker of Holland is one of the top pros in the sport. There are others, less good, less well known, but perhaps the future will produce names to be proud of.

One of the greatest Jewish names in sports—that of Mark Spitz—emerged as a result of what happened in the swimming competition in the 1972 Olympic Games in Munich. Spitz won seven gold medals, the first time this feat has ever been accomplished in the long history of the Games. In 1968, Mark Spitz was considered to be a coming champion, but he was young and im-

Benny Leonard

Sid Luckman

Barney Ross

mature and failed to do well. By 1972, he had become battle-hard, for he already had competed in the Maccabiah Games in Israel* and was ready for top competition. His first championship race was for the 200-meter butterfly. He broke his own world record in this event and immediately placed his foes on the watch for his later achievements. That same evening he won his second gold medal, the 400-meter free-style relay. He was one of a group, but his own contribution was a record time race. The next evening, he took part in the 200-meter free-style. He had to come from behind with a burst of speed to win. But he did. That made it three gold medals and Spitz had become the talk of the Olympic Games. He won five gold medals in three days. More were to come. In the end, he had seven, was named the Male Athlete of the Year by the Associated Press and he had gone into sports history.

Chess, which is considered a sport, has boasted scores of Jewish chess masters all over the world, as well as in the United States. William Steinitz and Emmanuel Lasker held the world title successively for fifty-seven years. Mikhail Botvinnik and Mikhail Tal, both Soviet chess masters, also where world champions. Samuel Reshevsky and Bobby Fischer held many American championships and have ranked high on the world scene.

In other lands, too, Jewish athletes are active and making their mark in all types of competition. There were Jewish sports clubs in Europe, called Maccabi. Today, the Maccabi is potent in Israel, and in the Jewish State sports are of very great interest to the people of Israel. The Israelis have sent athletes to the Olympic Games and to the Asian Games. Israel invites the finest Jewish amateur athletes in the world to compete in Israel in the Maccabiah, a kind of Jewish Olympics.

At the Munich Olympics in August, 1972, Arab terrorists entered the Israeli quarters at the Olympic Village and held members of the Israeli Olympic team as hostages, demanding the release of fellow Arab terrorists jailed in Israel. The Israeli government refused to meet their demand, and after nightfall the German police took the terrorists and their hostages to a nearby airfield from where they expected to fly out of Germany. The police opened fire on the terrorists in an attempt to release the prisoners. Eleven Israeli sportsmen perished in the melee. The entire Olympiad came to a halt with a memorial in honor of the victims, after which the games were resumed.

In the 1984 Los Angeles Olympics, the Israeli Olympic team participated in such sports as gymnastics, weightlifting, yachting, shooting, and track and field.

SPRINZAK, JOSEPH (1885-1959). Political leader in Israel. Born in Russia, educated in Russian and Swiss universities, Sprinzak was a founder and member of the Elected Assembly and of the National Council of Palestine Jews during the British mandatory period in Palestine.* He was successively, the president of the Zionist General Council, the secretary-general of Histadrut,* Israel's General Federation of Labor (1945-49), and speaker of the Knesset (Israel parliament) from February 1949 until his death.

STAMPS. Stamp collecting, one of the world's most popular hobbies, reached a high peak of interest among Jews with the establishment of Israel* and that nation's issuance of attractive postage stamps, but it was not until Israel undertook to print stamps reflecting Jewish and Israeli history, religion, and traditions, that the theme of Jews on stamps became internationally popular.

Countries all over the world have not hesitated to honor prominent Jewish scientists, writers, statesmen, political leaders and other noted personalities on their stamps. The United States, for example, has issued a stamp in tribute to Samuel Gompers* the labor leader; another to four chaplains who died heroically during the Second World War, one of whom, Alexander D. Goode, was a rabbi; a third to Joseph Pulitzer, the newspaper publisher who is considered Jewish, although he was not a full Jew. The Soviet Union has commemoratives for Isaac Levitan, the painter, and Anton Rubinstein, the musician. Ludwig Zamenhof,* the creator of the international language Esperanto, has been honored on stamps by the Soviet Union, Brazil,* Austria,* the Netherlands,* Yugoslavia,* and Bulgaria.* The actress Sarah Bernhardt is on a French stamp. Walter Rathenau,* the statesman assassinated by Germans in Germany also has had a stamp—by West Germany—issued in his memory. Hungary* has recognized David Schwarz as the inventor of the zeppelin, and West Germany has similarly honored the scientist Paul Ehrlich.* Poland,* too, has recalled a tragic but glorious moment in Jewish history by issuing a stamp commemorating the Warsaw* Ghetto* uprising, when trapped Jews chose to fight with small arms against the mechanized might of the German army.

Nearly all the Israeli stamps are, naturally, more directly concerned with Jewish history and tradition. Today, it is a Jewish education in miniature to know the background of each stamp issued by the State of Israel. Many of the symbols and themes reproduced on the stamps were resurrected from Israel's proud and valiant past. Some of the stamps, which commemorate individuals, offer the collector a chance to study the lives of the great scholars and idealists who did so much to influence the course of Jewish history. There are, for example, stamps of Albrt Einstein,* of

Maimonides,* of Chaim Weizmann,* of Theodor Herzl,* and of Baron Edmond de Rothschild.*

The story of the development of the Jewish State can also be studied from the stamps of Israel. There are stamps marking the birth of various **kibbutzim,** or settlements; there is a stamp of Tel Aviv,* and one of Jerusalem,* another stamp pays tribute to the Hebrew linguists who helped bring about a rebirth of Hebrew as a modern, living tongue. And, of course, many of Israel's remarkable institutions (the Hebrew University,* the Haifa* technion, the Red Magen David,* the Israel Red Cross) are commemorated in stamps. Some of the decisive battles against the Arab invaders during the Israel War of Independence are marked in stamps released for each Independence Day; one—dedicated to the parachutists who helped save Jewish lives during the Second World War—has been especially popular. Some stamps celebrate the Jewish holidays, taking their inspiration from the Bible* and from Jewish festivals. To collect stamps of Jewish interest—particulary those from Israel—is to absorb something of the spirit of the Jewish people.   H.R.

STAR OF DAVID. See MAGEN DAVID.

STERN COLLEGE FOR WOMEN. See VESHIVA UNIVERSITY.

Magen David

STERN GROUP (LEHI: Hebrew acronym for Fighters for the Freedom of Israel). Extremist splinter faction which split off from the Irgun Z'vai L'umi* in 1940. It was formed by Abraham (Yair) Stern, who was killed by the British in 1942. Believing that the Irgun was not sufficiently aggressive in its fight against British rule in Palestine,* the Stern Group resorted to terror tactics, including assassinations, to drive the British out of the country. It dissolved after the establishment of the Jewish state. Some of its leaders have become prominent in Menahem Begin's* Herut party **(see** REVISIONIST ZIONISM). One of them, Yitzhak Shamir,* was speaker of the Knesset during the period of Israel's peace negotiations with Egypt, and served as Prime Minister of Israel.

STRAUS, NATHAN (1848-1931). Merchant and philanthropist. Born in Germany,* Nathan Straus served as president of the New York City Board of Health in 1898. He came to hold this office out of a deep interest in public health. In 1890 he had established a system for the sterilization and distribution of milk to the poor of New York. He installed his own laboratory and distributed pasteurized milk in many cities in the United States and abroad. During the panic of 1893-94, he started a chain of groceries to distribute coal and groceries to the needy. Straus retired from R. H. Macy and Co. in 1914; during World War I, he became a one-man society to relieve the suffering of people all over the world. Deeply interested in Palestine,* he joined the Zionist movement, repeatedly visited Palestine, and founded the Nathan and Lina Straus Health Centers of Hadassah,* in Tel Aviv* and Jerusalem. His self-sacrifice and generosity won him the love and respect of millions.

STRAUS OSCAR (1870-1954). Composer. Oscar Straus studied music in his native Vienna and Berlin, and began his musical career as a conductor in theaters and cabarets. Although he wrote serious music as well, Straus made his mark as a master of light opera. He composed the music for over fifty operettas, including the much-produced **Waltz Dream** (1907) and **Chocolate Soldier.** Fleeing Nazism, he settled first in France and then in the United States (1940).

STRAUS, OSCAR SOLOMON (1850-1926). Diplomat and philanthropist. A brother of Nathan Straus* he became active in the business enterprises run by his family. He served as U.S. Minister (later Ambassador) to Turkey* from 1887 to 1890, 1898 to 1900, and again from 1909 to 1910. From 1906 to 1909 he served as U.S. Secretary of Commerce and Labor, the first Jew to hold a position in th U.S. Cabinet. He was active also in Jewish communal affairs and had contacts with Zionist leaders.

STRUMA. The Struma was one of the doomed "coffin ships" of the period of "illegal immigration" to Palestine* during the 1940's. In the beginning of 1941, 769 Jews boarded the tiny unseaworthy cargo boat to escape from Nazi brutalities in Rumania.* The **Struma** took them first to Turkey, where they were refused permission to land. They waited for two months on board the rotting, rat-infested vessel for permission to go to Palestine. The British mandatory government refused such permission. Ordered to

leave by the Turks, refused readmission to Rumania, the **Struma** cast aimlessly out to sea. Not far from the harbor of Istanbul, it struck a mine and sank in the Black Sea on February 24, 1941, with all its human cargo, including many children, aboard.

STYBEL, ABRAHAM JOSEPH (1885-1946). Publisher and patron of Hebrew literature. Born in a small town in Poland,* he acquired in his youth a love of Hebrew literature. During the First World War, Stybel became the largest leather merchant and importer in Russia.* Then possessing the means to realize his life-long ambition, in 1917, he established the Stybel Publishing House, in Moscow. Soon after the Russian Communist Revolution, Stybel was forced to transfer his literary activities to Poland and Germany.* In 1919 he founded the Hebrew monthly **Miklat** ("Refuge") in New York.* By the end of the 1920's a branch of the Stybel Publishing House was established in Palestine. In Warsaw,* in addition to publishing hundreds of books, Stybel founded (1917) the outstanding Hebrew quarterly **Ha-Tekufah** ("The Epoch"), edited by David Frischmann.* When the Nazis occupied Poland in 1939, Stybel fled Warsaw and immigrated to America. Despite wars, revolution and migration, Stybel succeeded in making the literary treasures of the world available to the Hebrew reader, engaging many writers, linguists, and translators for this task.

SUKKOT (the Feast of Booths). Five days after Yom Kippur,* Jews observe Sukkot, the Feast of Booths, or Tabernacles. This holiday is celebrated for seven days in Palestine * and eight days in the Diaspora. During the festival the family gathers for meals in booths erected for the occasion. Beautifully decorarated and covered with greenery which permits the stars to shine through, the booths recall the times when Israel wandered in the wilderness after the Exodus* from Egypt.* Sukkot is also the Harvest Festival, recalling the days when Israelite farmers went to the fields and lived in lean-tos until the harvest was in. Also associated with the harvest are the **lulav**—a palm-branch flanked with sprigs of willow and myrtle—and the **etrog** ("citron"). Together, these are the Biblical "four species," over which a blessing is recited daily during the holiday. They are also carried during **Hakafot,** a ceremonial march around the synagogue.

Sukkot is one of the **shalosh regalim,** the three pilgrimage festivals observed in ancient times with pilgrimages to Jerusalem.* (The other two are Passover* and Shavuot,* the Feast of Weeks, which, like Sukkot, were also harvest festivals.) In

olden days, in the Temple, the high point of the Sukkot festivities was **simhat bet ha-Shoevah** ("the ceremony of water drawing"). The importance of this ceremony was seasonal, for Sukkot comes in the fall, after the long dry summer and just before the rainy season in Israel. Therefore, prayers of thanksgiving were offered for the rains which had made the year's crops grow.

On Shemini Atzeret, which immediately follows Sukkot, prayers for rain during the coming season are chanted. The preceding day is known as Hoshana Rabba, after the prayers beginning with **Hoshana,** which means "Save us." Many such prayers are said, because it is believed that on Hoshana Rabba the Books of Judgment, sealed on Yom Kippur, are put away until the following year. During the Hoshana Rabba service, willow branches are beaten until all the leaves have fallen off. This is associated both with the rituals of penitence and the seasonal festivities. The beaten

One of the rabbis taking part in the Hakhel ceremony in Jerusalem. Hakhel commemorated the ancient ritual of the reading of a portion of the Torah by a reigning king during the intermediary days of Sukkot after every Sabbatical year.

willows symbolize the suffering man inflicts upon himself in the search for forgiveness. They also represent the hope that after the trees and plants lose their greenery God will provide new warmth and moisture for the renewal of nature, as well as for man's strength and his trust in God.

Shemini Atzeret and Simhat Torah are associated with Sukkot, but are not properly part of that festival. The former dates from Biblical times. Because it was the occasion of the crucial prayers for rain, it was marked with great solemnity. Simhat Torah ("The Rejoicing of the Law") is a joyous holiday. It arose after the Rabbis instituted the practice of reading through the entire Torah* (Five Books of Moses) in the synagogue each year. On Simhat Torah the last portion of one year's cycle is read, and a new cycle is begun with the reading of the first portion of Genesis.* **Hakafot,** an "encircling" procession with Torah scrolls, is the special mark of the day. Special attention is paid to children, who join in the Hakafot with flags and singing.   B.H.

SULZBERGER FAMILY. Distinguished American Jewish family, originating in Sulzberg in southern Germany. Four branches of the family emigrated to the United States in the nineteenth century.

Mayer Sulzberger (1843-1923), brought to Philadelphia in 1849, became one of that city's leading judges. He was a scholar of Jewish history, publishing studies on the legal and political institutions of ancient Judea. **Cyrus Leo Sulzberger** (1858-1932), his cousin, settled in New York* and prospered in the textile trade. Entering municipal politics as a liberal, he maintained a life-long interest in Jewish communal affairs, serving as president of the Jewish Agricultural and Industrial Aid Society and of the United Hebrew Charities. Although opposed to Jewish nationalism, he was vice-president of the Federation of American Zionists. Cyrus's son, Arthur Hays Sulzberger, studied at Columbia University, and joined **The New York Times** in 1919. He became its publisher in 1935. A supporter of the New Deal, he campaigned for active United States participation in world affairs. Other well-known Sulzbergers include Cyrus L., foreign correspondent, and Marion B., leading dermatologist.

SURA. See BABYLONIA.

SURINAM (DUTCH GUIANA). Dutch possession on the northeastern coast of South America. Surinam is the home of the Jewish community with the longest continuous history in the Western Hemisphere. Established in 1630, it was augmented in the 1650's and 1660's by Jews from Brazil* and England.* In 1665, the English, who held the territory for a time, granted full religious freedom to "the Hebrew Nation" residing there. The Dutch confirmed this freedom when Surinam was returned to them two years later. In 1682, the Brazilian Jews, who had prospered in the cultivation of sugar, founded a colony at Joden Savanne ("Savannah of the Jews"). This community survived until 1832, when fire destroyed the village. Most if its inhabitants moved to Paramaribo, where German Jews had settled in the eighteenth century. The present Jewish community, numbering about 200, is concentrated in the capital. Some of its members are refugees who arrived from Europe during World War II. The community is organized in Sephardic* and Ashkenazic* congregations, both of which are represented in the Central Committee for Jewish Affairs.

SWEDEN. One of the Scandinavian countries. Few Jews lived there until the late eighteenth century. The Jews have since played an important

Old etching of Hasidim dancing, on a Simhat Torah flag.

part in the life of the country, especially in the arts, and the old residents are well integrated in Swedish life. The rate of intermarriage is probably higher in Sweden than in any other country in Europe.

Sweden received a large number of refugees from the Nazi Holocaust. The current (1984) Jewish population of 15,000 is more than double that of 1933. About 6,000 live in Stockholm and vicinity, 2,000 each in Goteborg and Malmo, 350 in Boras, and 250 in Narrkoping. There is a central Council of Mosaic Communities. The Jewish community as a whole, including the "Vikings," as the old families are called, are keenly interested in Israel.

SWITZERLAND. Located between Germany, Italy and France. It had some Jewish inhabitants during the Middle Ages. At the time of the Black Death, Jews were viciously massacred, and 1622 the Swiss Diet expelled all Jews. There was a gradual return, beginning in the late seventeenth century. The federal constitution of 1874 finally abolished Jewish disabilities.

During World War II, Switzerland gave shelter to a limited number of refugees, some of whom have remained. In 1984 there were about 29,000 Jews in Switzerland of whom about 6,000 were in Zurich, 4,100 in Geneva, and 2,100 in Basle, with the rest scattered in other communities.

SYNAGOGUE (from Greek, meaning "assembly"). The Bet Knesset ("House of Meeting"—the Hebrew equivalent for synagogue) can be traced back to the period following the destruction of the First Temple* in 586 B.C.E. The exiled Jews in Babylonia* gathered at first in private homes, later in special buildings, to read from the Scriptures* and to observe holidays. Even when the Temple was rebuilt in 537 B.C.E., the number of houses of worship continued to increase. Following the destruction of the Second Temple in 70 A.D., the synagogue assumed a central place in Jewish religious and communal life. Wherever Jews settled, they established a place of worship and study. During the Middle Ages, the synagogue was the hub from which the religious, educational, social and charitable spokes of community life radiated. Wherever the Jewish communities moved, the synagogue moved with them and flourished.

The structure and magnificence of the synagogue varied depending upon the degree of religious freedom. In countries where the Jews were oppressed their building was often restricted. But where the Jews were permitted some measure of freedom, especially in the ancient East, beautiful structures were erected. Excavations in Dura Europos (Syria), Capernaum, and Bet Alpha

Synagogue in Turin, destroyed by the Nazis, was one of the most beautiful in Europe. It has been rebuilt since the war.

in Palestine* have uncovered the remains of highly ornate houses of prayer.

Traditionally, the worshippers in the synagogue face east, toward Jerusalem.* Into the eastern wall of the structure is built the Holy Ark,* where the Torah* Scrolls are kept. This Ark is often lavishly decorated and ornamented with symbolic paintings of lions, eagles, and ceremonial objects such as the ram's horn, Menorah,* and musical instruments. The two tablets of the covenant inscribed with the Ten Commandments* and surmounted by the Torah crown are generally placed above the Ark. A richly embroidered velvet or satin curtain is draped before the Ark. Suspended from the ceiling nearby hangs the **Ner Tamid,** the eternal light, which, as the name suggests, must never be extinguished. Traditionally, the **Bimah,** or pulpit, is located in the center of the house of prayer. The **Amud,** or reader's stand, which is directly in front of the Ark, is decorated by a tall seven-branched candelabrum. In Orthodox synagogues, a separate seating section is provided for the women.

SYRIA. The Aram of the Old Testament, called Syria in the Septuagint. It became a free Arab republic in 1946, and, with Lebanon,* covers most of the northwest horn of the Fertile Crescent. Syria's present area is 66,046 square miles, extending from Israel* in the south to Turkey* in the north, and from Lebanon in the west to Iraq* in the east. Its location on the main trade routes has always tempted invaders, and Syria has never been free of foreign influence since the coming of the Assyrians in 842 B.C. During the Hellenistic period, particularly in the time of Herod* the Great (36-4 B.C.E.), a considerable Jewish community gathered in Syria. Jews were accorded equal rights, but in the course of the wars in Israel many were massacred (66 B.C.). With the advance of Christianity many Jews were forcibly baptized. The invasion of the Arabs in the seventh century

Mount Zion Temple, St. Paul, Minnesota.
Eric Mendelsohn, architect

brought the Jews greater religious toleration but placed them in an inferior status. The Jews congregated mainly in the large cities, Damascus, the capital, Aleppo, and Tripoli, largely as traders and craftsmen. They numbered about 18,000 but never became a strong cultural community. In 1840, the Syrian Jews suffered the effects of the Damascus* blood libel. World Jewry intervened, and rescued the Damascus Jews from mob violence.

Since the Six-Day War* Syrian Jews have suffered constant harassment and persecution officially sponsored by the government and carried out by the police, as a result of which a world-wide movement has been established to help reduce the number of Syrian Jews and bring them out of Syria. As of 1984, hopes that Syria would enter into peace negotiations with Israel have not materialized. In 1982, Israel's Operation Peace for Galilee sought to challenge and defeat Syria's pro-PLO military base in Lebanon. Despite a resounding defeat, the Syrians were rearmed by the USSR and were influential in forcing the abrogation of the Israel-Lebanese peace treaty concluded in 1983. In 1984, an unprecedented exchange of Syrian and Israeli prisoners of war occurred; 291 Syrian soldiers and officers were exchanged for 6 Israelis (3 soldiers and 3 civilians). The present (1984) Jewish population is between 3,500 and 4,000.

SYRKIN, NACHMAN (1867-1924). Labor Zionist leader. As a boy in Russia, he was active in the Hibbat Zion* movement. A brilliant student, he was nevertheless expelled from gymnasium or high school, for talking back to the principal, who had made an anti-Semitic remark. Syrkin went to Berlin to study, and became a Zionist leader among the students. At the age of twenty, in 1888, he was already trying to unify his two ideals— Zionism and socialism. He came to reject many of the ideas of Karl Marx,* and saw Socialist Zionism as a modern expression of the Hebrew prophets' teachings of justice for all men. Syrkin became one of the earliest founders of the Labor Zionist party (**see LABOR ZIONISM**). Returning to Russia, he took part in the 1905 revolution against the oppressive, corrupt Tsarist government. The suffering of Russian Jewry also led him to seek an immediate solution for the Jewish problem in territorialism.* Quickly disillusioned, he returned to Zionism.

Nachman Syrkin came to America in 1908, where he continued his Zionist work, and also became active in the American Jewish Congress.* After World War I, he helped organize the Jewish delegation to the Versailles Peace Conference,* and served as one of its delegates. A biography of Syrkin was published in 1960 by his daughter Marie Syrkin (1899-   ), a noted Zionist writer and lecturer.

SZOLD, HENRIETTA (1860-1945). Founder of Hadassah.* She was born in Baltimore, the eldest daughter of Rabbi Benjamin Szold, a scholar and leader of Conservative Judaism. Rabbi Szold guided his daughter's education, and from early youth, Henrietta Szold became a companion and an assistant to her father in his complex tasks. Broad sympathy and understanding for all manner of human beings were a part of her environment. In her home she became acquainted with work for the liberation of the American Negro. When the flood of Jewish immigration from Eastern Europe poured into America, the Szold home gave shelter, aid, and guidance to all within its reach. Henrietta Szold, teaching at the time at a fashionable girls' school, founded, managed, and taught in one of the first night schools for immigrants in the United States.

Editor, translator and writer. Henrietta Szold had shared in her father's scholarly interests and had written articles for periodicals since she was seventeen. When the Jewish Publication Society of America* (JPS) was organized in 1888, she became a volunteer member of its publication committee, and from 1893 to 1916 was its paid literary secretary. In this capacity, her translation labors included editing a five-volume translation of Graetz's* **History of the Jews.** She also translated and edited the seven-volume **Legends of the Jews** by Louis Ginzberg.* In addition, she edited, together with Cyrus Adler,* the **American Jewish Year Book.**

Henrietta Szold

Zionist work. Miss Szold's Zionism* was a natural development. It grew out of the home atmosphere, and was nourished by her scholarly preoccupation with Jewish history and literature. Its germ appeared in her 1889 essay, **A Plea for Custom.** This essay was not only a plea for the preservation of Jewish culture and way of life, but also an early expression of what later became known as "cultural pluralism" in America. In 1893 she joined the Hevrat Zion, or Zionist Association of Baltimore, one of the earliest Zionist societies on the continent. In 1895 Miss Szold made her first Zionist speech before the Baltimore section of the National Council of Jewish Women.*

In 1909, she went to Europe with her mother. The trip included a visit to Palestine* from where she wrote: "If not Zionism, then nothing," and, "there are heroic men and women here doing valiant work. If only they could be more intelligently supported by the European and American Jew." What she saw of disease and suffering in Palestine, and her own dislike of holding theories without translating them into action, bore fruit in 1912. The Hadassah Study Circle, to which Henrietta Szold had belonged since 1907, was transformed into a national women's organization that undertook the practical task of fund raising for health work in Palestine. Its first goal, a system of visiting nurses, began modestly in 1913 with the arrival of two American-trained nurses who set up a small welfare station in Jerusalem.*

That same year, Miss Szold began a series of tours of the United States* for Hadassah; Hadassah grew in strength and membership. During the First World War, in 1917, Supreme Court Justice Louis D. Brandeis,* head of the Provisional Zionist Committee, entrusted Henrietta Szold with the responsibility for organizing the American Zionist Medical Unit for Palestine. In the autumn of 1918, equipment for a fifty-bed hospital and a group of forty-four doctors, nurses, dentists, sanitary engineers and administrators arrived in Palestine. Miss Szold joined them in 1920, and from then until 1927, she divided her time between Hadassah's work in Palestine and in the United States. Even after she had settled permanently in Palestine and undertook other major responsibilities, she remained dedicated to Hadassah's work. She was elected honorary president of Hadassah in 1926. In 1933, Miss Szold laid the foundation stone for the Rothschild Hadassah-University Hospital in 1933. When the Second World War broke out, she served on the Hadassah Emergency Committee that was engaged in solving the problems created by the war. As a result of her survey and recommendations, Hadassah established the Alice Seligsberg Trade School for Girls in Jerusalem.

Serving the Yishuv.* In 1927, Miss Szold had been elected one of the three members of the Palestine Executive Committee of the World Zionist Organization,* the first woman ever to serve in this capacity. Her portfolios were education and health. Since, however, the other two members of the Executive (Harry Sacher and Colonel Frederick Kisch) were frequently abroad for long periods, the task of political work and of negotiations with the Palestine government in behalf of the Yishuv fell upon her. The prevailing Oriental attitude toward women added to the delicacy of the task. The Yishuv had to learn how to accept guidance from a woman. How successful she was may be recognized from her election in 1930 to serve on the Vaad Leumi—the National Council of Jews in Palestine. The Vaad Leumi placed the responsibility for social welfare in her hands. She trained social workers for the whole country and in 1941 initiated an educational and correctional system for young offenders.

Youth Aliyah.* When Henrietta Szold was seventy-three years old, she wanted to return to America "to be coddled by my sisters," but her deep sense of responsibility made her shoulder a new undertaking. In 1933, Nazism had come to power in Germany, and German Jews began to migrate to Palestine. The year before had seen the

Scroll recording establishment by the Hebrew University of scholarships for Youth Aliyah students in the name of Henrietta Szold on her eightieth birthday.

onset of a youth immigration into Palestine. Inevitably, Miss Szold assumed the task of developing the Youth Aliyah movement initiated by Recha Freier.* As organizer and leader of Youth Aliyah, she first worked out a program of education that would give individual attention to each child. Afterward, she guided the immigration, re-education, and resettlement of these children, straining to establish a personal contact at some point with each child.

In 1942, her concern for the problem of Arab-Jewish relations led her to join the Ihud ("Unity") movement, an organization for the promotion of good relations between Arabs and Jews and for the formation of a bi-national Arab-Jewish state in Palestine. Henrietta Szold received many honors from Jews and non-Jews alike. Not the least of these was the enduring deep regard of her close associates and co-workers for the astonishing variety of her endeavors to help humanity.   N.B.-A.

SZYK, ARTHUR (1894-1951). Artist, born in Poland,* studied in Paris,* came to America in 1940. Noted for his book illuminations, including the Passover* Haggadah* and the U.S. and Israel Declarations of Independence.

T

TABERNACLE. The Hebrew **ohel moed,** or "tent of meeting", also referred to as **mishkan,** the sanctuary which was a symbol of God's presence among the Children of Israel. According to the Bible,* the Tabernacle was built by the Israelites in the wilderness, after their exodus from Egypt.* (Ex. 25, 26, 27.) It was the first sanctuary where sacrifices were offered and services were conducted by priests and Levites.* Bezalel and Oholiab were the principal artists in charge of building and decorating it. The Tabernacle, a square portable tent, stood on the western side of its forecourt, pointed in the direction of the Promised Land. The forecourt was enclosed by wooden columns draped with blue, purple, and scarlet hangings. At the entrance to the Tabernacle stood the laver, a copper basin where the priests washed before they brought the sacrifices on the altar. The acacia-wood altar was overlaid with copper and had four horns. Within the Tabernacle, in the Holy Place, stood the gold overlaid wooden table holding the twelve shewbreads. There, too, was the seven-branched candelabrum, which was approached by way of stairs. The gilded incense altar was centered in front of the veil that hung from four gilded pillars and hid the Holy of Holies. The Holy of Holies held nothing save the Ark of the Covenant* with the stone tablets of the Ten Commandments.* A dark cloud rested upon the Tabernacle by day, a fiery one by night. Its place was a square in the center of the camp, and, forming a living square around it, the twelve tribes of Israel marched on their forty-year journey to the Promised Land.

When the Children of Israel settled in Canaan,* the Tabernacle rested at Shiloh, almost in the center of the Land. In the time of King David,* the service in the sanctuary took on a new importance in the life of the people as the favored center of worship. After an overwhelming victory over the Philistines,* the king built a splendid new Tabernacle on Mt. Zion. Then, dancing at the head of a procession of Levites who played musical instruments, David brought the Holy Ark to its new sanctuary in the capital, and Jerusalem* became the holy city in Israel. Until King Solomon* built the Temple, the Tabernacle on Mt. Zion was the place of worship for the nation.   N.B.-A.

TABLETS OF THE LAW. See MOSES; **also** TEN COMMANDMENTS.

TAF. Twenty-second letter of the Hebrew alphabet; numerically, four hundred.

TALLIT. Prayer shawl, usually of silk or wool, sometimes banded with silver or gold thread, and fringed at each of the four corners in accordance with the Biblical law (Num. 15:38). The wearing of the **tallit** at worship is obligatory only for married men, but it is customarily worn also by males of bar mitzvah age and over. Occasionally it is spread over the marriage canopy, or used as a burial shroud.

TALMID HAKHAM (Hebrew for "disciple of the wise"). Any scholar or authority on the Talmud came to be known as a Talmid Hakham. For long centuries of Jewish life, the Talmid Hakham was respected as the social aristocrat. In contrast to him was the Am Ha-Aretz* or ignoramus, at the opposite end of the social ladder. During the Middle Ages, the Talmid Hakham was consulted as an authority on worldly as well as religious affairs, even when he held no official position in the community.

Numerous pithy sayings in the Talmud reflect the position of the scholar in Jewish life. Perhaps the most typical and most frequently quoted is: "Talmidei Hakhamim (pl.) strengthen peace in the world." Another frequent quotation mirroring the same attitude is the Biblical proverb: "The learning of the wise man is a source of life." (Proverbs 13:14.)

TALMUD. (From the Hebrew, meaning "study" or "teaching.") Legal code whose compilation extended over almost a thousand years. Based on the teachings of the Bible,* the Talmud interprets Biblical laws and commandments, and branches out into many fields of knowledge. Although dealing primarily with law, the Talmud also contains a rich store of historic facts and traditions. In its pages are found scientific discussions, ethical teachings, legends, and profound observations on all phases of human experience.

Studying has never stopped for this aged Jew.

The Talmud is composed of two basic divisions the Mishnah and the Gemarah. The Mishnah is mainly the interpretation of the Biblical law as handed down over the generations as the "Oral Tradition." The Gemarah represents a commentary on the Mishnah by a group of later scholars, the Amoraim.*

Mishnah. The Mishnah had its origin in the period following the return of the Jews from Babylonian captivity (537 B.C.E.). Ezra the Scribe* is believed to have founded the Great Assembly—a supreme Jewish religious and legislative authority. The distinguished schloars of this learned body set certain basic rules for the interpretation of Jewish law. They instituted the prayer of **Shmoneh Esreh** ("The Eighteen Benedictions"), and edited some of the books of the Bible. Out of the Great Assembly arose a group of men, called Scribes. The Scribes represented the official copyists of the Bible and taught its laws. They were followed by the Tannaim,* sages who continued for several generations to develop methods of interpreting the laws contained in the Bible. As life progressed, new problems and situations arose that demanded a broader

First page of the Talmud—the text of the Mishnah and Gemarah, found in the center column, is surrounded by the commentaries of Rashi, Tosafot and others.

and clearer defining of Biblical law. The schools of the Tannaim dealt with the urgent legal needs of their time. The discussions, arguments, ordinances, and interpretations of the Tannaim are known as the Oral Tradition, as distinguished from the Written Law—that is, the Bible itself.

The oral traditions of the Tannaim, from the days of the great scholars, Hillel* and Shammai,* needed classification and editing. Some of the laws were systematized by the great scholars Rabbi Akiba* and his pupil Rabbi Meir. The major task of arranging the **halachot,** or laws, fell to Judah ha-Nasi or the Prince.* He was head of the Sanhedrin,* the highest court of Jewis' law, about 200 C.E.

The final form of the Mishnah consists of six sections, or orders. They include all the laws and customs which govern traditional Jewish religious life to the present day. The six sections are divided into sixty-three tractates or treatises; each tractate is subdivided into chapters and each chapter is further divided into paragraphs.

The following are the six sections of the Mishnah.

1. **Zeraim** (''Seeds'') contains laws relating to agriculture. The first treatise in this section, Berachot, deals mainly with prayers.

2. **Moed** (''Appointed Time'') refers to laws involving the Sabbath, festivals, feasts, and fast days. A separate treatise is devoted to each impor-

tant festival: Rosh ha-Shanah, Sukkot, Passover, and others.

3. **Nashim** ("Women") deals with laws concerning family life.

4. **Nezikim** ("Damages") a section studied most often, discusses civil and criminal laws. This section includes the treatise **Avot (Ethics of the Fathers*)**, a collection of moral teachings, epigrams, and acute observations on human conduct.

5. **Kodashim** ("Holy Objects"), concerned mainly with sacrificial rites, laws dealing with **shehitah*** ("ritual slaughter"), kosher and non-kosher foods, etc. **(See also** DIETARY LAWS.)

6. **Tahorot** ("Purity") states all the laws of "cleanliness" and "uncleanliness," or ritual purity **(see** PURITY LAWS).

The Mishnah is written in Hebrew. Its style is expressive, forceful, exact, and terse. It is a development of the Biblical Hebrew, enriched by new words and forms, assimilating Aramaic* and some Greek and Latin terms.

The opinions of the Tannaim which were not included in the Mishnah are called **baraitot,** or external traditions. These opinions were assembled separately, and are quoted in the text of the Gemarah. Similarly, the **Tosefta** (literally "additions,") contains discussions of the laws by the Tannaim and is written in the style of the Mishnah.

Actually, there are two Talmuds: a Palestinian and a Babylonian Talmud. Some time after the Mishnah was edited in its final form, or canon, the Amoraim,* scholars in Palestine and Babylonia,* began an intensive study of the Mishnah. In the course of interpreting and discussing the laws and decisions of their predecessors, the Tannaim, they often found obscure passages and contradictory opinions in the Mishnah. The Amoraim sought to reconcile the varying opinions, and to draw clear conclusions from the mass of conflicting material. For over two hundred years after the completion of the Mishnah, this intellectual activity continued, (c. 200-c.50). The commentaries on the Mishnah by the Amoraim are known as the Gemarah, the Hebrew for "completed."

Among the foremost Amoraim was Johanan bar Napaha, the son of a blacksmith. He rose to fame as the head of a famous academy, and as a teacher of hundreds of scholars. His brother-in-law, Simeon bar Lakish, was once a gladiator and a highwayman. Rabbi Johanan won him over to the study of the Law, and bar Lakish became a brilliant Talmudic scholar.

The editing of the Palestinian Talmud took place during the period when Christianity was becoming entrenched in the Roman Empire. The Jews of Palestine were driven by the Roman persecutions to escape to Babylonia. The centers of Jewish learning in Palestine deteriorated. The scholars who remained, concerned with the decline in the study of the Law, compiled the work of the Palestinian Amoraim. Of their interpretations of the Mishnah only four sections have come down: Zeraim, Moed, Nashim, Nezikin. The Palestinian, or Jerusalem, Talmud, although rich in legal, moral and aggadic* material, bears the mark of incompleteness. It is written in the Aramaic mixed with Hebrew that was spoken in Palestine at that time.

Like the Palestinian Talmud, the Babylonian Talmud, the work of the Babylonian Amoraim, consists of the Mishnah and its commentary, the Gemarah. It is much wider in scope, embracing the religious, communal and social life of the Jews for many centuries. As the source-book of Jewish law, it became the most important guide and companion of the Jewish people throughout the ages. The Babylonian Talmud is also an encyclopedic work, embodying all that was known of medicine, agriculture, history, geography, astronomy, etc., at the time of its creation.

The Babylonian Talmud is the monumental work of approximately two thousand scholars. Among the foremost Amoraim were Rav and Samuel. Rav was born in Babylonia and studied at the academy of Judah ha-Nasi in Palestine. When he returned to Babylonia, in about 220 C.E., he established the famous academy of Sura. A great scholar of the Law, he was also the author of masterly liturgical poems, legends, and parables. Rav's comrade, Samuel was also a pupil of Judah ha-Nasi. Upon his return to Babylonia, he too became head of another famous academy, that of Nehardea. Thoroughly learned in medicine, astronomy, and the natural sciences, Samuel's opinions were decisive in all laws involving monetary matters.

Studying the Talmud—woodcut by Joseph Budko.

306

Six generations of Amoraim contributed to the interpretation and clarification of the law. The last of the Amoraim, Rav Ashi, who revived the Academy of Sura, assembled all the works of his predecessors dealing with law, ethics, religious thought, legends, and the general knowledge of the day. He systematized the vast accumulation of material, accomplishing a task equal to that of Judah ha-Nasi, editor of the Mishah. The work of Rav Ashi, who died in 427 C.E., was continued by Rabbina and Jose. They completed the final editing of the Babylonian Gemarah in the year 500. The scholars who lived in the beginning of the sixth century, the Saboraim,* clarified further the text of the Talmud and helped to give it the form which it has retained to this day.

The Babylonian Talmud follows the order arrangement of the Mishnah. However, only thirty-six treatises of the sixty-three contained in the Mishnah are supplemented by the comments of the Amoraim, or the Gemarah.

The two fundamental elements of the Talmud are **Halakhah,*** or legal discussions of the law and **Aggadah,*** which, consisting of legends, tales, fables, are almost always poetical and moving; the **aggadot** attempt to teach a moral lesson.

Among the great codifiers of Talmudic law were Issac Alfasi and Maimonides.* The aggadic part of the Talmud was compiled and published separately by Rabbi Jacob Haviv (1460-1516) under the name En Yaakov.

It can be safely said that the Talmud served as the greatest force in preserving the unity and integrity of the Jewish people in the Diaspora.

Jewish religious life revolved around it. The Talmud regulated every act and every hour of the Jew's day. Its lofty moral teachings sustained the Jewish spirit in the dark days of persecution. As soon as the Jewish child had some grounding in the Bible and its commentaries, especially Rashi,* he dived into the "Sea of Talmud." Many emerged eventually as scholars of Jewish law, fortified by the high ideals and wisdom of the sages. The Talmud and its commentaries are a most fascinating and significant product of the Jewish religious genius.   H.L.

TAM, RABBENU (Jacob ben Meir) (1100-1171). Talmudic scholar. Grandson of the famous commentator, Rashi,* he was the head of a school of Talmudists whose works are called **Tosafot** ("additions"). These scholars or Tosafists analyzed the opinions in the Talmud.* Their comments and discussions are characterized by keen and critical examination of Talmudic law. They also dealt with problems arising in their time, and rendering important decisions which influenced Jewish life and institutions throughout the Middle Ages.

Rabbenu Tam, whose byname "Tam" means "perfect," was rich and influential, but he was a modest and forthright man. On the festival of Shavuot* in 1147, he was attacked by Crusaders and nearly killed. He was saved by a knight who took him under his protection. From his native town of Rameru, he moved to Troyes, where he opened an important Talmudical academy. Rabbenu Tam became the spiritual leader of all the Jewish communities of France.* He called for assemblies of rabbis to discuss new decisions. As many as 150 rabbis participated in these assemblies, which helped strengthen Jewish unity and regulate religious life for many generations.

TANNAIM (Aramaic, meaning "those who repeat"). The teachers and scholars of the first two centuries C.E. who set down the laws of the Talmud.* They were called **Tannaim** because they were teachers who taught their students to rehearse the Oral Tradition, based on the Written Law of the Bible, for the purpose of memorization. The group of laws taught by a Tanna was called his Mishnah, or "repetition." The famous rabbis Johanan ben Zakkai,* Akiba,* Meir,* Joshua ben Hananyah, Nahum of Gimzo, Eliezer ben Hyracanus, Eleazar ben Azaryah, and Judah the Prince* were among the nearly three hundred Tannaim. (**See also** TALMUD.)

TANYA. A Hasidic classic. (**See** HASIDISM.)

TARBUT (Hebrew, meaning "culture"). After

The well-known title page of the Vilna Shas.

the first Russian revolution in 1917, Hebrew culture flourished for a time among the Jews of Russia.* An organization called Tarbut was founded; it established cultural institutions, teachers' seminaries, and schools. Tarbut published Hebrew newspapers for adults and children, and contributed to the revival of Hebrew as a spoken language. However, the Tarbut movement was short-lived. As soon as the Soviet regime was established, it banned all of the widespread Tarbut activities. Tarbut organizations then sprang up in other Eastern European countries, especially in Poland* and Lithuania.* They made an important contribution to modern Hebrew education. On the eve of the Second World War, 70,000 pupils were enrolled in Tarbut schools. These were destroyed by the Nazis, together with the vast majority of Eastern European Jewry.

TARGUM (Hebrew, meaning "translation"). Usually applied to the Aramaic* translation of the Bible, of which the best known is Targum Onkelos.*

An Aramaic translation was necessary to make the Bible be understood by the large numbers of Jews who spoke Aramaic for many generations during and following the period of the Second Temple. Targum Onkelos is an excellent, almost literal translation. To this day, many editions of the Bible carry the Targum Onkelos, which, in many instances, enables us to interpret more correctly the original Hebrew text. **(See also ONKELOS.)**

TASHLIKH. See ROSH HA-SHANAH.

TECHNION, ISRAEL INSTITUTE OF TECHNOLOGY IN HAIFA.* The Technion is the oldest educational institution of university rank in Israel.* It was founded in 1912 by a group of farsighted men from many lands, including K.Z. Wissotsky of Moscow, Jacob H. Schiff* of New York,* Julius Rosenwald of Chicago and Dr. Paul Nathan of Berlin. The outbreak of the First World War delayed the opening of the Technion till 1924. Since then its graduates have supplied more than half of the technically trained manpower for the scientific and industrial development programs of Israel.

The original institute was built at the foot of Mt. Carmel and was intended to accommodate about 300 students. Today close to 9,000 students are enrolled in the Technion, the affiliated Junior Technical College and Technical High School. A new campus ("Technion City"), consisting of 300 acres on the slopes of Mount Carmel, was deeded to the school by the Government of Israel. The campus, still growing, currently consists of more than a score of buildings which include aeronautical, hydraulics, building research, soil research and other laboratories; classroom, library and workshop buildings; and dormitories providing living accommodations for students.

The Technion's College of Engineering, with its faculties of civil, mechanical, chemical, agricultural, and aeronautical engineering, and departments of architecture and town planning, currently supplies Israel with engineers, applied scientists, and high-level technicians. Its various research laboratories are engaged in solving some of the manifold problems of Israel's pioneering economy. Since 1940, the American Technion Society has been aiding the Technion with funds and scholarships, and making it possible for selected graduates to come to the United States for a year of practical experience in American industrial plants.   S.S.B.

Technion City on the Slopes of Mt. Carmel.

TEFILLIN (PHYLACTERIES). The law of Tefillin is derived from the Biblical commandment: "And thou shalt bind them for a sign upon thy hand, and they shall be as frontlets between thine eyes" (Deut. 6:8). The tefillin, or phylacteries, consist of two leather boxes containing four selections from the Bible (Exod. 13:1-10, 11-16 and Deut. 6:4-9, 11:13-21), inscribed on parchment, which proclaim the existence and unity of God and serve as a reminder of the liberation from Egypt.

One of the boxes, called "Shel Rosh," is placed upon the head, hanging over the center of the forehead; the other box, called "Shel Yad," is placed on the large muscle of the left upper arm. Straps of leather are attached to each box. The straps of the arm phylactery are wound around the arm seven times, and three times around the middle finger.

The prayer which is recited before putting on the phylacteries describes their significance: "He hath commanded us to lay the phylacteries upon the hand as a memorial of his outstretched arms; opposite the heart, to indicate the duty of subjecting the longings and designs of out heart to His service, blessed be He; and upon the head over against the brain, thereby teaching that the mind, whose seat is in the brain, together with all senses and faculties, is to be subjected to His service."

Phylacteries are thus represented as a sign of dedication to the Creator. Every Jewish male who has reached the age of bar mitzvah* is commanded to wear them during the morning prayers on each weekday, and during the afternoon service on the Ninth of Ab. Sabbaths and festivals being themselves "signs," no phylacteries are worn on these days.　　　　　　　　　　　　H.L.

TEL AVIV (Hebrew, meaning "Hill of Spring"). Largest city in Israel, with a population, including that of its twin city Jaffa,* of over 316,700 in 1984. Tel Aviv was founded in 1909, when a group of Jewish residents of Jaffa decided to leave the squalor and high rents of that overwhelming Arab town. They bought two stretches of sand-dunes and built a garden suburb which they called Tel Aviv, after Sokolow's* translation of Herzl's* Jewish utopia **Altneuland.** By 1914, this all-Jewish town boasted 1,416 inhabitants. Most of them were expelled by the Turks as "enemy aliens" during the First World War. After the Balfour Declaration* and the British occupation of the country in 1918, Tel Aviv grew swiftly. The Third Aliyah (wave of immigration) from Eastern Europe, and refugees from Jaffa itself during the Arab riots of 1921, swelled its population.

Twenty years after its founding, Tel Aviv had a population of 40,000, and was on its way to the cultural and industrial leadership of the country. But its expansion was greatest in the 1930's when immigrants from Germany* streamed in. Houses and streets multiplied at a rapid rate. It became consolidated as a dynamic urban center, the heart of the country's trade and light industry. During the 1936 disturbances, it built its own port almost overnight. In the days of chaos and terror that marked the end of the British Mandate, Tel Aviv was the heart of underground immigration and defense movement operated by Haganah.* In 1948, the independence of Israel was declared in Tel Aviv's Museum. Jerusalem* being then under siege. Since then Tel Aviv has developed rapidly, spreading out in many directions. Its vitality is expressed in many modern apartment houses, public buildings, and educational institutions. Art galleries, chamber music, the Israel Philharmonic Orchestra, the Habimah, Ohel and Kameri theatres, and innumerable well-stocked bookshops are focal centers of an intense cultural life. The broad boulevards, stores and hotels attract a considerable tourist "industry," and outdoor and sea-front cafes serve the citizens who come to Israel from the highways and byways of the world. It is the home of Tel Aviv University* founded in 1956.

S. and T.B.

Tefillin (phylactery), cases, Poland, 19th century—engraved silver.　　　　Courtesy The Jewish Museum, New York City.

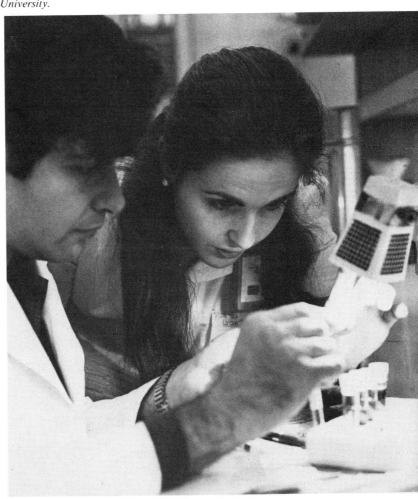

Cancer research at the Dept. of Micro-Biology at Tel Aviv University.

TEL AVIV UNIVERSITY.

Founded in 1956, it has (1984) an enrollment of almost 27,000 and a faculty of more than 3,600. The equipment of the University includes the most advanced electron microscope, telescope, computer, film-lane digitizer and language laboratory in Israel.

Subjects taught range from A-Z—Archaeology to Zoology—in 90 departments and over 50 research institutes. Its many schools include Arts and Communication, Music Academy, Social Work, Business Administration, Space Sciences, Engineering, Medicine, Law, Educational Sciences, Exact Sciences, Life Sciences, Social Sciences, Physical Education, Dentistry, Veterinary Medicine, Nursing and Humanities, Judaic Studies, History, Linguistics and Psychology.

The research institutes engage in advanced study of cancer, heart and 16 other medical specialties, urban studies, Middle Eastern and African Studies, petroleum, space and planetary science, nature preservation, labor studies, Soviet studies, developing countries and many others.

The American Friends of Tel Aviv University maintain an office in New York City.

TEMPLE: FIRST AND SECOND.

The First Temple was planned by King David* and erected by King Solomon* (965-925 B.C.E.). It took seven years to build the sanctuary; its walls were made

"Planning King Solomon's Temple," by Jack Levine.

men to build it. For the Temple roof, cedars and cypresses were hewn in the forests of Lebanon,* floated down in rafts from Phoenicia* to Joppa (Jaffa),* and then borne up, log by log, to the heights of Jerusalem. The Temple was surrounded by courts and auxiliary buildings. It had three divisions: the vestibule before which were freestanding pillars, Jahin and Boaz; the holy place containing the altar of incense, the table of the shewbread and the sevenbranched **Menorah;*** and the Holy of Holies, which held only the Ark of the Covenant* and the Ten Commandments.* The altar for the sacrifices was in the Temple court. The services in the Temple were impressive and accompanied by singing and instrumental music. For 380 years, this shrine was the heart of the nation. To it the people went up in pilgrimage three times a year, on the festivals of Pesach,* Shavuot,* and Sukkot.* The Temple was destroyed on the ninth day of Ab, in 586 B.C.E., by Nebuchadnezzer, King of Babylonia, who deported the people of Judah and made it a Babylonian colony.

The Second Temple was completed seventy years later by the people who had returned from the Babylonian exile. Many of the original Temple vessels, plundered by the conqueror, had disappeared. The Ark of the Covenant was gone, and the Holy of Holies stood quite empty. When the sacredness of the Temple was defiled in 168 B.C.E. at the command of the Syrian King Antiochus, the people revolted. After the Maccabean victory, the Temple was restored, but did not reach its full magnificence till Herod* rebuilt it (20-19 B.C.E.). Ninety years later, the Roman legions, under Titus, set fire to the Temple (again on the ninth day of Ab), and left it a heap of ruins (70 C.E.). Since then, the day of the destruction has been remembered by Jews with fasting and with prayer, and historic events are mentioned as having occurred "in the days of the First Temple" of "in the time of the Second Temple."   N.B-A.

of huge blocks of granite, quarried, dressed and dovetailed in the hills surrounding Jerusalem.* On the Temple site itself, no iron tools were used because implements of war were made of iron—and the Temple was a symbol of peace (I Kings 6:7). Solomon imported Phoenician crafts-

Model of King Solomon's Temple, built by Joseph Doctorowitz. Based on text from the Bible.
Courtesy The Jewish Museum, New York City.

TEN COMMANDMENTS. According to the Bible, the divine laws spoken by God to Moses* and written on two tablets of stone. (Exod. 20:2-17; and Deut. 5:6-21). The Greek word for them is Decalogue. They are the highest laws in Judaism, and the source of all Jewish law and ethics. Christianity and Islam* also have accepted them. The Ten Commandments cover the whole religious and moral life of man. They teach the unity of God, and prescribe the fundamental ways of behavior between man and man.

TEN LOST TRIBES. See LOST TRIBES.

TEN MARTYRS. See MARTYRS, TEN.

TERRITORIALISM. A movement to found a Jewish state or autonomous Jewish community in some territory other than Palestine:* Zionism* differed from territorialism chiefly in its emphasis on Zion (Palestine) as the only suitable area for Jewish colonization. Some of the great Zionist leaders leaned toward territorialism at some time in their careers. In his revolutionary pamphlet, **Auto-Emancipation** (1881), Leo Pinsker* called for the establishment of a Jewish state without specific reference to Palestine. Theodor Herzl,* the father of political Zionism, did not at first think of Palestine alone as the home of his Jewish state. After failing to obtain a charter for Jewish settlement in Palestine, Herzl presented the Sixth Zionist Congress* with a proposal for Jewish settlement in East Africa. Known as the ''Uganda Plan,'' it had been proposed by the English government. Herzl himself dropped the plan, but a group of Zionists headed by Israel Zangwill* continued to support it. They formed the independent Jewish Territorial Organization (ITO), and proceeded to investigate the possibilities for Jewish settlement in Angola, Cyrenaica, Mesopotamia, Mexico,* Canada,* Australia, Siberia and other countries. These efforts had no success and the movement soon directed its efforts to the encouragement of Jewish farming in various countries. After the Balfour Declaration*

(1917), stating the support of the English government for a Jewish National Home in Palestine, the movement lost much of its force. It was disbanded in 1925, only to be revived as the ITO in Berlin, and the Freeland League, in London,* after Hitler's rise to power.   B.H.

TESTAMENT, OLD. See OLD TESTAMENT.

TET. Ninth letter of the Hebrew alphabet; numerically, nine.

TIBERIAS. A city on the Sea of Galilee (Kineret),* famous for its healing hot springs. It was built by Herod Antipas in 18 B.C.E. in honor of the reigning Roman emperor, Tiberius Caesar. Notwithstanding its pagan origin and alien style of architecture, it soon became Judaized. In the second century C.E., after the failure of Bar Kokhba's* revolt, the Sanhedrin* moved to Tiberias, and the Mishnah and Masorah* were edited here. During the following centuries, Tiberias attracted many pilgrims and scholars as one of the four Holy Cities, and as the burial place of Rabbi Meir Baal Hanes, as well as of Maimonides.* In 1560, Don Joseph Nasi, a Marrano* from Spain,* received permission from the Turkish sultan to rebuild Tiberias as a Jewish agricultural and industrial center. His project failed,

Tomb of Rabbi Meir Baal Hanes at Tiberias.
Zionist Archives and Library, New York City.

Torah dressed with mantle, crown, breastplate and pointer.
Mantle: Brocade and velvet, Germany, 1765.
Crown: Silver, Poland, 18th century.
Pointer: Silver, Galicia, early 19th century.

however, and Tiberias lay in ruins until 1740, when the Bedouin sheikh, Daher el Omer, restored the city with the help of Rabbi Aboulafia of Izmir. Today, as in ancient times, it is the economic center and metropolis of Lower Galilee, and Israel's principal health resort and spa.

TISHRI. First month of the Jewish civil calendar. It is during this month that the High Holidays occur.

TORAH (Hebrew, meaning "teaching"). Though originally Torah may have applied to the Ten Commandments only, and later to the Pentateuch,* it was from an early period employed as a general term to cover all of Jewish law, including the vast mass of teachings recorded in the Talmud* and other rabbinical works. This latter literature was called Oral Torah, or Tradition, as opposed to Written Torah or Written Law. To the pious Jew, both Torahs are sacred and inviolable. The Torah guided God in the creation of the world, says the Talmud, and if men were not to observe it, the universe would cease to exist.

A scribe (sofer) in Israel carries on an ancient craft as he inscribes the Pentateuch onto parchment.
Joint Distribution Committee.

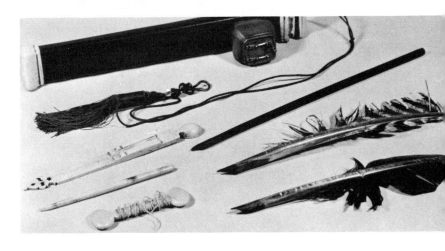

Implements of a sofer (scribe) for writing a Torah—European Jews wrote with a quill; Oriental Jews with a reed, which formed heavier lines.

TORAH UMESORAH. Orthodox Jewish educational agency whose aim is to found **yeshivot**—Hebrew Day Schools—providing religious and secular studies under the same auspices, in the Jewish communities of the United States, particularly in small towns and suburban communities. It was founded in 1944 by Rabbi Feivel Mendlowitz. At that time there were only thirty-three day schools in the United States, only seven situated outside of New York and its environs.

At the beginning of the 1978 school year, there were 516 Hebrew day schools located in 37 states and five Canadian provinces. Of these 254 were located outside of the New York Metropolitan area. In the New York area there were 209 schools. There were 150 high schools functioning in the United States.

Torah Umesorah tries to maintain high standards in existing yeshivot through curriculum study and evaluation, supervisory visits by staff members, and regular consultation with principals and boards of education. It also carries on a program of teacher placement and interviews. Other activities include: publication of textbooks coordinated with the school program, including the children's magazine, **Olomeinu-Our World;** the organization and maintenance of a network of parent-teacher groups affiliated with the National Association of Hebrew Day School Parent-Teacher Associations.

During the past few years, Torah Umesorah has been concentrating upon the training of teachers. It conducts such programs in five major seminaries. It has, as well, its own teacher-training program called Aish Dos (the "Fire of Faith").

TORONTO. See CANADA.

TOSAFOT. See TAM, RABBENU.

TOSEFTA. See TALMUD.

TOURO, JUDAH (1775-1854). Philanthropist. Born in Newport, R.I., where his father was a cantor, Touro was educated in Boston by his uncle, Moses Michael Hays. Touro prospered as a merchant in New Orleans, amassing a huge fortune which was distributed at his death to many worthy causes in the United States* and in Jerusalem.* When a Universalist church was foreclosed and sold at auction, Touro bought the property and turned it back to its congregation. His name is honored in many places, notably in the Touro Synagogue at Newport, which was named a national religious shrine in 1947.

TRANSJORDAN. See JORDAN HASHEMITE KINGDOM OF; **also** ZIONISM.

TRUMPELDOR, JOSEPH (1880-1920). Zionist pioneer leader, soldier and founder of the pioneer movement Hechalutz. He was born in the Caucasus, Russia,* and spent his childhood away from the great Russian Jewish centers, in a completely Russified family. Shortly after he completed a course in dentistry, the Russo-Japanese War broke out (1904), and Trumpeldor joined the Russian Army as a volunteer. He lost his left arm in the siege of Port Arthur, and was decorated four times for conspicuous bravery. He emerged from the army with the unheard of distinction of being the only Jewish officer in the Tsar's forces. Then, Trumpeldor, the Russian patriot, was jarred out of his patriotism and bitterly hurt by the wave of pogroms that broke over Russian Jewry. He became a Zionist and went to Palestine as a chalutz—a pioneer. With his one arm he learned to till the soil in the settlement of Degania.*

At the outbreak of World War I, the Turkish rulers of Palestine became very suspicious of the Jewish settlers and many were jailed or exiled. Trumpeldor was one of the refugees who came to Alexandria,* Egypt.* There he made every effort to organize a Jewish fighting unit for service with

Judah Touro

Joseph Trumpeldor

the British in Palestine. The British at first bitterly opposed this idea, but later relented and permitted Trumpeldor to organize a transport unit—the Zion Mule Corps. Trumpeldor served as Captain under Colonel Patterson in the Gallipoli Expeditionary Force. The record of bravery of the Corps was helpful in breaking down British resistance, and around its remnants the Jewish Legion* was finally formed in 1917. Trumpeldor was refused a commission in the British army, and turned his energies to the realization of another dream. The Tsarist government had fallen and Trumpeldor returned to Russia hoping to organize an army of 10,000 Jews and to lead them over the Caucasus and Anatolia to Palestine. The Bolshevik revolution broke out and his plan failed. Instead, he organized the young Zionists of Russia in the Hechalutz pioneer movement and succeeded in getting a group of them out of Russia. Back in Palestine he plunged into self-defense work. At the end of World War I, the borderline between Syria* and Palestine was unsettled. Three small Jewish settlements were in this disputed area. The British and French forces had withdrawn, and Metulla, Ayelet Hashachar, and Tel Hai lay exposed to the bands of hostile Bedouins. Trumpeldor realized the importance of defending these settlements and holding them within the boundaries of Palestine. With a small band of men and women, Trumpeldor defended the area until he was killed in March 1920, by an act of trickery perpetrated by a treacherous sheikh. He died defending Tel Hai, but the area he fought for remained a part of Israel. When a new settlement was opened near the border of Syria, it was named Tel Joseph, in honor of Joseph Trumpeldor.

The **Betar** (Brith Trumpeldor) organization **(see** REVISIONIST ZIONISM) is named after him.

N.B-A.

TSCHERNICHOWSKY, SAUL (1875-1943). Hebrew poet. Together with Chaim N. Bialik,* he was one of the two leading modern Hebrew poets. Tschernichowsky's education did not include Talmudic training, but the Bible left a deep impression upon him, as did Greek philosophy and culture. He became a practicing physician in St. Petersburg and continued this work after he settled in Palestine.*

Tschernichowsky's poetry is distinguished by a vigorous sense of beauty, and a closeness to nature. His idylls, or pastoral poems, possess wonderful charm and humor. They reflect the wholesome and happier phases of Eastern European Jewish traditional life. His sonnets are works of art, skillfully designed and executed.

Tschernichowsky identified himself with the Jewish national revival. He wrote some of his first poems on the Palestine landscape and on its historical themes. In addition to his original works, he made a great contribution to Hebrew letters by outstanding translations of Homer, Sophocles, Shakespeare, Goethe, Longfellow (**Evangeline** and **Hiawatha**), and many other great writers.

Saul Tschernichowsky

TU BISHEVAT (New Year of Trees). The fifteenth day of the month of Shevat is also known as the "New Year of Trees." It marks the end of winter and the beginning of spring, and in ancient times people thought of it as the day in which sap

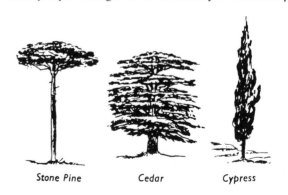

Stone Pine   Cedar   Cypress

Tu Bishevat celebration at Ramat Gan, Israel.

begins again to flow in the trees. Before the Jews were driven from their land, it was celebrated with the festive planting of saplings. This custom has been revived in modern Israel,* and is joyously observed in a land that centuries of neglect have denuded of green things. In the Diaspora, Tu Bishevat was also celebrated by eating such Palestinian fruits as figs, dates, and "boxer"—the fruit of the carob-tree.

TUNISIA. The Jewish community of Tunisia dates back to the destruction of the Second Temple. Since that time the settlement has felt the yoke of both Muslim and Christian domination, in a history marked by alternating periods of peaceful development and bitter persecution. Tunisian Jews knew their darkest days under Spanish domination (1535-1575), but they had also felt the lash under Moslem leaders. Despite the hardships they underwent, Tunisian Jewry maintained the Jewish tradition intact; during the eighteenth century Tunisia became an important seat of Talmudic learning. A bright era began in 1881, when France,* assumed the protectorate over the country. Jews received equal citizenship rights along with Muslims, and for the first time were permitted to enter the fields of commerce and industry. The Alliance Israelité Universelle then organized schools which are still in operation. In 1956, Tunisia gained its independence from France. The Jews of Tunisia had been perhaps the most secure Jewish community in all the Muslim lands. Their religious, cultural and communal life was close-knit, active and well-organized. But recent Tunisian participation in the Arab League has led to increasing unease about their future. Emigration since 1947, mainly to Israel and France, has left (1984) a Jewish population of about 3,000 which is still decreasing. Communications between Tunisia and Israel have been severed.

TURKEY. When Ottoman forces crossed over into Europe in the fourteenth century, conquering the Byzantine Empire and taking over Thrace, Thessaly and Asia Minor, comprising present-day Turkey, they found Jewish communities which could trace their origin back to Roman times. The Turkish Jews welcomed the Ottoman invasion for their lot had been hard under Christian Byzantine rule. Under the rule of Islam,* they were granted religious liberty, security against attack, and the right to own land. This period of prosperity and calm lasted several centuries. During this time Turkey became a haven for persecuted Jews throughout Europe. Jews played an important role in the courts of the sultans as ministers, scholars, advisers, and physicians; often they were able to intervene on behalf of their less fortunate brethren in other countries.

In 1453, Sultan Mohammed II conquered Constantinople, and that city became a center of Jewish cultural and political life. In 1492, Sultan Bayazid II welcomed the Jews who had been expelled from Spain* and Portugal.* Many of these settled in Palestine,* which fell under Turkish rule in 1516, and was held by Turkey until the end of the First World War. A great influx of Sephardic* Jews who brought with them a highly developed cultural tradition, as well as many of Europe's foremost scholars and physicians, enriched Turkey. The great Sephardic spiritual centers at Salonica and Smyrna flowered in the sixteenth and seventeenth centuries. There was also an influx of Ashkenazic Jews from Germany,* Austria,* Hungary,* Poland,* and Russia.* Turkish Jews attained their greatest prominence during the reigns of Suleiman the Magnificent (1520-1556) and Selim II (1556-1574). Don Joseph Nasi, a former Marrano,* became Sultan Selim's chief adviser, and exerted great influence over European affairs. During the sixteenth century, Turkey became a center of Talmudic and Kabbalistic teaching. The works of Joseph Karo,* Isaac Luria, and Hayyim Vital had a great influence on Jewish learning and mysticism. Sabbatai Zevi,* the messianic pretender, attracted a fanatical following among thousands of Jews in Turkey and Europe.

The end of Salim II's reign saw the beginning of Turkey's decline as an important power, and with it, Jewish fortunes. Later sultans enacted discriminatory measures against the Jews. At the end of the nineteenth century, Turkey played a crucial role in the history of political Zionism.* In 1899, Theodor Herzl* tried to obtain a colonization charter from the Turkish Sultan which would allow unlimited immigration to Palestine. His efforts were unsuccessful due to the Turkish suspicions of Zionist political aims. After the First World War, the government of Kemal Pasha began a policy of Ottomanization of Turkey. Jewish autonomy was weakened in 1923, when Turkish became the only language of instruction permissible in Jewish schools. The Chief Rabbi of Turkey no longer served as official representative of the Jewish minority, under a strict interpretation of separation of Church and State. In 1925, the rights of non-Muslims to travel both within Turkey and abroad were sharply curtailed.

In 1934, thousands of Jews were forcibly evacuated from Thrace and the Dardanelles; it was feared that Turkey was under German influence in her treatment of Jewish nationals. With the outbreak of of the Second World War, however, Turkey was firm in her refusal to return Jewish refugees to Germany. Since 1947, about 45,000 Turkish Jews left for Israel. An estimated 21,000 Jews still (1984) remain. They are concentrated in the three major cities of Instanbul, Ismir, and Ankara. The Turkish government has been friendly to Israel,* and put no obstacles in the way

Turkish Jew of the sixteenth century.

of emigration. In 1952, after a lapse of twenty-two years, the post of Chief Rabbi of Turkey was once again filled and the old Council of Jewish Communities revived.

TWELVE TRIBES. Descended from Jaco 's sons—Reuben,* Simeon,* Levi,* Judah,* Issachar,* Zebulun,* Gad,* Asher,* Dan,* Naphtali,* Joseph* and Benjamin.* While the tribe of Levi was set apart to serve in the Holy Temple, the sons of Joseph—Ephraim* and Manasseh*—were each given the status of an independent tribe at the time of the possession and distribution of the land of Israel.

TZADE. Eighteenth letter of Hebrew alphabet; numerically, ninety.

TZADIK. Hasidic saint. **(See HASIDISM.)**

TZEDAKAH. See CHARITY.

TZITZIT. Ritual fringes on the Tallit.*

U

UGANDA. See TERRITORIALISM.

ULPAN (Hebrew: "house of learning"). Israeli adult education program to give newcomers an accelerated, intensive course in the Hebrew* language and the Israeli way of life. Ulpanim using the same intensive method for the study of the Hebrew language have been set up in other countries as well.

UNION OF AMERICAN HEBREW CONGREGATIONS. The Union of American Hebrew Congregations (UAHC) is an association of Reform or Liberal congregations in the Western Hemisphere. It was founded in 1873 by Rabbi Isaac Mayer Wise. Wise's primary purpose was to establish a seminary for the training of American rabbis; this was accomplished two years later with the founding of the Hebrew Union College* in Cincinnati. The UAHC maintained its headquarters in Cincinnati until 1951, when the Berg Memorial-House of Living Judaism, in New York,* was opened as headquarters for the organization and all its affiliates.

The UAHC maintained the Board of Delegates of American Israelites from 1878 until 1925, when it ceased to exist. The Board published the first census of Jews in the United States, in 1880. It concerned itself throughout with the rights of Jews in foreign countries.

But the primary purpose of the UAHC and its affiliates was and is to service the constituent synagogues and temples. Currently there are over 700 congregations, with a total membership of about 1,100,000.

The chief legislative authority of the UAHC is its Biennial General Assembly. Between assemblies, the executive board (120 persons) and the administrative committee of that board carry on the policy-making functions of the organization. Various commissions deal with such programs as Jewish education, synagogue activities, and interfaith activities.

The UAHC has organized three national affiliates: The National Federation of Temple Sisterhoods (1913), the National Federation of Temple Brotherhoods (1916), and the National Federation of Temple Youth (1939). Each carries on a full program of religious, cultural, educational, and social activities. In addition, the UAHC has, affiliated with it, the National Association of Temple Secretaries (1943), an organization of professional temple executives, and the National Association of Temple Educators (1955).

The UAHC and its affiliates publish the quarterlies **American Judaism,** and **Jewish Teacher,** and **Synagogue Service,** a bi-monthly.

E.L.

UNION OF ORTHODOX JEWISH CONGREGATIONS. On June 8, 1898, representatives of fifty Orthodox congregations met in New York* to organize the Union of Orthodox Jewish Congregations of America. The affiliate synagogues of the UOJCA list approximately 500,000 individuals on their membership rolls. The Union also serves as a representative body for an additional 250,000 Orthodox Jews who comprise other elements of Orthodoxy.

The UOJCA holds a biennial general convention, which sets the policies of the organization and at which are discussed the status and problems of Orthodox Judaism. The day-to-day work is carried on by national commissions. Some of these have been: Armed Forces, communal relations, community activities, education, Israel and overseas, **Orthodox Jewish Life** magazine (monthly), **kashruth,** law and legislation, Orthodox Union Association, public relations, religious standards, synagogue relations, youth activities. By far the most famous and wide-spread activity of the UOJCA is its program of **kashruth.**

UNION OF ORTHODOX JEWISH CONGREGATIONS OF AMERICA, WOMEN'S BRANCH. The national organization representing the women affiliated with Orthodox synagogues in the United States. It was organized in 1923 to spread the understanding and observance of Orthodoxy, to instill an appreciation of traditional Judaism in young people, and to give the Jewish woman an understanding of her role in the home, the synagogue, and the community. The Women's Branch formed a **kashruth** committee, which sought to make kosher products available to the public. The Women's Branch helped raise funds for dormitories at Yeshiva University,* and established the Hebrew Teachers Training School for Girls, now housed in the Stern College for Women of Yeshiva University.

UNION OF SOVIET SOCIALIST REPUBLICS. See RUSSIA.

UNITED HIAS SERVICE. The Hebrew Sheltering Society and the Hebrew Immigrant Aid Society united in 1909 to form HIAS, the Hebrew Sheltering and Immigrant Aid Society. They had been established to meet the needs of Jewish immigrants to the United States. In 1954, HIAS, the United Service for New Americans, and the migration services of the American Jewish Joint

These 8 American university students who were chosen as national winners of the United Jewish Appeal-Kaplun Foundation 1983 University Essay contest on the theme "Jewish Experience as a source of Survival Strategies" are pictured above at the Israel Museum during their prize winning trip. Left to right: Ellen Resnick, 19, Brookline, MA; Michael Berger, 21, Brooklyn, NY; Bonnie Morris, 22, Bethesda, MD; Samuel Fleischacker, 22, Gibsonia, PA; Diane Steinberg, 24, Los Angeles, CA; Barry Paul Mann, 23, West Palm Beach, FL; Steven Schnipper, 23, Roslyn Heights, NY; Harman Grossman, 24, Brooklyn, NY.

Distribution Committee,* consolidated into a single international migration agency. United Hias Service. United Hias Service is maintained by funds from Federations, Welfare Funds, membership, and individual contributions.

The Service locates friends and relatives through its global network of offices. It assists the immigrant at every step in his journey—with preparing documents and arranging transportation, with personal welcome and shelter upon his arrival, and with a plan for resettlement. It further helps the newcomer comply with government regulations and with preparation for naturalization. The Service intervenes with government authorities in cases of unjustified detention and deportation, and presses constantly for relaxation of immigration barriers all over the world.

UNITED JEWISH APPEAL. An organization which raises money in the United States* for the resettlement and rehabilitations of Jews in Israel* and throughout the world, and for humanitarian programs benefiting needy and troubled Jews in Israel and in thirty other countries. Since its founding in 1939, the UJA has contributed to the rescue and resettlement of well over three million men, women and children, about half of them immigrants brought to Israel. To accomplish this, since its inception the UJA has collected some $10.6 billion and distributed it to its beneficiary agencies.

Through United Israel Appeal, Inc., the UJA supported the Jewish Agency's programs of immigrant absorption and human support services designed to improve the quality of life in Israel. These include initial resettlement services to new immigrants, such as Hebrew-language instruction, vocational training, and subsidized housing; special programs for disadvantaged youth; support of pre-school and higher education; health and welfare aid; and the establishment of kibbutzim* and moshavim,* and their support to the point of self-sufficiency. In 1979, the Jewish Agency also began a program called Project Renewal for the physical and social rehabilitation of the lives of immigrant families in distressed urban neighborhoods.

Another UJA beneficiary body is the American Jewish Joint Distribution Committee* (JDC), which operates in Israel and in 33 other countries throughout the world. In Israel, it provides services for the physically and mentally handicapped and supports extensive programs on behalf of the elderly, as well as special day-care programs for infants and toddlers. Its life-support services among remnant Jewish communities in other countries include food and clothing parcels, kosher meals, medical care, nursery and day schools, centers for senior citizens, and relief-in-transit for Jewish migrants from areas of distress. It also supports worldwide vocational training for Jewish youth through the Organization for

Stamp issued by Israel to commemorate the UJA's 40th anniversary.

Rehabilitation through Training (ORT). The Hebrew Immigrant Aid Society (HIAS) also receives allocations from the UJA. In its 100 years HIAS has resettled more than 4 million Jewish refugees from countries of oppression in the U.S. and other free lands.

In American Jewish communities, the annual fund raising campaigns support local and national programs as well as UJA-funded overseas services. Local programs include Jewish day schools, day-care centers, Y's and community centers, vocational workshops, medical care, family counseling, youth guidance, home and institutional care for the elderly, aid to the indigent and a full range of resettlement services for the incoming Jewish immigrants. Some 700 communities throughout the United States conduct annual fund raising campaigns on behalf of the UJA. A portion of the money is used for local need and a portion goes to support the UJA's overseas services.

UNITED KINGDOM. See ENGLAND.

UNITED STATES, HISTORY OF JEWS IN.

American Jewish history has its background in the work of the scientists and explorers of the fifteenth century. Individual Jews landed in what is now the United States between the years 1621, when Elias Legardo came to Virginia, and 1654, when Jacob Barsimson came to New Amsterdam from Holland, and they scattered along the Atlantic seaboard region of North America.

By common consent, however, American Jewish history began in September, 1654, when a group of twenty-three Jewish refugees from Brazil,* pursued by the Inquisition,* arrived in New Amsterdam. They were penniless, their belongings had been sold to pay for their passage, and three of them were thrown in jail while they awaited financial help from the Jews in Holland. Faced with official hostility and every hardship known to a pioneering community, these refugees in New Amsterdam fought for their rights courageously. The Dutch governor, Peter Stuyvesant, and his officials barred them from participation in the obligations and civil rights of the New Amsterdam citizens. These obligations included the duty of standing guard for the protection of the town. Asser Levy* fought for and secured this right. Jews also wrung from Stuyvesant the privilege of laying out a cemetery for the new Jewish community. The struggle continued till 1664, when the English assumed control of New Amsterdam and recognized the right of public worship for all creeds. As this right spread among the colonies, Jewish community life became normalized. In 1729, the New York Congregation Shearith

Leaders of the United Jewish Appeal convene at the Annual National Leadership Conference to begin the UJA/community fundraising campaign. Left to right: Alexander Grass of Harrisburg, PA, 1985 National Chairman; Herschel W. Blumberg, outgoing Chairman of the Board of Trustees; Stanley B. Horowitz, UJA President and Chief Professional Officer; and Robert E. Loup, incoming Chairman of the Board of Trustees and 1984 National Chairman.

Israel*—after many years of worshipping in private or rented dwellings—built a synagogue.

For the next century, Jews filtered into other seaboard settlements. Among the colonies in New England, Rhode Island provided a most congenial climate for Jewish settlers. Under the guiding genius of Roger Williams, this colony secured a charter in 1663 that provided full religious freedom. As a result, a thriving Jewish community

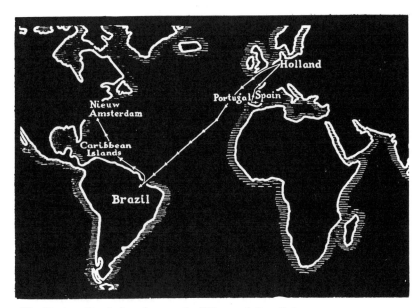

The Western Hemisphere became the "Shores of Hope" for European Jewry, beginning with the 17th century.
Columbia University Press. *An Old Faith in the New World* by David and Tamar de Sola Pool.

Grace Seixas Nathan (1752-1831) and Simon Nathan (1746-1822) were prominent citizens of colonial New York.

flourished in Newport more than a hundred years before the American Revolution. In Pennslyvania, in South Carolina, and in Georgia, freedom-loving men pressed for religious toleration, and Jews came and settled in these colonies. In 1750 there were enough Jews in Charleston, S.C., to organize a religious community. In Georgia, the Jews of Savannah established a congregation in 1734, two years after the colony was settled by Oglethorpe. By the time of the Revolutionary War, the Jews, concentrated chiefly in a half-dozen seaboard centers, were deeply rooted in their adopted land. When the colonies revolted against England, launching the American Revolution, the Jews threw themselves into the cause of the revolution whole-heartedly and with few exceptions. Jewish patriots served in the armed forces, and helped finance and provision the armies. In New York, outspoken patriot members of Congregation Shearith Israel, led by their **hazzan,** Gershom Mendes Seixas, fled the city rather than fall into Tory hands. In Philadephia Haym Salomon* worked ceaselessly to help finance the revolutionary cause. Jews were sent as confidential messengers to European governments, and their names in the lists of the prisoners, the dead and the wounded tell the story of their participation in this period of American history.

Throughout this period, culminating in the establishment of the Republic, and in the adoption of the American constitution in 1789, there were within the population no more than 2,000 to 3,000 Jews. Among these were a number of German Jews and even a sprinkling of East European Jews. An overwhelming majority, however, were descendants of Sephardic* exiles from the Mediterranean area. With Asser Levy's act of wresting from Peter Stuyvesant the right to stand

guard duty, the Sephardim established the pattern characteristic of American Jewry—integration into American political life by achieving civic, political, and economic equality without giving up their Jewishness.

Because they had fought to create the new nation, American Jews were jealous of their rights and ever vigilant in resisting encroachments or violations of them. The Virginia constitution establishing religious liberty, was widely followed, and it was reflected in the Northwest Ordinance, in the constitutions of Pennsylvania, of New York, and finally in the Constitution of the United States. Disabilities remained and had to be removed by legal action. In Maryland, Thomas Ken-

First synagogue building erected in North America. Drawn from contemporary illustrations by Esther H. Oppenheim.

Touro Synagogue, Newport, Rhode Island, the oldest synagogue building in the United States. Dedicated in 1763, it was designated as a national monument in 1946.

nedy led the fight for extending equal rights to Jews, finally won in 1826. North Carolina lagged in this respect until 1868. The Board of Delegates of American Israelites (1865-1878) labored to obtain the removal of the remaining relics of legal discrimination against Jews from several state constitutions. They were equally watchful in calling attention to the infringement of Jewish rights abroad. During the Civil War, when more than 700 Jews fought with both Confederate and Union armies, after persistent effort rabbis were permitted to serve as chaplains.

The regional history of the Jews in America followed the general pattern of development. As the westward movement followed the water and overland routes to the Mississippi River, and as it opened up the verdant valleys to settlers, individual Jews moved westward. They became landowners and traded with the Indians. Jewish peddlers, known as "hawkers and walkers," brought much-needed goods to the most distant pioneer outposts. At first they went as solitary travelers, but gradually families moved westward and congregations began to dot the land.

The nineteenth century brought many changes. A period of expansion unique in the annals of history opened in the United States. This growth was paralleled in the Jewish community as well. During the two decades preceding the Civil War, about 200,000 German Jews settled in America. Some of them settled on the Atlantic coast, establishing the first German Jewish congregation in Philadelphia in 1802. Others moved into the interior, founding or developing such Jewish communities as those of Chicago, Cincinnati, Memphis, and St. Paul. During the forty years from 1840 to 1880, these German Jewish immigrants assumed leadership, and founded the religious, philanthropic, and fraternal organizations that are still basic to Jewish communal life in America. In Philadelphia, Rabbi Isaac Leeser* pioneered, by introducing the English sermon as a regular part of the synagogue service and by founding the Hebrew Education Society and institutions of higher Jewish education. At first the German Jews encountered the patronizing attitude of the American-born Sephardim, who had by this time achieved social prominence, wealth, and considerable influence. There were religious differences among them as well. German Jews, Isaac Mayer Wise* outstanding among them, introduced the Reform movement in the United States, while the Sephardim clung largely to strict observance and to their particular ritual in the synagogue. Soon, however, the German Jews who had started out in the main as peddlers, with packs on their backs, opened retail stores, went on to establish great merchandising firms and became quickly absorbed in the American middle class. When mass Jewish immigration from Eastern Europe began in the 1880's, the German Jewish element in turn felt superior to the new immigrants, poverty-stricken and foreign in their ways of life. Nevertheless, the German Jews established philanthropic organizations to aid and assist their brethen.

For the third time, Jewish immigrants repeated the cycle of economic, political, and social adjustment in America. Between 1880 and 1920, two million Jews came to America from Eastern Europe. They came out of a Tsarist Russia that had inaugurated pogroms and persecutions as instruments of goverment; they came out of Galician poverty and Romanian oppression. They took to peddling, they poured into sweat shops, till gradually, painfully, they established themselves in this country and made their own contributions to its color and fabric. They created trade unions in the garment industries and emerged from the sweat shops. They established light industries and businesses in the large cities, took to education in large numbers, and entered the professions. Within their communities they created secular organizations. Out of their need for self-help and for comfort and warmth in their new environment, they organized **landsmannschaften**

From George Washington's letter to the Newport Synagogue.

and various social and cultural Jewish movements and labor organizations. They established a vital Zionist movement. The Yiddish literature, press, and theatre were their creation, as were Hebrew literature and Jewish literature in English. They built up religious institutions and a complex Jewish educational system culminating in great **yeshivot** and seminaries. Under the leadership of Solomon Schechter* the Conservative movement took root and developed. Reconstruction* was fathered by Mordecai M. Kaplan.

Jewish life in the United States is largely urban. For this reason, and because the Jews came mainly from lands that deprived them of equality, American Jews have prized citizenship deeply, and their participation in American political life has been marked by an awareness of major issues. They have been not merely voters, but also candidates for office. They have been members of Congress and have held state offices, including that of Governor. They have held important diplomatic posts; Henry Kissinger* was Secretary of State. On the Supreme Court, the figures of Brandeis,* Cardozo* and Frankfurter* are outstanding by any measure. Throughout American history, the identification of Jews with their adopted country has run deep.

Since 1920, a number of changes have taken place in the American Jewish community. The process of integration into all phases of American life has been greatly accelerated. With immigration restricted by the quota system, American Jewry has become largely native-born. Before World War I, the majority of American Jews were laborers. Since then, the occupational pattern has changed, and most Jews have become middle class professional and business men. A more affirmative attitude toward religious observance and Jewish identification has become generally evident in education, in religious and cultural activity. Since the Nazi destruction of six million Jews in Europe, American Jewry has become the largest Jewish body in the world, and has accepted correspondingly great responsibilities. Rescue, relief, and reconstruction are shouldered by American Jews under the leadership of such organizations as the United Jewish Appeal* the American Jewish Joint Distribution Committee,* the Organization for Rehabilitation through Training (ORT*), and the United HIAS Service.* Dedicated to safeguarding Jewish rights at home and abroad are the American Jewish Congress,* Bnai B'rith,* and the American Jewish Committee.* Before and since the establishment of the State of Israel,* the Zionist Organization of America* and Hadassah,* the Women's Zionist Organization of America, have lent assistance to Israel in absorbing a million Jewish newcomers onto its soil and into its industry.

A.L.I.

UNITED SYNAGOGUE OF AMERICA. An organization of Conservative synagogues; it is also known as the Association of Conservative Synagogues in the United States and Canada. The United Synagogue was founded in 1913 by a group of rabbis and educators under the leadership of Solomon Schechter.* Through a series of departments and commissions it aids affiliated congregations in solving religious, educational, cultural and administrative problems. These include the department of education, the department of youth activities, the National Academy for Adult Jewish Studies, the department of regional activities, the department of programs, the Commission on Social Action, the National Ramah Commission and the department of synagogue administration.

Some 850 congregations, serving over 1,500,000 people, are affiliated with the United Synagogue. As the representative of Conservative Jewry in the United States, it participates with delegates of Orthodox and Reform organizations in the Synagogue Council of America. The United Synagogue is closely associated with the Jewish Theological Seminary of America* and the Rabbinical Assembly of America. Its national headquarters are in the buildings of the Jewish Theological Seminary in New York. Regional offices are maintained in Boston, Philadelphia, Newark, Baltimore, Kansas City, Chicago, Miami Beach, Los Angeles, and Toronto.

The Women's League for Conservative Judaism (see NATIONAL WOMEN'S LEAGUE OF THE UNITED SYNAGOGUE OF AMERICA) is the organization of Conservative synagogue sisterhoods.

The United Synagogue Youth is the national organization of teenagers (thirteen through seventeen inclusive) affiliated with Conservative congregations, launched in December, 1951. It presently consists of about 25,000 members in over 500 chapters and seventeen regions, United Synagogue Youth sponsors twenty regional conferences, ten local summer camps, leadership training institutes and a national convention annually. A two-month Israel Pilgrimage is conducted each summer.

United Synagogue Youth's purpose is to provide high school youth with "an awareness of the essential harmony between the ideals and traditions of Judaism and American democracy," as expressed by the Conservative movement.

The National Youth Commission of the United Synagogue of America guides and supervises United Synagogue Youth activity.

The Atid is an organization of students affiliated with the Conservative Movement launched in the early 1960's with chapters in most of the states. It seeks to develop a program of religious, cultural and social activities leading to Jewish self-fulfillment and to participation in the life of the synagogue and the Jewish community.

URUGUAY. Located on the Atlantic coast, between Brazil* and Argentina,* Uruguay is the smallest of the South American republics. Its Jewish community, however, is the third largest—and one of the most highly organized—in Latin America. It now (1984) numbers about 30,000 in a total population of 2,900,000. The majority live in Montevideo, where they are engaged in the manufacture and sale of furs, furniture, clothing, and oil. A considerable number have entered the professions as well, some of them holding posts in government service. As in Argentina, the cooperative and credit banks established by Jewish citizens play an important role in the economic life of the country.

The Jewish community achieved its high degree of organization during World War II. At that time Germany* was interested in gaining control of Uruguay, and Nazi agents began to spread effective anti-Semitic propaganda in the country. The Jews were forced to unite in order to combat this menace. Uruguay's break with Germany in 1943 put a stop to the anti-Semitic agitation, and the peaceful conditions of this most democratic of South American republics were restored. Uruguayan Jewry did not relax, however, and its energies were channeled to work within the community.

One of the results of its efforts is an extensive educational system, which includes eleven schools in Montevideo and three in the provinces. Over 1,000 Jewish children attend these institutions. Zionist activity, too, is vigorous. The Zionist Council, which represents all Zionist parties, raises funds, conducts an extensive cultural program, and maintains **hakhsharah** training farms for youth who wish to emigrate to Israel.*

Montevideo's Jewish press is widely read. Two Yiddish dailies, as well as periodicals of Jewish interest, in Spanish and German, are published. Two of these, in Spanish, are for younger readers. Many organizations maintain libraries and arrange cultural activities. A Jewish daily radio program and a weekly program devoted to Jewish scholars, writers, and artists are broadcast.

Although the community is organized in separate East European, German, and Sephardic* sectors, all sectors are represented in the Central Jewish Committee of Uruguay. The Central Committee is the government-recognized spokesman for Uruguayan Jewry.
C.M.

Menachem M. Ussishkin

USSISHKIN, MENACHEM MENDEL (1863-1941). Zionist leader. A very strong personality, Menachem Ussishkin never thought it possible to do a thing in more than one way. His training as an engineering strengthened his native realism, yet he gave himself completely to the Zionist idea at a time when the overwhelming majority considered it impossible to realize. Ussishkin was one of the leaders of the Hibbat Zion ("Love of Zion")* movement from his youth on, and one of the founders of the Odessa Committee (1890) which guided the Lovers of Zion toward settlement on the soil in Palestine. When Theodor Herzl* proposed that Uganda, in British East Africa, be used as a temporary asylum for the persecuted Jews of Russia, Ussishkin was one of the Russian Jewish leaders in violent opposition. He would suffer no distraction from the straight road of return to Palestine.* After World War I, Ussishkin was a member of the Zionist delegation to the Versailles Peace Conference* though this political action also seemed to him of lesser importance than settlement on the soil of the Holy Land. In 1920, Ussishkin himself settled in Palestine, and as chief of the Zionist Commission, he forced the purchase of the Emek, or Valley, of Jezreel swamplands—now lush farms and orchards. This lifelong fixed interest in agricultural settlement of the Land of Israel became Ussishkin's duty in 1923, as president, of the Keren Kayemet—the Jewish National Fund.* Until his death, eighteen years later, the Keren Kayemet, under his guidance, raised large sums of money and bought large tracts of land in Israel, now teeming with life. (**See also** JEWISH NATIONAL FUND.)

N.B-A.

V

VAV. Sixth letter of the Hebrew alphabet; numerically, six.

VENEZUELA. Republic, the northernmost state in South America. Italian Jews who wandered from Cayenne to Curacao finally settled at Tucaca in Venezuela in 1693. Since the nineteenth century, the commercially prosperous Jewish community has been concentrated in Caracas, the capital. Numbering (1984) over 20,000 in a total population of 14,313,000, the Jewish community is made up of an old Sephardic* settlement and more recent Eastern European immigrants. The latter predominate. Zionist organizations are active within the community, and religious education is on the increase. In 1947, the Escuela General Herzl-Bialik, a day school combining general and Jewish studies, was established. A central committee to represent the entire community is being formed.

VERSAILLES PEACE CONFERENCE (1919). After the First World War, representatives of the nations met at Versailles to work out the terms of the peace. A Jewish delegation made up of representatives of the European and American

Members of the Committee of Jewish Delegations in Paris at the time of the Versailles Peace Conference. Left to right, front row: Julian W. Mack (U.S.), E. Braunstein (Rumania), Louis Marshall (U.S.), Harry Cutler (U.S.), Nahum Sokolow (Poland), Michel Ringel (Galicia), Joshua Thon (Poland), Jacob Niemirower (Rumania), Marcus Braude (Poland), L. Sarage (Rumania), Joseph Barondess (U.S.), Chaim Weizmann (Zionist Organization), Bernard G. Richards (U.S.), Wilhelm Fildermann (Rumania), Emil Reich (Galicia), M. M. Ussishkin (Ukraine), Nachman Syrkin (U.S.) Joseph Tenenbaum (Galicia). Back row, left to right: Leon Lewite (Poland), Isaac Viklansky, Elia Berlin, David Yellin, Aaron Eisenberg (Palestine), Leopold Benedict (U.S.)

Courtesy Dr. Joseph Tenenbaum.

Jewish communities came to the peace conference to present the Zionist claims on Palestine,* and the claims for minorty rights for the Jews of Poland,* Rumania,* Bulgaria,* and Yugoslavia.* On February 27, 1919, Nahum Sokolow,* Menahem Ussishkin,* Chaim Weizmann,* and André Spire presented the Zionist claims. At a later session, another committee headed by Louis Marshall* presented the claims for Jewish minority rights. The peace conference accepted the validity of these claims, extended them to other groups, and wrote them into the peace treaties. These stated that minority rights "shall be recognized as fundamental law and shall be placed under the guarantee of the League of Nations."

VIENNA. See AUSTRIA.

VILNA. City of Lithuania,* famous as a center of Talmudic learning, cultural institutions, and traditional Judaism. It was the cradle of modern Hebrew and Yiddish literature, and a stronghold of Zionism* and Jewish socialism from the nineteenth century on.

Old synagogue—Vilna.

Jews settled in Vilna in the fourteenth and fifteenth centuries and were, for the most part, tradesmen. In the beginning they were on good terms with their Christian neighbors. As the Jewish community grew and prospered, the gentile population became more hostile. The Jews of Vilna suffered great losses at the hands of the invading Cossacks in 1654. The remaining Jews were expelled by the Russian king, Alexis, a year later, but returned once more after the victory of the Polish army in 1661. Early in the seventeenth century, Vilna again changed hands. It was occupied in turn by the Russian and Swedish armies. During this time, 4,000 Jews perished from famine.

Known as the "Jerusalem of Lithuania," the Jewish community of Vilna rose to prominence through its renowned scholars, the most famous of them being Elijah, Gaon of Vilna.* It was also one of the centers of the Enlightenment (Haskalah*) movement. In the early 1860's, the scholar Samuel Joseph Finn published the Hebrew periodical, **Ha-Carmel** in Vilna. Vilna was the seat of the well-known Romm Publishing house, printer of the Talmud.*

Between the two World Wars, the Jewish population of Vilna was close to 60,000. The city had many **yeshivot,** Hebrew and Yiddish teachers' training schools, and numerous newspapers. It housed the famous Strashun Library and the YIVO* Yiddish Scientific Institute.

During the Second World War, Vilna was occupied first by Soviet Russia and later, in 1941, by the Nazis. The extermination of the Jews extended through 1942-43. All the historic landmarks and institutions were destroyed. Only a few of Vilna's Jews managed to escape the Nazi slaughter, among them several hundred who fought as partisans in nearby forests. In 1977, it was estimated that several thousand Jews were living in Vilna.

H.L.

VIRGIN ISLANDS. A group of islands in the eastern Caribbean Sea. The three largest, St. Thomas, St. John, and St. Croix, are inhabited. These islands, formerly the Danish West Indies, were purchased by the United States* from Denmark* in 1917.

In 1977, there were over 250 Jewish families. St. Thomas has had a Jewish population since 1764. The Jewish settlers, mainly sailors and merchants, came from the nearby island of St. Eustatius, one of the Dutch West Indies. By 1850, about 500 Jews lived in St. Thomas. The flourising commercial and maritime settlement built a number of synagogues successively, Orthodox-Sephardic in character except for a brief period of Reform. The economic decline, resulting from the abolition of slavery (1848) and the removal of the Royal Mail Steamship Company (1855) to Barbados, led many Jews to leave the island. Jews figured prominently in the public life of the Virgin Islands. Among important Americans descended from Jewish families of the Virgin Islands was Judah P. Benjamin, distinguished lawyer and Secretary of State for the Southern Confederacy.

VITAL, HAYIM. See KABBALAH.

VOLOZHIN YESHIVA. Lithuania* was the cradle of the **yeshiva** movement, and the Yeshiva of Volozhin was the first and most influential of the Lithuanian **yeshivot.** Under the influence of its founder, Rabbi Haim of Volozhin, the Yeshiva took over the teaching method of Rabbi Elijah, the beloved Gaon of Vilna,* who had been Rabbi Haim's rabbi and teacher. The method, briefly, consisted of intensifying and broadening, while at the same time simplifying, the study of the Talmud.* The heads of the Yeshiva, who included Rabbi Naphtali Zvi Berlin, Rabbi Joseph Baer Soloveichik, and his son Rabbi Hayim Soloveichik of Brest-Litovsk, were among the most revered Talmudists of their time. Their students later founded **yeshivot** patterned after the Yeshiva of Volozhin throughout Lithuania.

The history of the Yeshiva of Volozhin was a stormy one. Founded in 1803, it was closed by Russian edict in 1824, to be reopened later. In 1858 its doors were once again barred, but again it was reopened for study. In 1892, it was closed for the last time—there was no appealing the decision. But ''illegal'' study continued until the First World War. Volozhin left its mark on all the great **yeshivot** of Lithuania and has strongly influenced the development of present systems of study in the United States* and Israel.*

WAKSMAN, SELMAN ABRAHAM (1883-1973). Scientist, educator, author. Born in Priluka, the Ukraine, in Russia, Waksman came to America in 1910 to escape Tsarist persecution. After receiving his degree from Rutgers University School of Agriculture, he became research assistant in soil bacteriology at the New Jersey Agricultural Experiment Station. By 1938, he was recognized as one of the world's authorities on soil micro-biology. With the outbreak of the Second World War, Waksman's interest shifted from soil study to disease causes in humans and animals, and began intensive work on the development of antibiotics, substances which destroy or arrest the growth of certain disease-causing microbes. In 1952, Waksman was awarded the Nobel Prize in Physiology and Medicine for work in antibiotics and for the development of streptomycin, an antibiotic of invaluable aid in fighting tuberculosis. He donated all royalties from his discoveries to Rutgers University, for the creation of the Institute of Microbiology, of which he was director. He was the holder of a number of honorary degrees. In 1952, Waksman travelled to Israel on the invitation of the government, to advise upon construction of a new antibiotic center there.

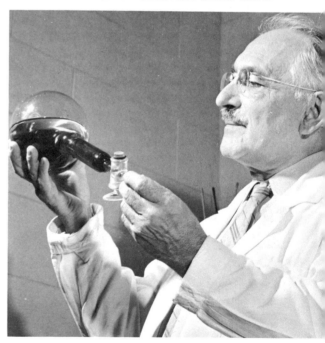

Dr. Selman A. Waksman
Courtesy Rutgers University, New Jersey.

WALD, LILLIAN D. (1867-1940). Social worker. A native of Cincinnati, Ohio, she left a sheltered existence to enter the field of nursing and organized the first city school nursing program in the world. Moved by the appalling conditions on New York's Lower East Side, Lillian Wald became a pioneer social worker, and founded the Henry Street Settlement in 1893. In 1908, she organized the Federal Children's Bureau, and her labors in behalf of the underprivileged earned her gratitude and an enduring place in the history of American social service. Her book describing the Nurses' Settlement, **The House on Henry Street,** was published in 1915.

WAR OF INDEPENDENCE. See ISRAEL, STATE OF.

WARBURG, FELIX M. (1871-1937). Banker, philanthropist, and communal leader. Born in Hamburg, Germany, of a noted banking family, Warburg settled in New York City* in 1895, and joined one of the city's leading brokerage firms. From the time of his arrival he took an active interest in local charities, especially those caring for immigrants. Concerned with education, he made important contributions to educational institutions, both general and Jewish. He served as chairman of the Young Men's Hebrew Association in New York for many years, and was chairman of the American Jewish Joint Distribution Committee* from its establishment in 1914 to 1932. In 1917 Warburg was instrumental in forming the Federation of Jewish Philanthropies in New York. Although opposed to Jewish nationalism, he supported agencies concerned with the economic development of Jews in Palestine,* and mobilized support for the Hebrew University* in Jerusalem.* As a non-Zionist, he participated in the Jewish Agency for Palestine, and took part in the political struggle against British anti-Zionist policy. He was the son-in-law of Jacob H. Schiff.*

WARSAW. The oldest records that mention the presence of Jews in Warsaw date to the fourteenth century, when this city was the capital of Mazovia, a principality later united with Poland.* After 1453, the Jews are known to have been banished by official decree. When Warsaw became the capital of the Polish Kingdom, at the close of the sixteenth century, Jews were brought into the city by the senators and delegates to the Polish parliament. In the eighteenth century, many Jews were permitted to settle in Warsaw on the condition that they pay a special tax. Two small Jewish towns were founded on the outskirts of Warsaw, by the Poles Potocki and Sulkowski. However, the existence of these towns was challenged by the native Polish population and they were destroyed in 1775. Jews finally received full permission to settle in Warsaw in 1788. They were not popularly

Felix Warburg
Courtesy The Jewish Theological Seminary of America.

accepted, however, and suffered intermittently from the hostile outbursts of their Christian countrymen. Nevertheless, the Jews helped defend the city against the Russians in 1794 and organized a regiment of light cavalry. Three years later the Jews were compelled to adopt surnames and to pay a poll tax.

During the time of Napoleon, a Duchy of Warsaw was set up and chartered by a constitution that included full civil and political rights for the Jews. In 1808, these rights were suspended by the Duke of Warsaw upon the instigation of anti-Semitic noblemen. In the course of the nineteenth century, the Jews of Warsaw gradually received greater official acceptance. In 1863, many Jews participated in the Polish uprising against the Russians.

Pogroms drove thousands of Russian Jews to Warsaw at the close of the nineteenth century. At the same time, anti-Semitism* in Poland, and especially in Warsaw, began to grow as the new Polish middle class found itself in competition with Jewish merchants and industrial workers. When the Russian government convened the Dumas, or legislatures, at the beginning of the twentieth century, the Jews of Warsaw supported liberal labor candidates in opposition to the reactionary and anti-Semitic candidates of the National Democratic Party. The resulting anti-Jewish agitation in Warsaw was very great.

328

By the time of the First World War, Warsaw had become a spiritual, economic, and political center for the Jews of Eastern Europe. The Jews had built a compact community, which included Orthodox, assimilationist, Zionist,* and Bundist (socialist) sectors. When Poland received its independence in 1919, Warsaw contained the headquarters of all these Jewish "parties," as well as commercial and cultural organizations, **yeshivot,** and seminaries. A flourishing and influential Jewish press had appeared: there were seven Yiddish daily newspapers and numerous periodicals. There were also two Jewish dailies in the Polish language, and, intermittently, one in Hebrew. In addition, the Jewish community in Warsaw produced and supported numerous prosperous publishing houses, theaters, art exhibits, and professional organizations. In the political sphere, the Jews of Warsaw saw many of their numbers elected to the Polish parliament. Nevertheless, anti-Semitism never completely abated, and economic discriminations against the Jews continued to exist up to the outbreak of the Second World War.

At the time of the Nazi invasion in 1939, there were approximately 330,000 Jews in Warsaw, or 10 per cent of the total Jewish population of Poland. By October 1940, the Germans had herded the entire Jewish population of Warsaw into a ghetto the size of about one hundred square city blocks, surrounded by walls and barbed wire. Until July 1942, the Germans were content to make life difficult for the Jews by keeping them on starvation rations and denying them medical care. Then the Nazis began systematically deporting the

Detail of the Monument of the Warsaw Ghetto.

Jews from the Warsaw ghetto; told that they were being taken to labor camps, the Jews actually were sent to death camps where millions of Jews were to perish. In the spring of 1943, the leaders of the Jewish underground of Warsaw rose up against the Germans—much to the latter's surprise. By April 1943, the Germans had ordered the complete evacuation of the ghetto. Only lightly armed, the remaining Jews of the ghetto put up a gallant struggle against the heavily armed Germans sent to destroy them. The Jewish resistance, led by the young commander in chief Mordecai Anielewicz,* fought to the last man, until September 1943. The story of the ghetto fighter of Warsaw has been retold many times; John Hersey's **The Wall** is a notable example.

The postwar period saw the return of a small number of Jews to Warsaw—survivors of the concentration camps and death camps, as well as those who had somehow managed to hide under the protection of non-Jewish friends. Conditions for Jewish development in Warsaw were unfavorable in the country where, under Communist domination, the official policy was anti-religious and anti-Zionist. An estimated 4,500 Jews lived in Warsaw in 1979.

The famous Warsaw Synagogue, later destroyed by Nazis during the uprising of the Warsaw Ghetto.

WASSERMANN, AUGUST VON (1866-1925). German Jewish scientist. He did important research into immunity and in the field of bacteriology. In 1906, he discovered serodiagnosis in syphilis (the so-called ''Wasserman Reaction''), which made him famous. Wasserman was very much interested in Jewish affairs, and was president of the Jewish Academy of Science in Berlin.

WASSERMANN, JAKOB (1873-1934). Novelist. A writer of international repute, Wasserman strove all his life to reconcile his Jewishness with his love for German culture. Opposed both to assimilation* and to Jewish nationalism, he sought to fuse the two cultures. Disillusionment with his quest was expressed in **My Way as a German and a Jew,** written in 1921. His stories often deal with Jewish characters; his chief works are **The Jews of Zirndorf** (1897), **Casper Hauser** (1908), **The Gooseman** (1915), and **The Maurizius Case** (1928).

WEBER, MAX (1881-1961). Artist. Born in Russia, he was brought to the U.S. as a boy of ten. His bold and free brushwork, and his refusal to paint figures and objects naturalistically, at first brought the anger of critics down on him, but eventually Weber came to be recognized as one of America's most vigorous artists. In 1954, he was elected to membership in the National Institute of Arts and Letters. Among contemporary American artists, none has struck his roots more deeply into the spiritual soil of Judaism then he. He has painted rich, harmonious flower pieces; sombre and melancholy landscapes; musicians who make you hear their music; and sweating workmen struggling with structural steel. But his best works are those which deal with Jewish topics. Favorite subjects are the Talmudists Weber saw in downtown Manhattan and Brooklyn; he has painted them sitting around the table, using their eloquent hands to underline an argument. He often elongates and even distorts their faces and figures, to indicate the highest pitch of emotional and spiritual experience.

WEIZMANN, CHAIM (1874-1952). Scientist, Zionist statesman, first President of Israel.* Chaim Weizmann's childhood was spent in the tiny Russian village of Motol, and the deeply traditional Jewish education he received gave him a love of the prophets and a lasting interest in Hebrew literature. At the age of eleven he left for Pinsk to study at a Russian high school. There the school boy joined the Hibbat Zion movement; his twin passions for science and Zionism* developed

"Still Life," by Max Weber.

and absorbed Weizmann's whole life. At eighteen he went to Western Europe for his education at German and Swiss universities. When Weizmann was still quite young, he made an important discovery in the chemistry of dyes, and in 1904, Weizmann became an instructor in chemistry at the University of Manchester in England. During World War I, Weizmann served as the head of the British Admiralty Laboratories, and developed a process for manufacturing acetone out of starches—a vital link in the production of the explosives needed in the war effort. Lloyd George records in his memoirs that, when asked how the British government might repay him, Weizmann answered: "There is only one thing I want—a national home for my people."

Weizmann's international Zionist role began in 1901, at the fifth Zionist Congress.* Influenced by Ahad Ha-am,* the philosopher of cultural Zionism, he led a group that demanded that the Zionist Organization, in addition to its political

work, set up a program of cultural work in Palestine and among the Jewish masses throughout the world. In 1903, Weizmann was found among those who opposed Theodor Herzl.* The issue of the time was Uganda, an East African territory the British had offered for Jewish settlement. Herzl proposed Uganda as a temporary asylum for the pogrom-ridden Jews of Russia,* and Weizmann was among those Russian Jews who would not be diverted from Palestine—their only and ultimate goal. At the Zionist Congress in 1907, Weizmann pleaded for uniting the political work for obtaining Palestine* as a Jewish homeland with the practical work of immediate colonization. Throughout his Zionist career, Weizmann strove to join political, cultural, and practical Zionism in one effort.

His greatest triumph came in the midst of World War I. The good will he had gained through his scientific achievements and his war efforts helped bring about the Balfour Declaration* (November 2, 1917) supporting the establishment of a Jewish National Home in Palestine. In 1918, as head of a Zionist commission to Palestine, Weizmann visited Emir Feisal of Transjordan and discussed with him the idea of peacful relations between the Jews in Palestine and the Arab world. The same year he began the realization of an old Zionist dream when he laid the cornerstone for the Hebrew University* on Jerusalem's Mt. Scopus. In 1919, Weizmann appeared before the Versailles Peace Conference* together with other Zionist leaders to ask endorsement of a Jewish National Home. He was elected president of the World Zionist Organization* in 1920. Anxious to obtain wide support for Zionism, Weizmann proposed, in 1923, that the World Zionist Executive be enlarged to include non-Zionists. This idea was opposed vigorously for fear of weakening the Zionist movement. By 1929, however, Weizmann had won, and the enlarged Jewish Agency* came into being, with Weizmann as its president. Weizmann headed the Zionist movement as president, continuously except for the break between 1931-1935, until the British mandate began to crumble in 1946, two years before the birth of the State of Israel. Meanwhile his scientific interests continued without interruption. He served the Hebrew University in Jerusalem (inaugurated 1925) as chairman of the board of governors and later as honory president. He was instrumental in the establishment of the Daniel Sieff Research Institute, which later developd into the Weizmann Institute of Science.* During World War II, he was invited by President Franklin D. Roosevelt to come to the United States* to work on developing synthetic rubber needed for the vast war effort.

The last years of Weizmann's life were spent in two battles. On the political front he fought for a Jewish State before the various commissions investigating Palestine and before the United Nations. His other struggle was with growing blindness and failing health. The first battle was successful. The UN voted to partition Palestine into an Arab and a Jewish state, and on the day that the British left Palestine, the State of Israel was proclaimed. Weizmann lived to witness Israel's victory over the Arab invaders, and to open the first session of the Knesset, Israel's parliament, on February 14, 1949. Two days later, the Knesset elected Chaim Weizmann the first president of the reborn State of Israel. At his death he was honored by the world and mourned by his people.

N.B-A.

WEIZMANN, EZER (1924-   ). Israeli soldier and public servant. Born in Tel Aviv,* he is a nephew of Chaim Weizmann.* Known as the father of Israel's Air Force, he served as chief of operations of Israel's army general staff during the Six-Day War* of 1967. He was Minister of Transport from 1969 to 1970 and was appointed Minister of Defense in 1977. He played a key role in Israel's negotiations with Egypt since Anwar el-Sadat's visit to Israel in November, 1977.

WEIZMANN INSTITUTE OF SCIENCE. Located in Rehovot, Israel, the Institute is a city of science with 19 departments, embraced in five faculties—Mathematics; Physics; Chemistry; Biophysics-Bio-chemistry; Biology—devoted to fundamental research in the natural sciences, related to human welfare. Its primary task is the discovery of new knowledge and the training of new generations of scientists. It was first conceived in 1944 in honor of the 70th birthday of Chaim Weizmann.*

Relevance of Science Research. Engaged in some several hundred research projects, Weizmann Institute scientists are studying the elements which constitute the life forces of man, in animals and their environs to fathom how they function, and thereby to learn how birth, congenital defects, disease, aging can be controlled; and how the energies of the earth, of the ocean tides, and the atmosphere can be deflected from destruction and harnessed for mankind's welfare.

Status of Institute. It is in the forefront of research in the life sciences (cell biology, experimental biology, biological ultrastructure, biodynamics, biophysics, genetics, plant genetics, chemical immunology, biochemistry, polymer research); in physics; in chemistry and in mathematics. It has become an important scientific resource, not only for Israel, but for the world.

Contributions to the State of Israel. Institute scientists are principal advisors to the Israel government on science, new resources, water economy, industry, education, population of and development of the desert, agriculture, new food potentials, mineral exploitation and the like.

Aid to Science Education. The Weizmann Institute is serving the educational and scientific manpower needs of Israel on two levels—the graduate student through the Feinberg Graduate School; the high school student through its Science Teaching Department.

The Feinberg Graduate School is a multidisciplinary school for the training of independent researchers both in the natural sciences and in modern science technology. It is accredited as an American school abroad by charter from the New York State University Regents. In 1968, the Institute set up a Science Teaching Department, the first of its kind in Israel.

As a further stimulus to science learning, the Institute sponsors an Annual Science Fair, a Mathematics Olympiad, science clubs, special courses for gifted children and a Summer Science Youth Camp.

In May 1973, a Weizmann Institute scientist, Professor Ephraim Katchalsky-Katzir,* world renowned authority on protein research, was inaugurated as the fourth President of Israel. Founder and head of the Institute's Biophysics Department for 25 years, President Katzir continued his reasearch while in office.

The Weizmann Institute has been ranked by Nobel Laureate Dr. Arthur Kornberg as among the top ten research institutes in the world.

WEST BANK. Area west of the Jordan river, part of Palestine.* Assigned in 1947 by the United Na-

Aerial view of Weizmann Institute.

Israeli soldiers immediately after the liberation of Western Wall, Jerusalem.

tions as a separate Arab state, it was annexed by the Hashemite Kingdom of Jordan in 1948 and occupied by Israel* in 1967.

WESTERN WALL. The last relic of the western defense wall of the First and Second Temples* in Jerusalem.* The Western Wall is holy to Jews, who have prayed and wept over its stones since the destruction of Jerusalem in 70 C.E. almost continuously, except during periods when this was prohibited on pain of death. Since the fall of the Old City of Jerusalem to the Arab forces of Jordan,* in 1948, it had been inaccessible to Jews. On June 7, 1967, during the Six-Day War,* the Israeli Army recaptured the Old City of Jerusalem and since then Jews have had free access to the Wall. Since then, the Wall is officially referred to as the Western Wall, or in Hebrew, **Kotel Ma'aravi.** Shortly after the area was liberated, the Government of Israel* started extensive archaeological excavations in the vicinity of the Wall. The Wall is

about fifty-four feet high and eighty-five feet long, and has about twenty-four layers of immense uncut grey stones. This section of the wall belongs to the Second Temple; however, buried beneath the surface are almost as many layers of stones which are the remains of the First Temple. Prayers are recited at the Wall day and night, but pilgrimages usually take place on Tisha B'ab, the anniversary of the razing of the temple.

WIESEL, ELIE (1928-   ). Novelist and journalist. Born in Rumania* and raised in a Hasidic environment, he was deported by the Nazis and was in the death camps of Birkenau, Auschwitz,* Buna and Buchenwald. For several years following World War II he lived in Paris;* later, he settled in New York.* His novels, which he originally wrote in French and which were subsequently translated into English, brought him fame not only as a writer on Jewish themes but also as a major French novelist. Most of his novels are concerned with the Holocaust. Among his best known works are **The Town Beyond the Wall** (1964); **The Gates of the Forest** (1966); **Legends of Our Time** (1968), **The Jews of Silence** (an eyewitness report of the plight of Soviet Jewry; 1968), **A Beggar in Jerusalem** (1970), **One Generation After** (1970), **Souls on Fire** (1972), and **The Oath** (1973). He has also written two plays, **Zalman,** or the **Madness of God** and **The Trial of God.**

WINGATE, MAJOR GENERAL ORDE CHARLES (1903-1944). Wingate is renowned as the creator of the long-range penetration technique, by which his Burma campaign (1943-44) saved India* from the Japanese in World War II. He had earlier, in 1941, used a similar method to drive the Italians* out of Abyssinia and had restored Haile Selassie to his throne in Addis Ababa. But it was in Palestine* that Wingate achieved his early fame; under his training, special night squads broke the grip of the Arab terror in 1938. And, throughout his later career, his heart was fixed on returning to the Holy Land.

The deeply idealistic and fiercely individualist personality of Orde Charles Wingate, a non-Jew, was shaped by the twin influences of the Bible* and of military service. He came to Palestine in 1936 as an intelligence officer to the British Forces stationed there. His lifelong absorption in the Bible made Wingate feel at home in the Holy Land. He traveled to all the Holy Places, learned Hebrew, sought out the Jews in Haifa,* where he was stationed, and got to know the leaders in Jerusalem* and the young **halutzim*** in the **kibbutzim.***

The Arab terror that had broken out in 1936 was aided by German and Italian subsidies, and was making life difficult in Palestine. Arab guerrillas filtered in from Syria,* Lebanon,* and Transjordan. They attacked settlements and road traffic, and instigated the local Arabs of town and village to join them in looting, killing, and in sabotaging the oil pipelines that led from Iraq* to the British-controlled refineries in Haifa. Wingate found that the British police and troops were ineffectual in controlling the situation because of their tradition-bound methods, and because of the prevailing anti-Zionist policy. The British administration drove the Jewish self-defense militia underground and actually arrested those caught defending Jewish settlements with arms.

Wingate obtained official permission to investigate the ways and methods of Arab infiltrators; unofficially, he got assistance from members of the Haganah* in carrying out this task. His report to General Wavell included a plan for wiping out the Arab terrorists and a request for permission to carry it out. Despite considerable official opposition, Wingate was granted permission and set up headquarters at En Harod, a kibbutz in the shadow of Mount Gilboa. In the same countryside where Gideon* had chosen his warriors, Wingate chose and trained his special night squads. They were composed mainly of 400 selected members of the **kibbutzim,** with about 200 equally handpicked British soldiers. Within three months, Wingate had a highly trained commando force. These he led in swift nightly attacks on Arab rebel centers and points of infiltration. In six months, the back of the Arab terror was broken. Wingate's achievement brought him the Distinguished Service Order but the intense dislike of the local anti-Jewish British officials. Moreover, the Palestine administration did not like to see military skills developed in the Jews, and shortly after his success in 1938, Wingate was recalled to London.

Wingate's brilliant contributions to Allied victories in World War II ended tragically while he was touring his forward bases in the Burma jungle. During a severe storm, his plane crashed against a mountainside and Wingate died at the age of forty-one. In Israel, Orde Charles Wingate has become a legend. He is remembered gratefully in many ways. A Wingate Forest was planted near En Harod on the southern slopes of Mt. Gilboa. A normal school for physical training has been named for him, and Yemin Orde—a Youth Aliyah* village on the slopes of his well-loved Mt. Carmel—was established as a living memorial to him.   N.B-A.

Stephen S. Wise

WISE, STEPHEN SAMUEL (1874-1949). Rabbi, author, and Zionist leader. Born in Budapest and brought to the United States* as an infant, Stephen Wise was educated in New York City,* where he studied at City College and Columbia University and prepared privately for the rabbinate. He took his first pulpit at nineteen, and from 1900 to 1906 served in Portalnd, Ore. In 1907 Wise returned to New York and founded the Free Synagogue, which he led to the end of his life. Fifteen years later he established the Jewish Institute of Religion, a rabbinical seminary dedicated to the liberal ideals Wise embodied as rabbi and citizen. In 1950 this institution merged with the Hebrew Union College.

Wise's brilliant gifts as orator and administrator early gained him a distinguished position in the two areas that were to preoccupy him throughout his career: social reform and Zionist affairs. while still in Portland, he spoke out on behalf of labor reform. Later, he became a prominent advocate of civil rights, labor legislation, and Franklin D. Roosevelt's New Deal program. An early Zionist, he was a founder of the Federation of American Zionists in 1898, the year of the second Zionist Congress.* During the half-century that followed, he worked passionately within the community to gain adherents for the movement. But Zionism was only one facet of Wise's concern with Jewish life. To provide democratic representation for American Jewry as a body, he joined with Justice Louis Brandeis* and Felix Frankfurter* in founding the American Jewish Congress* (1917), whose interests, as well as those of Zionism,* he represented at the Versailles Peace Conference* in 1919. In 1936, to provide an agency for contact between Jewish communities the world over, he organized the World Jewish Congress.

WIZO. Women's International Zionist Organization, founded in 1920. Wizo developed from the Federation of Women Zionists in great Britain* (1918) as a welfare organization for the care of women and children in Eretz Israel. With headquarters in Tel Aviv,* it has branches in 54 countries with a total membership of about 220,000. Some 13,000 children are in the care of 197 Wizo child welfare institutions in Israel, ranging from homes for babies through pre-school day centres to clubs and playgrounds for schoolchildren. In the field of education, Wizo maintains six agricultural and vocational training schools in Israel with a total of 3,000 pupils. The services for women and families maintained by Wizo in Israel number 260 and range from mending and sewing courses to a mobile library. Wizo activity in Israel is not centralized but covers social services for women and children from the cradle to the grave, in the whole area from Dan to Eilat, wherever there are underprivileged in need of help.

S.J.G.

WOLFSON, SIR ISAAC (1897-   ). British businessman and philanthropist. Born in Glasgow, Scotland, of Eastern European immigrant parents. He has worked since the age of 14 and now heads a chain of 2,600 retail stores in Great Britain,* Canada* and South Africa; he controls the largest mail-order enterprise outside the United States.* Wolfson is active in innumerable Jewish organizations, and has contributed over $1,000,000 to the Weizmann Institute of Science,* as well as considerable funds to Youth Aliyah and other institutions. Heichal Shlomo, a religious center in Jerusalem,* was built by him as a memorial to his father. In 1955 he set up the Isaac Wolfson Foundation which has since donated more than $15,000,000 to worthy British causes. He was created a baronet in 1962 "for philanthropic services." Wolfson is an observant Jew, and serves currently as president of the United Synagogue. In March 1963, Sir Isaac made a contribution of rare munificence in the sum of $2,000,000 to help develop community projects in Acre,* Israel. The unparalleled extent and variety of his benefactions places him in the foremost ranks of philanthropists in Jewish history.

WOMEN'S AMERICAN ORT. See ORT.

WOMEN'S LEAGUE FOR CONSERVATIVE JUDAISM. See NATIONAL WOMEN'S LEAGUE OF THE UNITED SYNAGOGUE OF AMERICA.

Workmen's Circle members at a memorial demonstration on the New York City Hall steps in August, 1984, for the Jewish writers and artists of the Soviet Union murdered in Lubianka Prison in Moscow in 1952.

WORKMEN'S CIRCLE. Jewish fraternal order organized in 1892 to protect working immigrants in the United States, and assist them in times of illness or unemployment. These arrivals, mainly in New York's East Side, who became needleworkers, carpenters, painters, laundrymen, and cleaners, were immediate beneficiaries of the new order. In 1984 there is a membership throughout the United States and Canada of 50,000, in more than 280 functioning branches. The Circle operates a system of medical aid, hospitalization, and various forms of insurance and direct benefits. It has summer camps, women's clubs, homes for the aged, burial grounds, high schools and teachers' seminaries, educational publications, and other periodicals in English and Yiddish. Aid has been extended to Yiddish schools in South America and other centers. Notably, the Circle supports Jewish and non-Jewish victims of need and discrimination in the Americas and abroad.

WORLD FEDERATION OF BERGEN BELSEN ASSOCIATIONS. An organization dedicated to perpetuate the memory of the martyrs exterminated at Bergen Belsen* and all other concentration camps in Europe by creating and maintaining public movements and memorial libraries throughout the free world, and publishing materials and preserving books, artifacts, and other memorabilia relating to the Nazi Holocaust.

The federation sponsors the International Remembrance Award for Excellence and Distinction in the Literature of the Holocaust, and allocates grants to universities for research projects in the history of the Holocaust.

The founder and first president of the federation was the late Joseph Rosensaft.

WORLD JEWISH CONGRESS. Founded at Geneva in August, 1936, the World Jewish Congress (WJC) assumed responsibility for consultations on behalf of persecuted Jews in various countries and in the councils of the League of Nations. It was active in the planning of the Evian Conference on Refugees in 1938. Following the failure of that conference, it continued to work to save Jews from the clutches of the Nazis and their allies. At the end of World War II, the WJC worked with and on behalf of the survivors of Nazi terror, the Jewish displaced persons all over Europe and Africa. During the Nuremberg war crimes trials the WJC served in a consultative capacity, supplying factual dossiers from its files. The WJC has consistently helped the Jewish community of Israel.*

Representatives of the WJC attented the founding conference of the United Nations (UN) at San Francisco in 1945. They worked for the inclusion of rights planks in the UN charter, and for the most democratic structure possible for the UN. The WJC serves as a consulting organization for the UN and its specialized agencies, concerning itself with such matters as human rights, genocide and cultural affairs.

The WJC was active in the negotiations which resulted in the agreements by Germany* and Austria* to pay collective restitution to the Jewish people for damages done by the Nazis. It is a member of the Conference on Jewish Material Claims Against Germany.

WJC offices in various countries represent Jews individually and Jewish communities collectively in negotiations with governments with regard to various political and related problems.

In 1979, sixty-six countries had affiliates of the

World Jewish Congress. There were regional councils in the Americas and Europe. Full Congress meetings were held at Montreux, Switzerland* in 1948 and in Geneva in 1953.

The official aims of the World Jewish Congress are: coordination of the efforts of its affiliated organizations in respect to the political, economic, social and cultural problems of the Jewish people; securing and defending the rights, status and interests of Jews and Jewish communities throughout the world; assisting their creative development, and representing and acting on their behalf before governmental, inter-governmental and international authorities   E.L.

WORLD ZIONIST ORGANIZATION. Organized in 1897, the 204 delegates to the first Congress* represented many Zionist societies in 17 countries. The Congress elected Theodor Herzl* as the first president of the World Zionist Organization, and worked out a constitution with the Basle Program* as its basic plank. The constitution provided that any Jew could become a member of the World Zionist Organization by subscribing to the Basle Program and by paying the minimal dues, called a shekel.* The Zionists of each country elected one delegate to the Zionist Congress for each unit of 1,500 shekel holders. The Congress in session served as the governing body of the Zionist movement. Each Congress elected two bodies: the general council, or actions committee, to determine Zionist policy between sessions, and the executive, to carry on day-to-day Zionist affairs. As the movement grew, right- and left-wing parties developed programs reflecting the times, conditions, and the thinking of the various groups within the Jewish communities. These parties, advocating their particular programs for the upbuilding of Palestine, became constituent organizations, elected delegates to the Congress and were represented on the Actions Committee and on the Executive. (**See** GENERAL ZIONISM, MIZRACHI, and LABOR ZIONISM.)

YADIN, YIGAEL (1917-1984). Soldier, archaeologist. A son of the late Eliezer I. Sukenik, Professor of Archaeology in the Hebrew University* of Jerusalem,* Yigael Yadin has shared his father's love for rediscovering the secrets of the past. A brilliant student of military tactics, he applied his knowledge of ancient battle strategy effectively to defeat the superior Egyptian forces in the Negev during the Israel War of Independence in 1948.

As soon as he could be relieved from his military duties, Yadin returned to his first love—archaeology. Yadin's gift for deciphering the past led him to the study of the famous Dead Sea Scrolls.* His introduction and commentary to **The Scroll of the War of the Sons of Light Against the Sons of Darkness** won him the Israel Prize for scholarly achievement. In 1965 he reported a number of significant archaeological finds in Masada.* A founder and the leader of the middle-of-the-road Democratic Movement for Change (DASH) in Israel, he became Israel's deputy prime minister in 1977.

YAD VASHEM. Israel's memorial to the Jewish communities and people who perished in the Nazi Holocaust. The name means ''Monument and Memorial.'' Located on the Mount of Remembrance near Jerusalem,* the Yad VaShem building includes a library, an archives building, many exhibits and a memorial chamber. Foreign statesmen visiting Israel* are taken to visit Yad VaShem, and schools organize regualr visits by students so that the new generation born and raised in Israel may learn about one of the most tragic episodes in the history of their people.

YAVNEH (Jamnia in Greek). An old Palestinian city on the Mediterranean coast between Jaffa* and old Ashdod.* At the time of the Second Temple,* Yavneh was a well-populated, well-fortified city, and was fast becoming a great Jewish center. During the Roman siege of Jerusalem, it is said that Rabbi Johanan Be Zakkai* escaped the city and made his way to the camp of the Roman general, Vespasian. He told Vespasian he would soon become Emperor of Rome, which indeed happened. After the fall of Jerusalem, Vespasian, in gratitude, granted Ben Zakkai's request to let him gather a small community of sages and organize a school. The Sanhedrin* was reestablished at Yavneh, and Ben Zakkai became its head. Yavneh remained the seat of scholarship and culture until the Bar Kokhba revolt (132-35 C.E.), when the Sanhedrin was disbanded, and

many of the Jewish inhabitants of the city fled. Before the Israel War of Independence (1948) Yavneh was an Arab market-town known as Yebneh. Today (1979) there is a religious kibbutz* near the abandoned site of the old Yavneh. Recently the inhabitants of the kibbutz built a **yeshiva,** and the tradition of scholarship for which ancient Yavneh was famed is now carried on by the modern settlers.

YEHOASH (1871-1927). Solomon Bloomgarden, Yiddish poet. He was born in Lithuania,* and came to the United States in 1890. Yehoash contributed to the modernization of Yiddish leterature* in America and cultivared in his readers a taste for the best in world literature, by his translations into Yiddish. His major achievement was his masterly translation of the Bible* into Yiddish. This work combines a deep scholarly understanding of the Hebrew original with poetic skill. Yehoash's translation of the Bible became one of the most popular works in Yiddish literature.

YELLIN, DAVID (1864-1942). Hebrew scholar. Born in Jerusalem,* Yellin became one of the first active supporters of Eliezer Ben Yehudah* in his efforts to revive Hebrew as a spoken language. Yellin helped found the Hebrew Language Academy and wrote important works on Maimonides,* Hebrew poetry of the Middle Ages, and Hebrew grammar. He established a Teachers' Institute in Jerusalem, and in his later years taught at the Hebrew University* of Jerusalem.

YEMEN. Muslim kingdom in the southwest corner of the Arabian peninusla, 75,000 square miles in area, made up of plateaus and hills rising to 10,000 feet. This altitude gives Yemen enough rain to supply a population of about 7,000,000 with corn, vegetables, fruit, and wheat, and enough of its famous mocha coffee to export. In ancient times, Yemen traded with Africa and the Far East, but since adopting Islam,* in 628, the country has been fearful of strangers, isolated, and poor. The Jewish community of Yemen is thought to be the oldest in the world, dating back to Solomon's* time. In the fifth century C.E., Jewish influence was so great that the Himyaritic kings adopted Judaism; however, the Ethiopian invasions ended this dynasty. When Yemen adopted Islam, the Jews were degraded to the status of second-class citizens; they were not, for example, permitted to walk on the pavement or ride on a donkey—lest the Jew look down upon a Muslim pedestrian. Jewish orphans were forcibly converted to Islam. Nevertheless, through centuries of oppression, the Yemenite Jews preserved

their traditional religion. In 1172, Maimonides* wrote his famous **Epistle to the Yemenites,** in which he expressed his sympathy for the Jews of Yemen in their martyrdom and exhorted them to remain true to their faith. Their yearning for Zion led the Yemenite Jews to place their faith in a number of false Messiahs—a danger Maimonides had warned them to guard against. Despite their isloation, the Yemenite Jews were in contact with Jewish spiritual and creative life during the Middle Ages. Kabbalah* was a popular study among them and they had Kabbalist writers, poets, and scholars. In 1517 Yemen became a part of the Ottoman (Turkish) empire. Periodic clashes between Arab and Turk followed; the Turks were driven out of Yemen, but returned to reoccupy the country. Each change worsened the position of the Jews. This situation, and their ancient love of the Holy Land, induced them to begin to migrate to Israel* in 1881. This migration reached its climax after the establishment of the State of Israel, when the entire community of 40,000 Yemenite Jews was transported within a year or so via air lift. To the Yemenite Jews, these flights were the "eagle's wings" in the prophecy of redemption. In 1977 there were about 1,000 Jews still in the country.

S. and T.B.

A Yemenite Jew.

YESHIVA (plural: Yeshivot; Hebrew, means "Academy"). A traditional Orthodox institution where young men devote themselves to the study of Talmudic law. Some graduates receive rabbinic ordination; others remain for varying periods and then leave to enter a secular vocation. Some yeshivot have **kollelim,** schools of advanced Talmudic study where married students receive support for their families while they concentrate on their studies. More recently the term has been used also for all-day Orthodox schools where both Jewish and secular subjects are taught. **Yeshiva Ketanah** ("little yeshiva") is an Orthodox all-day school on the elementary level.

YESHIVA UNIVERSITY. First founded in New York,* in 1886, as a small Talmudical school named Yeshiva Etz Chaim. Ten years later, another Yeshiva was founded and named after the great Lithuanian rabbi, Rabbi Isaac Elchanan Spector.* In 1915, the two institutions merged, under the head of a leading scholar, Bernard Revel.* Recognizing the need for combined religious and secular training, the Yeshiva opened the Talmudical Academy, the first academic high school under Jewish auspices in the United States. In 1921, a Teachers' Institute (originally founded in 1917 by the Mizrachi Organization of America*) was added to the Yeshiva. The Teachers' Institute has provided hundreds of principals and teachers for Hebrew schools throughout the country. Yeshiva University's rabbinical graduates are organized in the Rabbinical Council of America.

In 1928, the first college of liberal arts and sciences in America under Jewish auspices—Yeshiva College—opened its doors. Under the name "Rabbi Isaac Elchanan Theological Seminary and Yeshiva College," the expanding institution moved the following year to the present Main Center, Amsterdam Avenue and 186th Street, in New York's Washington Heights. Since 1977, it has been headed by Dr. Norman Lamm. In 1945, the institution attained university status.

In addition to its rabbinical seminary, Yeshiva University in 1979 had a total of eighteen schools and divisions, including four High Schools (for boys and girls), Stern College for Women, Albert Einstein College of Medicine, Wurzweiler School of Social Work, Ferkauf Graduate School of Humanities and Social Sciences, and Belfer Graduate School of Science. In addition, the University maintained twenty-four special programs and services, among them the Community Service Division, Israel Rogosin Center for Ethics and Human Values, Information Retrieval Center on the Disadvantaged, Inservice Institute in Science and Mathematics for Secondary School Teachers, and Albert Einstein College Hospital.

YETZER HA-RAH (Hebrew, meaning "evil inclination"). The impulse within man to do wrong. Judaism believes that the impulse to do evil is part of man's human nature, just as is the impulse to do good **(Yetzer Ha-tov).** However, man is not born to do evil, and by exercising his willpower he can conquer his Yetzer Ha-Rah. The rabbis suggested the study of Torah* as one way of conquering the evil impulse.

YIDDISH. The language spoken by East European Jewry, Yiddish is approximately one thousand years old. Jews have always spoken the language of the land where they lived. Babylonian Jews spoke Aramaic,* the Jews who lived under Arab dominion spoke Arabic, and those of France* spoke French in their daily lives. The language of Jewish religious life was Hebrew.* Yiddish began to develop when Jews from France settled along the Rhine, and their vocabulary was augmented by many words from the various medieval German dialects of their new neighbors.

Expulsions and persecutions forced the Jews to move from place to place, increasing the difference between their speech and that of the surrounding population. When the German Jews migrated to Bohemia, Poland,* and Lithuania,* they took their medieval German dialect with them, at the same time adapting more Hebrew and Slavic words. The Jew in the ghetto was cut off from the cultural life of the surrounding peoples; this isolation, added to the special Jewish way of life, was also a basic factor in the development of the Yiddish language. Also, Yiddish refelcts the

Dr. Bernard Revel, first president.   *Dr. Norman Lamm, President.*

Yeshiva University.

East European Jews' concentration in cities, and consequent separation from nature. There are not too many terms for flowers and trees, birds, animals and fishes in Yiddish. On the other hand, Yiddish may be pungent, colorful, and even sentimental—but it is rarely pompous. There was little room for sham in the ghetto.* The Jews continued to move eastward, and Ukrainian, White Russian, and Russian elements entered the Yiddish language. When Yiddish-speaking immigrants moved westward, to the New World, the vocabulary of Yiddish expanded to include English terms in the United States, Spanish words in Argentina.* All this has enriched the language. In all, Yiddish has a vocabulary of approximately 150,000 words.

Yiddish is the creation of Ashkenazic* Jewry. Even before 1500, Yiddish was spoken in Ashkenazic communities. Beginning with the thirteenth century, as the role of the Ashkenazic Jews in Jewish history became more and more prominent, the Yiddish language gained in importance. From the sixteenth through the eighteenth century, it was the spoken language of Ashkenazic Jews everywhere. Yiddish is still the language of communication among Jews in the various centers of the world. It is heard wherever Jews from diverse countries meet (for example, at Zionist Congresses). There are approximately 130 Yiddish periodicals the world over.

For many generations, Yiddish was the language of Jewish education. In the heder,* the Bible* was interpreted in Yiddish; in the yeshiva,* Yiddish was used to study the Talmud.* The twentieth century saw the development of secular Yiddish schools. On the North American continent there have been Yiddish afternoon schools since 1910. There are Yiddish day schools in Canada,* Mexico,* and other countries. In the United States, Yiddish is taught at several colleges and universities.

It is estimated that before World War II, between ten and eleven million Jews spoke Yiddish. Of the six million Jews who perished at Hitler's hands, at least five and a half million spoke Yiddish. To this loss must be added the linguistic assimilation* in America and other countries. It is difficult to estimate the number of Jews who speak Yiddish today.

Y.M.

YIDDISH LITERATURE. The history of Yiddish literature may conveniently be divided into five periods:

1) From the beginning to approximately 1500;
2) The flourishing years of the sixteenth and the first half of the seventeenth century;
3) The period of stagnation during the second half of the seventeenth and the first half of the eighteenth century;
4) The era of Hasidism and Haskalah (the second half of the eighteenth century to 1864);
5) Modern Yiddish literature since 1864.

Before 1500, Yiddish literature was based on Jewish folklore, religious Hebrew literature, and the secular literary output of the European peoples among whom Jews lived. There were three types of professionals making this literature popular: copyists, who prepared anthologies and who were themselves frequently anonymous authors; minstrels who sang or recited ballads and poems at public gatherings; and the jesters who gave brief performances. The best known work of this first period is the **Shmuel-Bukh** (Samuel Book), which describes the life of King David* in poetic form. In this early period, Yiddish literature already served as a medium of entertainment and education for all segments of the Jewish people, particularly for the women and the uneducated. The sixteenth century saw a dramatic upsurge in Yiddish literature, similar to that which took place in a number of European literatures. Printing became widespread, and since Jews were the most literate people in Europe, Yiddish books could be mass-produced. At the beginning of the sixteenth century the **Bova Bukh,** a romantic adventure novel, became tremendously popular. However, the most widely read book appeared at the close of the sixteenth century: **Tsena Urena,** a retelling of the Pentateuch,* interwoven with various legends, stories, and parables. For three hundred years Jewish women read from this book every Sabbath.*

In this period, Yiddish literature made use of all the narrative and a large part of the poetic materials of the earlier centuries in the history of the Jewish people. The popular **Maase Bukh** (1602) contained a number of interesting stories from various periods of Jewish history. At this time there was close contact between the readers of Yiddish in Eastern Europe and in the Germanic countries. Yiddish books and authors circulated from east to west and from west to east. Yiddish literature made possible close contact among all Ashkenazic* Jews. Prague* and a number of other Eastern European communitites became centers of Yiddish literature.

The Thirty Years War in Western Europe, and the bloody persecutions of Jews in the Ukraine and Poland (1648-49) ushered in a period of intellectual stagnation. No new important works appeared. Many books were published in Amsterdam and there was a great demand for Yiddish books, but the spirit of the times was not conducive to the appearance of talented new writers.

The advent of Hasidism* in the middle of the

eighteenth century brought with it a spiritual revival among the masses of the Jewish people in Eastern Europe. At the same time the Haskalah* (Enlightenment) movement developed in Germany,* and a generation or two later, in Galicia, the Ukraine, and Lithuania.* These two opposing movements were represented in the renewed literary activity of this period. The Enlighteners utilized Yiddish literature to write satiric works criticizing the negative aspects of rigid Judaism; the Hasidim created legends and stories dealing with the great achievements of the rabbis. Many of the Hasidim were talented narrators, poets and writers of parables. The most interesting of these was Rabbi Nahman of Bratzlav.* In Eastern Europe the Enlighteners included a number of able writers, the most important of whom were Shlomo Ettinger, a poet and dramatist, and the popular writer of the mid-nineteenth century, and Isaac Meyer Dick, whose hundreds of stories were published in tens of thousands of copies.

Modern Yiddish Literature.

Modern Yiddish Literature is about one hundred years old, dating back to 1864, the year when Mendele Mocher Sefarim* published his first book. His works reflect the whole Jewish way of life in his time. Mendele was a realist and created a literary framework for narrative Yiddish prose. He had a number of followers and imitators. His greatest disciple was the famous humorist Sholom Aleichem.* The latter, with Mendele and J. L. Peretz,* are known as the three classic writers of modern Yiddish literature. Peretz, in turn, influenced a whole group of younger writers; some of them later became outstanding: e.g. the novelist Sholem Asch,* and the poet and short story writer Abraham Reisen.* The classic period in Yiddish literature lasted for fifty years, from 1864 to 1914. The 1880's saw the beginnings of the Yiddish theatre, which was pioneered by Abraham Goldfaden.* This was the period of large-scale immigration to the United States,* and Yiddish

Distinguished Yiddish writers in America: first row, left to right: S. Niger, H. Leivick, J. Opatoshu, H. Raisin, A. Glantz, P. Schwartz, H. Novak. Second row: J. Patt, H. Poupko, S. Tabachinsky Courtesy A. Glantz.

literature developed in America as well. Of the American Yiddish writers of that time, Morris Rosenfeld,* the poet who described and protested against the life of the sweatshop worker, is outstanding. In the twenty years between the two World Wars there were distinct centers of Yiddish literary activity; Warsaw,* Moscow, and New York. The Russian center was, of course, out of contact with the others. Its greatest writers were the novelist David Bergelson and the poet Peretz Markish. In Poland, the classic tradition was followed; there was also a good deal of experimentation with various literary froms and trends. A number of the Yiddish writers from Poland emigrated to America. Almost all of those who remained in Eastern Europe perished in the Hitler holocaust. In 1948, Yiddish literature was liquidated in the Soviet Union;* the most prominent writers were arrested and later executed.

Since 1914, New York has been the most important Yiddish literary center. There, Abraham Liesin, the editor of the magazine **Zukunft,** wrote his nationalistic poetry; and Yehoash* made an excellent Yiddish translation of the Bible. There were many fine poets, such as M. L. Halperin, Mani Leib, and I. J. Schwartz. The best Yiddish novelists (Zalman Shneur,* I. Bashevis Singer*), published in the New York Yiddish dailies. Here, J. Opatoshu,* the novelist, spent all of his creative years. The greatest living Yiddish poet, H. Leivick,* has written many poems, and dramas in both symbolic and realistic styles. After the Second World War, the Rumanian-Polish master of the ballad, Itzik Manger, and the Lithuanian poet Chaim Grade migrated to New York, together with many other poets and writers. Yiddish literary criticism, which had previously reached its zenith in Eastern Europe in the writings of Baal

340

Makhshovess, became significant in New York, largely because of the influence of Shmuel Niger.

There is now a lively literary center in Buenos Aires, and another in Montreal. There is an active group of Yiddish writers in Israel, of whom the most important is A. Sutzkever, the editor of **Di Goldene Keyt.**

During the last ninety years there has been a considerable development in essay writing, in scientific prose, children's literature, and many other branches of creative writing. Modern Yiddish literature reflects all aspects of Jewish life and all facets of the Jewish personality. Most recently, Yiddish literature has concentrated on the description and commemoration of the destruction of Eastern Eruopean Jewry. In all, there are approximately two thousand Yiddish poets and prose writers.   Y.M.

YISHUV. "Settlement." Term used for the Jewish community of Palestine* before the founding of the State of Israel.*

YIVO INSTITUTE OF JEWISH RESEARCH. Founded in Vilna* in 1925 for the purpose of studying the Yiddish language and literature, Jewish folklore and history, particularly the history of East European Jewry, contemporary Jewish social problems, Jewish psychology, education, and related subjects. Since 1940, the main office of YIVO, which has branches in many countries, has been located in New York.* YIVO has a library of approximately 170,000 volumes in all areas of Jewish knowledge, and the largest Jewish archives in the world. The archives contain at least two million documents. Much of the YIVO library and archives was rescued from the Nazi-pillaged Vilna collection with the aid of the United States government. YIVO has published such Yiddish periodicals as **Yivo-Bletter, Yiddishe Shprakh, Yiddisher Folklore,** and the English language **Yivo Annual.** YIVO'S branch in Argentina* publishes **Argentiner Yivo Bletter.** Recently, YIVO has been concentrating on an intensive study of Jewish life in the United States.

YIZKOR. Memorial prayer for the dead recited at the synagogue on the major Jewish holidays.

YOD. Tenth letter of the Hebrew alphabet; numerically, ten.

YOM KIPPUR (Day of Atonement). Regarded as the holiest day in the year and known as "the Sabbath of Sabbaths" **(Shabbat Shabbaton).** A day of appeal for the forgiveness of sins, it is marked by fasting from sundown of the ninth of Tishri to

sunset of the tenth. Because the rituals of repentance can absolve man only of sins committed against God and His law, the eve of the holiday is the appropriate time for asking the forgiveness of men whom one has offended. It is also customary among traditional Jews to offer **kapparot** ("atonement") on the eve of the fast. In the past, this was a colorful ceremony, in which a live rooster or hen was swung around the head of each member of the family to recall the ancient sin-offerings. Today, a special money gift to charity is mostly used instead. During the ceremony, the head of the house recites the words. "This is my atonement, this is my forgiveness."

The Yom Kippur service is the longest in the Jewish liturgy. It begins with the chanting of the mournful **Kol Nidre** just before sunset on the eve of the holiday. This prayer, composed before the ninth century C.E., asks for release from vows or promises made that cannot be kept. Prayers con-

Praying Jews, by Maurice Gottlieb.

tinue throughout the next day. Famous portions of the service include the **Viddui,** or confession of sins, and the **Seder Avodah** ("Order of Worship"), attributed to the poet Yosi ben Yosi of Palestine, during the fourth or fifth century C.E. This long narrative describes the Yom Kippur service in the Temple.* It reaches its climax with the entrance of the High Priest to the Holy of Holies to beg forgiveness for his own sins and those of the entire people. The Yom Kippur service concludes with the **Neilah** ("closing"), so called because it refers to the closing of the gates of heaven at the end of the day. A single shofar* blast and the words "Next year in Jerusalem!*" terminate the fast.

YOM KIPPUR WAR. Despite Isarael's* overwhelming victory in the Six-Day War* of 1967, and her oft-repeated offers of peace, her Arab neighbors refused to enter into negotiations with her or even to recognize her existence. On Yom Kippur, 5734 (October 6, 1973), the Egyptian and Syrian armies crossed the 1967 cease-fire lines on the Suez Canal and the Golan Heights, respectively. Israel was caught off balance, since she had not expected her neighbors to launch an all-out war at that time. Also, in contrast to the situation in 1967, Israel's air force was greatly hampered by new, highly effective anti-aircraft missiles with which Russia* had supplied both Egypt* and Syria* over the years since the Six-Day War. Egypt succeeded in establishing bridgeheads east of the Canal, and Syria captured Mt. Hermon and the city of Kuneitra. Until Israel was able to mobilize her reserves, the outcome of the war was in doubt. On October 12, however, the tide of battle began to turn in Israel's favor. Israeli forces recaptured all the territory taken by Syria, pushed the Syrian armies behind the 1967 cease-fire lines and eventually advanced to positions about 20 miles away from Damascus.* On October 17, the Israelis crossed the Suez Canal, eventually coming within about 50 miles of Cairo. All this time, Russia was constantly sending arms shipments to Syria and Egypt to replace the vast quantities of airplanes and tanks they had lost. Under the circumstances, and in view of Israel's heavy losses, particularly in airplanes, the United States began a massive airlift of weapons to Isreal.

As long as the Arabs appeared to be winning the war, Russia did not seek an end to the fighting. But with Israel gaining the upper hand, Russia summoned Secretary of State Henry Kissinger* to Moscow and began to press for a cease-fire. On October 24, finally, all fighting ceased. Israel had lost almost 3,000 soldiers; total Arab losses were close to 20,000. On November 11, 1973, Israel and Egypt signed a cease-fire agreement at Kilometer 101 on the Suez-Cairo highway, and four days later, the two sides began to exchange prisoners of war.

On May 29, 1974, Syria, the most implacable of Israel's enemies, agreed to sign a disengagement pact with Israel under terms to those agreed upon by Israel and Egypt. One June 5, 1974, the agreement between Israel and Syria was signed in Geneva.

Although fighting had officially ceased on Israel's northern and southern fronts, she was still (as of 1979) harassed by attacks from Palestinian guerillas who crossed into Israel from neighboring Lebanon.* In the summer of 1979, the Palestinian Liberation Organization, whose charter calls for the dismantling of the Jewish state, was clamoring for a voice in the peace conferences that were being planned between Israel and her Arab neighbors.

YOUNG ISRAEL. In 1912 a group of fifteen young men and women in New York City* established the first Young Israel organization. Their purpose was to make traditional Judaism attractive to Jewish youth, and to increase their Jewish education and awareness. In 1915, Young Israel opened its first model synagogue. The new synagogue featured decorum during services, a sermon in English, and congregational participation and singing. By 1979 Young Israel had one hundred six affiliated branches in the United States,* Canada,* the Netherlands,* and Israel,* serving 100,000 members. Each Young Israel branch conducts services in its own synagogue, strictly in conformance with traditional requirements. All branches offer an educational program for all age groups, one that lays particular emphasis on traditional Judaism. The National Council of Young Israel maintains the Young Israel Institute for Jewish Studies. Its youth department trains the future leaders of the movement and sponsors the Young Israel Boy Scout Troop. Its employment bureau specializes in securing positions for Sabbath observers and part-time or vacation jobs for youngsters in school. Its armed forces division extends material and spiritual aid to Orthodox boys in the armed services of the United States. Young Israel supports major Jewish relief agencies throughout the world and the rebuilding of Israel. The official publication of the organization is the Young Israel Viewpoint.

YOUNG JUDEA. Organized in 1909 to help young American Jews develop healthy attitudes toward themselves, the Jewish people, and Israel.

Its first president was Israel Friedlaender and such prominent Zionists as Henrietta Szold* and Emanuel Newmann have held positions of leadership. Under the auspices of Hadassah Zionist Youth Commission, Young Judea is provided with funds and administration, as well as with supervision and guidance. Young Judea provides cultural, religious, and recreational programs for Jewish young people up to the age of eighteen. It supports a youth farm in Israel* for the benefit of Jewish scouts and those young Judeans who visit Israel. Young Judea maintains Tel Yehuda, a camp for high school youngsters which offers training in leadership. Young Judea sponsors both a summer-in-Israel course for seniors and a more intensive year-in-Israel course.

YOUNG MEN'S AND YOUNG WOMEN'S HEBREW ASSOCIATION.

Popularly known as Y.M. and Y.W.H.A., a recreational and cultural Jewish institution throughout the United States. The first Y.M.H.A. was established in New York in 1874. It was patterned on the Young Men's Christian Association, and was geared to serve the social and recreational needs of the individual. At the height of Jewish mass immigration into the United States, the "Y" movement grew swiftly and devoted much of its program to Americanization work. Some of its tendencies were assimilationist during this period.

In 1913, the Y.M.H.A. and kindred organizations united to form one national association. Eight years later, this association merged with the National Jewish Welfare Board,* which has guided the work of the movement since then. In the last few decades, the nature of the Y.M.H.A. has changed, becoming dedicated to the service of the family unit rather than to that of the individual. This change is also reflected in the name and program of the affiliated institutions. A large proportion of them are called Jewish Community Centers, and Jewish cultural and educational programs are an integral part of their work. Three hundred and fifty-two such centers in the United States and Canada are currently affiliated with the National Jewish Welfare Board.

YOUTH ALIYAH

(Hebrew, meaning "youth immigration"). An organization for the resettlement, education, and rehabilitation of Jewish youth in Israel.* Youth Aliyah was founded in 1934, the year after Hitler's seizure of power in Germany. Its purpose was to save German Jewish youth from imminent doom under the Nazi system. In the desperate days of 1932, the idea for youth immigration from Germany to Palestine came to Recha Freier, the wife of a rabbi in Berlin. She represented this idea to a gathering of children about to complete their elementary education, and the repsonse was tremendous. The youth themselves organized Juedische Jugendhilfe ("Jewish Youth Aid"), which was soon joined by Ahava ("Love"), an orphanage in Berlin. For years Ahava had been transferring children to Ben Shemen, a children's village in Palestine.* Under the leadership of Henrietta Szold,* these spontaneous beginnings were organized into the Youth Aliyah movement. Selected adolescents were brought to Israel. There, in groups of twenty to thirty, they were given two years of intensive training to enable them to settle on the land. During the Second World War, when communications with Europe were cut off, Youth Aliyah agents worked behind enemy lines, endangering their lives to spirit children out of Europe and bring them to Palestine. The greatest challenge, however, came after the war. At that time thousands of children, wandering parentless over the face of a war-ravaged continent, had to be given homes and security. After the establishment of the State of Israel in 1948, and the beginning of mass immigration, the number of young people needing training and care increased still further. Many of them came from Oriental countries, and had to be helped to bridge the thousand-year gap between the lives they had led in their backward lands or origin and the lives they were about to lead in modern, westernized Israel. In time, other problems arose. Whereas at first Youth Aliyah cared for youths spearated from their parents, in recent years they have had to aid youngsters living with their families in underprivileged surroundings. It has therefore undertaken a program of vocational training for immigrant youth, and is founding a chain of clubs and youth centers in immigrant settlements. It has also taken under its wing underprivileged Israel-born youth; among its latest projects is an agricultural training course for Israel Arabs. At the same time, Youth Aliyah is continuing to receive hundreds of youngsters each month in the 270 settlements throughout Israel; there, full-time educational programs are conducted under the guidance of specially trained counselors, many of whom are Youth Aliyah "graduates." Special centers are maintained for disturbed children, and for those needing medical treatment. The organization, has cared for a total of over 160,000 Jewish youths from 80 different countries in its 45 years of existence. The majority of Youth Aliyah wards have gone into agriculture, making a sizeable contribution to the farm community of Israel. There is at present scarcely an agricultural settlement without its Youth Aliyah "graduates." Others have become skilled craftsmen, teachers, soldiers, artists, and social workers.

The Youth Aliyah program is conducted and partly financed by the Jewish Agency.* Hadassah,* which has taken a special interest in the project from its inception, is the official representative of Youth Aliyah in the United States,* and provides about 35 per cent of its funds.

YUGOSLAVIA. This nation in southeast Europe, established as an independent state after World War I, was inhabited by Jews in early Roman times. In 1492 refugees expelled from Spain settled about Belgrade and Sarajevo. They preserved the Sephardi traditions in the new land. Although for many years they were ill-treated, the new Serbia of 1878 carried out the stipulations of the Berlin Treaty regarding religious liberty. After World War II only 10,500 Jews remained of 72,000. 8,000 of these migrated to Israel. There are now 6,000 Jews in Yugoslavia.

Israel Zangwill

Z

ZACUTO, ABRAHAM BEN SAMUEL (c. 1450-c.1510). Astronomer, scientist, professor, rabbinical scholar. A native of Spain,* Zacuto lived in Portugal* after the expulsion of the Jews from Spain in 1492. Fleeing the Inquisition,* he left Portugal for Tunis and Turkey.* Zacuto perfected the astrolabe (the forerunner of the sextant) used by Vasco da Gama. He was the author of the **Almanach Perpetuum,** nautical tables, and works on astronomy.

ZACUTO, MOSES. See HEBREW LITERATURE.

ZAMENHOF, LAZARUS LUDWIG (1859-1917). Linguist. Born in Bialystok, Zamenhof practiced medicine in Warsaw. Intent on solving the problem of national conflicts, he thought that a simple international language might hasten the solution. He, therefore, created an auxiliary language called Esperanto (literally, "Hopeful"). Esperanto, which brought its creator world fame, uses all the letters of the Roman alphabet, except Q, W, X, and Y. It is spelled as pronounced, its rules have no exceptions, and its guiding principle is to use roots common to the main languages of Europe. More than 10,000 publications have appeared in Esperanto; more than 100 Esperanto periodicals are regularly published.

ZANGWILL, ISRAEL (1864-1926). Writer, satirist, and founder of the Jewish Territorialist Organization.* Zangwill was born and raised in London's East End, amid the struggles of the East European Jewish immigrants to adjust to new surroundings. He understood the ghetto folk and saw their sorrow when the children left their parents' way of life for the new ways of modern London. In his **Children of the Ghetto** (1892), he brought these people to life with realism, sympathy, and humor, His journalistic essays were cruelly witty, his non-Jewish novels brought him passing success and are now forgotten. But **Children of the Ghetto** is Zangwill's first claim on lasting fame, followed closely by the **King of Schnorrers** and **Dreamers of the Ghetto.**

Theodor Herzl* won Zangwill over to Zionism* in 1895, and for a number of years he worked actively for Zionism. When the Zionist movement rejected Uganda in British East Africa as a "temporary asylum" for the persecuted Jews of Russia,* Zangwill left the Zionist organization. He wanted to find a land in which the Jews could settle immediately and have their own state. For this purpose he founded the Jewish Territorialist

Emblem of the tribe of Zebulun

Organization* (JTO), which searched for a Jewish homeland in other countries, from Africa to Australia.* After the Balfour Declaration,* which promised "the establishment in Palestine of a national home for the Jewish people," Zangwill returned to the Zionist fold and worked for Zionism till the end of his life.

ZAYIN. Seventh letter of the Hebrew alphabet; numerically, seven.

ZEBULUN (from the Hebrew, "he dwelled"). Sixth son of Jacob and Leah. Zebulun was the only tribe to settle near the coast and its land was a sliver in the center of Canaan.

ZECHARIAH (c.520 B.C.E.). Eleventh of the Minor Prophets. Like his contemporary, the prophet Haggai, Zechariah lived and preached in Jerusalem* after the return from the Babylonian exile. He too urged the rebuilding of the Temple* and prophesied the coming of the Messiah. His visions are mystic revelations replete with symbolic figures: horses, craftsmen, a golden candlestick, a flying scroll, and Satan in the role of an accusing angel.

ZEITLIN, HILLEL (1872-1942). Hebrew and Yiddish writer and thinker. Born in a small town in White Russia, his early youth was steeped in the study of the Talmud* and Hasidism.* He later contributed to the Hebrew and Yiddish press, and became editor of a Yiddish daily, **Moment,** in Warsaw,* Poland.* In his books and numerous articles, Zeitlin dealt with the philosophical problems of good and evil; he also wrote extensively on the Kabbalah* and on Hasidism. Deeply religious, his fine poetic essays expressed his love of nature, its harmony and beauty.

Zeitlin died a martyr's death at the hands of the Nazis in the Warsaw* ghetto, while absorbed in

prayer. He is survived by his son Aaron Zeitlin, a Hebrew and Yiddish poet and essayist who died in New York.

ZEPHANIAH, BOOK OF. Zephaniah, ninth of the Minor Prophets, lived toward the end of the seventh century B.C.E., and prophesied the downfall of Nineveh and the Assyrian empire. He warned the people that "a great and dreadful day of the Lord, a day of darkness and obscurity" would come upon them and they would be punished for evildoing. After this punishment, salvation would come to Israel and to all the world.

ZERUBBABEL. Princely descendant of the House of David,* who governed Judea* in the sixth century B.C.E., Zerubbabel was the grandson of Jehoiachin, the last king of Judea, who ended his life a captive in Babylonia.* Cyrus, the Median prince, having conquered Babylonia in 539 B.C.E., permitted Zerubbabel to lead a group of returning exiles back to Judea. With the aid of the high priest Joshua, Zerubbabel set up an altar, restored the celebration of the holidays, and began the rebuilding of the city walls and the Temple. Internal difficulties and hostile neighbors interrupted this work. About 520 B.C.E., Zerubbabel was appointed governor of Judea and, encouraged by the prophets Haggai* and Zechariah,* resumed the labor of reconstruction.

ZIONISM. The modern political movement for the return of the Jewish people to Zion, the old prophetic name for Palestine.* This movement began in the nineteenth century with the thinking and writings of a number of men in various parts of Europe, and was followed by the founding of several Jewish agricultural settlements in Palestine. Zionism received its political form from the work of Theodor Herzl,* and its clearly defined program at the first Zionist Congress,* held in Basle, Switzerland,* in 1897.

The History.

Although the term Zionism did not come into use until the 1890's, the desire to reunite the Jewish people with its ancient homeland began eighteen centuries earlier, when the might of Rome destroyed Judea and exiled the Jews from Palestine. At that movement, the Jewish people turned passionately to the vision of their prophets that a Messiah, an anointed son of the House of David,* would appear "at the end of days" and lead them home to Zion. The mystical longing for the Messiah and the Return entered the people's dreams and prayers. It was so intense that, from time to time, persons who felt themselves to be either the "messiah" or his forerunner would appear, and announce themselves as such. Always

Hillel Zeitlin

these "messiahs" found followers, whom they sometimes led to open rebellion against their rulers. Some "messiahs" who started out as mystic believers ended up as crude impostors. The tragic, dangerous trail of Messianism* runs through Jewish history, from the eighth-century warlike tailor, Abu Isa of Persia, to the eighteenth-century mystic poet, Moses Hayim Luzzato* of Italy.*

The love of Zion expressed itself in the people's daily life and in its literature. After the first exile, the people sang:

By the rivers of Babylon, there we sat down,
Yea we wept when we remembered Zion.

They did more than weep and remember; when they were given the opportunity, they left Babylon and returned to their homeland. Six hundred years later, they were exiled from Palestine a second time and scattered across the continents. Life became very difficult, and survival uncertain; yet the Jewish people continued to turn in the direction of Zion thrice daily when they prayed. A thousand years after the second dispersion, the great poet Yehuda Ha-Levi* sang in majestic poems of his love of Zion and his longing for Zion's restoration. Pious pilgrims made their way to the Holy Land throughout the centuries of exile, some to live there, and some to die and be buried in its sacred soil.

Forerunner of Modern Zionism.

In the nineteenth century, when the nations of Europe were achieving their independence, the Jewish people felt that the time was ripe to resettle in their ancient homeland. Yehuda Alkalai* agitated for colonization among the Hasidim* in Europe and among the pious recipients of Halukkah* in Palestine. In 1862, Rabbi Z'vi Hirsch Kalischer* published a book, **The Quest for Zion,** that urged the people to help themselves by forming a settlement society for the purpose of buying land in Palestine and settling on it. At about the same time, Moses Hess,* a German Jewish Socialist living in Paris,* published a little book called **Rome and Jerusalem.** This booklet discussed the Jewish problem, emancipation, anti-Semitism,* and the Reform movement. The Jewish people, said Hess, would never lose its special character. Mankind was made up of many nations and small peoples, like the Jews, each of which had something special to contribute to world civilization. The only way to solve the Jewish problem was "through the creation of a national center in Palestine" under the protection of some European power.

When **The Quest for Zion** and **Rome and Jerusalem** were published, few people accepted the ideas expressed in them. For at that time many Jews thought to solve the problems of discrimination and anti-Semitism by becoming "enlightened"—that is, by obtaining a modern education and adopting the language and manners of their non-Jewish countrymen. This was the Enlightenment or Haskalah* movement, which absorbed the energies and thought of the intellectual leaders of the Jewish people. Among the first to turn the Haskalah movement away from assimilation* and toward a Jewish national revival was the novelist Peretz Smolenskin.* Smolenskin inspired the forming of the Kadimah Zionist students' societies in Vienna. In his book, **Am Olam** (1872), Smolenskin called the Jewish people an "eternal people" that must keep the eternal idea of Zion before it. According to Smolenskin, only the eternal Hebrew language embodied the Zionist ideal; and only by settlement on the soil of Palestine could the Jewish people maintain its uniqueness.

Another voice called the Jewish people to action. An Odessa* physician, Leo Pinsker,* had lost his faith in the struggle for Jewish emancipation in Russia under Tsarist persecution and pogroms.* Pinsker diagnosed anti-Semitism as an incurable disease, and prescribed the treatment for it in an essay called "Auto-Emanciaption" (setting one's self free). Published in 1882, "Auto-Emancipation" diagnosed the Jewish sickness as homelessness. "The world sees in the Jewish people a ghost, a corpse that walks among the living. This ghost of a people without unity or organization, without a land of its own...is yet walking about among the living." Because the "living" peoples of the world cannot understand this "walking ghost" of the Jewish people, they fear and hate it. The nations of the world never have to deal with the Jews as another nation, but only as individuals—hence they cannot respect us. To achieve this respect, Pinsker claimed, "We must have a home, a land, a territory." "Now or never!" was his cry, and he called for a congress of Jewish leaders.

The Lovers of Zion.

Pinsker's call was heard by the Hoveve Zion* ("Lovers of Zion"), a movement of scattered societies that had begun to spring up in the 1860's. These groups got together at a conference in Kattowitz, Silesia, in November 1884, formed a federation, and elected Pinsker as their president. Their aim was to restore Jewish national life by settling Palestine. About two years earlier, a group of young university students who belonged to the Hoveve Zion had gotten together, and had emigrated to Palestine. They called themselves

BILU,* from the Hebrew initials of the Biblical verse "O House of Jacob, come let us go!" The BILU group was determined to work only on the land, and as a cooperative body. City-bred and soft, they came to Palestine and heroically struggled to settle on the soil despite the hostility of Turkish rulers and Arab neighbors, overcoming the hardships of swampy valleys, stony hillsides, and burning sand. Such pioneering, which came to be known as "practical Zionism" was performed by idealists too impractical to recognize the impossible. The BILU were the vanguard of the First Aliyah,* or migration. They were to be followed in time by the famous Second Aliyah (1904-1914), whose principles set a lasting pattern for pioneering on the land of Israel. In the meantime, the example of the First Aliyah, and the influence of the writings of Kalischer, Hess, Smolenskin, and Pinsker were the indispensable preliminaries for the political Zionism which appeared in 1896.

Theodor Herzl and Political Zionism.

Theodor Herzl,* the founder of political Zionism, knew nothing of the early Zionist movement or its literature. He was a successful Viennese journalist and playwright who apparently thought of his Jewishness only now and again when he was disturbed by anti-Semitism. In Paris,* as correspondent of the famous **Neue Freie Presse,** Herzl was aroused by the Dreyfus* case, and deeply shocked by its effect on the French people. In a spiritual turmoil, he grappled with the Jewish problem and arrived at a solution: the Jewish people must have a Jewish State. A "charter" for such a state in Palestine must be obtained from Turkey.* A Jewish society must be formed to engineer the mass movement of the Jewish people to Palestine.

In 1896, Herzl published his program in his book **Judenstaat** ("The Jewish State"), and began to search for a leader to translate his ideas into action. The philanthropist Baron Maurice de Hirsch already engaged in Jewish settlement projects in Argentina,* refused to assume leadership. Albert Rothschild of Vienna did not even answer Herzl's letter. The ultra-Orthodox Jews saw in his scheme an interference with the will of the Almighty, who, according to the traditional view, would send the Messiah to restore the Jews to their land. The leaders of the Reform movement opposed Zionism because, they claimed, the Jews represented only a religion, not a nation. Socialists said that the Jewish problem would be solved only when the world became one utopian classless society.

In January, 1897, Herzl issued a call for a con-

Nordau greeting Herzl at first Zionist Congress in Basle—1897.

gress, and on August 27 of that year the first Zionist Congress met in Basle, Switzerland.* Herzl appeared before the delegates, a magnetic, majestic figure. He caught their imagination, and held it as long as he lived, and long afterwards. The first Zionist Congress formulated the Basle Program,* which announced to the world that: "Zionism aims to create for the Jewish people a home in Palestine secured by public law." In subsequent Congresses, the World Zionist Organization* was given form and function. Herzl established **Die Welt,** a publication to speak for the Zionist movement. In 1899, the Zionist bank, called the Jewish Colonial Trust, was founded in London.* A commission to further the colonization work in Palestine was set up, and the Keren Kayemet, or Jewish National Fund* was organized to purchase land in Palestine. Men and ideas matured as the issues were debated at the various Congresses. From the beginning, Max Nordau,* physician and writer, was Herzl's closest supporter and the master orator who gave winged words to the Zionist movement. Herzl's tireless negotiations with European governments for a charter to Palestine were not successful during his short life. But they did prepare the way for the future. In 1902, Great Britain offered to open up first the Sinai peninusla* for Jewish settlement, and then the territory of Uganda in East Africa for autonomous Jewish settlement. The sixth and seventh Zionist Congresses debated the Uganda project and rejected it, even though Herzl pleaded for its acceptance as a temporary asylum for the hard-pressed Jews of Russia.

The death of Herzl, in 1904, at the age of forty-four, was a severe blow to the Zionist movement. For a while the work slowed down, but it did not halt. Disagreement arose between two Zionist schools of thought. The followers of Herzl, the "political Zionists," believed that Zionist energy must be concentrated on the **political** work of obtaining a charter to establish a Jewish state in Palestine. They held that the **practical** work of mass settlement would come after this legal guarantee for the colonizers had been achieved. On the other hand, "practical Zionists," supported by the old Lovers of Zion, were convinced that settlement must go on, since a larger Jewish settlement in Palestine would lend greater weight to the political efforts of the Zionist movement. A rising young leader, Chaim Weizmann,* tried for years to convince the two factions that a combination of both approaches would benefit Zionism most.

Cultural Zionism.

Still another important school urged Zionists to take yet a different road to their goal. This school was headed by the writer and philosopher. Ahad Ha-Am* (Asher Ginzberg); the course he charted was "cultural Zionism." The cultural Zionists maintained that it was not enough for the driven and harassed among the Jewish people to find a national home in Palestine. Palestine had to be restored as a spiritual center for the whole Jewish people. Such a center, wrote Ahad Ha-am, could be accomplished, gradually, only by those who were imbued with the Hebrew prophetic ideals. The cultural Zionists feared that concentration on political and practical Zionism might overlook the spiritual and cultural starvation among the Jewish people—and the results would be disastrous.

World War I put an end to these debates and opened a new chapter in Jewish history. Zionism was faced with the splitting of its forces between the hostile powers of Germany* and Austria* on one side, and Britain, France* and Russia* on the other. The World Zionists Organization, therefore, adopted a policy of neutrality, and opened a central office in neutral Copenhagen. An important result of this policy came when the German government influenced the Turkish administration to soften to some extent its cruel treatment of the Jewish community in Palestine. The Turks were particularly suspicious of those Palestinian Jews who had come from Russia. (Russia fought on the side of the Allies, while Turkey was leagued with Germany.) Since they were in danger of imprisonment by the Turks as enemy aliens, a large number of Jewish refugees fled from Palestine to Alexandria,* Egypt.* Their pressure in Egypt complemented Zionist political activity among the Allies. Joseph Trumpeldor* and Vladimir Jabotinsky* urged British military authorities in Alexandria and Cairo for permission to organize a Jewish Legion* to fight on the side of the Allies. At first sharply opposed, the British at last relented somewhat and permitted Trumpeldor to form a transport unit, the Zion Mule Corps, which served with the British in the Gallipoli Expeditionary Force. By June 1917, Jabotinsky had succeeded in breaking down British resistance, and the Jewish Legion* was finally formed; it fought with the British forces for the liberation of Palestine from the Turks.

The Balfour Declaration.

Beginning in 1915, Chaim Weizmann,* together with a few other leaders of British Jewry, began negotiations with the British government to obtain the charter that Herzl had so vainly sought. For nearly three years these negotiations inched forward. Nahum Sokolow* became Zionism's roving ambassador to the war-locked capitals of the Allies, returning again and again till their consent was won. When the United States* entered the war in 1917, Justice Louis D. Brandeis* led the drive to obtain President Woodrow Wilson's backing for Zionist aims. Finally, on November 2, 1917, the Balfour Declaration* was issued in a letter to Lord Lionel Walter Rothschild, president of the British Zionist Federation. The declaration stated in part that: "His Majesty's Government view with favor the establishment in Palestine of a national home for the Jewish people."

A few weeks after the Balfour Declaration, British troops entered Jerusalem.* A few months later, a commission headed by Weizmann came to Palestine. Major W. Ormsby-Gore, representing the British government, was attached to the commission, whose responsibility it was to find out how the promise of the declaration could best be fulfilled. While in Palestine, Weizmann went to Amman to visit Prince Feisal, son of King Hussein of Hedjaz, and discussed with him the idea of peaceful relations between the Jews in Palestine and the Arab world. This discussion resulted in an agreement signed by Feisal and Weizmann in London* in January 1919, backing the Balfour Declaration and safeguarding the rights of the Arabs in Palestine. In America President Wilson expressed his approval of the Balfour Declaration and said that he was "persuaded ... our own Government and people, are agreed that in Palestine shall be laid the foundation of a Jewish Commonwealth." On February 27, 1919, a Zionist delegation consisting of Weizmann, Sokolow, Ussishkin,* and Andre Spire appeared before the Versailles Peace Conference,* and presented the Zionist claims based on "the historic claims of the Jewish people to Palestine." The Peace Conference accepted the Balfour Declaration, and entrusted the mandate for Palestine to England.* the Allied Supreme Council meeting at San Remo in April 1920, included the Declaration in its treaty with Turkey, and two years later, the League of Nations affirmed the British mandate for Palestine. Finally, President Warren Harding and the Congress of the United States approved the Balfour Declaration on September 21, 1922.

Retreat from the Mandate.

But, while international approval was making the Jewish National Home in Palestine legally more secure, the British government was doing the opposite. The British systematically stalled on and blocked the execution of their mandate. Thus, they gave away a tract of state lands to Bedouin nomads who did not cultivate it, and by numerous similar actions administered Palestine in a manner intended primarily to hinder the development of a Jewish national home. The rivalry between Britain and France for control in the Near East, budding Arab nationalism, and the rival ambitions of Arab leaders, all served to arouse Arab unrest and incite violence. In 1920 and again in 1921, there were Arab attacks on Jewish agricultural settlements and on the Jews of Jerusalem,* Jaffa,* and Tel Aviv.* The British administration in Palestine hampered Jewish self-defense, arresting defenders and attackers alike. The mandate was further weakened by the Churchill White Paper of 1922. This, the first of the white papers on the mandate, diminished the area of Jewish Palestine by removing Transjordan and making it a separate Arab territory. The political activity to counter these British actions in which the Zionist movement engaged led to lasting internal divisions. (See REVISIONIST ZIONISM.)

Internal Difficulties.

Other difficulties developed. In 1921, at the first Zionist Congress held after World War I, the Keren Hayesod, or Palestine Foundation Fund was created to finance the development of Palestine. The Keren Hayesod was entrusted with the task of obtaining from world Jewry donations as well as investments to develop industry and agriculture, to bring immigrants to Palestine, and to care for their health and education. Supreme Court Justice Louis D. Brandeis and his followers among American Zionists differed from the

Zionists under Weizmann's leadership on whether it was advisable to use this method to finance the work in Palestine. Brandeis objected to setting up the Keren Hayesod as an umbrella fund to accept both investments and donations; he stressed the need to stimulate and to rely on large-scale private investment. When his point of view was not accepted, Justice Brandeis retired from the leadership of American Zionism. **(See also ZIONIST ORGANIZATION OF AMERICA.)** In 1924, the movement of create an enlarged Jewish Agency,* within which non-Zionists would serve together with the Zionists, led to still other divisions of opinion. These were not settled until August 1929, when the enlarged Jewish Agency came into being at the sixteenth Zionist Congress held in Zurich.

This Congress marked a decade of Zionist growth since the end of World War I. World Zionism had reached out for support and membership to every corner of the globe. In Palestine the growth of Zionist settlements on the land and in the cities was remarkable, despite the economic crisis between 1925 and 1928. The Jewish National Fund had purchased the Emek and the Haifa Bay area. The Palestine Foundation Fund had provided the credit and the various other forms of assistance needed by the pioneers of the Second and Third aliyot. The arab riot of 1929, which took many Jewish lives and destroyed much Jewish property, failed to wipe out the Jewish settlement of Palestine or to deter the Zionist effort.

Arab Riots. White Paper Commissions and Partition Proposal.

The Arab riots did, however, lead the British to renew their efforts to nullify the Balfour Declaration. The major provisions of the Passfield White Paper, issued in October 1930, aimed to reduce Jewish immigration to a trickle, and to stop altogether the purchase of agricultural lands by Jews. On the day this White Paper was published, Chaim Weizmann resigned his presidency of the World Zionist Organization and of the Jewish Agency for Palestine in protest. This was the first in a series of protests and cries of indignation uttered by Jews and non-Jews alike. The result was a full-dress debate in the British parliament during which the government was severely attacked. In its wake, Prime Minister Ramsay MacDonald wrote a letter to Weizmann modifying the worst features of the White Paper.

The Arabs in Palestine quieted down, and there were no more serious disturbances till 1936. Yet the situation was not radically changed. As Hitler and the Nazis rose to power in Germany,* persecutions sent a stream of German Jews to Palestine. The Arabs reacted with new riots. From 1936 to 1938, terrorist attacks on Jewish settlements, the setting of fire to fields and forests, and the murder and intimidation of Arabs friendly to Jews, went on unchecked. British action to eradicate the terror was neither consistent nor forceful enough to accomplish its aim. But Britain did pursue vigorously another form of action. In November 1936, a new British Royal Commission headed by Lord William Robert Peel came to Palestine to investigate the causes of the Arab terror. The Peel Commission stayed till January 1937; it reported that the mandate had become unworkable, recommended further restriction of Jewish immigration and land purchase, and the partition of Palestine into an Arab state and a tiny Jewish state. The Arabs flatly rejected partition; the Zionist Congress held in August 1937 offered a compromise. The Zionist Executive was authorized to negotiate with the British to find out "the precise terms of his Majesty's Government for the proposed establishment of a Jewish State."

Balfour Declaration Scrapped.

In 1938, a British commission went to Palestine to work out the partition boundaries. The report of this commission was negative. It found no boundaries possible which might make practical "the establishment of self-supporting Arab and Jewish states." Another White Paper announced that the partition plan had been abandoned as unrealistic. The British then called a round table conference of Jews and Arabs in London to find another solution to the Palestine problem. This conference failed, because the Arab delegation refused to sit down at the same table with the Jews, and insisted on the termination of the mandate. In May 1939, the final White paper appeared. It scrapped the Balfour Declaration with its promise of a Jewish National Home. To freeze the Jewish population as a permanent minority in Palestine, it limited Jewish immigration to 75,000 over a period of five years. The sale of land to Jews was severely restricted. Finally, the White Paper proposed that in ten years Palestine be made into an independent Arab state allied to Britain. This White Paper appeared at the very time when Nazi Germany occupied Czechoslovakia* and the Hitler regime began to murder Jewish victims, whose numbers were to mount into the millions in the next few years. The Zionist Congress met to act on this new British policy on the eve of World War II. Rejecting the White Paper unanimously, the Congress pledged its full support to the democracies in their fight against Nazism.

World War II and Jewish Brigade.

Immediately after their return from the Congress, Zionist leaders began strenuous efforts to rescue European Jewry. During the years of World War II, the World Zionist Organization protested vehemently against British policy in Palestine, and made every effort to mobilize public opinion against it. At the same time Weizmann pressed the British government to accept his offer to establish a fighting force of Palestine Jews for service with the British Army. For two years he met with no success. Then the dangerous situation in the Mediterranean campaign brought partial agreement. Selected Jewish units totaling 33,000 were permitted to serve with the British Forces in the Near and Middle East and elsewhere. In 1944, the British finally agreed to the formation of a Jewish Brigade. When the victorious Allied armies swept into Austria and Germany, the Jewish Brigade under its own blue-white flag was a part of these Forces.

The Blockade and "Illegal Immigration."

At the end of World War II, it was discovered that six million Jews, one-third of all the Jewish people in the world, had been destroyed by Hitler. It seemed only just that the pitiful survivors of Nazi concentration camps should be admitted freely to Palestine to be cared for by their own people. But the British government disagreed. The British White Paper and the British fleet blockaded the Jewish National Home. The "illegal immigration" begun before the war by Palestine Jewry was, therefore, resumed and increased. In London and Washington, Zionist leaders used every form of pressure acceptable in democratic countries to change British policy and open the doors of Palestine to Jewish immigration. In April 1946, an Anglo-American Committee of Inquiry visited Palestine and the concentration camps in Europe. On its return, the Committee recommended that 100,000 survivors should be admitted to Palestine immediately. United States President Harry S. Truman gave this proposal his emphatic support. Nevertheless, the new Labor government in England vetoed this recommendation. The tiny Jewish community of Palestine increased its defiant resistance to the British Empire. In this unequal battle, the world Zionist movement acted to enlist public opinion and to increase its own strength. The disaster that wiped out European Jewry, and the passionate struggle against British policy in Palestine brought hundres of thousands of new members into Zionist ranks. Millions of dollars for reconstruction were poured into Palestine.

Meanwhile, the most powerful political and resistance weapon of the Palestine Jewish community, "illegal immigration," continued to bring in shiploads of refugees who preferred to run the British blockade rather than remain in the displaced persons camps of Germany. Many ships were caught by the British Navy, and thousands of refugees were deported to detention camps in Cyprus. Public opinion was outraged; finally, Foreign Minister Ernest Bevin, in London, gave up and in February 1947, announced to the House of Commons his intention to refer the problem to the United Nations (UN).

"Palestine Problem" before the United Nations.

On April 28, 1947, the UN Assembly met in special session to consider the situation in Palestine and to find a solution for it. A series of passionate and bitter debates began. The Arab side was represented by the delegates of six member states, and by the members of the Arab Higher Committee. The Jewish side was presented by the leaders of the Jewish Agency: Abba Hillel Silver,* head of its American section, Moshe Shertok (Sharett)*, head of its political department, and David Ben Gurion,* its chairman. When debate was completed, the UN Assembly appointed an eleven-member Special Committee of Inquiry on Palestine (UNSCOP) "to investigate all questions and issues relevant to the problem of Palestine." UNSCOP was instructed to bring back its report to the regular session of the assembly in September 1947.

UNSCOP visited Beirut and listened to the representatives of the Arab states; they went to Jerusalem and listened to all parties of the Yishuv —the Jewish community of Palestine. They went to Europe and visited the survivors of Hitler's horror, who were still fenced in camps and waiting for a home and freedom. The UNSCOP members were all deeply moved by these pitiful victims; two of them, Jorge Garcia Granados of Guatemala* and Enrique Fabregat of Uruguay,* became ardent Zionists. The UNSCOP report, published on August 31, 1947, recommended unanimously the termination of the mandate, the preservation of economic unity of Palestine, and the safeguarding of the Holy Places. On the political future of the country UNSCOP was divided. The majority suggested the partition of Palestine into a Jewish state, an Arab state, and an international authority for governing Jerusalem. A minority of three recommended a Federal Arab-Jewish state.

Partition Voted by U. N.

For two months this report was debated by the UN Assembly. On November 29, 1947, the final vote was taken, and the partition resolution based on the UNSCOP majority report was approved by a UN majority. Political Zionism had reached its goal of a publicly recognized, legally secured Jewish state in Palestine, and a wave of joy spread over all the Jewish communities of the world.

Five months later, the British withdrew from Palestine, and the State of Israel* was proclaimed. Zionism shouldered the new task of supporting the infant state that was immediately attacked by its Arab neighbors. (See ISRAEL.) But the need for economic support continued after the Arabs had been repelled; for Israel opened wide its doors and absorbed about a million Jewish refugees from Europe and the Arab countries.   N.B-A.

ZIONIST ORGANIZATION OF AMERICA.

The history of the Zionist movement in the United States begins in the early 1880's when Hoveve Zion* ("Lovers of Zion") societies were formed by Russian immigrants in New York,* Baltimore, and Chicago. Dr. Joseph I. Bluestone, who practiced medicine and wrote poetry, was the founder of the New York Lovers of Zion group. Dr. Bluestone believed that Zionism should serve a spiritual purpose and safeguard American Jewry against assimilation.* In 1897, the two-year-old Zion Society of Chicago was the only such group to send a delegate to the First Zionist Congress* held in Basle.

Stimulated by the reports from this Congress, the Federation of American Zionists was organized in 1898 at a national conference in New York. Professor Richard Gottheil* was the first president of the federation, and Rabbi Stephen S. Wise* its first secretary. The following year, a young journalist, Louis Lipsky,* founded the **Maccabean**; this monthly became the official Zionist publication. The periodical later changed its name to **The New Palestine** and finally to **The American Zionist.** By 1900, there were over one hundred societies all over the country. In addition to those already mentioned, a brilliant group of men including Harry Friedenwald and Benjamin Szold of Baltimore, and Judah L. Magnes* of New York, were the leaders of the infant movement. yet, until the First World War, its growth was rather slow. Young Judaea* was organized in 1907 as the youth department of the federation, and Hadassah,* the Women's Zionist Organization of America, was founded in 1912. When the First World War broke out in 1914, the role of

Leaders of American Zionism after World War I. Seated left to right: Miss Henrietta Szold, Dr. Stephen S. Wise, Jacob de Haas, R. Kesselman, Louis Lipsky, Charles Cowen, Dr. Shmaryahu Levin, Rabbi Meir Berlin (later Bar-Ilan).

American Zionism assumed new importance. The American Zionists were practically cut off from the European Zionist headquarters. Louis Lipsky,* then chairman of the Zionost Federation, and Shmaryahu Levin* (member of the World Zionist Executive then visiting in America) called an extraordinary conference to cope with the emergency. This conference established the Provisional Committee for Zionist Affairs under the chairmanship of Louis D. Brandeis.* In its Berlin headquarters, the World Zionist Executive acted to avoid the splitting of Zionist forces between the contending hostile powers of the war by transferring its authority to the Provisional Committee. The Committee functioned until 1918, managing the Zionist institutions in Palestine, and financing Zionist political activities in various war zones. Most important were the negotiations conducted by Brandeis and the Committee which contributed so largely to the issuance of the Balfour Declaration,* and were so responsible for obtaining American backing for it.

In 1917, the Mizrachi* and Poale Zion groups, representing the religious and labor Zionists,* withdrew from the Provisional Committee, and all the General Zionist* groups united to form the Zionist Organization of America, replacing the Provisional Committee. The following year, the Zionist Organization met at a conference in Pittsburgh. There it adopted what came to be called the Pittsburgh Program which was liberal and appealed strongly to the Jewish love for social justice. Brandeis, appointed to the United States Supreme Court, withdrew from public Zionist leadership. He became the honorary president of the Zionist Organization of America, while Judge Julian W. Mack was elected president. At the Cleveland Zionist Convention in 1921, the Brandeis program stressed private initiative in preference to the use

of public funds in the economic development of Palestine. This brought about a serious difference of opinion between the followers of Brandeis and Mack, and the followers of Chaim Weizmann,* president of the World Zionist Organization. Finally, Brandeis and his colleagues withdrew from active Zionist responsibility. Louis Lipsky and the men who led the opposition to the Brandeis group were entrusted with the leadership. Until 1931, Lipsky served as president of the Zionist Organization of America.

The Keren Hayesod* was established as the principal agency to support the development of Palestine. The Zionist Organization began to grow in membership, particularly after president Harding and the United States Congress approved the Balfour Declaration on September 21, 1922. Eventually, the breach between the two factions in American Zionism was healed, and most of the members of the Brandeis group, including Judge Mack, Stephen S. Wise,* and Abba Hillel Silver,* returned to active leadership. Between 1921 and 1929, approximately $10,000,000 was raised for the keren Hayesod. The Arab riots in Palestine in 1929, and the world economic depression set back Zionist activity. However, the rising tide of Nazism in Germany* was followed by a wave of anti-Semitism* in the United States; the result was an increase in Zionist membership.

When the Second World War broke out in 1939, representatives of the Zionist Organization, Hadassah, Mizrachi, and the Labor Zionist movement came together in the American Emergency Committee for Zionist Affairs to meet the crisis facing the Jewish communities of Europe and Palestine.

Since 1948, with the rebirth of Israel, the Zionist Organization established and supports the ZOA House in Tel Aviv, Kfar Silver, and the technical

Delegates of the ZOA to the 30th Zionist Congress in Jerusalem.

high school in Ashkelon which trains over 750 Israeli, American and foreign high school youth.

Within the Jewish community, ZOA is committed to work vigorously on behalf of education and Aliyah.* To contribute to these efforts, ZOA established four Institutes in the 1980's. They are the *Jacob Goodman Institute for Middle East Relations and information, The Ivan J. Novick Institute for Israel-Diaspora Relations, The George Rothman Institute on U.S. Foreign Policy in the Middle East,* and the *Greenwald-Tarnepol Foundation for the Advancement of Zionism.*

With over 20 regional offices and 200 Zionist districts country-wide, ZOA maintains a growing membership of over 120,000 family members.

ZOA's Masada movement is the second largest Zionist youth movement in the United States. Through Masada, ZOA's Women's Division, Young Zionist Leadership groups and Regions and Districts, public affairs programs, ZOA remains a strong and vital Zionist institution in America.

ZOHAR (Hebrew, meaning "light" or "splendor"). The holiest book of the Kabbalah,* actually called the "Holy Zohar." Written in Aramaic,* the Zohar first appeared in the thirteenth century, when it was published by Moses de Leon. De Leon attributed the Zohar to Rabbi Simeon Ben Yohai,* who lived in the second century, and together with his son Eliezer, hid for thirteen years in caves to escape Roman persecution. During this time, the Kabbalists believe, Ben Yohai occupied himself with composing mystical interpretations of the Bible.

The Zohar dwells on the mystery of Creation, and explains the stories and events in the Bible in a symbolic manner. It finds hidden meanings in common statements of facts. The Zohar describes God, "the Infinite One." God makes himself known to the world through ten "spheres of emanation." The Zohar also contains wonderful stories, discourses by the ancient masters, ethical pronouncements, and some most moving prayers.

The Zohar has exerted a profound influence on the religious thought of large groups of Jews, including the Hasidim.*

ZOLA, EMILE (1840-1902). French novelist and founder of the naturalistic school of writing. During the Dreyfus affair,* he published his famous pamphlet **J'Accuse** (1901), and was an important champion of this Jewish army officer falsely accused of selling French secret documents to the German government. In addition to **J'Accuse,** Zola wrote a parable on the Dreyfus affair in his book **Verite.**

ZWEIG, STEFAN (1881-1942). Critic, biographer and dramatist. Best known for his play, **Jeremiah,** and a biography of **Marie Antoinette.** He brought to his subjects great learning and a talent for breathing life into far-off places, persons and times. An impassioned pacifist as well as a Jew, Zweig was forced to leave his native Austria when Hitler came to power. Although they had become British subjects, he and his wife fled to the New World during World War II. Overwhelmed by despair at the triumph of Nazism, Stefan Zweig and his wife committed suicide in Brazil* in 1942.

Emile Zola